D0324904

Eastern Europe

Estonia p159

Russia p333

Latvia p211

Russia (Kaliningrad Region) p354

Lithuania p227

Belarus p57

Poland p279

Ukraine p411

Czech Republic p135

Slovakia p375

Moldova p255

Slovenia p395

Hungary p177

Romania p311

Croatia p107

Serbia p359

Bosnia & Hercegovina p69

Montenegro p267

Kosovo p201

Bulgaria p85

Albania p43

Macedonia p241

THIS EDITION WRITTEN AND RESEARCHED BY

Mark Baker, Marc Di Duca, Peter Dragicevich, Mark Elliott, Steve Fallon,
Tom Masters, Anja Mutić, Simon Richmond, Tamara Sheward,
Luke Waterson

DISCARD

PLAN YOUR TRIP

ON THE ROAD

HVAR ISLAND P124,
CROATIA

KYIV P414, UKRAINE

Contents

LAKE OHRID P248,
MACEDONIA

ON THE ROAD

RED SQUARE P338,
MOSCOW, RUSSIA

CHARLES BRIDGE P141,
PRAGUE, CZECH REPUBLIC

Contents

WALTER BIBIKOW / GETTY IMAGES ©

RĪGA P213, LATVIA

K-KING PHOTOGRAPHY MEDIA CO. LTD / GETTY IMAGES ©

GELLÉRT BATHS P181, BUDAPEST, HUNGARY

Welcome to Eastern Europe

Surreal, exciting and constantly surprising, Eastern Europe is an amazing warehouse of culture, history and architecture as well as mind-blowing scenery.

Cultural Explosion

Crossing Prague's 14th-century Charles Bridge at dawn; marvelling at Kraków's preserved Rynek Główny (Main Market Sq); viewing an unrivalled cross-section of art history at the Hermitage in St Petersburg; and hearing Liszt in his native Hungary: these are just a few of the cultural and architectural highlights on offer in Eastern Europe. Cities such as Moscow, Budapest and Warsaw groan under the weight of their heritage. It's not all about high culture though – the people you'll meet in the region's many small towns and charming villages are just as much of an attraction.

Spectacular Scenery

Anything but grey and predictable, this is also a region of exciting and unexpected landscapes: take a boat ride on the blue Danube; discover incredible beaches on the Croatian or Albanian riviera; hike your way through Poland and Slovakia's High Tatras, Romania's Bucegi Mountains and Albania's simply incredible Accursed Mountains. Even more surprising are the vast sand dunes of Curonian Spit in Lithuania and Kaliningrad, beautiful Lake Ohrid in Macedonia, the Great Masurian Lakes of Poland and the racing river gorges of Slovenia, and Bosnia & Hercegovina.

Historic Overload

Eastern Europe's dramatic past is tangibly present in its amazingly preserved palaces, haunting castles, magnificent churches and grandiose plazas. Cross the bridge where Archduke Ferdinand was assassinated in Sarajevo; stand in the room in the Livadia Palace where 'the Big Three' divided up postwar Europe at the 1945 Yalta Conference; feel the echo of the Romanian Revolution on Bucharest's Piaţa Revoluţiei (Revolution Square) or the even more recent tragic events on Kyiv's Maydan Nezalezhnosti. Going further back there's St Basil's Cathedral on Moscow's Red Square, a legacy of Ivan the Terrible's terrifying reign, and the remains of Diocletian's Palace in Split, Croatia.

Folklore & Festivals

This is the heartland of Orthodox Christianity, with the religion's rites and traditions permeating many aspects of cultural life, particularly so in countries such as Russia and Ukraine, where celebrations for Easter are not to be missed. Roman Catholic, Muslim and Jewish communities are also alive and kicking, as are older pagan rituals in events such as the Baltica International Folklore Festival or Slovakia's Východná festival – a chance to gain a contemporary insight into age-old Europe.

Why I Love Eastern Europe

By Simon Richmond, Writer

What has always impressed me about Eastern Europe is how communally minded the locals can be and how this makes for such a friendly experience for the traveller. Falling into conversation with locals on a train or at a cafe is commonplace. You'll likely end up sharing food and drinks with them, listening to folk songs, learning a new card game or even being invited home for dinner where you could be treated to delicacies such as Croatian truffles and Hungarian *gulyás* (goulash) as well as delicious staples such as Polish *pierogi* (dumplings) and Russian bliny.

For more about our writers, see page 478

Above: Prague (p137), Czech Republic

Eastern Europe

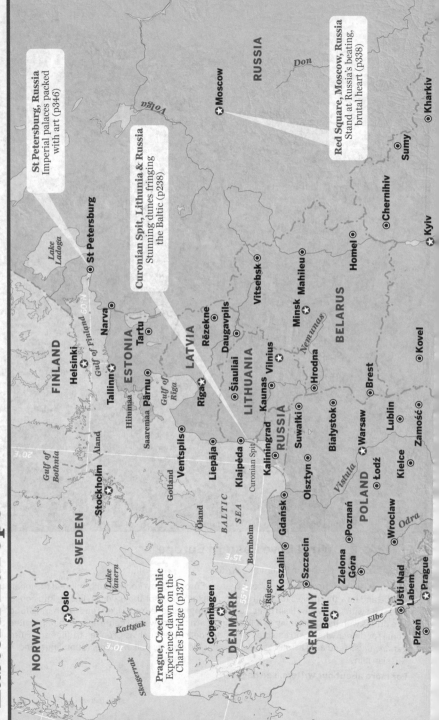

St Petersburg, Russia
Imperial palaces packed with art (p346)

Curonian Spit, Lithuania & Russia
Stunning dunes fringing the Baltic (p238)

Red Square, Moscow, Russia
Stand at Russia's beating, brutal heart (p338)

Prague, Czech Republic
Experience dawn on the Charles Bridge (p137)

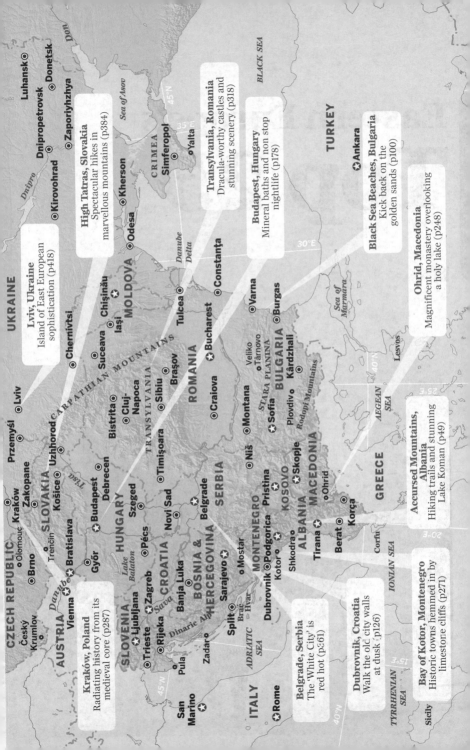

Eastern Europe's
Top 25

1

Prague, Czech Republic

1 The Czech capital (p137) is a near-perfectly preserved museum of European architecture through the ages. From the Old Town Square, across the Charles Bridge and up to Prague Castle, it's almost as if a 14th-century metropolis has been transported in time and plunked down in the heart of modern Europe. After you've meandered the alleyways, neck sore from craning to spy the statues and gargoyles, retire to a local pub for some Czech beer – the country's pride and joy. Charles Bridge

The Hermitage, St Petersburg, Russia

2 Standing proudly at the end of Nevsky Prospekt, Russia's most famous palace (p347) houses its most famous museum. Little can prepare most visitors for the scale of the exhibits, nor for their quality, comprising an almost unrivalled history of Western art, including a staggering number of Rembrandts, Rubens, Picassos and Matisses. In addition, there are superb antiquities, sculpture and jewellery on display, and if that's not enough, simply content yourself with wandering through the private apartments of the Romanovs, for whom the Winter Palace was home until 1917. State Hermitage Museum

3

LI KIM GOH / GETTY IMAGES ©

Budapest, Hungary

3 Straddling both sides of the romantic Danube River, with the Buda Hills to the west and the start of the Great Plain to the east, Budapest (p178) is perhaps the most beautiful city in Central Europe. Parks brim with attractions, the architecture is second to none and museums are filled with treasures. Add to that pleasure boats sailing up and down the scenic Danube Bend, Turkish-era thermal baths belching steam and a nightlife throbbing till dawn most nights, and it's easy to see why the Hungarian capital is one the continent's most delightful, fun cities to visit. Széchenyi Baths (p183)

Moscow's Red Square, Russia

4 With the gravitational pull of a black hole, Red Square (p338) sucks in every visitor to Russia's capital, leaving them slack-jawed with wonder. Standing on the rectangular cobblestoned expanse – surrounded by the candy-coloured swirls of the cupolas atop St Basil's Cathedral, the red-startipped towers of the Kremlin, Lenin's squat granite mausoleum, the handsome red-brick facade of the State History Museum, and GUM (a grand emporium of consumption) – you are literally at the centre of Russia's modern history.

Hiking the High Tatras, Slovakia

5 The rocky, alpine peaks of the High Tatras (p384) in Slovakia are the highest in the Carpathians, with 25 peaks soaring over 2500m. But hiking this impressive little range needn't require an Olympian effort. In the morning, ride a cable car up to 1800m and you can hike along midelevation trails, stopping at a log-cabin hikers' hut with a restaurant for lunch. A few hours more and you're at the Hrebienok funicular terminus that will take you down to turn-of-the-20thcentury Starý Smokovec below, well in time for dinner. Velka Studena Valley (p385)

Black Sea Beaches, Bulgaria

6 Home to almost 400km of sensational Black Sea coastline, the so-called Bulgarian Riviera (p100) is lined with beautiful beaches and ripper resorts, all at a fraction of the cost of others on the continent. There's a stretch of sand to suit every taste; party-hard playgrounds like Sunny Beach attract international tourists keen on water sports and wild nightlife, cosmopolitan Varna offers long, white-sand beaches and pleasant parks, while the heritage-rich harbours of Nesebâr and Sozopol dish up culture by the spadeful. Beach near Varna

Bay of Kotor, Montenegro

7 There's a sense of secrecy and mystery to the Bay of Kotor (p271). Grey mountain walls rise steeply from steely blue waters, getting higher as you progress through their folds to the hidden reaches of the inner bay. Here, ancient stone settlements hug the shoreline, with the old alleyways of Kotor concealed in its innermost reaches behind hefty stone walls. Talk about drama! But you wouldn't expect anything else of the Balkans, where life is exuberantly Mediterranean and lived full of passion on these time-worn streets. Perast, Bay of Kotor

8

9

10

Accursed Mountains, Albania

8 Albania's natural landscape is its greatest drawcard, and it's best experienced in the country's north, where the Accursed Mountains (p49) offer superb hiking, traditional mountain villages that still look like they're living in the 19th century, and the ferry ride across stunning Lake Koman. The most popular hike is the gorgeous and only moderately challenging day trek from Valbona to Theth, which shouldn't be missed. But for keen walkers there are dozens of opportunities to walk in the raw near-wilderness of high Albania.

Waterfall near Theth village

Dubrovnik's Old City Walls, Croatia

9 In Croatia, get up close and personal with Dubrovnik by walking its spectacular city walls (p126), as history is unfurled from the battlements. No visit is complete without a leisurely stroll along these ramparts, the finest in the world and Dubrovnik's main claim to fame. Built between the 13th and 16th centuries, they are still remarkably intact and the vistas over terracotta rooftops and the Adriatic Sea are sublime, especially at dusk when the sunset turns the hues dramatic and the panoramas unforgettable.

Kraków, Poland

10 As popular as it is, Poland's former royal capital (p287) never disappoints. It's hard to pinpoint why it's so special, but there's an aura of history radiating from the sloping stone buttresses of medieval buildings in the Old Town that makes its streets seem just right. Throw in the extremes of a spectacular castle and the low-key, oh-so-cool bar scene situated within the tiny worn buildings of the Kazimierz back streets, and it's a city you'll want to seriously get to know.

Miejsce Bar (p291)

Prizren, Kosovo

11 Kosovo's most charming town is pretty little Prizren (p208), nestled in the valley of the Bistrica river and dominated by the minarets and church towers of its old town. Despite the dark legacy of war, Prizren today is progressively run, with one of Eastern Europe's best film festivals, Dokufest, bringing a splash of international sophistication every summer. The rest of the year you can explore the town's rich heritage in the form of its hilltop fortress, grand mosques and ancient churches.
Ottoman Bridge

Belgrade Nightlife, Serbia

12 Brassy Belgrade (p361) may be a million light years away from hedonistic hot spots like Barcelona and Berlin, but somehow the gritty city has morphed into one of the top party destinations in the world. Perhaps it's an enduring live-for-the-moment phenomenon (the city was repeatedly bombed in 1999) or simply the sociable Serbian spirit: whatever the reason, Belgrade by night (and well past dawn) throbs to the beat of countless clubs, bars and *splavovi* (floating pleasure pontoons). Ask a local for their favourite haunt, or just follow the crowds.

DAVE LONG / GETTY IMAGES ©

WESTEND61 / GETTY IMAGES ©

Transylvania's Castles & Mountains, Romania

13 The Romanian region (p318) that so ghoulishly inspired Irish writer Bram Stoker to create his *Dracula* has some seriously spooky castles. Monumental Bran Castle (p320), south of Braşov, is suitably vampiric, but our favourite haunt has to be the 13th-century Râşnov fortress just down the road. The castles are nestled high amid the Carpathians, a relatively underexplored mountain range that's ideal for all manner of outdoor activity, including hiking, trekking, mountain biking and skiing. Bran Castle

Cycling Curonian Spit, Lithuania

14 Allegedly created by the sea goddess Neringa, the fragile, narrow sliver of land that is Curonian Spit (p238) juts out into the Baltic Sea, its celestial origins giving it a somewhat otherworldly ambience and its giant sand dunes earning it the nickname of 'Lithuania's Sahara'. The best way to explore it is by bicycle, riding through dense pine forest from one cheerful fishing village to the next, stopping to sample freshly smoked fish, or – if you're lucky – to glimpse the spit's elusive wildlife: elk, deer and wild boar.

Lviv, Ukraine

15 A pleasant island of Eastern European sophistication in a post-Soviet sea, Ukraine's great hope for tourism is a moody city (p418) of arabica-scented coffee houses, verdant old parks, trundling trams and Austro-Hungarian manners. Melodiously accented Ukrainian provides the soundtrack while incense billows through medieval churches that miraculously avoided their dates with Soviet dynamite, and violin-toting schoolchildren compete for seats on buses with smiling nuns and West Ukrainian hippies. Tourists now flock to Lviv, but the city seems admirably determined not to do a Prague or a Kraków. Market Square

Mostar, Bosnia & Hercegovina

16 If the 1993 bombardment of the iconic 16th-century stone bridge in Mostar (p79) underlined the pointlessness of Yugoslavia's brutal civil war, its reconstruction has proved symbolic of a peaceful post-conflict era. The charming Ottoman quarter has been convincingly rebuilt and is once again a patchwork of stone mosques, souvenir peddlers and inviting cafes. In summer it is tourists rather than militias that besiege the place. *Stari Most*

Tallinn, Estonia

17 The Estonian capital (p161) is famous for its two-tiered chocolate-box Old Town with its intertwining alleys, picturesque courtyards and red-rooftop views from medieval turrets. But be sure to step outside the Old Town walls and experience the other treasures of Tallinn: its stylish restaurants plating up oh-so-fashionable New Nordic cuisine, the buzzing Scandinavian-influenced design community, its ever-growing number of museums and its progressive contemporary architecture.
A restaurant in Tallinn

Ohrid, Macedonia

18 Whether you come to sublime, hilly Ohrid (p248) for its sturdy medieval castle, to wander the stone laneways of its Old Town or to gaze at its restored Plaošnik, every visitor pauses for a few moments at the Church of Sveti Jovan at Kaneo, set high on a bluff overlooking Lake Ohrid and its popular beaches. It's the prime spot for absorbing the town's beautiful architecture, idling sunbathers and distant fishing skiffs – all framed by the rippling green of Mt Galičica to the southeast and the endless expanse of lake stretching out elsewhere. Sunrise, Lake Ohrid

Mt Triglav & Vršič Pass, Slovenia

19 For such a small country, Slovenia has got it all: charming towns, great wines, a Venetian-inspired seashore and, most of all, mountains. The highest peak, Mt Triglav (p402; 2864m), stands particularly tall in local lore. Indeed, the saying goes that you're not really Slovene until you've climbed to the top. If time is an issue and you're driving, head for the high-altitude Vršič Pass, which crosses the Julian Alps and leads down to the sunny coastal region in one hair-raising, spine-tingling hour. Mt Triglav

Wine Tasting, Moldova

20 Moldova's soil and climate are ideal for growing grapes and the country offers some of Eastern Europe's best wines. Whites include Chardonnay, Riesling and the local Fetească Albă, while Cabernet Sauvignon, Merlot and Fetească Neagră are all popular for reds. Cricova and Mileştii Mici wineries (p261) have underground storage cellars stretching on for hundreds of kilometres that you can tour by car. Tasting room, cellar, Cricova

21

22

23

Island-Hopping in the Adriatic, Croatia

21 From short jaunts between nearby islands to overnight rides along the length of the Croatian coast, travelling by sea is a great and inexpensive way to experience the Croatian side of the Adriatic. Take in the scenery of this stunning coastline as you whiz past some of Croatia's 1244 islands and explore hidden beaches like those on the Pakleni Islands (p124). And if you have cash to splash, take it up a couple of notches and charter a sailboat to see the islands in style, propelled by winds and sea currents. Bay, Adriatic Coast

Art Nouveau Architecture in Rīga, Latvia

22 Latvia's impressive and surprising capital, Rīga (p213) boasts a superb architectural heritage known locally as *style moderne,* but better known to the world as art nouveau. Over 750 buildings (more than any other city in Europe) boast this style – a menagerie of mythical beasts, screaming masks, twisting flora, goddesses and goblins. Much of the city's personality can be gleaned through its architecture. Many of its elaborate apartments stand next to weathered, crumbling facades. Facade on Alberta Iela Street

Minsk, Belarus

23 Minsk (p59) is no typical Eastern European capital. Almost totally destroyed in WWII, the ancient city underwent a Stalinist rebirth in the 1950s, and is now a masterpiece of socialist architecture and the perfect place to discover the Soviet time capsule that is modern Belarus. While its initial appearance is severe and austere, a few days in Minsk allows you to break through to the fun-loving heart of this green and pleasant city. National Library of Belarus, designed by architects Mihail Vinogradov and Viktor Kramarenko

Český Krumlov, Czech Republic

24 Showcasing quite possibly Europe's most glorious Old Town, Český Krumlov (p149) is a popular day trip from Prague for many travellers. But a rushed few hours navigating the town's meandering lanes and audacious clifftop castle sells short the CK experience. Stay at least one night to lose yourself in the Old Town's shape-shifting after-dark shadows and get cosy in riverside restaurants, cafes and pubs.

Lake Balaton, Hungary

25 Hungary's 'sea' (and continental Europe's largest lake) is where the populace comes to sun and swim in summertime. The quieter side of Lake Balaton (p190) mixes sizzling beaches and oodles of fun on the water with historic waterside towns such as Keszthely and Balatonfüred. Tihany, a protected peninsula jutting 4km into the lake, is home to a stunning abbey church, and Hévíz boasts a thermal lake where you can bathe even when it's snowing.

Need to Know

For more information, see Survival Guide (p423)

Currency
Euro (€) in Estonia, Kosovo, Latvia, Lithuania, Montenegro, Slovakia and Slovenia; local currency elsewhere.

Language
Apart from national languages, Russian, German and English also widely understood.

Visas
EU, US, Canadian, Australian and NZ passport holders do not require a visa to visit the majority of Eastern Europe. Visas needed by all for Russia and Belarus.

Money
ATMS are common, credit and debit cards are accepted in cities and major towns. Always carry cash though.

Mobile Phones
The GSM 900 network is used in the region. Coming from outside Europe it's usually worth buying a prepaid local SIM.

Time
Most of Eastern Europe (GMT plus two hours), Russia (GMT plus three hours).

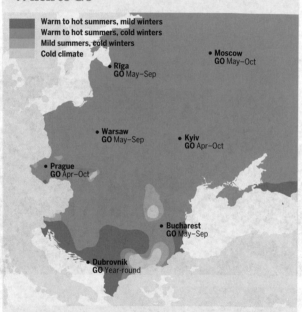

When to Go

- Warm to hot summers, mild winters
- Warm to hot summers, cold winters
- Mild summers, cold winters
- Cold climate

Moscow GO May–Oct
Riga GO May–Sep
Warsaw GO May–Sep
Kyiv GO Apr–Oct
Prague GO Apr–Oct
Bucharest GO May–Sep
Dubrovnik GO Year-round

High Season
(Jul & Aug)

➡ Expect high temperatures and long evenings.

➡ Hotels will be up to 30% more expensive and you'll need to book rooms in advance.

➡ Big draws such as Prague, Budapest and Kraków will be very crowded.

Shoulder Season
(May & Jun, Sep & Oct)

➡ Crowds and prices drop off.

➡ The weather remains very pleasant.

➡ Overall the best time to travel in Eastern Europe.

Low Season
(Nov–Apr)

➡ Hotel prices drop to their lowest.

➡ Weather can be decidedly cold and days short.

➡ Some places, such as resort towns, are like ghost towns.

Useful Websites

Lonely Planet (www.lonely planet.com/thorntree) Ask other travellers questions.

Deutsche Bahn (www.bahn.de) The best online train timetable for the region.

Like a Local (www.likealocal guide.com) Free online guides to cities across the region, written by locals.

Hidden Europe (www.hidden europe.co.uk) Fascinating magazine and online dispatches from all the continent's corners.

VisitEurope (www.visiteurope. com) Information about travel in 33 member countries.

Spotted by Locals (www. spottedbylocals.com) Insider tips for cities across Europe.

What to Take

Flip-flops (thongs) Useful on overnight train rides, in hostel bathrooms and for the beach.

Hiking boots To experience Eastern Europe's fantastic and easy walking.

Ear plugs Especially if you plan to sleep in hostels or on trains.

European plug adaptors To juice up your electronic devices.

An unlocked mobile phone Insert a local SIM card to make cheap calls.

Exchange Rates

AU	A$1	€0.72	R46.32
CAN	C$1	€0.74	R46.97
JPN	¥100	€0.78	R49.10
NZ	NZ$1	€0.70	R45.03
UK	UK£1	€1.37	R87.95
US	US$1	€0.95	R58.81

For current exchange rates see www. xe.com

Daily Costs

**Budget:
Less than €40**

➡ Hostel beds for as little as €10

➡ Admission to museums €1 to €15

➡ Beer €1.50 to €3

**Midrange:
€40–€150**

➡ Midrange hotels are everywhere, averaging €40 a night

➡ Meals in decent restaurants are about €10 per person

➡ Short taxi trip €10 to €20

**Top End:
More than €150**

➡ Top-end hotel rooms start at €100 per night

➡ In big cities top restaurant prices start at about €25 per person

➡ Hire cars start at about €30 per day

Accommodation

Hotels From Soviet-era dinosaurs to five-star pamper palaces.

Guesthouses & Pensions Small, family-run, generally provide good value.

Hostels From super basic to hipster cool.

Homestays & Farmstays A great way to really find out how locals live.

Camping & Couchsurfing Cheap, with Couchsurfing (www. couchsurfing.org) free. Note that wild camping is usually forbidden.

Arriving in Eastern Europe

Many travellers will arrive overland by train, bus or car from other European transport hubs such as Frankfurt, Berlin or İstanbul.

Domodedovo Airport Moscow (Домодедово; www.domode dovo.ru) and **Sheremetyevo Airport Moscow** (Шереметьево, SVO; www.svo.aero; ☑495-578 6565) Trains (R340–400) run 6am to midnight, every 30 minutes and take 40 minutes. Taxis cost R2000 to R2200 (R1500 to R1800 if booked in advance) but are best avoided because of traffic.

Václav Havel Airport Prague (Prague Ruzyně International Airport; www.prg.aero; K letišti 6, Ruzyně; ☑220 111 888) Airport Express buses cost 60Kč and run from 5am to 10pm, every 30 minutes and take 35 minutes. Taxi cost from 500Kč to 650Kč depending on your central Prague destination.

Getting Around

Train Connects nearly all major cities. Overnight trips are fantastic experiences.

Bus Covers most of Eastern Europe; particularly useful for reaching more remote areas.

Car Drive on the right. Roads are generally good, but be aware that many hire companies limit which countries their cars can be taken to.

Ferry International services connect the Balkans to Italy, Albania to Corfu, and Estonia and Russia to Finland.

Plane International flights connect most capitals to neighbouring countries and European hubs.

Bicycle Hired in big cities where cycling is generally quite safe.

For much more on
getting around,
see p436.

If You Like...

Old Towns

Kraków, Poland Arguably Eastern Europe's finest old town; the incredible Rynek Główny cannot be missed. (p287)

Prague, Czech Republic It's hard not to fall instantly in love with the incredibly preserved Staré Město. (p137)

Dubrovnik, Croatia Walk the marble-paved streets of the Stradun and the fantastical city walls. (p126)

Vilnius, Lithuania Europe's largest baroque old town offers cobbled streets, artists' workshops and countless church steeples. (p228)

Lviv, Ukraine A charmingly multicultural town that's a repository of culture and a must-see on any Eastern European trip. (p418)

Tallinn, Estonia As chocolate box as they come, but nevertheless an utterly charming place to explore. (p161)

Berat, Albania White Ottoman houses on a rugged mountainside in this 'town of a thousand windows'. (p50)

Beaches & Islands

Curonian Spit, Lithuania World Heritage sand dunes slide into bracing waters that are the best place to swim in the Baltic. (p238)

Drymades beach, Albania Legendary white-sand beach on Albania's fast-disappearing undeveloped coastline remains the one to head for. (p52)

Black Sea Coast, Bulgaria The best beaches on the Black Sea, with big resorts around Varna, and less hectic spots like Sozopol to the south. (p100)

Hvar Island, Croatia Covered with lilac fields, this luxurious, sunny island is the jumping-off point for the wooded Pakleni Islands. (p124)

Jūrmala, Latvia Dip into the spa scene at the Soviet-era sanatoriums along the Baltic Riviera. (p221)

Lake Bled, Slovenia A picture-postcard church on a tiny island punctuates this crystal blue-green lake. (p403)

Castles & Palaces

Bran Castle, Romania This Transylvanian beauty is straight out of a horror movie, even if it has little to do with Dracula himself. (p320)

Karlštejn Castle, Czech Republic A true piece of fairy tale Gothic, this Bohemian beauty near Prague makes for a great day trip. (p146)

Catherine Palace, Tsaskoe Selo, Russia Marvel at this glittering baroque palace, restored to tsarist splendour after destruction in WWII. (p352)

Bojnice Castle, Slovakia Stunning fairy-tale fortress with soaring towers and landscaped grounds, setting for countless fantasy films.

Ljubljana Castle, Slovenia Amazing views from the watchtower and gourmet food in one of the city's top restaurants. (p397)

Kamyanets-Podilsky, Ukraine On the Smotrych River, this gorgeous castle town is backed by dramatic natural beauty. (p419)

Mir Castle, Belarus Straight out of Disney, this painstakingly restored castle offers attractive grounds and impressively renovated interiors. (p63)

Historical Sites

Butrint, Albania Ruins of an ancient Greek fortified city in a tranquil national-park location. (p53)

Diocletian's Palace, Croatia Imposing Roman ruin occupying the heart of Split with 220 ancient buildings within its boundaries. (p120)

Rila Monastery, Bulgaria Heavenly, Unesco-listed monastery, dating back over 1000 years and long a stronghold of Bulgarian culture. (p93)

Kremlin, Moscow, Russia The seat of power to medieval tsars and modern presidents alike is packed with incredible sights. (p335)

Mountains & Hiking

Slovenský Raj National Park, Slovakia Waterfalls, gorges and thick forests decorate Slovakia's outstanding national park. (p389)

Bulgarian mountains Don't miss the trails around stunning Rila Monastery or the beautiful Rodopi Mountains. (p93)

Carpathian Mountains, Poland Use Zakopane as a base for your walks, including around wonderful emerald green Lake Morskie Oko. (p295)

Zlatibor, Serbia The rolling hills and spectacular views in this corner of Southern Serbia are ideal for gentle hikes. (p369)

Tatra Mountains, Slovakia Europe's easternmost Alpine mountain range bisected by one of Europe's loveliest long-distance hikes. (p383)

Relics of Communism

Lenin's Mausoleum, Moscow, Russia A waxy Lenin continues to lay in state on impressive Red Square. (p338)

Stalinist Minsk, Belarus Rebuilt in the 1950s in monolithic Stalinist style following destruction in WWII, Minsk has barely changed since. (p59)

Transdniestr, Moldova This still-communist slice of Moldova is a self-proclaimed country and living relic of the Soviet past. (p262)

Grūtas Park, Druskininkai, Lithuania Hundreds of communist-era statues set in grounds designed to resemble a Siberian concentration camp. (p234)

Palace of Culture & Science, Warsaw, Poland Take in the view from Poland's tallest building, a

Top: Double helix staircase, Ljubljana Castle, Slovenia (p397)
Bottom: Diving from Stari Most, Mostar, Bosnia & Hercegovina (p79)

1950s 'gift of friendship' from the Soviet Union. (p283)

Maršal Tito's Grave, Belgrade, Serbia Gigantic marble mausoleum, also displaying hundreds of wonderfully kitsch birthday batons presented by young 'Pioneers'. (p363)

Great Food & Drink

Hungarian cuisine Try the national dish, goulash, just one option in a country offering the best cuisine and wines in the region. (p200)

Istrian delights, Croatia Truffles, wild asparagus and fresh seafood are on the menu in Istria; there's also a superb local wine scene. (p117)

Nordic cuisine, Estonia Dip into Tallinn's excellent dining scene with cutting-edge Nordic cuisine at Ö and seasonal delights at Neh. (p176)

Wine tasting, Moldova For something totally different check out the great and largely undiscovered viniculture of plucky little Moldova. (p266)

Museum of Wine, Melnik, Bulgaria Learn about winemaking, explore the dirt vault and work your way through a tasting menu. (p93)

Activities & Sports

Bovec, Slovenia Along with neighbouring Bled, this is the region's unrivalled location for extreme sports, offering everything from canyoning to hydrospeeding. (p405)

Rafting and kayaking, Bosnia & Hercegovina Ride the fast-flowing rivers in the Vrbas Canyons between Jajce and Banja Luka.

Sigulda, Latvia Come here to bobsleigh, bungee jump from

a moving cable car and even try out 'aerodium' air blasting. (p222)

Bridge diving, Mostar, Bosnia & Hercegovina Locals will teach you how to dive from Mostar's terrifyingly high bridge to the river below. (p79)

Caving, Slovakia The Slovenský Raj National Park includes one of only three aragonite caves in the world as well as the Dobšinská Ice Cave. (p389)

Iron Curtain Cycling Route Pedal 9600km through 20 countries from Russia to Turkey along the old dividing line between East and West Europe.

Belavezhskaya Pushcha National Park, Belarus Cycle or hike around Europe's oldest wildlife refuge, home to 300-odd European bison. (p65)

Spectacular Scenery

Train from Belgrade to Bar Eastern Europe's most impressive train journey, through the spectacular canyons of Montenegro. (p277)

Lake Koman Ferry, Albania See part of the world few foreigners ever make it to on this beautiful ferry ride in Albania's remote and mountainous north. (p50)

Slovak Karst National Park, Slovakia See central Europe's biggest cave system in this Unesco-listed national park in southeast Slovakia.

Danube Delta, Romania This sprawling, wild wetland where the Danube meets the Black Sea is all reeds and birds as far as the eye can see. (p328)

Art Collections

Hermitage, St Petersburg, Russia One of the world's greatest art collections, stuffed full of treasures, from Egyptian

mummies to a superb cache of Picassos. (p347)

Mucha Museum, Prague, Czech Republic Be seduced by the sensuous art nouveau posters, paintings and decorative panels of Alfons Mucha. (p142)

Art Museum Rīga Bourse, Rīga, Latvia The old stock exchange is a worthy showcase for the city's art treasures. (p213)

State Tretyakov Gallery, Moscow, Russia This fabulous repository of Russian culture covers it all, from religious icons to contemporary sculpture. (p339)

Jewish Heritage

Prague's Jewish sights, Czech Republic Europe's oldest still-functioning synagogue, the 16th-century Jewish Town Hall and the Old Jewish Cemetery. (p141)

New Synagogue, Szeged, Hungary Spectacular reborn synagogue being used as a place of worship rather than simply another museum. (p195)

Auschwitz-Birkenau Memorial & Museum, Oświęcim, Poland These notorious death camps are chilling sites and a bleak document to the Holocaust. (p292)

Museum of the History of Polish Jews, Warsaw, Poland Newly opened high-tech marvel with a permanent exhibition tracing a millennium of Jewish history. (p284)

Great Synagogue, Budapest, Hungary The largest synagogue in the world outside New York City also includes a museum on the Holocaust. (p181)

Jewish Vilnius, Lithuania Visit the Tolerance Centre, Holocaust Museum and Choral Synagogue in this age-old centre of Jewish life. (p233)

Hill of Crosses (p236), Lithuania

Vitsebsk, Belarus A major centre of old European Jewish culture, immortalised by the paintings of Marc Chagall. (p66)

Contemporary Architecture

Museum of Contemporary Art, Zagreb, Croatia Sleek stunner, designed by Igor Franić, that's a stellar example of clever use of light and space. (p113)

Kumu, Tallinn, Estonia A world-class concrete-and-glass building that holds an excellent art collection. (p165)

Košice, Slovakia Buildings here, including an art nouveau swimming pool and an old military base, have been renovated to create an arts and culture hub. (p390)

Garage Museum of Contemporary Art, Russia In Moscow's revitalised Gorky Park, this

museum occupies a 1960s pavilion redesigned by Rem Koolhaas. (p342)

Nightlife

Romkertek, Budapest, Hungary These pop-up clubs in abandoned buildings have put the Hungarian capital's nightlife on a par with that of Berlin or London. (p178)

Moscow, Russia Evolving into an essential stop on the clubber's world map, with a slew of new democratically run bars and clubs. (p335)

Belgrade, Serbia The Serbian capital is one of the most exciting, vibrant and affordable places to party the night away. (p361)

Cluj-Napoca, Romania Cluj's historic backstreets house perhaps the friendliest bunch of student party animals anywhere in the world. (p325)

Folk & Traditional Culture

Trubači, Serbia Ragtag *trubači* (brass bands) wander the streets of many Serbian cities and villages year-round. (p367)

Museum of Devils, Kaunas, Lithuania Diabolical collection of 2000-odd devil statuettes in this museum which outlines their connection to Lithuanian folklore. (p235)

Hill of Crosses, Lithuania Awe-inspiring sight of thousands of crosses, 12km north of Šiauliai, many finely carved folk-art masterpieces. (p236)

Spa and bathing culture Dip into Budapest's Turkish baths, the spas of Karlovy Vary (Karlsbad) in the Czech Republic and Russia's *bani* (traditional saunas).

Month by Month

January

January is a great time to experience the region's winter-wonderland appearance, with everything under blankets of snow. You'll find most towns relatively tourist free and hotel prices are rock-bottom.

🏃 Great-Value Skiing

Head to Eastern Europe's ski slopes for wallet-friendly prices. After the first week of January most hotels offer their lowest annual rates, making skiing affordable to all. Try the resorts near Sarajevo in Bosnia & Hercegovina or Bulgaria's Mt Vitosha range. (p94)

☆ Küstendorf Film & Music Festival, Serbia

Created and curated by Serbian director Emir Kusturica, this international indie-fest (http://kustendorf-filmand musicfestival.org) in the town of Drvengrad, near Zlatibor in Serbia, eschews traditional red-carpet glitz for oddball inclusions vying for the 'Golden Egg' prize.

February

Still cold, but with longer days, February is when colourful carnivals are held across the region. Low hotel prices and the off-season feel also remain.

🍷 Golden Grape Festival, Bulgaria

Held on the second weekend of February in Melnik, at this festival you can get merry on vino tastings, music and all manner of wine-centric wassailing.

March

Spring arrives in the southern parts of the region, while further north the rest of Eastern Europe continue to suffer the dregs of winter, though days are often bright and the sun shines.

🍴 Pancake Week (Maslenitsa), Russia

The Russian for this Shrovetide festival comes from the word *masla* (butter). Folk shows and games celebrate the end of winter, with lots of pancake eating before Lent (pancakes were a pagan symbol of the sun).

🏃 Vitranc Cup, Slovenia

Anyone who enjoys watching thrilling acrobatics on the ski slopes should not miss the excitement of this men's slalom and giant slalom competition (www.pokal-vitranc.com) in Kranjska Gora.

🎊 Paganism, Poland

Head to Poland in March for the quirky rite of the Drowning of Marzanna, a surviving pagan ritual in which an effigy of the goddess of winter is immersed in water at the advent of spring. The festival features lots of delicious blini to boot.

🏃 Ski-Jumping World Cup, Slovenia

Held on the third weekend in March, this exciting international competition (www.planica.si) in Planica is the place to catch world-record-making jumps and is a must for all adrenalin junkies.

April

Spring has well and truly arrived by April – across the region there are warm, sunny days and, after months of snow, even

Russia has finally seen a thaw. Hotel prices outside the Easter holiday period remain low.

⭐ Alexander Nevsky Festival, Russia

The second weekend of April sees this celebration in Veliky Novgorod honouring Russia's best-known prince. Members of historical clubs dress up as knights, engage in mock battle and storm the Kremlin walls.

⭐ Budapest Spring Festival, Hungary

One of Europe's top classical music events is this two-week festival (www.spring festival.hu) in mid-April. Concerts are held in a large number of beautiful venues, including several stunning churches, the Hungarian State Opera House and the National Theatre.

⭐ Easter Festival of Sacred Music, Czech Republic

Six thematic concerts (www.mhf-brno.cz) with full orchestras take place in three of the oldest churches in Brno, Czech Republic,

including the beautiful Cathedral of Sts Peter & Paul, in the two weeks following Palm Sunday.

⭐ Music Biennale Zagreb, Croatia

Held since 1961, the Music Biennale Zagreb (www.mbz. hr/eng) is Croatia's most important contemporary music event. It takes place in various venues around the capital over 10 days during mid-April in odd years.

May

An excellent time to visit Eastern Europe. May is sunny and warm and full of things to do, and while never too hot or too crowded, you can still expect the big destinations to feel busy.

⭐ International Labour Day, Russia

Once bigger than Christmas in the communist world, International Labour Day may have dropped in status since the fall of the Wall, but it's still a national holiday in Russia and several other former Soviet republics. You'll find fireworks, concerts and even

a huge military parade on Moscow's Red Square.

🍷 Czech Beer Festival, Czech Republic

An event most travellers won't want to miss is the Czech Beer Festival (www. ceskypivnifestival.cz), where lots of food, music and – most importantly – over 150 beers from around the country are on offer in Prague from mid- to late May.

🚣 Rafting, Bosnia & Hercegovina

After the spring rains May is the time for experienced rafters to head to the fast-flowing river gorges of Bosnia & Hercegovina, such as Foča, Bihać or Banja Luka. If you're a beginner, stay well away until summer, when conditions are more suitable.

⭐ Performances in Prague, Czech Republic

The three-week Prague Spring International Music Festival (www.festival.cz) sees international stars descend for major classical-music events. The Khamoro World Roma Festival (www.khamoro.cz/en) showcases the musical traditions of Europe's Roma people. And the Prague Fringe Festival (www.praguefringe.com) presents theatre, comedy and music with an irreverent tone, much of it in English.

June

The shoulder season is well under way – it's already summer in southeastern Europe and the sun is barely setting in the Baltic

---

ORTHODOX CHRISTMAS & EASTER

Eastern Orthodox Christianity uses the Julian calendar for its religious festivals and events, not the Gregorian calendar as is the case for the West. Hence Christmas Day falls on 7 January. On Christmas Eve (6 January) special masses are held in churches at midnight and the religious fast from morning to nightfall. Russians then have a feast that includes roast duck and porridge.

Easter (falling on 1 May 2016, 16 April 2017 and 8 April 2018) begins with midnight services on Easter Sunday. Afterwards, Russians have a tradition of eating *kulich* (traditional dome-shaped bread) and *paskha* (cheesecake) and exchanging painted wooden Easter eggs.

as the solstice approaches. This is definitely one of the best times to travel, if not the cheapest.

Rose Festival, Bulgaria

Bulgarians celebrate the harvest of their famously fragrant roses over a week of pageantry, parades and the crowning of the Rose Queen in Kazanlâk. (p100)

Exposition of New Music, Czech Republic

The streets, gardens, parks and buildings of Brno are filled with the sounds of contemporary music for this creative festival (www. mhf-brno.cz/expozice-nove-hudby) in mid-June.

Mikser Festival, Serbia

Belgrade's hyper-hipster Mikser Festival (http:// festival.mikser.rs) brings the supercool Savamala district into the spotlight, with a program devoted to the latest in music, design and quirky creativity.

White Nights, Russia

The barely setting sun across the Baltic encourages locals to party through the night. The best place to join the fun is the imperial Russian capital, St Petersburg, where classical concerts, an international music festival (http://wnfestival.com) and other summer events keep spirits high.

St John's Eve & St John's Day, Baltic Countries

The Baltic region's biggest annual night out is a celebration of midsummer

on 23 and 24 June. It's best experienced out in the country, where huge bonfires flare for all-night revellers.

Jewish Culture Festival, Poland

Kraków rediscovers its Jewish heritage during a packed week of music, art exhibitions and lectures (www.jewishfestival.pl) in late June/early July. Poland's festival is the biggest and most exciting Jewish festival in the region.

Moscow International Film Festival, Russia

Russia's premier film festival (www.moscowfilm festival.ru) runs for 10 days at the end of the month and includes retrospective and documentary film programs as well as the usual awards.

July

The middle of summer sees Eastern Europe packed with both people and things to do. Temperatures and prices soar by the end of July, but hotel room rates remain reasonable early in the month.

Východná, Slovakia

Slovakia's top folk festival (www.festivalvychodna. sk) is held over the first weekend of July each year in the tiny Tatra Mountain village of Východná. Over a thousand performers descend here to celebrate traditional music, dance, arts and crafts.

Ultra Europe, Croatia

Held over three days in Split's Poljud Stadium (www.ultraeurope.com), this electronic music fest includes a huge beach party.

EXIT Festival, Serbia

Eastern Europe's most talked-about music festival (www.exitfest.org) takes place each July within the walls of the Petrovaradin Fortress in Serbia's second city, Novi Sad. Book early for tickets as big international headlining acts attract music lovers from all over the continent. (p370)

Baltica International Folklore Festival, Baltic Countries

This triennial festival (www.cioff.org/events-festival.cfm/en/762/ Estonia-International_ Folklore_Festival_Baltica) consists of five days of traditional Baltic folk music and dance. It rotates between the three capitals of the Baltic states; it will be in Tallinn (Estonia) in 2016, Vilnius (Lithuania) in 2019 and Rīga (Latvia) in 2022.

Slavyansky Bazaar, Belarus

Held in the old Russian city of Vitsebsk (in modern Belarus), this festival (http://fest-sbv.by/en) is one of the biggest cultural events in the former Soviet Union, featuring theatrical performances, music concerts and exhibits from all over the Slavic world.

☆ Dubrovnik Summer Festival, Croatia

From 10 July to 25 August, Croatia's most prestigious summer festival (www.dubrovnik-festival.hr) presents a program of theatre, opera, concerts and dance on open-air stages throughout the city. (p128)

☆ Belgrade Summer Festival, Serbia

BELEF is a dynamic sampling of innovative music, dance, theatre and visual arts displays, takes over the Serbian capital for a month from mid-July.

☆ Karlovy Vary International Film Festival, Czech Republic

Held in one of the most beautiful spa towns in the Czech Republic, the region's own version of Cannes is a far smaller affair than its French cousin, but it still shows hundreds of movies in its packed program (www.kviff.com).

☆ Bažant Pohoda, Slovakia

Slovakia's largest music and arts festival (www.pohoda festival.sk), held in Trenčín, represents all genres of music from rock to orchestral over multiple stages. It is firmly established now as one of Europe's biggest and best summer music festivals.

☆ Ivana Kupala, Ukraine

On 7 July, Ukraine's exhilarating pagan celebration of midsummer involves fire jumping, maypole dancing, fortune telling, wreath floating and strong overtones of sex. Head for the countryside for the real deal.

☆ Medieval Festival of the Arts, Romania

During July the beautiful Romanian city of Sighişoara hosts open-air concerts, parades and ceremonies, all glorifying medieval Transylvania and taking the town back to its fascinating 12th-century origins.

☆ Ohrid Summer Festival, Macedonia

The month-long Ohrid Summer Festival (www.ohridsummer.com.mk) comprises a wealth of performances ranging from classical, opera and rock acts to theatre and literature, all celebrating Macedonian culture. The best events are held in the town's magical open-air Roman Classical Amphitheatre.

☆ International Music Festival, Czech Republic

Thousands of music lovers congregate in Český Krumlov for classical concerts, as well as jazz, rock and folk music, at this impressive month-long festival (www.festivalkrumlov.cz), which runs from mid-July to mid-August.

August

It's easy enough to get away from the crowds and expense, even at summer's height. There's a huge amount to see and do in August, and the weather – from the Baltic coast to the Adriatic – is hot, hot, hot!

☆ Dragačevo Trumpet Assembly, Serbia

Guča's Dragačevo Trumpet Assembly (www.guca.rs) is one of the most exciting and bizarre events in all of Eastern Europe. Hundreds of thousands of revellers descend on the small Serbian town of Guča to damage their eardrums, livers and sanity over four cacophonous days of revelry. (p367)

☆ Sziget Music Festival, Hungary

A weeklong, great-value music festival (www.sziget.hu) held all over Budapest. Sziget features bands from around the world playing at more than 60 venues.

☆ Kaliningrad Jazz City, Russia

Going now for over a decade, this jazz event (www.jazzfestival.ru) in Kaliningrad attracts performers from across Europe. It's held over three days around the city, with nightclub jams, big concerts and even free open-air sessions.

☆ Sarajevo Film Festival, Bosnia & Hercegovina

This globally acclaimed festival (www.sff.ba) that grew out of the ruins of the '90s civil war screens commercial and art-house movies side by side in the Bosnian capital. (p74)

☆ Nišville International Jazz Festival, Serbia

The sprawling Niš Fortress hosts this jazz festival (www.nisville.com) each August with acts from around the world on the program.

September

The summer crowds have dropped off somewhat and prices are no longer sky high, but great weather remains across the entire region, making September a fantastic time to head for Eastern Europe.

Cow's Ball, Slovenia

This Slovenian mid-September weekend of folk dancing, music, eating and drinking in Bohinj marks the return of the cows from their high pastures to the valleys in typically ebullient Balkan style.

Dvořák Autumn, Czech Republic

This classical music festival honours the work of the Czech Republic's favourite composer, Antonín Dvořák. The event is held over three weeks in the spa town of Karlovy Vary.

Lviv Coffee Festival, Ukraine

It's no surprise that Eastern Europe's first coffee festival (www.coffeefest.lviv.ua) takes place in charming Lviv, where the central European coffee culture is really thriving. Come and taste coffees from all over the world as the city goes even more caffeine mad than usual.

October

October is still wonderfully warm in the south of the region but already getting cold in the north. Prices remain low and crowds lessen with each passing day, making it a good time to visit.

National Wine Day, Moldova

Winemakers, wine tasting, wine buying and wine-enriched folkloric performances (www.moldovawineday.md) in and around Chişinău draw oenophiles and anyone that wants to take advantage of the 10-day visa-free arrangement Moldova introduces during the festival dates.

Tirana International Film Festival, Albania

From the last week of October to the first week of November Tirana, holds a short- and feature-film festival (www.tiranafilmfest.com), the only one of its kind in tiny Albania. It's a great way to take stock of Eastern European film-making.

November

The days are short and the weather is cold, but you'll have most of Eastern Europe's attractions all to yourself and accommodation is cheap. If you want any chance of sunshine, you'll need to head south to the Balkans.

Sarajevo International Jazz Festival, Bosnia & Hercegovina

Held in Sarajevo in early November, this festival (http://jazzfest.ba) showcases local and international jazz musicians.

Martinje in Zagreb, Croatia

The Feast of St Martin is an annual wine festival held in Zagreb to celebrate the end of the grape harvest as Croatian wineries begin the crushing process. Expect lots of wine, good food and a generally upbeat mood.

December

December is a magical time to visit Eastern Europe: Christmas decorations brighten up the dark streets and, despite the cold across much of the region, as long as you avoid Christmas and New Year's Eve, prices remain surprisingly low.

Christmas Markets

Throughout December Eastern Europe heaves with German-style Christmas markets. You'll find these in many cities in the region, though we recommend Bratislava's for its Slovakian charm and beautiful setting.

Christmas

Most countries celebrate on Christmas Eve (24 December) with an evening meal and midnight Mass. However, in Russia, Ukraine and Belarus, Christmas falls in January.

New Year's Eve

Even back when communist officials frowned on Christmas, New Year's Eve remained a big holiday in Eastern Europe. Join the party wherever you are and see in the new year with locals.

Itineraries

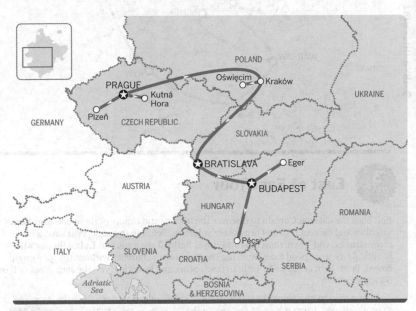

2 WEEKS Essential Eastern Europe

Combine highlights of the Czech Republic, Poland, Slovakia and Hungary for a quintessential introduction to the charms of Eastern Europe. Start in **Prague**, spending several days absorbing the Staré Město (Old Town), Malá Strana (Lesser Quarter) and the magnificent Prague Castle. Don't miss nearby towns such as beer-lovers' mecca **Plzeň** and beautiful **Kutná Hora**.

On day five head by train into Poland and regal **Kraków**, with its gob-smacking Old Town and the vast Rynek Główny (Main Sq). Spending three nights here allows you to get to know the Wawel Castle complex, offbeat Kazimierz and take a day trip to **Oświęcim** (Auschwitz).

On day eight head south to Slovakia, where you'll pass through magnificent scenery in the High Tatras before arriving in **Bratislava**, with its grand castle and wonderful Danube views.

On day 10 take a boat down the Danube to **Budapest**, where you can spend hours in luxurious sulphur baths, explore the famous coffee houses and take in the dazzling art and architecture of the forward-looking Hungarian capital. From here visit the Hungarian countryside – try the baroque city of **Eger**, or **Pécs**, full of relics from the Turkish occupation.

East of East Tour

Pull back the old Iron Curtain to discover the history and beauty of these one-time Soviet satellites and current regional heavyweight Russia. Begin in dynamic **Warsaw**, with its reconstructed Old Town, museums and Royal Parks. Take a train to **Lviv**, Ukraine's most beautiful city, and spend a day enjoying the Old Town's churches without the tour-group crowd. From Lviv, continue by train to fascinating and historic **Kyiv**, the Jerusalem of East Slavonic culture.

After a few days enjoying the sights in the Ukrainian capital, including the awesome Kyevo-Pecherska Lavra (Caves Monastery), take the sleeper train to the megalopolis **Moscow**, Europe's biggest city and a place of striking extremes, dazzling wealth and gridlocked traffic. Drink in the history of the Kremlin, see Lenin's Mausoleum, St Basil's Cathedral and Red Square, and sample the nightlife and fashion for which the city is now rightly famous. On day 10 get out of Moscow and visit picturesque **Veliky Novgorod** en route to the beautiful baroque and neoclassical architecture of mind-blowing **St Petersburg**. You can easily spend three or four days in the city itself, although there are abundant sights outside it as well, such as the tsarist palaces of Petrodvorets or Tsarskoe Selo.

From Russia take the train to Estonia's magical capital, **Tallinn**, where you can soak up the medieval Old Town. Relax on the golden-sand beaches of **Pärnu** before heading south to the Latvian capital **Rīga**, which boasts Europe's finest collection of art nouveau architecture and is a delightful place to spend a few days. Latvia has plenty of other highlights to offer though, such as the caves and medieval castles of **Sigulda** and the breathtaking Baltic coastline around **Ventspils**. Cross into Lithuania, where a couple of nights in charming **Vilnius** will reveal the Baltic's most underrated capital as well as Europe's largest collection of baroque architecture. From Vilnius make a trip to the huge sand dunes and fragile ecological environment of the amazing **Curonian Spit**. If you've arranged a double-entry visa for Russia, you can cross over into the exclave of **Kaliningrad** here. Alternatively, if you've sorted a Belarus visa, take the train to this isolated republic with its Stalinist-style, but surprisingly pleasant capital **Minsk** before re-entering Poland and heading back to Warsaw.

Breezing Through the Balkans

Taking its name from the Balkan Mountains, this is a fascinating, beautiful region of Eastern Europe lapped by several different seas and including spectacular countryside and awesome towns and cities. Begin in lively little Slovenia, where the charming capital **Ljubljana** is a pedestrian delight with a castle, beautiful buildings and bridges, and top-class museums to view. Indulge in superb scenery and adrenaline-rush mountain sports in the **Julian Alps** before heading south to the Croatian coast and working your way through the beaches along the **Dalmatian coast**. Stop in **Dubrovnik** to explore the Old Town, its vast ramparts and the surrounding islands, which shouldn't be missed.

Detour into Bosnia – perhaps a day trip to **Mostar** to see the legendary bridge and the interesting multiethnic community that has enjoyed rejuvenation since the Balkan War, or a night or two in the bustling capital of **Sarajevo**. Continue south into Montenegro, to visit the historic walled city of **Kotor**, see the wonderful coastline, and enjoy some of the country's beautiful beaches around the walled island village of **Sveti Stefan** before heading into Albania. From the northern city of **Shkodra** take a bus straight on to **Tirana**, a mountain-shrouded ramshackle capital on the rise. Make an excursion to the gorgeous Unesco-listed heritage town of **Berat** before taking a bus through the mountains into little-explored Macedonia, ending up in beautiful **Ohrid**. Spend at least two days here, enjoying the wonderful monastery and swimming in the eponymous lake.

Make your way to **Skopje**, Macedonia's fun capital where an abundance of newly minted structures are redefining the city for the 21st century. Take the train to **Pristina**, Kosovo's optimistic capital, from where it's an easy hop to **Prizen**, a charming mosque-filled old town. To reach Serbia's audacious and gritty capital **Belgrade**, you'll need to backtrack to Skopje and board the international train. Don't miss the city's ancient Kalemegdan Citadel and wild clubbing scene. Another cross border train will take you on into Bulgaria where the capital **Sofia** is a little-known gem. Continue east to **Veliko Târnovo**, the awesome ancient capital and a university town with a dramatic setting over a fast-flowing river. From here it's an easy bus to the beach at **Varna**, complete with marvellous museums, Roman ruins and open-air nightclubs.

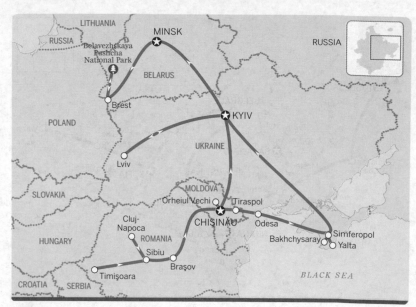

4 WEEKS · On the Edge

Covering the eastern edge of the region up to the border with Russia, this itinerary balances the charm of old towns and thrill of Gothic castles with the quirky, time-stood-still qualities of oddballs Transdniestr and Belarus. Start in **Timişoara** or **Cluj-Napoca** in Romania before getting medieval in **Sibiu** and/or **Braşov** from where you can make a day trip to 'Dracula's Castle', properly known as Bran Castle. Cross into Moldova where the real adventure starts. Get into the groove in the entertaining capital, **Chişinău**, where partying is a way of life and the excellent local wine is plentiful and cheap, including that from the must-visit vineyards of Cricova. Make a day trip to the stunning cave monastery at **Orheiul Vechi**. Travel into Transdniestr, a country that doesn't officially exist. In the fascinating 'capital' **Tiraspol** little appears to have changed since the Soviet era of the mid-80s.

Entering Ukraine, make a beeline for **Kyiv**, which demands several days' attention. This eclectic capital city is the ancient seat of Slavic and Orthodox culture as well as a modern and pleasant metropolis that played a starring role in the 2014 Maidan Revolution, which toppled the last of the post-Soviet dictators. Don't miss the Kyevo-Pecherska Lavra (Caves Monastery) and St Sophia's Cathedral, as well as ousted ex-president Viktor Yanukovych's opulent mansion Mezhyhirya. For a complete contrast, detour to the western edge of the country where Unesco World Heritage–listed **Lviv** is a charming central European town of quaint cobbles, aromatic coffee houses and rattling trams, which feels a continent away from the war-torn badlands of Ukraine's east.

The final stops on this tour through the most remote parts of the region take you to Belarus, Europe's so-called 'last dictatorship'. Have a blast in monolithic **Minsk** and find a surprising amount going on in a city dominated by huge Stalinist avenues and Soviet memorials. Heading southwest, stop at **Brest** on the border and use it as a base to visit **Belavezhskaya Pushcha National Park**, where you'll be able to see the *zoobr* (European bison), Europe's largest mammal, as well as a host of other wild beauties before crossing back into the EU.

Top: Lviv (p418), Ukraine

Bottom: Minsk (p59), Belarus

4 WEEKS The Ionian to the Baltic

This Ionian to Baltic Sea itinerary, covering eight countries, will enlighten you to a vast variety of things to do and see in the region. Arrive in mountainous Albania by ferry from Corfu at the busy port of **Saranda**, then stay the night and try to see the glorious ruins of **Butrint** right on the Greek border. Continue up through Albania to **Tirana** via either **Gjirokastra** or **Berat** – two of Albania's loveliest old towns. Spend a day or two exploring the Albanian capital before taking the bus to **Shkodra** and journeying on to Montenegro.

Base yourself in lovely **Kotor**, soaking up its spectacular setting and Old Town. Make day trips to Venice lookalike **Perast** and **Budva** with its atmospheric Old Town and lively beach scene. Head north to the extraordinary cliff-face-hugging **Ostrog Monastery**, and on to **Durmitor National Park**, a great place for hiking, rafting and canyoning.

From Montenegro's capital **Podgorica** catch an overnight train to the vibrant Serbian capital **Belgrade** that's definitely worth a couple of days, then continue north to con-vivial **Novi Sad**. Cross into Hungary at pretty **Szeged** and head for **Lake Balaton** for some sublime swimming. Keep surging north into Slovakia, aiming for plucky traveller favourite **Bratislava**, where it's perfectly acceptable to kick back and enjoy the good food and nightlife for a few days before going on to the incredible scenery of **Slovenský Raj National Park**. Crossing the Tatra Mountains into Poland, travel via **Kraków** to unsung gem **Wrocław**, spending a few days in both before dropping in on beautifully restored **Poznań**. From here, head for the Baltic coast and the bustling Hanseatic city of **Gdańsk** (formerly the German Free City of Danzig), a thriving port city where WWII broke out and the Solidarity social movement was born. From here you can make day trips to nearby beaches as well as **Malbork**, famed for Europe's biggest Gothic castle.

Next up is the intriguing Russian exclave of **Kaliningrad** (remember to sort your visa ahead of your arrival), which combines elements of old Prussia, the USSR and modern Russia. Return to the coast to travel though Kaliningrad's **Kurshskaya Kosa National Park** across into the Lithuanian section of the Curonian Spit, aiming for **Klaipėda**, Lithuania's main port. End your trip in baroque **Vilnius**, Lithuania's beautiful capital.

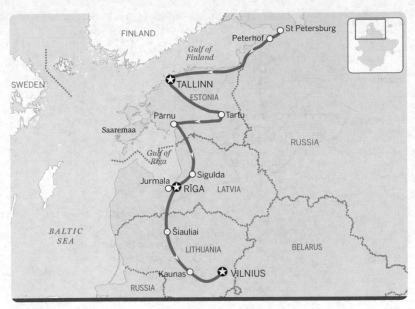

Baltic Blast

2 WEEKS

This trip along the Baltic coast takes you through four very different countries and across a region that few travellers ever get to know beyond the universally loved capital cities of Tallinn, Rīga and Vilnius. In Russia, set aside three nights for the gloriously beautiful Baltic city of **St Petersburg** to see the Hermitage, vast Nevsky Prospekt's mansions and the amazing Church on the Spilled Blood. Head to the superbly restored out-of-town **Peterhof**, which belonged to Peter the Great and is positioned with glorious views over the Baltic.

Take a bus or train to the Estonian capital **Tallinn** for two days and wander the charmingly chocolate-box streets of the 14th- and 15th-century Old Town before heading to the university town of **Tartu**, which lays claim to being the nation's cultural capital and is packed with interesting museums. On the Baltic coast is the inviting Estonian beach resort of **Pärnu** where you can indulge in Eastern European holidaymaking (think mud baths, Bacchanalian youth and golden-sand beaches) before continuing south into Latvia.

Stop off in cheerful, castle-rich **Sigulda** and spend a day or two walking in the tranquil landscapes and thick forests of the Gauja National Park. Continue on to **Rīga**, Latvia's delightful capital, where you can soak up the fantastic architecture, the Old Town and friendly atmosphere over several days. Consider a day trip to the opulent Rundāle Palace. If you'd prefer a day or two's rest, there's the lovely beaches and gracious wooden houses of **Jūrmala**.

Lithuania is next up – and it greets you straight away with its astounding Hill of Crosses in **Šiauliai**, a must-see even if there's no reason to dawdle. Charming university town **Kaunas** is Lithuania's second city and boasts a leafy old centre and friendly locals, as well as being just a short distance away from the chilling Ninth Fort concentration camp. Finally, end your journey in beautiful **Vilnius**, the country's crowning glory, which boasts the biggest Old Town in the Baltic and is still relatively undiscovered by tour groups.

Eastern Europe 101

Time-challenged travellers need not fret – this zippy itinerary gives you the best of five Eastern European gems. Start off by flying to the Polish capital **Warsaw** for one night, seeing the beautifully restored Old Town and eating delicious *pierogi* (dumplings) before taking the train south to **Kraków** for two nights, giving you time to see the Old Town, Wawel Castle and Kazimierz, and to do a day trip to **Oświęcim** (Auschwitz) before taking the overnight train to **Prague** for two days of intensive sightseeing: Prague Castle, Charles Bridge, wandering the Malá Strana (Lesser Quarter) and the Staré Město (Old Town) and tasting genuine Czech beer in a local brewery.

Take another overnight train to **Budapest** for two nights in Hungary. Soak in the city's glorious Gellért Baths, take a cruise on the Danube, see the magnificent Hungarian Parliament building and wander Castle Hill before yet another overnight train to Romania's much underrated capital, **Bucharest**. With a one-night stay you can cover the main sights (including the amazing Palace of Parliament), wander the small historic centre and pick up a sense of the city's energy in its bars and clubs.

Continue by train to wonderful and much-overlooked **Veliko Târnovo** in Northern Bulgaria for one night; it's a stunning and unusually located university town and a far more 'everyday' Eastern European town than most national capitals. While here, find the time to see the ancient Tsarevets Fortress (and stick around for the nightly summer light show). Finish up your two weeks by taking the train to **Sofia** for two final nights that will give you a taste of the plucky Bulgarian capital, including the wonderful golden-domed Aleksander Nevski Church and the subterranean museum housing an ancient necropolis beneath the Sveta Sofia Church.

On your last day take a day trip through the Rila Mountains to the unmissable **Rila Monastery**, the country's holiest site and one of the most important monasteries in Eastern Europe. From here you can fly out of Sofia or continue to bigger air hubs such as nearby Athens or İstanbul to get a flight home.

On the Road

Albania

Best Places to Eat

➜ Kujtimi (p54)
➜ Da Pucci (p47)
➜ Tradita G&T (p49)
➜ Pastarella (p47)
➜ Mare Nostrum (p53)

Best Places to Stay

➜ Tradita G&T (p49)
➜ Hotel Rilindja (p50)
➜ Trip N Hostel (p47)
➜ Gjirokastra Hotel (p54)
➜ Hotel Mangalemi (p51)

Why Go?

Albania has natural beauty in such abundance that you might wonder why it's taken a full 20 years for the country to take off as a tourist destination after the end of a particularly brutal strain of communism in 1991. So backward was Albania when it emerged blinking into the bright light of freedom that it needed two decades just to catch up with the rest of Eastern Europe. Now that it arguably has done so, Albania offers a remarkable array of unique attractions, not least due to this very isolation: ancient mountain behaviour codes, forgotten archaeological sites and villages where time seems to have stood still are all on the menu.

With its stunning mountain scenery, a thriving capital in Tirana and beaches to rival anywhere else in the Mediterranean, Albania has become the sleeper hit of the Balkans. But hurry here, as word is well and truly out.

When to Go
Tirana

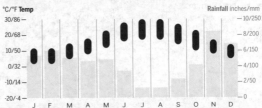

Jun Enjoy the perfect Mediterranean climate and deserted beaches.

Aug Albania's beaches may be packed, but this is a great time to explore the mountains.

Dec See features and shorts at the Tirana Film Festival, while the intrepid can snowshoe to Theth.

Albania Highlights

1 Catch the **Lake Koman Ferry** (p50) through stunning mountain scenery, then continue to **Valbona** (p50) and trek through the 'Accursed Mountains' to **Theth** (p50).

2 Explore the Unesco World Heritage–listed museum town of **Berat** (p50), the so-called 'city of a thousand windows'.

3 Catch some sun at **Drymades**, (p52), just one of the many beaches on the south's dramatic Ionian Coast.

4 Travel back in time to the ruins of **Butrint** (p53), hidden in the depths of a forest in a serene lakeside setting.

5 Feast your eyes on the wild colour schemes and experience Blloku cafe culture in **Tirana** (p45).

6 Take a trip to the traditional Southern Albanian mountain town of **Gjirokastra** (p54), with is spectacular Ottoman-era mansions and impressive hilltop fortress.

ITINERARIES

One Week

Spend a day in busy **Tirana**, checking out the various museums as well as the Blloku bars and nightclubs. On day two, make the three-hour trip to the Ottoman-era town of **Berat**. Spend a night there, before continuing down the coast for a couple of days on the beach in **Drymades**. Loop around for one last night in charming **Gjirokastra** before returning to Tirana.

Two Weeks

Follow the first week itinerary and then head north into Albania's incredible 'Accursed Mountains'. Start in **Shkodra**, from where you can get transport to **Koman** for the stunning morning ferry ride to **Fierzë**. Continue the same day to the charming mountain village of **Valbona** for a couple of nights, before trekking to **Theth** and spending your last couple of nights in the beautiful **Theth National Park**.

TIRANA

☑ 04 / POP 802,000

Lively, colourful Tirana is the beating heart of Albania, where this tiny nation's hopes and dreams coalesce into a vibrant whirl of traffic, brash consumerism and unfettered fun. Having undergone a transformation of extraordinary proportions since it awoke from its communist slumber in the early 1990s, Tirana's centre is now unrecognisable, with its buildings painted in primary colours, and public squares and pedestrianised streets a pleasure to wander.

Trendy Blloku buzzes with the well-heeled and flush hanging out in bars or zipping between boutiques, while the city's grand boulevards are lined with fascinating relics of its Ottoman, Italian and communist past – from delicate minarets to loud socialist murals. Tirana's traffic does daily battle with both itself and pedestrians in a constant scene of unmitigated chaos. Loud, crazy, colourful and dusty – Tirana is never dull.

◉ Sights & Activities

Sheshi Skënderbej   SQUARE

(Skanderbeg Sq) Skanderbeg Sq is the best place to start witnessing Tirana's daily goings-on. Until it was pulled down by an angry mob in 1991, a 10m-high bronze statue of Enver Hoxha stood here, watching over a mainly car-free square. Now only the **equestrian statue of Skanderbeg** remains.

★ National History Museum   MUSEUM

(Muzeu Historik Kombëtar; Sheshi Skënderbej; adult/ student 200/60 lekë; ⊙10am-5pm Tue-Sat, 9am-2pm Sun) The largest museum in Albania holds many of the country's archaeological treasures and a replica of Skanderbeg's massive sword (how he held it, rode his horse and fought at the same time is a mystery). The excellent collection is almost entirely signed in English and takes you chronologically from ancient Illyria to the postcommunist era. One big highlight of the museum is a terrific exhibition of icons by Onufri, a renowned 16th-century Albanian master of colour.

★ National Art Gallery   GALLERY

(Galeria Kombëtare e Arteve; www.gka.al; Blvd Dëshmorët e Kombit; adult/student 200/100 lekë; ⊙10am-6pm Wed-Sun) Tracing the relatively brief history of Albanian painting from the early 19th century to the present day, this beautiful space also has temporary exhibits that are worth a look. Downstairs there's a small but interesting collection of 19th-century paintings depicting scenes from daily Albanian life, while upstairs the art takes on a political dimension with some truly fabulous examples of Albanian socialist realism.

Et'hem Bey Mosque   MOSQUE

(Sheshi Skënderbej; ⊙8am-11am) To one side of Skanderbeg Sq, the 1789–1823 Et'hem Bey Mosque was spared destruction during the atheism campaign of the late 1960s because of its status as a cultural monument. Small and elegant, it's one of the oldest buildings left in the city. Take your shoes off to look inside at the beautifully painted dome.

Palace of Culture   NOTABLE BUILDING

(Pallate Kulturës; Sheshi Skënderbej) To the east of Sheshi Skënderbej is the white stone Palace of Culture, which has a theatre, shops and art galleries. Construction of the palace began as a gift from the Soviet people in 1960 and was completed in 1966, years after the 1961 Soviet–Albanian split.

Tirana

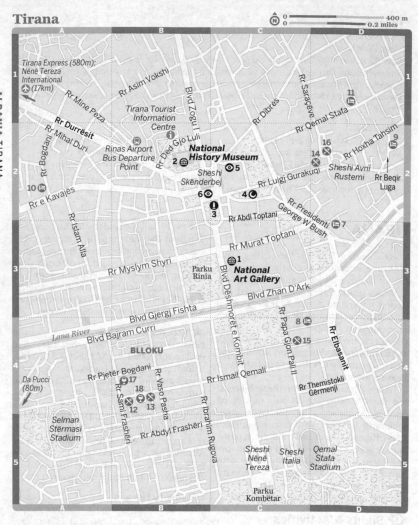

0 400 m
0 0.2 miles

ALBANIA TIRANA

Tirana

🛏 Sleeping

⭐ Trip N Hostel
HOSTEL €

(📞 068 2055 540, 068 3048 905; www.tripn hostel.com; Rr Musa Maci 1; dm/d €10/30) Tirana's coolest hostel is this recently opened place, housed in a large design-conscious house in a residential neighbourhood, with a garden out the back and a cool bar-hangout area. Dorms have handmade fixtures, curtains between beds for privacy and private lockable drawers, while there's also a roof terrace strewn with hammocks. There's a great vibe and a cool crowd as well.

⭐ Tirana Backpacker Hostel
HOSTEL €

(📞 068 4682 353, 068 3133 451; www.tiranahostel. com; Rr e Bogdaneve 3; dm €10-11, s/d €28/35, cabin per person €14; ✴@📶) Albania's first ever hostel has now moved to an ever better location and remains one of the best value and most enthusiastically run places to stay in the country. Housed in a charmingly decorated house with a garden in which there are several cute cabins for those wanting something more than a dorm room, though there are also great private rooms available.

Hostel Albania
HOSTEL €

(📞 067 6748 779; www.hostel-albania.com; Rr Beqir Luga 56; dm €10-12 d €32; @📶) Voted the best hostel in Albania in 2014, this friendly place has small four- and six-person dorms, though the basement's 14-bed dorm (€11.50) is the coolest spot in summer and dividers hide the fact that there are so many bunks down there. Zen space is in the outdoor shoes-off oriental lounge, and a filling breakfast with filter coffee is included.

⭐ Brilant Antik Hotel
HOTEL €€

(📞 04 2251 166; www.hotelbrilant.com; Rr Jeronim de Rada 79; s/d €60/90; ✴📶) This charming house-cum-hotel has plenty of character, a central location and welcoming English-speaking staff to ease you into Tirana life. Rooms are spacious, decently furnished with the odd antique, and breakfast downstairs is a veritable feast each morning.

Green House
BOUTIQUE HOTEL €€€

(📞 04 4521 015, 068 2072 262; www.greenhouse. al; Rr Jul Variboba 6; s/d €90/100; ✴📶) In a cool spot in Tirana sits this modern 10-room hotel with downlit, stylish rooms that might be the city's coolest. Its sprawling downstairs terrace restaurant is a friendly expat hangout with a varied menu and a long wine list. It looks up at one of Tirana's quirkiest buildings.

🍴 Eating

Era
ALBANIAN, ITALIAN €€

(📞 04 224 3845; www.era.al; Rr Ismail Qemali; mains 400-800 lekë; ⏱ 11am-midnight; 🍴) This local institution serves traditional Albanian and Italian fare in the heart of Blloku. The inventive menu includes oven-baked veal and eggs, stuffed eggplant, pizza, and pilau with chicken and pine nuts. Be warned: it's sometimes quite hard to get a seat as it's fearsomely popular, so you may have to wait. Delivery and takeaway are both available.

Oda
ALBANIAN €€

(Rr Luigj Gurakuqi; mains 350-650 lekë; ⏱ noon-11pm; 🍴) This tourist favourite is stuffed full of traditional Albanian arts and crafts, and while its popularity with travellers means you won't feel like you've discovered a truly authentic slice of the country, the delicious menu and pleasant atmosphere make it well worth a visit. You can choose from two brightly lit dining rooms or an atmospheric terrace.

⭐ Da Pucci
ITALIAN €€€

(📞 069 3434 999; Rr Mustafa Qosja; mains 500-800 lekë; ⏱ noon-midnight; 📶🍴) A surprise find in a rather out-of-the-way residential district (a short wander beyond the busy streets of Blloku) is this cosily decked out, need-to-know-about-it subterranean space that feels rather like somebody's living room. The menu, which changes daily, is brought to you on a chalkboard and waiters just about manage a basic English translation. The classic Italian home cooking is divine though. Reservations are a good idea for the evenings.

Stephen Centre
CAFE €€

(Rr Hoxha Tahsim 1; mains 400-700 lekë; ⏱ 8am-8pm Mon-Sat; 📶) Looking better than ever after a 2014 refit, this Tirana classic is where to come for a great burger, fantastic Tex-Mex and enormous, great value breakfasts. Run by Christian missionaries to Albania who work with local orphans, Roma and the disabled, the Centre has no booze on the menu, but is a super friendly and relaxed hang out.

⭐ Pastarella
ITALIAN €€€

(www.pastarellarestaurant.com; Rr Mustafa Matohiti 18; mains 500-1200 lekë; ⏱ 8am-midnight; 📶🍴) The seafood is fresh here, and forms the centre of the menu, but there's also a large range of pastas (as you'd expect), risotti and grilled meats on offer, and all are superb. There's a charming terrace to dine on, or a

ALBANIA TIRANA

rather more formal inside dining room. Staff are polite and English speaking.

Hola! SPANISH €€€
(Rr Ismail Qemali; mains 600-1300 lekë; ☺11am-11pm; 🛜) The Spanish owner here was a finalist on *Masterchef Albania* who went on to found one of Tirana's most popular restaurant as a hobby, and, as the name suggests, he'll greet you at the door on most evenings. The menu here is wonderfully creative Spanish fare, ranging from delicious tapas to a splash-out paella.

🍷 Drinking

Radio BAR
(Rr Ismail Qemali 29/1; ☺9am-1am; 🛜) This place remains one of the city's coolest bars and attracts a young and alternative crowd. Set back from the street, you have to know it's here, but once inside this understated and friendly place be sure to check out the owner's collection of antique Albanian-made radios.

Nouvelle Vague BAR
(Rr Pjetër Bogdani; ☺9am-midnight; 🛜) A Blloku hotspot favoured by a cool crowd, Nouvelle Vague is one of the places to head any night of the week for a great atmosphere, full cocktail list and interesting music.

☆ Entertainment

★Tirana Express GALLERY, CONCERT VENUE
(www.tiranaekspres.com; Rr Dritan Hoxha) This fantastic nonprofit arts project is a unique arts space that hosts revolving temporary exhibits, concerts, installations and other events that appeal to Tirana's arty, alternative crowd. Go along and see what's on during your visit. Opening hours vary depending on what's on.

ℹ️ Information

Tirana Tourist Information Centre (📞04 2223 313; www.tirana.gov.al; Rr Ded Gjo Luli; ☺9am-6pm Mon-Fri, to 2pm Sat) Friendly English-speaking staff make getting information easy at this government-run initiative just off Skanderbeg Sq.

ℹ️ Getting There & Around

AIR
The modern **Nënë Tereza International Airport** (Mother Teresa Airport; 📞04 2381 800; www.tirana-airport.com) is at Rinas, 17km northwest of Tirana. The Rinas Express airport bus operates an hourly (8am to 7pm) service from Rr Mine Peza a few blocks from the National History Museum

for 250 lekë one way. The going taxi rate is 2000 to 2500 lekë.

BUS
Most international services depart from various parts of Blvd Zogu I, with multiple services to Skopje, Macedonia (€20, eight hours) and Pristina, Kosovo (€20, five hours) leaving from near the Tirana International Hotel, and services to Ulcinj in Montenegro (€20, four hours) leaving from in front of the Tourist Information Centre.

Services to Shkodra (300 lekë, two hours, hourly until 5pm) leave from the Zogu i Zi Roundabout at the intersection of Rr Durrësit and Rr Muhamet Gjollesha. *Furgons* (shared minibuses) to Bajram Curri (1000 lekë, 5½ hours, hourly 5am-2pm), the jumping off point for Valbona on the far side of Lake Koman, leave from here too – you'll find them outside the Logos University building.

Departures to the south leave from Rr Myhedin Llegami near the corner with Blvd Gjergj Fishta. These include services to Berat (400 lekë, three hours, every 30 min until 6pm), Saranda (1300 lekë, 6½ hours, roughly hourly 5am-midday) and Gjirokastra (1000 lekë, 6 hours, regular departures until midday, also at 2.30pm & 6.30pm). Services to Saranda will drop you off at any of the coastal villages along the way.

TAXI
Taxi stands dot the city, and taxis charge 300 to 400 lekë for a ride inside Tirana, and 500 to 600 lekë at night and to destinations outside the city centre.

NORTHERN ALBANIA

Northern Albania is a scenic wonderland where the incredible landscape of the 'Accursed Mountains' dominates and the rich and independent mountain culture strongly flavours all journeys.

Shkodra
📞022 / POP 111,000
Shkodra, the traditional centre of the Gheg cultural region, is one of the oldest cities in Europe. The ancient Rozafa Fortress has stunning views over the nearby lake, while a concerted effort to renovate the buildings in the Old Town has made wandering through Shkodra a treat for the eyes.

👁 Sights

Rozafa Fortress CASTLE
(admission 200 lekë; ☺10am-8pm) With spectacular views over the city and Lake Shkodra, the Rozafa Fortress is the most interesting

sight in the town. Founded by the Illyrians in antiquity and rebuilt much later by the Venetians and then the Turks, the fortress takes its name from a woman named Rozafa, who was allegedly walled into the ramparts as an offering to the gods so that the construction would stand.

Marubi Permanent
Photo Exhibition
GALLERY

(Rr Muhamet Gjollesha; admission 100 lekë; ⊙8am-4pm Mon-Fri) The Marubi Permanent Photo Exhibition has fantastic photography by the Marubi 'dynasty', Albania's first and foremost photographers. It's poorly signposted: look for the sign Galeria e Arteve Shkodër, and once in the courtyard go through a further small gate and look for the sign in Albanian with the word Marubi in it.

🛏 Sleeping & Eating

Mi Casa Es Tu Casa
HOSTEL €

(☎069 3812 054; www.micasaestucasa.it; Blvd Skenderbeu; dm/d/apt €12/30/40; @🖤) Shkodra's best established hostel is run by the helpful, English-speaking Alba, and has a great location in the centre of town, opposite the Millenium Cinema. There's a proper hostel vibe with lots of space, bright colour schemes and a garden where you can also pitch a tent. Bike hire is available for €5 and the dorms are bright and clean.

★Tradita G&T
BOUTIQUE HOTEL €€

(☎068 2086 056, 022-240 537; www.traditagt. com; Rr Edith Durham 4; s/d/tr €35/50/55; P🖤) By far the best choice in town, this innovative, well-managed guesthouse is a delight. Housed in a painstakingly restored 17th-century mansion that once belonged to a famous Shkodran writer, the Tradita heaves with Albanian arts and crafts and has traditional yet very comfortable rooms

with terracotta-roofed bathrooms and locally woven bed linen.

ℹ Information

The **Tourist Information Centre** (☎022 240 242; Sheshi Nënë Tereza; ⊙9am-4pm Mon-Fri 10am-noon Sat & Sun) at the intersection of Bul Skënderbeg and Rr Kolë Idromeno is run as a public-private partnership and has helpful, English-speaking staff on hand to answer your questions.

ℹ Getting There & Away

BUS

There are hourly furgons (400 lekë) and buses (300 lekë) to Tirana (two hours, 6am to 5pm), which depart from outside Radio Shkodra near Hotel Rozafa. There are three daily buses to Ulcinj in Montenegro that leave at 9am, 2.15pm and 4pm (€5, two hours) from outside the Tourist Information Centre. Catch the 6.30am bus to Lake Koman (500 lekë, two hours) in time for the wonderful ferry trip along the lake to Fierzë near Kosovo; most hotels can call ahead and get the furgon to pick you up on its way out of town. Several furgons depart daily for Theth between 6am and 7am (700 lekë, four hours) from outside Cafe Rusi.

TAXI

It costs between €40 and €50 for the trip from Shkodra to Ulcinj in Montenegro, depending on your haggling skills.

The Accursed Mountains

The 'Accursed Mountains' (Bjeshkët e Namuna) offer some of Albania's most impressive scenery and have exploded in recent years as a popular backpacker destination. The reason that most people come here is to do the popular hike between Valbona and Theth, which takes roughly five to six hours.

BUNKER LOVE

On the hillsides, beaches and generally most surfaces in Albania, you will notice small concrete domes (often in groups of three) with rectangular slits. Meet the bunkers: Enver Hoxha's concrete legacy, built from 1950 to 1985. Weighing in at 5 tonnes of concrete and iron, these little mushrooms are almost impossible to destroy. They were built to repel an invasion and can resist full tank assault – a fact proved by their chief engineer, who vouched for his creation's strength by standing inside one while it was bombarded by a tank. The shell-shocked engineer emerged unscathed, and tens of thousands were built. Today, some are creatively painted, one houses a tattoo artist, and some even house makeshift hostels.

In late 2014, a private bunker built for Hoxha himself was opened for the first time just outside Tirana. Built 100m below ground and designed to withstand a nuclear attack, the bunker is to open in 2015 as a museum and exhibition space.

THE LAKE KOMAN FERRY

One of Albania's undisputed highlights is this superb three-hour ferry ride across vast Lake Koman, connecting the towns of Koman and Fierzë.

The best way to experience the journey is to make a three-day, two-night loop beginning and ending in Shkodra, and taking in Koman, Fierzë, Valbona and Theth. To do this, arrange to have the morning 6.30am *furgon* (shared minibus) from Shkodra to Koman (500 lekë, two hours) pick you up at your hotel, which will get you to the departure point for the boats by 8.30am. There are two ferries daily in the summer months – both leave from Koman at 9am and arrive in Fierzë around 1pm.

On arrival in Fierzë the boats are met by *furgons* that will take you to either Bajram Curri (200 lekë) or to Valboa (400 lekë). There's no real reason to stay in Bajram Curri though, unless you plan to head to Kosovo. Hikers will want to head straight for Valbona, where you can stay for a night or two before doing the stunning day hike to Theth. After the hike you can stay for another night or two in Theth before taking a *furgon* back to Shkodra.

Valbona

Most travellers just spend a night here before trekking to Theth, though there are a wealth of other excellent hikes to do in the area – ask for guides or information at Hotel Rilindja, or check out the excellent www.journeytovalbona.com website, a DIY-kit for the entire area.

🛏 Sleeping & Eating

★ **Hotel Rilindja**   GUESTHOUSE €€
(☎ 067 3014 637; www.journeytovalbona.com; Quku i Valbonës; per tent €6, dm per person €12, r s/d/t €30/40/50) Pioneering tourism in Valbona since 2005, the Albanian-American run Rilindja is hugely popular with travellers who love the comfortable accommodation and excellent food. The simple five rooms in the atmospheric farmhouse share a bathroom, except for one that has private facilities. The new Rezidenca up the road offers a far more upscale experience with ensuite singles, double and triples.

❶ Getting There & Away

Valbona can be reached from Shkodra via the Lake Koman Ferry, and a connecting *furgon* from Fierzë (400 lekë, 1 hour). Alterrnatively it can be reached by *furgon* from Bajram Curri (200 lekë, 45 minutes).

Theth

This unique mountain village has traditional houses, an imposing church and a riverside setting dominated by a rare surviving example of a lock-in tower, where in the past locals under a blood feud could retreat to safety.

🛏 Sleeping & Eating

★ **Guesthouse Rupa**   GUESTHOUSE €€
(☎ 068 2003 393, 022-244 077; rorupaog@yahoo.com; r per person full board €23) This wonderful option is run by the formidable Roza, who speaks good English and is a great source of information about the area. There are only five rooms, but rarely for Theth, all have private facilities. The excellent meals are taken communally around a big table, so there's a very sociable vibe.

❶ Getting There & Around

The daily *furgon* (1000 lekë) leaves from Shkodra at 7am and will pick you up from your hotel if your hotel owner calls ahead for you. It returns between 1 and 2pm, arriving late afternoon in Shkodra.

CENTRAL ALBANIA

Berat

☑ 032 / POP 71,000

Berat weaves its own very special magic, and is easily a highlight of visiting Albania. Its most striking feature is the collection of white Ottoman houses climbing up the hill to its castle, earning it the title of 'town of a thousand windows' and helping it join Gjirokastra on the list of Unesco World Heritage sites in 2008. Its rugged mountain setting is particularly evocative when the clouds swirl around the tops of the minarets, or break up to show the icy top of Mt Tomorri. Berat today is now a big centre for tourism in Albania, though it has managed to retain its easy-going charm and friendly atmosphere. Don't miss it.

⊙ Sights

★ Kalaja
CASTLE

(admission 100 lekë; ⊘ 24hr) The neighbourhood inside the castle's walls still lives and breathes; if you walk around this busy, ancient neighbourhood for long enough you'll invariably stumble into someone's courtyard thinking it's a church or ruin (no one seems to mind, though). In spring and summer the fragrance of camomile is in the air (and underfoot), and wildflowers burst from every gap between the stones.

★ Onufri Museum
GALLERY

(admission 200 lekë; ⊘ 9am-1pm & 4-7pm Tue-Sat, to 2pm Sun May-Sep, to 4pm Tue-Sun Oct-Apr) Kala was traditionally a Christian neighbourhood, but fewer than a dozen of the 20 churches remain. The quarter's biggest church, **Church of the Dormition of St Mary** (Kisha Fjetja e Shën Mërisë), is the site of the Onufri Museum. The church itself dates from 1797 and was built on the foundations of a 10th-century church. Onufri's spectacular 16th-century artworks are displayed on the ground level along with a beautifully gilded iconostasis.

Ethnographic Museum
MUSEUM

(admission 200 lekë; ⊘ 9am-1pm & 4-7pm Tue-Sat, to 2pm Sun May-Sep, to 4pm Tue-Sun Oct-Apr) Down from the castle, this museum is in an 18th-century Ottoman house that's as interesting as the exhibits. The ground floor has displays of traditional clothes and the tools used by silversmiths and weavers, while the upper storey has kitchens, bedrooms and guest rooms decked out in traditional style.

Mangalem Quarter
NEIGHBOURHOOD

Down in the traditionally Muslim Mangalem quarter, there are three grand mosques. The 16th-century **Sultan's Mosque** (Xhamia e Mbretit) is one of the oldest in Albania. The **Helveti teqe** behind the mosque has a beautiful carved ceiling and was specially designed with acoustic holes to improve the quality of sound during meetings. The Helveti, like the Bektashi, are a dervish order, or brotherhood, of Muslim mystics.

🛏 Sleeping & Eating

Berat Backpackers
HOSTEL €

(☑ 069 7854 219; www.beratbackpackers.com; Gorica; tent/dm/r €6/12/30; ⊘ mid Mar-Nov; @ 🛜) This transformed traditional house in the Gorica quarter (across the river from Mangalem) houses one of Albania's friendliest and best-run hostels. The vine-clad establishment contains a basement bar, alfresco drinking area and a cheery, relaxed atmosphere that money can't buy. There are two airy dorms with original ceilings, and one excellent-value double room that shares the bathroom facilities with the dorms.

There's also a shaded camping area on the terrace and cheap laundry available.

★ Hotel Mangalemi
HOTEL €€

(☑ 068 2323 238; www.mangalemihotel.com; Rr Mihail Komneno; s/d from €30/40; P ❄ @ 🛜) A true highlight of Berat is this gorgeous place inside two sprawling Ottoman houses where all the rooms are beautifully furnished in traditional Berati style and balconies give superb views. Its terrace restaurant (mains 400 lekë to 600 lekë; reserve in the evening) is the best place to eat in town and has great Albanian food with bonus views of Mt Tomorri.

It's on the left side of the cobblestone road leading to the castle.

Hotel Muzaka
HOTEL €€

(☑ 231 999; www.hotel-muzaka.com; Gorica; s/d from €50/65; P ❄ 🛜) This gorgeous Gorica hotel is a careful restoration of an old stone mansion on the riverfront, just over the footbridge from the centre of town. Wooden floorboards, gorgeous bathrooms and beautifully chosen pieces of furniture in the 10 spacious rooms make this a good option for those looking for some style as well as tradition in their accommodation.

There's also a pleasant restaurant here, open to the public for lunch and dinner (mains 400 lekë to 800 lekë).

White House
ITALIAN €€

(Rr Antipatrea; mains 300-600 lekë; ⊘ 8am-11pm) On the main road that runs north of the river, this place has a superb roof terrace with sweeping views over Berat, and serves up a mean pizza to boot. There's also a classier dining room downstairs with air-conditioning, perfect for a blowout meal.

ⓘ Getting There & Away

Buses and *furgons* run between Tirana and Berat (400 lekë, three hours, half-hourly until 3pm). Services arrive in and depart from Sheshi Teodor Muzaka next to the Lead Mosque in the centre of town. There are also buses to Vlora (300 lekë, 2 hours, hourly until 2pm), Durrës (300 lekë, 2 hours, six per day) and Saranda (1200 lekë, six hours, two daily at 8am and 2pm), one of which goes via Gjirokastra (800 lekë, four hours, 8am).

SOUTHERN COAST

With rough mountains falling headfirst into bright blue seas, the coastal drive between Vlora and Saranda is easily one of the most spectacular in Eastern Europe and shouldn't missed by any visitor to Albania. While beaches can be jam-packed in August, there's plenty of space, peace and happy-to-see-you faces in the low season.

Drymades

As you zigzag down the mountain from the Llogaraja Pass National Park, the white crescent-shape beaches and azure waters lure you from below. The first beach before the alluvial fan is Palasa, and it's one of the best, and least developed beaches around, perfect for chilling out for a night or two if you have a tent. The next beach along is Drymades beach. To get here leave for main road for Dhërmi, then take the first right (signposted for the Turtle Club) and you'll reach the rocky white beach in 20 mins via the sealed road that twists through olive groves.

🛏 Sleeping

★ **Sea Turtle**　　　　　　CAMPGROUND €
(☑069 4016 057; Drymades; per person incl half-board from 1000 lekë; ☉ Jun-Sep; ☜) This great little set-up is run by two brothers. Each summer they turn the family orange orchard into a vibrant tent city, and the price includes the tent (with mattresses, sheets and pillows), breakfast and a family-cooked dinner (served up in true camp style). Hot showers are under the shade of old fig trees, or it's a short walk to the beach.

Saranda

☑0852 / POP 37,700
Saranda has grown rapidly in the past decade; skeletal high-rises crowd around its horseshoe shape and hundreds more are being built in the outlying region. Saranda is bustling in summer – buses are crowded with people carrying swimming gear and the weather means it's almost obligatory to go for a swim. A daily stream of Corfu holidaymakers take the 45-minute ferry trip to Albania, add the Albanian stamp to their passports and hit Butrint or the Blue Eye Spring before heading back.

🛏 Sleeping

SR Backpackers　　　　　　HOSTEL €
(☑069 4345 426; www.backpackerssr.hostel.com; Rr Mitat Hoxha 10; dm from €12; @☜) The hostel with the most central location in Saranda, this is also the cheapest option. Housed in an apartment and hosted by the gregarious English-speaking Tomi, the 14 beds here are spread over three dorms, each with its own balcony. There's one shared bathroom, a communal kitchen and a friendly atmosphere.

Hotel Porto Eda　　　　　　HOTEL €€
(www.portoeda.com; Rr Jonianët; r €55; P❀☜) Referencing the temporary name given to Saranda during the fascist occupation, this hotel is nevertheless a charming place and

---

THE ALBANIAN RIVIERA

The Albanian Riviera was a revelation a decade or so ago, when travellers began to discover the last virgin stretch of the Mediterranean coast in Europe. Since then, things have become significantly less pristine, with overdevelopment blighting many of the once charming coastal villages. But worry not: while Dhërmi and Himara may be well and truly swarming, there are still spots to kick back and enjoy the empty beaches the region was once so famous for.

One such place is **Vuno**, a tiny hillside village above picturesque Jal Beach. Each summer Vuno's primary school is filled with blow-up beds and it becomes **Shkolla Hostel** (☑068 4063 835; www.tiranahostel.com; Vuno; tent/dm €4/7; ☉late Jun-Sep). What it lacks in infrastructure and privacy it makes up for with its goat-bell soundtrack and evening campfire. From Vuno, walk over the bridge and follow the rocky path to your right past the cemetery. It's a challenging 40-minute signed walk through olive groves to picturesque **Jal**, or a 5km walk along the main beach road.

Jal has two beaches; one has free camping while the other has a camping ground set back from the sea (including tent 2000 lekë). Fresh seafood is bountiful in Jal and there are plenty of beachside restaurants in summer.

about as central as you can get, overlooking the bay. The 24 rooms are comfortably and stylishly laid out, all with balconies and sea-views, and the welcome is warm. From September to June rooms cost just €45.

✗ Eating

Gërthëla
SEAFOOD €€

(Rr Jonianët; mains 300-1000 lekë; ⊙11am-midnight; ☎) One of Saranda's original restaurants, 'the crab' is a long-standing taverna that only has fish and seafood on the menu, and locals will tell you with certainty that it offers the best prepared versions of either available in town. The charming glass-fronted dining room is full of traditional knickknacks and there's a big wine selection to boot.

★ Mare Nostrum
INTERNATIONAL €€€

(Rr Jonianët; mains 700-1200 lekë; ⊙7am-midnight Mar-Dec) This sleek new restaurant immediately feels different to the others along the seafront: here there's elegant decor that wouldn't look out of place in a major European capital, the buzz of a smart in-the-know crowd and an imaginative menu that combines the seafood and fish you'll find everywhere else with dishes such as Indonesian chicken curry and burgers.

ℹ Information

Saranda's tiny but excellent **ZIT information centre** (☑069 324 3304; Rr Skënderbeu; ⊙9am-9pm Jul-Aug, to 4pm Mon-Fri Sep-Jun) provides information about transport and local sights and is staffed by friendly and helpful English speaking staff.

ℹ Getting There & Away

The ZIT information centre opposite the synagogue ruins has up-to-date bus timetables.

BUS

Most buses leave just uphill from the ruins on Rr Vangjel Pando, right in the centre of town. Buses to Tirana (1300 lekë, eight hours) go inland via Gjirokastra (30 lekë) and leave at 7am, 8.30am, 10.30am, 2pm, and 10pm. The 5.30am Tirana bus takes the coastal route (1300 lekë, eight hours). In addition to the Tirana buses, there are buses to Gjirokastra's new town (300 lekë, 1½ hours) at 11.30am and 1pm – they all pass the turn-off to the Blue Eye Spring. Buses to Himara (400 lekë, two hours) leave around four times a day.

FERRY

Finikas (☑085 226 057, 067 2022 004; www.finikas-lines.com; Rr Mithat Hoxha) at the port sells hydrofoil tickets for Corfu (Jul-Aug/Sep-Jun €24/19, 45 minutes) with a daily departure at 9am, 10.30am and 4pm in the summer months. See the website for timings, which vary year round. From Corfu there are three ferries per day in summer: 9am, 1pm and 6.30pm. Note that Greek time is one hour ahead of Albanian time.

TAXI

Taxis wait for customers at the bus stop and opposite Central Park on Rr Skënderbeu. A taxi to the Greek border at Kakavija costs 4000 lekë.

Around Saranda

Butrint

The ancient ruins of **Butrint** (www.butrint.al; admission 700 lekë; ⊙8am-dusk), 18km south of Saranda, are renowned for their size, beauty and tranquillity. They're in a fantastic natural setting and are part of a 29-sq-km national park. Set aside at least two hours to explore this fascinating place.

Although the site was inhabited long before, Greeks from Corfu settled on the hill in Butrint (Buthrotum) in the 6th century BC. Within a century Butrint had become a fortified trading city with an acropolis. The lower town began to develop in the 3rd century BC, and many large stone buildings had already been built by the time the Romans took over in 167 BC. Butrint's prosperity continued throughout the Roman period, and the Byzantines made it an ecclesiastical centre. The city then went into a long decline and was abandoned until 1927, when Italian archaeologists arrived. These days Lord Rothschild's UK-based Butrint Foundation helps maintain the site.

As you enter the site the path leads to the right, to Butrint's 3rd-century-BC Greek theatre, secluded in the forest below the acropolis. Also in use during the Roman period, the theatre could seat about 2500 people. Close by are the small public baths, where geometric mosaics are buried under a layer of mesh and sand to protect them from the elements.

ℹ Getting There & Away

The municipal bus from Saranda to Butrint costs 50 lekë and leaves hourly from 8.30am to 5.30pm, and then comes back from Butrint hourly on the hour.

EASTERN ALBANIA

Gjirokastra

📞 084 / POP 43,000

Defined by its castle, roads paved with chunky limestone and shale, imposing slate-roofed houses and views out to the Drina Valley, Gjirokastra is an intriguing hillside town described beautifully by Albania's most famous literary export and locally born author, Ismail Kadare (b 1936), in *Chronicle in Stone*. There has been a settlement here for 2500 years, though these days it's the 600 'monumental' Ottoman-era houses in town that attract visitors.

◉ Sights

★ **Gjirokastra Castle** — CASTLE
(admission 200 lekë; ⊘ 9am-7pm) Gjirokastra's eerie hilltop castle is one of the biggest in the Balkans and easily the town's best sight, most definitely worth the steep walk up from the Old Town. Inside there's an eerie collection of armoury, two good museums, a shot-down US Air Force jet and a hilariously hard-to-use audiotour that is included in your entry fee.

★ **Zekate House** — HISTORIC BUILDING
(admission 200 lekë; ⊘ 9am-6pm) This incredible three-storey house dates from 1811 and has twin towers and a double-arched facade. It's fascinating to nose around the almost totally unchanged interiors of an Ottoman-era home, especially the upstairs galleries, which are the most impressive. The owners live next door and collect the payments; to get here, follow the signs past the Hotel Kalemi and keep zigzagging up the hill.

🛌 Sleeping

Kotoni B&B — B&B €
(📞 084-263 526, 069 2366 846; www.kotonihouse.com; Rr Bashkim Kokona 8; s/d from €25/30; 🅿 ✳ 🛜) Hosts Haxhi and Vita look after you in true Albanian style here: they love Gjirokastra and are happy to pass on information, as well as pack picnics for guests' day trips. The fact that these rooms are 220 years old makes up for their small size, while the astonishing views and friendly cats further sweeten the deal.

★ **Gjirokastra Hotel** — HOTEL €€
(📞 068 4099 669, 084-265 982; Rr. Sheazi Çomo; s/d €25/35, ste €40; ✳ 🛜) A great option that combines modern facilities with traditional touches, this lovely family-run hotel inside a 300-year-old house has rooms that boast huge balconies and beautifully carved wooden ceilings. The suite is gorgeous, with a long Ottoman style sofa, original wooden doors and ceiling and magnificent stone walls.

Hotel Kalemi — HOTEL €€
(📞 084-263 724, 068 2234 373; www.hotelkalemi.tripod.com; Lagjia Palorto ; r €40; 🅿 ✳ @ 🛜) This delightful, large Ottoman-style house has spacious rooms adorned with carved ceilings, antique furnishings and large communal areas, including a broad verandah with Drina Valley views. Some rooms even have fireplaces, though bathrooms can be on the cramped side. Breakfast (juice, tea, a boiled egg and bread with delicious fig jam) is an all-local affair.

🍴 Eating

★ **Kujtimi** — ALBANIAN €€
(mains 200-800 lekë; ⊘ 11am-11pm) This wonderfully laid-back outdoor restaurant, run by the Dumi family is an excellent choice. Try the delicious *trofte* (fried trout; 400 lekë), the *midhje* (fried mussels; 350 lekë) and *qifqi* (rice balls fried in herbs and egg, a local speciality). The terrace here is the perfect place to absorb the charms of the Old Town with a glass of local wine.

Taverna Kuka — TRADITIONAL €€
(Rr Astrit Karagjozi; mains 300-800 lekë; ⊘ 11am-midnight; 🛜) Just beyond Gjirokastra's old mosque, this largely outdoor terrace restaurant has a wonderful location and a menu full of delicious traditional Albanian cooking including *qofte* (meatballs), Saranda mussels, pork pancetta and grilled lamb.

ℹ Getting There & Away

Buses stop at the ad hoc bus station just after the Eida petrol station on the new town's main road. Services include Tirana (1200 lekë, seven hours, every 1-2 hours until 5pm), Saranda (300 lekë, one hour, hourly) and Berat (1000 lekë, four hours, 9.15am & 3.45pm). A taxi between the Old Town and the bus station is 200 lekë.

SURVIVAL GUIDE

ℹ Directory A–Z

BUSINESS HOURS
Banks 9am to 3.30pm Monday to Friday
Cafes & Bars 8am to midnight

EATING PRICE RANGES

The following price categories for the cost of a main course are used in the listings in this chapter.

€ less than 200 lekë

€€ 200 lekë to 500 lekë

€€€ more than 500 lekë

Offices 8am to 5pm Monday to Friday

Restaurants 8am to midnight

Shops 8am to 7pm; siesta time can be any time between noon and 4pm

INTERNET ACCESS

Free wi-fi is ubiquitous in all but the most basic hotels. In larger towns many restaurants also offer free access.

INTERNET RESOURCES

Albania (www.albania.al)

Balkanology (www.balkanology.com/albania)

Journey to Valbona (www.journeytovalbona.com)

MONEY

The lekë is the official currency, though the euro is widely accepted; you'll get a better deal for things in general if you use lekë. Albanian lekë can't be exchanged outside the country, so exchange or spend them before you leave.

Credit cards are accepted only in the larger hotels, shops and travel agencies, and few of these are outside Tirana.

POST

The postal system is fairly rudimentary – there are no postcodes, for example – and it certainly does not enjoy a reputation for efficiency.

PUBLIC HOLIDAYS

New Year's Day 1 January

Summer Day 16 March

Nevruz 23 March

Catholic Easter March or April

Orthodox Easter March or April

May Day 1 May

Mother Teresa Day 19 October

Independence Day 28 November

Liberation Day 29 November

Christmas Day 25 December

TELEPHONE

Albania's country phone code is ☑ 355. Mobile numbers begin with ☑ 06. To call an Albanian mobile number from abroad, dial +355 then either ☑ 67, ☑ 68 or ☑ 69 (ie drop the 0 before the 6).

VISAS

Visas are not required for citizens of EU countries or nationals of Australia, Canada, New Zealand, Japan, South Korea, Norway, South Africa or the USA. Travellers from other countries should check www.mfa.gov.al.

☉ Getting There & Away

Albania has good connections in all directions: daily buses go to Kosovo, Montenegro, Macedonia and Greece. The southern seaport of Saranda is a short boat trip from Greece's Corfu, while in summer ferries also connect Himara and Vlora to Corfu. Durrës has regular ferries to Italy.

AIR

Nënë Tereza International Airport (p48) is 17km northwest of Tirana and is a modern, well-run terminal. There are no domestic flights within Albania. The following airlines fly to and from Albania:

Adria Airways (www.adria.si)

Air One (www.flyairone.it)

Alitalia (www.alitalia.com)

Austrian Airlines (www.austrian.com)

British Airways (www.britishairways.com)

Lufthansa (www.lufthansa.com)

Olympic Air (www.olympicair.com)

Pegasus Airlines (www.flypgs.com)

Turkish Airlines (www.turkishairlines.com)

LAND
Border Crossings

There are no passenger trains into Albania, so your border-crossing options are buses, *furgons*, taxis or walking to a border and picking up transport on the other side.

Montenegro The main crossings link Shkodra to Ulcinj (Muriqan) and to Podgorica (Hani i Hotit).

COUNTRY FACTS

Area 28,748 sq km

Capital Tirana

Country Code ☑ 355

Currency lekë

Emergency Ambulance ☑ 127, fire ☑ 128, police ☑ 129

Language Albanian

Money ATMs in most towns

Population 2.77 million

Visas Nearly all visitors can travel visa free to Albania

SLEEPING PRICE RANGES

The following price categories for the cost of a double room in high season are used in the listings in this chapter.

€ less than €30

€€ €30 to €80

€€€ more than €80

Kosovo The closest border crossing to the Koman Ferry terminal is Morina, and further south is Qafë Prush. Near Kukës use Morinë for the highway to Tirana.

Macedonia Use Blato to get to Debar, Qafë e Thanës or Sveti Naum, each to one side of Pogradec, for accessing Ohrid.

Greece The main border crossing to and from Greece is Kakavija on the road from Athens to Tirana. It's about half an hour from Gjirokastra and 250km west of Tirana, and can take up to three hours to pass through during summer. Kapshtica (near Korça) also gets long lines in summer. Konispoli is near Butrint in Albania's south.

Bus

From Tirana, regular buses head to Pristina, Kosovo; to Skopje in Macedonia; to Ulcinj in Montenegro; and to Athens and Thessaloniki in Greece. *Furgons* and buses leave Shkodra for Montenegro, and buses head to Kosovo from Durrës. Buses travel to Greece from Albanian towns on the southern coast as well as from Tirana.

Car & Motorcycle

To enter Albania with you own vehicle you'll need a Green Card (proof of third-party insurance, issued by your insurer); check that your insurance covers Albania.

SEA

Two or three boats per day ply the route between Saranda and Corfu, in Greece, and there are plenty of ferry companies making the journey to Italy from Vlora and Durrës, as well as additional ferries from Vlora to Corfu in the summer.

ⓘ Getting Around

BICYCLE

Cycling in Albania is tough but certainly feasible. Expect lousy road conditions including open drains, some abysmal driving from fellow road users and roads that barely qualify for the title. Organised groups head north for mountain biking, and cyclists are even spotted cycling the long and tough Korça–Gjirokastra road. Shkodra, Durrës and Tirana are towns where you'll see locals embracing the bike, and Tirana even has bike lanes and its own bike-sharing scheme.

BUS

Bus and *furgon* are the main form of public transport in Albania. Fares are low, and you either pay the conductor on board or when you hop off, which can be anywhere along the route.

Municipal buses operate in Tirana, Durrës, Shkodra and Vlora, and trips cost 30 lekë.

CAR & MOTORCYCLE

Car Hire

There are lots of car-hire companies operating out of Tirana, including all the major international agencies. Hiring a small car costs as little as €35 per day.

Road Rules

Drinking and driving is forbidden, and there is zero tolerance for blood-alcohol readings. Both motorcyclists and passengers must wear helmets. Speed limits are as low as 30km/h in built-up areas and 35km/h on the edges, and there are plenty of traffic police monitoring the roads. Keep your car's papers with you, as police are active checkers.

HITCHING

Though never entirely safe, hitchhiking is quite a common way for travellers to get around – though it's rare to see locals doing it.

TRAIN

Albanians prefer bus and *furgon* travel, and when you see the speed and the state of the (barely) existing trains, you'll know why.

ESSENTIAL FOOD & DRINK

In coastal areas the calamari, mussels and fish will knock your socks off, while high-altitude areas such as Llogaraja have roast lamb worth climbing a mountain for.

➡ **Byrek** Pastry with cheese or meat.

➡ **Fergesë** Baked peppers, egg and cheese, and occasionally meat.

➡ **Midhje** Wild or farmed mussels, often served fried.

➡ **Paçë koke** Sheep's head soup, usually served for breakfast.

➡ **Qofta** Flat or cylindrical minced-meat rissoles.

➡ **Sufllaqë** Doner kebab.

➡ **Tavë** Meat baked with cheese and egg.

Belarus

Best Places to Eat

➡ Grand Cafe (p62)

➡ Bistro de Luxe (p62)

➡ Food Republic (p61)

➡ Strawnya Talaka (p62)

➡ Jules Verne (p65)

Best Places to Stay

➡ Hotel Manastyrski (p60)

➡ Hermitage Hotel (p65)

➡ Revolucion Hostel (p59)

➡ Semashko (p64)

Why Go?

Eastern Europe's outcast, Belarus (Беларусь) lies at the edge of the region and seems determined to avoid integration with the rest of the continent at all costs. Taking its lead from the Soviet Union rather than the European Union, this little-visited dictatorship may seem like a strange choice for travellers, but its isolation lies at the heart of its appeal.

While the rest of Eastern Europe has charged headlong into capitalism, Belarus allows the chance to visit a Europe with minimal advertising and no litter or graffiti. Outside the monumental Stalinist capital of Minsk, Belarus offers a simple yet pleasing landscape of cornflower fields, thick forests and picturesque villages. The country also offers two excellent national parks and is home to Europe's largest mammal, the zoobr (or European bison). While travellers will always be subject to curiosity, they'll also be on the receiving end of warm hospitality and genuine welcome.

When to Go
Minsk

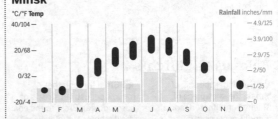

Jun–Aug Come to Belarus to escape the crowds elsewhere in Eastern Europe.

Early Jul On 6 July watch locals celebrate *Kupalye*, a fortune-telling festival with pagan roots.

Mid-Jul Join in Vitsebsk's superb Slavyansky Bazaar festival and celebrate all things Slavic.

Belarus Highlights

1 Get under the skin of **Minsk**, the showpiece of Stalinist architecture and a friendly, accessible city.

2 Spot a European bison, a brown bear or a wolf at **Belavezhskaya Pushcha National Park** (p65).

3 Stroll through the mellow pedestrian streets of cosmopolitan Brest to the epic WWII memorial that is **Brest Fortress** (p64).

4 Discover the childhood home of painter **Marc Chagall** (p66) in Vitsebsk.

5 See the fairy-tale 16th-century **castle** (p63) that presides over the tranquil town of Mir.

6 Explore one of the few historical complexes to have survived WWII at Nyasvizh, at the gloriously restored **Radziwill Palace Fortress** (p63).

Three Days

Spend two days getting to know **Minsk** – its Stalinist architecture belies a lively and friendly city – before taking a day trip to **Mir** to get a feel for the lovely Belarusian countryside.

One Week

Begin with two nights in **Brest**, including a day trip to the **Belavezhskaya Pushcha National Park**, then take a train to **Minsk**, allowing yourself time for a day trip to **Mir** before continuing on to historic and charming **Vitsebsk**.

MINSK   MИHCK

☑ 017 / POP 1.9 MILLION

Minsk will almost certainly surprise you. The capital of Belarus is, despite its thoroughly dreary-sounding name, a progressive and modern place quite at odds with its own reputation. Fashionable cafes, impressive restaurants and crowded nightclubs vie for your attention, while sushi bars and art galleries have taken up residence in a city centre once totally remodelled to the tastes of Stalin. Despite the strong police presence and obedient citizenry, Minsk is a thoroughly pleasant place that's not hard to become fond of.

Razed to the ground in WWII, Minsk has almost no buildings remaining from the prewar years, and there are relatively few traditional sights in the city, save two excellent museums. Instead though, there are myriad places of interest to anyone fascinated by the Soviet period and a smattering of cosmopolitan pursuits to keep you entertained come the evening.

◉ Sights

Oktyabrskaya Pl   SQUARE

(pl Kastrychnitskaya) The city's main square is referred to universally by its Russian name, Oktyabrskaya pl (October Sq; in Belarusian, it's pl Kastrychnitskaya). This is where opposition groups gather to protest against President Alexander Lukashenko from time to time, and is where the infamous 2010 presidential election protests ended in violence. The failed Denim Revolution of March 2006 was attempted here as well.

★ Museum of the Great Patriotic War   MUSEUM

(☑ 017-203 0792; www.warmuseum.by; pr Peremozhtsau 8; adult/student BR40,000/20,000, guided tour BR120,000; ☺ 10am-6pm Tue & Thu-Sat, 11am-7pm Wed & Sun) Housed in a garish new building after leaving its severely outdated premises on Oktyabrskaya pl, Minsk's best museum houses an excellent display detailing Belarus' suffering and heroism during the Nazi occupation. With English explanations throughout, atmospheric dioramas and a range of real tanks, airplanes and artillery from WWII, it's a big improvement on its fusty predecessor. Its section on concentration camps is particularly disturbing: an incredible 2.3 million people in Belarus were killed during the war, including 1.5 million civilians.

Belarusian State Art Museum   MUSEUM

(vul Lenina 20; adult/student BR50,000/25,000; ☺ 11am-7pm Wed-Mon) This excellent state museum has been renovated and now includes a light-bathed extension out the back that features local art from the 1940s to the 1970s. Don't miss Valentin Volkov's socialist realist *Minsk on July 3, 1944* (1944–5), depicting the Red Army's arrival in the ruined city. Yudel Pen, Chagall's teacher, is well represented, including his 1914 portrait of Chagall.

Traetskae Pradmestse   OLD TOWN

In lieu of any real remaining Old Town is Traetskae Pradmestse ('Trinity Suburb'), a pleasant – if tiny – re-creation of Minsk's pre-war buildings on a pretty bend of the river just a little north of the centre. It's worth strolling through for its little cafes, restaurants and shops, though the towering monoliths of modern Minsk are never very far away.

🛏 Sleeping

If you're in the city for more than a night or two, an alternative is renting an apartment. Several agencies offer this service, including **Belarus Rent** (www.belarusrent.com), **Belarus Apartment** (www.belarusapartment.com) and **Minsk4rent** (☑ 29 111 4817; www.minsk4rent. com). Rates range from €40 to €120 per night.

★ Revolucion Hostel   HOSTEL €

(☑ 029 614 6465; www.revolucion.by; vul Revalyutsiynaya 16; dm €9-12, d €27-35; ☎) Right in the heart of town, this friendly and pleasingly

Minsk

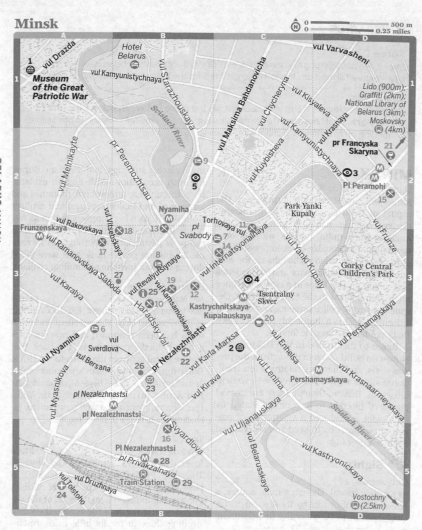

quirky hostel is festooned with photographs of various revolutionaries and even has a pet tortoise called Marseillaise. Dorms run from 4- to 12-bed, and there are a couple of double rooms as well. Extras include a roof terrace, bike hire (BR100,000 per day) and the free use of an espresso machine.

Trinity Hostel
HOSTEL €

(☑ 029 311 2783; www.hostel-traveler.by; Starovilenskaya vul 12; dm/d €17/40; 🛜) Right in the heart of Minsk, this new hostel is a great option. It's located in the Disney-esque 'Old Town', and has small dorms with 4 to 6 beds. There's a no

alcohol rule, and a strict ban on making noise after 10pm, so it's not a place to come to party.

★ Hotel Manastyrski
HISTORIC HOTEL €€€

(☑ 017-329 0300; www.vtroitskaya.by; vul Kirilla i Mefodya 9; s/d from €95/122; 🛜) This much-needed, relatively affordable, new top-end hotel in the centre of Minsk has considerable charm and great, proactive management. Housed in the converted remains of a Benedictine monastery, the 48 rooms are smart and comfortably furnished with dark wood fittings, while the impressive corridors are decorated with frescoes (found during the renovation) and wrought iron chandeliers.

Minsk

Buta Boutique Hotel BOUTIQUE HOTEL €€

(☏029 152 2555; www.hotel-buta.by; vul Myasnikova 7; s/d from €75/80; P❄🖥) Minsk's first boutique hotel looks like the kind of place Louis XIV would stay had he been travelling for business; think flat-screen TVs in golden frames on the wall and lots of bling. That said, with rain showers, great views, plenty of space and quality furnishings, this is actually a good deal for the price. Location is also good, and staff are attentive and professional. Breakfast costs an extra €20.

✖ Eating

Minsk has a decent eating scene and plenty of choice – don't believe the hype about food in Belarus; in the capital, at least, you'll eat well. Consider reserving tables at weekends.

Stolle PIE SHOP €

(www.stolle.by; vul Rakovskaya 23; pies from BR25,000; ⊙10am-11pm; 🖥📷) Stolle is a great option with delicious, freshly baked sweet and savoury pies to eat in or take away. This is the most central location of the many now open in the city and, unlike the others, there's also a full non-pie menu serving up traditional Russian and Belarusian cuisine. Other central branches include **vul Internatsyonalnaya 23** (⊙10am-10pm; 🖥📷), **vul Sverdlova 22** (⊙10am-10pm; 🖥📷) and **pr Nezalezhnastsi 38** (⊙10am-9pm; 🖥📷).

Gurman RUSSIAN €

(pr Peremozhtsau 1; mains BR20,000-100,000; ⊙8am-11pm; 🖥) This Minsk institution specialises in many varieties of delicious, freshly made *pelmeni* (Russian-style ravioli stuffed with meat) and also offers a wide selection of pastas, curries and other international cuisine. The light and airy new central premises and the consistently friendly staff are other reasons to come.

★Food Republic FOOD COURT €€

(www.foodrepublic.by; vul Yanki Kupaly 25; ⊙10am-midnight; ⊜🖥) This brand new restaurant complex is a real turn up for the books in dusty old Minsk: 10 different eateries and a number of food shops all under one huge industrial-style roof, with cuisine running from sushi, burgers, Italian and Turkish to a steakhouse, deli, fish restaurant and patisserie. To top it off, there's a fantastic terrace overlooking the river. This is the best place in Minsk for sheer choice and variety, and quality and service are also good.

Tapas Bar SPANISH €€

(vul Internatsyanalnaya 9/17; mains BR70,000-150,000; ⊙11am-midnight; 🖥📷) This stylish joint with olive-coloured walls, friendly service and bright dining areas serves up good tapas from a large menu. All the classics are present, as well as a range of meaty *platos calientes* (hot dishes) and excellent paella. With its good wine selection and lovely atmosphere, it's also a great place to come for a drink in the evenings.

★ Bistro de Luxe
BISTRO €€€

(Haradsky Val 10; mains BR100,000-300,000; ⊘8am-midnight Mon-Fri, 11am-midnight Sat & Sun; 🛜) Housed in a gorgeous space with chandeliers, sleek brasserie-style furnishings, a chessboard floor and aspirational toilets, Bistro de Luxe has charm and atmosphere that's hard to find elsewhere in Minsk. The food is excellent – leaning towards Italian – and service is impeccable. Breakfast served daily until midday.

Grand Cafe
ITALIAN €€€

(vul Lenina 2; mains BR150,000-400,000; ⊘noon-midnight; 🛜) This classy place has great service from waiters in tuxedos, and white-linen tablecloths starched enough to cause an injury. The interesting menu is big on seasonal Italian classics, with plenty of choice and a few non-Italian variations. Alternatively, just sit at the glamorous bar and drink sensational cocktails.

Strawnya Talaka
TRADITIONAL €€€

(vul Rakovskaya 18; mains BR160,000-400,000; ⊘10am-6am) This relaxed and cosy basement place is unashamedly aimed at tourists, but it also happens to be one of the best restaurants in Minsk for an authentic local meal. Try the hare in bilberry sauce, the mushroom soup served in a loaf of bread or just a bowl of their fantastic beer snacks and the fabulous *draniki* (potato pancakes).

🍷 Drinking

★ Ý Bar
WINE BAR

(www.ybar.by; pr Nezalezhnastsi 37A; ⊘noon-midnight, until 2am Fri & Sat) Hidden in the courtyard of a building just off pl Peramohi, this sleek wine bar is attached to the contemporary art gallery of the same name and is the current favoured watering hole of Minsk's creative classes. There's a dazzling wine list, with a huge choice of wine by the glass, as well as delicious cakes and bar food.

My English Granny
CAFE

(vul Karla Marksa 36; ⊘9am-midnight; 🛜) This place has pulled off the incredible feat of making kitschy Victoriana look trendy in its bizarre but very cosy basement location. You'll get a good pot of tea and some gorgeous cakes here, as well as meals with a strong British bias and a great breakfast selection.

ℹ Information

INTERNET ACCESS

Free wi-fi can be had at nearly all hotels and several, but by no means all, cafes and restaurants.

MEDICAL SERVICES

24-hour Pharmacy (pr Nezalezhnastsi 16)
EcoMedservices (☑017-207 7474; www.ems. by; vul Tolstoho 4; ⊘8am-9pm) The closest thing to a reliable, Western-style clinic. Dental services are offered here, too. Just south of the train station.

MONEY

ATMs can be found throughout the city and often dispense US dollars and euros as well as Belarusian roubles. Exchange bureaux dot the centre, while most banks and hotels can change euros and US dollars.

POST

Central Post Office (pr Nezalezhnastsi 10; ⊘7am-11pm) In the centre of town.

TOURIST INFORMATION

Minsk Tourist Information Centre (☑017-203 3995; www.minsktourism.by; vul Revalyutsiynaya 16-24; ⊘8.45am-1pm & 2-6pm Mon-Fri) Minsk's tourist office is central but well hidden. The entrance is in the courtyard behind building 13 on vul Revalyutsiynaya.

ℹ Getting There & Away

AIR

Flights entering and departing Belarus do so at the **Minsk-2 International Airport** (☑017-279 1300; www.airport.by), about 40km east of Minsk. There are daily flights to many major European cities, and Minsk remains surprisingly well connected to the rest of Europe. There are no domestic flights.

BUS

There are three main bus stations in Minsk, but most long-distance and international services leave from the Tsentralny Bus Station in the city centre.

Tsentralny Bus Station (☑017-227 0473; vul Bobruyskaya 6) The main bus station is next to the train station in the centre of Minsk. Buses to Mir (Novgrorodok), Vitsebsk, Brest, Hrodna and Nyasvizh depart from here, as well as international departures.

CAR

As well as outlets at the airport, both **Avis** (☑017-334 7990; www.avis.by) and **Europcar** (☑017-209 9009; www.europcar.by) can be found at Hotel Minsk (pr Nezalezhnastsi 11).

COMRADE LEE

Just across the bridge over the Svislach River, on the west bank, is the **former residence of Lee Harvey Oswald** (vul Kamyunistychnaya 4) – it's the bottom left apartment. The alleged assassin of former US president John F Kennedy lived here for a couple of years in his early 20s. He arrived in Minsk in January 1960 after leaving the US Marines and defecting to the USSR. Once here, he truly went native: he got a job in a radio factory, married a Minsk woman, had a child – and even changed his name to Alek. But soon he returned to the United States and...you know the rest.

TRAIN

The busy and modern **Minsk train station** (☑105, 017-225 7000; Privakzalnaya pl; ☉24hr) is pretty easy to deal with. You can buy domestic and CIS (Commonwealth of Independent States) tickets here. Downstairs is a well-signed **left luggage office** (lockers BR1000, luggage room BR2000; ☉24hr).

You can buy tickets for non-CIS destinations at the **international train ticket office** (vul Kirova 2; ☉8am-8pm), located across the main road in front of the train station.

ℹ Getting Around

TO/FROM THE AIRPORT
From Minsk-2 airport, a 40-minute taxi ride into town should cost around BR300,000, depending on your bargaining skills. Bus 300Э (BR6000) goes from outside the airport terminal into the city centre, via pr Nezalezhnastsi and ends at the Tsentralny Bus Station. It leaves between every 30 minutes and one hour, tapering off to every two hours during the night.

PUBLIC TRANSPORT
Minsk's metro is simple: just two lines with one transfer point at the Kastrychnitskaya-Kupalauskaya interchange on pr Nezalezhnastsi. A third line is under construction, but at present the system isn't hugely useful to travellers. It's open daily from dawn until just after midnight. One token (zheton) costs BR4000.

Buses, trams and trolleybuses also cost BR4000 per ride and you can buy tickets on board in most cases.

TAXI
For taxis, dial ☑035 or ☑007. Operators usually won't speak English, however. You can also hail taxis from the street.

AROUND MINSK

Nyasvizh   Нясвіж
☑01770 / POP 15,000

The magical old buildings of Nyasvizh make it a great place to get in touch with Belarus' past – one that elsewhere has all too often been destroyed as the military campaigns of WWII flattened the country. This quiet but green and attractive town 120km southwest of Minsk is one of the oldest in the country, dating from the 13th century.

◉ Sights

★**Radziwill Palace Fortress**   PALACE
(adult/student BR80,000/40,000; ☉9.30am-5.30pm) Over a causeway leading away from the town, with lovely lakes on either side, lies the beautiful Radziwill Palace Fortress (1583), the main sight in Nyasvizh. In Soviet times it was turned into a sanatorium but it has been fully restored in recent years and is looking superb.

With over 30 fully refurbished state rooms now open, a very impressive inner courtyard and clearly labelled displays, you can easily spend a couple of hours looking around.

ℹ Getting There & Away

From Minsk's Tsentralny Bus Station, there are four daily buses to and from Nyasvizh (BR63,000, 2½ hours).

Mir   Мір
☑01596 / POP 2500

The charming small town of Mir, 85km southwest of Minsk, is dominated by the impossibly romantic 16th-century castle that overlooks a small lake at one end of the town. It was once owned by the powerful Radziwill princes and has been under Unesco protection since 1994.

◉ Sights

★**Mir Castle**   CASTLE
(☑01596 23 035; www.mirzamak.by/ru; adult/student BR70,000/35,000; ☉10am-6pm) The 16th century Mir Castle rises above the town majestically and looks like something straight out of Disney. A painstaking renovation over the past decade has been completed and the place is looking simply lovely, with gorgeous grounds, impressively restored interiors and a huge display on the life and times of the Radziwills.

HRODNA ГРОДНА

If you're entering Belarus from northern Poland, or if you have extra time here, think about visiting Hrodna (Grodno in Russian). It was one of the few Belarusian cities that *wasn't* bombed during WWII, so it's rife with old wooden homes and, although it's a major city, it definitely has a 'big village' sort of feel to it. The city's best hotel by far is the privately run, super-friendly **Semashko** (☑0152-75 02 99; www.hotel-semashko.ru/en; vul Antonova 10; s/d incl breakfast from BR200,000/280,000; @✉), which you should reserve in advance due to its popularity. The room price includes use of the Oasis sauna and its small pool. Trains between Minsk and Hrodna leave five times a day (BR24,000, six hours), although *marshrutky* from Minsk's Vostochny Bus Station do the trip much faster and far more regularly (BR36,000, three hours).

ⓘ Getting There & Away

From Minsk's Tsentralny Bus Station, there are buses to Navahrudak (Novogrudok in Russian) that stop in Mir (BR55,000, 2½ hours, hourly).

SOUTHERN BELARUS

Brest Брэст

☑0162 / POP 330,000

This prosperous and cosmopolitan border town looks far more to the neighbouring EU than to Minsk. It has plenty of charm and has performed a massive DIY job on itself over the past few years in preparation for its millennial celebrations in 2019.

◉ Sights

Brest Fortress FORTRESS

(Brestskaya krepost; pr Masherava) FREE Very little remains of Brest Fortress. Certainly don't come here expecting a medieval turreted affair – this is a Soviet WWII memorial to the devastating battle that resulted when German troops advanced into the Soviet Union in the early days of Operation Barbarossa in 1941. The large complex occupies a beautiful spot at the confluence of the Bug and Mukhavets Rivers, a 20-minute walk from the town centre or a short hop on bus 17 from outside Hotel Intourist.

The fortress was built between 1838 and 1842, but by WWII it was used mainly as a barracks. The two regiments bunking here when German troops launched a surprise attack in 1941 defended the fort for an astounding month and became venerated as national legends thanks to Stalin's propaganda machine.

The Brest Fortress main entrance is its most iconic building – a huge socialist star formed from concrete. Sombre music accompanies you through the tunnel and as you leave it; on the left and past a small hill, you'll see some tanks. Straight ahead is the stone **Thirst statue**, which depicts a water-starved soldier crawling for a drink. After you cross a small bridge, to your right are the brick ruins of the **White Palace**, where the 1918 Treaty of Brest-Litovsk was signed, marking Russia's exit from WWI. Further to the right is the **Defence of Brest Fortress Museum** (adult/student BR25,000/12,500, audioguide BR20,000; ⊙9am-6pm Tue-Sun). Its extensive and dramatic exhibits demonstrate the plight of the defenders. There's also a small collection of weaponry from 18th- to 20th-century warfare, for which a separate ticket is required (BR10,000).

★**Museum of Railway Technology** MUSEUM

(pr Masherava 2; adult/student BR15,000/10,000; ⊙8.30am-5.30pm Tue-Sun) One of Brest's most popular sights is the outdoor Museum of Railway Technology, where there's a superb collection of locomotives and carriages dating from 1903 (the *Moscow–Brest Express* with shower rooms and a very comfy main bedroom) to 1988 (far more proletarian Soviet passenger carriages). You can go inside many of them, so train enthusiasts and children tend to love it here.

🛏 Sleeping

Dream Hostel HOSTEL €

(☑033 361 0315, 0162-531 499; www.dreamhostel. by; vul Mayakaskaha 17, bldg 1, apt 5; dm €13-15; ☎) Brest's first hostel is housed in a modern apartment building right in the middle of town. To get here go through the entrance between Tez Tour and Colombia Sportswear Company, and follow the footpath around to the right. The entry code is 5K, and it's otherwise unsigned. The hostel has three dorms with modern, clean bunks, a large TV room and kitchen.

Hotel Molodyozhnaya
HOTEL €

(🖉 0162-216 376; www.molodezhnaya.by; vul Kamsamolskaya 6; s/d €32/42; 🛜) This small and very centrally located place is a short walk from the station and has been steadily improving its facilities for the past few years. The rooms are comfortable and clean, all have private facilities and the welcome is warm. Breakfast is an extra BR70,000 per person.

★ Hermitage Hotel
HOTEL €€

(🖉 0162-276 000; www.hermitagehotel.by; vul Chkalova 7; s/d incl breakfast from €90/115; P ❋ 🛜) This fantastic hotel is streets ahead of even the nearest competition locally, although frankly that's not saying too much. Housed in a sensitively designed modern building, there's more than a little old-world style here, with spacious, grand and well-appointed rooms as well as impressive public areas. Multilingual staff are charming and there's good food available, including a great breakfast.

✗ Eating & Drinking

★ Jules Verne
FINE DINING €€

(vul Hoholya 29; mains BR100,000-170,000; ⊙ noon-midnight; 🛜 🖉) It's almost a miracle that such a great restaurant exists in Brest. Decked out like a gentleman's club and with a travel theme, this dark, atmospheric joint manages to be refined without being stuffy. It serves up cracking dishes – from mouthwatering curries and a range of French cooking to sumptuous desserts and the best coffee in town. Don't miss it.

Time's Cafe
EUROPEAN €€

(vul Savetskaya 30; mains BR60,000-140,000; ⊙ 8.30am-11pm Mon-Fri, 11am-11pm Sat & Sun; 🛜) Finally somewhere a little self-consciously cool in Brest, this friendly and smart place has a jazz-and-blues soundtrack, charming staff and a summer terrace with views onto pedestrianised vul Savetskaya. Food runs from steak in a balsamic reduction to caramelised cod with potato purée – quite different from the offerings of most places nearby. Breakfast is also served.

Information

24-Hour Pharmacy (vul Hoholya 32; ⊙ 24 hrs)
Brest In Tourist (🖉 0162 225 571, 310-8304522; www.brestintourist.com; Hotel In Tourist, pr Masherava 15; ⊙ 9am-6pm Mon-Fri) Inside Hotel In Tourist; the English-speaking staff can arrange

city tours including 'Jewish Brest' and trips to the Belavezhskaya Pushcha National Park.
Post Office (pl Lenina; ⊙ 8am-6pm Mon-Sat)

ℹ Getting There & Around

BUS

The **bus station** (🖉 114, 004; vul Mitskevicha) is in the centre of town and has left-luggage lockers and an internet cafe. There are five daily buses to Minsk (BR40,000 to BR70,000, five hours), 10 to Hrodna (BR50,000 to BR80,000, five hours) and services to Vilnius in Lithuania on Friday and Sunday (BR120,000, eight hours).

TAXI

For a taxi, call 🖉 061 or have your hotel call for you.

TRAIN

Trains leave for Minsk (platzkart/kupe (3rd/2nd class) BR60,000/82,000, four hours) several times daily. To get to the city from the train station, you'll have to mount a steep flight of steps from the platform; once you're up, go right on the overpass. It's a short walk, but a taxi into town should be no more than BR30,000.

Around Brest

Belavezhskaya Pushcha National Park
PARK

(🖉 01631-56 370) A Unesco World Heritage Site some 60km north of Brest, Belavezhskaya Pushcha National Park is the oldest wildlife refuge in Europe and is the pride of Belarus. Half the park's territory lies in Poland, where it's called Białowieża National Park. Some 1300 sq km of primeval forest survives here. It's all that remains of a canopy that eight centuries ago covered northern Europe.

The area is most celebrated for its 300 or so European bison, the continent's largest land mammal. These free-range zoobr – slightly smaller than their American cousins – were driven to near extinction (the last one living in the wild was shot by a hunter in 1919) and then bred back from 52 animals that had survived in zoos.

It's entirely possible (and a great deal cheaper) to see the national park without taking a guided tour, although if you don't speak Russian you may miss some interesting commentary on trips through the woods and in the museum. From Brest take one of the six daily *marshrutky* or buses to Kamyanyuki (BR30,000, one hour 20 minutes) and walk from the village to the clearly visible reserve buildings. Once there you can walk around the park yourself, or even better, hire a bike from the museum (BR20,000 per hour). An altogether easier option is to book a day trip with Brest In Tourist.

NORTHERN BELARUS

Vitsebsk   Віцебск

[☏] 0212 / POP 363,000

The historic city of Vitsebsk (known universally outside Belarus by its Russian name, Vitebsk) lies a short distance from the Russian border and almost 300km from Minsk. Vitsebsk was an important centre of Jewish culture when it was one of the major cities of the 'Pale of Settlement', where Jews were allowed to live in the Russian Empire.

◉ Sights

★**Chagall Museum**   MUSEUM

(www.chagall.vitebsk.by; vul Punta 2; adult/student BR15,000/10,000, tours BR30,000; ⊘11am-7pm Tue-Sun Jun-Sep, Wed-Sun Oct-May) The first museum on every itinerary should be the excellent Chagall Museum, which was established in 1992 and displays collections of Chagall lithographs (his illustrations for the Bible; 1956–60), designs to accompany Gogol's *Dead Souls* (1923–25) and graphic representations of the 12 tribes of Israel (1960).

★**Marc Chagall House Museum**   MUSEUM

([☏] 0212-363 468; vul Pokrovskaya 11; adult/student BR15,000/10,000; ⊘11am-7pm Tue-Sun Jun-Sep, Wed-Sun Oct-May) Across the town's river, a good 20-minute walk away from the Chagall Museum, is the Marc Chagall House Museum, where the artist lived as a child for 13 years between 1897 and 1910 – a period beautifully evoked in his autobiography, *My Life*. The simple, small house contains photographs of Chagall and his family, various possessions of theirs and some period furniture. It leads out into a garden and is very evocative of a simple Jewish-Russian childhood. Call ahead to arrange a tour of the house in English.

✯⁣ Festivals & Events

Slavyansky Bazaar   FESTIVAL

(Slavic Bazaar; www.festival.vitebsk.by) This popular festival is held in mid-July and brings in dozens of singers and performers from Slavic countries for a week-long series of concerts. The annual event attracts tens of thousands of visitors, creating a huge party.

🛏 Sleeping

X.O. Hostel   HOSTEL €

([☏] 029 718 4554, 0212-236 626; www.xostel.by; vul Suvorova 10/2; dm €8-13, d €30; ☞) Right in the centre of the old town, Vitsebsk's first hostel is a great addition to the accommodation scene, with a well-equipped kitchen, comfortable doubles and a range of dorms. The only disappointment is the mildewy smell of the bathrooms. To find it, go into the courtyard of vul Suvorova 10/2. Laundry costs BR40,000 per load.

★**Hotel Eridan**   HOTEL €€

([☏] 0212-604 499; www.eridan-vitebsk.com; vul Savetskaya 21/17; r/ste from €60/79; 🅿☞) The best-value hotel in Vitsebsk is handy for the Chagall Museum and well located in the middle of the Old Town. With pleasant wooden furniture, art, antiques and old photos of Vitsebsk on the walls, there's a certain clunky post-Soviet makeover charm. Rooms are well equipped (albeit rather gaudy) and there's lots of space and light.

✗ Eating & Drinking

Zolotoy Lev   BELARUSIAN €€

(vul Suvorova 20/13; mains BR50,000-150,000; ⊘noon-midnight; ☞) The smartest place in town is the expansive 'Golden Lion'. There's a charming interior (when the TV is off) spread over no fewer than six dining areas, a large menu offering traditional Belarusian cuisine, and a spacious outdoor area serving up *shashlyk* and beer. You'll find it on the pedestrianised main street parallel to vul Lenina.

Vitebsky Traktir   INN €€

(vul Suvorova 4; mains BR40,000-100,000; ⊘noon-midnight; ☞) This decent place has lots of charm, even if it is a little too dark for its own good. A traditional Belarusian menu is complimented by European dishes and sushi.

ⓘ Getting There & Away

BUS

There are approximately hourly buses or *marshrutky* to Minsk (BR120,000 to 150,000, four to five hours). The city's bus station can be found next to the train station on vul Zamkovaya.

TRAIN

There are two or three daily trains to Minsk (BR55,000 to BR75,000, 4½ to six hours) and one to St Petersburg (BR630,000, 13 hours). There's also a daily train to both Moscow (BR595,000, 11 hours) and Brest (BR135,000, 11 hours).

SURVIVAL GUIDE

🛈 Directory A–Z

ACCOMMODATION
Rooms have private bathrooms unless otherwise indicated, but many do not include breakfast.

BUSINESS HOURS
Banks 9am to 5pm Monday to Friday
Office hours 9am to 6pm Monday to Friday
Shops 9am/10am to 9pm Monday to Saturday, to 6pm Sunday (if at all)

INSURANCE
Most visitors to Belarus are required to possess medical insurance to cover the entire period of their stay. Evidence of having purchased medical insurance with specific reference to coverage in Belarus for a minimum of €10,000 is now asked for as part of the visa application, so there's no way around this. If you have travel insurance already, ask your insurance company for a letter stating that you are covered in Belarus and for what amount. If you haven't got insurance already, you can simply buy one of the Belarus government's officially endorsed policies: check the embassy website in the country you're applying from.

INTERNET ACCESS
Internet provision is generally very good in Belarus. In major towns wireless is easy to find, and it's now totally standard in all hotels and hostels. It's also hassle free to buy a local SIM card with data at a mobile phone shop, you'll just need your passport and the address of your hotel.

INTERNET RESOURCES
Belarus Embassy in the UK (www.uk.mfa.gov.by)
Belarus Tourism (http://eng.belarustourism.by)

COUNTRY FACTS
Area 207,600 sq km
Capital Minsk
Country Code ☑375
Currency Belarusian rouble (BR)
Emergency Ambulance ☑03, fire ☑01, police ☑02
Language Belarusian and Russian
Money ATMs taking international cards are widely available
Population 9.46 million
Visas Needed by almost everybody

SLEEPING PRICE RANGES
The following price ranges refer to the cost of a double room:
€ less than €50
€€ €50 to €120
€€€ more than €120

MONEY
The Belarusian rouble (BR) is the national currency and the money's wide spectrum of bill denominations is overwhelming to the newcomer. Ensure you change any remaining roubles before leaving Belarus, as it's impossible to exchange the currency outside the country. ATMs and currency-exchange offices are not hard to find in Belarusian cities. Major credit cards are accepted at many of the nicer hotels, restaurants, and supermarkets in Minsk, but travellers cheques are not worth the effort.

POST
The word for post office is *pashtamt* in Belarusian, or *pochta* in Russian. You can mail important, time-sensitive items via the Express Mail Service (EMS) at most main post offices.

PUBLIC HOLIDAYS
New Year's Day 1 January
Orthodox Christmas 7 January
International Women's Day 8 March
Constitution Day 15 March
Catholic & Orthodox Easter March/April
Unity of Peoples of Russia and Belarus Day 2 April
International Labour Day (May Day) 1 May
Victory Day 9 May
Independence Day 3 July
Dzyady (Day of the Dead) 2 November
Catholic Christmas 25 December

VISAS
Nearly all visitors require a visa and arranging one before you arrive is usually essential. Belarusian visa regulations change frequently, so check the website of your nearest Belarusian embassy for the latest bureaucratic requirements.

Applications
Visa costs vary depending on the embassy you apply at and your citizenship. Americans pay more, but typically transit visas cost around €65, single-entry visas cost about €90 and to get either of those in 48 hours rather than five working days, count on paying double.

Registration

If you are staying in Belarus for more than five working days, you must have your visa officially registered. Hotels do this automatically and the service is included in the room price. They will stamp the back of your white landing card, which you keep and show to immigration agents upon departure. Note that if you're staying for fewer than five working days, there is no need to register.

ℹ Getting There & Away

Once you have your visa in your passport, the process of entering Belarus is relatively simple. Ensure you fill out one of the white migration cards in duplicate before presenting your passport to the immigration officer. Keep the half of the slip that the immigration officer returns to you, as you'll need it to leave the country.

AIR

Belarus' national airline is **Belavia** (☑ 017-220 2555; www.belavia.by; vul Nyamiha 14, Minsk), which has a good safety record and modern planes. Belavia has regular flights to London,

---

EATING PRICE RANGES

Price ranges are based on the average cost of a main course.

€ less than BR50,000

€€ BR50,000 to BR100,000

€€€ more than BR100,000

Paris, Frankfurt, Berlin, Vienna, Rome, Milan, Barcelona, Kyiv, Istanbul, Tel Aviv, Warsaw, Prague, Rīga and many Russian cities, including Moscow and St Petersburg.

The other main airlines that fly to Minsk:

Aeroflot (www.aeroflot.com)

Air Baltic (www.airbaltic.com)

Austrian Airlines (www.aua.com)

Czech Airlines (www.csa.cz)

El Al (www.elal.co.il)

Estonian Air (www.estonian-air.ee)

Etihad Airways (www.etihad.com)

LOT Polish Airlines (www.lot.com)

Lufthansa (www.lufthansa.com)

Turkish Airlines (www.turkishairlines.com)

LAND

Belarus has good overland links to all neighbouring countries. Daily trains from Minsk serve Moscow and St Petersburg in Russia, Vilnius in Lithuania, Warsaw in Poland and Kyiv in Ukraine. Bus services, which tend to be less comfortable, connect Minsk to Moscow, St Petersburg, Kyiv, Warsaw and Vilnius; Vitsebsk to Moscow and St Petersburg; and Brest to Terespol in Poland.

ℹ Getting Around

BUS

Bus services cover much of the country and are generally a reliable, if crowded, means of transportation.

CAR & MOTORCYCLE

It's perfectly possible to hire a car in Minsk, with competition and thus standards improving in recent years. That said, there are still some pretty poor cars out there: look them over carefully and check the spare tyre before you drive off.

TRAIN

Train is a popular and scenic way to travel between the major towns of Belarus. Though the bus network is far more extensive, train travel times tend to be faster and prices are similar.

ESSENTIAL FOOD & DRINK

Belarusian cuisine rarely differs from Russian cuisine, although there are a few uniquely Belarusian dishes.

➡ **Belavezhskaya** A bitter herbal alcoholic drink.

➡ **Draniki** Potato pancakes, usually served with sour cream (smetana).

➡ **Khaladnik** A local variation on cold borsch, a soup made from beetroot and garnished with sour cream, chopped up hard-boiled eggs and potatoes.

➡ **Kindziuk** A pig-stomach sausage filled with minced pork, herbs and spices.

➡ **Kletsky** Dumplings stuffed with mushrooms, cheese or potato.

➡ **Kolduni** Potato dumplings stuffed with meat.

➡ **Kvas** A mildly alcoholic drink made from black or rye bread and commonly sold on the streets in Belarus.

➡ **Manchanka** Pancakes served with a meaty gravy.

Bosnia & Hercegovina

Best Places to Eat

➡ Mala Kuhinja (p76)

➡ Hindin Han (p81)

➡ Park Prinčeva (p77)

Best Places to Stay

➡ Muslibegović House (p81)

➡ Colors Inn (p75)

➡ Shangri-La (p81)

➡ Hotel Lula (p75)

Why Go?

This craggily beautiful land retains some lingering scars from the heartbreaking civil war in the 1990s. But today visitors will more likely remember Bosnia & Hercegovina (BiH) for its deep, unassuming human warmth and for the intriguing East-meets-West atmosphere born of fascinatingly blended Ottoman and Austro-Hungarian histories.

Major drawcards are the reincarnated antique centres of Sarajevo and Mostar, where rebuilt historical buildings counterpoint fashionable bars and wi-fi–equipped cafes. Fascinating Sarajevo is an architectural gem, with countless minarets amid the tile-roofed houses that rise steeply up its river flanks. Mostar is world famous for its extraordinary arc of 16th-century stone bridge, photogenically flanked by cute mill-house restaurants. The town is set at the heart of Hercegovina's sun-baked wine country, with waterfalls, a riverside sufi-house and an Ottoman fortress all nearby.

When to Go

Sarajevo

Apr–Jun & Oct Beat the heat, especially when exploring in Hercegovina from Mostar.

Jul & Aug Accommodation fills up as the cities sizzle in the summer sun.

Mid-Jan–mid-Mar Skiing gets cheaper after the New Year holidays.

Bosnia & Hercegovina Highlights

1 Potter around the timeless Turkish- and Austrian-era pedestrian lanes of old **Sarajevo** (p71).

2 Discover more about the hopes and horrors of the 1990s civil war at the intensely moving **Tunnel Museum** (p74).

3 Nose about Mostar's atmospheric Old Town, seeking ever-new angles from which to photograph young men throwing themselves off the magnificently rebuilt **Stari Most** (Old Bridge; p79).

4 Make a satisfyingly varied day trip from Mostar to **Kravice Waterfalls** (p82) and other gems of Hercegovina.

ITINERARIES

Three Days

Roam **Mostar's** Old Town and dine overlooking the famous bridge. Next day take the morning train to **Sarajevo**. Do a free walking tour to get a sense of the old town and dine with a panoramic view at Park Prinčeva. On the third day head for the History and Tunnel Museums in Sarajevo's southern suburbs.

Five Days

Extend the three day itinerary by joining a day tour ex-Mostar to visit historic **Počitelj**, quaint **Blagaj** and the impressive **Kravice** waterfalls. In Sarajevo cafe-hop around Baščaršija's *caravanserais* and extend your wanderings to the Svrzo House and the fascinating, less-visited citadel area of **Vratnik**.

SARAJEVO

📞 033 / POP 419,000

The capital city's antique core has a Turkic feel, delighting visitors with narrow bazaar alleys and a plethora of 1530s Ottoman buildings. Bosnia's later annexation by Austria-Hungary is evident in surrounding groups of neo-Moorish Central European buildings, notably the recently reconstructed City Hall from which Archduke Franz Ferdinand was returning when assassinated in 1914. That shooting ultimately triggered WWI.

The city's north and south flanks are steep valley sides fuzzed with red-roofed Bosnian houses and prickled with uncountable minarets rising to green-topped mountain ridges. Westward, Sarajevo sprawls for over 10km through bland but busy Novo Sarajevo and dreary Dobrijna. Here, dismal ranks of apartment blocks remain bullet-scarred from the 1990s Yugoslav civil war, in which the capital's centuries-long history of religious harmony seemed to evaporate during almost four years of brutal siege. Many fascinating tours still focus on the civil war horrors but today the city is once again remarkably peaceful, non-threatening and photogenic.

⊙ Sights & Activities

⊙ Old Sarajevo

Baščaršija AREA

Sarajevo's bustling old quarter, Baščaršija (pronounced *bash-CHAR-shi-ya*) is a delightful warren of marble-flagged pedestrian courtyards and laneways full of Ottoman-era mosques, copper workshops, jewellery shops, *caravanserai*-cafes and inviting little restaurants. Start your explorations at the Sebilj, an 1891 ornamental gazebo-style water fountain on central 'Pigeon Sq'.

Franz Ferdinand's Assassination Spot HISTORIC SITE

(cnr Obala Kulina Bana & Zelenih Beretki) On 28 June 1914, Archduke Franz Ferdinand, heir to the Habsburg throne of Austria-Hungary, was shot by 18-year-old Gavrilo Princip. This assassination, which would be the fuse that ultimately detonated WWI, happened by an odd series of coincidences on a street corner outside what is now the Sarajevo 1878–1918 museum.

Bezistan ARCHITECTURE

(http://vakuf-gazi.ba/english/index.php/objects/ottoman-era/bezistan-tasli-han; ⊘ 8am-8pm Mon-Fri, 9am-2pm Sat) The 16th-century stone-vaulted covered bazaar is little more than 100m long, but squint and you could be in Istanbul. Most of the 50+ shops sell inexpensive souvenirs, scarves, cheap handbags and knock-off sunglasses.

Sarajevo City Hall ARCHITECTURE

(Vijećnica; www.nub.ba; adult/child 2KM/free; ⊘ 8am-5pm Mon-Fri) Storybook neo-Moorish facades make the 1898 Vijećnica Sarajevo's most beautiful Austro-Hungarian-era building. Seriously damaged during the 1990s siege, it has been laboriously restored and was reopened in 2014. As yet the only exhibits are a small collection of photos about the building's history, but it's well worth the modest entry fee to enjoy the sheer grandeur of its colourful multi-arched interior and stained-glass ceiling.

Gazi-Husrevbey Mosque MOSQUE

(www.vakuf-gazi.ba; Saraći 18; admission 2KM; ⊘ 9am-noon, 2.30-3.30pm & 5-6.15pm May-Sep, closed Ramadan) Bosnia's second Ottoman governor, Gazi-Husrevbey, funded a series of splendid 16th-century buildings of which this 1531 mosque forms the greatest centrepiece.

Central Sarajevo

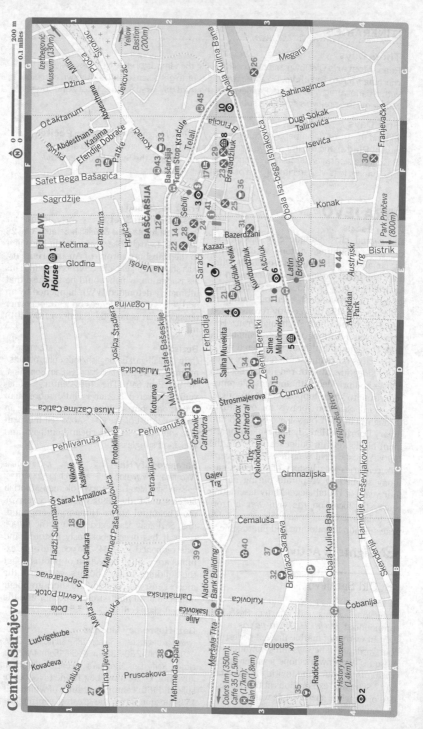

200 m
0.1 miles

Izetbegović
Museum (130m)

Yellow
Bastion
(200m)

Megara

Šahinaginca

Dugi Sokak
Talirovića

Isevića

Franjevačka

Park Prinčeva
(800m)

Bistrik

Austrijski
Trg

Atmejdan
Park

Miljacka River

Colors Inn (350m);
Caffe 35 (1.5km);
(1.7km);
Main (1.8km)

History Museum
(1.4km)

Central Sarajevo

The exterior might appear somewhat plain but there's a beautiful courtyard fountain, a 45m minaret and a splendidly proportioned interior.

Sahat Kula　　　　　TOWER
(off Mudželeti Veliki) This elegant 1529 stone tower sports a half-speed 19th-century prayer-clock with Arabic numerals. It is adjusted daily so that dusk is the moment when the hands appear to show 12 o'clock.

Despića Kuća　　　　　MUSEUM
(☎033-215531; http://muzejsarajeva.ba; Despićeva 2; adult/child 3/1KM, guide 5KM; ◷10am-6pm Mon-Fri (till 4pm winter), 10am-3pm Sat) The Despića Kuća is one of the oldest surviving residential buildings in central Sarajevo, though you'd never guess so from the ho-hum facade. Inside, however, it's a house within a house, the original 1780 section retaining even the prison-style bars on stone window frames.

**★Academy of
Fine Arts Sarajevo**　　　ARCHITECTURE
(Likovna Akademija; www.alu.unsa.ba; Obala Maka Dizdara 3) Originally built in 1899 as an evan-gelical church, the Gothic Revival–style Academy of Fine Arts Sarajevo has a fine facade looking like a mini version of Budapest's magnificent national parliament building. Inside the small Alu Gallery hosts occasional exhibitions.

◉ Vratnik & Around

If you're looking for accessible but less touristed parts of the city to explore, try wandering up the (sometimes steep) lanes to the north and east of the old city centre.

★Svrzo House　　　　　MUSEUM
(Svrzina Kuća; ☎033-535264; http://muzejsarajeva.ba; Glođina 8; admission 3KM; ◷10am-6pm Mon-Fri (till 4pm mid-Oct–mid-Apr), 10am-3pm Sat) An oasis of white-washed walls, cobbled courtyards and partly vine-draped dark timbers, this 18th-century house-museum is brilliantly restored and appropriately furnished, helping visitors imagine Sarajevo life in eras past.

Vratnik　　　　　AREA
Built in the 1720s and reinforced in 1816, Vratnik Citadel once enclosed a whole area of the

upper city. Patchy remnants of wall fragments, military ruins and gatehouses remain. The urban area is appealingly untouristed with many small mosques and tile-roofed houses, and there are several superb viewpoints. Start a visit with a 3KM taxi hop up to the graffiti-daubed Bijela Tabija fortress ruin-viewpoint (or take buses 52 or 55 to Višegradski Kapija gatehouse) then walk back.

Yellow Bastion   HISTORIC SITE
(Žuta Tabija; Jekovac bb) FREE Part-way between upper Vratnik and Kovaći Cemetery, a simple summer cafe places chairs between the trees on this overgrown former citadel bastion. Gaze out from here across the red-roofed cityscape.

Izetbegović Museum   MUSEUM
(www.muzejalijaizetbegovica.ba; Ploča bb; admission 2KM; ☉10am-6pm Mon-Fri, to 3pm Sat) Located in two 1730s stone towers linked by a section of former city wall, this two-room museum explores the background to the 1990s conflict and the role played by BiH's first president, Alija Izetbegović, in 'saving' the country.

◉ Novo Sarajevo

For the History Museum take tram 3 and get off when you see the superb but sadly still-closed National Museum. The tram route follows Zmaja od Bosne, the city's wide east-west artery road that was dubbed 'sniper alley' during the 1990s siege because Serb gunmen in surrounding hills could pick off civilians as they tried to cross it.

History Museum   MUSEUM
(☎033-226098; www.muzej.ba; Zmaja od Bosne 5; admission 5KM; ☉9am-7pm Mon-Fri, 10am-2pm Sat & Sun, shorter hours in winter) Around half of the small but engrossing History Museum 'non-ideologically' charts the course of the 1990s conflict. Affecting personal exhibits include examples of food aid, stacks of Monopoly-style 1990s dinars and a makeshift siege-time 'home'. The exhibition's maudlin effect is emphasised by the museum building's miserable and still partly war-damaged 1970s architecture.

◉ Butmir & Ilidža

Around 35 minutes after leaving Baščaršija, tram 3 reaches Ilidža, its western terminus. From there the very moving Tunnel Museum is some 3km southeast, around 8KM by metered taxi. Alternatively, from the tram ter-

minus, switch to Kotorac-bound bus 32 (10 minutes). Get off at the last stop, walk across the Tilava bridge, then turn immediately left down Tuneli for 500m. The bus runs around twice hourly weekdays but only every 90 minutes on Sundays so it's often faster to walk from Ilidža. Many city tours include a Tunnel Museum visit, saving the hassle.

★ Tunnel Museum   MUSEUM
(Tunel Spasa; http://tunelspasa.ba; Tuneli bb 1; adult/student 10/5KM; ☉9am-5pm, last entry 4.30pm, to 3.30pm Nov-Mar) The most visceral of Sarajevo's many 1990s war-experience 'attractions', this unmissable museum's centrepiece and raison d'être is a short section of the 1m wide, 1.6m high hand-dug tunnel under the airport runway which acted as the city's lifeline to the outside world during the 1992–95 siege, when Sarajevo was virtually surrounded by Serb forces.

⚲ Tours

Various companies run a range of tours in and beyond Sarajevo, many including the otherwise awkward-to-reach Tunnel Museum. Reliable operators include **Sarajevo Funky Tours** (☎062 910546; www.sarajevofunky tours.com; Besarina Čikma 5) and **Insider** (☎061 190591; www.sarajevoinsider.com; Zelenih Beretki 30; ☉9am-6pm Mon-Fri, 9.30am-2pm Sat & Sun), which also offers a tips-only walking tour daily at 4.30pm in season starting outside its office-museum.

✲ Festivals & Events

Sarajevo Film Festival   FILM
(www.sff.ba; ☉mid-Aug) During this globally acclaimed film fest, the whole city turns into a giant party with countless concerts and many bars opening street counters.

⏢ Sleeping

Hostels are multiplying at an incredible rate, with several great options on or near the narrow 'party street', Muvekita.

Hostel For Me   HOSTEL €
(☎062 328658, 033-840135; www.hostelforme.com; 4th fl, Prote Bakovica 2; dm/breakfast €10/3; ❉🛜) One of Sarajevo's best-appointed new hostels sits right within the Old Town, albeit hidden away up four flights of stairs. It's worth the climb for good-headroom bunks, huge lockers, a decent lounge area and a two-table kitchen with fine views across the Old Town roofs to the Gazi Husrevbegov Mosque.

Franz Ferdinand Hostel
HOSTEL €

(☎ 033-834625; http://franzferdinandhostel.com/; Jelića 4; dm 19-27KM, d 62-82KM; ☺ 24hr; ✳ @ 🛜) Giant sepia photos and a floor timeline recall characters and scenes related to Sarajevo WWI history. Bunks have private powerpoints and ample headroom, and the comfortably stylish kitchen-lounge is well designed to encourage conversation between travellers.

Residence Rooms
HOSTEL €

(☎ 033-200157, 061 159886; www.residencerooms. ba; 1st fl, Muvekita 1; dm 25-30KM, s/d/tr 50/80/90KM; ✳ @ 🛜) High ceilings and widely spaced dorm beds are complemented by a somewhat 1930s-flavoured lounge, with piano and ample seating space. The lively bars directly outside can be a blessing or a curse, depending on your party plans.

★ Hotel Lula
HOTEL €€

(☎ 033-232250; www.hotel-lula.com; Luledžina 14; s/d/tr €35/60/80; ✳ 🛜) The facade of this cute seven-room hotel is designed to harmonise with its perfect Old Town location, and there's even a mini 'cottage' in the basement dining-room area. Guest rooms are comfortably contemporary if mostly rather small; several have eaves reducing headroom. Fine value.

Villa Wien
GUESTHOUSE €€

(☎ 033-972800, 062 416507; www.villa-wien.ba; Ćurčiluk Veliki 3; s/d 103/146KM; ☺ 7am-10pm; ✳ 🛜) Six well-equipped rooms come with engraved wooden furniture, kilims on parquet floors, wrought-iron bedsteads and attractive bowl-lamp chandeliers. Walls have partly exposed brick-and-timber sections and little luxuries include trouser press and a fridge pre-loaded with a few free soft drinks. There's no reception: check in at the Wiener Café downstairs before that closes (at 10.30pm).

Hotel Latinski Most
HOTEL €€

(☎ 033-572660; www.hotel-latinskimost.com; Obala Isabega Isakovića 1; s/d/tr 117/158/178KM, off-season 99/138/158KM) This cosy hotel is ideal for WWI aficionados who want to survey the Franz Ferdinand assassination spot from directly across the river. Three of the smaller rooms have small balconies offering just that, and their double-glazing works remarkably well against street noise.

Hotel Safir
HOTEL €€

(☎ 033-475040; www.hotelsafir.ba; Jagodića 3; s/d €50/72, off season walk-in €35/60; ✳ 🛜) For a place in this price range, the Safir goes that

---

ENTITIES & AREAS

Getting your head around the divisions within Bosnia & Hercegovina (BiH) takes a bit of head-scratching. Geographically there's Bosnia in the north and Hercegovina (pronounced her-tse-GO-vina) in the south, although the term 'Bosnian' refers to anyone with BiH nationality. ('Bosniak' refers specifically to Muslim Bosnians, while simplistically put, Bosnian Croats are Catholics and Bosnian Serbs are Orthodox Christians.)

Then there are two quite different political 'entities'. Most of south and central BiH falls within the **Federation of Bosnia & Hercegovina**, which is itself subdivided into 10 cantons (five run by Bosniaks, three run by Bosnian Croats, two 'mixed'). Meanwhile, a territory comprising most of the north and arching around as far as Trebinje forms the semi-autonomous **Republik Srpska** (RS). That's predominantly Serb but certainly not in Serbia. Then there's the anomalous **Brčko District**, which falls in neither entity. Confused yet?

---

bit further than the competition. Off stairways featuring vibrantly colour-suffused flower photos, the eight rooms come with little mirror 'windows', big-headed showers, coffee, kettle and kitchenette (in most), free bottles of mineral water and even a little posy of flowers. Obliging 24-hour receptionists.

Hotel Michele
BOUTIQUE HOTEL €€€

(☎ 033-560310; www.hotelmichele.ba; Ivana Cankara 27; s/d €55/65, apt €120-150; ✳ 🛜) Behind the exterior of an oversized contemporary townhouse, this offbeat guesthouse-hotel welcomes you into a lobby-lounge full of framed portraits and elegant fittings. Antique-effect elements are in evidence in the 12 new standard rooms, but what has drawn celebrity guests like Morgan Freeman and Kevin Spacey are the vast, indulgently furnished apartments with antique (if sometimes mismatching) furniture.

★ Colors Inn
BUSINESS HOTEL €€€

(☎ 033-276600; www.hotelcolorsinnsarajevo.com; Koševo 8; s/d from 162/212KM; P ✳ 🛜) Modernist white-grey-lime decor is given a dramatic twist with vast wall-sized black and white photos of 20th-century Sarajevo. The 37 comfortably fashion-conscious rooms come with

WORTH A TRIP

THE WORLD'S BIGGEST PYRAMID?

The otherwise forgettable leather-tanning town of Visoko, 30km northwest of Sarajevo, is overlooked by an unusually shaped hill that Semir Osmanagić, a Bosnian-American Indiana Jones–style researcher, claims is the **'World's Biggest Pyramid'** (Piramida Sunca; www.piramidasunca.ba). Osmanagić also claims that **Tunnel Ravne** (guided tour per person 10KM; ⊙ 9am-5.45pm Apr–mid-Nov) is a 12,000-year-old subterranean labyrinth built by the same mysterious lost culture as the pyramid.

The claims have been dismissed by the European Association of Archaeologists as a 'cruel hoax' with 'no place in the world of genuine science', but that doesn't seem to have detered visitors and volunteers.

If you want to check it out for yourself, the **Pyramid of the Sun Foundation** (☑ 061 994821, 033-259935; www.bosnianpyramidofthesun.com; Bravadžiluk 17; admission free, tours for 1/2/5 people 110/120/125KM; ⊙ 10am-10pm summer, 11am-7pm winter) organises private tours ex-Sarajevo, or you can reach Visoko independently and cheaply by taking a Sarajevo–Kakanj bus (at least hourly).

kettle, coffee and a Ferrero Rocher or three. A good buffet breakfast is laid out in a 24-hour basement dining room that's designed like a stylised birch forest. Pay 20KM extra for a substantially larger 'luxury' room.

Hotel Central HOTEL €€€
(☑ 033-561800; www.hotelcentral.ba; Ćumurija 8; s/d/ste 200/240/300KM; ✴ ☎ ⊠) Behind a grand Austro-Hungarian facade, most of this snazzily renovated 'hotel' is in fact an amazing three-floor gym complex with professional-standard weight rooms, saunas and a big indoor pool staffed by qualified sports training staff. The 15 huge, fashionably appointed guest rooms lead off corridors painted a lugubriously deep purple.

✗ Eating

For inexpensive snack meals look along Bradžiluk or nearby Kundurdžiluk: **Buregdžinica Bosna** (Bravadžulik; 250g portions 2-3.50KM; ⊙ 7am-11pm) is excellent for cheap, fresh *burek* sold by weight. Locals argue whether **Hodžić** (Sebilj Sq; ćevapi 3-6KM; kajmak 1.5KM; ⊙ 8am-11pm), **Mrkva** (www.mrkva.ba; Bravadžulik 15; ćevapi from 3.5KM; ⊙ 8am-10pm) or **Željo** (Kundurdžiluk 17 & 20; ćevapi 3.5-10KM; kajmak 1.5KM; ⊙ 8am-10pm) serves the best *ćevapi*.

Barhana PIZZA, BOSNIAN €
(Đugalina 8; mains 5-10KM, steak 18-20KM, pizza 5-12KM, beer/rakija (fruit brandy) 2/3KM; ⊙ 10am-midnight, kitchen till 11.30pm) Barhana's remarkably reasonable prices pair unbeatably with its charming part-wooden cottage interior, whose centrepiece is the large brick pizza oven and open kitchen, partly masked by collections of bottles and candles.

★ **Mala Kuhinja** FUSION €€
(☑ 061 144741; www.malakuhinja.ba; Tina Ujevića 13; veg/chicken/beef/surprise meals 12/17/22/25KM, wine per glass/bottle 6/30KM; ⊙ 10am-11pm Mon-Sat, kitchen closes around 9.30pm; ☎ ✎) Run by former TV celebrity chefs, the novel concept here is that staff forget menus and simply ask you what you do/don't like. Spicey? Vegan? Gluten free? No problem. And armed with this knowledge the team sets about making culinary magic in the show-kitchen. Superb.

Dveri EUROPEAN €€
(☑ 030-537020; www.dveri.co.ba; Prote Bakovića 12; meals 10-20KM; ⊙ 8am-11pm; ☎ ✎) This tourist-friendly 'country cottage' eatery is densely hung with loops of garlic, corn cobs and gingham-curtained 'windows'. Classic European meat-based dishes are supplemented by inky risottos, veggie-stuffed eggplant and garlic-wine squid.

Pivnica HS INTERNATIONAL €€
(☑ 033-239740; www.sarajevska-pivara.com; Franjevačka 15; pasta 6-10KM, mains 10-20KM, beer from 2KM; ⊙ 10am-1am, kitchen 10.30am-midnight) Wild West saloon, Munich bierkeller, Las Vegas fantasy or Willy Wonka masterpiece? However you describe its decor, Pivnica HS is a vibrant place for dining on well-presented (mainly meat-based) dishes and ideal for sampling the full range of Sarajevskaya tap beers brewed next door. Try the rare unfiltered.

Morića Han BOSNIAN €€
(☑ 033-236119; Saraći 77; mains 8-17KM, tea/coffee 1.5/2KM; ⊙ 8am-11pm) Settle into cushioned wicker chairs as a single tree filters the sunlight or, at night, as lamps and lanterns glow magically between the hanging fabrics and

wooden beams of a gorgeous, historic *caravanserai* courtyard. The menu features typical Bosnian home fare including *klepe*, a vampire-slaying garlic ravioli. Cafe section but no alcohol served.

Inat Kuća
BOSNIAN €€

(Spite House; 🕿 033-447867; www.inatkuca.ba; Velika Alifakovac 1; mains 8-15KM, steak 25KM; ⊗ 10am-10pm; 🕸) This Sarajevo institution occupies a classic Ottoman-era house that's a veritable museum piece with central stone water-trough, a case of antique guns and fine metal-filigree lanterns. A range of Bosnian specialities are served using pewter crockery at glass-topped display tables containing traditional local jewellery.

Park Prinčeva
BALKAN, EUROPEAN €€€

(🕿 033-222708; www.parkprinceva.ba; Iza Hidra 7; meals 16-32KM; ⊗ 9am-11pm; 🚍 56) It's well worth the 3.50KM taxi-ride from Latinski Most to gaze out over a superb city panorama from this hillside perch, like Bono and Bill Clinton before you. From the open-sided terrace the City Hall is beautifully framed between rooftops, mosques and twinkling lights. The main chandelier-decked dining room sports a white piano, and a folk trio playing from 7.30pm.

🍷 Drinking & Entertainment

Sarajevo is chock full of appealing bars and pubs, and great cafes for coffee, cakes, ice cream and narghile (hubble-bubble) water pipes.

★ Zlatna Ribica
BAR

(Kaptol 5; beer/wine from 4/5KM; ⊗ 9am-1am or later) Sedate and outwardly grand, this tiny bar is inspiringly eccentric, adding understated humour to a cosy treasure trove of antiques and kitsch, all mixed together and reflected in big art-nouveau mirrors.

Cheers
PUB, PIZZA

(Muvekita 4; beer/pizza from 2.50/5.50KM; ⊗ 24hr) Look for the London Routemaster double-decker bus then turn the corner to find central Sarajevo's most consistently popular boozer, with music blaring and tipsy travellers bopping well after most other places have shut.

Cafe Barometar
BAR

(www.facebook.com/CafeBarometar; Branilaca Sarajeva 23; ⊗ 8am-midnight) Like an image of HG Wells' *Time Machine*, this cafe-bar weaves together dials, pipes and wacky furniture

crafted from axles, compressors and submarine parts.

Pink Houdini
BAR

(www.facebook.com/JazzBluesClubPinkHoudini; Branilaca Sarajeva 31; light/dark beer 3/3.50KM; ⊗ 24hr) One of Sarajevo's relatively rare 24-hour drinking spots, this quirky basement jazz bar has live gigs at 10pm on Fridays and Sundays.

Dekanter
WINE BAR

(🕿 033-263815; Radićeva 4; ⊗ 8am-midnight Mon-Sat, noon-midnight Sun) Sample from around 60 local and world vintages in this wine bar decorated with decanter shapes dangling from intertwined vine stems on the ceiling.

Caffe 35
BAR

(Avaz Twist Tower, 35th fl; coffee/cake/beer 2/3/4KM, sandwiches 3-5KM; ⊗ 8am-11pm) If you're waiting for a train, what better place to do so than admiring a full city panorama from the 35th floor cafe of 'The Balkans' Tallest Tower', just three minutes' walk away from the station.

Čajdžinica Džirlo
TEAHOUSE

(www.facebook.com/CajdzinicaDzirlo; Kovači 16; tea 4.50-6KM, coffee & sherbet 3KM; ⊗ 8am-10pm) Minuscule but brimming with character, Džirlo offers 45 types of tea, many of them made from distinctive Bosnian herbs, served in lovely little pots.

Kuća Sevdaha
CAFE

(www.artkucasevdaha.ba/en/; Halači 5; tea/coffee/sherbet from 2/2/3KM; ⊗ 10am-11pm) Sip Bosnian coffee, juniper sherbet, rose water or herb-tea infusions while nibbling local sweets and listening to the lilting wails of *sevdah* (traditional Bosnian music). The ancient building that surrounds the cafe's fountain courtyard is now used as a museum celebrating great 20th-century *sevdah* performers (admission 3KM, open 10am to 6pm Tuesday to Sunday).

Sloga
CLUB

(www.cinemas.ba; Mehmeda Spahe 20; ⊗ 9pm-5am) This cavernous, club-disco-dance hall caters to an excitable, predominantly student crowd. Monday nights see Latin dance, Thursday is party night, Friday is disco and Saturday is live music. At least in principle. Modest cover charge, cheap beer.

Underground
LIVE MUSIC

(www.facebook.com/undergroundclubsarajevo; Maršala Tita 56; beer 3KM; ⊗ 7pm-late) On Friday and Saturday nights, talented bands give classic rock songs a romping rework in this medium-sized basement venue. Concerts some Thursdays, too.

❶ Information

Destination Sarajevo (www.sarajevo.travel)
Extensive listings and information website.
Kapitals (Bascarsija 34; commission 2%,
minimum 2KM; ☺9am-11pm) Helpfully central
money changers, open till late.
Sarajevo Tourism Association (www.
sarajevo-tourism.com; Saraĉi 58; ☺9am-8pm
Mon-Fri, 10am-6pm Sat & Sun, varies season-
ally.) Helpful tourist information centre.

❶ Getting There & Away

BUS

From Sarajevo's **main bus station** (☑033-
213100; www.centrotrans.com; Put Života 8;
☺6am-10pm), beside the train station, there
are frequent buses to Mostar (18KM, 2½ hours),
several daily services to Zagreb and Split in
Croatia, plus early-morning buses to Dubrovnik
(Croatia) and Belgrade (Serbia). There are five
more Belgrade services from the inconveniently
distant **East Sarajevo (Lukovica) Bus Station**
(Autobuska Stanica Istočno Sarajevo; ☑057-
317377; www.balkanexpress-is.com; Nikole Tesle
bb; ☺6am-11.15pm), 400m beyond the western
terminus of trolleybus 103 or bus 31E. That
bus station also has buses to Podgorica and
Herceg Novi in Montenegro.

TRAIN

Mostar 11KM, 2¾ hours, 6.51am and 6.57pm
Zagreb (Croatia) 61KM, nine hours via Banja
Luka, 10.46am

For Budapest (Hungary) take the 12.30pm bus
from Lukovica Bus Station to Belgrade (arrives
8pm) then switch to the 9.45pm overnight train
from there (couchette 1960DIN ie €17, 8¼ hours).

❶ Getting Around

TO/FROM THE AIRPORT

Taxis charge around 20KM for the 12Km drive to
Bašĉaršija.

The nearest centre-bound bus stop is around
700m from the terminal: turn right out of the airport following black-backed 'Hotel' signs. Take
the first left, shimmy right-left-right past Hotel
Octagon, then turn third right at Braĉe Mulića
17. Before the Mercator Hypermarket (Mimar
Sinana 1) cross the road and take trolleybus 103
heading back in the direction you've just come.

BICYCLE RENTAL

Gir (☑033-213687; www.gir.ba; Zelenih Berekti
14a; per hr/day/5 days city bike 3/15/25KM,
mountain bike from 4/20/35KM; ☺10am-6pm
Mon-Sat, 11am-5pm Sun) Bicycle rental, sales
and repairs.

PUBLIC TRANSPORT

Single-ride tickets for bus, tram or trolleybus
cost 1.60KM from kiosks, 1.80KM from drivers.
Tickets must be stamped once aboard.

TAXI

Paja Taxis (☑1522, 033-412555) Reliable taxi
company charging on-the-metre fares (2KM
plus about 1KM per kilometre).

BOSNIA & HERCEGOVINA & THE 1990S CONFLICT

Today's Bosnia & Hercegovina (BiH) remains deeply scarred by the 1990s civil war that
began when post-Tito-era Yugoslavia imploded. Seen very simply, the core conflict was a
territorial battle between the Bosnians, Serbs and Croats. The war that ensued is often
portrayed as 'ethnic', but in fact all sides were Slavs, differing only in their (generally secu-
larised) religious backgrounds. Indeed, many Bosniaks (Muslims), Serbs (Orthodox Christians) and Croats (Catholics) had intermarried or were friends. Yet for nearly four years a
brutal and extraordinarily complex civil war raged, with atrocities committed by all sides.

Best known is the campaign of 'ethnic' cleansing in northern and eastern BiH, which
aimed at creating a Serb republic. Meanwhile in Mostar, Bosnian Croats and Bosniaks
traded fire across a 'front line', with Croat bombardment eventually destroying the city's
world-famous Old Bridge. Sarajevo endured a long siege and, in July 1995, Dutch peace-
keepers monitoring the supposedly 'safe' area of Srebrenica proved unable to prevent a
Bosnian Serb force from killing an estimated 8000 Muslim men in Europe's worst mass
killings since WWII. By this stage, Croats had renewed their own offensive, expelling Serbs
from western BiH and the Krajina region of Croatia.

Finally two weeks of NATO air strikes in September 1995 added force to an ultimatum
to end the Serbs' siege of Sarajevo and a peace conference was held in Dayton, Ohio. The
resultant accords maintained BiH's pre-war external boundaries but divided the country
into a complex jigsaw of semi-autonomous 'entities' and cantons to balance 'ethnic' sensi-
bilities. This succeeded in maintaining the fragile peace but the complex political structure
resulting from the war has led to bureaucratic tangles and economic stagnation.

MOSTAR

🎵 036 / POP 113,200

Mostar's world-famous 16th-century stone bridge is the centrepiece of its alluring, extensively restored old town where, at dusk, the lights of numerous mill-house restaurants twinkle across streamlets. Further from the centre a scattering of shattered building shells remain as moving testament to the terrible 1990s conflict that divided the city. The surrounding sun-drenched Herzegovinian countryside produces excellent wines and offers a series of tempting day-trip attractions.

⊙ Sights & Activities

Stari Most   BRIDGE
The world-famous Stari Most (Old Bridge) is Mostar's indisputable visual focus. Its pale stone arch magnificently throws back the golden glow of sunset or the tasteful nighttime floodlighting. The bridge's swooping stone arch was originally built between 1557 and 1566 on the orders of Suleyman the Magnificent. The current structure is a very convincing 2004 rebuild following the bridge's 1993 bombardment during the civil war. Numerous well-positioned cafes and restaurants tempt you to sit and savour the splendidly restored scene.

Bridge Diving   SPECTACLE
In summer, young men leap over 20m from Stari Most's parapet. That's not a suicide attempt but a professional sport – donations are expected from spectators. Daredevil tourists can try jumping for themselves but only after paying 50KM and doing a brief training. Enquire at the Bridge-Divers' Clubhouse and listen very carefully to their advice: diving badly can prove fatal.

Crooked Bridge   BRIDGE
(Kriva Ćuprija) Resembling Stari Most but in miniature, the pint-sized Crooked Bridge crosses the tiny Rabobolja creek amid a layered series of picturesque millhouse-restaurants.

Kajtaz House   MUSEUM
(Gaše Ilića 21; admission 4KM; ⊙9am-7pm Apr-Oct) Hidden behind tall walls, Mostar's most historic old house was once the harem section of a larger homestead built for a 16th-century Turkish judge. Full of original artefacts, it still belongs to descendents of the original family.

Bišćevića Ćošak   HOUSE
(Turkish House; Bišćevića 13; adult/student 4/3KM; ⊙8.30am-6.30pm mid-Apr–Oct, winter by tour only) Built in 1635, Bišćevića Ćošak is a one of very few traditional Turkic-styled houses to retain its original appearance. Off the small entrance courtyard, three rooms are colourfully furnished with rugs, metalwork and carved wooden furniture.

Spanski Trg   AREA
Over 20 years ago Croat and Bosniak forces bombarded each other into the rubble across a 'front line' which ran along the Bulevar and Alese Šantića St. Even now, several shell-pocked skeletal buildings remain in ruins around Spanski Trg, notably the triangular nine-storey tower that was once **Ljubljanska Banka** (Kralja Zvonimira bb).

☞ Tours

Several homestay-hostels offer well-reputed walking tours around town and/or full-day trips visiting Blagaj, Međugorje, Počitelj and the Kravice Waterfalls (around €30).

i-House Travel   TOUR AGENCY
(📱063 481842, 036-580048; www.ihouse-mostar.com; Onešćukova 25; ⊙10.30am-7.30pm Mar-Dec, 10am-10pm peak season) A wide and imaginative series of small group tours (minimum two customers) including an evening vineyard wine tasting trip (four hours) and a 'Death of Yugoslavia' trip (two hours including a 'secret' base). Paragliding (€35) and rafting (€35) are also possible.

🛏 Sleeping

There are numerous small hostels, though some are dormant between November and April.

Backpackers   HOSTEL €
(📱036-552408, 063 199019; www.backpackersmostar.com; Braće Felića 67; dm/d/tr €10/30/45; ◉✳🛜) With its graffiti-chic approach and music-till-late sitting area, this is Mostar's party hostel. It's above a main-street shop and currently quite small, but owner Ermin has big plans for expansion.

Hostel Nina   HOSTEL €
(📱061 382743; www.hostelnina.ba; Čelebica 18; dm/d without bathroom €10/30; ✳@) This popular homestay-hostel is run by an obliging English-speaking lady whose husband, a war survivor and former bridge jumper, runs regional tours.

Mostar

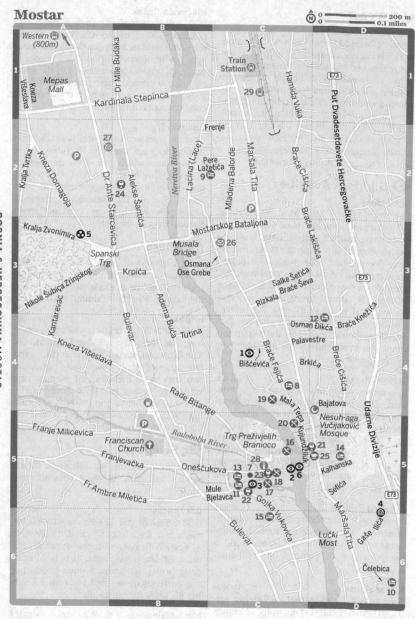

Hostel Majdas

HOSTEL €

(☎061 382940; www.facebook.com/Hostel MajdasMostar; Pere Lažetića 9; dm 20-23KM; ✳@🛜) Mostar's cult traveller getaway, Majdas now has a garden where breakfast is served, and a loveable cat. It still offers the classic multisite around-Mostar day tours which manager-guide Bata pioneered.

Pansion Oskar

GUESTHOUSE €

(☎061 823649, 036-580237; Onešćukova 33; d/tr €45/60, off-peak €35/50, s/d/tr/q without bathroom

Mostar

from €20/30/50/60; ⊞ ⟨⟩) Oskar is essentially a pair of family homes above a delightful open-air garden bar-restaurant slap bang in the historic centre. Room sizes and standards vary considerably between the nine rooms.

★ **Muslibegović House** HISTORIC HOTEL €€
(⟨⟩036-551379; www.muslibegovichouse.com; Osman Đikća 41; s/d/ste €60/90/105; ⊘ museum 10am-6pm mid-Apr-mid-Oct; ⊞⟨⟩) In summer, tourists pay 4KM to visit this beautiful, late-17th-century Ottoman courtyard house (extended in 1871). But it's also an extremely charming boutique hotel. Room sizes and styles vary significantly, mixing excellent modern bathrooms with elements of traditional Bosnian, Turkish or even Moroccan design.

★ **Shangri-La** GUESTHOUSE €€
(⟨⟩061 169362; www.shangrila.com.ba; Kalhanska 10; d Apr-mid-Oct €41-55, s/d mid-Oct-Mar €35/39; ⊞⊞⟨⟩) Behind a pseudo-19th-century facade, eight invitingly contemporary rooms are better appointed than those of most Mostar hotels. Stari Most is three minutes' walk away past some war-ruined historic buildings, yet the location is wonderfully peaceful.

Kriva Ćuprija 1 BOUTIQUE HOTEL €€
(⟨⟩036-550953; www.hotel-mostar.ba; r 70-130KM, apt 100-180KM; ⊞⟨⟩) Kriva Ćuprija 1 presents an idyllic blend of perfect Old Town location, soothing sounds of gushing streams and well-furnished rooms within a sensitively extended cluster of mill-house stone buildings.

Villa Anri HOTEL €€
(⟨⟩036-578477; www.motel-mostar.com; Braće Đukića 4; s/d/tr/q €35/40/60/80, peak season d/tr/q €70/95/115; ⊞⊞⟨⟩) The star attraction of this new four-storey hotel is the great Stari Most view from the open rooftop terrace. Two small, cosy rooms have the same views, but most other rooms are larger with modern bathrooms and an ecclectic taste in arts that ranges from tasteful to downright odd.

✗ Eating

Cafes and restaurants with divine views of Stari Most cluster along the riverbank. Along Mala Tepa and the main central commercial street Braće Fejića you'll find supermarkets, a **vegetable market** (⊘ 6.30am-2pm) and several inexpensive places for *ćevapi* and other Bosnian snacks.

★ **Hindin Han** BALKAN €€
(⟨⟩036-581054; Jusovina bb; mains 7-20KM, wine per litre 15KM; ⊘ 11am-11pm; ⟨⟩) Hindin Han is a rebuilt historic building with several layers of summer terrace perched pleasantly above a side stream. Locals rate its food as better than most other equivalent tourist restaurants. The stuffed squid we tried (13KM) was perfectly cooked and generously garnished.

Šadrvan BALKAN €€
(Jusovina 11; mains 7-25KM; ⊘ 8am-11pm, closed Jan) On a vine- and tree-shaded corner where the pedestrian lane from Stari Most divides, this delightful tourist favourite has tables

BOSNIA & HERCEGOVINA MOSTAR

WORTH A TRIP

AROUND MOSTAR

Many Mostar agencies and hostels combine the following for a satisfying day trip:

Blagaj A village whose signature sight is a half-timbered sufi-house (*tekija*) standing beside the surreally blue-green Buna River, where it gushes out of a cliff-cave.

Počitelj A steeply layered Ottoman-era fortress village that's one of BiH's most picture-perfect architectural ensembles.

Međugorje Curious for its mixture of pilgrim piety and Catholic kitsch ever since the Virgin Mary was reputedly spotted in a series of 1981 visions.

Kravice Waterfalls BiH's splendid 25m mini Niagara. Some tours give you several hours here to swim in natural pools.

set around a trickling fountain made of old Turkish-style metalwork. Obliging costumed waiters can help explain a menu that covers all bases and takes a stab at some vegetarian options. Meat-free *đuveč* (KM8) tastes like ratatouille on rice.

Babilon   BALKAN €€
(Tabhana; mains 8-20KM; ☺9am-10pm summer, 11am-4pm winter) The Babilon has stupendous terrace views across the river to the Old Town and Stari Most.

Urban Grill   BOSNIAN €€
(Mala Tepa 26; mains 8-27KM; ☺8am-11pm Mon-Sat, 9am-11pm Sun) From the street level Urban Grill seems to be a slightly up-market Bosnian fast-food place. But the menu spans a great range and the big attraction is the seven-table lower terrace with unexpectedly perfect framed views of the Old Bridge.

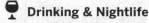 Drinking & Nightlife

Black Dog Pub   PUB
(Crooked Bridge; beer/wine from 2/4KM; ☺10am-late) Old Mostar's best hostelry features four specially brewed draft beers, happy hours and live acoustic music on Monday nights.

Caffe Marshall   BAR
(Oneščukova bb; ☺8am-1am) This minuscule box bar has a ceiling draped with musical instruments and is often the latest to be active in the Old Bridge area.

Terasa   CAFE
(Maršala Tita bb; coffee from 2KM; ☺weather-dependent) Half a dozen tables on an open-air perch-terrace survey Stari Most and the Old Town towers from altogether new angles. Enter beside MUM, crossing through the little roof garden of art studio Atelje Novalić.

OKC Abrašević   BAR
(☑036-561107; www.okcabrasevic.org; Alekse Šantića 25; coffee/beer 1/2KM; ☺9am-midnight) This understatedly intellectual smoky box of a bar offers Mostar's most vibrantly alternative scene and has an attached venue for off-beat gigs. It's hidden away in an unsigned courtyard on the former front line.

Ali Baba   BAR
(Kujundžiluk; cocktails 10KM; ☺24hr Jun-Sep, 7am-7pm Oct, closed winter) Take a gaping cavern in the raw rock, add beats and colourful low lighting and hey presto, you've got this one-off party bar. A dripping tunnel leads out to a second entrance on Maršala Tita.

ℹ️ Information

Bosniak Post Office (Braće Fejića bb; ☺8am-8pm Mon-Fri, 8am-3pm Sat)

Croat Post Office (Dr Ante Starčevića bb; ☺7am-7pm Mon-Sat, 9am-noon Sun)

Tourist Information Centre (☑036-397350; Preživjelih Branioco Trg; ☺9am-7pm May-Sep, closed Oct-Apr) Limited info, city tours sold (25KM).

COUNTRY FACTS

Area 51,129 sq km

Capital Sarajevo

Country code ☑387

Currency Convertible mark (KM, BAM)

Emergency Ambulance ☑124, fire ☑123, police ☑122

Language Spoken Bosnian (Bosanski, 48%), Serbian (Српски, 37%) and Croatian (Hrvatski, 14%) are all variants of the same language.

Money Visa & MasterCard ATMs widely available

Population 3.79 million (2.37 million in the Federation, 1.33 million RS, 93,000 Brčko)

Visas Not required for most visitors (see www.mfa.ba)

ⓘ Getting There & Around

BUS

The **main bus station** (☏ 036-552025; Ivana Krndelja Trg) beside the train station handles half a dozen daily services to Sarajevo, Split and Zagreb plus morning departures to Belgrade, Herceg Novi, Kotor and Vienna. For Dubrovnik there are direct buses (38KM, 4½ hours) at 7am and 10am, or you could take one of three daily buses to attractive Trebinje (21KM, four hours), from where there's a 10am bus to Dubrovnik (not Sundays). Three extra Split-bound buses use the **Western Bus Station** (☏ 036-348680; Autobusni Kolodvor; Vukovarska bb), 800m beyond Mepas Mall.

TRAIN

Sarajevo 11KM, 2¼ hours, 7.05am and 7.10pm
Zagreb 74.60KM, 13¼hours, 7.05am

SURVIVAL GUIDE

ⓘ Directory A–Z

BUSINESS HOURS

Banks 8am to 6pm Monday to Friday, 8.30am to 1.30pm Saturday
Office hours 8am to 4pm Monday to Friday
Restaurants 11.30am to 10.30pm, varying by customer demand
Shops 8am to 6pm daily

INTERNET ACCESS

Most hotels and some cafes offer free wi-fi.

INTERNET RESOURCES

BiH Tourism (www.bhtourism.ba)
Bosnian Institute (www.bosnia.org.uk)
Office of the High Representative (www.ohr.int)

MONEY

Bosnia's convertible mark (KM or BAM), pronounced *kai-em* or *maraka*, is tied to the euro at approximately €1=1.96KM. For minor purchases, many businesses unblinkingly accept euros using a slightly customer-favourable 1:2 rate.

POST

BiH has three parallel postal organisations, each issuing their own stamps: **BH Pošta** (Federation; www.posta.ba), **Pošte Srpske** (RS; www.poste srpske.com) and **HP Post** (Croat areas, western Mostar; www.post.ba).

PUBLIC HOLIDAYS

Nationwide holidays:

New Year's Day 1 January
Independence Day 1 March
May Day 1 May
National Statehood Day 25 November

Additional holidays in the Federation:
Kurban Bajram (Islamic Feast of Sacrifice) 23 September 2015, 11 September 2016, 1 September 2017
Ramazanski Bajram (end of Ramadan) 7 July 2016, 26 June 2017, 15 June 2018
Gregorian Easter 28 March 2016, 17 April 2017, 2 April 2018
Gregorian Christmas 25 December

Additional holidays in the RS:
Orthodox Easter April/May
Orthodox Christmas 6 January

SAFE TRAVEL

Landmines and unexploded ordnance still affect 2.4% of BiH's area (see www.bhmac.org). In affected areas stick to asphalt/concrete surfaces or well-worn paths. Avoid exploring war-wrecked buildings.

VISAS

Stays of less than 90 days are visa-exempt for most European nationals, Australians, Canadians, Israelis, Japanese, Malaysians, Kiwis, Singaporians, South Koreans, Turks and US citizens. Other nationals should check www.mfa.ba for details.

Transit through Neum (coastal BiH between Split and Dubrovnik) is possible without a Bosnian

ESSENTIAL FOOD & DRINK

➡ **Bosanski Lonac** Slow-cooked meat-and-veg hotpot.

➡ **Burek** Bosnian *burek* are cylindrical or spiral lengths of filo-pastry filled with minced meat. *Sirnica* is filled instead with cheese, *krompiruša* with potato and *zeljanica* with spinach. Collectively these pies are called *pita*.

➡ **Ćevapi (Ćevapčići)** Minced meat formed into cylindrical pellets and served in fresh bread with melting *kajmak*.

➡ **Hurmastica** Syrup-soaked sponge fingers.

➡ **Pljeskavica** Patty-shaped *ćevapi*.

➡ **Kajmak** Thick semi-soured cream.

➡ **Klepe** Small ravioli-like triangles served in a butter-pepper drizzle with grated raw garlic.

➡ **Kljukuša** Potato-dough-milk dish cooked like a pie then cut into slices.

➡ **Ligne** Squid.

➡ **Pastrmka** Trout.

➡ **Rakija** Grappa or fruit brandy.

➡ **Ražnjići** Barbequed meat skewers.

➡ **Sogan Dolma** Slow-roasted onions filled with minced meat.

➡ **Sač** Traditional cooking technique using a metal hood loaded with hot charcoals.

➡ **Sarma** Steamed dolma-parcels of rice and minced meat wrapped in cabbage or other green leaves.

➡ **Tufahija** Whole stewed apple with walnut filling.

➡ **Uštipci** Bready fried dough-balls.

---

visa, assuming you have a double- or multiple-entry Croat visa.

ⓘ Getting There & Away

Around a dozen airlines fly to/from Sarajevo's compact little **international airport** (Aerodrom; www.sia.ba; Kurta Schorka 36; ⊘ closed 11pm-5am).

Air Serbia (☏ 033-289 265; www.airserbia.com) connects to Banja Luka from/via Belgrade.

Mistral Air (www.mistralair.it) operates seasonal Mostar–Rome charters.

BiH cities have plenty of international bus services (notably to Belgrade, Dubrovnik, Munich, Split, Vienna and Zagreb), but the only international train is the daily Zagreb–Sarajevo–Mostar service.

Bulgaria

Best Places to Eat

➡ Manastirska Magernitsa (p90)

➡ Mehana Chavkova House (p94)

➡ Han Hadji Nikoli (p99)

➡ Grazhdanski Klub (p96)

➡ Panorama (p104)

Best Places to Stay

➡ Red B&B (p90)

➡ Sofia Residence (p90)

➡ Hostel Old Plovdiv (p96)

➡ Hotel-Mehana Gurko (p99)

➡ Graffit Gallery Hotel (p101)

Why Go?

There's a lot to love about Bulgaria: just ask the Greeks, Romans, Byzantines and Turks, all of whom fought to claim it as their own. Billed as the oldest nation on the continent – it preceded ancient Greece by at least 1500 years – Bulgaria is rich with ancient treasure: stories abound of locals planting gardens only to have them ripped up by archaeologists after a turn of the spade unearthed priceless antiquities. The past has been preserved to remarkable effect; everything from Thracian tombs and Hellenic hoards to Roman ruins and medieval fortresses are easily accessible.

Centuries later, this Balkan beauty still beguiles, with a come-hither coastline, voluptuous mountain ranges and lush, fertile valleys laden with vines and roses. Plovdiv is the European Capital of Culture for 2019, Sofia has cool cred to rival any major metropolis, and the lively resorts of the Black Sea coast teem with modern-day pleasure pilgrims.

When to Go
Sofia

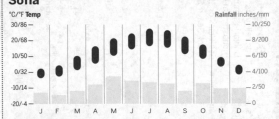

Feb Pop your cork at Melnik's Golden Grape Festival.

Jun Celebrate the sweetest harvest at Kazanlâk's Rose Festival.

Jul–Sep Spend lazy days on the Black Sea beaches and nights at Bulgaria's best clubs.

Bulgaria Highlights

1 Soak up the ancient ambience of **Plovdiv's** awesome Old Town (p95).

2 Sip a glass or two of Bulgarian vino in the wine town of **Melnik** (p93).

3 Explore the artistic and religious treasures of Bulgaria's most revered monastery at **Rila** (p93).

4 Relax on the sands of the Black Sea at **Sozopol** (p104).

5 Go clubbing, have a splash, and stroll through Primorski Park in cosmopolitan **Varna** (p101).

6 Head back in time through the National Revival houses in **Koprivshtitsa** (p97).

7 Visit the Tsars' medieval stronghold in **Veliko Tărnovo** (p98).

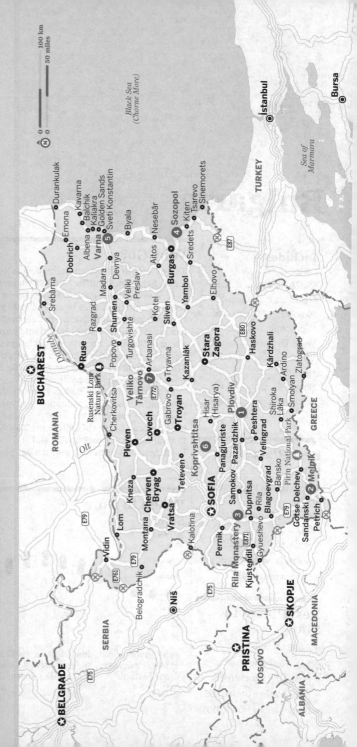

ITINERARIES

One Week

Take a full day to hit **Sofia's** main attractions, then take the bus to **Veliko Târnovo** for a few days of sightseeing and hiking. For the rest of the week, head to **Varna** for some sea and sand, or veer south to the ancient beach towns of **Nesebâr** and **Sozopol**.

Two Weeks

Spend a few extra days in Sofia, adding in a day trip to Rila Monastery, then catch a bus to **Plovdiv** to wander the cobbled lanes of the Old Town. From there, take the mountain air in majestic Veliko Târnovo. Make for the coast, with a few nights in Varna and lively Sozopol.

SOFIA   СОФИЯ

♫ 02 / POP 1.2 MILLION

Sofia (So-fia) is no Paris or Prague, but Bulgaria's capital and biggest city has a Balkan beguilement all its own. The old east-meets-west feel is still here, with a scattering of onion-domed churches, Ottoman mosques and stubborn Red Army monuments, and the city's grey, blocky architecture adds a lingering, interesting Soviet flavour to the place. Vast, leafy parks and manicured gardens offer welcome respite from the busy city streets and the ski slopes and hiking trails of mighty Mt Vitosha are right on the doorstep. With many of Bulgaria's finest museums and art galleries to explore and plenty of excellent bars, restaurants and entertainment venues, you may well end up sticking around for longer than you imagined.

◉ Sights

◉ Ploshtad Aleksander Nevski

★ **Aleksander Nevski Church**   CHURCH
(pl Aleksander Nevski; ⊘7am-7pm) FREE One of *the* symbols not just of Sofia but of Bulgaria itself, this massive, awe-inspiring church was built between 1882 and 1912 in memory of the 200,000 Russian soldiers who died fighting for Bulgaria's independence during the Russo-Turkish War (1877–78).

Aleksander Nevski Crypt   GALLERY
(Museum of Icons; pl Aleksander Nevski; adult/student 6/3 lv; ⊘10am-5.30pm Tue-Sun; 🚌1) Originally built as a final resting place for Bulgarian kings, this crypt now houses Bulgaria's biggest and best collection of icons, stretching back to the 5th century. Enter to the left of the eponymous church's main entrance.

Sveta Sofia Church   CHURCH
(ul Parizh; museum adult/student 6/2 lv; ⊘7am-7pm Apr-Oct, to 6pm Nov-Mar, museum 9am-5pm

Tue-Sun; 🚌9) Sveta Sofia Church is the capital's oldest, and gave the city its name. A newly opened subterranean **museum** houses an ancient necropolis, with 56 tombs and the remains of four other churches. Outside are the Tomb of the Unknown Soldier and an eternal flame, and the grave of Ivan Vazov, Bulgaria's most revered writer.

◉ Sofia City Garden & Around

Royal Palace   PALACE
(ul Tsar Osvoboditel; 🚌20) Originally built as the headquarters of the Ottoman police force, it was here that Bulgaria's national hero, Vasil Levski, was tried and tortured before his public execution in 1873. After the liberation, the building was remodelled to become the official residence of Bulgaria's royal family. It houses the National Art Gallery and the Ethnographical Museum.

Ethnographical Museum   MUSEUM
(Royal Palace; adult/student 3/1 lv; ⊘10am-3.30pm Tue-Sun; 🚌20) Displays on regional costumes, crafts and folklore are spread over two floors of the palace, and many of the rooms, with marble fireplaces, mirrors and ornate plasterwork, are worth pausing over themselves.

Archaeological Museum   MUSEUM
(www.naim.bg; pl Nezavisimost; adult/student 10/2 lv; tours in English 20 lv; ⊘10am-6pm May-Oct, to 5pm Tue-Sun Nov-Apr; 🚌10) Housed in a former mosque built in 1496, this museum displays a wealth of Thracian, Roman and medieval artefacts. Highlights include a mosaic floor from the Church of Sveta Sofia, a 4th-century BC Thracian gold burial mask, and a magnificent bronze head, thought to represent a Thracian king.

Sveti Georgi Rotunda   CHURCH
(Church of St George; www.svgeorgi-rotonda.com; bul Dondukov 2; ⊘daily services 8am, 9am & 5pm; 🚌10) Built in the 4th century AD, this tiny

Sofia

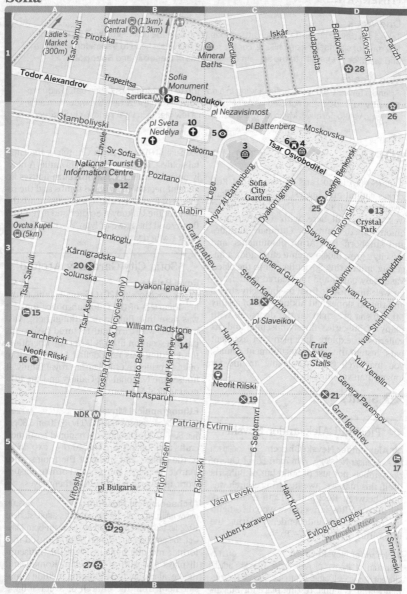

Central (1.1km);
Central (1.3km)

Ladie's
Market
(300m)

Tsar Samuil
Pirotska

Serdika

Iskâr

Budapeshta

Benkovski

Rakovski

Parizh

Mineral
Baths

28

Todor Alexandrov

Trapezitsa

Stamboliyski

Sofia
Monument

Serdica **8** Dondukov

pl Nezavisimost

26

Lavele

pl Sveta
Nedelya

Sv Sofia

National Tourist
Information Centre

10

7

Sâborna

5

pl Battenberg

Moskovska

6 4

Tsar Osvoboditel

3

Pozitano

Lege

12

Knyaz Al Battenberg

Sofia
City
Garden

Dyakon Ignatiy

Georgi Benkovski

25

Rakovski

13
Crystal
Park

Ovcha Kupel
(5km)

Denkoglu

Alabin

Graf Ignatiev

Dyakon Ignatiy

Slavyanska

Kârnigradska

20
Solunska

Dyakon Ignatiy

General Gurko

6 Septemvri

Ivan Vazov

Dobrudzha

Tsar Samuil

Tsar Asen

Vitosha (trams & bicycles only)

Stefan Karadzha

Ivan Shishman

Yuli Venelin

15

Parchevich

Neofit Rilski

16

Hristo Belchev

Angel Kânchev

William Gladstone

14

Han Krum

18

pl Slaveikov

Fruit
& Veg
Stalls

General Parensov

Han Asparuh

22
Neofit Rilski

19

21

Graf Ignatiev

17

NDK

Patriarh Evtimii

Fritjof Nansen

Rakovski

6 Septemvri

Han Krum

pl Bulgaria

Vasil Levski

Evlogi Georgiev

Perlovska River

Hr Smirneski

29

Lyuben Karavelov

27

---

red-brick church is Sofia's oldest preserved building. The murals inside were painted between the 10th and 14th centuries. It's a busy, working church, but tourists are welcome.

President's Building NOTABLE BUILDING

(pl Nezavisimost; 10) The Bulgarian president's office isn't open to the public, but the **changing of the guard** ceremony (on the hour) is a spectacle not to be missed; for the full ceremony, replete with music, weapons

BULGARIA SOFIA

city's major landmarks, noted for its rich, Byzantine-style murals. It was blown up by communists on 16 April 1925 in an attempt to assassinate Tsar Boris III.

Sveta Petka
Samardzhiiska Church   CHURCH
(bul Maria Luisa; Ⓜ Serdika) This tiny church was built during the early years of Ottoman rule (late 14th century), which explains its sunken profile and inconspicuous exterior. Inside are some 16th-century murals. It's rumoured that the Bulgarian national hero Vasil Levski is buried here.

and all manner of pomp, be there on the first Wednesday of the month at noon.

Sveta Nedelya Cathedral   CHURCH
(pl Sveta Nedelya; Ⓜ Serdika) Completed in 1863, this magnificent domed church is one of the

☞ Tours

Free Sofia Tour WALKING TOUR
(✉ 088 699 3977; www.freesofiatour.com; ⏱ 11am & 6pm) **FREE** Explore Sofia's sights in the company of friendly and enthusiastic English-speaking young locals on this guided walk. No reservation is needed, just show up outside the Palace of Justice on bul Vitosha, at 11am or 6pm. Walks take around two hours.

New Sofia Pub Crawl TOUR
(✉ 087 761 3992; www.thenewsofiapubcrawl.com; tour 20 lv; ⏱ 9pm-1am) Explore Sofia's secret haunts on this nightly knees-up. Expect lots of insights into the social side of the city (plus the odd free drink). Meet by the statue of Stefan Stambolov in Crystal Park.

City Sighteeing Bus Tour BUS TOUR
(www.citysightseeing.bg; 20 lv; ⏱ hourly btwn 10am-1pm Wed-Sun) Get your bearings on this hop-on hop-off bus tour that takes in over 30 sights across Sofia. Starts on the hour at Aleksander Nevski Cathedral. Reservations required between October and March; just show up the rest of the year.

🛏 Sleeping

Accommodation in Sofia tends to be more expensive than anywhere else in Bulgaria, with prices comparable to those in Western European cities. Good-quality budget hotels are a rarity, and cheaper places that do exist are often either squalid dives or in awkward-to-reach locations; hostels are a better deal.

Art Hostel HOSTEL €
(✉ 02-987 0545; www.art-hostel.com; ul Angel Kânchev 21a; dm/s/d from 20/47/66 lv; 🛜; 🚐 12) This bohemian hostel stands out from the crowd with its summertime art exhibitions, live music, dance performances and more. Dorms are appropriately arty and bright; private rooms are airy and welcoming. There's a great basement bar and peaceful little garden.

Canapé Connection HOSTEL €
(✉ 02-441 6373; www.canapeconnection.com; ul William Gladstone 12a; dm/s/d from 16/40/52 lv; @🛜; 🚐 1) Run by three young travellers, Canapé is a homely place with eight- and four-bed dorms featuring wide bunks and wooden floors, as well as private rooms. Homemade *banitsa* (cheese pastry) and croissants are on the breakfast menu.

★ Red B&B B&B €€
(✉ 088 922 6822; www.redbandb.com; ul Lyuben Karavelov 15; s/d from 40/70 lv; @; Ⓜ Vasil Levski,

🚐 10) Attached to the Red House cultural centre in a wonderful '20s building once home to Bulgaria's most famous sculptor, this six-room hotel offers digs with a difference. All rooms are individually decorated, and the general air is one of boho bonhomie. Shared bathrooms.

Hotel Niky HOTEL €€
(✉ 02-952 3058; www.hotel-niky.com; ul Neofit Rilski 16; r/ste from 80/120 lv; 🅿😊❄🛜🚗; 🚐 1) Offering excellent value and a good city-centre location, Niky has comfortable rooms and gleaming bathrooms, and smart little suites come with kitchenettes. It's very popular and frequently full; be sure to book ahead.

★ Sofia Residence BOUTIQUE HOTEL €€€
(✉ 02-814 4888; www.residence-oborishte.com; ul Oborishte 63; s/d/ste from 176/195/215 lv; 😊❄🛜; 🚐 9, 72) A luxurious salmon-pink '30s-era home with its own bistro, the Residence has nine rooms and sumptuous suites with cherry-wood flooring, antique-style furnishings and lots of space. The penthouse (254 lv) has a view over the Aleksander Nevski Church. Prices drop by 20% at weekends.

🍴 Eating

Compared with the rest of Bulgaria, Sofia is gourmet heaven, with an unrivalled range of international cuisine and new, quality restaurants springing up all the time. If you're on a budget, there are plenty of kiosks where you can buy fast food like *banitsa* and *palachinki* (pancakes).

K.E.V.A BULGARIAN €
(✉ 087 731 3233; School for Performing Arts, ul Rakovski 112; mains 5-15 lv; ⏱ 11am-midnight; Ⓜ Sofia Universitet) All is not as it seems at K.E.V.A, a simple-looking place with a cheap menu: this restaurant offers five-star cuisine at cafeteria prices. A favourite hang-out of Sofia's arty elite and students from the attached School for Performing Arts, it also hosts regular mealtime theatrical performances.

★ Manastirska Magernitsa BULGARIAN €€
(✉ 02-980 3883; www.magernitsa.com; ul Han Asparuh 67; mains 6-10 lv; ⏱ 11am-2am; 😊; ⓂNDK) This traditional *mehana* (tavern) is among the best places in Sofia to sample authentic Bulgarian cuisine. The enormous menu features recipes collected from monasteries across the country, with dishes such as 'drunken rabbit' stewed in wine as well as salads, fish, pork and game options. Portions are generous and service attentive.

The Little Things
INTERNATIONAL €€

(☑ 088 249 0030; ul Tsar Ivan Shishman 37; mains 7-18 lv; ⊙ noon-midnight; 🖵 1) It's the little things – knickknacks, toys, books, flowers – that give this charming spot its name, but it's the large portions of delightful, home-style food that keep locals coming back for more. Mains includes handmade meatballs, sinful pastas and creamy fish dishes; whatever you do, try the fig cheesecake.

Pastorant
ITALIAN €€€

(☑ 02-981 4482; www.pastorant.eu; ul Tsar Asen 16; mains 11-28 lv; ⊙ noon-10.30pm; ⊜ 🖉; Ⓜ NDK) This charming pea-green restaurant provides an intimate setting for high-quality Italian cuisine, including some inventive pasta and risotto dishes as well as traditional favourites like saltimbocca and pesto chicken.

🍷 Drinking & Nightlife

One More Bar
BAR

(☑ 088 253 9592; ul Shishman 12; ⊙ 8am-2am; Ⓜ Sofia Universitet) Inside a gorgeous old house, this shabby-chic hotspot wouldn't be out of place in Melbourne or Manhattan: an extensive cocktail list, delightful summer garden and jazzy background music add to its cosmopolitan appeal.

Raketa Rakia Bar
BAR

(☑ 02-444 6111; ul Yanko Sakazov 17; ⊙ 11am-midnight; 🖵 11) Unsurprisingly, this rakish retro bar has a huge selection of *rakia* (fiery fermented fruit brandy) on hand; before you start working your way down the list, line your stomach with their meat-and-cream-heavy snacks and meals.

Bar Up
BAR

(☑ 087 654 1641; ul Neofit Rilski 55; ⊙ 9am-midnight Mon-Thu, 9am-2am Fri-Sat, 11am-1am Sun; Ⓜ NPK) As you'd expect from a place that serves cocktails in jars and has furniture made from shipping pallets, this is a laid-back and arty place, with a regular roster of changing exhibitions to seal the deal.

Yalta
CLUB

(www.yaltaclub.com; bul Tsar Osvoboditel 20; ⊙ 24hr; Ⓜ Sofia Universitet) Shake it with Sofia's trendy types and local and international DJ stars at this hip, hyper spot that's been going strong since 1959 (it was Bulgaria's first nightclub).

☆ Entertainment

If you read Bulgarian, *Programata* is a comprehensive source of entertainment listings; otherwise check out its English-language website, www.programata.bg.

Live Music

Rock It
LIVE MUSIC

(www.rockit.bg; ul Georgi Benkovski 14; ⊙ 7pm-4am Mon-Sat; Ⓜ Serdika) If you're into rock and metal, get your horns up here. This huge, two-level building shakes beneath the weight of heavy live bands, DJs and lots and lots of hair.

Sofia Live Club
LIVE MUSIC

(www.sofialiveclub.com; pl Bulgaria 1; ⊙ 9pm-5am Wed-Sat; Ⓜ NDK) This slick venue is the city's largest live-music club. All swished up in cabaret style, it hosts local and overseas jazz, alternative, world music and rock acts.

Bulgaria Hall
CLASSICAL MUSIC

(☑ 02-987 7656; www.sofiaphilharmonie.bg; ul Georgi Benkovski 1; ⊙ ticket office 9am-8pm Mon-Fri, to 3pm Sat; 🖵 9) Home of the excellent Sofia Philharmonic Orchestra.

Performing Arts

National Opera House
OPERA

(☑ 02-987 1366; www.operasofia.bg; bul Dondukov 30, entrance on ul Vrabcha; ⊙ ticket office 9am-2pm & 2.30-7pm Mon-Fri, 11am-7pm Sat, 11am-4pm Sun; 🖵 9, 🖵 20) Opened in 1953, this monumental edifice is the venue for grand opera and ballet performances, as well as concerts.

National Palace of Culture
CONCERT VENUE

(NDK; ☑ 02-916 6300; www.ndk.bg; pl Bulgaria; ⊙ ticket office 10am-8pm; 🖉; Ⓜ NDK) The NDK (as it's usually called) has 15 halls and is the country's largest cultural complex. It maintains a regular program of events throughout the year, including film screenings, trade shows and big-name international music acts.

🛍 Shopping

Bulevard Vitosha is Sofia's main shopping street, featuring international brand-name boutiques interspersed with restaurants; the charming, rambling ul Pirotska is a central pedestrian mall lined with cheaper shops selling clothes, shoes and household goods.

Ladies' Market
MARKET

(Zhenski Pazar; ul Stefan Stambolov; ⊙ dawn-dusk; 🖵 20) Stretching several blocks between ul Ekzarh Yosif and bul Slivnitsa, this is Sofia's biggest fresh-produce (and everything else) market. Beware pickpockets.

Ot Manastira
FOOD

(From the Monastery; ☑ 088 775 8093; www.ot manastira.com; ul Ivan Asen II 54; ⊙ 10am-2pm &

3-7.30pm Mon-Fri, 10am-5.30pm Sat-Sun; ⓂSofia Universitet) This small shop sells super-fresh fruit, vegetables, honey, relish and – on Fridays – fish (including caviar) all produced by the Kyustendil Monastery, 100km southwest of the city.

❶ Information

National Tourist Information Centre (☑02-987 9778; www.bulgariatravel.org; ul Sveta Sofia; ☉9am-5pm Mon-Fri; ᮀ5) Helpful, English-speaking staff and glossy brochures for destinations around Bulgaria.

Pirogov Hospital (☑02-915 4411; www.piro gov.bg; bul General Totleben 21; ᮀ4, 5) Sofia's main public hospital for emergencies.

Sofia Tourist Information Centre (☑02-491 8345; www.info-sofia.bg; Sofia University underpass; ☉8am-8pm Mon-Fri, 10am-6pm Sat-Sun; ⓂKliment Ohridski) Lots of free leaflets and maps, and helpful English-speaking staff.

❶ Getting There & Away

AIR

Sofia Airport (☑02-937 2211; www.sofia-airport.bg; off bul Brussels; minibus 30) is 12km east of the city centre. The only domestic flights within Bulgaria are between Sofia and the Black Sea. **Bulgaria Air** (☑02-402 0400; www.air.bg; ul Ivan Vazov 2; ☉8.30am-5pm Mon-Fri; ᮀ20) flies daily to Varna, with two or three daily flights between July and September; the airline also flies to Burgas.

BUS

Sofia's **central bus station** (Tsentralna Avtogara; www.centralnaavtogara.bg; bul Maria Luisa 100; 24hr; ᮀ7) is 100m south of the train station. There are dozens of counters for individual private companies, an information desk and an **OK-Supertrans taxi desk** (www.oktaxi.net; ☉6am-10pm). Departures are less frequent between November and April. Frequent buses depart Sofia for Plovdiv (14 lv, 2½ hours), Veliko Târnovo (22 lv, four hours), Varna (33 lv, seven hours) and more; the easy-to-navigate www.bgrazpisanie.com has full local and international timetable and fare listings.

TRAIN

The **central train station** (bul Maria Luisa; ᮀ1, 7) is finally undergoing some much-needed renovations, scheduled to culminate in a shiny, user-friendly station in 2015. It's still operational, though travellers may find it easier to purchase tickets online (www.bdz.transportinfo.bg; you'll need to register) than battle the disruptions and typically chaotic ticket queues. Whatever you do, don't wait until the last minute to buy your tickets.

Destinations for all domestic and international services are listed on timetables in Cyrillic, but departures (for the following two hours) and arrivals (for the previous two hours) are listed in English on a large screen on the ground floor.

Sample fast train routes include Sofia to Plovdiv (12 lv, 2½ hours) and Varna (31 lv, seven hours): see www.bgrazpisanie.com (click on 'timetable') or www.bdz.bg for all domestic and international routes.

❶ Getting Around

TO/FROM THE AIRPORT

At the time of research, Sofia Airport was linked to the city by minibus 30 (to and from pl Nezavisimost, 1.50 lv) and the slower, meandering buses 84 and 384 (from Terminals 1 and 2, respectively). These buses may be phased out once a new direct metro line – planned for completion in April 2015 – is opened.

CAR & MOTORCYCLE

Frequent public transport, cheap taxis and horrendous traffic provide little or no incentive to drive around Sofia. If you wish to explore further afield, though, renting a car is a great idea. Most majors (and cheaper local options) have offices at the airport; see www.sofia-airport.bg for a full list of companies.

PUBLIC TRANSPORT

Public transport – trams, buses, minibuses and trolleybuses, as well as the underground metro – run from 5.30am to 11pm every day.

Many buses, trams and trolleybuses are fitted with on-board ticket machines; all tickets in Sofia cost 1 lv. It's far easier and quicker, especially during peak times, to buy tickets from kiosks at stops along the route before boarding.

If you plan to use public transport frequently, buy a one-day/10-trip/one-month transit card (4/8/50 lv), valid for all lines (a monthly card just for the metro is 35 lv). All tickets must be validated by inserting them in the small machine on-board; once punched, tickets are nontransferable. Inspectors will issue on-the-spot fines (10 lv) if you don't have a ticket.

See www.sofiatraffic.bg for more information on public transport.

TAXI

By law, taxis must use meters, but those that wait around the airport, luxury hotels and within 100m of pl Sveta Nedelya will often try to negotiate an unmetered fare – which, of course, will be considerably more. All official taxis have fares per kilometre displayed in the window, and have obvious taxi signs (in English or Bulgarian) on top. **OK-Supertrans** (☑02-973 2121; www.oktaxi. net) or **Yellow Taxi** (☑02-91 119; www.yellow333. com) are reliable operators.

SOUTHERN BULGARIA

Some of Bulgaria's most precious treasures are scattered in the towns, villages and forests of the stunning south. The must-visit medieval Rila Monastery is nestled in the deep forest but easily reached by bus; tiny Melnik is awash in ancient wine; and the cobbled streets of Plovdiv, Bulgaria's second city, are lined with timeless reminders of civilisations come and gone.

The region is a scenic and craggy one; the **Rila Mountains** (www.rilanationalpark.bg) are just south of Sofia, the **Pirin Mountains** (www.pirin-np.com) rise towards the Greek border, and the Rodopi Mountains loom to the east and south of Plovdiv. There's great hiking to be had, and the south is also home to three of Bulgaria's most popular ski resorts: **Borovets, Bansko** and **Pamporovo**; see www.bulgariaski.com for information.

Rila Monastery
Рилски Манастир

Many Bulgarians say you haven't really been to Bulgaria until you've paid your respects to the truly heavenly, Unesco-listed **Rila Monastery** (www.rilamonastery.pmg-blg.com; ☉7am-9pm) `FREE`, 120km south of Sofia. Built in 927 and heavily restored in 1469, the monastery was a stronghold of Bulgarian culture and language during Ottoman rule. Set in a magnificent forested valley ideal for hiking, the monastery is rightfully famous for its mural-plastered Nativity Church dating from the 1830s. The attached **museum** (Rila Monastery; 8 lv; ☉8am-5pm) is home to the astonishing Rila Cross, with biblical scenes painstakingly carved in miniature. Visitors should dress modestly.

If you have time, hike up to the **Tomb of St Ivan**, the hermit founder of the monastery. The 15-minute walk begins along the road 3.7km east behind the monastery.

You can stay in simple **rooms** (☎089 687 2010; www.rilamonastery.pmg-blg.com; r 30-60 lv) at the monastery, or for something slightly more upmarket, try **Gorski Kut** (☎07054-2170; d from 50 lv; 🅿❋), an easy 5km away.

From Sofia's **Ovcha Kupel** (☎02-955 5362; bul Ovcha Kupel 1, also called 'Zapad,' or 'West' station), one daily morning bus (12 lv, 2½ hours) goes to the monastery and returns in the afternoon. Five daily buses go to and from Rila village (4 lv). Otherwise, the **Rila Monastery Bus** (☎02-489 0883; www.rilamonasterybus.com;

€25; ☉Apr-Nov) departs Sofia at 9am, takes in the monastery and Boyana, and returns at 5pm.

Melnik   Мелник
📞 07437 / POP 385

Officially Bulgaria's smallest town, Melnik is one of the country's most famous wine centres. Family-run *mehanas* boast their own barrels of blood-red Melnik, the unique local varietal, which is sold in plastic jugs on the dirt streets.

◉ Sights

The major sights here, unsurprisingly, are wineries. Melnik's wines, celebrated for more than 600 years, include the signature dark red, Shiroka Melnishka Loza; it was a favourite tipple of Winston Churchill. Shops and stands dot Melnik's cobblestone paths, with reds and whites for 3 lv to 4 lv and up.

Museum of Wine   MUSEUM
(www.muzei-na-vinoto.com; ul Melnik 91; admission 5 lv; ☉10am-7pm) Learn the history of wine-making in Melnik, ogle the 400-plus bottles of wine on display (the dirt vault is especially cool), and work your way through a tasting menu at this fun museum attached to the Hotel Bulgari. Once you find one (or four) wines that you like, fill a bottle and they'll personalise a label for you.

Mitko Manolev Winery   WINERY
(Shestaka; ☎07437-2215; www.shestaka.com; admission incl tasting 2 lv; ☉9am-dusk) For the most atmospheric adventures in *degustatsia* (wine tasting), clamber up the cobblestones to this winery, also known as Shestaka ('six-fingered'); it's named after the founder, who had an extra digit (as does his modern-day descendant Mitko). This place is basically a cellar dug into the rocks, plus a hut with tables and chairs outside. It's along the hillside trail between the Bolyaskata Kâshta ruins and the Kordopulov House. Accommodation is also available (double 35 lv).

Kordopulov House   MUSEUM
(☎07437-2265; www.kordopulova-house.com; admission 3 lv; ☉8am-8pm) Built in 1754, this four-storey former home of a prestigious wine merchant is an impressive structure. The sitting rooms have been carefully restored, and boast 19th-century murals, stained-glass windows and exquisitely carved wooden ceilings. An enormous wine cellar (tasting

MT VITOSHA & BOYANA

At the southern edge of Sofia, Mt Vitosha is popular for skiing and hiking at a cheaper rate than the ski resorts (it's about 30 lv for a lift ticket). The mountain is part of the 227-sq-km **Vitosha Nature Park** (www.park-vitosha.org), the oldest of its kind in Bulgaria (created in 1934). The highest point is Mt Cherni Vrâh (Black Peak; 2290m), the fourth-highest peak in Bulgaria.

Chairlifts, starting around 3km from the village of **Dragalevtsi**, run all year up to Goli Vrâh (1837m); another option is the six-person gondola at Simeonovo (Friday to Sunday only).

A trip out here could be combined with a visit to **Boyana**, home to the fabulous, Unesco-listed **Boyana Church** (www.boyanachurch.org; ul Boyansko Ezero 3; adult/student 10/1 lv, combined ticket with National Historical Museum 12 lv, guide 10 lv; ⊘9.30am-5.30pm Apr-Oct, 9am-5pm Nov-Mar; 🚌 64, minibus 21), built between the 11th and 19th centuries. Its interior is adorned with colourful murals painted in 1259 that are considered among the most important examples of medieval Bulgarian art.

The decent **National Historical Museum** (www.historymuseum.org; bul Vitoshko Lale 16; adult/student 10/1 lv, combined ticket with Boyana Church 12 lv, guide 20 lv; ⊘9.30am-6pm Tue-Sun Apr-Oct, to 5.30pm Nov-Mar) is also found in Boyana. It's worth a look for the Thracian artefacts and 19th-century costumes and weapons, although many are reproductions.

Minibus 21 runs to Boyana from the city centre (hop on at bul Vasil Levski), and will drop you at the gates of the museum; it also connects the museum with the church. Alternatively, take bus 64 from Hladilnika terminal on ul Srebârna, or a taxi (about 8 to 10 lv one-way); for the museum, ask for 'Residentsia Boyana'.

available) includes 180m of illuminated labyrinthine passageways; look out for the wall full of glittering coins. The house is on the cliff face at the street's end, south of the creek: you can't miss it.

✨ Festivals & Events

Golden Grape Festival   WINE
Vino tastings, music and all manner of wine-centric wassailing. Held on the second weekend of February.

🛏 Sleeping

Most wineries offer accommodation; also look out for the 'rooms to sleep' (стаи за спане) signs in windows.

Hotel Bulgari   HOTEL €
(☑7437-2215; www.hotelbulgari.net; ul Melnik 91; s/d/apt from 30/50/80 lv; 🛜) This imposing building seems out of place in little old Melnik but its shiny, sleek and spacious rooms go down a treat. While the cavernous restaurant is more suitable for banquets than intimate dining, the attached wine museum is a great spot for a tipple.

★**Hotel Bolyarka**   HOTEL €€
(☑07437-2383; www.melnikhotels.com; ul Melnik 34; s/d/apt incl breakfast 40/60/100 lv; 🅿❄@🛜)

The spiffy Bolyarka has elegant and well-decorated rooms, and apartments with fireplaces. Sauna and massage treatments are available, but the authentic Ottoman-era hammam (Turkish bath) is for viewing only. The on-site restaurant is excellent.

🍴 Eating

All wine and no dine can make for delirious days; thankfully Melnik also excels in eateries. Try the traditional *banitsa*, a local speciality, and the mountain river trout.

★**Mehana Chavkova House**   BULGARIAN €€
(☑089 350 5090; ul Melnik 112; 5-10 lv) Sit beneath the 500-year-old trees and watch Melnik meander past at this superb spot. Like many places in town, grilled meats and Bulgarian dishes are specialities (try the 'sach', a sizzling flat pan of meat and vegetables); the atmosphere and super-friendly service gives it that extra nudge above the rest.

**Mehana Mencheva
Kâshta**   BULGARIAN €€
(☑07437-2339; mains 6-11 lv; ⊘10am-11.30pm) This tiny tavern has a lovely upper porch overlooking the main street down towards the end of the village. It's popular with locals and does the full run of Bulgarian dishes.

ℹ Getting There & Away

One daily direct bus connects Melnik with Sofia (17 lv, four hours) though times vary. One daily direct bus serves Blagoevgrad (9 lv, two hours) near the border with Macedonia.

Plovdiv   Пловдив

📞 032 / POP 341.040

Awash in art galleries, bohemian cafes, museums and highbrow house museums, it's little wonder Plovdiv has been named the European Capital of Culture for 2019. A smaller, less stressful city than Sofia, pretty Plovdiv is an ideal walking city; as a lively university town, it's also on the fun frontline, with laid-back bars galore.

The past lives on in Plovdiv's atmospheric Old Town, largely restored to its mid-19th-century appearance and marked by winding cobblestone streets. Lined with historic homes, antique shops and creative salons, Plovdiv differs from 'Old Towns' in that eminent artists still live and work within its tranquil confines. The neighbourhood boasts Thracian, Roman, Byzantine and Bulgarian antiquities, most impressive being the Roman amphitheatres – the best-preserved in the Balkans and still used for performances.

◎ Sights

Most of Plovdiv's main sights are in and around the fantastic Old Town. Its meandering cobblestone streets, overflowing with atmospheric house museums, art galleries and antique stores, are also home to welcoming nooks for eating, drinking and people-watching.

★ Roman Amphitheatre   HISTORIC SITE

(ul Hemus; adult/student 5/2 lv; ⊙9am-6pm) Plovdiv's magnificent 2nd-century-AD amphitheatre, built during the reign of Emperor Trajan, was only uncovered during a freak landslide in 1972. It could hold about 6000 spectators. Now largely restored, it's one of Bulgaria's most magical venues, once again hosting large-scale special events and concerts. Visitors can admire the amphitheatre for free from several lookouts along ul Hemus, or pay admission for a scarper around.

Roman Stadium   HISTORIC SITE

(www.ancient-stadium-plovdiv.eu; ⊙9am-6pm) While the once-huge 2nd-century Roman Stadium is mostly hidden under the pedestrian mall, there are stairways from different sides allowing for at-your-leisure exploration. A new on-site 3D movie (adult/student 6/3 lv; 10 showings daily) offers an immersive experience into the stadium's glory days as a venue for gladiator matches.

Roman Odeon   RUIN

Constructed between the 2nd and 5th centuries AD, the Odeon was once the seat of the city council. It now hosts occasional performances in its tiny reconstructed amphitheatre: check out the original columns. It's adjacent to the tourist information centre.

Ethnographical Museum   MUSEUM

(📞 032-626 328; www.ethnograph.info; ul Dr Chomakov 2; adult/student 5/2 lv; ⊙9am-6pm Tue-Sun May-Oct, 9am-5pm Tue-Sun Nov-Apr) This museum houses 40,000 exhibits, including folk costumes, musical instruments, jewellery and traditional craftworks such as winemaking and beekeeping. Built in 1847, it's Plovdiv's most renowned National Revival–period home; the gorgeous garden and exquisite exterior are reasons enough to make a visit.

Church of Sveti Konstantin & Elena   CHURCH

(ul Sâborna 24; ⊙8am-7pm) This is Plovdiv's oldest church and one of its most beloved: the riotous frescoes and gilded iconostasis within belie its broody exterior. The original church – dedicated to Emperor Constantine the Great and his mother, Helena – was built in AD 337; what stands today dates to 1832.

Dzhumaya Mosque   MOSQUE

(pl Dzhumaya; ⊙6am-11pm) This, the second-oldest working mosque in Europe, was originally built in 1364, then demolished and rebuilt in the mid-15th century. With a 23m-high minaret, it was the largest of Plovdiv's more than 50 Ottoman mosques.

☞ Tours

Free Plovdiv Tours   WALKING TOUR

(www.freeplovdivtour.com; ⊙6pm May-Sep, 2pm Oct-Apr) FREE Free two-hour-long walks taking in Plovdiv's prime attractions. Meet under the clock at the central post office in pl Tsentralen.

🛏 Sleeping

Hikers Hostel   HOSTEL €

(📞 089 676 4854; www.hikers-hostel.org; ul Sâborna 53; dm/tw from 14/50 lv; @🖤) With a mellow, central location in the Old Town, Hikers has standard dorms and facilities, but bonuses such as a garden lounge, hammocks and mega-friendly staff make it a worthy option. They also have off-site private rooms available; ask when booking.

9th Kilometre Complex
CAMPGROUND €

(☎ 088 814 8174; www.9km.bg; Pazardzhiko shose; camping per person from 4 lv, caravan 6 lv, summer-only bungalow 22 lv, r renovated/unrenovated 35/30 lv; ⊙ year-round; P 🛜 🛏) This snazzy, family-friendly campground features a restaurant, 24-hour bar, playground and large outdoor pool. A taxi out here should cost about 12 lv. It's best to phone for bookings, rather than go through the website.

★ Hostel Old Plovdiv
HOSTEL €€

(☎ 032-260 925; www.hosteloldplovdiv.com; ul Chetvarti Yanuari 3; dm/s/tw/tr/q €12/25/35/39/45; P 🛜) This marvellous old building (1868) is more akin to a boutique historical hotel than a run-of-the-mill hostel. Remarkably restored by charismatic owner Hristo Giulev and his wife, this genial place – in the middle of the Old Town – is about warm welcomes and old-world charm. Every room features local antiques (from the decor to the beds themselves), and the courtyard is desperately romantic with a history all its own (Hristo will fill you in over a glass of their special iced tea).

Hotel Dafi
HOTEL €€

(☎ 032-620 041; www.hoteldafi.com; ul Giorgi Benkovski 23; s/d/ste 49/69/120 lv; P ❄ 🛜) With its mirrored tower and bland facade, the Dafi looks a bit like a small office tower from the outside, but its location in the Kapana district, comfortable rooms and astonishingly friendly staff ensure that mediocrity doesn't get a look-in. There's a good little cafe attached.

Hotel Globus
HOTEL €€

(☎ 032-686 464; www.hotelglobus-bg.com; bul 6 Septemvri 38; d/tr/apt 69/90/120 lv; P ❄ 🛜) A short walk from the Old Town and surrounded by lots of shops and cafes, the Globus has English-speaking staff and a popular restaurant attached. Rooms are sparkling; the huge, oddly windowless apartment – with over-the-top furniture, full-length heart-shaped mirror and a bear rug – must be seen to be believed.

Hotel Odeon
BOUTIQUE HOTEL €€€

(☎ 032-622 065; www.hotelodeon.net; ul Otets Paisii 40; s/d/apt 94/117/205 lv; P ❄ 🛜) Aptly named (it's across from the Roman Odeon), this restored home/hotel keeps the theme going with Roman-style columns in some rooms and an elegant old-world feel throughout.

The attached restaurant has a creative and extensive vegan menu, as well as sophisticated options for carnivores.

✖ Eating

King's Stables
BULGARIAN €

(☎ 088 981 4255; ul Sâborna 40; mains 4-7 lv; ⊙ 9am-2am) The sprawling, summer-only King's Stables occupies a rolling hill ending in Roman walls. Offerings range from breakfast crepes to hearty meat dishes: be prepared to be shaken down for whatever you're eating by the trillion (clean) kittens roaming the joint. It's a lively spot, with local bands playing most nights.

Rahat Tepe
GRILL €

(☎ 087 845 0259; ul Dr Chomakov 20; mains 4-8 lv; ⊙ 10am-midnight) Way up in the Old Town, the alfresco Rahat Tepe serves simple meals such as salads, beef kebabs and fried fish. Suitably rustic with great city views, it's an ideal spot for a nosh after clambering around Nebet Tepe (Nebet Hill).

★ Grazhdanski Klub
BULGARIAN €€

(Citizens Club; ul Stoyan Chalukov 1; mains 5-12 lv; ⊙ 8am-1am Mon-Fri, 10am-1am Sat & Sun; 🛜) A locals' favourite, this fabulous, friendly nook is just a totter down the hill from the Roman Amphitheatre. Its cool, green courtyard is a haven in hotter months. The food – mostly Bulgarian staples and sinful salads – is moreish: thankfully, portions are huge! It's attached to the endearing, free-to-enter Vazrazdane Gallery (open 10am to 6.30pm Monday to Saturday, 11am to 5pm Sunday).

Dayana
GRILL €€

(☎ 032-623 027; ul Dondukov Korsakov 2; mains 5-9 lv; ⊙ 24hr; 🛜) This big, popular place has a huge (and colourful) menu strong on grilled meats. Portions are fit to feed an army.

Hemingway
INTERNATIONAL €€€

(☎ 032-267 350; www.hemingway.bg; ul Gurko 10; mains 5-22 lv; ⊙ noon-1am) Papa would approve. This atmospheric spot near the Odeon comes across all 1920s Paris; it even smells like freshly baked baguettes. Seafood is a speciality, though posh takes on meaty Bulgarian classics get a good run, too. Unobtrusive live music provides a classy soundtrack to your meal.

🍷 Drinking & Nightlife

There are some great haunts in the Kapana district; the name means 'the trap', referring to its tight streets (north of pl Dzhumaya, between ul Rayko Daskalov to the west and bul Tsar Boris Obedinitel to the east).

★ **Art Club Nylon** BAR
(📞 088 949 6750; ul Giorgi Benkovski 8, Kapana; ⊙ noon-4am Mon-Sat; 🛜) A bastion of bohemia, this damp, bare-bones but somehow wonderful place often hosts rock and indie bands playing to Plovdiv's cool kids.

Apartment 101 BAR
(ul William Gladston 8; ⊙ 10am-1am Sun-Thu, to 2am Fri & Sat) A hip – but not painfully so – spot in a wonderfully ramshackle building with chill-out music and occasional live acts. The interior is op-shop chic; you'll have to be crowbarred out of the eminently hangoutable courtyard.

Petnoto CLUB
(ul Ioakim Gruev 36, Kapana; ⊙ 8am-6am; 🛜) Meet the locals at this happy honkytonk, which hosts frequent music, literary, art and cinema events; it's a great place for a tipple even if nothing's on.

Club Infi CLUB
(📞 088 828 1431; Bratya Pulievi 4, Kapana; ⊙ 9pm-6am; 🛜) Packed with students, this dancey place parties until dawn...and then some.

ℹ Information

Tourist Information Centre (www.visitplovdiv. com; pl Tsentralen 1; ⊙ 8.45am-noon & 12.45-6pm Mon-Fri, 10am-2pm Sat & Sun) Helpful centre near the post office providing maps and info. There's another office (ul Sâborna 22; ⊙ 9am-12.30pm & 1-5.30pm Mon-Fri, 10am-2pm Sat & Sun) in the Old Town.

ℹ Getting There & Away

BUS

Plovdiv's main station is **Yug bus station** (📞 032-626 937; bul Hristo Botev 47). Yug is diagonally opposite the train station and a 15-minute walk from the centre. Taxis cost 5 to 7 lv; local buses 7, 20 and 26 stop across the street. Frequent routes include Plovdiv to Sofia (12 lv, 2½ hours), Burgas (20 lv, five hours) and Varna (26 lv, seven hours). Check out www.bgrazpisanie.com for full destination and fare info.

The **Sever bus station** (ul Dimitar Stambolov 2), in the northern suburbs, serves destinations to the north of Plovdiv, including Veliko Târnovo (18 lv, four hours).

TRAIN

Daily direct services from the **train station** (bul Hristo Botev) include trains to Sofia (9 lv, three hours) and Burgas (14.60 lv, five hours); see www. bgrazpisanie.com or www.bdz.bg for all fares and timetables.

CENTRAL BULGARIA

The historic heart of Bulgaria beats its strongest in the country's mountainous centre. The country's past is played out in scenic settlements on both sides of the dramatic Stara Planina range; to the west, the museum village of Koprivshtitsa is renowned for its 18th- and 19th-century National Revival houses, while the lowlands town of Kazanlâk is the jumping-off point for visiting both the ancient Thracian tombs of the Valley of the Kings and the famously fragrant Valley of the Roses. The centre's hub is the magnificent Veliko Târnovo, former capital of the Bulgarian tsars; built into steep hills and bisected by a river, its medieval Tsarevets Fortress is among Europe's most spectacular citadels.

Koprivshtitsa
Копривщица

📞 07184 / POP 2540

This romantic museum village, nestled in wooded hills between Karlovo and Sofia, is a perfectly preserved hamlet filled with Bulgarian National Revival–period architecture, cobblestone streets, and bridges that arc gently over a lovely brook. Nearly 400 buildings of architectural and historical significance are protected by government decree.

⦿ Sights

Koprivshtitsa boasts six house museums. Some are closed either on Monday or Tuesday; all keep the same hours (9.30am to 5.30pm April to October, 9am to 5pm November to March). To buy a combined ticket for all (adults/students 5/3 lv), visit the souvenir shop **Kupchinitsa**, near the tourist information centre (p98).

Oslekov House HISTORIC BUILDING
(ul Gereniloto 4; ⊙ 9.30am-5.30pm Apr-Oct, 9am-5pm Nov-Mar, closed Mon) The Oslekov House (1853–6) was built by a rich merchant killed in the line of duty during the 1876 April Uprising. It's arguably the best example of Bulgarian National Revival–period architecture in Koprivshtitsa.

Kableshkov House HISTORIC BUILDING
(ul Todor Kableshkov 8; ⊙ 9.30am-5.30pm Apr-Oct, 9am-5pm Nov-Mar, closed Mon) Todor Kableshkov is revered as having (probably) been the

person who fired the first shot in the 1876 uprising against the Turks. This, his glorious former home (1845), has exhibits about the April Uprising.

🛏 Sleeping & Eating

Hotel Kozlekov   HOTEL €
(📞07184-3077; www.hotelkozlekov.com; ul Georgi Benkovski 8; d/studio from 50/60 lv; 🅿 @) Rustic as it gets but with amazingly modern service, this hilltop hotel is attached to a superb restaurant serving hearty Bulgarian classics. Staff speak English; some rooms have balconies.

Hotel Astra   HOTEL €
(📞07184-2033; www.hotelastra.org; bul Hadzhi Nencho Palaveev 11; d/apt 50/70 lv; 🅿) Set beautifully in a garden, the hospitable Astra is a popular place with large, well-kept rooms.

Dyado Liben   BULGARIAN €€
(📞07184-2109; bul Hadzhi Nencho Palaveev 47; mains 4-9 lv; ⊙11am-midnight; 🛜) This traditional restaurant housed in a huge 1852 mansion is a wonderfully atmospheric – and inexpensive – place for a hearty evening meal. It's just across the bridge leading from the main square inside the facing courtyard.

ℹ Information

There are ATMs and a post office/telephone centre in the village centre.

Tourist Information Centre (www.koprivshtitza. com; pl 20 April; ⊙10am-1pm & 2-7pm) This helpful, friendly centre in a small maroon building on the main square provides local information.

ℹ Getting There & Away

Getting to Koprivshtitsa is a bit of a challege. Being 9km north of the village, the train station requires a shuttle bus (2 lv, 15 minutes), which isn't always timed to meet incoming trains. Trains do come from Sofia (6 lv, 2½ hours, eight daily) and Burgas (19 lv, five hours, two daily). Koprivshtitsa's bus stop is more central; there are four daily buses to Sofia (13 lv, two hours) and one to Plovdiv (12 lv, two hours).

Veliko Târnovo
Велико Търново

📞062 / POP 68,780

The evocative capital of the medieval Bulgarian tsars, sublime Veliko Târnovo is dramatically set amid an amphitheatre of forested hills, divided by the ribboning Yantra River. Commanding pride of place is the magisterial Tsarevets Fortress, citadel of the Second Bulgarian Empire. It's complemented by scores of churches and other ruins, many still being unearthed. As the site of Bulgaria's most prestigious university, Veliko Târnovo also boasts a revved-up nightlife that many larger towns would envy. Top-notch city restaurants offer commanding views of the river and castle; head to the Varosha quarter and the impossibly quaint Samovodska Charshiya to grab a bite (and a bargain) in olde worlde surrounds.

◉ Sights

★Tsarevets Fortress   FORTRESS
(adult/student 6/2 lv, scenic elevator 2 lv; ⊙8am-7pm Apr-Oct, 9am-5pm Nov-Mar) The inescapable symbol of Veliko Târnovo, this reconstructed fortress dominates the skyline, and is one of Bulgaria's most beloved monuments. The former seat of the medieval tsars, it boasts the remains of more than 400 houses, 18 churches, the royal palace, an execution rock and more. Watch your step: there are lots of potholes, broken steps and unfenced drops. The fortress morphs into a psychedelic spectacle with a magnificent night-time sound-and-light show, held on public holidays.

Tsarevgrad Tarnov
Wax Museum   WAX MUSEUM
(ul Nikola Pikolo 6; adult/child 10/5 lv; ⊙9am-7pm) En route to the Fortress is this new wax museum showcasing the medieval glory days of Veliko Târnovo. Explore the well-crafted figures (everyone from kings to craftsmen get a look-in), catch an explanatory film, or get in the mood playing dress-up in period costume (5 lv).

Sarafkina Kâshta   MUSEUM
(ul General Gurko 88; adult/student 6/2 lv; ⊙9am-6pm Tue-Sat) Built in 1861 by a rich Turkish moneylender, this fine five-storey National Revival–style house-museum displays antique ceramics, metalwork, woodcarvings, traditional costumes and jewellery.

Veliko Târnovo
Archaeological Museum   MUSEUM
(ul Ivanka Boteva 2; adult/student 6/2 lv; ⊙9am-6pm Tue-Sun) Housed in a grand old building with a courtyard full of Roman sculptures, the museum contains Roman artefacts and medieval Bulgarian exhibits including a huge mural of the tsars, plus some ancient gold from nearby neolithic settlements.

Samovodska Charshiya   HISTORIC AREA
This atmospheric, cobblestoned historical quarter was Veliko Târnovo's biggest market

square in the 1880s, and remains the place to come to shop, stroll and admire the town's many National Revival–era houses.

Ulitsa Gurko
HISTORIC SITE

The oldest street in Veliko Tårnovo, ul Gurko is a must-stroll. Overlooking the River Yantra, its charmingly crumbling period houses – which appear to be haphazardly piled on one another – provide a million photo-ops and conversations that start with 'Imagine living here...' Sturdy shoes a must.

🛏 Sleeping

Hotel Comfort
HOTEL €

(☏088 777 7265; www.hotelcomfortbg.com; ul P Tipografov 5; d/apt from 40/100 lv; P❄🅿🛜) With jaw-dropping views of the fortress and surrounding hills, plus a stellar location just around the corner from the Samovodska Charshiya market square, this family-owned hotel is a winner. English is spoken by the amiable staff.

Hikers Hostel
HOSTEL €

(☏0889 691 661; www.hikers-hostel.org; ul Rezervoarska 91; dm/d from 14/20 lv; @🛜) Tårnovo's most laid-back hostel, Hikers has an unassuming location high in Varosha's old quarter (a 10-minute walk from downtown). Owner Toshe Hristov does free bus/train station pick-ups and runs trips. Dorms are spartan but clean.

★Hotel-Mehana Gurko
HISTORIC HOTEL €€

(☏062-627 838; www.hotel-gurko.com; ul General Gurko 33; s/d/apt from 50/90/100 lv; ❄@🛜) You can't miss this gorgeous place, with riotous blooms and ye olde curios bedecking its restored 19th-century facade. Sitting pretty on Veliko Tårnovo's oldest street, the Gurko is one of the best places to sleep (and eat) in town; rooms are spacious and soothing, each individually decorated and offering great views.

Old Town Apartment
APARTMENT €€

(☏087 867 5356, 087 888 1281; ul Rakovski 4, Samovodska Charshiya; whole apt 90 lv, price drops by 10% after the 1st night; ❄@🛁) One of the best, and best-located, digs in town, this private apartment has two balconies – one directly atop the cobblestoned Samovodska Charshiya, the other taking in a sweeping view of the entire city – a well-equipped kitchen, and a wonderful bedroom. Charming owner Tsvetelina arranges parking, baby paraphernalia and whatever else you need for a great stay.

Hotel Bolyarski
HOTEL €€€

(☏062-613 200; www.bolyarski.com; ul Stefan Stambolov 53a; s/d incl breakfast from 70/130 lv; P❄🅿🛜🏊) The schmick Bolyarski has a phenomenal location on the bluff on ul Stambolov, with magical views of the town and river. Its modern, well-kept rooms are pitched at business travellers. Great on-site restaurant.

🍴 Eating & Drinking

Shtastlivetsa
BULGARIAN €€

(☏062-600 656; ul Stefan Stambolov 79; mains 7-17 lv; ⊙11am-1am; 🛜) A local institution, the 'Lucky Man' (as the impossible-to-pronounce name means in Bulgarian) has an ideal location overlooking the river's bend and a long menu of inventive meat dishes, baked-pot specials, superb pizzas and lunchtime soups – every visitor to Veliko Tårnovo comes here at least once.

Hunter
INTERNATIONAL €€

(☏088 821 0960; ul Aleksandar Stamboliyski 2; mains 5-18 lv; ⊙8am-midnight; 🛜) As the name suggests, they do love their meat at Hunter. It's set in a pleasant garden (the woodsman's house interior is cosy in colder months) with the requisite resident cats angling for a bite of melt-in-your-mouth barbecue ribs or the ever-popular *shkembe chorba* (tripe soup). It's a mellow location for a beer or 10 as well.

★Han Hadji Nikoli
INTERNATIONAL €€€

(☏062-651 291; www.hanhadjinikoli.com; ul Rakovski 19; mains 17-30 lv; 🛜) Veliko Tårnovo's finest restaurant, Han Hadji Nikoli occupies a beautifully restored 1858 building with an upstairs art gallery. High-end treats include escargots bourguignon, mussels sautéed in white wine and exquisitely prepared pork neck. A 'gourmet room' out the back has a secret menu for extreme epicures.

Tequila Bar
BAR

(ul Stefan Stambolov 30; ⊙noon-3am) Overlooking the main street and around the corner from Samovodska Charshiya, Tequila Bar is a festively painted, as-fun-as-you'd-expect student bar with good cocktails and cheap beer.

☆ Entertainment

Konstantin Kisimov Dramatic Theatre
THEATRE

(☏062-623 526; www.teatarvtarnovo.com; ul Vasil Levski) Hosts regular international performances and Bulgarian plays.

WORTH A TRIP

TOMBS & BLOOMS: KAZANLÂK

Kazanlâk might not look like much, but this rough 'n' ready town is the perfect base for exploring two of Bulgaria's most important and iconic (if not very imaginatively named) regions: the Valley of the Roses and the Valley of the Thracian Kings.

The **Valley of the Roses** is as the name suggests; kilometres of fat, fragrant roses (the *Rosa damascena* to be precise) carefully cultivated for their delicate oils for use in everything from pricey perfumes to cooking. About 70 per cent of the world's rose oil comes from here. The annual **Rose Festival** – replete with parades, picking displays and Queen of the Roses pageant – celebrates the harvest every June. In Kazanlâk itself, the **Museum of the Roses** (☑0431-64 057; www.muzei-kazanlak.org; ul Osvobozhdenie 49; adult/child 3/1 lv; ⊙9am-5pm) gives a deeper insight into the fabulous history and many uses of the flower.

Millenniums before a single seed was sown, the Thracians, a fierce Indo-European tribe, ruled the roost. Archaeologists believe there are at least 1500 Thracian burial mounds and tombs in the vicinity; the most famous is the remarkably preserved, brightly embellished **Tomb of Kazanlâk** (Tyulbe Park; admission 20 lv; ⊙10am-5pm May-Nov, by reservation Nov-Apr), dating back to the 4th century BC. Kazanlâk also boasts a **museum** (☑0431-64 750; www.muzei-kazanlak.org; Tyulbe Park; adult/child 3/1 lv; ⊙9am-5pm May-Nov, by reservation Nov-Apr) housing a full-scaled Thracian tomb replica. More temples and tombs – including that of the great Thracian priest-king Seuthes III – are accessible via tour bus or with your own vehicle. Day trips taking in both regions can be arranged at the Kazanlâk **tourist information centre** (ul Iskra 4; ⊙8am-1pm & 2-6pm Mon-Fri).

Buses run between Kazanlâk and Sofia (20 lv, 3½ hours), Plovdiv (13 lv, two hours) and Veliko Târnovo (17 lv, 2½ hours). See www.bdz.bg for train schedules.

Melon Live Music Club LIVE MUSIC
(☑062-603 439; bul Nezavisimost 21; ⊙6pm-2am) Popular spot for live music from rock and R&B to Latin jazz. It's tucked halfway up the main street.

🛍 Shopping

Samovodska Charshiya ANTIQUES
(ul Rakovski) Veliko Târnovo's charming historic quarter is a true centre of craftsmanship, with genuine blacksmiths, potters and cutlers, among other artisans, still practising their trades here. Wander the cobblestone streets to discover bookshops and purveyors of antiques, jewellery and art housed in appealing Bulgarian National Revival houses.

ℹ Information

Hospital Stefan Cherkezov (☑062-626 841; ul Nish 1) Modern hospital with an emergency room and English-speaking doctors.
Tourist Information Centre (☑062-622 148; www.velikoturnovo.info; ul Hristo Botev 5; ⊙9am-6pm Mon-Fri, Mon-Sat Apr-Oct) English-speaking staff offering local info and advice.

ℹ Getting There & Away

BUS
Three bus stations serve Veliko Târnovo. **Zapad** (☑062-640 908; ul Nikola Gabrovski 74), about

4km southwest from the centre, is the main station. From here, buses serve Plovdiv (24 lv, four hours, at least two daily), Burgas (23 lv, four hours, three daily), Kazanlâk (10 lv, two hours, three daily) and elsewhere.

The more central **Yug bus station** (☑062-620 014; ul Hristo Botev 74) has many daily buses to Sofia (22 lv, three hours), Varna (17 lv, four hours) and Burgas (23 lv, four hours). **Etap Adress** (☑062-630 564; Hotel Etâr, ul Ivailo 2), right by the tourist information centre, also runs hourly buses to Sofia and Varna.

TRAIN
Gorna Oryakhovitsa station (☑062-826 118), 8.5km from town, and the smaller **Veliko Târnovo train station** (☑062-620 065), 1.5km west of the centre, both run frequent trains to Plovdiv (23 lv, five hours), Burgas (19 lv, five hours), Varna (14 lv, five hours) and Sofia (21 lv, five hours). The latter station may be closer, but many trains require a change at Gorna Oryakhovitsa anyway. Get there on bus 10.

BLACK SEA COAST

The Black Sea coast is the country's summer playground, attracting fun 'n' sun seekers from across Bulgaria and the world. Nicknamed 'the Red Riviera' during communism, the almost 400km-long sandy stretch is today dotted with resorts to rival Spain and Greece, though independent travellers will find plenty to explore away from the parasols and jet skis. With its rich museums and happening beachside bars, the maritime capital of Varna offers an intriguing mix of history and hedonism, while to the south, beautiful Nesebâr and Sozopol revel in their Hellenic heritage.

Varna Варна

📞 052 / POP 335,000

Cosmopolitan Varna is by far the most interesting town on the Black Sea coast. A combination of port city, naval base and seaside resort, it's an appealing place to while away a few days, packed with history yet thoroughly modern, with an enormous park to amble around and a lengthy, white-sand beach to lounge on. In the city centre you'll find Bulgaria's largest Roman baths complex and its finest archaeological museum, as well as a dynamic cultural and restaurant scene.

⊙ Sights & Activities

Varna's main attractions are **swimming** and **strolling**; there are plenty of opportunities for both at the 8km-long **city beach**. The popular southern end has a pool complex, water slides and cafes; the central beach has thinner sand patches and is dominated by clubs. The rocky north beach is lined with restaurants; if you go further north you'll find beautiful stretches of sand plus an alfresco **thermal pool** with year-round hot water. Just in from the beach is the huge, green **Primorski Park**, dotted with cafes, statues and popcorn vendors.

Archaeological Museum MUSEUM
(www.archaeo.museumvarna.com; ul Maria Luisa 41; adult/student 10/2 lv; ⊙10am-5pm Tue-Sun Apr-Sep, Tue-Sat Oct-Mar; 📮3, 9, 109) Exhibits at this vast museum, the best of its kind in Bulgaria, include 6500-year-old bangles, necklaces and earrings said to be the oldest worked gold found in the world. You'll also find Roman surgical implements, Hellenistic tombstones and touching oddments including a marble plaque listing, in Greek, the names of the city's school graduates for AD 221.

Roman Thermae RUIN
(cnr ul Han Krum & ul San Stefano; adult/student 4/2 lv; ⊙10am-5pm Tue-Sun May-Oct, Tue-Sat Nov-Apr) The well-preserved ruins of Varna's 2nd-century-AD Roman Thermae are the largest in Bulgaria, although only a small part of the original complex still stands.

🛏 Sleeping

Flag Hostel HOSTEL €
(📞089 740 8115; www.varnahostel.com; ul Bratya Shkorpil 13a; dm incl breakfast 22 lv; 📮😊📶; 📮3, 9) The Flag is a long-established, sociable spot with a party atmosphere. The three dorms are basic with comfortable single beds (no bunks). Free pick-ups from the bus and train stations.

Yo Ho Hostel HOSTEL €
(📞088 472 9144; www.yohohostel.com; ul Ruse 23; dm/s/d/tw incl breakfast from 14/30/40/40 lv; @📶; 📮109) Shiver your timbers at this pirate-themed place, with four- and 11-bed dorm rooms and private options. Staff offer free pick-ups and can organise camping and rafting trips.

Hotel Astra HOTEL €€
(📞052-630 524; www.hotelastravarna.com; ul Opalchenska 9; s/d 50/60 lv; ❄📶; 📮9) A real bargain by Varna standards, this central, cheerful family-run hotel has 10 spacious rooms, all with terraces and basic but good-sized bathrooms.

★ Graffit Gallery Hotel BOUTIQUE HOTEL €€€
(📞052-989 900; www.graffithotel.com; bul Knyaz Boris I 65; s/d from 168/185 lv; 📮😊❄📶; 📮9) With its own art gallery and themed rooms, this modern designer hotel is one of Varna's more colourful options. Super-efficient staff, a chic spa and gym and superb on-site dining options make this a top option if you're looking to splurge.

Grand Hotel London LUXURY HOTEL €€€
(📞052-664 100; www.londonhotel.bg; ul Musala 3; s/d Mon-Thu from 150/176 lv, Fri-Sun from 170/210 lv; 📮😊❄📶) Varna's grandest and oldest hotel opened in 1912. Rooms are spacious and elegantly furnished, if a little chintzy; the restaurant is especially good.

✗ Eating

★ Stariya Chinar BULGARIAN €€
(📞052-949 400; ul Preslav 11; mains 7-19 lv; ⊙8am-midnight) This is upmarket Balkan soul food at its best. Try the baked lamb, made to an old Bulgarian recipe, or the divine barbecue pork ribs; they also create some rather ornate salads. Outdoors is lovely in summer; park yourself in a traditional interior when the cooler weather strikes.

Balkanska Skara Nashentsi BULGARIAN €€
(☑052-630 186; ul Tsar Simeon 1 27; mains 5-10lv;
☺11am-1am Mon-Sat, 6pm-1am Sun) This big, riotous restaurant is popular with locals for its prodigious portions of grilled meats, live music and fun atmosphere. Set menus are available.

Bistro Dragoman SEAFOOD €€
(☑052-621 688; ul Dragoman 43; mains 4-16 lv;
☺10am-11.30pm) This welcoming little place specialises in delicious takes on seafood and locally caught fish. This being the Balkans, grilled meats are also on the menu.

🍷 Drinking & Nightlife

Some of Varna's best bars exist only during the summer; head down to Kraybrezhna aleya by the beach and take your pick.

Pench's COCKTAIL BAR
(ul Dragoman 25; ☺2pm-2am) Want cocktails? Oh, they've got cocktails: Pench's is a two-time world record holder for having the largest number of cocktails available at a single bar. Choosing one may be the hardest decision you'll ever make. They also have a summer location by the beach at Kraybrezhna aleya.

Sundogs BAR
(☑088 951 3434; ul Koloni 1; ☺9am-midnight; 🛜) Big with expats and locals, this very friendly watering hole is a great place to make new friends, chase down excellent pub grub with a good selection of beers, or show off your smarts at the every-second-Sunday pub quiz (summer only).

4aspik CLUB
(☑088 911 0202; Kraybrezhna aleya; ☺10pm-4am) This wild summertime club specialises in Bulgarian folk-pop.

☆ Entertainment

Varna Opera House OPERA
(☑052-650 555; www.operavarna.bg; pl Nezavisimost 1; ☺ticket office 11am-1pm & 2-7pm Mon-Fri, 11am-6pm Sat) Varna's grand opera house hosts performances by the Varna Opera and Philharmonic Orchestra all year, except July and August, when some performances are staged at the Open-Air Theatre in Primorski Park.

ℹ️ Information

Tourist Information Centre (☑052-820 689; www.varnainfo.bg; pl Kiril & Metodii; ☺9am-7pm; 🖥3) Plenty of free brochures and maps, and helpful multilingual staff.

ℹ️ Getting There & Away

AIR
Varna's international **airport** (☑052-573 323; www.varna-airport.bg; 🖥409) is 8km northwest of town. There are regular flights across Europe and to/from Sofia.

BUS
Varna's **central bus station** (bul Vladislav Varenchik 158; 🖥148, 409) is about 2km northwest of the city centre. There are regular buses to Sofia (33 lv, seven hours), Burgas (14 lv, two hours) and all the major destinations in Bulgaria: see www.bgrazpisanie.com for fares and schedules.

TRAIN
Trains depart Varna's **train station** (☑052-662 3343; pl Slaveikov) for Sofia (23.60 lv, seven hours, seven daily), Plovdiv (22.20 lv, seven hours, three daily) and Veliko Târnovo (13.80 lv, four hours, one daily).

Nesebâr   Несебър

☑0554 / POP 11,620

Postcard-pretty Nesebâr (Ne-*se*-bar) – about 40km northeast of Burgas – was settled by Greek colonists in 512 BC, though today it's more famous for its (mostly ruined) medieval churches. Though beautiful, Nesebâr is heavily commercialised, and transforms into one huge, open-air souvenir market during the high season. The Sunny Beach megaresort is 5km to the north.

🅾️ Sights & Activities

All of Nesebâr's main sights are in the Old Town; around 1.5km west from there is **South Beach**, where all the usual water sports are available, including **jet-skiing** and **waterskiing**.

Archaeological Museum MUSEUM
(www.ancient-nessebar.com; ul Mesembria 2; adult/child 5/3 lv; ☺9am-8pm Mon-Fri, 9.30am-1.30pm & 2-7pm Sat-Sun Jul-Aug) Explore the rich history of Nesebâr – formerly Messembria – at this fine museum. Greek and Roman pottery, statues and tombstones as well as Thracian gold jewellery and ancient anchors are displayed here. There's also a collection of icons recovered from Nesebâr's numerous churches.

Sveti Stefan Church CHURCH
(ul Ribarska; adult/student 5/3 lv; ☺9am-7pm Mon-Fri, 9am-1pm & 1.30-6pm Sat & Sun) Built in the 11th century and reconstructed 500 years later, this is the best-preserved church in town. Its beautiful 16th- to 18th-century murals

cover virtually the entire interior. Come early, as it's popular with tour groups.

🛏 Sleeping & Eating

⭐ Hotel Tony
GUESTHOUSE €

(☎0554-42 403, 088 926 8004; ul Kraybrezhna 20; r from 40 lv; ☺Jun-Sep; ❋) Thanks to its low prices and excellent location overlooking the sea, the Hotel Tony books out quickly: be sure to reserve in advance. Rooms are simple but clean, and the chatty host is very helpful.

Old Nesebâr
SEAFOOD €€

(☎0554-42 070; ul Ivan Alexander 11; mains 7-15 lv; ☺noon-11pm) With two tiers of seating offering splendid sea views, and a menu crammed with splendid seafood dishes, this is the go-to place for a dinner (or lunch) to remember.

❶ Getting There & Away

Nesebâr is well connected to coastal destinations by public transport; its bus station is on the small square just outside the city walls. The stop before this on the mainland is for the New Town. There are buses to Sunny Beach (1 lv, 10 minutes, every 15 minutes), Burgas (6 lv, 40 minutes, every 30 minutes), Varna (15 lv, two hours, seven daily) and Sofia (37 lv, seven hours, several daily).

Fast Ferry (www.fastferry.bg) operates a high-speed hydrofoil service to Sozopol (one way/return 27/50 lv, 30 minutes, three daily in summer, one per day on Tuesday, Wednesday, Thursday and Saturday in winter).

Burgas   Бургас
☑ 056 / POP 200,270

For most visitors, the port city of Burgas (sometimes written as 'Bourgas') is no more than a transit point for the more obviously appealing resorts and historic towns further up and down the coast. If you do decide to stop over, you'll find a well-kept city with a neat, pedestrianised centre, a long, uncrowded beach and some small but interesting museums.

Burgas is also the jumping-off point for visits to **St Anastasia Island** (www.anastasia-island.com; return boat trip adult/child 9/6 lv; ☺10am-5.30pm summer), the only inhabited island off the Bulgarian Black Sea coast. Throughout its long history, it's served as a religious retreat, a prison and pirate bait (according to legend, a golden treasure is buried in its sands), and is today dominated by a lighthouse and a monastery, where visitors can sample various healing herb po-

tions. It's also possible to spend the night in a monastic cell (rooms from 50 to 120 lv).

🛏 Sleeping & Eating

⭐ Old House Hostel
HOSTEL €

(☎087 984 1559; www.burgashostel.com; ul Sofroniy 2; dm/d 17/33 lv; ❋❋) This charming hostel makes itself right at home in a lovely 1895 house. Dorms are airy and bright (and bunk-free!), while doubles have access to a sweet little courtyard. Right downtown and only 400m to the beach, this place is a winner.

Hotel California
BOUTIQUE HOTEL €€

(☎056-531 000; www.burgashotel.com; ul Lyuben Karavelov 36; s/d incl breakfast 55/65 lv; P❋❋❋; ❋4) This appealing boutique hotel has large, colourful rooms and especially soft mattresses. Guests get a 20% reduction in the excellent restaurant. It's on a quiet side street about five minutes' walk west of the city centre.

⭐ Ethno
SEAFOOD €€

(☎088 787 7966; ul Aleksandrovska 49; 7-20 lv; ☺11am-11.30pm) This downtown restaurant does splendid things with seafood: the Black Sea mussels alone are worth a trip to Burgas. With ambient blue-and-white surrounds that recall the city's Greek heritage, the superb (English-speaking) service and a summery vibe, Ethno is classy without being uptight.

❶ Getting There & Away

AIR
Bulgaria Air links **Burgas Airport** (☎056-870 248; www.bourgas-airport.com; ☐15), 10km northeast of town, with Sofia three times a day (April to October).

BUS
Yug bus station (pl Tsaritsa Yoanna), outside the train station at the southern end of ul Aleksandrovska, is where most travellers arrive or leave. There are regular buses to coastal destinations, including Nesebâr (6 lv, 40 minutes), Varna (14 lv, 2½ hours) and Sozopol (4.50 lv, 40 minutes). Buses also go to and from Sofia (30 lv, five to six hours) and Plovdiv (17 lv, four hours). Departures are less frequent outside summer.

TRAIN
The **train station** (ul Ivan Vazov) has ticket windows (8am to 6pm) on the right, where you can buy advance tickets for domestic and international services, while same-day tickets can be bought at the windows (24 hours) on the left. Trains run to Varna (19 lv, five to six hours, five to seven daily) and Sofia (23.60 lv, seven to eight hours, six daily).

Sozopol Созопол

⌨ 0550 / POP 5000

With a curling peninsula of cobbled streets, sandy beaches and reminders of its ancient Greek heritage at every turn, stunning Sozopol is one of the highlights of the coast. It's not as crowded as Nesebâr, but its happening cultural scene, wonderful Old Town and lively street life are attracting more visitors every summer. Archaeologists, too, are drawn to Sozopol – formerly known as Apollonia – where it seems that every casual turn of a gardener's spade unearths new treasures.

◉ Sights & Activities

Sozopol has two great beaches: **Harmani Beach** has all the good-time gear (water slides, paddle boats, beach bars), while to the north, the smaller **Town Beach** packs in the serious sun-worshippers. Stone sarcophagi – part of the ancient **Apollonia necropolis** – have been unearthed at the southern end of Harmani.

Archaeological Museum   MUSEUM
(ul Han Krum 2; adult/child 8/3 lv; ⊙ 9am-6pm, closed Sat & Sun Oct-Apr) Housed in a drab concrete box near the port, this museum has a small but fascinating collection of local finds from its Apollonian glory days and beyond. In addition to a wealth of Hellenic treasures, the museum occasionally exhibits the skeleton of a local 'vampire', found with a stake driven through its chest.

Southern Fortress Wall
& Tower Museum   RUIN, MUSEUM
(ul Milet 40; museum admission 3 lv; ⊙ 9.30am-8pm Jul-Aug, to 5pm May & Jun, Sep & Oct) The reconstructed walls and walkways along the rocky coastline, and a 4th-century BC well that was once part of a temple to Aphrodite, are free to explore; the views are glorious. The attached museum is a bit of an anticlimax.

✦ Festivals & Events

Apollonia Arts Festival   MUSIC, ART
(www.apollonia.bg; ⊙ end Aug–mid-Sep) This is the highlight of Sozopol's cultural calendar, with concerts, theatrical performances, art exhibitions, film screenings and more held across town.

▟ Sleeping & Eating

Hotel prices drop considerably in the off-season, when visitors will have Sozopol all to themselves. Cheap eats abound along the harbourfront ul Kraybrezhna in the Old Town; more upmarket restaurants are found on ul Morski Skali.

★**Hotel Radik**   HOTEL €€
(⌨ 055-023 706; ul Republikanska 4; d/studio/apt from 68/75/95 lv; 🅿❄🛜🛜❄) Run by a lovely English/Bulgarian couple, the Radik is cheap, cheerful and perfectly located 100m from the Old Town and a quick stagger to the beach. Rooms have sea views and balconies; studios and apartments have good kitchenettes.

Art Hotel   HOTEL €€
(⌨ 0550-24 081; www.arthotel-sbh.com; ul Kiril & Metodii 72; d/studio Jul-Sep 70/90 lv, Oct-Jun from 50/60 lv; ❄🛜) This peaceful old house, belonging to the Union of Bulgarian Artists, is within a walled courtyard towards the tip of the peninsula, away from the crowds. It has a small selection of bright, comfortable rooms with balconies, most with sea views; breakfast is served on the terraces over the sea.

★**Panorama**   SEAFOOD €€
(ul Morski Skali 21; mains 8-20 lv; ⊙ 10am-1am) This lively place has an open terrace with fantastic views towards Sveti Ivan Island. Fresh, local fish is a mainstay of the menu. It's one of the best of many seafood spots on the street.

ⓘ Getting There & Away

The small public **bus station** (ul Han Krum) is just south of the Old Town walls. Buses leave for Burgas (4.50 lv, 40 minutes) about every 30 minutes between 6am and 9pm in summer, and about once an hour in the low season. Buses run up to three times a day to Sofia (32 lv, seven hours).

Fast Ferry (⌨ 088 580 8001; www.fastferry. bg; Fishing Harbour) runs three ferries per day

---

COUNTRY FACTS

Area 110,910 sq km

Capital Sofia

Country Code ⌨ 359

Currency Lev (lv)

Emergency ⌨ 112

Language Bulgarian

Money ATMs are everywhere

Population 7.35 million

Visas Not required for citizens of the EU, UK, USA, Canada, Australia and New Zealand for stays of less than 90 days

EATING PRICE RANGES

The following price ranges refer to a typical main course:

€ less than 5 lv

€€ 5 lv to 15 lv

€€€ more than 15 lv

to/from Nesebâr (single/return from 27/50 lv, 40 minutes) between June and September.

SURVIVAL GUIDE

ℹ Directory A–Z

ACCOMMODATION

Sofia, Plovdiv, Veliko Târnovo, Varna and Burgas all have hostels; for cheap accommodation elsewhere, look out for signs reading 'стаи под наем'  (rooms for rent). Many hotels offer discounts for longer stays or on weekends; prices may rise during summer.

FOOD

Eating out in Bulgaria is remarkably cheap, and even if you're on a tight budget, you'll have no problem eating well.

GAY & LESBIAN TRAVELLERS

Homosexuality is legal in Bulgaria, though opinion polls suggest a majority of Bulgarians have a negative opinion of it. Attitudes among younger people are slowly changing, and there are a few gay clubs and bars in Sofia and in other major cities. Useful websites include **Bulgayria** (www.gay.bg) and **Gay Bulgaria Ultimate Gay Guide** (www.gay-bulgaria.info).

INTERNET RESOURCES

Beach Bulgaria (www.beachbulgaria.com)
BG Maps (www.bgmaps.com)
Bulgaria Travel (www.bulgariatravel.org)

MONEY

The local currency is the lev (plural: leva), comprised of 100 stotinki. It is almost always abbreviated as lv. Bulgaria has no immediate plans to adopt the euro.

PUBLIC HOLIDAYS

New Year's Day 1 January
Liberation Day (National Day) 3 March
Orthodox Easter Sunday & Monday March/April; one week after Catholic/Protestant Easter
May Day 1 May
St George's Day 6 May
Cyrillic Alphabet Day 24 May
Unification Day (National Day) 6 September

Bulgarian Independence Day 22 September
National Revival Day 1 November
Christmas 25 and 26 December

TELEPHONE

To call Bulgaria from abroad, dial the international access code, add ☑ 359 (the country code for Bulgaria), the area code (minus the first zero) and then the number. Mobile phone numbers can be identified by the prefixes ☑ 087, ☑ 088 or ☑ 089.

TRAVELLERS WITH DISABILITIES

Bulgaria is not an easy destination for travellers with disabilities. Uneven and broken footpaths are common in towns and wheelchair-accessible toilets and ramps are rare outside the more expensive hotels.

VISAS

Citizens of other EU countries, as well as Australia, Canada, New Zealand, the USA and many other countries do not need a visa for stays of up to 90 days. Other nationals should contact the Bulgarian embassy in their home country for current visa requirements.

ℹ Getting There & Away

AIR

Most international visitors come and/or go via **Sofia Airport** (☑ 02-937 2211; www.sofia-airport.bg); there are frequent flights between Sofia and other European cities. The national carrier is **Bulgaria Air** (www.air.bg); the airport website has a full list of other carriers who service it.

LAND

Although Sofia has international bus and train connections, it's not necessary to backtrack to the capital if you're heading to, for example, Budapest, Athens or İstanbul: Plovdiv offers regular buses to all three. Heading to Belgrade by train means going through Sofia; for Skopje, you'll need to catch a bus from there, too.

Bus

Most international buses arrive in Sofia. You'll have to get off the bus at the border and walk through customs to present your passport. When travelling out of Bulgaria by bus, the cost of entry visas for the countries concerned are not included in the prices of the bus tickets.

SLEEPING PRICE RANGES

Price ranges are based on the cost of a double room with a bathroom.

€ less than 60 lv

€€ 60 lv to 120 lv (to 200 lv in Sofia)

€€€ more than 120 lv (200 lv in Sofia)

ESSENTIAL FOOD & DRINK

Fresh fruit, vegetables, dairy produce and grilled meat form the basis of Bulgarian cuisine, which is heavily influenced by Greek and Turkish cookery. Pork and chicken are the most popular meats, while tripe also features on traditional menus. You will also find recipes including duck, rabbit and venison, and fish is plentiful along the Black Sea coast.

➡ **Banitsa** Flaky cheese pastry, often served fresh and hot.

➡ **Kebabche** Thin, grilled pork sausage, a staple of every *mehana* (tavern) in the country.

➡ **Tarator** On a hot day there's nothing better than this delicious chilled cucumber and yoghurt soup, served with garlic, dill and crushed walnuts.

➡ **Beer** You're never far from a cold beer in Bulgaria. Zagorka, Kamenitza and Shumensko are the most popular nationwide brands.

➡ **Wine** They've been producing wine here since Thracian times and there are some excellent varieties to try.

➡ **Kavarma** This 'claypot meal', or meat stew, is normally made with either chicken or pork and is one of the country's most popular dishes.

➡ **Shkembe chorba** Traditional stomach soup is one of the more adventurous and offbeat highlights of Bulgarian cuisine.

➡ **Mish Mash** Summer favourite made from tomatoes, capsicum, eggs, feta and spices.

➡ **Shishcheta** Shish kebab consisting of chunks of chicken or pork on wooden skewers with mushrooms and peppers.

➡ **Musaka** Bulgarian moussaka bears more than a passing resemblance to its Greek cousin and it's a delicious staple of cheap cafeteria meals.

Car & Motorcycle

In order to drive your own car on Bulgarian roads, you will need to purchase a vignette, sold at all border crossings into Bulgaria, petrol stations and post offices. For a car, this costs 10/25 lv for one week/month.

Train

There are a number of international trains from Bulgaria, including services to Serbia, Greece and Turkey. Sofia is the main hub, although trains stop at other towns.

ⓘ Getting Around

AIR

The only scheduled domestic flights within Bulgaria are between Sofia and Varna and Sofia and Burgas. Both routes are operated by **Bulgaria Air** (www.air.bg).

BICYCLE

➡ Many roads are in poor condition; some major roads are always choked with traffic and bikes aren't allowed on highways.

➡ Many trains will carry your bike for an extra 2 lv.

➡ Spare parts are available in cities and major towns, but it's better to bring your own.

BUS

Buses link all cities and major towns and connect villages with the nearest transport hub. See www.bgrazpisanie.com/en/transport_companies for a comprehensive list of bus companies.

CAR & MOTORCYCLE

Bulgaria's roads are among the most dangerous in Europe and the level of fatalities each year is high. The worst time is between July and September, with drink-driving, speeding and poor road conditions contributing to accidents.

The **Union of Bulgarian Motorists** (☎02-935 7935, road assistance 02-91146; www.uab.org; pl Positano 3, Sofia) offers 24-hour road assistance.

Road Rules

➡ Drive on the right.

➡ Drivers and passengers in the front must wear seat belts; motorcyclists must wear helmets.

➡ Blood-alcohol limit is 0.05%.

➡ Children under 12 are not allowed to sit in front.

➡ From November to March, headlights must be on at all times.

➡ Speed limits are 50km/h within towns, 90km/h on main roads and 140km/h on motor-ways.

TRAIN

Bâlgarski Dârzhavni Zheleznitsi – **Bulgarian State Railways** (BDZh; www.bdz.bg) – boasts an impressive 4278km of track across the country, linking most towns and cities. Most trains tend to be antiquated and not especially comfortable, with journey times slower than buses. On the plus side you'll have more room in a train compartment and the scenery is likely to be more rewarding. Trains are classified as *ekspresen* (express), *bârz* (fast) or *pâtnicheski* (slow passenger). Unless you absolutely thrive on train travel or want to visit a more remote town, use a fast or express train.

Croatia

Best Places to Eat

➜ Mundoaka Street Food (p114)

➜ Kantinon (p118)

➜ Konoba Menego (p125)

➜ Konoba Matejuška (p122)

Best Places to Stay

➜ Studio Kairos (p114)

➜ Goli + Bosi (p122)

➜ Hotel Lone (p118)

➜ Karmen Apartments (p129)

Why Go?

If your Mediterranean fantasies feature balmy days by sapphire waters in the shade of ancient walled towns, Croatia is the place to turn them into reality.

The extraordinary Adriatic coastline, speckled with 1244 islands and strewn with historic towns, is Croatia's main attraction. The standout is Dubrovnik, its remarkable Old Town ringed by mighty defensive walls. Coastal Split showcases Diocletian's Palace, one of the world's most impressive Roman monuments, where dozens of bars, restaurants and shops thrive amid the old walls. In the heart-shaped peninsula of Istria, Rovinj is a charm-packed fishing port with narrow cobbled streets. The Adriatic isles hold much varied appeal, from glitzy Hvar Town on its namesake island to the secluded naturist coves of the Pakleni Islands just offshore.

Away from the coast, Zagreb, Croatia's lovely capital, has a booming cafe culture and art scene, while Plitvice Lakes National Park offers a verdant maze of turquoise lakes and cascading waterfalls.

When to Go
Zagreb

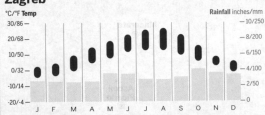

May & Sep Good weather, less tourists, full events calendar, great for hiking.

Jun Best time to visit: beautiful weather, fewer people, lower prices, the festival season kicks off.

Jul & Aug Lots of sunshine, warm sea and summer festivals; many tourists and highest prices.

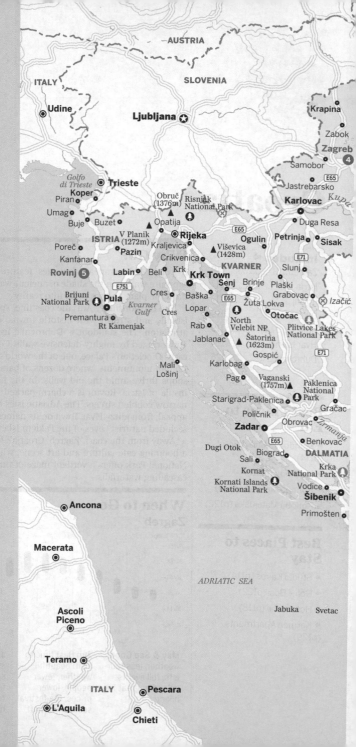

Croatia Highlights

1 Gape at the Old Town wall of **Dubrovnik** (p126), which surrounds luminous marble streets and finely ornamented buildings.

2 Admire the Venetian architecture and experience the vibrant nightlife of **Hvar Town** (p125).

3 Indulge in the lively and historic delights of Diocletian's Palace in **Split** (p119).

4 Take in the remains of failed romances at the **Museum of Broken Relationships** (p110) in Zagreb.

5 Roam the steep cobbled streets and piazzas of **Rovinj** (p117), Istria's showpiece coastal town.

Three Days

Spend a day in dynamic **Zagreb**, delving into its vibrant cafe culture and nightlife, and fascinating museums, then head down to **Rovinj** in Istria to spend a couple of days unwinding by the sea, wandering the cobbled streets and sampling the celebrated Istrian cuisine.

One Week

Start with a weekend in Zagreb, then head south to take in one of the region's best sights: the Roman ruins of Diocletian's Palace in **Split** are a living part of this exuberant seafront city. Base yourself here for two days of sightseeing, beach fun and nightlife action. Next, take the winding coastal road to **Dubrovnik**, a magnificent walled city whose beauty is bound to blow you away with the jaw-dropping sights of its Old Town.

ZAGREB

◪ 01 / POP 792,900

Zagreb has culture, arts, music, architecture, gastronomy and all the other things that make a quality capital city – it's no surprise that the number of visitors has risen sharply in the last couple of years. Croatia's coastal attractions aside, Zagreb has finally been discovered as a popular city-break destination in its own right.

Visually, Zagreb is a mixture of straight-laced Austro-Hungarian architecture and rough-around-the-edges socialist structures, its character a sometimes uneasy combination of the two. This mini metropolis is made for strolling the streets, drinking coffee in the permanently full cafes, popping into museums and galleries, and enjoying the theatres, concerts and cinema. It's a year-round outdoor city: in spring and summer everyone scurries to Jarun Lake in the southwest to swim, boat or dance the night away at lakeside discos, while in autumn and winter Zagrebians go skiing and hiking at nearby mountains.

◉ Sights

As the oldest part of Zagreb, the Upper Town (Gornji Grad) offers landmark buildings and churches from the earlier centuries of Zagreb's history. The Lower Town (Donji Grad) has the city's most interesting art museums and fine examples of 19th- and 20th-century architecture.

◎ Upper Town

**Museum of
Broken Relationships** MUSEUM
(www.brokenships.com; Ćirilometodska 2; adult/concession 25/20KN; ◷9am-10.30pm) Explore

mementos that remain after a relationship ends at Zagreb's quirkiest museum. The innovative exhibit toured the world until it settled here in its permanent home. On display are donations from around the globe, in a string of all-white rooms with vaulted ceilings and epoxy-resin floors.

Dolac Market MARKET
(◷6.30am-3pm Mon-Fri, to 2pm Sat, to 1pm Sun) Zagreb's colourful fruit and vegetable market is just north of Trg Bana Jelačića. Traders from all over Croatia come to sell their products at this buzzing centre of activity. Dolac has been heaving since the 1930s, when the city authorities set up a market space on the 'border' between the Upper and Lower Towns.

**Cathedral of the
Assumption of the
Blessed Virgin Mary** CATHEDRAL
(Katedrala Marijina Uznešenja; Kaptol 31; ◷10am-5pm Mon-Sat, 1-5pm Sun) Kaptol Sq is dominated by this cathedral, formerly known as St Stephen's. Its twin spires – seemingly permanently under repair – soar over the city. Although the cathedral's original Gothic structure has been transformed many times over, the sacristy still contains a cycle of **frescoes** dating from the 13th century. An earthquake in 1880 badly damaged the cathedral; reconstruction in a neo-Gothic style began around the turn of the 20th century.

Lotrščak Tower HISTORIC BUILDING
(Kula Lotrščak; Strossmayerovo Šetalište 9; adult/concession 20/10KN; ◷9am-9pm) This tower was built in the middle of the 13th century in order to protect the southern city gate. Climb it for a sweeping 360-degree view of

the city. Near the tower is a **funicular railway** (www.zet.hr/english/funicular.aspx; ticket 4KN; ⊙ 6.30am-10pm), constructed in 1888, which connects the Lower and Upper Towns.

St Mark's Church
CHURCH

(Crkva Svetog Marka; Trg Svetog Marka 5; ⊙ mass 7.30am & 6pm Mon-Fri, 7.30am Sat, 10am, 11am & 6pm Sun) This 13th-century church is one of Zagreb's most emblematic buildings. Its colourful tiled roof, constructed in 1880, has the medieval coat of arms of Croatia, Dalmatia and Slavonia on the left side, and the emblem of Zagreb on the right. The Gothic portal, composed of 15 figures in shallow niches, was sculpted in the 14th century. The interior contains sculptures by Ivan Meštrović. You can enter the anteroom only during opening hours; the church itself is open only at Mass times.

Croatian Museum of Naïve Art
MUSEUM

(Hrvatski Muzej Naivne Umjetnosti; ☎ 01-48 51 911; www.hmnu.org; Ćirilometodska 3; adult/concession 20/10KN; ⊙ 10am-6pm Tue-Fri, to 1pm Sat & Sun) If you like Croatia's naive art – a form that was highly fashionable locally and worldwide during the 1960s and 1970s and has declined somewhat since – this small museum will be a feast. It houses around 1900 paintings, drawings and some sculptures by the discipline's most important artists, such as Generalić, Mraz, Rabuzin and Smajić.

Meštrović Atelier
GALLERY

(☎ 01-48 51 123; Mletačka 8; adult/concession 30/15KN; ⊙ 10am-6pm Tue-Fri, to 2pm Sat & Sun) Croatia's most recognised artist is Ivan Meštrović. This 17th-century building is his former home, where he worked and lived from 1922 to 1942; the excellent collection it houses has some 100 sculptures, drawings, lithographs and pieces of furniture from the first four decades of his artistic life. Meštrović, who also worked as an architect, designed many parts of the house himself.

City Museum
MUSEUM

(Muzej Grada Zagreba; ☎ 01-48 51 926; www.mgz.hr; Opatička 20; adult/concession/family 30/20/50KN; ⊙ 10am-6pm Tue-Fri, 11am-7pm Sat, 10am-2pm Sun; 🚼) Since 1907, the 17th-century Convent of St Claire has housed this historical museum, which presents the history of Zagreb through documents, artwork and crafts, as well as interactive exhibits that fascinate kids. Look for the scale model of old Gradec. Summaries of the exhibits are posted in English.

Lower Town

Trg Bana Jelačića
SQUARE

Zagreb's main orientation point and its geographic heart is Trg Bana Jelačića – it's where most people arrange to meet up. If you enjoy people-watching, sit in one of the cafes and watch the tramloads of people getting out, greeting each other and dispersing among the newspaper and flower sellers.

Museum Mimara
MUSEUM

(Muzej Mimara; ☎ 01-48 28 100; www.mimara.hr; Rooseveltov trg 5; adult/concession 40/30KN; ⊙ 10am-7pm Tue-Fri, to 5pm Sat, to 2pm Sun) This is the diverse private art collection – Zagreb's best – of Ante Topić Mimara, who donated over 3750 priceless objects to his native Zagreb (even though he spent much of his life in Salzburg, Austria). Housed in a neo-Renaissance former school building (1883), the collection spans a wide range of periods and regions.

Art Pavilion
GALLERY

(Umjetnički Paviljon; ☎ 01-48 41 070; www.umjetnicki-paviljon.hr; Trg Kralja Tomislava 22; adult/concession 30/15KN; ⊙ 11am-7pm Tue-Sat, 10am-1pm Sun) The yellow Art Pavilion presents changing exhibitions of contemporary art. Constructed in 1897 in stunning art nouveau style, the pavilion is the only space in Zagreb that was specifically designed to host large exhibitions. In some years, the gallery shuts its doors from mid-July through August; check the website for details.

---

24 HOURS IN ZAGREB

Start your day with a stroll through Strossmayerov trg, Zagreb's oasis of greenery, and then walk to Trg Bana Jelačića, the city's centre. Head up to Kaptol Sq for a look at the cathedral (p110), the centre of Zagreb's religious life. While in the Upper Town, pick up some snacks at the Dolac Market (p110). Next pop into the quirky Museum of Broken Relationships (p110) and take in a view of the city from the top of Lotrščak Tower (p110) just a few steps away, then spend the evening bar crawling along Tkalčićeva.

CROATIA ZAGREB

Zagreb

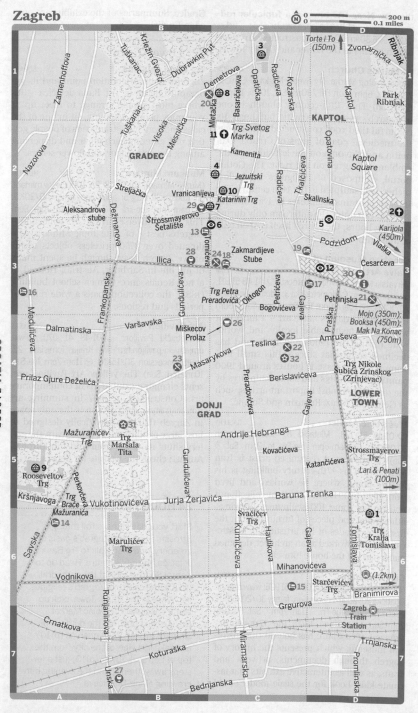

Zagreb

Outside the Centre

**Museum of
Contemporary Art** MUSEUM
(Muzej Suvremene Umjetnosti; ☎01-60 52 700; www.msu.hr; Avenija Dubrovnik 17; adult/concession 30/15KN; ☉11am-6pm Tue-Fri & Sun, to 8pm Sat) Housed in a stunning city icon designed by local star architect Igor Franić, this swanky museum displays both solo and thematic group shows by Croatian and in-

ternational artists in its 17,000 sq metres. The permanent display, called *Collection in Motion,* showcases 620 edgy works by 240 artists, roughly half of whom are Croatian. There's a packed schedule of film, theatre, concerts and performance art year-round.

⟲ Tours

Funky Zagreb GUIDED TOUR
(www.funky-zagreb.com) Personalised tours that range in theme from wine tasting (340KN for 2½ to three hours) to hiking in Zagreb's surroundings (from 720KN per person for a day trip).

Blue Bike Tours BIKE TOUR
(☎098 18 83 344; www.zagrebbybike.com) To experience Zagreb on a bike, book one of the tours – choose between Lower Town, Upper Town or Novi Zagreb – departing daily at 10am and 2pm from Trg Bana Jelačića 15. Tours last around two hours and cost 175KN.

🛏 Sleeping

Zagreb's accommodation scene has been undergoing a noticeable change with the arrival of some of Europe's budget airlines. Hostels have mushroomed in the last few years; as of writing, there are over 30 in Zagreb, from cheap backpacker digs to more stylish hideaways. The city's business and high-end hotels are also in full flow.

Prices usually stay the same in all seasons, but be prepared for a 20% surcharge if you arrive during a festival or major event, in particular the autumn fair.

With the rise of Airbnb.com, short-term apartment rentals are becoming increasingly popular, and a good way to experience the city like a local. Recommended options include **ZIGZAG Integrated Hotel** (☎01-88 95 433; www.zigzag.hr; Petrinjska 9; r/apt from 450/720KN; [P][✳][🛜]) and **Main Square Apartment** (☎098 494 212; www.apartmentmainsquare.com; Trg Bana Jelačića 3; 2 people 608KN, 3-4 people 684KN; [✳][🛜]).

**Chillout Hostel
Zagreb Downtown** HOSTEL $
(☎01-48 49 605; www.chillout-hostel-zagreb.com; Tomićeva 5a; dm 105-125KN; s/d 300/350KN; [P][✳][@][🛜]) Located in the tiny pedestrian street with the funicular, this cheerful spot has no less than 170 beds just steps away from Trg Bana Jelačića. The trimmings are plentiful, and the vibe friendly. Breakfast is available.

Hobo Bear Hostel
HOSTEL **$**

(☑ 01-48 46 636; www.hobobearhostel.com; Medulićeva 4; dm from 153KN, d from 436KN; ✳ @ 🛜) Inside a duplex apartment, this sparkling five-dorm hostel has exposed brick walls, hardwood floors, free lockers, a kitchen with free tea and coffee, a common room and book exchange. The three doubles are across the street. Take tram 1, 6 or 11 from Trg Bana Jelačića.

★ Studio Kairos
B&B **$$**

(☑ 01-46 40 680; www.studio-kairos.com; Vlaška 92; s 340-420KN, d 520-620KN; ✳ ✷ 🛜) This adorable B&B in a street-level apartment has four well-appointed rooms decked out by theme – Writers', Crafts, Music and Granny's – and there's a cosy common space where a delicious breakfast is served. The interior design is gorgeous and the friendly owners are a fountain of info. Bikes are also available for rent.

Hotel Jägerhorn
HOTEL **$$**

(☑ 01-48 33 877; www.hotel-jagerhorn.hr; Ilica 14; s/d/apt 835/911/1217KN; P ✳ @ 🛜) A charming, and little, recently renovated hotel that sits right underneath Lotrščak Tower (p110), the 'Hunter's Horn' has friendly service and 18 spacious, classic rooms with good views (you can gaze over leafy Gradec from the top-floor attic rooms). The downstairs terrace cafe is charming.

★ Esplanade Zagreb Hotel
HOTEL **$$$**

(☑ 01-45 66 666; www.esplanade.hr; Mihanovićeva 1; s/d 1385/1500KN; P ✳ @ 🛜) Drenched in history, this six-storey hotel was built next to the train station in 1925 to welcome the *Orient Express* crowd in grand style. It has hosted kings, artists, journalists and politicians ever since. The art-deco masterpiece is replete with walls of swirling marble, immense staircases and wood-panelled lifts.

Hotel Dubrovnik
HOTEL **$$$**

(☑ 01-48 63 555; www.hotel-dubrovnik.hr; Gajeva 1; s/d from 740/885KN; P ✳ 🛜) Smack on the main square, this glass New York–wannabe is a city landmark, and the 245 well-appointed units have old-school classic style. It buzzes with business travellers who love being at the centre of the action – try to get a view of Jelačić square and watch Zagreb pass by under your window. Inquire about packages and specials.

Eating

You can pick up excellent fresh produce, cheeses and cold cuts at Dolac market (p110). The city centre's main streets, including Ilica, Teslina, Gajeva and Preradovićeva, are lined with fast-food joints and inexpensive snack bars. Note that many restaurants close in August for the summer holiday, which typically lasts anywhere from two weeks to a month.

Karijola
PIZZA **$**

(Vlaška 63; pizzas from 42KN; ⊙ 11am-midnight Mon-Sat, to 11pm Sun) Locals swear by the crispy, thin-crust pizza churned out of a clay oven at this newer location of Zagreb's best pizza joint. Pizzas come with high-quality ingredients, such as smoked ham, olive oil, rich mozzarella, cherry tomatoes, rocket and shiitake mushrooms.

Tip Top
SEAFOOD **$**

(Gundulićeva 18; mains from 40KN; ⊙ 7am-11pm Mon-Sat) How we love Tip Top and its waitstaff, who still sport old socialist uniforms and scowling faces that eventually turn to smiles. But we mostly love the excellent Dalmatian food. Every day has a different set menu.

Pingvin
SANDWICHES **$**

(Teslina 7; sandwiches from 15KN; ⊙ 10am-4am Mon-Sat, 6pm-2am Sun) This quick-bite institution, around since 1987, offers tasty designer sandwiches and salads, which locals savour on a couple of bar stools.

Vincek
BAKERY **$**

(Ilica 18; pastries from 6KN; ⊙ 8.30am-11pm Mon-Sat) This institution of a *slastičarna* (pastry shop) serves some of Zagreb's creamiest cakes. They have some serious competition, however, with **Torte i To** (Nova Ves 11, 2nd fl, Kaptol Centar; pastries from 3KN; ⊙ 8am-11pm Mon-Sat, 9am-11pm Sun) on the 2nd floor of Kaptol Centar, and the recently opened **Mak Na Konac** (Dukljaninova 1; pastries from 8KN; ⊙ 9am-9pm Mon-Sat).

★ Mundoaka Street Food
INTERNATIONAL **$$**

(☑ 01-78 88 777; Petrinjska 2; mains from 45KN; ⊙ 8am-midnight Mon-Thu, to 1am Fri, 9am-1am Sat) This adorable new eatery clad in light wood, with tables outside, serves up American classics – think chicken wings and pork ribs – and a global spectrum of dishes, from Spanish tortillas to *shakshuka* eggs. Great breakfasts, muffins and cakes, all prepared by one of Zagreb's best-known chefs. Reserve ahead.

★ Vinodol
CROATIAN $$

(www.vinodol-zg.hr; Teslina 10; mains from 56KN; ☺ noon-11pm) The well-prepared Central European fare here is much-loved by local and overseas patrons. On warm days, eat on the covered patio (entered through an ivy-clad passageway off Teslina); the cold-weather alternative is the dining hall with vaulted stone ceilings. Highlights include the succulent lamb or veal and potatoes cooked under *peka* (domed baking lid) as well as *bukovače* (local mushrooms).

Lari & Penati
MODERN CROATIAN $$

(Petrinjska 42a; mains from 60KN; ☺ noon-11pm Mon-Fri, to 5pm Sat) Small stylish bistro that serves up innovative lunch and dinner specials – they change daily according to what's market-fresh. The food is fab, the music cool and the few sidewalk tables lovely in warm weather. Closes for two weeks in August.

Didov San
DALMATIAN $$

(☑ 01-48 51 154; www.konoba-didovsan.com; Mletačka 11; mains from 60KN; ☺ 10am-midnight) This Upper Town tavern features a rustic wooden interior with ceiling beams and tables on the streetside deck. The food is based on traditional cuisine from the Neretva River delta in Dalmatia's hinterland, such as grilled frogs wrapped in prosciutto. Reserve ahead.

Zinfandel's
INTERNATIONAL $$$

(☑ 01-45 66 644; www.esplanade.hr/cuisine/; Mihanovićeva 1; mains from 170KN; ☺ 6am-11pm Mon-Sat, 6.30am-11pm Sun) The tastiest, most creative dishes in town are served with flair in the dining room of the Esplanade Zagreb Hotel (p114). For a simpler but still delicious dining experience, head to French-flavoured Le Bistro (www.esplanade.hr/french-chic/; Mihanovićeva 1; mains from 95KN; ☺ 9am-11pm), also in the hotel – and don't miss its famous *štrukli* pastry.

🍷 Drinking & Nightlife

In the Upper Town, the chic Tkalčićeva is throbbing with bars and cafes. In the Lower Town, there's bar-lined Bogovićeva and Trg Petra Preradovića (known locally as Cvjetni trg), the most popular spot in the Lower Town for street performers and occasional bands.

One of the nicest ways to see Zagreb is to join in on the *špica* – Saturday-morning pre-lunch coffee drinking on the terraces along Bogovićeva, Preradovićeva and Tkalčićeva.

Clubs are mainly located around the Lower Town. Entry ranges from 20KN to 100KN, and things don't get lively until around midnight.

Stross
BAR

(Strossmayerovo Šetalište; ☺ from 9.30pm daily Jun-Sep) A makeshift bar is set up most nights in summer at the Strossmayer promenade in the Upper Town, with cheap drinks and live music. The mixed-bag crowd, great city views and leafy ambience make it a great spot to while away your evenings.

Booksa
CAFE

(www.booksa.hr; Martićeva 14d; ☺ 11am-8pm Tue-Sun; 🛜) Bookworms and poets, writers and performers, oddballs and artists...basically anyone creative in Zagreb comes here to chat and drink coffee, browse the library, surf with free wi-fi and hear readings at this lovely, book-themed cafe. There are English-language readings here, too; check the website. Closes for three weeks from late July.

Kino Europa
CAFE, BAR

(www.kinoeuropa.hr; Varšavska 3; ☺ 8.30am-midnight Mon-Thu, to 4am Fri & Sat, 11am-11pm Sun; 🛜) Zagreb's oldest cinema, from the 1920s, now houses a splendid cafe, wine bar and *grapperia*. At this glass-enclosed space with an outdoor terrace, you can enjoy great coffee, over 30 types of grappa and free wi-fi. The cinema hosts film screenings and occasional dance parties.

Mojo
BAR

(Martićeva 5; ☺ 7am-2am Mon-Fri, 8am-2am Sat, 8am-midnight Sun) Smoky basement hang-out where live music and DJ-spun tunes are on every night. On warm nights, take your pick among 70 *rakijas* (grappas) and liqueurs and sample them on the sidewalk tables out front.

Basement Wine Bar
WINE BAR

(Tomićeva 5; ☺ 9am-2am Mon-Sat, 4pm-midnight Sun) A city-centre hot spot for sampling Croatian wines by the glass, this basement bar (with a few sidewalk tables) sits right by the funicular. Pair the tipple with meat and cheese platters.

VIP Club
CLUB

(www.vip-club.hr; Trg Bana Jelačića 9; ☺ 8pm-5am Tue-Sat, closed summer) This newcomer on the nightlife scene has quickly become a local favourite. A swank basement place on the main square, it offers a varied program, from jazz to Balkan beats. It closes in summer months.

Masters

CLUB

(Ravnice bb) Zagreb's smallest club also has the most powerful sound system, the feel of a private party and top-notch local and international DJ acts spinning deep house, tech-house, dub and reggae.

Pepermint

CLUB

(www.pepermint-zagreb.com; Ilica 24; ⊙ 10pm-5am Tue-Sat, closed Aug) Small and chic city centre club clad in white wood, with two levels and a well-to-do older crowd. Programs change weekly, ranging from vintage rockabilly and swing to soul and house.

Aquarius

CLUB

(www.aquarius.hr; Aleja Matije Ljubeka bb, Jarun Lake) Past its heyday but still fun, this lakeside club has a series of rooms that open onto a huge terrace. House and techno are the standard fare but there are also hip-hop and R&B nights. During summer, Aquarius sets up shop at Zrće on Pag.

KSET

CLUB

(www.kset.org; Unska 3; ⊙ 9am-4pm & 8pm-midnight Mon-Thu, 9am-4pm & 8pm-1am Fri, 10pm-3am Sat) Zagreb's top music venue, with everyone who's anyone performing here, from ethno to hip-hop acts. Saturday nights are dedicated to DJ music, when youngsters dance till late. You'll find gigs and events to suit most tastes.

☆ Entertainment

Zagrebačko Kazalište Mladih

THEATRE

(☑ 01-48 72 554; www.zekaem.hr; Teslina 7; ⊙ box office 10am-8pm Mon-Fri, to 2pm Sat & Sun, plus 1hr before the show) Zagreb Youth Theatre, better known as ZKM, is considered the cradle of Croatia's contemporary theatre. It hosts several festivals and many visiting troupes from around the world.

Croatian National Theatre

THEATRE

(☑ 01-48 88 418; www.hnk.hr; Trg Maršala Tita 15; ⊙ box office 10am-7pm Mon-Fri, to 1pm Sat & 1hr before the show) This neobaroque theatre, established in 1895, stages opera and ballet performances. Check out Ivan Meštrović's sculpture *The Well of Life* (1905) standing out front.

ⓘ Information

There are ATMs at the bus and train stations, the airport, and at numerous locations around town. Some banks in the train and bus stations accept travellers cheques. Several cafes around town offer free wi-fi.

Atlas Travel Agency (☑ 01-48 07 300; www. atlas-croatia.com; Zrinjevac 17) Tours around Croatia.

KBC Rebro (☑ 01-23 88 888; Kišpatićeva 12; ⊙ 24hr) East of the city; provides emergency aid.

Main Tourist Office (☑ information 0800 53 53, office 01-48 14 051; www.zagreb-tourist info.hr; Trg Bana Jelačića 11; ⊙ 8.30am-9pm Mon-Fri, 9am-6pm Sat & Sun Jun-Sep, 8.30am-8pm Mon-Fri, 9am-6pm Sat, 10am-4pm Sun Oct-May) Distributes free city maps and leaflets, and sells the 24- (60KN) or 72-hour (90KN) **Zagreb Card** (www.zagrebcard. fivestars.hr).

ⓘ Getting There & Away

AIR

Zagreb Airport (☑ 01-45 62 222; www. zagreb-airport.hr) Located 17km southeast of Zagreb, this is Croatia's major airport, offering a range of international and domestic services.

BUS

Zagreb's **bus station** (☑ 060 313 333; www. akz.hr; Avenija M Držića 4) is 1km east of the train station. If you need to store bags, there's a **garderoba** (left luggage; bus station; per hr 5KN; ⊙ 24hr). Trams 2 and 6 run from the bus station to the train station. Tram 6 goes to Trg Bana Jelačića. Frequent domestic departures include: Dubrovnik (205KN to 250KN, 9½ to 11 hours, nine to 12 daily), Rovinj (150KN to 195KN, four to six hours, nine to 11 daily) and Split (115KN to 205KN, five to 8½ hours, 32 to 34 daily).

International destinations include Belgrade (220KN, six hours, five daily), Sarajevo (160KN to 210KN, seven to eight hours, four to five daily) and Vienna (225KN to 247KN, five to six hours, three daily).

TRAIN

The **train station** (☑ 060 333 444; www.hznet. hr; Trg Kralja Tomislava 12) is in the southern part of the city; there's a **garderoba** (train station; lockers per 24hr 15KN; ⊙ 24hr). It's advisable to book train tickets in advance because of limited seating.

Domestic trains head to Split (197KN to 208KN, five to seven hours, four daily). There are international departures to Belgrade (188KN, 6½ hours, daily), Ljubljana (127KN, 2½ hours, four daily), Sarajevo (238KN, eight to 9½ hours, daily) and Vienna (520KN, six to seven hours, two daily).

ⓘ Getting Around

Zagreb is a fairly easy city to navigate. Traffic is bearable and the tram system efficient.

OTHER PLACES WORTH A VISIT

Istria Don't miss the peninsula's main city, **Pula**, with its wealth of Roman architecture. The star of the show is the remarkably well-preserved amphitheatre dating back to the 1st century. About 10km south along the indented shoreline, the **Premantura Peninsula** hides a spectacular nature park, the protected cape of Kamenjak with its lovely rolling hills, wild flowers, low Mediterranean shrubs, fruit trees and medicinal herbs, and around 30km of virgin beaches and coves.

South Dalmatia The island of **Korčula**, rich in vineyards and olive trees, is the largest island in an archipelago of 48, with plenty of opportunities for scenic drives, many quiet coves and secluded beaches, as well as Korčula Town, a striking walled town of round defensive towers, narrow stone streets and red-roofed houses that resembles a miniature Dubrovnik.

Around Dubrovnik A great excursion from Dubrovnik is the seductive island of **Mljet**, its northwestern half showcasing Mljet National Park, where the lush vegetation, pine forests and spectacular saltwater lakes are exceptionally scenic. It's an unspoiled oasis of tranquillity that, according to legend, captivated Odysseus for seven years.

TO/FROM THE AIRPORT
Bus

The Croatia Airlines bus to the airport (30KN) leaves from the bus station every half-hour or hour from about 4.30am to 8pm, and returns from the airport on the same schedule.

Taxi

Taxis cost between 110KN and 200KN.

PUBLIC TRANSPORT

Public transport (www.zet.hr) is based on an efficient network of trams, although the city centre is compact enough to make them almost unnecessary. Tram maps are posted at most stations, making the system easy to navigate.

Buy tickets at newspaper kiosks or from the driver for 10KN. Tickets can be used for transfers within 90 minutes, but only in one direction.

A *dnevna karta* (day ticket), valid on all public transport until 4am the next morning, is available for 30KN at most newspaper kiosks.

Make sure you validate your ticket when you get on the tram by inserting it in the yellow box.

TAXI

For short city rides, **Taxi Cammeo** (☎ 060 71 00, 1212) is typically the cheapest, the 15KN start fare includes the first two kilometres (it's 6KN for every subsequent kilometre).

ISTRIA

☎ 052

Continental Croatia meets the Adriatic in Istria (Istra to Croats), the heart-shaped 3600-sq-km peninsula just south of Trieste in Italy. While the bucolic interior of rolling hills and fertile plains attracts artsy visitors to its hilltop villages, rural hotels and farmhouse restaurants, the verdant indented coastline is enormously popular with the sun'n'sea set. Vast hotel complexes line much of the coast and its rocky beaches are not Croatia's best, but the facilities are wide-ranging, the sea is clean and secluded spots are still plentiful.

The coast gets flooded with tourists in summer, but you can still feel alone and undisturbed in 'Green Istria' (the interior), even in mid-August. Add acclaimed gastronomy (starring fresh seafood, prime white truffles, wild asparagus, top-rated olive oils and award-winning wines), sprinkle it with historical charm and you have a little slice of heaven.

Rovinj

POP 14,365

Rovinj (Rovigno in Italian) is coastal Istria's star attraction. While it can get overrun with tourists in summer, it remains one of the last true Mediterranean fishing ports. Wooded hills and low-rise hotels surround the old town, which is webbed with steep cobbled streets and piazzas. The 14 green islands of the Rovinj archipelago make for a pleasant afternoon away; the most popular islands are Sveta Katarina and Crveni Otok (Red Island), also known as Sveti Andrija.

The old town is contained within an egg-shaped peninsula. About 1.5km south is the

Punta Corrente Forest Park and the wooded cape of Zlatni Rt (Golden Cape), with its age-old oak and pine trees and several large hotels. There are two harbours: the northern open harbour and the small, protected harbour to the south.

◎ Sights

★ Church of St Euphemia
CHURCH

(Sveta Eufemija; Petra Stankovića; ⊙10am-6pm Jun-Sep, to 4pm May, to 2pm Apr) The town's showcase, this imposing church dominates the old town from its hilltop location in the middle of the peninsula. Built in 1736, it's the largest baroque building in Istria, reflecting the period during the 18th century when Rovinj was its most populous town. Inside, look for the marble **tomb of St Euphemia** behind the right-hand altar.

Batana House
MUSEUM

(Pina Budicina 2; adult/concession 10/5KN, with guide 15KN; ⊙10am-2pm & 7-11pm) On the harbour, Batana House is a museum dedicated to the *batana,* a flat-bottomed fishing boat that stands as a symbol of Rovinj's seafaring and fishing traditions. The multimedia exhibits inside the 17th-century town house have interactive displays, excellent captions and audio with *bitinada,* which are typical fishers' songs. Check out the *spacio,* the ground-floor cellar where wine was kept, tasted and sold amid much socialising (open on Tuesday and Thursday).

Grisia
STREET

Lined with galleries where local artists sell their work, this cobbled street leads uphill from behind the Balbi Arch to St Euphemia. The winding narrow backstreets that spread around Grisia are an attraction in themselves. Windows, balconies, portals and squares are a pleasant confusion of styles – Gothic, Renaissance, baroque and neoclassical. Notice the unique *fumaioli* (exterior chimneys), built during the population boom when entire families lived in a single room with a fireplace.

Punta Corrente Forest Park
PARK

(Zlatni Rt) Follow the waterfront on foot or by bike past Hotel Park to this verdant area, locally known as Zlatni Rt, about 1.5km south. Covered in oak and pine groves and boasting 10 species of cypress, the park was established in 1890 by Baron Hütterott, an Austrian admiral who kept a villa on Crveni

Otok. You can swim off the rocks or just sit and admire the offshore islands.

⌖ Sleeping

Porton Biondi
CAMPGROUND $

(☑052-813 557; www.portonbiondi.hr; Aleja Porton Biondi 1; campsites per person/tent 53/40KN; ⊙mid-Mar–Oct; ⊛) This beachside campground, which sleeps 1200, is about 700m north of the old town.

Villa Baron Gautsch
GUESTHOUSE $$

(☑052-840 538; www.baron-gautsch.com; IM Ronjgova 7; s/d incl breakfast 293/586KN; ⊛⊚) This German-owned *pansion* (guesthouse), up the leafy street leading up from Hotel Park, has 17 spick-and-span rooms, some with terraces and lovely views of the sea and the old town. Breakfast is served on the small terrace out the back. It's cash (kuna) only.

★ Hotel Lone
DESIGN HOTEL $$$

(☑052-632 000; www.lonehotel.com; Luje Adamovića 31; s/d 1800/2300KN; ⓟ⊛⊚⊚) Croatia's first design hotel, this 248-room powerhouse of style is a creation of Croatia's starchitects 3LHD. It rises over Lone bay like a ship dropped in the forest. Light-flooded rooms come with private terraces and five-star trimmings. Facilities include a couple of restaurants, an extensive spa and a brand-new beach club.

✕ Eating

Male Madlene
TAPAS $

(☑052-815 905; Svetog Križa 28; snacks from 30KN; ⊙11am-2pm & 7-11pm May-Sep) Adorable spot in the owner's tiny living room hanging over the sea, where she serves up creative finger food with market-fresh ingredients, based on old Italian recipes. Think tuna-filled zucchini, goat-cheese-stuffed peppers and bite-size savoury pies and cakes. A 12-snack plate for two is 100KN. Great Istrian wines by the glass. Reserve ahead, especially for evenings.

Da Sergio
PIZZA $

(Grisia 11; pizzas 28-71KN; ⊙11am-3pm & 6-11pm) It's worth waiting in line to get a table at this old-fashioned two-floor pizzeria that dishes out Rovinj's best thin-crust pizza, which locals swear by. The best is Gogo, with fresh tomato and arugula (rocket) and prosciutto.

★ Kantinon
SEAFOOD $$

(Alda Rismonda bb; mains from 70KN; ⊙noon-11pm) Recently unveiled in its new incarnation,

PLITVICE LAKES NATIONAL PARK

The absolute highlight of Croatia's Adriatic hinterland, this glorious expanse of forested hills and turquoise lakes is exquisitely scenic – so much so that in 1979 Unesco proclaimed the **park** (☑053-751 015; www.np-plitvicka-jezera.hr; adult/child Jul & Aug 180/80KN, Apr-Jun, Sep & Oct 110/55KN, Nov-Mar 55/35KN; ☺7am-8pm) a World Heritage Site.

Sixteen crystalline lakes tumble into each other via a series of waterfalls and cascades, while clouds of butterflies drift above. It takes upwards of six hours to explore the 18km of wooden footbridges and pathways which snake around the edges of the rumbling water on foot, but you can slice two hours off by taking advantage of the park's free boats and buses (departing every 30 minutes from April to October).

While the park is beautiful year-round, spring and autumn are the best times to visit. In spring and early summer the falls are flush with water, while in autumn the changing leaves put on a colourful display. Winter is also spectacular, although snow can limit access and the free park transport doesn't operate. If possible, avoid the peak months of July and August, when the falls reduce to a trickle, parking is problematic and the sheer volume of visitors can turn the walking tracks into a conga line.

this top eating choice is headed up by a stellar team – one of Croatia's best chefs and an equally amazing sommelier. The food is 100% Croatian, with ingredients as local and fresh as they get, and lots of seafood based on old-fashioned fishers' recipes. Don't miss their sardines *na savor*.

Monte MEDITERRANEAN $$$
(☑052-830 203; Montalbano 75; mains from 190KN; ☺noon-2.30pm & 6.30-11pm) Rovinj's top restaurant, right below St Euphemia Church, is worth the hefty cost. Enjoy beautifully presented dishes on the elegant glassed-in terrace. Don't want to splurge? Have a pasta or risotto (from 124KN). Try the fennel ice cream. Reserve ahead in high season.

🍷 Drinking & Nightlife

Limbo CAFE, BAR
(Casale 22b; ☺10am-1am) Cosy cafe-bar with small candlelit tables and cushions laid out on the stairs leading to the old town's hilltop. It serves tasty snacks and good *prosecco* (sweet dessert wine).

Valentino COCKTAIL BAR
(Svetog Križa 28; ☺6pm-midnight) Premium cocktail prices at this high-end spot include fantastic sunset views from cushions scattered on the water's edge.

❶ Getting There & Away

The bus station is just to the southeast of the old town, and offers a **garderoba** (per day 10KN; ☺6.30am-8pm). There are daily services to Zagreb (145KN to 180KN, four to five hours), Split (444KN, 11 hours) and Dubrovnik (628KN, 15 to 16 hours).

DALMATIA

Roman ruins, spectacular beaches, old fishing ports, medieval architecture and unspoilt offshore islands make a trip to Dalmatia (Dalmacija) unforgettable. Occupying the central 375km of Croatia's Adriatic coast, Dalmatia offers a matchless combination of hedonism and historical discovery. The jagged coast is speckled with lush offshore islands and dotted with historic cities.

Split

☑ 021 / POP 178,200

The second-largest city in Croatia, Split (Spalato in Italian) is a great place to see Dalmatian life as it's really lived. Always buzzing, this exuberant city has just the right balance of tradition and modernity. Step inside Diocletian's Palace (a Unesco World Heritage Site and one of the world's most impressive Roman monuments) and you'll see dozens of bars, restaurants and shops thriving amid the atmospheric old walls. To top it off, Split has a unique setting: the turquoise waters of the Adriatic backed by dramatic coastal mountains.

The Old Town is a vast open-air museum and the information signs at the important sights explain a great deal of Split's history. The seafront promenade, Obala Hrvatskog

Central Split

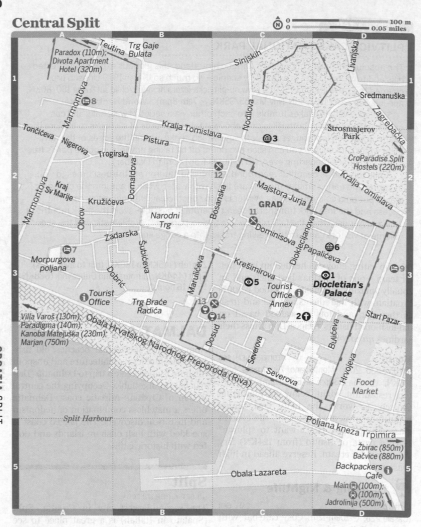

Narodnog Preporoda, better known as Riva, is the best central reference point.

◉ Sights

◉ Diocletian's Palace

Facing the harbour, **Diocletian's Palace** is one of the most imposing Roman ruins in existence. Don't expect a palace though, nor a museum – this is the living heart of the city, its labyrinthine streets packed with people, bars, shops and restaurants.

It was built as a military fortress, imperial residence and fortified town, with walls reinforced by square corner towers. There are 220 buildings within the palace boundaries, which is home to about 3000 people.

Town Museum   MUSEUM

(Muzej Grada Splita; www.mgst.net; Papalićeva 1; adult/concession 20/10KN; ⊙9am-9pm Tue-Fri, to 4pm Sat-Mon) Built by Juraj Dalmatinac for one of the many noblemen who lived within the palace in the Middle Ages, Papalić Palace is considered a fine example of late-Gothic

Central Split

style, with an elaborately carved entrance gate that proclaimed the importance of its original inhabitants. The interior has been thoroughly restored to house this museum.

Cathedral of St Domnius   CATHEDRAL
(Katedrala Svetog Duje; Duje 5; cathedral/treasury/belfry 15/15/10KN; ☉8am-7pm Mon-Sat, 12.30-6.30pm Sun) FREE Split's octagonal-shaped cathedral was originally built as Diocletian's mausoleum, encircled by 24 columns, that is almost completely preserved to this day. Its round domed interior has two rows of Corinthian columns and a frieze showing Emperor Diocletian and his wife. Note that admission to the cathedral also gets you free access to the Temple of Jupiter and its crypt. For 35KN, you can get a ticket that includes access to all these highlights.

Temple of Jupiter   TEMPLE
(admission temple/temple & cathedral 10/35KN; ☉8am-7pm Mon-Sat, 12.30-6.30pm Sun) The headless sphinx in black granite guarding the entrance to the temple was imported from Egypt at the time of the temple's construction in the 5th century. Of the columns that supported a porch the temple once had, only one remains. Take a look at the barrel-vaulted ceiling and a decorative frieze on the walls. You can also pop into the crypt, which was used as a church back in the day.

⊙ Outside the Palace Walls

Gregorius of Nin   MONUMENT
(Grgur Ninski) The 10th-century Croatian bishop Gregorius of Nin fought for the right to use old Croatian in liturgical services. Sculpted by Ivan Meštrović, this powerful work is one of the defining images of Split. Notice that his left big toe has been polished to a shine – it's said that rubbing the toe brings good luck and guarantees that you'll come back to Split.

Gallery of Fine Arts   GALLERY
(Galerija Umjetnina Split; www.galum.hr; Kralja Tomislava 15; adult/concession 20/10KN; ☉11am-4pm Mon, to 7pm Tue-Fri, to 3pm Sat) In the building that once housed the city's first hospital, this gallery exhibits nearly 400 works of art spanning almost 700 years. Upstairs is the permanent collection of mainly paintings and some sculpture, a chronological journey that starts with the old masters and continues with works of modern Croatian art by the likes of Vlaho Bukovac and Ignjat Job. Temporary exhibits downstairs change every few months. The pleasant cafe has a terrace overlooking the palace.

🏃 Activities

Bačvice   SWIMMING
A flourishing beach life gives Split its aura of insouciance in summer. The pebbly Bačvice is the most popular beach, awarded with a Blue Flag eco label. You'll find good swimming, lively ambience and picigin (beach-ball) games galore. There are showers and changing rooms at both ends of the beach. Bačvice is also a popular summer bar and club area for Split's younger crowd and for visitors.

Marjan   WALKING TRAIL
For an afternoon away from the city buzz, Marjan (178m) is the perfect destination. Considered the lungs of the city, this hilly nature reserve offers trails through fragrant pine forests, scenic lookouts and ancient chapels.

🛏 Sleeping

Hostels have sprouted all around Split in the last couple of years. Private accommodation is still a great option; expect to pay between 300KN and 500KN for a double room; in the cheaper ones you will probably share the bathroom with the proprietor. Split has

CROATIA SPLIT

quite a few boutique hotels popping up in the old town.

CroParadise Split Hostels HOSTEL $

(☑ 091 444 4194; www.croparadise.com; Čulića Dvori 29; dm 200KN, s/d 250/500KN, apt from 500KN; ✳ @ 🔊) A great collection of three hostels – Blue, Green and Pink – inside converted apartments in the neighbourhood of Manuš. The shared bar Underground (open June to September) is a starting point for pub crawls (Monday to Saturday nights). Other facilities include laundry, bike and scooter rental. Five apartments are also available.

Silver Central Hostel HOSTEL $

(☑ 021-490 805; www.silvercentralhostel.com; Kralja Tomislava 1; dm 190KN; ✳ @ 🔊) In an upstairs apartment, this light-yellow-coloured boutique hostel has four dorm rooms and a pleasant lounge. It has a two-person apartment nearby (250KN to 520KN) and another hostel, Silver Gate (☑ 021-322 857; www.silvergatehostel.com; Hrvojeva 6; dm per person 180KN, d with kitchen 525KN), near the food market.

★ Goli + Bosi HOSTEL $$

(☑ 021-510 999; www.gollybossy.com; Morpurgova Poljana 2; dm/s/d 240/700/800KN) Split's design hostel is the premier destination for flashpackers, with its sleek futuristic decor, hip vibe and a cool lobby cafe-bar-restaurant. For 1130KN you get the superior double (called Mala Floramy), with breakfast included and gorgeous views.

Villa Varoš GUESTHOUSE $$

(☑ 021-483 469; www.villavaros.hr; Miljenka Smoje 1; d/ste 586/887KN; 🅿 ✳ 🔊) Midrangers are getting a better deal in Split nowadays, with places such as Villa Varoš around. Owned by a New Yorker Croat, Villa Varoš is central, the rooms are simple, bright and airy, and the apartment has a Jacuzzi and a small terrace.

★ Divota Apartment Hotel HOTEL $$$

(☑ 091 404 1199; www.divota.hr; Plinarska 75; s/d 761/823KN; ✳ 🔊) Scattered across the Varoš neighbourhood in eight restored fishers' houses, Divota, owned by an artsy Swiss-Croatian, provides a retreat from the nearby palace buzz. The six contemporary rooms, nine apartments (1508KN) and a stunning three-bedroom villa (5030KN) with a courtyard come with upscale amenities, original detail and unique features, like a bedroom inside a vaulted well.

Eating

★ Villa Spiza DALMATIAN $

(Kružićeva 3; mains from 50KN; ⊙ 9am-midnight Mon-Sat) Locals' favourite within the palace walls, this low-key joint offers great-quality Dalmatian mainstays that change daily – think calamari, risotto, stuffed peppers – at low prices. It's fresh home cooking served at the bar inside, or at a couple of benches outside. Service is slow but the food is prepared with care.

Figa INTERNATIONAL $

(☑ 021-274 491; Buvinina 1; mains from 50KN; ⊙ 8.30am-1am) A cool little restaurant and bar, with a funky interior and tables on the stairs outside, Figa serves nice breakfasts, seafood dishes and a wide range of salads. There's live music some nights and the kitchen stays open late. Service can be slow but comes with smiles and jokes.

Konoba Matejuška DALMATIAN $

(☑ 021-355 152; Tomića Stine 3; mains from 50KN; ⊙ noon-midnight) Cosy, rustic tavern in an alleyway minutes from the seafront, it specialises in well-prepared seafood that also happens to be well-priced. The waitstaff are friendly. Wash down your meal with a glass of *kujunduša,* a local white wine from Dalmatia's hinterland.

Paradigma MEDITERRANEAN $$

(☑ 021-645 103; Bana Josipa Jelačića 3; mains from 95KN; ⊙ 8am-midnight) Bringing culinary innovation to Split, this new restaurant sports modern interiors with hand-painted murals and a rooftop terrace featuring Riva views in an old building resembling a ship's bow. It's slightly hidden from the tourist scene. Highlights are its top-notch wine list and Mediterranean-inspired dishes, like olive oil *sorbetto,* sous vide steaks and *pršut* (prosciutto) powder.

UJE Oil Bar DALMATIAN $$

(Dominisova 3; mains from 70KN; ⊙ 9am-midnight) A restaurant and olive oil/delicatessen shop with a small selection of mains, several tapas-style dishes and olive-oil tasting options. Rustic light-wood interiors are charming, as are alfresco seats in the alley. Service can be spotty though. Their recently opened wine bar next door is set against the original stone walls of Diocletian's Palace.

☕ Drinking & Nightlife

Žbirac CAFE
(Šetalište Petra Preradovića 1b; ⊙7am-1am Sun-Thu, to 2am Fri-Sat) This beachfront cafe is like the locals' open-air living room, a cult hang-out with great sea views, swimming day and night, *picigin* games and occasional concerts.

Ghetto Club BAR
(Dosud 10; ⊙6pm-midnight Mon-Thu, to 2am Fri-Sat) Head for Split's most bohemian and gay-friendly bar, in an intimate courtyard amid flower beds, a trickling fountain, great music and a friendly atmosphere.

Fluid BAR
(Dosud 1; ⊙8am-midnight Mon-Thu, to 1am Fri-Sat) This chic little spot is a jazzy party venue, pretty low-key and cool. Great for people-watching.

Paradox WINE BAR
(Poljana Tina Ujevića 2; ⊙9am-1am Mon-Sat, 4pm-1am Sun) Stylish wine bar with cool wine-glass chandeliers inside, alfresco tables and a great selection of well-priced Croatian wines and local cheeses to go with them.

❶ Information

You can change money at travel agencies or the post office. There are ATMs throughout the city.

Backpackers Cafe (☑021-338 548; Kneza Domagoja bb; internet per hr 30KN; ⊙7am-8pm) Sells used books, offers luggage storage and internet access, and provides information for backpackers.

KBC Firule (☑021-556 111; Spinčićeva 1) Split's hospital.

Tourist Office (☑021-360 066; www.visit split.com; Hrvatskog Narodnog Preporoda 9; ⊙8am-9pm Mon-Sat, to 1pm Sun Jun-Sep) Has info on Split and sells the Split Card (35KN), which offers free and reduced prices to Split attractions and discounts on car rental, restaurants, shops and hotels. You get the card for free if you're staying in Split more than three nights.

Tourist Office Annex (☑021-345 606; www. visitsplit.com; Peristil bb; ⊙8am-9pm Mon-Sat, to 1pm Sun Jun-Sep) This tourist office annex on Peristil has shorter hours.

Turist Biro (☑021-347 100; www.turistbiro-split.hr; Hrvatskog Narodnog Preporoda 12) Its forte is private accommodation and excursions.

❶ Getting There & Away

AIR

Split Airport (www.split-airport.hr) is 20km west of town, just 6km before Trogir. **Croatia Airlines** (☑021-895 298; www.croatiaairlines. hr; Split Airport; ⊙5.15am-8pm) operates one-hour flights to and from Zagreb several times a day and a weekly flight to Dubrovnik (summer only).

A couple of low-cost airlines fly to Split, including **Easyjet** (www.easyjet.com), **germanwings** (www.germanwings.com) and **Norwegian** (www. norwegian.com).

BOAT

Jadrolinija (☑021-338 333; www.jadrolinija.hr; Gat Sv Duje bb) handles most of the coastal ferry lines and catamarans that operate between Split and the islands.

There is also a fast passenger boat, the **Krilo** (www.krilo.hr), that goes to Hvar Town (70KN, one hour) twice daily. There's also a new connection twice weekly to Dubrovnik from mid-May through mid-October (170KN, 4½ hour).

Car ferries and passenger lines depart from separate docks; the passenger lines leave from Obala Lazareta and car ferries from Gat Sv Duje. You can buy tickets from either the main Jadrolinija office in the large ferry terminal opposite the bus station, or at one of the two stalls near the docks. You can't reserve tickets ahead of time; they're only available for purchase on the day of departure. In summer it's usually necessary to appear several hours before departure for a car ferry, and put your car in the line for boarding. There is rarely a problem or a long wait obtaining a space off-season.

BUS

Advance bus tickets with seat reservations are recommended. Most buses leave from the main **bus station** (☑060 327 777; www.ak-split.hr) beside the harbour, which has a **garderoba** (1st hr 5KN, then per hr 1.50KN; ⊙6am-10pm), to the following destinations: Dubrovnik (115KN to 137KN, 4½ hours, 15 daily), Pula (308KN to 423KN, 10 to 11 hours, three daily) and Zagreb (144KN to 175KN, seven hours, 40 daily).

Note that Split–Dubrovnik buses pass briefly through Bosnian territory, so keep your passport handy for border-crossing points.

TRAIN

There are five daily trains (89KN, six to eight hours) between Zagreb and Split **train station** (☑021-338 525; www.hznet.hr; Kneza Domagoja 9), which is just behind the bus station; two are overnight. There's a **garderoba** (per day 15KN; ⊙6am-10pm) at the station.

PAKLENI ISLANDS

Most visitors to Hvar Town head to the Pakleni Islands (Pakleni Otoci), which got their name, 'Hell's Islands' in Croatian, from Paklina, the resin that once coated boats and ships.

This gorgeous chain of 21 wooded isles has crystal-clean seas, hidden beaches and deserted lagoons. Taxi boats leave regularly during the high season from in front of the Arsenal to the islands of **Jerolim** and **Stipanska** (40KN, 10 to 15 minutes), which are popular naturist islands (although nudity is not mandatory). They continue on to **Ždrilca** and **Mlini** (40KN) and, further out, **Palmižana** (60KN), which has a pebble beach and the **Meneghello Place** (www.palmizana.hr), a beautiful boutique complex of villas and bungalows scattered among lush tropical gardens. Run by the artsy Meneghello family, the estate holds music recitals, and features two excellent restaurants and an art gallery. Also on Palmižana are two top restaurant-cum-hang-out spots, Toto and Laganini.

Hvar Island

[image] 021 / POP 10,900

Hvar is the number-one carrier of Croatia's superlatives: it's the most luxurious island, the sunniest place in the country and, along with Dubrovnik, the most popular tourist destination. Hvar is also famed for its verdancy and its lilac lavender fields.

The island's hub and busiest destination is Hvar Town. Visitors wander along the main square, explore the sights on the winding stone streets, swim on the numerous beaches or pop off to strip off to their birthday suits on the Pakleni Islands, but most of all they party at night. There are several good restaurants and a number of top hotels, as well as a couple of hostels.

The interior of the island hides abandoned ancient hamlets, towering peaks and green, largely uncharted landscapes. It's worth exploring on a day trip.

◉ Sights & Activities

St Stephen's Square　　　SQUARE
(Trg Svetog Stjepana) The centre of town is this rectangular square, which was formed by filling in an inlet that once stretched out from the bay. At 4500 sq metres, it's one of the largest old squares in Dalmatia. The town first developed in the 13th century to the north of the square and later spread south in the 15th century. Notice the well at the square's northern end, which was built in 1520 and has a wrought-iron grill dating from 1780.

**Franciscan Monastery
& Museum**　　　MONASTERY
(admission 25KN; ◉9am-1pm & 5-7pm Mon-Sat) This 15th-century monastery overlooks a shady cove. The elegant **bell tower** was built in the 16th century by a well-known family of stonemasons from Korčula. The **Renaissance cloister** leads to a refectory containing lace, coins, nautical charts and valuable documents, such as an edition of *Ptolemy's Atlas*, printed in 1524.

Fortica　　　FORTRESS
(admission 25KN; ◉9am-9pm) Through the network of tiny streets northwest of St Stephen's Sq, climb up through a park to the citadel built on the site of a medieval castle to defend the town from the Turks. The Venetians strengthened it in 1557 and then the Austrians renovated it in the 19th century by adding barracks. Inside is a tiny collection of ancient amphorae recovered from the seabed. The view over the harbour is magnificent, and there's a lovely cafe at the top.

⌲ Tours

Secret Hvar　　　GUIDED TOUR
([image] 021-717 615; www.secrethvar.com) Don't miss the great off-road tour with Secret Hvar (600KN, with lunch in a traditional tavern), which takes in hidden beauties of the island's interior, including abandoned villages, scenic canyons, ancient stone huts, endless fields of lavender and the island's tallest peak, Sveti Nikola (626m). It also does wine tours (550KN, with snacks and samplings) and island tours (450KN).

⌸ Sleeping

Accommodation in Hvar is extremely tight in July and August; if you arrive without a booking, try the travel agencies for help. Expect to pay anywhere from 150KN to

300KN per person for a room with a private bathroom.

Helvetia Hostel
HOSTEL $

(☑091 34 55 556; hajduk.hvar@gmail.com; Grge Novaka 6; dm/d 230/500KN; ❄️🎧) Run by a friendly islander, this hostel inside his family's old stone house just behind Riva has three dorms and two doubles. The highlight is the giant rooftop terrace where guests hang out and enjoy undisturbed views of Hvar bay and the Pakleni Islands.

Hotel Croatia
HOTEL $$$

(☑021-742 400; www.hotelcroatia.net; Majerovica bb; s/d 962/1283KN; P❄️@🎧) Only a few steps from the sea, this medium-sized, rambling 1930s building sits among gorgeous, peaceful gardens. The rooms – with a yellow, orange and lavender colour scheme – are simple and old-fashioned. Many (pricier ones) have balconies overlooking the gardens and the sea. There's a sauna, too.

Hotel Adriana
HOTEL $$$

(☑021-750 200; www.suncanihvar.com; Fabrika 28; s/d 3032/3131KN; ❄️@🎧🏊) All of the bright, swanky rooms of this deluxe spa hotel overlook the sea and the medieval town. Facilities include Sensori Spa, a gorgeous rooftop pool next to the rooftop bar, a plush restaurant, 24-hour room service and more.

✖️ Eating

Konoba Menego
DALMATIAN $

(☑021-742 036; www.menego.hr; Kroz Grodu 26; mains from 60KN; ⊘11.30am-2pm & 5.30pm-midnight) This rustic old house on the stairway towards Fortica is kept as simple and authentic as possible. As they say: no grill, no pizza, no Coca-Cola. The place is decked out in Hvar antiques, the staff wear traditional outfits, the service is informative and the marinated meats, cheeses and vegetables are prepared the old-fashioned Dalmatian way.

Konoba Luviji
DALMATIAN $

(☑091 519 8444; Jurja Novaka 6; mains from 50KN; ⊘7pm-1am) Food brought out of the wood oven at this tavern is simple, unfussy and tasty, although portions are modestly sized. Downstairs is the *konoba* (tavern) where Dalmatian-style tapas are served, while the restaurant is upstairs on a small terrace, with old-town and harbour views.

Nonica
PASTRIES, CAKES $

(☑021-718 041; Burak 23; ⊘8am-2pm & 5-11pm Mon-Sat, 8am-2pm Sun) Savour the best cakes in town at this tiny storefront cafe right behind the Arsenal. Try the old-fashioned local biscuits such as *rafioli* and *forski koloc* and the Nonica tart with choco mousse and orange peel.

Divino
MEDITERRANEAN $$$

(☑021-717 541; www.divino.com.hr; Put Križa 1; mains from 130KN; ⊘10am-1am) The fabulous location and the island's best wine list are reason enough to splurge at this swank restaurant. Add innovative food (think rack of lamb with crusted pistachio) and dazzling views of the Pakleni Islands and you've got a winning formula for a special night out. Or have some sunset snacks and wine on the gorgeous terrace. Book ahead.

🍷 Drinking & Nightlife

★ Falko
BEACH BAR

(⊘8am-9pm mid-May–mid-Sep) A 3km walk from the town centre brings you to this adorable hideaway in a pine forest just above the beach. A great unpretentious alternative to the flashy spots closer to town, it serves yummy sandwiches and salads from a hut, as well as its own limoncello and *rakija*. Think low-key artsy vibe, hammocks and a local crowd.

Carpe Diem
LOUNGE BAR

(www.carpe-diem-hvar.com; Riva; ⊘9am-2am) Look no further – you have arrived at the mother of Croatia's coastal clubs. From a groggy breakfast to pricey late-night cocktails, there is no time of day when this swanky place is dull. The house music spun by resident DJs is smooth, there are drinks aplenty, and the crowd is of the jet-setting kind.

Hula-Hula
BEACH BAR

(www.hulahulahvar.com; ⊘9am-11pm) *The* spot to catch the sunset to the sound of techno and house music, Hula-Hula is known for its après-beach party (4pm to 9pm), where all of young trendy Hvar seems to descend for sundowner cocktails.

Kiva Bar
BAR

(www.kivabarhvar.com; Fabrika bb; ⊘9pm-2am) A happening place in an alleyway just off the Riva. It's packed to the rafters most nights, with a DJ spinning old dance, pop and rock classics that really get the crowd going.

ℹ Information

Del Primi (☎ 091 583 7864; www.del primi-hvar.com; Burak 23) Travel agency specialising in private accommodation. Also rents jet skis.

Hvar Adventure (☎ 021-717 813; www.hvar-adventure.com; Obala bb)

Luka Rent (Riva 24; per hr 10KN; ⊗ 9am-9pm) Internet cafe and call centre right on the Riva.

Tourist Office (☎ 021-741 059; www.tzhvar. hr; Trg Svetog Stjepana 42; ⊗ 8am-2pm & 3-9pm Jul & Aug, 8am-2pm & 3-7pm Mon-Sat, 8am-noon Sun Jun & Sep) Right on Trg Svetog Stjepana.

ℹ Getting There & Away

The local **Jadrolinija** (☎ 021-741 132; www. jadrolinija.hr) car ferry from Split calls at the island's main ferry port, the coastal town of Stari Grad (47KN, two hours) six times a day in summer. Jadrolinija also has three to five catamarans daily to Hvar Town (55KN to 70KN, one hour). **Krilo** (www.krilo.hr), the fast passenger boat, travels twice a day between Split and Hvar Town (70KN, one hour) in summer. You can buy tickets at **Pelegrini Tours** (☎ 021-742 743; www. pelegrini-hvar.hr; Riva bb).

ℹ Getting Around

Buses meet most ferries that dock at Stari Grad and go to Hvar Town (27KN, 20 minutes). There are 10 buses a day between Stari Grad and Hvar Town in summer, and services are reduced on Sunday and in the low season.

A taxi to Hvar Town costs around 275KN.
Radio Taxi Tihi (☎ 098 338 824) is cheaper if there are a number of passengers to fill up the minivan.

Dubrovnik

☎ 020 / POP 28,500

No matter whether you are visiting Dubrovnik for the first time or if you're returning to this marvellous city, the sense of awe and beauty when you set eyes on the Stradun (the Old Town's main street) never fades. It's hard to imagine anyone becoming jaded by the marble streets and baroque buildings, or failing to be inspired by a walk along the ancient city walls that once protected a civilised, sophisticated republic for five centuries and that now look out onto the endless shimmer of the peaceful Adriatic.

◉ Sights

All the sights are in the Old Town, which is entirely closed to cars. Looming above the city is Mt Srđ, which is connected by cable car to Dubrovnik. Pile Gate is the main entrance to the Old Town; the main street is Placa (better known as Stradun).

◉ Old Town

★**City Walls & Forts** FORT
(Gradske Zidine; adult/child 100/30KN; ⊗ 9am-6.30pm Apr-Oct, 10am-3pm Nov-Mar) No visit to Dubrovnik would be complete without a walk around the spectacular city walls, the finest in the world and the city's main claim to fame. From the top, the view over the old town and the shimmering Adriatic is sublime. You can get a good handle on the extent of the shelling damage in the 1990s by gazing over the rooftops: those sporting bright new terracotta suffered damage and had to be replaced.

★**War Photo Limited** GALLERY
(☎ 020-322 166; www.warphotoltd.com; Antuninska 6; adult/child 40/30KN; ⊗ 10am-10pm daily Jun-Sep, 10am-4pm Tue-Sun May & Oct) An immensely powerful experience, this gallery features intensely compelling exhibitions curated by New Zealand photojournalist Wade Goddard, who worked in the Balkans in the 1990s. Its declared intention is to 'expose the myth of war...to let people see war as it is, raw, venal, frightening, by focusing on how war inflicts injustices on innocents and combatants alike'. There's a permanent exhibition on the upper floor devoted to the wars in Yugoslavia, but the changing exhibitions cover a multitude of conflicts.

Franciscan Monastery & Museum MONASTERY
(Muzej Franjevačkog Samostana; Placa 2; adult/child 30/15KN; ⊗ 9am-6pm) Within this monastery's solid stone walls is a gorgeous mid-14th-century **cloister**, a historic **pharmacy** and a small **museum** with a collection of relics and liturgical objects, including chalices, paintings, gold jewellery and pharmacy items such as laboratory gear and medical books. Artillery remains that pierced the monastery walls during the 1990s war have been saved, too.

Dominican Monastery & Museum
MONASTERY

(Muzej Dominikanskog Samostana; off Sv Dominika 4; admission 30KN; ⊙9am-5pm) This imposing structure is an architectural highlight, built in a transitional Gothic-Renaissance style, and containing an impressive art collection. Constructed around the same time as the city wall fortifications in the 14th century, the stark exterior resembles a fortress more than a religious complex. The interior contains a graceful 15th-century **cloister** constructed by local artisans after the designs of the Florentine architect Maso di Bartolomeo.

Rector's Palace
PALACE

(Pred Dvorom 3; admission via multimuseum pass, adult/child 80/25KN; ⊙9am-6pm May-Oct, to 4pm Nov-Apr) Built in the late 15th century for the elected rector who governed Dubrovnik, this Gothic-Renaissance palace contains the rector's office, his private chambers, public halls, administrative offices and a dungeon. During his one-month term the rector was unable to leave the building without the permission of the senate. Today the palace has been turned into the **Cultural History Museum**, with artfully restored rooms, portraits, coats of arms and coins, evoking the glorious history of Dubrovnik.

Cathedral of the Assumption
CATHEDRAL

(Stolna Crkva Velike Gospe; Poljana M Držića; ⊙7.30am-6pm) Built on the site of a 7th-century basilica, Dubrovnik's original cathedral was enlarged in the 12th century, supposedly funded by a gift from England's King Richard I, the Lionheart, who was saved from a shipwreck on the nearby island of Lokrum. Soon after the first cathedral was destroyed in the 1667 earthquake, work began on this, its baroque replacement, which was finished in 1713.

Sponza Palace
PALACE

(Placa bb) This superb 16th-century palace is a mixture of Gothic and Renaissance styles beginning with an exquisite Renaissance portico resting on six columns. The 1st floor has late-Gothic windows and the 2nd-floor windows are in a Renaissance style, with an alcove containing a statue of St Blaise. Sponza Palace was originally a customs house, then a mint, a state treasury and a bank.

Church of the Annunciation
CHURCH

(Crkva Sv Blagovještenja; Od Puča 8; ⊙8am-7.30pm) The old town's sole Serbian Orthodox church provides an interesting contrast to the numerous Catholic churches scattered about. Dating from 1877, it suffered substantial damage during the most recent war and was only fully restored in 2009.

Synagogue
SYNAGOGUE

(Sinagoga; Žudioska 5; admission 35KN; ⊙10am-8pm May-Oct, to 3pm Nov-Apr) Dating to the 15th century, this is the second-oldest synagogue (the oldest Sephardic one) in the Balkans. Inside is a museum that exhibits religious relics and documentation on the local Jewish population, including records relating to their persecution during WWII.

Orlando Column
MONUMENT

(Luža Sq) Luža Sq once served as a marketplace, and this stone column – carved in 1417 and featuring the image of a medieval knight – used to be the spot where edicts, festivities and public verdicts were announced. The knight's forearm was the official linear measure of the Republic – the ell of Dubrovnik (51.1cm). Folk groups occasionally perform in the square.

⊙ East of the Old Town

★Cable Car
CABLE CAR

(www.dubrovnikcablecar.com; Petra Krešimira IV bb; adult/concession return 100/50KN; ⊙9am-5pm Nov-Mar, to 8pm Apr, May & Oct, to midnight Jun-Aug, to 10pm Sep) Dubrovnik's cable car whisks you from just north of the city walls to Mt Srđ in under four minutes. Operations cease if there are high winds or a thunderstorm brewing. At the end of the line there's a stupendous perspective of the city from a lofty 405m, taking in the terracotta-tiled rooftops of the old town and the island of Lokrum, with the Adriatic and distant Elafiti Islands filling the horizon.

Dubrovnik During the Homeland War
MUSEUM

(Dubrovnik u Domovinskom Ratu; adult/child 30/15KN; ⊙8am-10pm) Set inside a Napoleonic fort near the cable-car terminus, this permanent exhibition is dedicated to the siege of Dubrovnik during the 'Homeland War', as the 1990s war is dubbed in Croatia.

CROATIA DUBROVNIK

Dubrovnik

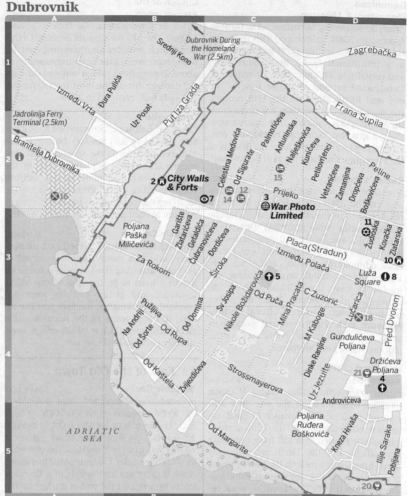

The local defenders stationed inside this fort ensured the city wasn't captured. If the displays are understandably one-sided, they still provide in-depth coverage of the events, including plenty of video footage.

The Coast

Banje Beach, around 300m east of the Ploče Gate, is the most popular city beach. A kilometre further on is **Sveti Jakov**, a good little beach that doesn't get rowdy and has showers, a bar and a restaurant. Buses 5 and 8 will get you there. **Lapad Bay** is brimming with hotel beaches that you can use without a problem; try the bay outside Hotel Kompas.

Festivals & Events

From 10 July to 25 August, the most prestigious summer festival in Croatia, the **Dubrovnik Summer Festival** (Dubrovačke ljetne igre; 020-326 100; www.dubrovnik-festival.hr; tickets 30-350KN; Jul-Aug), presents a program of theatre, opera, concerts and dance on open-air stages throughout the city. Tickets are available online, from the festival office on Placa, and on-site one hour before the beginning of each performance.

CROATIA DUBROVNIK

⊨ Sleeping

Dubrovnik is not a large city but accommodation is scattered all over the place; there's limited accommodation in the old town itself. Book all accommodation well in advance, especially in summer. It's the most expensive city in the country, so expect to pay more for a room here. Private accommodation is a good alternative; contact local travel agencies or the tourist office for options. In high season, expect to pay from 300KN for a double room, or from 500KN for an apartment.

⊨ Old Town

★ **Karmen Apartments**   APARTMENT **$$**
(☑ 098 619 282; www.karmendu.com; Bandureva 1; apt €95-175; ❋⊜) These four inviting apartments enjoy a great location a stone's throw from Ploče harbour. All have plenty of character with art, splashes of colour, tasteful furnishings and books to browse. Apartment 2 has a little balcony while apartment 1 enjoys sublime port views. Book well ahead.

Rooms Viceliċ   GUESTHOUSE **$$**
(☑ 095 52 78 933; www.rooms-vicelic.com; Antuninska 10; r €90-110; ❋⊜) Situated on one of the steeply stepped old town streets, this friendly, family-run place has four atmospheric stone-walled rooms with private bathrooms. Guests have use of a shared kitchenette with a microwave and a kettle.

Old Town Hostel   HOSTEL **$$**
(☑ 020-322 007; www.dubrovnikoldtownhostel. com; Od Sigurate 7; dm/s/d 325/350/650KN; ⊙ Mar-Nov; ⊜) Converted from a historic residence – some rooms even have ceiling paintings – this centrally located hostel isn't short on charm. Dorms range from four to

six beds (including a female-only one), and there's a small kitchen. There's no air-con, only fans.

Hotel Stari Grad HOTEL $$$
(020-322 244; www.hotelstarigrad.com; Od Sigurate 4; s/d 1650/2100KN; ❄ 🛜) The eight rooms at this well-located boutique hotel are smallish, but they're well presented and don't fall short on comfort. Staff are sweet and you'll enjoy the dramatic city views from the rooftop terrace. Note: there are many flights of stairs to negotiate (and no lift).

Outside the Old Town

★**Apartments Silva** GUESTHOUSE $
(098 244 639; silva.dubrovnik@yahoo.com; Kardinala Stepinca 62; s/d 220/440KN, apt from 440KN; ❄) Lush Mediterranean foliage lines the terraces of this lovely hillside complex, a short hop up from the beach at Lapad. The rooms are comfortable and well-priced but best of all is the spacious top-floor apartment (sleeping five). The charming host is happy to arrange free pick-ups from the bus station.

✖ Eating

Oliva Pizzeria PIZZERIA $
(020-324 594; www.pizza-oliva.com; Lučarica 5; mains 40-89KN; ⊘ noon-10pm) There are a few token pasta dishes on the menu, but this attractive little place is really all about pizza. And the pizza is worthy of the attention. Grab a seat on the street and tuck in.

Konoba Ribar DALMATIAN $$
(020-323 194; Kneza Damjana Jude bb; mains 60-120KN; ⊘ 10am-midnight) Serving local food the way locals like it, at more or less local prices, this little family-run eatery is a blissfully untouristy choice. They don't attempt anything fancy or clever, just big serves of traditional favourites such as risotto and stuffed squid. It's set in a little lane pressed hard up against the city walls.

Dubravka 1836 EUROPEAN $$
(020-426 319; www.dubravka1836.hr; Brsalje 1; mains 59-178KN; ⊘ 8am-11pm) Spilling on to a square right by the Pile Gate, this place is indisputably touristy. Still, it's a good spot for a light breakfast, and the locals rate the fresh fish, risotto, salads, pizza and pasta. The views are great, too.

★**Restaurant 360°** MODERN EUROPEAN $$$
(020-322 222; www.360dubrovnik.com; Sv Dominika bb; mains 240-320KN, 5-/7-course set menu 780/970KN; ⊘ 6.30-11pm Tue-Sun) Dubrovnik's glitziest restaurant offers fine dining at its finest, with flavoursome, beautifully presented, creative cuisine, and slick, professional service. The setting is unmatched, on top of the city walls with tables positioned so you can peer through the battlements over the harbour. If you can't justify a splurge, it's still worth calling in for a drink.

🍷 Drinking & Nightlife

Cave Bar More BAR
(www.hotel-more.hr; below Hotel More, Kardinala Stepinca 33; ⊘ 10am-midnight) This little beach bar serves coffee, snacks and cocktails to bathers reclining by the dazzlingly clear waters in Lapad. But that's not the half of it: the main bar is set in an actual cave. Cool off beneath the stalactites in the side chamber, where a glass floor exposes a water-filled cavern.

Buža BAR
(off Ilije Sarake; ⊘ 8am-late) Finding this ramshackle bar-on-a-cliff feels like a real discovery as you duck and dive around the city walls and finally see the entrance tunnel. Emerging by the sea, it's quite a scene with tasteful music (soul, funk) and a mellow crowd soaking up the vibes and views. Grab a cool drink in a plastic cup, perch on a concrete platform and enjoy.

Jazz Caffe Troubadour BAR
(Bunićeva Poljana 2; ⊘ 9am-1am) Tucked into a corner behind the cathedral, Troubadour looks pretty nondescript during the day. That all changes on summer nights, when jazz musicians set up outside and quickly draw the crowds.

ℹ️ Information

There are numerous ATMs in town, in Lapad and at the ferry terminal and bus station. Travel agencies and the post office will also exchange cash.

General Hospital Dubrovnik (Opća Bolnica Dubrovnik; 020-431 777; www.bolnica-du.hr; Dr Roka Mišetića bb; ⊘ emergency department 24hr) On the southern edge of the Lapad peninsula.

Tourist Office (www.tzdubrovnik.hr) Pile (020-312 011; Brsalje 5; ⊘ 8am-9pm Jun-Sep, 8am-7pm Mon-Sat, 9am-3pm Sun Oct-May); Gruž (020-417 983; Obala Pape Ivana

COUNTRY FACTS

Area 56,538 sq km

Capital Zagreb

Country Code 385

Currency Kuna (KN)

Emergency Ambulance ☑94, police ☑92

Language Croatian

Money ATMs are available; credit cards accepted in most hotels and many restaurants

Population 4.3 million

Visas Not required for most nationalities for stays of up to 90 days

---

Pavla II 1; ⊘8am-9pm Jun-Sep, to 3pm Mon-Sat Oct-May); Lapad (☑020-437 460; Kralja Tomislava 7; ⊘8am-8pm Jun-Sep, to 3pm Mon-Sat Oct-May) Maps, information and advice.

ⓘ Getting There & Away

AIR
Daily flights to/from Zagreb are operated by Croatia Airlines (p134). Dubrovnik Airport is served by more than a dozen other airlines from across Europe.

BOAT
The ferry terminal and the bus station are next to each other at Gruž, 3km northwest of the Old Town. A twice-weekly **Jadrolinija** (Obala Pape Ivana Pavla II 1) coastal ferry heads north to Hvar and Split.

BUS
Buses out of Dubrovnik **bus station** (☑060 305 070; Obala Pape Ivana Pavla II 44a) can be crowded, so book tickets ahead in summer. Split–Dubrovnik buses pass briefly through Bosnian territory, so keep your passport handy for border-crossing points.

All bus schedules are detailed at www.libertas-dubrovnik.hr.

ⓘ Getting Around

Dubrovnik Airport (Zračna Luka Dubrovnik; www.airport-dubrovnik.hr) is in Čilipi, 19km southeast of Dubrovnik. Atlas runs the airport bus service (35KN, 30 minutes), timed around flights. Buses to Dubrovnik stop at the Pile Gate and the bus station; buses to the airport pick up from the bus station and from the bus stop near the cable car.

A taxi to the old town costs about 250KN.

SURVIVAL GUIDE

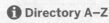

ⓘ Directory A–Z

ACCOMMODATION
Private accommodation is often great-value in Croatia plus it gets you a glimpse of Croatia's own brand of hospitality. Many of the owners treat their guests like long-lost friends. Some offer the option of eating with them, which is a great way to get to know the culture.

Note that many establishments add a 30% charge for stays of less than three nights and include 'residence tax', which is around 7KN per person per day. Prices quoted in this book do not include the residence tax.

Camping
Over 500 camping grounds are scattered along the Croatian coast. Most operate from mid-April to mid-September. The exact times change from year to year, so it's wise to call in advance if you're arriving at either end of the season.

Nudist camping grounds (marked FKK) are among the best, as their secluded locations ensure peace and quiet. A good site for camping information is www.camping.hr.

Hostels
The **Croatian YHA** (☑01-48 29 294; www.hfhs.hr; Savska 5, Zagreb) operates youth hostels in Dubrovnik, Zagreb and Pula. Nonmembers pay an additional 10KN per person per day for a stamp on a welcome card; six stamps entitle you to membership. The Croatian YHA can also provide information about private youth hostels in Hvar and Zagreb.

Hotels
In August, some hotels may demand a surcharge for stays of less than three or four nights, but this is usually waived during the rest of the year, when prices drop steeply.

Breakfast is included in the prices for all hotels.

Private Rooms
The best value for money in Croatia is a private room or apartment, often within or attached to a local home – the equivalent of small private

---

SLEEPING PRICE RANGES

The following price categories for the cost of a double room with bathroom are used in the listings in this chapter.

€ less than 450KN

€€ 450KN to 800KN

€€€ more than 800KN

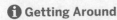

CROATIA DIRECTORY A–Z

ACTIVITIES

Croatia is a great destination for outdoor activities. Cycling is tops, especially in Istria, which has more than 60 marked trails through stunning scenery. Hiking is also incredible, particularly in the national parks such as Plitvice (p119). Croatia also has some great dive sites, including many wrecks; for more info, check out the **Croatian Diving Association** (www.diving-hrs.hr). Other activities worth trying in Croatia are kayaking and rafting; Zagreb-based **Huck Finn** (www.huckfinncroatia.com) is a good contact for sea and river kayaking packages, as well as rafting. For details on rock climbing and caving, contact the **Croatian Mountaineering Association** (www.hps.hr).

guesthouses in other countries. You'll pay a 30% surcharge for stays of less than four or three nights and sometimes 50% or even 100% more for a one-night stay; it may be waived in the low season. Some will even insist on a seven-night minimum stay in the high season.

Whether you rent from an agency or rent from the owners privately, don't hesitate to bargain, especially for longer stays.

If you land in a room or apartment without a blue *sobe* or *apartmani* sign outside, the proprietor is renting to you illegally (ie not paying residence tax). They will probably be reluctant to provide their full name or phone number and you'll have absolutely no recourse in case of a problem.

BUSINESS HOURS

Hours can vary across the year.

Banks 9am to 8pm Monday to Friday, 7am to 1pm or 8am to 2pm Saturday

Bars and cafes 8am to midnight

Offices 8am to 4pm or 8.30am to 4.30pm Monday to Friday

Restaurants noon to 11pm or midnight, closed Sunday out of peak season

Shops 8am to 8pm Monday to Friday, to 2pm or 3pm Saturday

INTERNET RESOURCES

Adriatica.net (www.adriatica.net)

Croatian National Tourist Board (www.croatia.hr)

Taste of Croatia (www.tasteofcroatia.org)

MONEY
Credit Cards

Amex, MasterCard, Visa and Diners Club cards are widely accepted in large hotels, stores and many restaurants, but don't count on cards to pay for private accommodation or meals in small restaurants. You'll find ATMs accepting MasterCard, Maestro, Cirrus, Plus and Visa in most bus and train stations, airports, all major cities and most small towns.

Currency

Croatia uses the kuna (KN). Commonly circulated banknotes come in denominations of 500, 200, 100, 50, 20, 10 and five kuna. Each kuna is divided into 100 lipa. You'll find silver-coloured 50- and 20-lipa coins, and bronze-coloured 10-lipa coins.

PUBLIC HOLIDAYS

New Year's Day 1 January

Epiphany 6 January

Easter Monday March/April

Labour Day 1 May

Corpus Christi 10 June

Day of Antifascist Resistance 22 June; marks the outbreak of resistance in 1941

Statehood Day 25 June

Homeland Thanksgiving Day 5 August

Feast of the Assumption 15 August

Independence Day 8 October

All Saints' Day 1 November

Christmas 25 and 26 December

TELEPHONE
Mobile Phones

If you have an unlocked 3G phone, you can buy a SIM card for about 20KN to 50KN. You can choose from three network providers: **VIP** (www.vip.hr), **T-Mobile** (www.hrvatskitelekom.hr) and **Tele2** (www.tele2.hr).

Phone Codes

➜ To call Croatia from abroad, dial your international access code, then ☑ 385 (the country code for Croatia), then the area code (without the initial 0) and the local number.

EATING PRICE RANGES

Prices in this chapter are based on a main course.

€ less than 70KN

€€ 70KN to 120KN

€€€ more than 120KN

ESSENTIAL FOOD & DRINK

Croatia's cuisine reflects the varied cultures that have influenced the country over the course of its history. You'll find a sharp divide between the Italian-style cuisine along the coast and the flavours of Hungary, Austria and Turkey in the continental parts.

Istrian cuisine has been attracting international foodies in recent years for its long gastronomic tradition, fresh ingredients and unique specialities. Istria-based **Eat Istria** (www.eatistria.com) offers cooking classes and wine tours around the peninsula.

Here are a few essential food and drink items to be aware of while in Croatia:

➡ **Ćevapčići** Small spicy sausages of minced beef, lamb or pork.

➡ **Ražnjići** Small chunks of pork grilled on a skewer.

➡ **Burek** Pastry stuffed with ground meat, spinach or cheese.

➡ **Rakija** Strong Croatian brandy comes in different flavours, from plum to honey.

➡ **Beer** Two top types of Croatian *pivo* (beer) are Zagreb's Ožujsko and Karlovačko from Karlovac.

➡ To call from region to region within Croatia, start with the area code (with the initial 0); drop it when dialling within the same code.

➡ Phone numbers with the prefix ☑060 are either free or charged at a premium rate, so watch out for the small print. Phone numbers that begin with ☑09 are mobile phone numbers.

TOURIST INFORMATION
Croatian National Tourist Board (www.croatia.hr) is a good source of info.

VISAS
Citizens of the EU, the USA, Canada, Australia, New Zealand, Israel, Ireland, Singapore and the UK do not need a visa for stays of up to 90 days. South Africans must apply for a 90-day visa in Pretoria. Contact any Croatian embassy, consulate or travel agency abroad for information.

🅘 Getting There & Away

AIR
There are direct flights to Croatia from a number of European cities; however, there are no nonstop flights from North America to Croatia.

Major airports in Croatia include:

Dubrovnik Airport (DBV; www.airport-dubrovnik.hr) Nonstop flights from Brussels, Cologne, Frankfurt, Hanover, London (Gatwick and Stansted), Manchester, Munich, Paris, Stuttgart and many more.

Pula Airport (PUY; www.airport-pula.com) Nonstop flights from London (Gatwick and Stansted), Manchester, Oslo, Stockholm, Munich, Edinburgh, Copenhagen and more.

Split Airport (SPU; www.split-airport.hr) Nonstop flights from Berlin, Cologne, Copenhagen, Frankfurt, London, Munich, Prague, Stockholm, Rome, Venice and many more.

Zagreb Airport (ZAG; www.zagreb-airport.hr) Direct flights from all European capitals, as well as Cologne, Doha, İstanbul, Hamburg, Madrid, Munich, Moscow and Tel Aviv.

LAND
Croatia is a convenient transport hub for southeastern Europe and the Adriatic, with border crossings with Hungary, Slovenia, Bosnia and Hercegovina (BiH), Serbia and Montenegro.

Zagreb is connected by train and/or bus to Venice, Budapest, Belgrade, Ljubljana and Sarajevo. Down south there are easy bus connections from Dubrovnik to Mostar and Sarajevo (BiH), and to Kotor (Montenegro).

From Austria, **Eurolines** (www.eurolines.com) operates buses from Vienna to several destinations in Croatia.

Bus services between Germany and Croatia are good, and fares are cheaper than the train. All buses are handled by **Deutsche Touring GmbH** (www.deutsche-touring.de); there are no Deutsche Touring offices in Croatia, but numerous travel agencies and bus stations sell its tickets.

SEA
There are a number of ferries linking Croatia with Italy, including routes from Dubrovnik to Bari, and Split to Ancona.

Blue Line (www.blueline-ferries.com)
Commodore Cruises (www.commodore-cruises.hr)
Jadrolinija (www.jadrolinija.hr)
SNAV (www.snav.com)
Venezia Lines (www.venezialines.com)

ⓘ Getting Around

AIR

Croatia Airlines (☎ 01-66 76 555; www.croatia airlines.hr) Croatia Airlines is the national carrier. There are daily flights between Zagreb and Dubrovnik, Osijek, Pula, Rijeka, Split and Zadar.

BOAT

Jadrolinija (p133) operates an extensive network of car ferries and catamarans along the Adriatic coast. Ferries are a lot more comfortable than buses, though somewhat more expensive.

Services operate year-round, though they are less frequent in winter. Cabins should be booked a week ahead. Deck space is usually available on all sailings.

You must buy tickets in advance at an agency or a Jadrolinija office. Tickets are not sold on board. In summer months, you need to check in two hours in advance if you bring a car.

BUS

Bus services are excellent and relatively inexpensive. There are often a number of different companies handling each route so prices can vary substantially. Luggage stowed in the baggage compartment under the bus costs extra (7KN a piece, including insurance).

At large stations, bus tickets must be purchased at the office, not from drivers. Try to book ahead to be sure of a seat, especially in the summer.

CAR & MOTORCYCLE

Croatia's motorway connecting Zagreb with Split is only a few years old and makes some routes much faster.

Car Hire

In order to rent a car you must be 21 or over, with a valid driving licence and a valid credit card.

Independent local companies are often much cheaper than the international chains, but the big companies offer one-way rentals.

Driving Licence

Any valid driving licence is sufficient to drive legally and rent a car; an international driving licence is not necessary.

The **Hrvatski Autoklub** (HAK, Croatian Auto Club; ☎ 01-46 40 800; www.hak.hr; Avenija Dubrovnik 44) offers help and advice. For help on the road, you can contact the nationwide **HAK road assistance** (Vučna Služba; ☎1987).

LOCAL TRANSPORT

The main form of local transport is bus. Buses in major cities such as Dubrovnik and Split run about once every 20 minutes, less on Sunday. A ride is usually around 10KN, with a small discount if you buy tickets at a *tisak* (newsstand).

Bus transport within the islands is infrequent since most people have their own cars.

TRAIN

Trains are less frequent than buses but more comfortable. For information about schedules, prices and services, contact **Croatian Railways** (Hrvatske Željeznice; ☎ 060 333 444; www.hznet.hr).

Zagreb is the hub for Croatia's less-than-extensive train system. No trains run along the coast and only a few coastal cities are connected with Zagreb.

Baggage is free on trains; most stations have left-luggage services, charging around 15KN a piece per day.

EU residents who hold an InterRail pass can use it in Croatia for free travel, but you're unlikely to take enough trains to justify the cost.

Czech Republic

Why Go?

Since the fall of communism in 1989 and the opening up of Central and Eastern Europe, Prague has evolved into one of Europe's most popular travel destinations. The city offers an intact medieval core that transports you back 500 years. The 14th-century Charles Bridge, traversing two historic neighbourhoods, is one of the continent's most beautiful sights.

The city is not just about history. It's a vital urban centre with a rich array of cultural offerings. Outside the capital, castles and palaces abound – including the audacious hilltop chateau at Český Krumlov – which illuminate the stories of powerful dynasties whose influence was felt throughout Europe.

Best Places to Eat

➡ Sansho (p144)

➡ Pavillon (p153)

➡ Kalina (p144)

➡ Moritz (p155)

Best Places to Stay

➡ Mosaic House (p143)

➡ Penzión Na Hradě (p154)

➡ Hotel Konvice (p151)

➡ Savic Hotel (p143)

When to Go
Prague

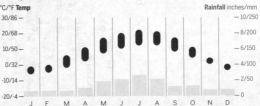

May Prague comes alive with festivals from classical music to fringe arts.

Jul Karlovy Vary shows off its arty side at the sleepy spa town's annual film festival.

Dec Prague's Christmas Market draws visitors from around the world.

Czech Republic Highlights

1 Stroll across the **Charles Bridge** (p141) in the early morning or late evening when the crowds thin out.

2 Enjoy an evening in an old-school Czech pub at **U Medvídků** (p144).

3 Join the appreciative throngs at Prague's **Astronomical Clock** (p140) at the top of the hour.

4 Repair to **Český Krumlov** (p149) to see the prettiest town in Central Europe.

5 Tour the **Pilsner Urquell Brewery** (p147) in Plzeň to see where it all started.

6 Amble through the stately town of **Olomouc** (p153), the most amazing place you've never heard of.

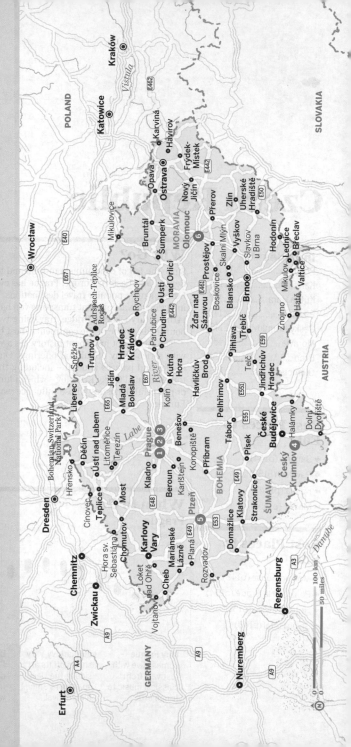

ITINERARIES

One Week

Experience the exciting combination of **Prague's** tumultuous past and energetic present. Top experiences include the grandeur of Prague Castle, Josefov's Prague Jewish Museum, and getting lost amid the bewildering labyrinth of the Old Town. Take an essential day trip to **Karlštejn**, and then head south to **Český Krumlov** for a few days of riverside R&R.

Two Weeks

Begin in **Prague** before heading west for the spa scene at **Karlovy Vary**. Balance the virtue and vice ledger with a few Bohemian brews in **Plzeň** before heading south for relaxation and rigour around **Český Krumlov**. Head east to the Renaissance grandeur of **Telč**, and to **Brno's** cosmopolitan galleries and museums. From the Moravian capital, it's just a skip to stately **Olomouc**.

PRAGUE

POP 1.24 MILLION

It's the perfect irony of Prague: you are lured here by the past, but compelled to linger by the present and the future. Fill your days with its illustrious artistic and architectural heritage – from Gothic and Renaissance to art nouveau and cubist. If Prague's seasonal legions of tourists wear you down, that's OK. Just drink a glass of the country's legendary lager, relax and rest reassured that quiet moments still exist: a private dawn on Charles Bridge, the glorious cityscape of Staré Město or getting lost in the intimate lanes of Malá Strana.

◉ Sights

Prague nestles on the Vltava River, separating Hradčany (the Castle district) and Malá Strana (Lesser Quarter) on the west bank, from Staré Město (Old Town) and Nové Město (New Town) on the east.

◉ Hradčany

Prague Castle
CASTLE

(Pražský hrad; Map p142; ☑224 372 423; www. hrad.cz; Hradčanské náměstí; grounds free, sights adult/concession long tour 350/175Kc, short tour 250/125Kc; ☺grounds 5am-midnight Apr-Oct, 6am-11pm Nov-Mar, gardens 10am-6pm Apr & Oct, to 7pm May & Sep, to 9pm Jun-Aug, closed Nov-Mar, historic buildings 9am-5pm Apr-Oct, to 4pm Nov-Mar; Ⓜ Malostranská, ⓐ22) Prague Castle – Pražský hrad, or just *hrad* to Czechs – is Prague's most popular attraction. Looming above the Vltava's left bank, its serried ranks of spires, towers and palaces dominate the city centre like a fairy-tale fortress. Within

its walls lies a varied and fascinating collection of historic buildings, museums and galleries that are home to some of the Czech Republic's greatest artistic and cultural treasures.

Old Royal Palace
PALACE

(Starý královský palác; Map p142; admission with Prague Castle tour ticket; ☺9am-5pm Apr-Oct, to 4pm Nov-Mar; ⓐ22) The Old Royal Palace is one of the oldest parts of Prague Castle, dating from 1135. It was originally used only by Czech princesses, but from the 13th to the 16th centuries it was the king's own palace. At its heart is the grand Vladislav Hall and the Bohemian Chancellery, scene of the famous Defenestration of Prague in 1618.

St Vitus Cathedral
CHURCH

(Katedrála Sv Víta; Map p142; ☑257 531 622; www. katedralasvatehovita.cz; Third Courtyard, Prague Castle; admission with Prague Castle tour ticket; ☺9am-5pm Mon-Sat, noon-5pm Sun Apr-Oct, to 4pm Nov-Mar; ⓐ22) It might appear ancient, but much of Prague's principal cathedral was completed just in time for its belated consecration in 1929. Its many treasures include the 14th-century mosaic of the Last Judgement above the Golden Gate, the baroque silver tomb of St John of Nepomuck, the ornate Chapel of St Wenceslas, and art nouveau stained glass by Alfons Mucha.

Lobkowicz Palace
MUSEUM

(Lobkovický palác; Map p142; ☑233 312 925; www.lobkowicz.cz; Jiřská 3; adult/concession/ family 275/200/690Kč; ☺10am-6pm; ⓐ22) This 16th-century palace houses a private museum which includes priceless paintings, furniture and musical memorabilia. You tour with an audioguide dictated by owner

Central Prague

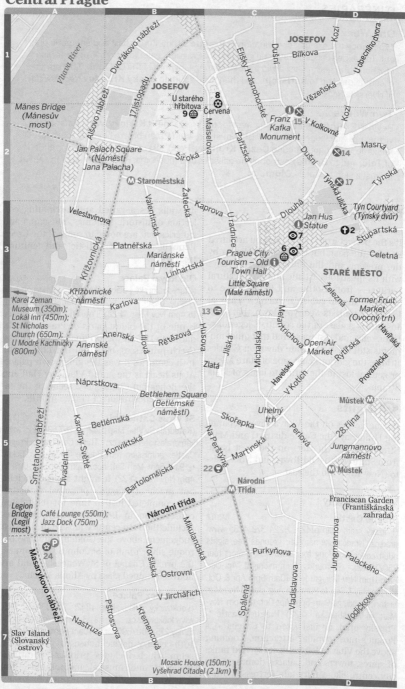

Vltava River

Mánes Bridge (Mánesův most)

JOSEFOV

Dvořákovo nábřeží

Alšovo nábřeží

17.listopadu

U starého hřbitova

9 Červená **8**

Jan Palach Square (Náměstí Jana Palacha)

Široká

Maiselova

Pařížská

Elišky Krásnohorské

Dušní

Bílkova

JOSEFOV

Kozí

U obecního dvora

Vězeňská

V Kolkovně

Franz Kafka Monument **15**

Kozí

Masná

Dušní **14**

17

Týnská ulička

Týnská

Masná

Staroměstská

Žatecká

Kaprova

U radnice

Valentinská

Veleslavínova

Platnéřská

Křižovnická

Mariánské náměstí

Linhartská

Dlouhá

Jan Hus Statue **7**

6 **1**

Prague City Tourism – Old Town Hall

Little Square (Malé náměstí)

Týn Courtyard (Týnský dvůr)

2

Štupartská

Celetná

STARÉ MĚSTO

Karel Zeman Museum (350m); Lokál Inn (450m); St Nicholas Church (650m); U Modré Kachničky (800m)

Křížovnické náměstí

Karlova

Anenská

Liliová

Řetězová

Husova

Jilská

Michalská

Melantrichova

Železná

Former Fruit Market (Ovocný trh)

Open-Air Market

Rytířská

Havlíská

Anenské náměstí

Zlatá

Havelská

V Kotcích

Provaznická

Náprstkova

Bethlehem Square (Betlémské náměstí)

Skořepka

Uhelný trh

Perlová

Můstek

28.října

Betlémská

Karolíny Světlé

Konviktská

Martinská

Na Perštýně

22

Jungmannovo náměstí

Můstek

Smetanovo nábřeží

Divadelní

Bartolomějská

13

Národní Třída

Národní třída

Legion Bridge (Legii most)

Café Lounge (550m); Jazz Dock (750m)

Franciscan Garden (Františkánská zahrada)

Masarykovo nábřeží

24

Voršilská

Ostrovní

Mikulandská

Purkyňova

Jungmannova

Palackého

Pštrossova

Křemencová

V Jirchářích

Spálená

Vladislavova

Vodičkova

Nastruze

Slav Island (Slovanský ostrov)

Mosaic House (150m); Vyšehrad Citadel (2.1km)

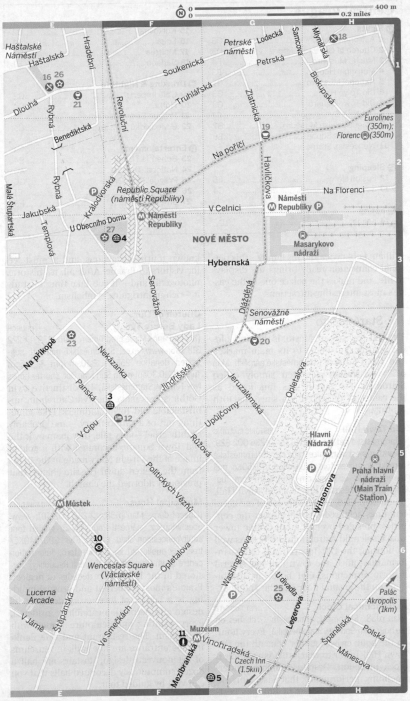

Central Prague

William Lobkowicz and his family – this personal connection really brings the displays to life, and makes the palace one of the castle's most interesting attractions.

◉ Staré Město

The Old Town (Staré Město) is the city's oldest quarter and home to its main market, **Old Town Square** (Staroměstské náměstí; Map p138; Ⓜ Staroměstská), often simply called Staromák. The square has functioned as the centre of the Old Town since the 10th century.

Old Town Hall   HISTORIC BUILDING
(Staroměstská radnice; Map p138; ☑ 236 002 629; www.staromestskaradnicepraha.cz; Staroměstské náměstí 1; guided tour adult/child 100/50Kč, incl tower 160Kč; ⊙ 11am-6pm Mon, 9am-6pm Tue-Sun; Ⓜ Staroměstská) Prague's Old Town Hall, founded in 1338, is a hotchpotch of medieval buildings acquired piecemeal over the centuries, presided over by a tall Gothic tower with a splendid Astronomical Clock. As well as housing the Old Town's main tourist information office, the town hall has several historic attractions, and hosts art exhibitions on the ground floor and the 2nd floor.

Astronomical Clock   HISTORIC SITE
(Map p138; Staroměstské náměstí; ⊙ chimes on the hour 9am-9pm; Ⓜ Staroměstská) Every hour, on the hour, crowds gather beneath the Old Town Hall Tower to watch the Astronomical Clock in action. Despite a slightly underwhelming performance that lasts only 45 seconds, the clock is one of Europe's best-known tourist attractions, and a 'must-see' for visitors to Prague. After all, it's historic, photogenic and – if you take time to study it – rich in intriguing symbolism.

Church of Our
Lady Before Týn   CHURCH
(Kostel Panny Marie před Týnem; Map p138; ☑ 222 318 186; www.tyn.cz; Staroměstské náměstí; suggested donation 25Kč; ⊙ 10am-1pm & 3-5pm Tue-Sat, 10.30am-noon Sun Mar-Oct, shorter hours Nov-Feb; Ⓜ Staroměstská) Its distinctive twin Gothic spires make the Týn Church an unmistakable Old Town landmark. Like something out of a 15th-century – and probably slightly cruel – fairy tale, they loom over the Old Town Square, decorated with a golden image of the Virgin Mary made in the 1620s from the melted down Hussite chalice that previously adorned the church.

Municipal House   HISTORIC BUILDING
(Obecní dům; Map p138; ☑ 222 002 101; www. obecnidum.cz; náměstí Republiky 5; guided tour adult/concession/child under 10yr 290/240Kč/ free; ⊙ public areas 7.30am-11pm, information centre 10am-8pm; ☎; Ⓜ Náměstí Republiky) Restored in the 1990s after decades of neglect, Prague's most exuberant and sensual building is a labour of love, every detail of its design and decoration carefully considered, every painting and sculpture loaded with symbolism. The restaurant and cafe flanking the entrance are like walk-in museums of art nouveau design; upstairs are half a dozen sumptuously decorated halls that you can visit by guided tour.

Malá Strana

Across the river from the Old Town are the baroque backstreets of Malá Strana (the Lesser Quarter), built in the 17th and 18th centuries by victorious Catholic clerics and noblemen on the foundations of their predecessors' Renaissance palaces.

Charles Bridge   BRIDGE
(Karlův most; ⊗ 24hr; ⊟ 17, 18 to Karlovy lázně, 12, 20, 22 to Malostranské náměstí) **FREE** Strolling across Charles Bridge is everybody's favourite Prague activity. However, by 9am it's a 500m-long fairground, with an army of tourists squeezing through a gauntlet of hawkers and buskers beneath the impassive gaze of the baroque statues that line the parapets. If you want to experience the bridge at its most atmospheric, try to visit it at dawn.

St Nicholas Church   CHURCH
(Kostel sv Mikuláše; ☑ 257 534 215; www.stnicholas. cz; Malostranské náměstí 38; adult/child 70/50Kč; ⊗ 9am-5pm Mar-Oct, to 4pm Nov-Feb; ⊟ 12, 20, 22) Malá Strana is dominated by the huge green cupola of St Nicholas Church, one of Central Europe's finest baroque buildings. (Don't confuse it with the other Church of St Nicholas on Old Town Square.) On the ceiling, Johann Kracker's 1770 *Apotheosis of St Nicholas* is Europe's largest fresco (clever trompe l'oeil technique has made the painting merge almost seamlessly with the architecture).

Karel Zeman Museum   MUSEUM
(Museum of Film Special Effects; ☑ 724 341 091; www.muzeumkarlazemana.cz; Saský dvůr, Saská 3; adult/child 200/140Kč; ⊗ 10am-7pm, last admission 6pm; ⊟ 12, 20, 22) Bohemia-born director Karel Zeman (1910–89) was a pioneer of movie special effects whose work is little known outside the Czech Republic. This fascinating museum, established by his daughter, reveals the many tricks and techniques he perfected, and even allows visitors a bit of hands-on interaction – you can film yourself on your smartphone against painted backgrounds and 3D models.

Nové Město

Nové Město (New Town) surrounds the Old Town on all sides and was originally laid out in the 14th century. Its main public area is **Wenceslas Square** (Václavské náměstí; Map p138; Ⓜ Můstek, Muzeum), lined with shops, banks and restaurants, and marked by a **statue of St Wenceslas** (sv Václav; Map p138; Václavské náměstí; Ⓜ Muzeum) on horseback. The **National Museum** (Národní muzeum; Map p138; ☑ 224 497 111; www.nm.cz; Václavské náměstí 68; Ⓜ Muzeum), which dominates the top of the square, is closed for long-term renovation.

PRAGUE'S JEWISH MUSEUM

The **Prague Jewish Museum** (Židovské muzeum Praha; Map p138; ☑ 222 317 191; www.jewishmuseum.cz; Reservation Centre, U starého hřbitova 3a; ordinary ticket adult/child 300/200Kč, combined ticket incl entry to Old-New Synagogue 480/320Kč; ⊗ 9am-6pm Sun-Fri Apr-Oct, to 4.30pm Nov-Mar; Ⓜ Staroměstská), a collection of four synagogues – the **Maisel**, **Pinkas**, **Spanish** and **Klaus** – and the former **Ceremonial Hall** and **Old Jewish Cemetery**, is one of the city's treasures. The monuments are clustered together in Josefov, a small corner of the Old Town that was home to Prague's Jews for some 800 years, before an urban-renewal project at the start of the 20th century and the Nazi occupation during WWII brought it all to an end.

The monuments cannot be visited separately but require a combined-entry ticket that is good for all of the sights and available at ticket windows throughout Josefov. A fifth synagogue, the **Old-New Synagogue** (Staronová synagóga; Map p138; www.jewish museum.cz; Červená 2; adult/child 200/140Kč; ⊗ 9am-6pm Sun-Fri Apr-Oct, to 4.30pm Nov-Mar; ⊟ 17), is still used for religious services, and requires a separate ticket or additional fee.

The museum was first established in 1906 to preserve objects from synagogues that were demolished during the slum clearance at the turn of the 20th century. The collection grew richer as a result of one of the most grotesquely ironic acts of WWII. During the Nazi occupation, the Germans took over management of the museum in order to create a 'museum of an extinct race'. To that end, they added objects from destroyed Jewish communities throughout Bohemia and Moravia.

Prague Castle

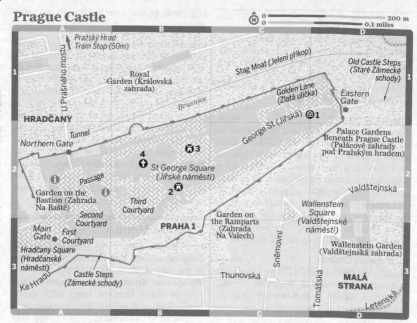

Prague Castle

◎ Sights

Mucha Museum   GALLERY
(Muchovo muzeum; Map p138; ☑ 221 451 333; www.mucha.cz; Panská 7; adult/child 240/140Kč; ◎ 10am-6pm; Ⓜ Můstek) This fascinating (and busy) museum features the sensuous art nouveau posters, paintings and decorative panels of Alfons Mucha (1860–1939), as well as many sketches, photographs and other memorabilia. The exhibits include countless artworks showing Mucha's trademark Slavic maidens with flowing hair and piercing blue eyes, bearing symbolic garlands and linden boughs.

Vyšehrad Citadel   FORTRESS
(☑ 261 225 304; www.praha-vysehrad.cz; information centre at V pevnosti 159/5b; admission to grounds free; ◎ grounds 24hr; Ⓜ Vyšehrad) FREE
The Vyšehrad Citadel refers to the complex of buildings and structures atop Vyšehrad Hill that have played a role in Czech history

for more than 1000 years. Although most structures date from the 18th century, the citadel is still viewed as the city's spiritual home. The sights are spread out over a wide area, with commanding views.

🎊 Festivals & Events

Prague Spring   CLASSICAL MUSIC
(www.festival.cz) The Czech Republic's biggest annual cultural event, and one of Europe's most important festivals of classical music.

Prague Fringe Festival   ARTS
(www.praguefringe.com) Eclectic action in late May and early June.

Christmas Market   SEASONAL FESTIVAL
From 1 to 24 December in the Old Town Square.

🛏 Sleeping

Fusion Hotel   HOSTEL, BOUTIQUE HOTEL €
(Map p138; ☑ 226 222 800; www.fusionhotels.com; Panská 9; dm from 400Kč, d/tr from 2100/2700Kč; @ 🛜; 🚌 3, 9, 14, 24) Billing itself as an 'affordable design hotel', Fusion certainly has style in abundance. From the revolving bar and spaceship-like UV corridor lighting, to the individually decorated bedrooms that

resemble miniature modern-art galleries, the place exudes 'cool'. You can choose from the world's most stylish backpacker dorm, private doubles, triples and family rooms, and there's a Skype booth in the lobby.

Czech Inn
HOSTEL, HOTEL €

(✆ 267 267 600; www.czech-inn.com; Francouzská 76, Vršovice; dm 260-450Kč; s/d 1320/1540Kč, apt from 3100Kč; P ✆ @ 🛜; 🚇 4, 22) The Czech Inn calls itself a hostel, but the boutique label wouldn't be out of place. Everything seems sculpted by an industrial designer, from the iron beds to the brushed-steel flooring and minimalist square sinks. It offers a variety of accommodation, from standard hostel dorm rooms to good-value private doubles (with or without private bathroom) and apartments.

★ Mosaic House
HOTEL, HOSTEL €€

(✆ 221 595 350; www.mosaichouse.com; Odborů 4; dm/tw from 370/2400Kč; ✆ ✱ @ 🛜; 🚇 Karlovo Náměstí) 🏊 A blend of four-star hotel and boutique hostel, Mosaic House is a cornucopia of designer detail, from the original 1930s mosaic in the entrance hall to the silver spray-painted tree branches used as clothes racks. The backpackers dorms are kept separate from the private rooms, but have the same high-quality decor and design, as does the in-house music bar and lounge.

Lokál Inn
INN €€

(✆ 257 014 800; www.lokalinn.cz; Míšeňská 12; d/ ste 3800/4900Kč; ✆ 🛜; 🚇 12, 20, 22) Polished parquet floors and painted wooden ceilings abound in this 18th-century house designed by Prague's premier baroque architect, Kilian Dientzenhofer. The eight rooms and four suites are elegant and uncluttered, and the rustic, stone-vaulted cellars house a deservedly popular pub and restaurant run by the same folk as Lokál, a popular Czech beer hall in Staré Město.

Savic Hotel
HOTEL €€€

(Map p138; ✆ 224 248 555; www.savic.eu; Jilská 7; r from 5200Kč; ✱ @ 🛜; 🚇 Můstek) From the complimentary glass of wine when you arrive to the comfy king-size beds, the Savic certainly knows how to make you feel pampered. Housed in the former monastery of St Giles, the hotel is bursting with character and full of delightful period details, including old stone fireplaces, beautiful painted timber ceilings and fragments of frescoes.

✖ Eating

Maitrea
VEGETARIAN €

(Map p138; ✆ 221 711 631; www.restaurace-maitrea. cz; Týnská ulička 6; mains 145-165Kč, weekday lunch 115Kč; ⏱ 11.30am-11.30pm Mon-Fri, noon-11.30pm Sat & Sun; ✆ ✱; 🚇 Staroměstská) Maitrea (a Buddhist term meaning 'the future Buddha') is a beautifully designed space full of flowing curves and organic shapes, from the sensuous polished-oak furniture and fittings to the blossom-like lampshades. The menu is inventive and wholly vegetarian, with dishes such as Tex-Mex quesadillas, spicy goulash with wholemeal dumplings, and pasta with smoked tofu, spinach and parmesan.

Lokál
CZECH €

(Map p138; ✆ 222 316 265; http://lokal-dlouha. ambi.cz; Dlouhá 33; mains 110-270Kč; ⏱ 11am-1am Mon-Fri, noon-1am Sat, noon-10pm Sun; 🚇 5, 8, 24) Who'd have thought it possible? A classic Czech beer hall (albeit with slick modern styling); excellent *tankové pivo* (tanked Pilsner Urquell); a daily-changing menu of traditional Bohemian dishes; smiling, efficient, friendly service; and a nonsmoking area! Top restaurant chain Ambiente has turned its hand to Czech cuisine, and the result has been so successful that the place is always busy, mostly with locals.

Café Lounge
CZECH €

(✆ 257 404 020; www.cafe-lounge.cz; Plaská 8; mains 120-390Kč; ⏱ 7.30am-10pm Mon-Fri, 9am-10pm Sat, 9am-5pm Sun; ✆ 🛜; 🚇 6, 9, 12, 20, 22) Cosy and welcoming, Café Lounge sports an art-deco atmosphere, superb coffee, exquisite pastries and an extensive wine list. The all-day cafe menu offers freshly made salads and cornbread sandwiches, while lunch and dinner extends to dishes such as beef cheeks braised in red wine, or roast pike-perch with caraway seeds. Great breakfasts, too (served until 11am weekdays, noon on weekends).

Kolkovna
CZECH €€

(Map p138; ✆ 224 819 701; www.vkolkovne.cz; V Kolkovně 8; mains 110-360Kč; ⏱ 11am-midnight; 🛜; 🚇 Staroměstská) Owned and operated by the Pilsner Urquell Brewery, Kolkovna is a stylish, modern take on the traditional Prague pub, with decor by top Czech designers, and posh (but hearty) versions of classic Czech dishes such as goulash, roast duck and Moravian sparrow, as well as the Czech favourite, roast pork knuckle. All washed down with exquisite Urquell beer, of course.

★**Sansho**　　　　　　ASIAN, FUSION €€
(Map p138; ☑222 317 425; www.sansho.cz; Petrská 25; lunch mains 110-225Kč, 6-course dinner 850-950Kč; ☺11.30am-3pm & 6-11pm Tue-Thu, to 11.30pm Fri, 6-11.30pm Sat, last orders 10pm; ☻☑; ☐3, 8, 24) ✒ Friendly and informal best describes the atmosphere at this groundbreaking restaurant where British chef Paul Day champions Czech farmers by sourcing all his meat and vegetables locally. There's no menu – the waiter will explain what dishes are available, depending on market produce – typical dishes include curried rabbit, pork belly with watermelon salad, and 12-hour beef rendang.

Kalina　　　　　　FRENCH €€€
(Map p138; ☑222 317 715; www.kalinarestaurant.cz; Dlouhá 12; mains 330-720Kč; ☺noon-3pm & 6-11.30pm Mon-Sat; ☻☎; ☐5, 8, 24) Setting a trend for taking the best of fresh Czech produce and giving it the French gourmet treatment, this smart but unfailingly friendly little restaurant offers dishes such as duck pâté with rowan berries, smoked eel with beetroot and hazelnut, and roast wild boar with red wine and juniper. The set two-course lunch menu costs 330Kč.

U Modré Kachničky　　　　CZECH €€€
(☑257 320 308; www.umodrekachnicky.cz; Nebovidská 6; mains 450-600Kč; ☺noon-4pm & 6.30pm-midnight; ☎; ☐12, 20, 22) A plush and chintzy 1930s-style hunting lodge hidden away on a quiet side street, 'At the Blue Duckling' is a pleasantly old-fashioned place with quiet, candlelit nooks perfect for a romantic dinner. The menu is heavy on traditional Bohemian duck and game dishes, such as roast duck with *slivovice* (plum brandy), plum sauce and potato pancakes.

🍷 Drinking & Nightlife

Czech beers are among the world's best. The most famous brands are Plzeňský Prazdroj (Pilsner Urquell), Budvar and Prague's own Staropramen. Independent microbreweries and regional Czech beers are also becoming more popular in Prague.

U Medvídků　　　　　BEER HALL
(At the Little Bear; Map p138; ☑224 211 916; www.umedvidku.cz; Na Perštýně 7; ☺beer hall 11.30am-11pm, museum noon-10pm; ☎; ☐Můstek, ☐6, 9, 18, 22) The most micro of Prague's microbreweries, with a capacity of only 250L, U Medvídků started producing its own beer in 2005, though its trad-style beer hall has been

around for many years. What it lacks in size, it makes up for in strength – the dark lager, marketed as X-Beer, is the strongest in the country, with an alcohol content of 11.8%.

Prague Beer Museum　　　　PUB
(Map p138; ☑732 330 912; www.praguebeer museum.com; Dlouhá 46; ☺noon-3am; ☎; ☐5, 8, 14) Although the name seems aimed at the tourist market, this lively and always-heaving pub is very popular with Praguers. There are no fewer than 30 Czech-produced beers on tap (plus a beer menu with tasting notes to guide you). Try a sample board – a wooden platter with five 0.15L glasses containing beers of your choice.

Café Imperial　　　　　CAFE
(Map p138; ☑246 011 440; www.cafeimperial.cz; Na poříčí 15; ☺7am-11pm; ☎; ☐Náměstí Republiky) First opened in 1914, and given a complete facelift in 2007, the Imperial is a tour de force of art nouveau tiling – the walls and ceiling are covered in original ceramic tiles, mosaics, sculptured panels and bas-reliefs, with period light fittings and bronzes scattered about. The coffee is good and there are cocktails in the evening.

Hoffa　　　　　COCKTAIL BAR
(Map p138; ☑601 359 659; www.hoffa.cz; Senovážné náměstí 22; ☺11am-2am Mon-Fri, 6pm-2am Sat & Sun; ☎; ☐5, 9, 26) One of Prague's first entirely smoke-free bars, Hoffa matches clean air with clean design: a long (12m long!) bar fronts a room with sleek, functional decor and a wall of windows looking out onto Senovážné náměstí's fountain of dancing sprites. Friendly staff, accomplished cocktails and good snacks – there's even homemade lemonade and iced tea at lunchtime.

★**Cross Club**　　　　　CLUB
(☑736 535 010; www.crossclub.cz; Plynární 23; admission free-150Kč; ☺cafe noon-2am, club 6pm-4am; ☎; ☐Nádraží Holešovice) An industrial club in every sense of the word: the setting in an industrial zone; the thumping music (both DJs and live acts); and the interior, an absolute must-see jumble of gadgets, shafts, cranks and pipes, many of which move and pulsate with light to the music. The program includes occasional live music, theatre performances and art happenings.

☆ Entertainment

From dance to classical music to jazz, Prague offers plenty of entertainment options. Try the following ticket agencies to see what might be on during your visit and to snag tickets online: **Bohemia Ticket** (Map p138; 224 215 031; www.bohemiaticket.cz; Na příkopě 16, Nové Město; 10am-7pm Mon-Fri, to 5pm Sat, to 3pm Sun) and **Ticketstream** (www.ticketstream.cz).

Performing Arts

National Theatre
OPERA, BALLET

(Národní divadlo; Map p138; 224 901 448; www.narodni-divadlo.cz; Národní třída 2; tickets 50-1100Kč; box offices 10am-6pm; 6, 9, 18, 22) The much-loved National Theatre provides a stage for traditional opera, drama and ballet by the likes of Smetana, Shakespeare and Tchaikovsky, sharing the program alongside more modern works by composers and playwrights such as Philip Glass and John Osborne. The box offices are in the Nový síň building next door, in the Kolowrat Palace (opposite the Estates Theatre) and at the State Opera.

Prague State Opera
OPERA, BALLET

(Státní opera Praha; Map p138; 224 901 448; www.narodni-divadlo.cz; Wilsonova 4; tickets 180-1190Kč; box office 10am-6pm; Muzeum) The impressive neo-rococo home of the Prague State Opera provides a glorious setting for performances of opera and ballet. An annual Verdi festival takes place here in August and September, and less conventional shows, such as Leoncavallo's rarely staged version of *La Bohème*, are also performed here.

Smetana Hall
CLASSICAL MUSIC

(Smetanova síň; Map p138; 222 002 101; www.obecnidum.cz; náměstí Republiky 5; tickets 300-600Kč; box office 10am-6pm; Náměstí Republiky) The Smetana Hall, centrepiece of the stunning Municipal House (p140; Obecní dům), is the city's largest concert hall, with seating for 1200. This is the home venue of the Prague Symphony Orchestra (Symfonický orchestr hlavního města Prahy), and also stages performances of folk dance and music.

Live Music

Palác Akropolis
LIVE MUSIC

(296 330 911; www.palacakropolis.cz; Kubelíkova 27, Žižkov; admission free-200Kč; club 7pm-5am; ; 5, 9, 26 to Lipanska) The Akropolis is a Prague institution, a smoky, labyrinthine, sticky-floored shrine to alternative music and drama. Its various performance spaces host a smorgasbord of musical and cultural events, from DJs to string quartets to Mace-

donian Roma bands to local rock gods to visiting talent – Marianne Faithfull, the Flaming Lips and the Strokes have all played here.

Roxy
LIVE MUSIC

(Map p138; 224 826 296; www.roxy.cz; Dlouhá 33; admission Fri & Sat free-300Kč; 7pm-5am; 5, 8, 14) Set in the ramshackle shell of an art-deco cinema, the legendary Roxy has nurtured the more independent and innovative end of Prague's club spectrum since 1987 – this is the place to see the Czech Republic's top DJs. On the 1st floor is NoD, an 'experimental space' that stages drama, dance, performance art, cinema and live music. Best nightspot in Staré Město.

Jazz Dock
JAZZ

(774 058 838; www.jazzdock.cz; Janáčkovo nábřeží 2, Smíchov; admission 150Kč; 4pm-3am; Anděl, 7, 9, 12, 14) Most of Prague's jazz clubs are smoky cellar affairs – this riverside club is a definite step up, with clean, modern decor and a decidedly romantic view out over the Vltava. It draws some of the best local talent and occasional international acts. Go early or book to get a good table. Shows normally begin at 7pm and 10pm.

ℹ Information

The major banks are best for changing cash, but using a debit card in an ATM gives a better exchange rate. Avoid *směnárna* (private exchange booths), which advertise misleading rates and have exorbitant charges.

Na Homolce Hospital (257 271 111; www.homolka.cz; 5th fl, Foreign Pavilion, Roentgenova 2, Motol; 167, 168 to Nemocnice Na Homolce) The best hospital in Prague, equipped and staffed to Western standards, with staff who speak English, French, German and Spanish.

Prague City Tourism – Old Town Hall (Prague Welcome; Map p138; 221 714 444;

WANT MORE?

For in-depth information, reviews and recommendations at your fingertips, head to the Apple App Store to purchase Lonely Planet's *Prague City Guide* and *Czech Phrasebook* iPhone apps.

Alternatively, head to www.lonelyplanet.com/czech-republic/prague for planning advice, author recommendations, traveller reviews and insider tips.

www.prague.eu; Old Town Hall, Staroměstské náměstí 5; ☺9am-7pm; M Staroměstská) The busiest of the Prague City Tourism branches occupies the ground floor of the Old Town Hall (enter to the left of the Astronomical Clock).

Relax Café-Bar (☑224 211 521; www. relaxcafebar.cz; Dlážděná 4; per 10min 10Kč; ☺8am-10pm Mon-Fri, 2-10pm Sat; ⧉; M Náměstí Republiky) A conveniently located internet cafe. Wi-fi is free.

❶ Getting There & Away

There are very efficient main overland and air routes to Prague and the Czech Republic. See p156 for more details.

❶ Getting Around

TO/FROM THE AIRPORT

To get into town from Prague airport, buy a full-price public transport ticket (32Kč) from the **Prague Public Transport Authority** (DPP; ☑296 191 817; www.dpp.cz; ☺7am-9pm) desk in the arrivals hall and take bus 119 (20 minutes, every 10 minutes, 4am to midnight) to the end of metro line A (Dejvická), then continue by metro into the city centre (another 10 to 15 minutes; no new ticket needed).

If you're heading to the southwestern part of the city, take bus 100, which goes to the Zličín metro station (line B).

There's also an Airport Express bus (AE; 60Kč, 35 minutes, every half-hour from 5am to 10pm) that runs to Praha hlavní nádraží (Prague main train station), where you can connect to metro line C (buy ticket from driver, luggage goes free).

AAA Radio Taxi operates a 24-hour taxi service, charging from 500Kč to 650Kč depending on the destination to get to central Prague. You'll find taxi stands outside both arrivals terminals. Drivers usually speak some English and accept credit cards.

PUBLIC TRANSPORT

Prague's excellent public-transport system combines tram, metro and bus services. It's operated by the Prague Public Transport Authority (DDP), which has information desks at Prague airport (7am to 10pm) and in several metro stations, including Muzeum, Můstek, Anděl and Nádraží Holešovice. The metro operates daily from 5am to midnight.

Tickets valid on all metros, trams and buses are sold from machines at metro stations (coins only), as well as at DPP information offices and many newsstands and kiosks. Tickets can be purchased individually or as discounted day passes valid for one or three days.

A full-price individual ticket costs 32/16Kč per adult/senior aged 65 to 70 and is valid for 90 minutes of unlimited travel. For shorter journeys, buy short-term tickets that are valid for 30 minutes of unlimited travel. These cost 24/12Kč per adult/senior. One-day passes cost 110/55Kč per adult/senior; three-day passes cost 310Kč (no discount for seniors).

TAXI

Taxis are frequent and relatively inexpensive. The official rate for licensed cabs is 40Kč flagfall plus 28Kč per kilometre and 6Kč per minute while waiting. On this basis, any trip within the city centre – say, from Wenceslas Square to Malá Strana – should cost around 170Kč. A trip to the suburbs, depending on the distance, should run from around 200Kč to 400Kč, and to the airport between 500Kč and 650Kč.

The following companies offer 24-hour service and English-speaking operators:

AAA Radio Taxi (☑14014, 222 333 222; www. aaataxi.cz)

City Taxi (☑257 257 257; www.citytaxi.cz)

AROUND PRAGUE

Karlštejn

Rising above the village of Karlštejn, 30km southwest of Prague, medieval **Karlštejn Castle** (Hrad Karlštejn; ☑tour booking 311 681 617; www.hradkarlstejn.cz; adult/child Tour 1 270/180Kč, Tour 2 300/200Kč, Tour 3 150/100Kč; ☺9am-6.30pm Jul & Aug, 9.30am-5.30pm Tue-Sun May, Jun & Sep, to 5pm Apr, to 4.30pm Oct, to 4pm Mar, reduced hours Sat & Sun only Dec-Feb) is in such good shape it wouldn't look out of place on Disneyworld's Main St. The crowds come in theme-park proportions as well, but the peaceful surrounding countryside offers views of Karlštejn's stunning exterior that rival anything you'll see on the inside.

The castle was born of a grand pedigree, originally conceived by Emperor Charles IV in the 14th century as a bastion for hiding the crown jewels. Run by an appointed burgrave, the castle was surrounded by a network of landowning knight-vassals, who came to the castle's aid whenever enemies moved against it.

Karlštejn again sheltered the Bohemian and the Holy Roman Empire crown jewels during the Hussite Wars of the 15th century, but fell into disrepair as its defences became outmoded. Considerable restoration work in the late-19th century returned the castle to its former glory.

Castle visits are by guided tour only. Some tours must be reserved in advance by phone or via the castle website.

There are three tours available: **Tour I** (50 minutes) passes through the Knight's Hall, still daubed with the coats-of-arms and names of the knight-vassals, Charles IV's Bedchamber, the Audience Hall and the Jewel House, which includes treasures from the Chapel of the Holy Cross and a replica of the St Wenceslas Crown. **Tour 2** (70 minutes, May to October only) takes in the Marian Tower, with the Church of the Virgin Mary and the Chapel of St Catherine, then moves to the Great Tower for the castle's star attraction, the exquisite Chapel of the Holy Cross. **Tour 3** (40 minutes, May to October only) visits the upper levels of the Great Tower, which provide stunning views over the surrounding countryside.

From Prague, there are frequent train departures daily from Prague's main station, *hlavní nádraží*. The journey takes 40 minutes and costs around 50Kč each way.

Kutná Hora

In the 14th century, Kutná Hora, 60km southeast of Prague, rivalled the capital in importance because of its rich deposits of silver ore. The ore ran out in 1726, leaving the medieval townscape largely unaltered. Now with several fascinating and unusual historical attractions, the Unesco World Heritage–listed town is a popular day trip from Prague.

Interestingly, most visitors come not for the silver splendour but rather to see an eerie monastery, dating from the 19th century, with an interior crafted solely from human bones. Indeed, the remarkable **Sedlec Ossuary** (Kostnice; ✍ information centre 326 551 049; www. ossuary.eu; Zámecká 127; adult/concession 90/60Kč; ⊙8am-6pm Mon-Sat, 9am-6pm Sun Apr-Sep, 9am-5pm Mar & Oct, 9am-4pm Nov-Feb), or better 'bone church', features the remains of no fewer than 40,000 people who died over the years from wars and pestilence.

Closer to the centre of Kutná Hora is the town's greatest monument: the Gothic **Cathedral of St Barbara** (Chrám sv Barbora; ✍ 775 363 938; www.khfarnost.cz; Barborská; adult/concession 60/40Kč; ⊙9am-6pm Apr-Oct, 10am-6pm Mon-Fri, 10am-6pm Sat & Sun Nov-Dec, 10am-4pm Jan-Mar). Rivalling Prague's St Vitus in size and magnificence, its soaring nave culminates in elegant, six-petalled ribbed vaulting, and the ambulatory chapels preserve original 15th-century frescoes. Other leading attractions include the **Hrádek** (České muzeum stříbra; ✍ 327 512 159; www. cms-kh.cz; Barborská 28; Tour 1 adult/concession 70/40Kč, Tour 2 120/80Kč, combined 140/90Kč; ⊙10am-6pm Jul & Aug, 9am-6pm May, Jun & Sep, 9am-5pm Apr & Oct, 10am-4pm Nov, closed Mon year-round) from the 15th century, which now houses the **Czech Silver Museum**.

Kutná Hora can be reached from Prague by either bus (68Kč, 1¾ hours) or train (101Kč, one hour). The bus station is located on the Old Town's northeastern edge, which is convenient to the central sites, but 3km from the ossuary. Kutná Hora's main train station, by contrast, is just 800m from the ossuary, but 3km from the Old Town.

BOHEMIA

The Czech Republic's western province boasts surprising variety. Český Krumlov, with its riverside setting and dramatic Renaissance castle, is in a class by itself. Big cities like Plzeň offer urban attractions like great museums and restaurants. The spa towns of western Bohemia, such as Karlovy Vary, were world famous in the 19th century and retain an old-world lustre.

Plzeň

POP 173,000

Plzeň, the regional capital of western Bohemia and the second-biggest city in Bohemia after Prague, is best known as the home of the Pilsner Urquell Brewery, but it has a handful of other interesting sights and enough good restaurants and night-time pursuits to justify an overnight stay. Most of the sights are located near the central square, but the brewery itself is about a 15-minute walk outside the city centre.

◉ Sights

★**Pilsner Urquell Brewery**   BREWERY
(Prazdroj; ✍ 377 062 888; www.prazdrojvisit.cz; U Prazdroje 7; guided tour adult/child 190/100Kč; ⊙8.30am-6pm Apr-Sep, to 5pm Oct-Mar, English tours 12.45pm, 2.15pm & 4.15pm) Plzeň's most popular attraction is the tour of the Pilsner Urquell Brewery, in operation since 1842 and arguably home to the world's best beer. Entry is by guided tour only, with three tours in English available daily. Tour highlights include a

trip to the old cellars (dress warmly) and a glass of unpasteurised nectar at the end.

Brewery Museum
MUSEUM

(☑377 224 955; www.prazdrojvisit.cz; Veleslavínova 6; guided tour adult/child 120/90Kč, English text 90/60Kč; ☉10am-6pm Apr-Dec, to 5pm Jan-Mar) The Brewery Museum offers an insight into how beer was made (and drunk) in the days before Prazdroj was founded. Highlights include a mock-up of a 19th-century pub, a huge wooden beer tankard from Siberia and a collection of beer mats. All have English captions and there's a good printed English guide available.

Underground Plzeň
UNDERGROUND

(Plzeňské historické podzemí; ☑377 235 574; www.plzenskepodzemi.cz; Veleslavínova 6; adult/child 100/70Kč; ☉10am-6pm Apr-Dec, to 5pm Feb-Mar, closed Jan, English tour 1pm daily Apr-Oct) This extraordinary tour explores the passageways below the old city. The earliest were probably dug in the 14th century, perhaps for beer production or defence; the latest date from the 19th century. Of an estimated 11km that have been excavated, some 500m of tunnels are open to the public. Bring extra clothing (it's a chilly 10°C underground).

★ Techmania Science Centre
MUSEUM

(☑737 247 585; www.techmania.cz; cnr Borská & Břeňkova, Areál Škoda; adult/concession incl 3D planetarium 180/110Kč; ☉8.30am-5pm Mon-Fri, 10am-6pm Sat & Sun; P♦🎧; 🚋15, 17) Kids will have a ball at this high-tech, interactive science centre, where they can play with infrared cameras, magnets and many other instructive and fun exhibitions. There's a 3D planetarium (included in the full-price admission) and a few full-sized historic trams and trains manufactured at the Škoda engineering works. Take the trolleybus; it's a hike from the city centre.

🛏 Sleeping

Hotel Roudna
HOTEL €

(☑377 259 926; www.hotelroudna.cz; Na Roudné 13; s/d 1150/1400Kč; P@🎧) Might very well be the city's best-value lodging. The exterior is not much to look at; but inside, rooms are well-proportioned, with high-end amenities such as flatscreen TV, minibar and desk. Breakfasts are fresh and ample. The reception is friendly. Note there's no lift. The hotel has an excellent steakhouse two doors down on the same street.

U Salzmannů
PENSION €

(☑377 235 476; www.usalzmannu.com; Pražská 8; s/d 1050/1450Kč, ste 2100Kč; ☺🎧) This pleasant pension, right in the heart of town, sits above a very good historic pub. The standard rooms are comfortable but basic; the more luxurious double 'suites' have antique beds and small sitting rooms, as well as kitchenettes. The pub location is convenient if you overdo it; to reach your bed, just climb the stairs.

🍴 Eating

Na Parkánu
CZECH €

(☑377 324 485; www.naparkanu.com; Veleslavínova 4; mains 100-200Kč; ☉11am-11pm Mon-Thu, to 1am Fri & Sat, to 10pm Sun; 🎧) Don't overlook this pleasant pub-restaurant, attached to the Brewery Museum. It may look a bit touristy, but the traditional Czech food is top rate, and the beer, naturally, could hardly be better. Try to snag a spot in the summer garden. Don't leave without trying the *nefiltrované pivo* (unfiltered beer). Reservations are an absolute must.

Aberdeen Angus Steakhouse
STEAK €€

(☑725 555 631; www.angussteakhouse.cz; Pražská 23; mains 180-400Kč; ☉11am-11pm; ☺🎧) For our money, this may be the best steakhouse in all of the Czech Republic. The meats hail from a nearby farm, where the livestock is raised organically. There are several cuts and sizes on offer; lunch options include a tantalising cheeseburger. The downstairs dining room is cosy; there's also a creekside terrace. Book in advance.

ℹ Information

City Information Centre
(Informační centrum města Plzně; ☑378 035 330; www.icpilsen.cz; Náměstí Republiky 41; ☉9am-7pm Apr-Sep, to 6pm Oct-Mar) Plzeň's well-stocked and -staffed tourist information office is a first port of call for visitors. Can advise on sleeping and eating options, hands out free city maps, and has a stock of brochures on what to see and do.

ℹ Getting There & Away

From Prague, eight trains (150Kč, 1½ hours) leave daily from the main station, *hlavní nádraží*. The train station is on the eastern side of town, 10 minutes' walk from nám Republiky, the Old Town Square. From Prague, the bus service to Plzeň (100Kč, one hour) is frequent (hourly), relatively fast and inexpensive.

WORTH A TRIP

A SPA STROLL THROUGH KARLOVY VARY

Karlovy Vary is the closest the Czech Republic has to a glam resort, but it is still only glam with a small 'g'. While the resort was famous across Europe in the 19th century as a health spa, these days the town attracts mostly short-term visitors, content to stroll the pretty spa area and to sip on allegedly health-restoring sulphuric compounds from ceramic, spouted drinking cups.

There are 15 mineral springs housed in or near the four main **colonnades** (kolonády) along the River Teplá. Each spring has its own purported medicinal properties and gushes forth at various temperatures, ranging from lukewarm to scalding hot.

The **Infocentrum** (Infocentrum Lázeňská; ☑ 355 321 176; www.karlovyvary.cz; Lázeňská 14; ⊗ 9am-5pm; ☜) has a chart of the springs and temperatures, and can advise on the various health benefits of the waters.

While frequent bus service from Prague makes this a possible day trip from Prague, there are plenty of excellent hotels for an overnight stay. **Hotel Romance Puškin** (☑ 353 222 646; www.hotelromance.cz; Tržiště 37; s/d 2450/3450Kč; ⊖☜) boasts a great location in the heart of the spa area and has fully renovated rooms with updated baths and comfortable beds.

Hospoda U Švejka (☑ 353 232 276; www.svejk-kv.cz; Stará Louka 10; mains 160-370Kč; ⊗ 11am-11pm) is a nice choice for lunch or dinner. Though the presentation borders on kitsch, the food is actually very good and the atmosphere not unlike a classic Czech pub.

Buses are the only practical way of reaching Karlovy Vary from Prague. **Student Agency** (☑ 353 176 333; www.studentagency.cz; TG Masaryka 58/34; ⊗ 9am-6pm Mon-Fri) runs frequent buses to/from Prague's Florenc bus station (from 160Kč, two hours, several daily) departing from the main bus station beside Dolní nádraží train station.

Český Krumlov

POP 14,050

Outside of Prague, Český Krumlov is arguably the Czech Republic's only other world-class sight and must-see. From a distance, the town looks like any other in the Czech countryside, but once you get closer and see the Renaissance castle towering over the undisturbed 17th-century townscape, you'll feel the appeal; this really is that fairy-tale town the tourist brochures promised. Český Krumlov is best approached as an overnight destination; it's too far for a comfortable day trip from Prague.

◉ Sights

Český Krumlov State Castle   CASTLE
(☑ 380 704 711; www.zamek-ceskykrumlov.eu; Zámek 59; adult/concession Tour 1 250/160Kč, Tour 2 240/140Kč, Theatre Tour 300/200Kč; ⊗ 9am-6pm Tue-Sun Jun-Aug, to 5pm Apr, May, Sep & Oct) Český Krumlov's striking Renaissance castle, occupying a promontory high above the town, began life in the 13th century. It acquired its present appearance in the 16th to 18th centuries under the stewardship of the noble Rožmberk and Schwarzenberg families. The interiors are accessible by guided tour only, though you can stroll the grounds on your own.

Castle Museum & Tower   MUSEUM, TOWER
(☑ 380 704 711; www.zamek-ceskykrumlov. eu; Zámek 59; combined entry adult/concession 130/60Kč, museum only 100/50Kč, tower only 50/30Kč; ⊗ 9am-6pm Jun-Aug, to 5pm Apr & May, to 5pm Tue-Sun Sep & Oct, to 4pm Tue-Sun Jan-Mar) Located within the castle complex, this small museum and adjoining tower is an ideal option if you don't have the time or energy for a full castle tour. Through a series of rooms, the museum traces the castle's history from its origins through the present day. Climb the tower for perfect photo-op shots of the town below.

Egon Schiele Art Centrum   MUSEUM
(☑ 380 704 011; www.schieleartcentrum.cz; Široká 71; adult/concession 120/70Kč; ⊗ 10am-6pm Tue-Sun) This excellent private gallery houses a small retrospective of the controversial Viennese painter Egon Schiele (1890–1918), who lived in Krumlov in 1911, and raised the ire of townsfolk by hiring young girls as nude models. For this and other sins he was eventually driven away. The centre also houses interesting temporary exhibitions.

Český Krumlov

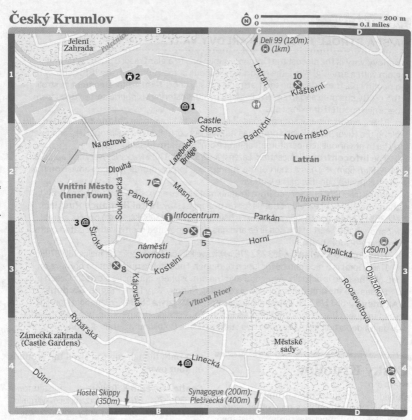

Museum

Fotoateliér Seidel MUSEUM
(☎ 380 712 354; www.seidel.cz; Linecká 272; adult/
concession 100/70Kč; ⊙ 9am-noon & 1-5pm daily
Apr & Oct-Dec, Tue-Sun Jan-Mar, 9am-noon & 1-6pm
daily May-Sep) This photography museum
presents a moving retrospective of the work
of local photographers Josef Seidel and his
son František. Especially poignant are the
images recording early-20th-century life
in nearby villages. In the high season you
should be able to join an English-language
tour; if not, let the pictures tell the story.

🛏 Sleeping

★ **Krumlov House** HOSTEL €
(☎ 380 711 935; www.krumlovhostel.com; Roosevel-
tova 68; dm/d/tr 300/1000/1350Kč; ⊕@⊜)
Perched above the river, Krumlov House is
friendly and comfortable, and has plenty of
books, DVDs and local information to feed
your inner wanderer. Accommodation is in
six-bed en suite dorms as well as private double and triple rooms or private, self-catered
apartments. The owners are English-speaking
and traveller-friendly.

U Malého Vítka

HOTEL €€

(📞 380 711 925; www.vitekhotel.cz; Radniční 27; s/d 1200/1500Kč; 🅿 🌐 🖰) We like this small hotel in the heart of the Old Town. The simple room furnishings are of high-quality, handcrafted wood, and each room is named after a traditional Czech fairy-tale character. The downstairs restaurant and cafe are very good, too.

Hotel Konvice

HOTEL €€

(📞 380 711 611; www.boehmerwaldhotels.de; Horní 144; s/d 1300/2000Kč; 🅿 🌐 🖰) Attractive old-fashioned hotel with romantic rooms and period furnishings. Many rooms, such as No 12, have impressive wood-beamed ceilings, and all have homey architectural quirks that lend atmosphere. The service is reserved but friendly. The cook at breakfast is more than happy to whip up an egg on request (to go with the usual cold cuts and cheeses).

✖ Eating

Nonna Gina

ITALIAN €

(📞 380 717 187; Klášteriní 52; pizza 100-170Kč; 🌐 11am-10pm; 🖰) Authentic Italian flavours from the Italian Massaro family feature in this pizzeria down a quiet lane. Grab an outdoor table and pretend you're in Naples. In winter the upstairs dining room is snug and intimate.

Hospoda Na Louži

CZECH €

(📞 380 711 280; www.nalouzi.cz; Kájovská 66; mains 90-170Kč; 🖰) Nothing's changed in this wood-panelled *pivo* (beer) parlour for almost a century. Locals and tourists pack Na Louži for huge plates of Czech staples such as chicken schnitzels or roast pork and dumplings, as well as dark (and light) beer from the Eggenberg brewery. Get the fruit dumplings for dessert if you see them on the menu.

★ Krčma v Šatlavské

CZECH €€

(📞 380 713 344; www.satlava.cz; Horní 157; mains 180-280Kč; 🌐 11am-midnight) This medieval barbecue cellar is hugely popular with visitors, and your tablemates are much more likely to be from Austria or Asia than from the town itself. But the grilled meats – served up with gusto in a funky labyrinth illuminated by candles – are excellent and perfectly in character with Český Krumlov. Advance booking is essential.

ℹ Information

Infocentrum (📞 380 704 622; www.ckrumlov.info; náměstí Svornosti 2; 🌐 9am-7pm Jun-Aug, to 6pm Apr, May, Sep & Oct, to 5pm Nov-Mar) One of the country's best tourist offices. Good source for transport and accommodation info, maps, internet access (per five minutes 5Kč) and audioguides (per hour 100Kč). A guide for disabled visitors is available.

ℹ Getting There & Away

From Prague (260Kč, 3½ hours), the train journey requires a change in České Budějovice. Buses are quicker and cheaper. From Prague, **Student Agency** (📞 841 101 101; www.student agency.cz) coaches (195Kč, three hours) leave regularly from the Na Knížecí bus station at Anděl metro station (Line B).

MORAVIA

The Czech Republic's eastern province, Moravia is yin to Bohemia's yang. If Bohemians love beer, Moravians love wine. If Bohemia is towns and cities, Moravia is rolling hills and pretty landscapes. The Moravian capital, Brno, has the museums, but the northern city of Olomouc has the captivating architecture.

Brno

POP 385,900

Among Czechs, Moravia's capital has a dull rep; a likeable place where not much actually happens. The reality, though, is different. Thousands of students ensure lively cafe and club scenes that easily rival Prague's. The museums are great, too. Brno was one of the leading centres of experimental architecture in the early 20th century, and the Unesco-protected Vila Tugendhat is considered a masterwork of functionalist design.

◎ Sights

Špilberk Castle

CASTLE

(Hrad Špilberk; 📞 542 123 611; www.spilberk.cz; Špilberk 210/1; combined entry adult/concession 400/240Kč, casemates only 90/50Kč, tower only 50/30Kč; 🌐 9am-5pm Tue-Sun Oct-Apr, 9am-5pm daily May & Jun, 10am-6pm daily Jul-Sep) Brno's spooky hilltop castle is considered the city's most important landmark. Its history stretches back to the 13th century, when it was home to Moravian margraves and later a fortress. Under the Habsburgs in the 18th and 19th centuries, it served as a prison. Today it's home to the **Brno City Museum**, with several temporary and permanent exhibitions.

Cathedral of Sts
Peter & Paul
CHURCH, TOWER

(katedrála sv Petra a Pavla; www.katedrala-petrov. cz; Petrov Hill; tower adult/concession 40/30Kč; ⊙11am-6pm Mon-Sat, from 11.45am Sun) This 14th-century cathedral atop Petrov Hill was originally built on the site of a pagan temple to Venus, and has been reconstructed many times since. The highly decorated 11m-high main altar with figures of Sts Peter and Paul was carved by Viennese sculptor Josef Leimer in 1891. You can also climb the **tower** for dramatic views.

Old Town Hall
HISTORIC BUILDING

(Stará radnice; ⊉542 427 150; www.ticbrno.cz; Radnická 8; tower adult/concession 50/30Kč; ⊙9am-5pm) Brno's atmospheric Old Town Hall dates from the early 13th century. The tourist office is here, plus oddities including a crocodile hanging from the ceiling (known affectionately as the Brno 'dragon') and a wooden wagon wheel with a unique story. You can also climb the **tower**.

Capuchin Monastery
CEMETERY

(Kapucínský klášter; www.kapucini.cz; Kapucínské náměstí; adult/concession 60/30Kč; ⊙9am-noon & 1-4.30pm Mon-Sat, 11am-11.45am & 1-4.30pm Sun May-Sep, closed Mon mid-Feb–Apr & Oct–mid-Dec, weekends only mid-Dec–mid-Feb) One of the city's leading attractions is this ghoulish cellar **crypt** that holds the mummified remains of several city noblemen from the 18th century. Apparently the dry, well-ventilated crypt has the natural ability to turn dead bodies into mummies. Up to 150 cadavers were deposited here prior to 1784, the desiccated corpses including monks, abbots and local notables.

Labyrinth under
the Cabbage Market
UNDERGROUND

(Brněnské podzemí; ⊉542 427 150; www.ticbrno. cz; Zelný trh 21; adult/concession 160/80Kč; ⊙9am-6pm Tue-Sun) In recent years the city has opened several sections of extensive underground tunnels to the general public. This tour takes around 40 minutes to explore several cellars situated 6m to 8m below the Cabbage Market, which has served as a food market for centuries. The cellars were built for two purposes: to store goods and to hide in during wars.

★**Vila Tugendhat**
ARCHITECTURE

(Villa Tugendhat; ⊉tour booking 515 511 015; www.tugendhat.eu; Černopolni 45; adult/concession basic tour 300/180Kč, extended tour 350/210Kč; ⊙10am-6pm Tue-Sun; ⊚3, 5, 11 to Černopolní) Brno had a reputation in the 1920s as a centre for modern architecture in the functionalist and Bauhaus styles. Arguably the finest example is this family villa, designed by modern master Mies van der Rohe in 1930. Entry is by guided tour booked in advance by phone or email. Two tours are available: a 60-minute basic tour and 90-minute extended visit.

🛏 Sleeping

In February, April, August, September and October, Brno hosts major international trade fairs, and hotel rates increase by 40% to 100%. Book ahead if possible.

★**Hostel Mitte**
HOSTEL €

(⊉734 622 340; www.hostelmitte.com; Panská 22; dm 500Kč, s/d 1000/1300Kč, all incl breakfast; ☻@☎) Set in the heart of the Old Town, this clean and stylish hostel smells and looks brand new. The rooms are named after famous Moravians (eg Milan Kundera) or famous events (Austerlitz) and decorated accordingly. There are dorms in six-bed rooms and private singles and doubles. Cute cafe on the ground floor.

Hotel Europa
HOTEL €€

(⊉515 143 100; www.hotel-europa-brno.cz; třída kpt Jaroše 27; s/d 1400/1800Kč; P☻☎) Set in a quiet neighbourhood a 10-minute walk from the city centre, this self-proclaimed 'art' hotel (presumably for the wacky futuristic lobby furniture) offers clean and tastefully furnished modern rooms in a historic 19th-century building. The lobby has free wi-fi, while the rooms have cable (ethernet) connections. There is free parking out the front and in the courtyard.

Barceló Brno Palace
LUXURY HOTEL €€€

(⊉532 156 777; www.barcelo.com; Šilingrovo nám 2; r from 3600Kč; P☻✳@☎) Five-star heritage luxury comes to Brno at the Barceló Brno Palace. The lobby blends glorious 19th-century architecture with thoroughly modern touches, and the spacious rooms are both contemporary and romantic. The location on the edge of Brno's Old Town is excellent.

Eating

Spolek
CZECH €

(☑774 814 230; www.spolek.net; Orlí 22; mains 80-180Kč; ☉9am-10pm Mon-Fri, 10am-10pm Sat & Sun; 🖘☑📶) You'll get friendly, unpretentious service at this coolly 'bohemian' (yes, we're in Moravia) haven with interesting salads and soups, and a concise but diverse wine list. Photojournalism on the walls is complemented by a funky mezzanine bookshop. It has excellent coffee, too.

Špaliček
CZECH €

(☑542 211 526; Zelný trh 12; mains 80-160Kč; ☉11am-11pm; ☻) Brno's oldest (and maybe its 'meatiest') restaurant sits on the edge of the Cabbage Market. Ignore the irony and dig into huge Moravian meals, partnered with a local beer or something from the decent list of Moravian wines. The old-school tavern atmosphere is authentic and the daily luncheon specials are a steal.

★ Pavillon
INTERNATIONAL €€

(☑541 213 497; www.restaurant-pavillon.cz; Jezuitská 6; mains 250-385Kč; ☉11am-11pm Mon-Sat, 11am-3pm Sun; ☻🖘) High-end dining in an elegant, airy space that recalls the city's heritage in functionalist architecture. The menu changes with the season, but usually features one vegetarian entree as well as mains with locally sourced ingredients, such as wild boar or lamb raised in the Vysočina highlands. Daily luncheon specials at 200Kč for soup, main and dessert are a steal.

☕ Drinking

★ Cafe Podnebi
CAFE

(☑542 211 372; www.podnebi.cz; Údolní 5; ☉8am-midnight Mon-Fri, from 9am Sat & Sun; 🖘📶) This homey, student-oriented cafe is famous citywide for its excellent hot chocolate, but it also serves very good espresso drinks. There are plenty of baked goods and sweets to snack on. In summer the garden terrace is a hidden oasis and there's a small play area for kids.

U Richarda
PUB

(☑775 027 918; www.uricharda.eu; Údolní 7; ☉11am-11pm Mon-Sat) This microbrewery is highly popular with students, who come for the great house-brewed, unpasteurised yeast beers, including a rare cherry-flavoured lager, and the good traditional Czech cooking (mains 109Kč to 149Kč). Book in advance.

☆ Entertainment

Stará Pekárna
LIVE MUSIC

(☑541 210 040; www.starapekarna.cz; Štefánikova 8; ☉5pm-late Mon-Sat; 🚊1, 6, 7) Old and new music with blues, world beats, DJs and rock. Catch the tram to Pionýrská. Gigs usually kick off at 8pm.

Brno Philharmonic Orchestra
CLASSICAL MUSIC

(Besední dům; ☑539 092 811; www.filharmonie-brno.cz; Komenského náměstí 8) The Brno Philharmonic is the city's leading orchestra for performing classical music. It conducts some 40 concerts a year, plus tours around the Czech Republic and Europe. It's particularly strong on Moravian-born, early-20th century composer Leoš Janáček. Most performances are held at Besední dům concert house. Buy tickets at the venue **box office** (☉9am-2pm Mon & Wed, 1-6pm Tue, Thu & Fri).

ℹ Information

Tourist Information Centre (TIC Brno; ☑542 211 090; www.ticbrno.cz; Old Town Hall, Radnická 8; ☉8am-6pm Mon-Fri, 9am-6pm Sat & Sun) Lots of great information on hand in English, including free maps. There's also a computer to check email for free.

ℹ Getting There & Away

Brno is easily reached from Prague by either bus (210Kč, 2½ hours) or train (220Kč, three hours). Bus service via the local coach service **Student Agency** (☑841 101 101; www.studentagency.cz; náměstí Svobody 17; ☉9am-6pm Mon-Fri) is especially good. Express trains run between Brno's train station and Prague's *hlavní nádraží* every couple of hours during the day.

Olomouc

POP 100,200

Olomouc (olla-moats) is one of the Czech Republic's most underrated destinations. There's great nightlife, fuelled by a cosmopolitan student population, and a gorgeous series of central squares that would rival any European city.

◉ Sights

Holy Trinity Column
MONUMENT

(Sloup Nejsvětější Trojice; Horní náměstí) **FREE** The town's pride and joy is this 35m-high (115ft) baroque sculpture that dominates the square and is a popular meeting spot for

WORTH A TRIP

UNESCO HERITAGE ARCHITECTURE IN TELČ

The Unesco-protected town of Telč, perched on the border between Bohemia and Moravia, possesses one of the country's prettiest and best-preserved historic town squares.

The main attraction is the beauty of the square, **Náměstí Zachariáše z Hradce**, itself, which is lined with Renaissance burghers' houses. Most of the structures were built in the 16th century after a fire levelled the town in 1530. Famous houses include No 15, which shows the characteristic Renaissance sgraffito. The house at No 48 was given a baroque facade in the 18th century.

Telč Chateau (Zámek; ☑ 567 243 943; www.zamek-telc.cz; náměstí Zachariáše z Hradce 1; adult/concession route A 110/70Kč, route B 90/60Kč, combined 170/100Kč; ⊘ 10am-4pm Tue-Sun Apr & Oct, to 5pm May, Jun & Sep, to 6pm Jul & Aug), another Renaissance masterpiece, guards the northern end of the square. Entry is by guided tour only.

If you decide to spend the night, **Pension Steidler** (☑ 721 316 390; www.telc-accommodation.eu; náměstí Zachariáše z Hradce 52; s/d 500/800Kč; ☻) offers rooms with skylights and wooden floors at a central location.

Around half-a-dozen buses make the run daily from Prague's Florenc bus station (175Kč, 2½ hours), with many connections requiring a change in Jihlava. Several daily buses run to Brno (100Kč, two hours). Check the online timetable at http://jizdnirady.idnes.cz for times.

local residents. The trinity column was built between 1716 and 1754 and is allegedly the biggest single baroque sculpture in Central Europe. In 2000 the column was awarded an inscription on Unesco's World Heritage list.

Archdiocesan Museum
MUSEUM

(Arcidiecézni muzeum; ☑ 585 514 111; www.olmuart.cz; Václavské náměstí 3; adult/concession 70/35Kč, free Sun; ⊘ 10am-6pm Tue-Sun) The impressive holdings of the Archdiocesan Museum trace the history of Olomouc back 1000 years. The thoughtful layout, with helpful English signage, takes you through the original Romanesque foundations of Olomouc Castle, and highlights the cultural and artistic development of the city during the Gothic and baroque periods.

Civil Defence Shelter
HISTORIC SITE

(Kryt Civilní Obrany; Bezručovy sady; admission 20Kč; ⊘ tours at 10am, 1pm & 4pm Thu & Sat mid-Jun-mid-Sep) Olomouc is all about centuries-old history, but this more recent relic of the Cold War is also worth exploring on a guided tour. The shelter was built between 1953 and 1956 and was designed to shelter a lucky few from the ravages of a chemical or nuclear strike. Tours are arranged by and begin at the Olomouc Information Centre.

🛏 Sleeping

Poet's Corner
HOSTEL €

(☑ 777 570 730; www.hostelolomouc.com; Sokolská 1; dm/s/d 350/700/900Kč; ☻ 🛜; 🚍 2, 4, 6) The Australian-Czech couple who mind this friendly and exceptionally well-run hostel are a wealth of local information. There are dorms in eight-bed rooms, as well as private singles and doubles. Bicycles can be hired for 100Kč per day. In summer there's sometimes a two-night minimum stay, but Olomouc is worth it, and there's plenty of day-trip information on offer.

★ Penzión Na Hradě
PENSION €€

(☑ 585 203 231; www.penzionnahrade.cz; Michalská 4; s/d 1290/1890Kč; ☻ ❄ 🛜) In terms of price/quality ratio, this is Olomouc's best deal. Worth the minor splurge if you can swing it. The location, tucked away in the shadow of St Michael's Church, is ideally central. The sleek, cool rooms have a professional design touch and there's a small garden terrace for relaxing at the back. Reserve in advance in summer.

🍴 Eating & Drinking

Drápal
CZECH €

(☑ 585 225 818; www.restauracedrapal.cz; Havlíčkova 1; mains 110-170Kč; ⊘ 10am-midnight Mon-Fri, 11am-midnight Sat, 11am-11pm Sun; 🛜) It's hard to go wrong with this big historic pub on a busy corner near the town centre. The unpasteurised 12° Pilsner Urquell is arguably the best beer in Olomouc. The smallish menu is loaded with Czech classics, such as the ever-popular *Španělský ptáček* (literally 'Spanish bird'), a beef roulade stuffed with smoked sausage, parsley and a hard-boiled egg.

Moritz CZECH €€
(☑585 205 560; www.hostinec-moritz.cz; Nešverova 2; mains 120-260Kč; ⊙11am-11pm; ⊜🔊) This microbrewery and restaurant is a local favourite. We reckon it's a combination of the terrific beers, good-value food, and a praise-worthy 'no smoking' policy. In summer the beer garden's the only place to be. Advance booking is a must. The location is about a 10-minute walk south of the town centre, across the busy street třída Svobody.

⭐ **Cafe 87** CAFE
(☑585 202 593; www.cafe87.cz; Denisova 47; coffee 40Kč; ⊙7.30am-9pm Mon-Fri, 8am-9pm Sat & Sun; 🔊) Locals come in droves to this funky cafe beside the Olomouc Museum of Modern Art for coffee and its famous chocolate pie (45Kč). Some people still apparently prefer the dark chocolate to the white chocolate. When will they learn? It's a top spot for breakfast and toasted sandwiches, too. Seating on two floors and a rooftop terrace.

☆ Entertainment

Jazz Tibet Club LIVE MUSIC
(☑585 230 399; www.jazzclub.olomouc.com; Sokolská 48; admission free-250Kč; ⊙box office 11am-2pm) Blues, jazz and world music, including occasional international acts, feature at this popular spot, which also incorporates a good restaurant and wine bar. Buy tickets in advance at the club box office or at the Olomouc Information Centre.

❶ Information

Olomouc Information Centre (Olomoucká Informační Služba; ☑585 513 385; www. tourism.olomouc.eu; Horní náměstí; ⊙9am-7pm) Olomouc's information centre is short on language skills, but very helpful when it comes to securing maps, brochures and tickets for events around town. It also offers regular daily sightseeing tours of the Town Hall (15Kč), and from mid-June to mid-September daily guided sightseeing tours of the city centre (50Kč).

❶ Getting There & Away

Olomouc has fast and frequent train service to Prague (220Kč, three hours). There is also regular rail and bus service to Brno (100Kč, 1½ hours).

SURVIVAL GUIDE

❶ Directory A–Z

ACCOMMODATION
The Czech Republic has a wide variety of accommodation options, from luxurious hotels to simple pensions and camping grounds. Prague, Brno and Český Krumlov all have decent backpacker-oriented hostels.

➡ In Prague hotel rates peak in spring and autumn, as well as around the Christmas and Easter holidays. Midsummer is considered 'shoulder season' and rates are about 20% lower.

➡ The capital is a popular destination, so be sure to book well in advance. Hotels are cheaper and less busy outside of Prague, but try to reserve ahead of arrival to get the best rate.

BUSINESS HOURS
Banks 8.30am to 4.30pm Monday to Friday
Bars 11am to midnight or later
Museums & castles Usually closed Monday year-round
Restaurants 11am to 10pm
Shops 8.30am to 6pm Monday to Friday, 8.30am to noon Saturday

GAY & LESBIAN TRAVELLERS
➡ Homosexuality is legal in the Czech Republic and attitudes are relatively open.

COUNTRY FACTS
....

Area 78,866 sq km

Capital Prague

Country Code ☑420

Currency Crown (Kč)

Emergency ☑112

Language Czech

Money ATMs are all over; banks open Monday to Friday

Population 10.5 million

Visas Schengen rules apply; visas not required for most nationalities

SLEEPING PRICE RANGES

The following price ranges refer to a double room in high season:

€ less than 1600Kč

€€ 1600Kč to 3700Kč

€€€ more than 3700Kč

➤ For online information including links to accommodation and bars see the **Prague Gay Guide** (www.prague.gayguide.net).

INTERNET RESOURCES

Czech Tourism (www.czechtourism.com)

National Bus & Train Timetable (http://jizdnirady.idnes.cz)

Prague City Tourism (www.praguecity tourism.cz)

Prague City Transport (www.dpp.cz)

Radio Prague News (www.radio.cz)

MONEY

➤ The best places to exchange money are banks or use your credit or debit card to withdraw money as needed from ATMs.

➤ Never exchange money on the street and avoid private exchange offices, especially in Prague, as they charge exorbitant commissions.

➤ Keep small change handy for use in public toilets and metro-ticket machines.

PUBLIC HOLIDAYS

New Year's Day 1 January

Easter Monday March/April

Labour Day 1 May

Liberation Day 8 May

Sts Cyril and Methodius Day 5 July

Jan Hus Day 6 July

Czech Statehood Day 28 September

Republic Day 28 October

Freedom and Democracy Day 17 November

Christmas 24 to 26 December

TELEPHONE

➤ All Czech phone numbers have nine digits. Dial all nine numbers for any call, local or long distance.

➤ The Czech Republic's country code is ☑ 420.

➤ Mobile-phone coverage (GSM 900/1800) is compatible with most European, Australian or New Zealand handsets (though generally not with North American or Japanese models).

➤ Purchase a Czech SIM card from any mobile-phone shop for around 500Kč (including 300Kč of calling credit).

➤ Local mobile numbers can be identified by prefix. Mobiles start with ☑ 601–608 or ☑ 720–779.

➤ Public phones operate via prepaid magnetic cards purchased at post offices or newsstands from 100Kč.

VISAS

➤ The Czech Republic is part of the EU's Schengen area, and citizens of most developed countries can spend up to 90 days in the country in a six-month period without a visa.

ℹ Getting There & Away

The Czech Republic is easily reached by air from key European hubs or overland by road or train from neighbouring countries. Lying along major European road and rail lines, it is a convenient hub for exploring surrounding countries. Prague has excellent rail connections to Berlin as well as Kraków, Bratislava, Budapest and Vienna.

Flights, tours and rail tickets can be booked online at www.lonelyplanet.com/travel_services.

AIR

Nearly all international flights arrive at Václav Havel Airport Prague.

Václav Havel Airport Prague (Prague Ruzyně International Airport; ☑ 220 111 888; www.prg.aero; K letišti 6, Ruzyně; 📶; ☑ 100, 119) Prague's main international gateway lies 17km west of the city centre. It's home to national carrier Czech Airlines and a regional hub for flights around Europe and to the Middle East (though at research time there were limited direct flights to North America). There are two main terminals: Terminal 1 handles flights outside the EU; Terminal 2 for flights within the EU.

LAND

The Czech Republic has border crossings with Germany, Poland, Slovakia and Austria. These are all EU member states within the Schengen zone, meaning there are no passport or customs checks.

Bus

➤ The main international terminal is Florenc bus station in Prague.

EATING PRICE RANGES

The following price ranges refer to a standard main meal:

€ less than 200Kč

€€ 200Kč to 500Kč

€€€ more than 500Kč

ESSENTIAL FOOD & DRINK

➠ **Beer** Modern *pils* (light, amber-coloured lager) was invented in the city of Plzeň in the 19th century, giving Czechs bragging rights to having the best beer (*pivo*) in the world.

➠ **Dumplings** Every culture has its favourite starchy side dish; for Czechs it's *knedliky* – big bread dumplings that are perfect for mopping up gravy.

➠ **Roast Pork** Move over beef, pork (*vepřové maso*) is king here. The classic Bohemian dish, seen on menus around the country, is *vepřo-knedlo-zelo*, local slang for roast pork, bread dumplings and sauerkraut.

➠ **Braised Beef** Look out for *svíčková na smetaně* on menus. This is a satisfying slice of roast beef, served in a cream sauce, with a side of bread dumplings and a dollop of cranberry sauce.

➠ **Becherovka** A shot of this sweetish herbal liqueur from Karlovy Vary is a popular way to start (or end) a big meal.

➠ **Carp** This lowly fish (*kapr* in Czech) is given pride of place every Christmas at the centre of the family meal. *Kapr na kmíní* is fried or baked carp with caraway seed.

➠ Leading international bus carriers include Student Agency and Eurolines.

Eurolines (☑ 245 005 245; www.elines.cz; ÚAN Praha Florenc, Křižíkova 2110/2b; ☺ 6.30am-10.30pm Mon-Fri, 6.30am-9pm Sat; ☎; Ⓜ Florenc) International bus carrier links Prague to cities around Europe. Consult the web page for a timetable and prices. Buy tickets online or at Florenc bus station.

Florenc Bus Station (ÚAN Praha Florenc; ☑ 900 144 444; www.florenc.cz; Křižíkova 2110/2b, Karlín; ☺ 4am-midnight, information counter 6am-10pm; ☎; Ⓜ Florenc) Prague's main bus station, servicing most domestic and long-haul international routes. There's an information counter, ticket windows, a left-luggage office, and a small number of shops and restaurants. You can also usually purchase tickets directly from the driver.

Student Agency (☑ bus information 841 101 101, nonstop info line 800 100 300; www.studentagency.cz; ÚAN Praha Florenc, Křižíkova 2110/2b) This modern, well-run company operates comfortable, full-service coaches to major Czech cities as well as 60 destinations around Europe. Buses usually depart from Florenc bus station, but may depart from other stations as well. Be sure to ask which station when you purchase your ticket.

Train

➠ The country's main international rail gateway is Praha hlavní nádraží (Prague main train station). The station is accessible by public transport on metro line C.

➠ There is regular rail service from Prague to and from Germany, Poland, Slovakia and Austria. Trains to/from the south and east, including from Bratislava, Vienna and Budapest, also stop at Brno's main train station.

➠ In Prague, buy train tickets at ČD Centrum, located on the lower level of the station. Credit cards are accepted. An adjoining travel agency, ČD Travel, can help work out complicated international connections.

➠ Both InterRail and Eurail passes are valid on the Czech rail network.

ČD Centrum (☑ 840 112 113; www.cd.cz; Praha hlavní nádraží, Wilsonova 8; ☺ 3am-midnight; Ⓜ Hlavní nádraží) The main ticket office for purchasing train tickets for both domestic (*vnitrostátní jízdenky*) and international (*mezinárodní jízdenky*) destinations is located on the lower (street) level of the station. It also sells seat reservations, as well as booking couchettes and sleeping cars.

ČD Travel (☑ 972 241 861; www.cdtravel.cz; Praha hlavní nádraží, Wilsonova 8; ☺ 9am-6pm Mon-Fri, 9am-2pm Sat Apr-Sep, 9am-5pm Mon-Fri Oct-Mar; Ⓜ Hlavní nádraží) ČD Travel is an affiliate of České dráhy (Czech Rail) and specialises in working out and booking international connections. It maintains a small office within the main ticketing area, ČD Centrum, on the lower level of Praha hlavní nádraží.

Praha hlavní nádraží (Prague main train station; ☑ 840 112 113; www.cd.cz; Wilsonova 8, Nové Město; Ⓜ Hlavní nádraží) Prague's main train station, handling most international and domestic arrivals and departures.

ℹ Getting Around

BUS

➠ Buses are often faster, cheaper and more convenient than trains.

➠ Many bus routes have reduced frequency (or none) on weekends.

➠ Check bus timetables and prices at http://jizdnirady.idnes.cz.

→ In Prague, many (though not all) buses arrive at and depart from Florenc bus station. Be sure to double-check the correct station.

→ Try to arrive at the station well ahead of departure to secure a seat. Buy tickets from the driver.

CSAD (☑ information line 900 144 444) The national bus company links cities and smaller towns. In Prague, CSAD buses normally arrive at and depart from Florenc bus station.

Student Agency (p157) A popular, private bus company operating convenient services between major cities.

CAR & MOTORCYCLE

→ For breakdown assistance anywhere in the country, dial ☑1230.

→ The minimum driving age is 18 and traffic moves on the right.

→ Children aged under 12 are prohibited from sitting in the front seat.

→ Drivers are required to keep their headlights on at all times.

→ The legal blood-alcohol limit is zero.

TRAIN

→ Czech Railways provides efficient train services to almost every part of the country.

→ For an online timetable, go to http://jizdnirady.idnes.cz or www.cd.cz.

Estonia

Best Places to Eat

➜ Ö (p168)

➜ Tchaikovsky (p168)

➜ Leib (p167)

➜ Von Krahli Aed (p167)

➜ Altja Kõrts (p170)

Best Places to Stay

➜ Antonius Hotel (p172)

➜ Hotel Telegraaf (p167)

➜ Yoga Residence (p167)

➜ Euphoria (p167)

➜ Tallinn Backpackers (p166)

Why Go?

Estonia doesn't have to struggle to find a point of difference; it's completely unique. It shares a similar geography and history with Latvia and Lithuania, but it's culturally very different. Its closest ethnic and linguistic buddy is Finland, yet although they both may love to get naked together in the sauna, 50 years of Soviet rule have separated the two cultures. For the past 300 years Estonia has been linked to Russia, but the two states have as much in common as a barn swallow and a bear (their respective national symbols).

In recent decades, and with a new-found confidence, Estonia has crept from under the Soviet blanket and leapt into the arms of Europe. The love affair is mutual: Europe has fallen for the chocolate-box allure of Tallinn and its Unesco-protected Old Town, while travellers seeking something different are tapping into Estonia's captivating blend of Eastern European and Nordic appeal.

When to Go
Tallinn

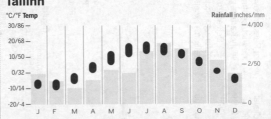

Apr & May See the country shake off winter's gloom.

Jun–Aug White nights, beach parties and loads of summer festivals.

Dec Christmas markets, mulled wine and long, cosy nights.

Estonia Highlights

1 Embark on a medieval quest for atmospheric restaurants and bars in the history-saturated lanes of Tallinn's **Old Town**.

2 Follow in the footsteps of Russian royalty within the rarefied confines of Tallinn's leafy **Kadriorg Park** (p165).

3 Delve into Estonia's history of foreign occupations in Tallinn's excellent **museums**, knowing there's the pay-off of a happy ending.

4 Stroll the broad golden sands and genteel streets of **Pärnu** (p173), Estonia's 'summer capital'.

5 Further your local education in the museums and bars of the university town of **Tartu** (p170), Estonia's second city.

6 Cycle between manor houses and discover your own slice of deserted coast in **Lahemaa National Park** (p170).

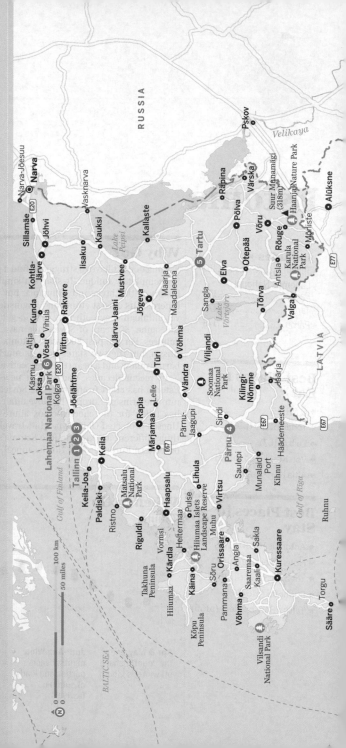

ITINERARIES

Three Days

Base yourself in **Tallinn** and spend your first day exploring all the nooks and crannies of Old Town. The following day, do what most tourists don't do – step out of Old Town. Explore Kadriorg Park for a first-rate greenery and art fix, then hit the wonderful Estonian Open-Air Museum. On your last day, hire a car or take a day tour to **Lahemaa National Park**.

One Week

Spend your first three days in Tallinn, then allow a full day to explore Lahemaa before bedding down within the national park. The following day, continue on to **Tartu** for a night or two, then finish up in **Pärnu**.

TALLINN

POP 412,000

If you're labouring under the misconception that 'former Soviet' means dull and grey, and that all tourist traps are soulless, Tallinn will delight in proving you wrong. This city has charm by the bucketload, fusing the modern and medieval to come up with a vibrant vibe all of its own. It's an intoxicating mix of church spires, glass skyscrapers, baroque palaces, appealing eateries, brooding battlements, shiny shopping malls, run-down wooden houses and cafes set on sunny squares – with a few Soviet throwbacks in the mix.

⊙ Sights & Activities

◉ Old Town

Tallinn's medieval Old Town (Vanalinn) is without doubt the country's most fascinating locality. It's divided into Toompea (the upper town) and the lower town, which is still surrounded by much of its 2.5km defensive wall.

Toompea

According to legend, Toompea is the burial mound of Kalev, the mythical first leader of the Estonians. When Tallinn was a German town (known as Reval), this large fortified hill was the preserve of the bishop and the feudal nobility, literally looking down on the traders and lesser beings below. A couple of wonderful lookouts offer sumptuous views across the Lower Town rooftops to the sea.

St Mary's Cathedral   CHURCH

(Tallinna Neitsi Maarja Piiskoplik Toomkirik; www.eelk.ee/tallinna.toom/; Toom-Kooli 6; tower adult/child €5/3; ⊗9am-5pm daily May-Sep, 9am-3pm Tue-Sun Oct-Apr) Tallinn's cathedral (now Lutheran, originally Catholic) was founded by at least 1233, although the exterior dates mainly from the 15th century, with the tower added in 1779. This impressive, austere building was a burial ground for the rich and titled, and the whitewashed walls are decorated with the coats-of-arms of Estonia's noble families. Fit viewseekers can climb the tower.

Alexander Nevsky Cathedral   CHURCH

(Lossi plats; ⊗9am-6pm) **FREE** The positioning of this magnificent, onion-domed Russian Orthodox cathedral (completed in 1900), opposite the parliament buildings, was no accident: the church was one of many built in the last part of the 19th century as part of a general wave of Russification in the empire's Baltic provinces. Orthodox believers come here in droves, alongside tourists ogling the interior's striking icons and frescoes.

Toompea Castle   HISTORIC BUILDING

(Lossi plats) **FREE** Toompea hill was topped by an early Estonian stronghold before the Danes invaded and built a castle here in 1219. Three towers have survived from the Knights of the Sword castle which replaced it, the finest of which is 14th-century Pikk Hermann (best viewed from the rear). In the 18th century the fortress underwent an extreme makeover at the hands of Russian empress Catherine the Great, converting it into the pretty-in-pink baroque palace that now houses Estonia's parliament (*riigikogu*).

Kiek in de Kök   CASTLE, MUSEUM

(☑644 6686; www.linnamuuseum.ee; Komandandi tee 2; adult/child €4.50/2.60; ⊗10.30am-6pm Tue-Sun) Built around 1475, this tall, stout fortress is one of Tallinn's most formidable cannon towers. Its name (amusing as it

ESTONIA TALLINN

sounds in English) is Low German for 'Peep into the Kitchen'; from the upper floors medieval voyeurs could peer into the houses below. Today it houses a branch of the City Museum, focusing mainly on the development of the town's elaborate defences.

Bastion Passages FORTRESS
(Bastionikäigud; ☑ 644 6686; www.linnamuuseum. ee; Komandandi tee 2; adult/child €5.80/3.20) Two-hour tours depart from Kiek in de Kök, exploring the 17th-centuring tunnels connecting the towers, built by the Swedes to help protect the city; bookings required.

Tallinn

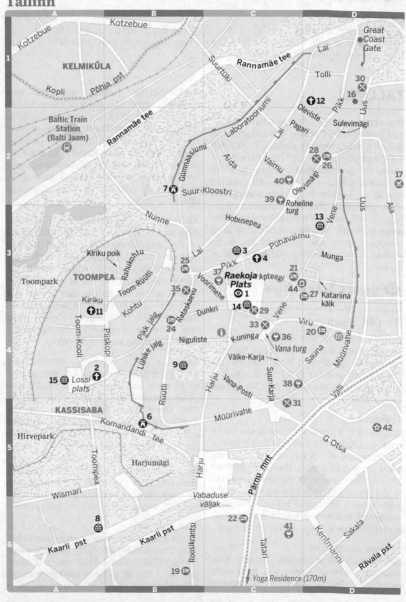

Museum of Occupations   MUSEUM
(Okupatsioonide Muuseum; www.okupatsioon.ee; Toompea 8; adult/child €5/3; ⊙10am-6pm Tue-Sun) Displays illustrate the hardships and horrors of five decades of occupation, under both the Nazis (briefly) and the Soviets. The photos and artefacts are interesting but it's

the videos (lengthy but enthralling) that leave the greatest impression – and the joy of a happy ending.

Lower Town

Picking your way along the lower town's narrow, cobbled streets is like strolling into the 15th century – not least due to the tendency of local businesses to dress their staff up in medieval garb. The most interesting street is Pikk (Long St), which starts at the Great Coast Gate and includes Tallinn's historic guild buildings.

⭐**Raekoja Plats**   SQUARE
(Town Hall Sq) Raekoja plats has been the heart of Tallinn life since markets began here in the 11th century. It's ringed by pastel-coloured buildings from the 15th to 17th centuries, and is dominated by the Gothic town hall. Throughout summer, outdoor cafes implore you to sit and people-watch; come Christmas, a huge pine tree stands in the middle of the square. Whether bathed in sunlight or sprinkled with snow, it's always a photogenic spot.

Tallinn Town Hall   HISTORIC BUILDING
(Tallinna Raekoda; ☑645 7900; www.tallinn.ee/raekoda; Raekoja plats; adult/student €5/2; ⊙10am-4pm Mon-Sat Jul-Aug, by appointment Sep-Jun) Completed in 1404, this is the only surviving Gothic town hall in northern Europe. Inside, you can visit the Trade Hall (housing a visitor book dripping in royal signatures), the Council Chamber (featuring Estonia's oldest woodcarvings, dating from 1374), the vaulted Citizens' Hall, a yellow-and-black-tiled councillor's office and a small kitchen. The steeply sloped attic has displays on the building and its restoration.

Holy Spirit Church   CHURCH
(Pühavaimu Kirik; www.eelk.ee/tallinna.puhavaimu/; Pühavaimu 2; adult/child €1/50c; ⊙noon-2pm Mon-Fri, 10am-3pm Sat Jan & Feb, 10am-3pm Mon-Sat Mar, Apr & Oct-Dec, 10am-5pm Mon-Sat May-Sep) The blue-and-gold clock on the facade of this striking 13th-century Gothic Lutheran church is the oldest in Tallinn, dating from 1684. Inside there are exquisite woodcarvings and painted panels, including an altarpiece dating to 1483 and a 17th-century baroque pulpit.

Estonian History Museum   MUSEUM
(Eesti Ajaloomuuseum; www.ajaloomuuseum.ee; Pikk 17; adult/child €5/3; ⊙10am-6pm, closed Wed Sep-Apr) The Estonian History Museum has filled the striking 1410 Great Guild building

0   200 m
0   0.1 miles

Linda Line (650m)

Admiraliteedi bassein

Moon (400m);
Lennusadam Seaplane
Harbour (1.4km)

Mere pst

Rannamäe tee

Kanuti

Neh (400m)

Ahtri

Roseni

Ahtri

32
34

ROTERMANN
QUARTER

Mere pst

Rotermanni väljak

10

Rotermanni

Hobujaama

Inseneri

18

23

Viru väljak

Central (1.7km);
Tallinn (4km);
Pirita beach
(5.5km)

5

Pärnu mnt

A Laikmaa

45

43

Tammsaare
Park

Estonia pst

Kaubamaja

Lahemaa
National Park
(Palmse, 80km)

5

Rävala pst

Islandi
väljak

Kauka

Lennuki

Lembitu

A Lauteri

Lembitu
Park

Tallinn

with a series of ruminations on the Estonian psyche, presented through interactive and unusual displays. Coin collectors shouldn't miss the display in the old excise chamber, while military nuts should head downstairs. The basement also covers the history of the Great Guild itself.

Lower Town Wall FORTRESS
(Linnamüür; Gümnaasiumi 3; adult/child €1.50/75c; ⏰11am-7pm Jun-Aug, 11am-5pm Fri-Wed Apr, May, Sep & Oct, 11am-4pm Fri-Tue Nov-Mar) The most photogenic stretch of Tallinn's remaining walls connects nine towers lining the western edge of Old Town. Visitors can explore the barren nooks and crannies of three of them, with cameras at the ready for the red-rooftop views.

St Olaf's Church CHURCH
(Oleviste Kirik; www.oleviste.ee; Lai 50; tower adult/child €2/1; ⏰10am-6pm Apr-Oct) From 1549 to 1625, when its 159m steeple was struck by lightning and burnt down, this (now Baptist) church was one of the tallest buildings in the world. The current spire reaches a still respectable 124m and you can take a tight, confined, 258-step staircase up the tower for wonderful views of Toompea over the Lower Town's rooftops.

Niguliste Museum MUSEUM
(www.nigulistemuuseum.ee; Niguliste 3; adult/student €3.50/2; ⏰10am-5pm Wed-Sun) Dating from the 13th century, St Nicholas' Church (Niguliste Kirik) is one of the city's Gothic treasures. It now houses a museum devoted to medieval religious art. The acoustics are first-rate, and organ recitals are held here most weekends.

Tallinn City Museum MUSEUM
(Tallinna Linnamuuseum; www.linnamuuseum.ee; Vene 17; adult/child €3.20/2; ⏰10.30am-5.30pm Wed-Mon) Tallinn's City Museum is actually split over 10 different sites. This, its main branch, is set in a 14th-century merchant's house and traces the city's development from its earliest days. The displays are engrossing and very well laid out, with plenty of information in English making the hire of the audioguide quite unnecessary.

Kalev Spa Waterpark SWIMMING, SPA
(www.kalevspa.ee; Aia 18; 2½hr visit adult/child
€12/10; ☺ 6.45am-9.30pm Mon-Fri, 8am-9.30pm
Sat & Sun) For serious swimmers there's an
indoor pool of Olympic proportions but
there are plenty of other ways to wrinkle
your skin here, including waterslides, spa
pools, saunas and a kids' pool. There's also a
gym, day spa and three private saunas, with
the largest holding up to 20 of your closest
hot-and-sweaty mates.

◉ City Centre

Hotel Viru KGB Museum MUSEUM
(🖉680 9300; www.viru.ee; Viru väljak 4; tour €9;
☺ daily May-Oct, Tue-Sun Nov-Apr) When the Hotel Viru was built in 1972, it was not only Estonia's first skyscraper, it was the only place
for tourists to stay in Tallinn – and we mean
that literally. Having all the foreigners in one
place made it much easier to keep tabs on
them and the locals they had contact with,
which is exactly what the KGB did from
their 23rd-floor spy base. The hotel offers
fascinating tours of the facility; bookings
essential.

Rotermann Quarter NEIGHBOURHOOD
(Rotermanni Kvartal) With impressive contemporary architecture wedged between old
brick warehouses, this development has
transformed a former factory complex into
the city's hippest new shopping and dining
precinct.

◉ Kadriorg Park

About 2km east of Old Town (take tram 1
or 3), this beautiful park's ample acreage is
Tallinn's favourite patch of green. Together
with the baroque Kadriorg Palace, it was
commissioned by the Russian tsar Peter the
Great for his wife Catherine I soon after his
conquest of Estonia (Kadriorg means Catherine's Valley in Estonian). Nowadays the oak,
lilac and horse chestnut trees provide shade
for strollers and picnickers, the formal pond
and gardens provide a genteel backdrop for
romantic promenades and wedding photos,
and the children's playground is a favourite
off-leash area for the city's youngsters.

Kadriorg Art Museum PALACE, GALLERY
(Kardrioru Kunstimuuseum; www.kadriorumuuse-
um.ee; A Weizenbergi 37; adult/child €4.80/2.80;
☺ 10am 5pm Tue & Thu-Sun, to 8pm Wed May-Sep,
closed Mon & Tue Oct-Apr) Kadriorg Palace, built
by Tsar Peter the Great between 1718 and

1736, now houses a branch of the Estonian
Art Museum, which is devoted to Dutch, German and Italian paintings from the 16th to
the 18th centuries, and Russian works from
the 18th to early 20th centuries (check out
the decorative porcelain with communist
imagery upstairs). The building is exactly as
frilly and fabulous as a palace ought to be
and there's a handsome French-style flower
garden at the back.

Kumu GALLERY
(www.kumu.ee; A Weizenbergi 34; all exhibitions
adult/student €5.50/3.20, permanent exhibitions
€4.20/2.60; ☺ 11am-6pm Tue & Thu-Sun, to 8pm
Wed May-Sep, closed Mon & Tue Oct-Apr) This
futuristic, Finnish-designed, seven-storey
building (2006) is a spectacular structure of
limestone, glass and copper, nicely integrated into the landscape. Kumu (the name is
short for *kunstimuuseum* or art museum)
contains the country's largest repository of
Estonian art as well as constantly changing
contemporary exhibits.

◉ Pirita

Pirita's main claim to fame is that it was
the base for the sailing events of the 1980
Moscow Olympics; international regattas
are still held here. It's also home to Tallinn's
largest and most popular beach.

Buses 1A, 8, 34A and 38 all run between
the city centre and Pirita, with the last two
continuing on to the TV Tower.

TV Tower VIEWPOINT
(Teletorn; www.teletorn.ee; Kloostrimetsa tee 58a;
adult/child €8/5; ☺ 10am-7pm) Opened in time
for the 1980 Olympics, this futuristic 314m
tower offers brilliant views from its 22nd
floor (175m). Press a button and frosted glass
disks set in the floor suddenly clear, giving a
view straight down. Once you're done gawp-
ing, check out the interactive displays in the
space-age pods. Daredevils can try the open-
air 'edge walk' (€20) or rappel their way
down (€49).

Maarjamäe Palace MUSEUM
(Maarjamäe Loss; www.ajaloomuuseum.ee; Pirita
tee 56; adult/child €4/2; ☺ 10am-5pm Wed-Sun) A
kilometre north of Kadriorg Park, Maarjamäe
is a neo-Gothic limestone manor house built
in the 1870s. It's now home to the Estonian
Film Museum and a less-visited branch of
the Estonian History Museum, detailing
the twists and turns of the 20th century.

Don't miss the Soviet sculpture graveyard at the rear of the building.

◎ Other Neighbourhoods

★ Lennusadam
Seaplane Harbour   MUSEUM
(www.lennusadam.eu; Vesilennuki 6, Kalamaja; adult/child €10/6; ⊘10am-7pm May-Sep, Tue-Sun Oct-Apr; P) When this triple-domed hangar was completed in 1917, its reinforced-concrete shell frame construction was unique in the world. Resembling a classic Bond-villain lair, the vast space was completely restored and opened to the public in 2012 as a fascinating maritime museum, filled with interactive displays. Highlights include exploring the cramped corridors of a 1930s naval submarine, and the icebreaker and minehunter ships moored outside.

Estonian Open-Air Museum   MUSEUM
(Eesti Vabaõhumuuseum; www.evm.ee; Vabaõhu-muuseumi tee 12, Rocca Al Mare; adult/child May-Sep €7/3.50, Oct-Apr €5/3; ⊘10am-8pm May-Sep, to 5pm Oct-Apr) If tourists won't go to the countryside, let's bring the countryside to them. That's the modus operandi of this excellent, sprawling complex, where historic buildings have been plucked and transplanted among the tall trees. In summer the time-warping effect is highlighted by staff in period costume performing traditional activities among the wooden farmhouses and windmills.

⏚ Tours

EstAdventures   WALKING, BUS
(☑53083731; www.estadventures.ee; from €15; ⊘May-Sep) Offers offbeat themed walking tours of Tallinn (Soviet, Legends, Spies, Haunted, Beer etc). Full-day excursions further afield include Lahemaa National Park and Tartu.

Tallinn Traveller Tours   WALKING, CYCLING
(☑58374800; www.traveller.ee) Entertaining, good-value tours – including a free, two-hour Old Town walking tour. There are also ghost tours (€15), pub crawls (€20), bike tours (€16) and day trips as far afield as Riga (€49).

City Bike   CYCLING, WALKING
(☑5111819; www.citybike.ee; Uus 33) Has a great range of Tallinn tours, by bike or on foot, as well as trips to Lahemaa National Park (€49). Two-hour cycling tours (€13 to €16) of Tallinn

run year-round and include Kadriorg and Pirita.

Tallinn City Tour   BUS
(☑627 9080; www.citytour.ee; 24hr-pass adult/child €19/16) Runs red double-decker buses that give you quick, easy, hop-on, hop-off access to the city's top sights. A recorded audio tour accompanies the ride. Buses leave from Mere pst, just outside Old Town.

🛏 Sleeping

⏚ Old Town

★ Tallinn Backpackers   HOSTEL €
(☑644 0298; www.tallinnbackpackers.com; Olevimägi 11; dm €12-15; @🛜) In an ideal Old Town location, this place has a global feel and a roll-call of traveller-happy features: free wi-fi and lockers, cheap dinners, a foosball table – one dorm even has it's own sauna! There's also a regular roster of pub crawls and day trips to nearby attractions.

Tabinoya   HOSTEL €
(☑632 0062; www.tabinoya.com; Nunne 1; dm/ s/d from €13/30/40; @🛜) The Baltic's first Japanese-run hostel occupies the two top floors of an old building, with dorms and a communal lounge at the top, and spacious private rooms, a kitchen and a sauna below.

Hotel Cru   HOTEL €€
(☑611 7600; www.cruhotel.eu; Viru 8; s/d from €100/135; 🛜) Behind its pretty powder-blue facade, this boutique 14th-century offering has richly furnished rooms with plenty of original features (timber beams and stone walls) scattered along a rabbit warren of corridors. The cheapest are a little snug.

Old House
Apartments   APARTMENTS €€
(☑641 1464; www.oldhouseapartments.ee; Rataskaevu 16; apt from €85; P🛜) Old House is an understatement for this wonderful 14th-century merchant's house. It's been split into eight beautifully furnished apartments (including a spacious two-bedroom one with traces of a medieval painted ceiling). There are a further 21 apartments scattered around Old Town in similar buildings, although the quality and facilities vary widely.

Villa Hortensia   APARTMENTS €€
(☑5046113; www.hoov.ee; Vene 6; s/d from €45/65; 🛜) Situated in the sweet, cobbled Masters'

Courtyard, Hortensia has four split-level studio apartments with kitchenettes and access to a shared communal lounge, but the two larger apartments are the real treats, with balconies and loads of character.

★ **Hotel Telegraaf**　　　HOTEL €€€
(☑600 0600; www.telegraafhotel.com; Vene 9; s/d from €145/165; P❄🐾🛜🏊) This upmarket hotel, in a converted 19th-century former telegraph station, delivers style in spades. It boasts a spa, a pretty courtyard, an acclaimed restaurant, swanky decor and smart, efficient service.

🛏 City Centre

★ **Euphoria**　　　HOSTEL €
(☑58373602; www.euphoria.ee; Roosikrantsi 4; dm/r from €12/40; P@🛜) So laid-back it's almost horizontal, this hostel, just south of Old Town, is an entertaining place to stay with a palpable sense of traveller community – especially if you like hookah pipes and impromptu late-night jam sessions (pack earplugs if you don't).

★ **Yoga Residence**　　　APARTMENTS €€
(☑5021477; http://yogaresidence.eu; Pärnu mnt 32; apt from €75; 🛜) It's a strange name for what's basically a block of very modern, fresh and well-equipped apartments, a short stroll from Old Town. You can expect friendly staff, a kitchenette and, joy of joys, a washing machine. There is a second block in an older building north of Old Town.

Hotell Palace　　　HOTEL €€
(☑680 6655; www.tallinnhotels.ee; Vabaduse Väljak 3; s/d from €115/125; ❄@🛜🏊) A recent renovation has swept through this architecturally interesting 1930s hotel, leaving comfortable, tastefully furnished rooms in its wake. It's directly across the road from Freedom Sq and Old Town, and the complex includes an indoor pool, spa, sauna and small gym.

Nordic Hotel Forum　　　HOTEL €€€
(☑622 2900; www.nordichotels.eu; Viru väljak 3; r from €135; P@🛜🏊) The Forum shows surprising personality for a large, business-style hotel – witness the artwork on the hotel's facade and the trees on the roof. Facilities include saunas and an indoor pool with an 8th-floor view.

🍴 Eating

🍴 Old Town

III Draakon　　　CAFE €
(Raekoja plats; mains €1.50-3; ⊘9am-11pm) There's bucketloads of atmosphere at this Lilliputian tavern below the Town Hall, and super-cheap elk soup, sausages and oven-hot pies. The historic setting is amped up – expect costumed wenches with a good line in tourist banter, and beer served in ceramic steins.

Must Puudel　　　CAFE €
(Müürivahe 20; mains €6-9; ⊘9am-11pm Sun-Tue, to 2am Wed-Sat; 🛜) Mismatched 1970s furniture, an eclectic soundtrack, courtyard seating, excellent coffee, cooked breakfasts (less than €5), tasty light meals, long opening hours and a name that translates as 'Black Poodle' – yep, this is Old Town's hippest cafe.

Chocolats de Pierre　　　CAFE €
(☑641 8061; www.pierre.ee; Vene 6; snacks €3-5; ⊘8am-midnight) Nestled inside the picturesque Masters' Courtyard and offering respite from Old Town hubbub, this snug cafe is renowned for its delectable (but pricy) handmade chocolates. It also sells pastries and quiches, making it a great choice for a light breakfast or lunch.

★ **Leib**　　　ESTONIAN €€
(☑611 9026; www.leibresto.ee; Uus 31; mains €15-17; ⊘noon-11pm) An inconspicuous gate opens onto a large lawn guarded by busts of Sean Connery and Robbie Burns. Welcome to the former home of Tallinn's Scottish club (really!), where 'simple, soulful food' is served along with homemade *leib* (bread). The slow-cooked meat and grilled fish dishes are exceptional.

★ **Von Krahli Aed**　　　MODERN EUROPEAN €€
(☑626 9088; www.vonkrahl.ee; Rataskaevu 8; mains €6-15; ⊘noon-midnight; 🍴) You'll find plenty of greenery on your plate at this rustic, plant-filled restaurant (*aed* means 'garden'). The menu embraces fresh flavours and wins fans by noting organic, gluten-, lactose- and egg-free options.

Chedi　　　ASIAN €€
(☑646 1676; www.chedi.ee; Sulevimägi 1; mains €14-23; ⊘noon-11pm) UK-based chef Alan Yau

(of London's Michelin-starred Hakkasan and Yauatcha) consulted on the menu of sleek, sexy Chedi, and some of his trademark dishes are featured here. The modern pan-Asian food is exemplary – try the delicious crispy duck salad and the artful dumplings.

Olde Hansa
ESTONIAN €€

(☑627 9020; www.oldehansa.ee; Vana turg 1; mains €10-40; ☉10am-midnight) Amid candlelit rooms with peasant-garbed servers labouring beneath large plates of game meats, medieval-themed Olde Hansa is the place to indulge in a gluttonous feast. If it all sounds a bit cheesy, take heart – the chefs have done their research in producing historically authentic, tasty fare.

★Tchaikovsky
RUSSIAN €€€

(☑600 0610; www.telegraafhotel.com; Vene 9; mains €23-26; ☉noon-3pm & 6-11pm Mon-Fri, 1-11pm Sat & Sun) Located in a glassed-in pavilion at the heart of the Hotel Telegraaf, Tchaikovsky offers a dazzling tableau of blinged-up chandeliers, gilt frames and greenery. Service is formal and faultless, as is the classic Franco-Russian menu, all accompanied by live chamber music.

City Centre

Sfäär
MODERN EUROPEAN €€

(☑56992200; www.sfaar.ee; Mere pst 6e; mains €9-16; ☉8am-10pm Mon-Wed, to midnight Thu & Fri, 10am-midnight Sat, 10am-10pm Sun) Chic Sfäär delivers an inventive menu highlighting the best Estonian produce in a warehouse-style setting that's like something out of a Nordic design catalogue. If you just fancy a tipple, the cocktail and wine list won't disappoint.

★Ö
MODERN ESTONIAN €€€

(☑661 6150; www.restoran-o.ee; Mere pst 6e; 4-/6-/8-course menu €46/59/76; ☉6-11pm Mon-Sat) Award-winning Ö (pronounced 'er') has carved a unique space in Tallinn's culinary world, delivering inventive degustation-style menus showcasing seasonal Estonian produce. The understated dining room nicely counterbalances the theatrical cuisine.

Neh
MODERN ESTONIAN €€€

(☑602 2222; www.neh.ee; Lootsi 4; mains €22-23; ☉6pm-midnight Mon-Sat Oct, daily Nov-Feb) Taking seasonal cooking to the extreme, Neh closes completely in summer and heads to the beach – well, Pädaste Manor on Muhu island – where it runs Estonia's best restaurant. In the low season it decamps back to the city, bringing the flavours of the Baltic islands with it.

Kalamaja

Moon
RUSSIAN €€

(☑631 4575; www.kohvikmoon.ee; Võrgu 3; mains €10-17; ☉noon-11pm Mon-Sat & 1-9pm Sun Aug-Jun) Despite its location in an an unlikely lane near the water, the food here is excellent – combining Russian and broader European styles to delicious effect. Save room for dessert.

🍷 Drinking & Nightlife

★DM Baar
BAR

(www.depechemode.ee; Voorimehe 4; ☉noon-4am) If you just can't get enough of Depeche Mode, this is the bar for you. The walls are covered with all manner of memorabilia, including pictures of the actual band partying here. And the soundtrack? Do you really need to ask?

Hell Hunt
PUB

(www.hellhunt.ee; Pikk 39; ☉noon-2am; 🐾) Billing itself as 'the first Estonian pub', this trusty old trooper boasts an amiable air and a huge beer selection – local and imported. Don't let the menacing-sounding name put you off – it actually means 'gentle wolf'. In summer, it spills onto the little square across the road.

Drink Bar & Grill
PUB

(Väike-Karja 8; ☉noon-11pm Mon-Thu, to 2am Fri & Sat) You know a bar means business when it calls itself Drink. This place takes its beer and cider seriously (its motto is 'no crap on tap'), and offers pub grub and long happy hours.

Kultuuriklubi Kelm
BAR

(Vaimu 1; ☉5pm-3am Mon-Thu, to 6am Fri, 7pm-6am Sat, 7pm-3am Sun) Hidden in a vaulted basement, as all good grungy rock bars should be, this hip little 'culture club' hosts art exhibitions and lots of live music.

Clazz
BAR

(www.clazz.ee; Vana turg 2; ☉6pm-midnight Mon, to 2am Tue-Thu, to 4am Fri, 2pm-4am Sat, 2pm-midnight Sun) Behind the cheesy name (a contraction of 'classy jazz') is a popular lounge bar featuring live music every night of the week (cover charge varies), ranging from jazz to soul, funk, blues and Latin.

X-Baar GAY, LESBIAN
(www.xbaar.ee; Tatari 1; ⊙4pm-1am Sun-Thu,
to 3am Fri & Sat) Tallinn holds the monop-
oly on visible gay life in Estonia and this
long-standing bar is the mainstay of the
local scene. It's a relaxed kind of place, entertaining a mixed crowd of gay men and
lesbians.

☆ Entertainment

Katusekino CINEMA
(www.katusekino.ee; L4 Viru Keskus, Viru Väljak 4/6;
⊙Jun-Aug) In the warmer months, an eclectic program of films (cult classics, as well as
interesting new releases) plays on the rooftop of the Viru Keskus shopping centre.

Estonia Concert Hall CLASSICAL MUSIC
(Eesti Kontserdisaal; ☑614 7760; www.concert.
ee; Estonia pst 4) The city's biggest classical
concerts are held in this double-barrelled
venue. It's Tallinn's main theatre and houses
the Estonian National Opera and National
Ballet.

🔒 Shopping

★Katariina Gild HANDICRAFTS
(Katariina käik; Vene 12) Lovely St Catherine's
Passage (Katariina Käik) is home to several artisans' studios where you can happily
browse ceramics, textiles, patchwork quilts,
hats, jewellery, stained glass and beautiful
leather-bound books.

Masters' Courtyard HANDICRAFTS
(Meistrite Hoov; Vene 6) Rich pickings here,
with the cobbled courtyard not only home
to a cosy cafe but also small stores and artisans' workshops selling quality ceramics,
glass, jewellery, knitwear, woodwork and
candles.

Viru Keskus SHOPPING CENTRE
(www.virukeskus.com; Viru väljak; ⊙9am-9pm)
Tallinn's showpiece shopping mall is home
to fashion boutiques and a great bookstore
(Rahva Raamat). At the rear it connects to
the upmarket Kaubamaja department store.

ℹ Information

East-Tallinn Central Hospital (Ida-Tallinna
Keskhaigla; ☑620 7040; www.itk.ee; Ravi 18)
Offers a full range of services, including a 24-
hour emergency room.
Tallinn Tourist Information Centre (☑645
7777; www.tourism.tallinn.ee; Kullassepa 4;
⊙9am-7pm Mon-Fri, to 5pm Sat & Sun May-
Aug, 9am-6pm Mon-Fri, to 3pm Sat & Sun

Sep-Apr) Brochures, maps, event schedules
and other info.

ℹ Getting There & Away

For international connections, see the transport
information (p175) at the end of this chapter.

BUS

The **Central Bus Station** (Autobussijaam;
☑12550; Lastekodu 46) is about 2km southeast of Old Town (tram 2 or 4). During the day,
buses leave at least hourly for Rakvere (from
€3.50, 1½ hours), Tartu (€11, 2½ hours) and
Pärnu (from €6.50, two hours). **TPilet** (www.
tpilet.ee) has times and prices for all national
bus services.

TRAIN

The **Central Train Station** (Balti Jaam; www.
elron.ee; Toompuiestee 35) is on the northwestern edge of Old Town. Destinations include
Rakvere (€5.50, three daily, 1¼ daily) and Tartu
(€10, two hours, eight daily).

ℹ Getting Around

TO/FROM THE AIRPORT

➡ **Tallinn Airport** (Tallinna Lennujaam; ☑605
8888; www.tallinn-airport.ee; Tartu mnt 101) is
4km from the centre.

➡ Bus 2 runs every 20 to 30 minutes (6am to
around 11pm) from the A Laikmaa stop, opposite the Tallink Hotel, next to Viru Keskus. From
the airport, bus 2 will take you to the centre.
Buy tickets from the driver (€1.60); journey
time depends on traffic but rarely exceeds 20
minutes.

➡ A taxi between the airport and the city centre
should cost less than €10.

PUBLIC TRANSPORT

Tallinn has an excellent network of buses, trams
and trolleybuses that run from around 6am to
11pm. The major local bus station is on the basement level of Viru Keskus shopping centre, just
east of Old Town. Local public transport timetables are online at www.tallinn.ee.

Public transport is free for Tallinn residents.
Visitors still need to pay, either with cash (€1.60
for a single journey) or by using the e-ticketing
system. Buy a plastic smartcard (€2 deposit)
and top up with credit, then validate the card
at the start of each journey using the orange
card-readers. Fares using the e-ticketing system
cost €1.10/3/5 for an hour/day/three days.

TAXI

Taxis are plentiful, but each company sets its
own fare. The base fare ranges from €2 to €5,
followed by 50c to €1 per kilometre. To avoid
suprises, try **Krooni Takso** (☑1212; www.

kroonitakso.ee; base fare €2.50, per km 55c) or **Reval Takso** (📞1207; www.reval-takso.ee; base fare €2.30, per km 50c).

LAHEMAA NATIONAL PARK

The perfect country retreat from the capital, Lahemaa takes in a stretch of coast indented with peninsulas and bays, plus 475 sq km of pine-fresh forested hinterland. Visitors are looked after with cosy guesthouses, remote seaside campgrounds and a network of pine-scented forest trails.

◉ Sights

★**Palmse Manor**   HISTORIC BUILDING
(www.palmse.ee; adult/child €6/4; ⊙10am-7pm) Fully restored Palmse Manor is the showpiece of Lahemaa National Park, housing the visitor centre in its old stables. The pretty manor house (1720, rebuilt in the 1780s) is now a museum containing period furniture and clothing. Other estate buildings have also been restored and put to new use: the distillery houses a hotel, the steward's residence is a guesthouse and the farm labourers' quarters became a tavern.

Sagadi Manor & Forest Museum   HISTORIC BUILDING
(📞676 7888; www.sagadi.ee; adult/child €3/2; ⊙10am-6pm May-Sep, by appointment Oct-Apr) This pretty pink-and-white baroque mansion was completed in 1753 and has been restored. The gardens are glorious (and free to visit), with the requisite lake, numerous modern sculptures, an arboretum and an endless view down a grand avenue of trees. The house ticket includes admission to the neighbouring Forest Museum, devoted to the forestry industry and the park's flora and fauna.

🛏 Sleeping & Eating

Toomarahva Turismitalu   GUESTHOUSE €
(📞5050850; www.toomarahva.ee; Altja; r from €40; 🛜) This farmstead comprises thatch-roofed wooden buildings and a garden full of flowers and sculptures. The converted stables contain four private rooms – two of which share bathrooms and one with kitchen facilities – or you can doss down in the hay in summer for €5. Signage is minimal – it's located opposite Swing Hill.

Sagadi Manor   HOTEL, HOSTEL €€
(📞676 7888; www.sagadi.ee; Sagadi; dm €15, s/d from €60/80; 📶🛜) Waking up within the rarefied confines of Sagadi Manor, with its gracious gardens at your disposal, is a downright lovely experience. There's a tidy 31-bed hostel in the former estate manager's house, while the hotel has fresh and comfortable rooms in the whitewashed stables block across the lawn.

★**Altja Kõrts**   ESTONIAN €
(Altja; mains €6-9; ⊙noon-8pm) Set in a thatched, wooden building with a large terrace, this uber-rustic place serves delicious plates of traditional fare (baked pork with sauerkraut etc) to candlelit wooden tables. It's extremely atmospheric and a lot of fun.

❶ Information

Lahemaa National Park Visitor Centre
(📞329 5555; www.lahemaa.ee; Palmse Manor; ⊙9am-6pm daily May-Oct, 9am-5pm Mon-Fri Oct-Apr) This excellent centre stocks the essential map of Lahemaa, as well as information on hiking trails, accommodation, island exploration and guiding services. It's worth starting your park visit with the free 17-minute film entitled *Lahemaa – Nature and Man*.

❶ Getting There & Away

Hiring a car will give you the most flexibility, or you could take a tour from Tallinn. Exploring the park using public transport requires patience and time. Buses to destinations within the park leave from the town of Rakvere (connected by bus to Tallinn, Tartu and Pärnu), which is 35km southeast of Palmse. Once you've arrived in the park, bike hire is easy to arrange.

TARTU

POP 98,500

Tartu was the cradle of Estonia's 19th-century national revival and lays claim to being the nation's cultural capital. Locals talk about a special Tartu *vaim* (spirit), created by the time-stands-still feel of its wooden houses and stately buildings, and by the beauty of its parks and riverfront. It's also Estonia's premier university town, with students making up nearly one fifth of the population – guaranteeing a vibrant nightlife for a city of its size.

◉ Sights

As the major repository of Estonia's cultural heritage, Tartu has an abundance of first-rate museums. We've listed the best of them here, but enquire at the tourist office if your interests extend to, say, farm machinery.

STUDENT LIFE IN TARTU

The world over, students gravitate to cheap meals and booze, and in Tartu it's no different.

Genialistide Klubi (www.genklubi.ee; behind Lai 37, enter from Magasini) The Genialists' Club is an all-purpose, grungy 'subcultural establishment' that's simultaneously a bar, cafe, alternative nightclub, live-music venue, cinema, specialist Estonian CD store and, just quietly, the hippest place in Tartu.

Möku (Rüütli 18; ⊗6pm-3am; 🛜) A popular student hangout, this tiny cellar bar spills out onto the pedestrian-only street on summer nights.

Zavood (Lai 30; ⊗7pm-5am) This battered cellar bar attracts an alternative, down-to-earth crowd with its inexpensive drinks and lack of attitude. Student bands sometimes play here.

Old Town

Raekoja plats SQUARE
Tartu's main square is lined with grand buildings and echoes with the chink of glasses and plates in summer. The centrepiece is the late-18th-century **Town Hall**, topped by a tower and weather vane, and fronted by a statue of students kissing under a spouting umbrella.

Tartu Art Museum GALLERY
(Tartu Kunstimuuseum; www.tartmus.ee; Raekoja plats 18; adult/student €3/2; ⊗11am-6pm Wed & Fri-Sun, to 9pm Thu) If you're leaving one of the plaza's pubs and you're not sure whether you're seeing straight, don't use this building as your guide. Foundations laid partially over an old town wall have given a pronounced lean to this, the former home of Colonel Barclay de Tolly (1761–1818) – an exiled Scot who distinguished himself in the Russian army. It now contains an engrossing gallery spread over three levels, the lowest of which is given over to temporary exhibitions.

Tartu University UNIVERSITY
(Tartu Ülikool; www.ut.ee; Ülikooli 18) Fronted by six Doric columns, the impressive main building of the university was built between 1803 and 1809. The university itself was founded in 1632 by the Swedish king Gustaf II Adolf (Gustavus Adolphus) to train Lutheran clergy and government officials. It was modelled on Uppsala University in Sweden.

University Art Museum MUSEUM
(Ülikooli Kunstimuuseum; www.kunstimuuseum. ut.ee; Ülikooli 18; adult/child €3/2; ⊗10am-6pm Mon-Sat May-Sep, 11am-5pm Mon-Fri Oct-Apr) Within the main university building, this collection comprises mainly plaster casts of ancient Greek sculptures made in the 1860s and 1870s, along with an Egyptian mummy. The rest of the collection was evacuated to Russia in 1915 and has never returned. Admission includes entry to the graffiti-covered attic **lock-up**, where students were held in solitary confinement for various infractions.

St John's Church CHURCH
(Jaani Kirik; www.jaanikirik.ee; Jaani 5; steeple adult/child €2/1.50; ⊗10am-6pm Tue-Sat) Dating to at least 1323, this imposing red-brick Lutheran church is unique for the rare terracotta sculptures placed in niches around its exterior and interior (look up). It lay in ruins and was left derelict following a Soviet bombing raid in 1944 and wasn't fully restored until 2005. Climb the 135 steps of the 30m steeple for a bird's-eye view of Tartu.

⭐**Toy Museum** MUSEUM
(Mänguasjamuuseum; www.mm.ee; Lutsu 8; adult/child €5/4; ⊗11am-6pm Wed-Sun) A big hit with the under-eight crowd (and you won't see too many adults anxious to leave), this is a great place to while away a few rainy hours. Set in a late 18th-century building, this excellent museum showcases dolls, model trains, rocking horses, toy soldiers and tons of other desirables. It's all geared to be nicely interactive, with exhibits in pull-out drawers and a kids' playroom.

Toomemägi

Rising to the west of the town hall, Toomemägi (Cathedral Hill) is the original reason for Tartu's existence, functioning on and off as a stronghold from around the 5th or 6th century. It's now a tranquil park, with walking paths meandering through the trees and a pretty-as-a-picture **rotunda** which serves as a summertime cafe.

Tartu University Museum MUSEUM
(Tartu Ülikool Muuseum; www.muuseum.ut.ee; Lossi 25; adult/child €4/free; ☉10am-6pm Tue-Sun May-Sep, 11am-5pm Wed-Sun Oct-Apr) Atop Toomemägi are the ruins of a Gothic cathedral, originally built by German knights in the 13th century. It was substantially rebuilt in the 15th century, despoiled during the Reformation in 1525, used as a barn, and partly rebuilt between 1804 and 1807 to house the university library, which is now a museum. Inside you'll find a reconstructed autopsy chamber and other exhibits chronicling student life.

◉ Other Neighbourhoods

★Science Centre AHHAA MUSEUM
(Teaduskeskus AHHAA; www.ahhaa.ee; Sadama 1; adult/child €12/9; ☉10am-7pm) Head under the dome for a whizz-bang series of interactive exhibits which are liable to bring out the mad scientist in kids and adults alike. Allow at least a couple of hours for button pushing, water squirting and knob twiddling. And you just haven't lived until you've set a tray of magnetised iron filings 'dancing' to Bronski Beat's *Smalltown Boy*. Upstairs there's a nightmarish collection of pickled organs and deformed foetuses courtesy of the university's medical faculty.

KGB Cells Museum MUSEUM
(KGB kongide muuseum; http://linnamuuseum. tartu.ee; Riia mnt 15b (entrance on Pepleri); adult/child €4/2; ☉11am-4pm Tue-Sat) What do you do when a formerly nationalised building is returned to you with cells in the basement and a fearsome reputation? In this case, the family donated the basement to the Tartu City Museum, which created this sombre and highly worthwhile exhibition. Chilling in parts, the displays give a fascinating rundown on deportations, life in the Gulag camps, the Estonian resistance movement and what went on in these former KGB headquarters, known as the 'Grey House'.

**Estonian National
Museum** MUSEUM
(Eesti Rahva Muuseum; www.erm.ee; Kuperjanovi 9; all/permanent collections €4/3; ☉11am-6pm Tue-Sun) Focused on Estonian life and traditions, this sweet little museum's permanent displays are split into four main themes: Everyday Life, Holidays & Festivals, Regional Folk Culture and 'To be an Estonian'. There are ambitious plans afoot to create a massive new home for the museum at Raadi Manor on the outskirts of town by October 2016.

🛏 Sleeping

Terviseks HOSTEL €
(☎5655382; www.terviseksbbb.com; top floor, Raekoja plats 10; dm €15-17, s/d €22/40; @🖘) In a perfect main-square location, this excellent 'backpacker's bed and breakfast' offers dorms (maximum four beds, no bunks), private rooms, a full kitchen and lots of switched-on info about the happening places in town.

★Antonius Hotel HOTEL €€
(☎737 0377; www.hotelantonius.ee; Ülikooli 15; s/d from €79/99; ❉🖘) Sitting plumb opposite the main university building, this first-rate 18-room boutique hotel is loaded with antiques and period features. Breakfast is served in the vaulted cellar and there's a lovely summertime terrace.

Tampere Maja GUESTHOUSE €€
(☎738 6300; www.tamperemaja.ee; Jaani 4; s/d/tr/q from €48/79/99/132; P❉@🖘) With strong links to the Finnish city of Tampere (Tartu's sister city), this cosy guesthouse features six warm, light-filled guest rooms in a range of sizes. Breakfast is included and each room has access to cooking facilities. And it wouldn't be Finnish if it didn't offer an authentic sauna (one to four people €13; open to non-guests).

Hotel Tartu HOTEL €€
(☎731 4300; www.tartuhotell.ee; Soola 3; s/d from €49/68; P❉🖘) In a handy position across from the bus station and Tasku shopping centre, this hotel offers rooms from the Ikea school of decoration – simple but clean and contemporary. A sauna's available for hire (per hour €25).

✖ Eating & Drinking

Crepp FRENCH €
(Rüütli 16; crepes €4.50; ☉11am-11pm) Locals love this place. Its warm, stylish decor belies its bargain-priced crepes (of the sweet or savoury persuasion, with great combos like cherry-choc and almonds). It serves tasty salads, too.

★Antonius EUROPEAN €€
(☎737 0377; www.hotelantonius.ee; Ülikooli 15; mains €18-22; ☉6-11pm) Tartu's most upmarket restaurant is within the romantic, candlelit nooks and crannies of the Antonius

Hotel's vaulted cellar, which predates the 19th-century building above it by several centuries. Expect a concise menu of meaty dishes, prepared from the finest Estonian produce.

Meat Market STEAKHOUSE €€
(☑ 653 3455; www.meatmarket.ee; Küütri 3; mains €13-18; ⊘ noon-midnight Mon-Thu, to 2am Fri & Sat, to 9pm Sun) The name says it all, with dishes ranging from elk carpaccio to nose-to-tail Livonian beef, to smoky Azeri-style *shashlyk* (skewered meat, delivered flaming to the table). The vegie accompaniments are excellent, too. It's open late for cocktails.

La Dolce Vita ITALIAN €€
(☑ 740 7545; www.ladolcevita.ee; Kompanii 10; mains €7-19; ⊘ 11.30am-11pm) Thin-crust pizzas come straight from the wood-burning oven at this cheerful, family-friendly pizzeria. It's the real deal, with a lengthy menu of bruschetta, pizza, pasta, grills etc and classic casual decor (checked tablecloths, Fellini posters – tick).

Püssirohukelder PUB
(Lossi 28; mains €8-17; ⊘ noon-2am Mon-Sat, to midnight Sun) Set in a cavernous 18th-century gunpowder cellar built into the Toomemägi hillside, this boisterous pub serves beer-accompanying snacks and meaty meals under a soaring 10m-high vaulted ceiling. There's regular live music and a large beer garden out front.

ℹ Information

Tartu Tourist Information Centre (☑ 744 2111; www.visittartu.com; Town Hall, Raekoja plats; ⊘ 9am-6pm Jun-Aug, 9am-5pm Mon-Fri, 10am-2pm Sat & Sun Sep-May) Stocks local maps and brochures, books accommodation and tour guides, and has free internet access.

ℹ Getting There & Away

BUS
From the **bus station** (☑ 12550; Turu 2 (enter from Soola)), buses run to and from Tallinn (€11, 2½ hours, at least hourly), Rakvere (€8, 2½ hours, seven daily) and Pärnu (€11, 2¾ hours, at least hourly).

TRAIN
Tartu's beautifully restored **train station** (☑ 385 7123; www.elron.ee; Vaksali 6) is 1.5km southwest of the old town (at the end of Kuperjanovi street). Eight trains a day make the journey to and from Tallinn (€10, two hours).

PÄRNU

POP 40,000

Local families, young party-goers and German, Swedish and Finnish holidaymakers join together in a collective prayer for sunny weather while strolling the golden-sand beaches, sprawling parks and picturesque historic centre of Pärnu (*pair*-nu), Estonia's premier seaside resort.

The main thoroughfare of the old town is Rüütli, lined with splendid buildings dating back to the 17th century.

⊙ Sights

★ **Pärnu Beach** BEACH
Pärnu's long, wide, golden-sand beach – sprinkled with volleyball courts, cafes and tiny changing cubicles – is easily the city's main drawcard. A curving path stretches along the sand, lined with fountains, park benches and an excellent playground. Early-20th-century buildings are strung along Ranna pst, the avenue that runs parallel to the beach. Across the road, the formal gardens of **Rannapark** are ideal for a summertime picnic.

Tallinn Gate GATE
(Tallinna Värav) The typical star shape of the 17th-century Swedish ramparts that surrounded the old town can easily be spotted on a colour map, as most of the pointy bits are now parks. The only intact section, complete with its moat, lies to the west of the centre. Where the rampart meets the western end of Kuninga, it's pierced by this tunnel-like gate that once defended the main road (it headed to the river-ferry crossing and on to Tallinn).

🏃 Activities

Tervise Paradiis Veekeskus SWIMMING, SPA
(www.terviseparadiis.ee; Side 14; adult/child 3hr €12/8, day €19/15; ⊘ 6.30am-10pm) At the far end of the beach, Estonia's largest water park beckons with pools, slides, tubes and other slippery fun. It's a big family-focused draw, especially when bad weather ruins beach plans. It's part of a huge resort complex. Also here are spa treatments, fitness classes and ten-pin bowling.

Hedon Spa DAY SPA
(☑ 449 9011; www.hedonspa.com; Ranna pst 1; ⊘ 9am-7pm Mon-Sat, to 2pm Sun) Built in 1927 to house Pärnu's famous mud baths, this

handsome neoclassical building has recently been fully restored and opened as a day spa. All manner of pampering treatments are offered, minus the mud.

🛏 Sleeping

In summer it's worth booking ahead; outside high season you should be able to snare a good deal (rates can be up to 50% lower).

Embrace
B&B, APARTMENTS €€

(☑58873404; www.embrace.ee; Pardi 30; r from €86; P ❄ ☎) Snuggle up in an old wooden house in a suburban street, close to the beach and water park. Rooms strike a nice balance between antique and contemporary, and there's a set of four modern self-contained apartments in a neighbouring annex.

Villa Johanna
GUESTHOUSE €€

(☑443 8370; www.villa-johanna.ee; Suvituse 6; s/d/ste €50/80/100; P ☎) Decorated with hanging flowerpots and planter boxes, this pretty place offers comfy pine-lined rooms on a quiet street near the beach. Some rooms have their own balconies. Not much English is spoken.

Villa Ammende
HOTEL €€€

(☑447 3888; www.ammende.ee; Mere pst 7; s/d from €165/220; P ☎) Luxury abounds in this refurbished 1904 art nouveau mansion, which lords it over handsomely manicured grounds. The gorgeous exterior – looking like one of the cooler Paris metro stops writ large – is matched by an elegant lobby and individually antique-furnished rooms. Rooms in the gardener's house are more affordable but lack a little of the wow factor.

✗ Eating

Piccadilly
CAFE €

(Pühavaimu 15; mains €4-7; ☺10am-6pm Sun, to 8pm Mon-Thu, to midnight Fri & Sat) Piccadilly offers a down-tempo haven for wine-lovers and an extensive range of coffee, tea and hot choc. Savoury options include delicious salads, sandwiches and omelettes, but really it's all about the sweeties, including moreish cheesecake and handmade chocolates.

★Supelsaksad
CAFE €€

(☑442 2448; www.supelsaksad.ee; Nikolai 32; mains €9-13; ☺8am-9pm Sun & Tue-Thu, 9am-11pm Fri & Sat) Looking like it was designed by Barbara Cartland on acid (bright pink and a riot of stripes and prints), this fabulous cafe serves an appealing mix of salads, pastas and meaty mains. If you eat all your vegies, make a beeline for the bountiful cake display.

Trahter Postipoiss
RUSSIAN €€

(☑446 4864; www.trahterpostipoiss.ee; Vee 12; mains €14-22; ☺noon-11pm Sun-Thu, to 2am Fri & Sat) Housed in an 1834 postal building, this rustic tavern has excellent Russian cuisine (ranging from the simple to sophisticated), a convivial crowd and imperial portraits watching over the proceedings. The spacious courtyard opens during summer and there's live music on weekends.

Mahedik
CAFE €€

(☑442 5393; www.mahedik.ee; Pühavaimu 20; breakfast €4-6, mains €7-15; ☺9am-7pm Sun-Thu, 10am-11pm Fri & Sat) The name roughly translates as 'organic-ish', and local, seasonal fare is the focus of this cosy all-day cafe. There are cooked breakfasts, locally caught fish and a divine array of cakes.

🍷 Drinking & Nightlife

Sweet Rosie
PUB

(Munga 2; ☺11am-midnight Sun-Thu, to 2am Fri & Sat) Revellers jam into the warm, darkwood interior of this fun Irish pub for a huge beer menu, pub grub, occasional live music and a raucous good time.

Puhvet A.P.T.E.K.
BAR

(www.aptek.ee; Rüütli 40; ☺noon-midnight Sun-Thu, to 3am Fri & Sat) Drop by the old 1930s pharmacy to admire the clever restoration that has turned it into a smooth late-night haunt. Fabulous decor (including original cabinets, vials and bottles) compete for your attention with cocktails and DJs.

Club Sunset
CLUB

(www.sunset.ee; Ranna pst 3; ☺11pm-6am Fri & Sat Jun-Aug) Pärnu's biggest and most famous summertime nightclub has an outdoor beach terrace and a sleek multifloor interior with plenty of nooks for when the dance floor gets crowded. Imported DJs and bands keep things cranked until the early hours.

ℹ Information

Pärnu Tourist Information Centre (☑447 3000; www.visitparnu.com; Uus 4; ☺9am-6pm daily Jun-Aug, 9am-5pm Mon-Fri & 10am-2pm Sat & Sun Sep-May) A very helpful centre stocking maps and brochures, and booking accommodation and rental cars for a small fee. There's a small gallery attached.

ⓘ Getting There & Away

Pärnu's **bus station** (Ringi 3) is right in the centre of town, with services to/from Tallinn (from €6.50, two hours, at least hourly), Rakvere (from €8.50, 2½ hours, three daily) and Tartu (€11, 2¾ hours, at least hourly).

SURVIVAL GUIDE

ⓘ Directory A–Z

ACCOMMODATION

In the budget category you'll find hostels, basic guesthouses (many with shared bathrooms) and camping grounds (generally open from mid-May to September). A dorm bed usually costs €12 to €15, and is usually a couple of euro more expensive on the weekends. Midrange options include family-run guesthouses and hotel rooms (private bathroom and breakfast generally included). At the top end there are spa resorts, historic hotels and modern tower blocks catering to the business set.

During the peak tourist season (June to August) you should try to book well in advance, particularly if you're looking for a bed in Tallinn on the weekend. There's a search engine at www.visitestonia.com for all types of accommodation.

GAY & LESBIAN TRAVELLERS

Today's Estonia is a fairly tolerant and safe home to its gay and lesbian citizens, but only Tallinn has any gay venues. Homosexuality was decriminalised in 1992 and since 2001 there has been an equal age of consent for everyone (14 years). In 2014 Estonia became the first former Soviet republic to pass a law recognising same-sex registered partnerships, coming into effect in 2016.

PUBLIC HOLIDAYS

New Year's Day 1 January
Independence Day 24 February
Good Friday March/April
Easter Sunday March/April
May Day 1 May
Pentecost Seventh Sunday after Easter; May/June

SLEEPING PRICE RANGES

The following price ranges refer to a high-season double room:

€ less than €50
€€ €50 to €140
€€€ more than €140

COUNTRY FACTS

Area 45,226 sq km
Capital Tallinn
Country Code ☑ 372
Currency Euro (€)
Emergency Ambulance & fire ☑ 112, police ☑ 110
Language Estonian
Money ATMs are all over
Visas Not required for citizens of the EU, USA, Canada, New Zealand and Australia

Victory Day (1919; Battle of Võnnu) 23 June
Jaanipäev (St John's Day; Midsummer's Day) 24 June
Day of Restoration of Independence 20 August
Christmas Eve 24 December
Christmas Day 25 December
Boxing Day 26 December

TELEPHONE

There are no area codes in Estonia. All landline numbers have seven digits; mobile numbers have seven or eight digits, beginning with ☑ 5.

TOURIST INFORMATION

Most major destinations have tourist offices. The national tourist board has an excellent website (www.visitestonia.com).

VISAS

EU citizens can spend unlimited time in Estonia, while citizens of Australia, Canada, Japan, New Zealand, the USA and many other countries can enter visa-free for a maximum 90-day stay over a six-month period. Travellers holding a Schengen visa do not need an additional Estonian visa. For information, see the website of the **Estonian Ministry of Foreign Affairs** (www.vm.ee).

ⓘ Getting There & Away

AIR

Fourteen European airlines fly in to Tallinn Airport, including the national carrier **Estonian Air** (www.estonian-air.ee). There are also direct flights from Helsinki to Tartu Airport.

LAND
Bus

Ecolines (☑ 606 2217; www.ecolines.net) Seven daily buses on the Rīga–Parnu–Tallinn route (€17, four to 4¾ hours) and two on the Rīga–Tartu route (€7, four hours).

EATING PRICE RANGES

These price ranges indicate the average cost of a main course. It's common to tip up to 10% for good service.

€ less than €10

€€ €10 to €20

€€€ more than €20

Lux Express & Simple Express (☑680 0909; www.luxexpress.eu) Eleven daily buses between Tallinn and Rīga, some of which stop in Pärnu; two continue on to Vilnius. Also nine daily buses between Tallinn and St Petersburg, and four daily buses on the St Petersburg–Tartu–Rīga route.

Train

Go Rail (☑ in Estonia 631 0044; www.gorail. ee) has two daily trains between Tallinn and St Petersburg (€34, 6½ hours) and an overnight between Tallinn and Moscow (from €86, 15¼ hours). There are no direct trains to Latvia; you'll need to change at Valga.

SEA

Eckerö Line (www.eckeroline.fi; Passenger Terminal A, Varasadam; adult/child/car from €19/15/19) Twice-daily car ferry from Helsinki to Tallinn (2½ hours).

Linda Line (☑ 699 9333; www.lindaliini.ee; Linnahall Terminal) Small, passenger-only

hydrofoils travel between Helsinki and Tallinn at least two times daily from late March to late December (from €25, 1½ hours). Weather dependent.

Tallink (☑ 640 9808; www.tallink.com; Terminal D, Lootsi 13) Four to seven car ferries daily between Helsinki and Tallinn (passenger/vehicle from €31/26). The huge *Baltic Princess* takes 3½ hours; newer high-speed ferries take two hours. They also have an overnight ferry between Stockholm and Tallinn, via the Åland islands (passenger/vehicle from €39/62, 18 hours).

Viking Line (☑ 666 3966; www.vikingline.com; Terminal A, Varasadam; passenger/vehicle from €29/26) Two daily car ferries between Helsinki and Tallinn (2½ hours).

ⓘ Getting Around

BUS

Buses are a good option domestically, as they're more frequent than trains and cover many destinations not serviced by the limited rail network. **TPilet** (www.tpilet.ee) has schedules and prices for all services.

TRAIN

Trains are handy for getting between Tallinn and Tartu, but services to Pärnu are extremely limited.

ESSENTIAL FOOD & DRINK

Estonian gastronomy mixes Nordic, Russian and German influences, and prizes local and seasonal produce.

➡ **Pork and potatoes** The traditional stodgy standbys, prepared a hundred different ways.

➡ **Other favourites** Include black bread, sauerkraut, black pudding, smoked meat and fish, creamy salted butter and sour cream, which is served with almost everything.

➡ **Desserts** On the sweet side, you'll find delicious chocolates, marzipan and cakes.

➡ **Seasonal** In summer, berries enter the menu in both sweet and savoury dishes, while everyone goes crazy for forest mushrooms in the autumn.

➡ **Favourite drinks** Õlu (beer) is the favourite alcoholic drink. Popular brands include Saku and A Le Coq, and aficionados should seek out the product of the local microbreweries such as Tallinn's Põhjala. Other tipples include vodka (Viru Valge and Saremaa are the best-known local brands) and Vana Tallinn, a syrupy sweet liqueur, also available in a cream version.

Hungary

Best Places to Eat

➜ Jókai Bisztró (p194)

➜ Erhardt (p189)

➜ Kisbuda Gyöngye (p184)

➜ Fő Tér (p197)

Best Places to Stay

➜ Hotel Palazzo Zichy (p184)

➜ Club Hotel Füred (p191)

➜ Bacchus (p192)

➜ Hotel Senator-Ház (p197)

Why Go?

Hungary is just the place to kick off a European adventure. Lying virtually in the centre of the continent, this land of Franz Liszt and Béla Bartók, paprika-lashed dishes, superb wines and the romantic Danube River continues to enchant visitors. The allure of Budapest, once an imperial city, is immediate at first sight, and it also boasts the hottest nightlife in the region. Other cities, too, like Pécs, the warm heart of the south, and Eger, the wine capital of the north, have much to offer travellers, as does the sprawling countryside, particularly the Great Plain, where cowboys ride and cattle roam. And where else can you laze about in an open-air thermal spa while snow patches glisten around you? That's at Hévíz at the western edge of Lake Balaton, continental Europe's largest lake and Hungary's 'inland sea', which offers innumerable opportunities for rest and recreation. In Hungary you'll find all the excitement and fun of Western Europe – at half the cost.

When to Go
Budapest

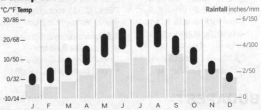

May Spring is in full swing, meaning reliable weather, cool temperatures and flowers.

Jul & Aug Sunny but often very hot; decamp to the hills or Lake Balaton (book ahead).

Sep & Oct Blue skies, mild temperatures and grape harvests – perhaps the best time to visit.

Hungary Highlights

1 Lose yourself in Europe's best nightlife – the 'ruin pubs' and 'garden clubs' of **Budapest**.

2 Learn about the bravery of **Eger** (p196) when it was under Turkish attack, and sample the region's famed Bull's Blood wine.

3 Watch cowboys ride at Bugac in **Kiskunság**

National Park (p195), the heart of the Great Plain.

4 Absorb the Mediterranean-like climate and historic architecture of **Pécs** (p193), including its iconic Mosque Church.

5 Take a pleasure cruise across **Lake Balaton** (p190), Central Europe's largest body of fresh water.

6 Ease your aching muscles in the warm waters of the thermal lake in **Hévíz** (p193).

7 Mill about with artists, freethinkers and day trippers at the too-cute-for-words town of **Szentendre** (p188).

BUDAPEST

✔1 / POP 1.75 MILLION

There's no other city in Hungary like Budapest. Home to almost 20% of the national population, Hungary's capital (*főváros*; 'main city') is the nation's administrative, business and cultural centre.

But it's the beauty of Budapest – both natural and man-made – that makes it unique. Straddling a gentle curve in the Danube, the city is flanked by the Buda Hills on the west bank and the beginnings of the Great Plain to the east. Architecturally it is a gem, with enough baroque, neoclassical and art nouveau elements to satisfy everyone.

In recent years Budapest has taken on the role of the region's party town. 'Pop-up' pubs and, in the warmer months, outdoor clubs are crammed with partygoers till the wee hours.

◉ Sights & Activities

◉ Buda

Castle Hill (Várhegy) is Budapest's biggest tourist draw and a first port of call for any visit to the city. Here, you'll find most of Budapest's remaining medieval buildings, the Royal Palace and sweeping views of Pest across the river.

You can walk to Castle Hill up the **Király lépcső**, the 'Royal Steps' that lead northwest off Clark Ádám tér, or else take the **Sikló** (Map p180; www.bkv.hu/en/siklojegy/ siklojegyek; I Szent György tér; one way/return adult 1100/1700Ft, child 650/1100Ft; ⊘7.30am-10pm, closed 1st & 3rd Mon of month; 🚌16, 🚌19, 41), a funicular railway built in 1870 that ascends from Clark Ádám tér to Szent György tér near the Royal Palace.

★ Royal Palace   PALACE
(Királyi Palota; Map p180; I Szent György tér; 🚌16, 16A, 116) The massive former royal seat, razed and rebuilt at least a half-dozen times over the past seven centuries, occupies the southern end of Castle Hill. Here you'll find two important museums: the **Hungarian National Gallery** (Nemzeti Galéria; Map p180; ☑1-201 9082; www.mng.hu; I Szent György tér 2, Bldgs A-D; adult/concession 1400/700Ft, audio guide 800Ft; ⊘10am-6pm Tue-Sun; 🚌16, 16A, 116), which traces Hungarian art from the 11th century to the present day, and the **Castle Museum** (Vármúzeum; Map p180; ☑1-487 8800; www.btm.hu; I Szent György tér 2, Bldg E; adult/ concession 1800/900Ft; ⊘10am-6pm Tue-Sun Feb-Oct, to 4pm Nov-Mar; 🚌16, 16A, 116, 🚌19, 41), which looks at 2000 years of the city's life.

★ Matthias Church   CHURCH
(Mátyás templom; Map p180; ☑1-355 5657; www. matyas-templom.hu; I Szentháromság tér 2; adult/ concession 1200/800Ft; ⊘9am-5pm Mon-Sat, 1-5pm Sun; 🚌16, 16A, 116) The pointed spire and the colourful tiled roof make neo-Gothic Matthias Church (so named because good King Matthias Corvinus held both his weddings here) a Castle Hill landmark. Parts date back some 500 years, notably the carvings above the southern entrance, but the rest of it was designed by the architect Frigyes Schulek in 1896.

★ Fishermen's Bastion   MONUMENT
(Halászbástya; Map p180; I Szentháromság tér; adult/concession 700/500Ft; ⊘9am-11pm mid-Mar–mid-Oct; 🚌16, 16A, 116) The bastion is a neo-Gothic folly built as a viewing platform in 1905. Its name comes from the medieval guild of fishermen responsible for defending this stretch of the castle wall.

Citadella   FORT
(Map p180; www.citadella.hu; 🚌27) **FREE** Built by the Habsburgs after the 1848–49 War of Independence to defend the city from further insurrection, the Citadella was obsolete by the time it was ready in 1851 and never saw battle. It is currently closed to the public.

HUNGARY BUDAPEST

ITINERARIES

One Week
Spend at least three days in **Budapest**, checking out the sights, museums, cafes and *kertek* (garden clubs). On your fourth day take a day trip to a Danube Bend town such as **Szentendre** or **Esztergom**. Day five can be spent getting a morning train to **Pécs** to see its lovely Turkish remains and to check out the many museums and galleries in town. If you've still got the travel bug, on day six head for **Eger**, a baroque town set in red-wine country. On your last day recuperate in one of Budapest's wonderful thermal baths.

Two Weeks
In summer make sure you spend some time exploring the towns and grassy beaches around **Lake Balaton**. **Tihany** is a rambling hillside village set on a protected peninsula, **Keszthely** is an old town with a great palace in addition to beaches, and **Hévíz** has a thermal lake. Try to see something of the **Great Plain** as well – **Szeged** is a splendid university town on the Tisza River, and **Kecskemét** a centre of Art Nouveau. Finish your trip in **Tokaj**, home of Hungary's famous sweet wine.

Buda

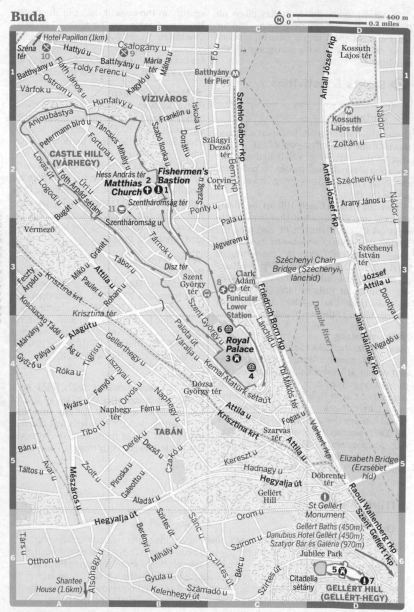

Map scale: N, 0 — 400 m / 0 — 0.2 miles

Liberty Monument

MONUMENT

(Szabadság szobor; Map p180; ☐27) The Liberty Monument, the lovely lady with the palm frond proclaiming freedom throughout the city from atop Gellért Hill, is to the east of the Citadella. Some 14m high, she was raised in 1947 in tribute to the Soviet soldiers who died liberating Budapest in 1945.

Memento Park

HISTORIC SITE

(☑1-424 7500; www.mementopark.hu; XXII Balatoni út 16; adult/student 1500/1000Ft; ⊙10am-dusk;

Buda

🚌150) Home to some 40 statues, busts and plaques of Lenin, Marx and 'heroic' workers like those that have ended up on trash heaps in other former socialist countries, Memento Park, 10km southwest of the city centre, is a mind-blowing place to visit. A direct bus (with park admission adult/child return 4900/3500Ft) departs from in front of the Le Meridien Budapest Hotel on Deák Ferenc tér at 11am year-round with an extra departure at 3pm in July and August.

★ **Gellért Baths**   BATHHOUSE
(Gellért Gyógyfürdő; 🚌1-466 6166; www.gellert bath.hu; XI Kelenhegyi út 4, Danubius Hotel Gellért; weekdays/weekends incl locker 4900/5100Ft, cabin 5300/5500Ft; ⊙6am-8pm; 🚋7, 86, Ⓜ M4 Szent Gellért tér, 🚋18, 19, 47, 49) Soaking in the art nouveau Gellért Baths, open to both men and women daily in mixed sections, has been likened to taking a bath in a cathedral. The eight thermal pools range in temperature from 26°C to 38°C.

◎ Margaret Island

Margaret Island   ISLAND
(Margit-sziget; 🚌26) FREE Neither Buda nor Pest, 2.5km-long Margaret Island in the middle of the Danube was the domain of one religious order or another in the Middle Ages and became a public park in the mid-19th century. The island's gardens and shaded walkways are lovely places to stroll or cycle around.

◎ Pest

★ **Parliament**   HISTORIC BUILDING
(Országház; Map p182; 🚌1-441 4904; www.parlament.hu; V Kossuth Lajos tér 1-3; adult/student & EU citizen 4000/2000Ft; ⊙8am-6pm Mon-Fri, to 4pm Sat & Sun Apr-Oct, 8am-4pm daily Nov-Mar; Ⓜ M2 Kossuth Lajos tér) You can visit a handful of the 691 sumptuously decorated rooms of the enormous riverfront Parliament (1902) on a guided tour and view the **Crown of St Stephen**, the nation's most important national icon.

★ **Great Synagogue**   SYNAGOGUE
(Nagy zsinagóga; Map p182; www.dohanystreet synagogue.hu; VII Dohány utca 2; adult/student & child incl museum 2850/2000Ft; ⊙10am-6pm Sun-Thu, to 4.30pm Fri Apr-Oct, reduced hours Nov-Mar; Ⓜ M2 Astoria) Budapest's stunning Great Synagogue (1859) is the largest Jewish house of worship in Europe. Inside, the **Hungarian Jewish Museum** (Magyar Zsidó Múzeum; Map p182; 🚌1-343 6756; www.zsidomuzeum.hu; VII Dohány utca 2; incl in admission to Great Synagogue, call ahead for guided tours; ⊙10am-6pm Sun-Thu, to 4pm Fri Mar-Oct, 10am-4pm Mon-Thu, to 2pm Fri Nov-Feb; Ⓜ M2 Astoria) contains objects relating to religious and every day life, as well as the harrowing **Holocaust Memorial Room**.

Heroes' Square   SQUARE
(Hősök tere; 🚌105, Ⓜ M1 Hősök tere) At the northern end of leafy Andrássy út, this huge public space holds a sprawling monument constructed in 1896 to honour the millennium of the Magyar conquest of the Carpathian Basin.

Museum of Fine Arts   MUSEUM
(Szépművészeti Múzeum; www.mfab.hu; XIV Dózsa György út 41; adult/concession 1800/900Ft, temporary exhibitions 3200/1600Ft; ⊙10am-6pm Tue-Sun; Ⓜ M1 Hősök tere) On the northern side of Heroes' Square, this gallery houses the nation's outstanding collection of foreign artworks in a building dating to 1906. The Old Masters collection includes seven paintings by El Greco.

City Park   PARK
(Városliget; Ⓜ M1 Hősök tere, M1 Széchenyi fürdő) Pest's green lung, this open space covers almost a square kilometre. It has boating on a small lake in summer and ice-skating there in winter.

Central Pest

N 0 ____ 400 m
0 ____ 0.2 miles

HUNGARY BUDAPEST

Parliament
3

Kossuth
Lajos tér

Nyugati
Train Station

Nyugati pu

TERÉZVÁROS

Heroes' Square (950m);
City Park (1km);
Museum of Fine
Arts (1.2km)

House of Terror
2

LIPÓTVÁROS

Szabadság
tér

Bank u

Arany
János u

ERZSÉBETVÁROS

Opera

Oktogon

Szent
István tér

József Attila u

Széchenyi
Chain Bridge
(Széchenyi
lánchíd)

Eötvös
tér

József
nádor tér

Erzsébet
tér

Deák
Ferenc tér

Danube River

Jane Haining rkp

Vörösmarty
tér

Deák Ferenc u

Vigadó
tér

Vigadó tér
Pier

Petőfi
tér

Great
Synagogue
1

Astoria

JÓZSEFVÁROS

Elizabeth Bridge
(Erzsébet
híd)

Ferenciek
tere

Kossuth Lajos u

Március
15 tér

Szabadsajtó út

Kálvin tér

Mahart
PassNave

International
Ferry Pier

Liberty Bridge
(Szabadság
híd)

Fővám
tér

Csarnok
tér

Central Pest

★ **House of Terror** MUSEUM
(Terror Háza; Map p182; www.terrorhaza.hu; VI Andrássy út 60; adult/concession 2000/1000Ft; ⊙10am-6pm Tue-Sun; Ⓜ M1 Oktogon) The former headquarters of the dreaded secret police now houses an evocative museum that focuses on the crimes and atrocities committed by both Hungary's fascist and communist regimes.

Basilica of St Stephen CHURCH
(Szent István Bazilika; Map p182; ☑06 30 703 6599; www.basilica.hu; V Szent István tér; requested donation 200Ft; ⊙9am-5pm Apr-Sep, 10am-4pm Oct-Mar; Ⓜ M2 Arany János utca) You can climb up to the dome at Budapest's colossal neoclassical cathedral (1905). The chapel to the left of the main altar contains the **Holy Right**, the mummified right hand of King St Stephen.

Hungarian National Museum MUSEUM
(Magyar Nemzeti Múzeum; Map p182; www.hnm.hu; VIII Múzeum körút 14-16; adult/concession 1600/800Ft; ⊙10am-6pm Tue-Sun; ☐47, 49, Ⓜ M3/4 Kálvin tér) The Hungarian National Museum houses the nation's most important collection of historical relics – from Roman finds to coronation regalia – in an impressive neoclassical building (1847).

Széchenyi Baths BATHHOUSE
(Széchenyi Gyógyfürdő; ☑1-363 3210; www.szechenyibath.hu; XIV Állatkerti körút 9-11; ticket incl locker/cabin Mon-Fri 4500/5000Ft, Sat & Sun 4700/5200Ft; ⊙6am-10pm; Ⓜ M1 Széchenyi fürdő) At the northern end of City Park, the immense Széchenyi Baths, open to both men and women at all times in mixed areas, counts 15 indoor and three outdoor thermal pools.

★☆ Festivals & Events

Budapest
Spring Festival PERFORMING ARTS
(www.springfestival.hu) The capital's largest and most important cultural festival; in late March/early April.

Sziget Festival MUSIC
(http://szigetfestival.com) One of Europe's biggest music festivals, held in mid-August on Budapest's Óbuda Island.

Formula One Hungarian Grand Prix CAR RACING
(www.hungaroring.hu) Hungary's prime sporting event, held in late July/early August in Magyoród, 24km northeast of Budapest.

🛏 Sleeping

🛏 Buda

Shantee House HOSTEL €
(☑1-385 8946; www.backpackbudapest.hu; XI Takács Menyhért utca 33; beds in yurt €10, dm large/small €13/16, d €38; ℗@⊕; ☐7, 7A, ☐19, 49) Budapest's first hostel has added two floors to its colourfully painted suburban 'villa' in south Buda. It's all good and the fun (and sleeping bodies in high season) still spills out into a lovely landscaped garden, with hammocks, yurt and gazebo. Two of the five doubles have private bathrooms.

Hotel Papillon HOTEL €€
(☑1-212 4750; www.hotelpapillon.hu; II Rózsahegy utca 3/b; s/d/tr €44/54/69, apt €78-90; P✱@🛜🏊; 🛗4, 6) One of Buda's best-kept accommodation secrets, this cosy hotel in Rózsadomb (Rose Hill) has a delightful back garden with a small swimming pool, and some of the 20 rooms have balconies. There are also four apartments available in the same building, one with a lovely roof terrace.

Danubius Hotel Gellért LUXURY HOTEL €€€
(☑1-889 5500; www.danubiusgroup.com/gellert; XI Szent Gellért tér 1; s/d/ste from €85/170/268; P✱@🛜🏊; Ⓜ M4 Szent Gellért tér, 🛗18, 19, 47, 49) Buda's *grande dame* is a 234-room art nouveau hotel completed in 1918. Prices depend on which way your room faces and what sort of bathroom it has. Use of the thermal baths is free for hotel guests.

🛏 Pest

Aventura Boutique Hostel HOSTEL €
(Map p182; ☑1-239 0782; www.aventurahostel. com; XIII Visegrádi utca 12; dm €9-19, d €29-56, apt €38-66; @🛜; Ⓜ M3 Nyugati pályaudvar, 🛗4, 6) This very chilled hostel has four themed rooms (India, Africa, Japan and – our favourite – Space). We love the colours and fabrics, the in-house massage, and the dorms with loft sleeping for four to eight.

KM Saga Guest Residence GUESTHOUSE €
(Map p182; ☑1-217 1934; www.km-saga.hu; IX Lónyay utca 17, 3rd fl; s €30-40, d €35-55; ✱@🛜; Ⓜ M4 Fővám tér) This unique place has five themed rooms, an eclectic mix of 19th-century furnishings, and hospitable, multilingual Hungarian-American owner Shandor. Two rooms share a bathroom.

Gerlóczy Rooms deLux BOUTIQUE HOTEL €€
(Map p182; ☑1-501 4000; www.gerloczy.hu; V Gerlóczy utca 1; r €80-95; ✱🛜; Ⓜ M2 Astoria) A stand-out choice, Gerlóczy hits the mark with an excellent combination of good value, decor, atmosphere and professional service. Set over four floors of an 1890s building on an attractive square, the individually designed and well-proportioned rooms all have king-size beds. The winding wrought-iron staircase, domed stained-glass skylight and etched glass are wonderful touches.

★Hotel Palazzo Zichy HISTORIC HOTEL €€€
(Map p182; ☑1-235 4000; www.hotel-palazzo-zichy.hu; VII Lőrinc pap tér 2; r/ste from €125/150; P●✱@🛜; Ⓜ M3 Corvin-negyed, M3/4 Kálvin tér, 🛗4, 6) Once the sumptuous

19th-century residence of an aristocratic family, the 'palace' has been transformed into a lovely hotel, with its original features, such as wrought-iron bannisters, blending seamlessly with the ultra-modern decor. The 80 rooms, all charcoals and creams, are enlivened by red glass–topped desks, the showers are terrific, and there's a sauna and fitness room in the cellar crypt.

🍴 Eating

🍴 Buda

Nagyi Palacsintázója HUNGARIAN €
(Granny's Crepe Place; Map p180; www.nagyipali. hu; I Hattyú utca 16; pancakes 190-680Ft, set menus 1090-1190Ft; ⊗24hr; ☑; Ⓜ M2 Széll Kálmán tér) This small eatery serves Hungarian pancakes – both savoury and sweet – round the clock and is always packed.

★Kisbuda Gyöngye HUNGARIAN €€
(☑1-368 6402; www.remiz.hu; III Kenyeres utca 34; mains 2780-4980Ft; ⊗noon-3pm & 7-10pm Tue-Sat; 🛗160, 260, 🛗17) Operating since the 1970s, this traditional yet very elegant Hungarian restaurant has an antique-cluttered dining room and attentive service, and manages to create a *fin-de-siècle* atmosphere. Try the excellent goose liver speciality plate with a glass of Tokaj (3980Ft), or a less complicated dish like roast duck with apples (2980Ft).

Csalogány 26 INTERNATIONAL €€€
(Map p180; ☑1-201 7892; www.csalogany26.hu; I Csalogány utca 26; mains 3600-5000Ft; ⊗noon-3pm & 7-10pm Tue-Sat; 🛗11, 39) This intimate restaurant with the unimaginative name and spartan decor turns its attention to its superb food. Try the suckling *mangalica* (a special type of Hungarian pork) with Savoy cabbage (4500Ft) or the free-range pullet with polenta (3800Ft). A three-course set lunch is a budget-pleasing 2500Ft.

🍴 Pest

The **Nagycsarnok** (Great Market; Map p182; www.piaconline.hu; IX Vámház körút 1-3; ⊗6am-5pm Mon-Fri, to 3pm Sat; Ⓜ M4 Fővám tér) is a vast historic market built of steel and glass. Head here for fruit, vegetables, deli items, fish and meat.

Kádár HUNGARIAN €
(Map p182; ☑1-321 3622; X Klauzál tér 9; mains 1250-2500Ft; ⊗11.30am-3.30pm Tue-Sat; 🛗4, 6)

Located in the heart of the Jewish district, Kádár is Budapest's most authentic *étkezde* (canteen serving simple Hungarian dishes) and attracts the hungry with its ever-changing menu.

Govinda
VEGETARIAN €
(Map p182; ☑1-473 1310; www.govinda.hu; V Vigyázó Ferenc utca 4; dishes 190-990Ft; ☺11.30am-9pm Mon-Fri, from noon Sat; ☑; ☐15, ☑2) This basement restaurant serves wholesome salads, soups and desserts as well as daily set-menu plates for 990/1890/2990Ft for one/two/three courses.

Da Mario
ITALIAN €€
(Map p182; ☑1-301 0967; www.damario.hu; V Vécsey utca 3; mains 2000-5500Ft; ☺11am-midnight; ☐15, Ⓜ M2 Kossuth Lajos tér) Owned and operated by three Italian *ragazzi* (lads) from southern Italy, Da Mario can't put a foot wrong in our book. While the cold platters, soups and meat and fish mains all look good, we stick to the house-made pasta dishes (2000Ft to 3500Ft) and pizzas (1250Ft to 3000Ft) from the wood-burning stove.

Pesti Disznó
HUNGARIAN €€
(Map p182; ☑1-951 4061; www.pestidiszno.hu; VI Nagymező utca 19; mains 1490-2890Ft; ☺11am-midnight Sun-Wed, to 1am Thu-Sat; Ⓜ M1 Oktogon) Punters would be forgiven for thinking that the 'Pest Pig' was all about pork. In fact, of the dozen main courses half are poultry, fish or vegetarian. It's a wonderful space, loft-like almost, with high tables and charming, informed service. Excellent wine list.

Borkonyha
HUNGARIAN €€€
(Wine Kitchen; Map p182; ☑1-266 0835; www.borkonyha.hu; V Sas utca 3; mains 3750-7150Ft; ☺noon-midnight Mon-Sat; ☐15, Ⓜ M1 Bajcsy-Zsilinszky út) One of four restaurants in Budapest with a Michelin star well and truly deserves the honour. Go for the signature foie gras appetiser wrapped in strudel pasty and a glass of sweet Tokaj wine. If *mangalica* (a special type of Hungarian pork) is on the menu, try it with a glass of dry Furmint. Warm and knowledgeable service.

🍸 Drinking

🍷 Buda

Ruszwurm Cukrászda
CAFE
(Map p180; ☑1-375 5284; www.ruszwurm.hu; I Szentháromság utca 7; ☺10am-7pm Mon-Fri, to 6pm Sat & Sun; ☐6, 6A, 116) This diminutive

cafe dating from 1827 is the perfect place for coffee and cakes (380Ft to 580Ft) in the Castle District.

Szatyor Bár és Galéria
BAR
(Carrier Bag Bar & Gallery; ☑1-279 0290; www.szatyorbar.com; XIII Bartók Béla út 36-38; ☺noon-1am Mon-Fri, 2pm-1am Sat & Sun; Ⓜ M4 Móricz Zsigmond körtér; ☐18, 19, 47, 49) Sharing the same building as a popular cafe and separated by just a door, the Szatyor is funky, with cocktails, street art on the walls and a Lada driven by the poet Endre Ady.

🍷 Pest

★Instant
CLUB
(Map p182; ☑06 30 830 8747; www.instant.co.hu; VI Nagymező utca 38; ☺4pm-6am Sun-Thu, to 11am Fri & Sat; Ⓜ M1 Opera) We still love this 'ruin bar' on Pest's most vibrant nightlife strip and so do all our friends. It has six bars on three levels with underground DJs and dance parties.

Gerbeaud
CAFE
(Map p182; ☑1-429 9001; www.gerbeaud.hu; V Vörösmarty tér 7; ☺9am-9pm; Ⓜ M1 Vörösmarty tér) Founded on the northern side of Pest's busiest square in 1858, Gerbeaud has been the most fashionable meeting place for the city's elite since the 19th century. And it doesn't come cheap. Cakes start at 1950Ft.

Csendes
CAFE, BAR
(Map p182; www.facebook.com/csendesvintagebar; V Ferenczy István utca 5; ☺10am-2am Mon-Fri, from 2pm Sat, 2pm-midnight Sun; 🛜; Ⓜ M2 Astoria) A quirky cafe just off the Little Ring Rd with junkyard chic decorating the walls and floor space, the 'Quietly' is just that until the regular DJ arrives and cranks up the volume.

★DiVino Borbár
WINE BAR
(Map p182; ☑06 70 935 3980; www.divinoborbar.hu; V Szent István tér 3; ☺4pm-midnight Sun-Wed, to 2am Thu-Sat; Ⓜ M1 Bajcsy-Zsilinszky út) Central and always heaving, DiVino is Budapest's most popular wine bar. Choose from 120 types of wine produced by some 30 winemakers, but be careful: those 0.1L glasses (650Ft to 2800Ft) go down quickly.

Morrison's 2
CLUB
(Map p182; ☑1-374 3329; www.morrisons.hu; V Szent István körút 11; ☺5pm-4am; ☐4, 6) Budapest's largest party venue, this cavernous club attracts a younger crowd with its five dance floors, half-dozen bars (including one

in a covered courtyard and one with table football). Great DJs.

Club AlterEgo
GAY

(Map p182; ☑06 70 345 4302; www.alteregoclub.hu; VI Dessewffy utca 33; ⊙10pm-6am Fri & Sat; ⚊4,6) Still Budapest's premier gay club, with the chicest crowd and the best dance vibe.

☆ Entertainment

Your best source of information in English for what's on citywide is the freebie **Budapest Funzine** (www.budapestfunzine.hu), available at hotels, bars, cinemas and wherever tourists congregate. The **Koncert Kalendárium** website, (www.muzsikalendarium.hu/), has more serious offerings: classical concerts, opera, dance and the like. You can book almost anything online from the following sites:

Jegymester (www.jegymester.hu)

Kulturinfo (www.kulturinfo.hu)

Ticket Express (www.tex.hu)

Performing Arts

Hungarian State Opera House
OPERA

(Magyar Állami Operaház; Map p182; ☑box office 1-353 0170; www.opera.hu; VI Andrássy út 22; ⊙box office 11am-5pm, from 4pm Sun; Ⓜ M1 Opera) Visit the the gorgeous neo-Renaissance opera house as much to admire the incredibly rich decoration inside as to take in a performance and hear the perfect acoustics. The ballet company performs here, too.

Liszt Academy
CLASSICAL MUSIC

(Liszt Zeneakadémia; Map p182; ☑1-321 0690; www.zeneakademia.hu; VI Liszt Ferenc tér 8; ⊙ticket office 11am-6pm; Ⓜ M1 Oktogon) Budapest's recently renovated premier venue for classical concerts is not just a place to hear music but also to ogle at the wonderful decorative Zsolnay porcelain and frescoes.

Aranytíz Cultural Centre
TRADITIONAL MUSIC

(Aranytíz Művelődési Központ; Map p182; ☑1-354 3400; www.aranytiz.hu; V Arany János utca 10; ⊙box office 2-9pm Mon & Wed, 9am-3pm Sat; ⚊15) The Kalamajka Táncház, one of the best folk music and dance shows in town, has programs at this cultural centre from 7pm on Saturday.

🛍 Shopping

★ Ecseri Piac
MARKET

(www.piaconline.hu; XIX Nagykőrösi út 156; ⊙8am-4pm Mon-Fri, 5am-3pm Sat, 8am-1pm Sun; ⚊54, 84E, 89E 94E) This is one of the biggest flea markets in Central Europe, and Saturday is the best day to go. Take bus 54 from Boráros tér in Pest or express bus 84E, 89E or 94E from the Határ út stop on the M3 metro line.

ℹ Information

There are ATMs everywhere, including in the train and bus stations and at the airport. Money-changers (particularly those along Váci utca) are best avoided.

Budapest Card (☑1-438 8080; www.budapestinfo.hu; per 24/48/72hr 4500/7500/8900Ft) Free admission to selected museums, unlimited travel on public transport, two free guided tours, and discounts for organised tours, car rental, thermal baths and selected shops and restaurants. Available at tourist offices but cheaper online.

Budapest Info (Map p182; V Sütő utca 2; ⊙8am-8pm; Ⓜ M1/M2/M3 Deák Ferenc tér) The best single source of information on Budapest.

FirstMed Centers (☑1-224 9090; www.firstmedcenters.com; I Hattyú utca 14, 5th fl; ⊙8am-8pm Mon-Fri, to 2pm Sat, urgent care 24hr; Ⓜ M2 Széll Kálmán tér) Round-the-clock emergency treatment, but expensive.

SOS Dent (☑1-269 6010, 06 30 383 3333; www.sosdent.hu; VI Király utca 14; ⊙8am-9pm) Dental practice.

Teréz Gyógyszertár (☑1-311 4439; VI Teréz körút 41; ⊙8am-8pm Mon-Fri, to 2pm Sat; Ⓜ M3 Nyugati pályaudvar) Central pharmacy.

ℹ Getting There & Away

BOAT

Mahart PassNave (Map p182; ☑1-484 4025; www.mahartpassnave.hu; V Belgrád rakpart; ⊙8am-6pm Mon-Fri; ⚊2) runs hydrofoils to Vienna from June to September, which arrive at and depart from the **International Ferry Pier** (Nemzetközi hajóállomás; Map p182; ☑1-318 1223; V Belgrád rakpart; ⚊2). See p199 for more information.

There are efficient ferry services (p188) to the towns of the Danube Bend.

BUS

Volánbusz (☑1-382 0888; www.volanbusz.hu), the national bus line, has an extensive list of destinations from Budapest. All international buses and some buses to/from western Hungary use **Népliget bus station** (☑1-219 8030; IX Üllői út 131; Ⓜ M3 Népliget). **Stadionok bus station** (☑1-219 8086; XIV Hungária körút 48-52; Ⓜ M2 Stadionok) generally serves places to the east of Budapest. Most buses to the Danube Bend arrive at and leave from the **Árpád Híd bus station** (☑1-412 2597; XIII Árbóc utca 1; Ⓜ M3 Árpád Híd), off XIII Róbert Károly körút, though some leave from the small suburban bus terminal next to **Újpest-Városkapu train station** (XIII Arva utca; Ⓜ M3 Újpest-Városkapu), off Váci út, which is also on the M3 blue metro line. All stations are on metro lines. If the ticket office is closed, you can buy your ticket on the bus.

CAR & MOTORCYCLE

All major international rental firms, including **Avis** (☑1-318 4240; www.avis.hu; V Arany János utca 26-28; ☺7am-6pm Mon-Fri, 8am-2pm Sat & Sun; Ⓜ M3 Arany János utca), **Budget** (☑1-214 0420; www.budget.hu; VII Krisztina körút 41-43, Hotel Mercure Buda; ☺8am-8pm Mon-Fri, to 6pm Sat & Sun) and **Europcar** (☑1-505 4400; www.europcar.hu; V Erzsébet tér 7-8; ☺8am-6pm Mon & Fri, to 4.30pm Tue-Thu, to noon Sat), have offices in the city and at the airport.

TRAIN

Hungarian State Railways (MÁV) runs the country's extensive rail network. Contact the **MÁV-Start passenger service centre** (☑1-512 7921; www.mav-start.hu; V József Attila utca 16; ☺9am-6pm Mon-Fri) for information on domestic train departures and arrivals. Its website has a useful timetable in English for planning routes.

Buy tickets at one of Budapest's three main train stations or the passenger service centre. **Keleti train station** (Eastern Train Station; VIII Kerepesi út 2-4) handles most international trains as well as domestic ones from the north and northeast. For some international destinations (eg Romania), as well as domestic ones to/from the Danube Bend and Great Plain, head for **Nyugati train station** (Western Train Station; VI Nyugati tér). For trains bound for Lake Balaton and the south, go to **Déli train station** (Southern Train Station; I Krisztina körút 37; Ⓜ M2 Déli pályaudvar). All three stations are on metro lines.

ⓘ Getting Around

TO/FROM THE AIRPORT

The cheapest way to get into the city centre from Ferenc Liszt International Airport is to take city bus 200E (350Ft; on the bus 450Ft), which terminates at the Kőbánya-Kispest metro station. From there, take the M3 metro into the city centre.

The **Airport Shuttle Minibusz** (ASM; ☑1-296 8555; www.airportshuttle.hu; one way/return 3200/5500Ft) ferries passengers from the airport directly to their accommodation. Tickets are available at a clearly marked desk in the arrivals hall, though you may have to wait while the van fills up.

Taxi fares to most locations in Pest are 6000Ft and in Buda 7000Ft.

PUBLIC TRANSPORT

Public transport is run by **BKK** (Budapesti Közlekedési Központ; Centre for Budapest Transport; ☑1-258 4636; www.bkk.hu). The three underground metro lines (M1 yellow, M2 red, M3 blue) meet at Deák tér in Pest; the new green M4 links with the M2 at Keleti train station and the M3 at Kálvin tér. The HÉV suburban railway runs north from Batthyány tér in Buda to Szentendre. Travel cards are only good on the HÉV within the city limits (south of the Békásmegyer stop).

There's also an extensive network of buses, trams and trolleybuses. Public transport operates from 4.30am until 11.30pm and some 40 night buses run along main roads. Tram 6 on the Big Ring Road runs round the clock.

A single ticket for all forms of transport is 350Ft (60 minutes of uninterrupted travel on the same metro, bus, trolleybus or tram line *without* transferring/changing); a book of 10 tickets is 3000Ft. A transfer ticket (530Ft) is valid for one trip with one validated transfer/ change within 90 minutes.

The three-day travel card (4150Ft) or the seven-day pass (4950Ft) make things easier, allowing unlimited travel inside the city limits. Keep your ticket or pass handy; the fine for 'riding black' is 8000Ft on the spot, or 16,000Ft if you pay later at the **BKK office** (☑1-461 6800; VII Akácfa utca 22; ☺6am-8pm Mon-Fri, 8am-1.45pm Sat; Ⓜ M2 Blaha Lujza tér).

TAXI

Reliable companies include **Fő Taxi** (☑1-222 2222; www.fotaxi.hu) and **City Taxi** (☑1-211 1111; www.citytaxi.hu). Note that rates are higher at night and early morning.

THE DANUBE BEND

North of Budapest, the Danube breaks through the Pilis and Börzsöny Hills in a sharp bend before continuing along the Slovak border. The Roman Empire had its northern border here and medieval kings ruled Hungary from majestic palaces overlooking the river at Esztergom and Visegrád. Szentendre, once a thriving art colony, is full of museums and galleries.

ⓘ Getting There & Away

BUS & TRAIN

Regular buses serve towns on the west bank of the Danube. Trains reach Szentendre and, on a separate line, Esztergom.

BOAT

The Danube is a perfect highway and regular boats ferry tourists to and from Budapest in the warmer months.

From May to September, a **Mahart PassNave** (☑1-484 4013; www.mahartpassnave.hu; Belgrád rakpart; ⊘8am-4pm Mon-Fri) ferry departs Pest's Vigadó tér at 10am (Buda's Batthány tér at 10.10am) Tuesday to Sunday bound for Szentendre (one way/return 2000/2500Ft, 1½ hours), returning at 5pm. They carry on to Visegrád (one way/return 2000/3000Ft, 3½ hours) in July and August, returning at 3.30pm. There is also an additional departure to Szentendre at 2pm (returning at 8pm) in July and August.

Hydrofoils travel to Visegrád (one way/return 4000/6000Ft, one hour) and Esztergom (one way/return 5000/7500Ft, 1½ hours) at 9.30am on Saturday and Sunday from early May to September. They return at 5pm from Esztergom and 5.30pm from Visegrád.

Szentendre

☑ 26 / POP 25,300

A a popular day-trip destination 19km north of Budapest, pretty little Szentendre (*sen-ten-dreh*) has narrow, winding streets and is a favourite with souvenir shoppers. The charming old centre around Fő tér (Main Square) has plentiful cafes and galleries, and there are a handful of noteworthy Serbian Orthodox churches dating from the time when Christian worshippers fled here to escape the Turkish invaders. The **Tourinform** (☑26-317 965; www.szentendreprogram.hu; Dumtsa Jenő utca 22; ⊘9am-5pm Mon-Fri, 10am-2pm Sat & Sun) office hands out maps and info about the town and region.

Just 5km to the northwest is the enormous **Hungarian Open-Air Ethnographical Museum** (Magyar Szabadtéri Néprajzi Múzeum; ☑26-502 500; www.skanzen.hu; Sztaravodai út; adult/student 1500/750Ft Apr-Oct, 1000/500Ft Nov-Mar; ⊘9am-5pm Tue-Sun Apr-Oct, 10am-4pm Sat & Sun Nov-early Dec & Feb-Mar). Walking through reassembled cottages, farms and workshops from around the country will show you what life was – and sometimes still is – like in rural Hungary. Reach it on bus 230 from bay/stop 7 at the bus station next to the train station.

The most convenient way to get to Szentendre is to take the HÉV suburban train from Buda's Batthyány tér metro station (660Ft, 40 minutes, every 10 to 20 minutes). There are efficient ferry services to Szentendre from Budapest.

Visegrád

☑ 26 / POP 1780

The spectacular vista from what remains of the 13th-century hilltop fortress in Visegrád (*vish*-eh-grahd), on a hilltop above a curve in the Danube, is what pulls visitors to this sleepy town.

After the 13th-century Mongol invasions, Hungarian kings built the mighty **Visegrád Citadel** (Visegrádi Fellegvár; ☑26-598 080; www.parkerdo.hu; Várhegy; adult/child & student 1700/850Ft; ⊘9am-5pm mid-Mar–Apr & Oct, to 6pm May-Sep, to 3pm Nov-Mar). It's a bit of a climb, but the views are well worth it. The **Royal Palace** (Királyi Palota; ☑26-597 010; www.visegradmuzeum.hu; Fő utca 29; adult/concession 1100/550Ft; ⊘9am-5pm Tue-Sun Mar-Oct, 10am-4pm Tue-Sun Nov-Feb) stands on the flood plain at the foot of the hills, closer to the centre of town. Seek information from **Visegrád Info** (☑26-597 000; www.palotahaz.hu; Dunaparti út 1; ⊘10am-6pm Apr-Oct, 10am-4pm Tue-Sun Nov-Mar).

No train line reaches Visegrád, but buses are very frequent (745Ft, 1¼ hours, hourly) to/from Budapest's Újpest-Városkapu train station, Szentendre (465Ft, 45 minutes, every 45 minutes) and Esztergom (465Ft, 45 minutes, hourly). Regular ferry services travel to Visegrád from Budapest.

Esztergom

☑ 33 / POP 28,400

It's easy to see the attraction of Esztergom – especially from a distance. The city's massive basilica, sitting high above the town and the Danube River, is an incredible sight rising magnificently from its rural setting.

But the historical significance of this town is even greater than its architectural appeal. The 2nd-century Roman emperor-to-be Marcus Aurelius wrote his famous *Meditations* while he camped here. In the 10th century, Stephen I, founder of the Hungarian state, was born here and crowned at the cathedral. From the late 10th to the mid-13th centuries Esztergom served as the Hungarian royal seat. In 1543 the Turks ravaged the town and much of it was destroyed, only to be rebuilt in the 18th and 19th centuries.

Hungary's largest church is **Esztergom Basilica** (Esztergomi Bazilika; ☑33-402 354; www.bazilika-esztergom.hu; Szent István tér 1; ⊘8am-6pm Apr-Oct, to 4pm Nov-Mar) FREE. At the southern end of the hill is the extensive **Castle Museum** (Vármúzeum; ☑33-415 986; www.mnmvarmuzeuma.

hu; Szent István tér 1; adult/student 1800/900Ft, courtyard only 500/250Ft, EU citizens free; ⊘ 10am-6pm Tue-Sun Apr-Oct, to 4pm Tue-Sun Nov-Mar), with archaeological finds from the 2nd and 3rd centuries. Below Castle Hill in the former Bishop's Palace, the **Christian Museum** (Keresztény Múzeum; ✆ 33-413 880; www.christian museum.hu; Mindszenty hercegprímás tér 2; adult/concession 900/450Ft; ⊘ 10am-5pm Wed-Sun Mar-Nov) contains the finest collection of medieval religious art in Hungary.

Frequent buses run to/from Budapest (930Ft, 1¼ hours), Visegrád (465Ft, 45 minutes) and Szentendre (930Ft, 1½ hours). Trains depart from Budapest's Nyugati train station (1120Ft, 1½ hours) at least hourly. Ferries travel regularly from Budapest to Esztergom (see opposite).

WESTERN HUNGARY

A visit to this region is a boon for anyone wishing to see remnants of Hungary's Roman legacy, medieval heritage and baroque splendour. Because it largely managed to avoid the Ottoman destruction of the 16th and 17th centuries, towns like Sopron retain their medieval cores; exploring their cobbled streets and hidden courtyards is a magical experience.

Sopron

✆ 99 / POP 61,250

Sopron (*showp*-ron) is an attractive border town with a history that stretches back to Roman times. It boasts some well-preserved ancient ruins and a fetching medieval square, bounded by the original town walls, that invite an hour or two of aimless meandering.

⊙ Sights

Fő tér SQUARE
(Main Square) Fő tér contains several museums, churches and monuments, including the massive **Firewatch Tower** (Tűztorony; ✆ 99-311 327; www.muzeum.sopron.hu; Fő tér; adult/student 1200/600Ft; ⊘ 10am-8pm Tue-Sun May-Sep, 10am-6pm Tue-Sun Apr & Oct, 9am-5pm Tue-Sun Nov & Dec, 10am-4pm Tue-Sun Jan-Mar), which can be climbed and houses a lovely new cafe. The 60m-high tower rises above the Old Town's northern gate and is visible from all around. In the centre of Fő tér is the 1701 **Trinity Column** (Szentháromság oszlop; Fő

tér). The **Castle Wall Walk** (⊘ 9am-9pm Apr-Sep, to 6pm Oct-Mar) **FREE** takes in ruins dating from the time when Sopron was a tiny Roman outpost known as Scarbantia.

★**Storno Collection** MUSEUM
(Storno Gyűjtemény; ✆ 99-311 327; www.muzeum.sopron.hu; Fő tér 8; adult/senior & student 1000/500Ft; h 10am-6pm Tue-Sun Apr-Oct, 9am-5pm Tue-Sun Nov & Dec, 10am-4pm Tue-Sun Jan-Mar) The Storno Collection is on the 2nd floor of **Storno House** (Storno Ház és Gyűjtemény; ✆ 99-311 327; www.muzeum.sopron.hu), home to the Swiss-Italian family of Ferenc Storno, chimney sweep turned art restorer, whose recarving of Romanesque and Gothic monuments throughout Transdanubia divides opinion to this day. The collection's highlights include a beautiful enclosed balcony with leaded windows and frescoes, an extensive collection of medieval weaponry, leather chairs with designs depicting the devil and dragons, and door frames made from pews taken from a nearby 15th-century church.

🛏 Sleeping

Jégverem Fogadó GUESTHOUSE €€
(✆ 99-510 113; www.jegverem.hu; Jégverem utca 1; s/d 7400/9800Ft; ☎) Booking ahead is essential since there are only five suite-like rooms at this 18th-century *fogadó* (inn). Even if you're not staying here, visit the terrace restaurant for enormous portions of pork, chicken and fish. And if you're wondering about the symbol of a little man with an ice pick perched on a giant cube, *jégverem* means 'ice house', which is what the place was in the 18th century.

Hotel Wollner HOTEL €€€
(✆ 99-524 400; www.wollner.hu; Templom utca 20; s/d/tr €75/90/110; ☎) This refined family-run hotel offers 18 spacious and tastefully decorated rooms in a 300-year-old villa in the heart of the Inner Town. It has a unique tiered garden, in which the reconstructed medieval walls of the castle can be seen, and a romantic wine cellar where you can sample some of the region's celebrated vintages.

✕ Eating & Drinking

★**Erhardt** INTERNATIONAL €€€
(✆ 99-506 711; www.erhardts.hu; Balfi út 10; mains 2600-3900Ft; ⊘ 11.30am-10pm Sun-Thu, to 11pm Fri & Sat; ✐) One of the best restaurants in Sopron, with a wooden-beamed ceiling and paintings of rural scenes complementing the

imaginative dishes, such as paprika catfish with oyster mushrooms, and crispy duck leg and duck breast slices. There's an extensive selection of Sopron wines to choose from (also available for purchase at its wine cellar), and the service is both informed and welcoming.

Museum Cafe
CAFE

(☑06 30 667 1394; www.museumcafesopron.hu/hu; Előkapu 2-7; ☺9am-11pm Mon-Thu, to 2am Fri & Sat, to 10pm Sun) This wonderful new venue at the foot of the Firewatch Tower has stunning views through oversized windows, cutting-edge decor, and is surrounded by a lapidary of Roman and medieval finds. And it's not just about coffee and tea here. There's also cocktails and *pálinka* (fruit-flavoured brandy) and, as blotter, sandwiches (420Ft to 880Ft) and pastries (390Ft to 690Ft).

❶ Information

Tourinform (☑99-517 560; http://turizmus. sopron.hu; Liszt Ferenc utca 1, Ferenc Liszt Conference & Cultural Centre; ☺9am-5pm Mon-Fri, to 1pm Sat, 9am-1pm Sun Mar-Sep only) Abundant information on Sopron and surrounds, including the local vintners.

❶ Getting There & Away

BUS
Bus travel to/from Budapest takes forever (six hours), involves at least one transfer/change and is not recommended. There are two direct buses a day each to Keszthely (2520Ft, three hours) and to Balatonfüred (3130Ft, 4¼ hours).

TRAIN
Trains run to Budapest's Keleti train station (4525Ft, three hours, up to 12 daily). Local trains run to Wiener Neustadt/Bécsújhely (2800Ft, 40 minutes, hourly) in Austria, where you change for Vienna.

LAKE BALATON

Lake Balaton, Central Europe's largest expanse of fresh water, covers an area of 600 sq km. The main activities at this 'inland sea' are swimming, sailing and sunbathing, but the lake is also popular with cyclists lured here by more than 200km of marked bike paths that encircle the lake.

Balatonfüred

☑ 87 / POP 13,300

Balatonfüred (*bal*-ah-ton-fuhr-ed) is the oldest and most fashionable resort on the lake. In its glory days in the 19th century the wealthy and famous built large villas along its tree-lined streets, hoping to take advantage of the health benefits of the town's thermal waters. More recently, the lake frontage received a massive makeover and now sports the most stylish marina on Balaton. It's a great base for exploring.

◉ Sights & Activities

Gyógy tér
SQUARE

(Cure Square; Gyógy tér) This leafy square is home to the **State Hospital of Cardiology** (Állami Szívkórház; Gyógy tér 2), which put Balatonfüred on the map. In the centre you'll encounter the **Kossuth Pump House** (1853), a natural spring that dispenses slightly sulphuric, but drinkable, thermal water. If you can ignore the water's pale-yellow hue, join the locals lining up to fill their water bottles. On the northern side of the square **Balaton Pantheon** (Gyógy tér), with memorial plaques from those who took the cure here.

Public Beaches
BEACH

Balatonfüred has several beaches open to the public of which **Kisfaludy Strand** (www.balatonfuredistrandok.hu; Aranyhíd sétány; adult/child 680/420Ft; ☺8.30am-7pm mid-Jun–mid-Aug, 8am-6pm mid-May–mid-Jun & mid-Aug–mid-Sep) off Aranyhíd sétány, the eastern continuation of Tagore sétány, is the best.

Cruises
CRUISE

(☑87-342 230; www.balatonihajozas.hu; ferry pier; adult/concession 1600/700Ft) One-hour pleasure cruises depart four to five times times a day from late late April to early October from the central ferry pier.

🛏 Sleeping

Hotel Blaha Lujza
HOTEL €€

(☑87-581 210; www.hotelblaha.hu; Blaha Lujza utca 4; s €40-50, d €55-80; ❋ ☎ ☜) This small hotel is one of the loveliest places to stay in Balatonfüred. Its 22 rooms are a little compact but very comfy, and the location, seconds from the town centre and the lake, is ideal. This was the summer home of the much-loved 19th-century actress-singer Lujza Blaha from

TIHANY

While in Balatonfüred, don't miss the chance to visit Tihany (population 1380), a small peninsula 14km to the southwest and the place with the greatest historical significance on Lake Balaton. Activity here is centred on the tiny settlement of the same name, which is home to the celebrated **Benedictine Abbey Church** (Bencés Apátság Templom; ☑ 87-538-200; http://tihany.osb.hu; András tér 1; adult/child incl museum 1400/700Ft; ⊙ 9am-6pm May-Sep, 10am-5pm Apr & Oct, 10am-4pm Nov-Mar), filled with fantastic altars, pulpits and screens carved in the mid-18th century by an Austrian lay brother; all are baroque-rococo masterpieces in their own right. The church attracts a lot of tourists, but the peninsula itself has an isolated, almost wild feel to it. Hiking is one of Tihany's main attractions; a good map outlining the trails is available from the helpful **Tourinform** (☑ 87-448 804; www.tihany.hu; Kossuth Lajos utca 20; ⊙ 9am-7pm Mon-Fri, 10am-6pm Sat & Sun mid-Jun–mid-Sep, 10am-4pm Mon-Fri mid-Sep–mid-Jun) office just down from the church. Buses bound for Tihany depart from Balatonfüred's bus/train station (310Ft, 30 minutes) at least hourly.

1893 to 1916. Its restaurant is very popular with locals.

★ **Club Hotel Füred**　　　　RESORT HOTEL €€€
(☑ 06 70 458 1242, 87-341 511; www.clubhotel fured.hu; Anna sétany 1-3; s/d €55/110, ste from €135; ❄ ☎ 🖥 ☲) This stunner of a resort hotel – right on the lake, about 1.5km from the town centre – has 43 rooms and suites in several buildings spread over 2.5 hectares of parkland and lush gardens. There's an excellent spa centre with sauna, steam room and pool, but the real delight is the private beach at the end of the garden. Stellar service, too.

✕ Eating & Drinking

Vitorlás　　　　　　　　HUNGARIAN €€
(☑ 06 30 546 0940; www.vitorlasetterem.hu; Tagore sétany 1; mains 2000-3300Ft; ⊙ 9am-midnight) This enormous wooden villa sits right on the lake's edge at the foot of the town's pier. It's a prime spot to watch the yachts sail in and out of the harbour while munching on Hungarian cuisine and sipping local wine on the terrace. A fish dish is de rigueur here. We recommend the fiery catfish stew (3100Ft).

Karolina　　　　　　　　CAFE, BAR
(☑ 87-583 098; http://karolina.hu; Zákonyi Ferenc utca 4; ⊙ 8am-midnight daily May-Sep, noon-9pm Sun-Fri, to midnight Sat Oct-Apr) Hands-down the most popular place in town to grab a drink or a quick bite (dishes 950Ft to 2500Ft), Karolina is a sophisticated cafe-bar with live music from 8pm on weekends. The interior, with its art nouveau wall hangings and subtle lighting, has a certain decadent air about it, while the terrace area with sofas couldn't be more laid-back.

Kedves　　　　　　　　CAFE
(☑ 87-343 229; Blaha Lujza utca 7; ⊙ 8am-7pm Sun-Thu, to 10pm Fri & Sat) Join fans of Lujza Blaha and take coffee and cake (cakes 240Ft to 450Ft) at the cafe where the famous actress used to while away the hours when not in residence across the street. It's also appealing for its location, away from the madding crowds.

ℹ Information

Tourinform (☑ 87-580 480; www.balatonfured. info.hu; Blaha Lujza utca 5; ⊙ 9am-7pm Mon-Sat, 10am-4pm Sun mid-Jun–Aug, 9am-5pm Mon-Fri, to 3pm Sat Sep–mid-Jun) Well-stocked tourist office run by helpful staff.

ℹ Getting There & Around

BUS

Buses to Tihany (310Ft, 30 minutes) leave every 30 minutes or so throughout the day. Eight buses a day head for Hévíz (1490Ft, 1¾ hours) via Keszthely (1300Ft, 1½ hours). Buses and trains to Budapest (both 2520Ft, three hours) are much of a muchness, though bus departures are more frequent.

TRAIN

From April to early October, half a dozen daily ferries ply the water between Balatonfüred and Tihany (1100Ft, 30 minutes).

Keszthely

☑ 83 / POP 20,200

At the very western end of Lake Balaton sits Keszthely (*kest*-hey), the lake's main town and a place of grand town houses and a gentle ambience. Its small, shallow beaches are well suited to families and the lavish Festetics Palace is a must-see.

◉ Sights & Activities

★ Festetics Palace PALACE
(FesteticsKastély; ☑ 83-312194;www.helikonkastely. hu; Kastély utca 1; Palace & Coach Museum adult/ concession 2300/1150Ft; ⊙ 9am-6pm Jun-Sep, 10am-5pm May, 10am-5pm Tue-Sun Oct-Apr) The glimmering white, 100-room Festetics Palace was begun in 1745; the two wings were extended out from the original building 150 years later. Some 18 rooms in the baroque south wing now contain the **Helikon Palace Museum** (Helikon Kastélymúzeum). Here too is the palace's greatest treasure, the **Helikon Library** (Helikon Könyvtár), with its 100,000 volumes and splendid carved furniture. Behind the palace in a separate building is the **Coach Museum** (Hintómúzeum; incl in admission to Festetics Palace; ⊙ 9am-6pm Jun-Sep, 10am-5pm May, 10am-5pm Tue-Sun Oct-Apr), which is filled with carriages and sleighs built for royalty.

Lakeside Area BEACH
The lakeside area centres on the long ferry pier. From late April to early October you can take a one-hour **pleasure cruise** (☑ 83-312 093; www.balatonihajozas.hu; ferry pier; ⊙ adult/ concession 1600/700Ft) on the lake between three and eight times daily. If you're feeling like a swim, **City Beach** (Városi Strand; adult/ child 900/650Ft; ⊙ 8am-6pm May–mid-Sept) is just to the southwest of the ferry pier, near plenty of beer stands and food booths. Reedy **Helikon Beach** (Helikon Strand; adult/child 500/350Ft; ⊙ 8am-6pm May–mid-Sept) is a further 200m south.

🛏 Sleeping

★ Bacchus HOTEL €€
(☑ 83-314 096; www.bacchushotel.hu; Erzsébet királyné útja 18; s 13,300Ft, d 16,400-21,400Ft, apt 26,000Ft; ✳ ☎) Bacchus' central position and immaculate rooms – each named after a grape variety – make it a popular choice with travellers and rightly so. The 26 rooms are simple but extra clean and inviting with solid wood furnishings; some even have terraces. Equally pleasing is its atmospheric cellar, which includes a lovely restaurant that includes wine tastings. Bacchus indeed.

Párizsi Udvar INN €€
(☑ 83-311 202; www.parizsi.huninfo.hu; Kastély utca 5; d 9400-10,500Ft, tr 11,400-13,400Ft; ☎)

There's no closer accommodation to the Festetics Palace than the 'Parisian Courtyard'. Rooms are a little too big to be cosy, but they're well kept and look on to a sunny and very leafy inner courtyard (a corner of which is taken over by a daytime restaurant and beer garden).

🍴 Eating & Drinking

Margareta HUNGARIAN €
(☑ 83-314 882, 06 30 826 0434; www.margareta-etterem.hu/; Bercsényi Miklós utca 60; mains 1600-2500Ft; ⊙ 11am-10pm) Ask any local where they like to eat and one answer dominates: Margareta. It's no beauty, but the wrap-around porch and hidden backyard terrace heave in the warm months, and the small interior packs them in the rest of the year. Food sticks to basic but hearty Hungarian staples. Set lunch is a snip at 990Ft.

Pelso Café CAFE
(☑ 06 30 222 2111, 83-315 415; Kossuth Lajos utca 38; ⊙ 9am-9pm Sun-Thu, to 10 pm Fri & Sat; ☎) This modern two-level cafe boasts a fantastic terrace overlooking the southern end of the main square. It does decent cakes and has a selection of teas from around the world plus the usual coffee concoctions (coffee and cake from 450Ft). But we like it best as a prime spot for an alfresco sundowner – the wine and beer list is small, but the vantage point is lovely.

ℹ Information

Tourinform (☑ 83-314 144; www.keszthely. hu; Kossuth Lajos utca 30; ⊙ 9am-7pm mid-Jun–Aug, 9am-5pm Mon-Fri, to 1pm Sat Sep–mid-Jun) An excellent source of information on Keszthely and the west Balaton area.

ℹ Getting There & Away

BUS
Buses link Keszthely with Hévíz (250Ft, 15 minutes, half-hourly), Balatonfüred (1300Ft, 1½ hours, eight daily) and Budapest (3410Ft, three hours, six daily).

TRAIN
Keszthely is on a railway branch line linking the lake's southeastern shore with Budapest (3705Ft, 3½ hours, six daily). To reach towns along Lake Balaton's northern shore, such as Balatonfüred (1640Ft, two hours) by train, you have to change at Tapolca (465Ft, 30 minutes, hourly).

HÉVÍZ

Hévíz (population 4685), just 8km northwest of Keszthely, is the most famous of Hungary's spa towns because of the **Gyógy-tó** (Hévíz Thermal Lake; 83-342 830; www.spaheviz.hu; Dr Schulhof Vilmos sétány 1; 3hr/4hr/whole day 2600/2900/3900Ft; 8am-7pm Jun-Aug, 9am-6pm May & Sep, 9am-5.30pm Apr & Oct, 9am-5pm Mar & Nov-Feb) – Europe's largest 'thermal lake'. A dip into this water lily-filled lake is essential for anyone visiting the Lake Balaton region.

It's an astonishing sight: a surface of almost 4.5 hectares in the Park Wood, covered for most of the year in pink and white lotuses. The source is a spring spouting from a crater some 40m below ground that disgorges up to 80 million litres of warm water a day, renewing itself every 48 hours or so. The surface temperature averages 33°C and never drops below 22°C in winter, allowing bathing throughout the year, even when there's ice on the fir trees. Do as the locals do: rent a rubber ring (600Ft) and just float.

Buses link Hévíz with Keszthely (250Ft, 15 minutes) every half-hour.

SOUTHERN HUNGARY

Southern Hungary is a region of calm; a place to savour life at a slower pace. It's only marginally touched by tourism and touring through the countryside is like travelling back in time.

Pécs

72 / POP 146,600

Blessed with a mild climate, an illustrious past and a number of fine museums and monuments, Pécs (pronounced *paich*) is one of the most pleasant and interesting cities to visit in Hungary. Many travellers put it second only to Budapest on their Hungary 'must-see' list.

👁 Sights & Activities

★ Mosque Church   MOSQUE
(Mecset templom; 72-321 976; Hunyadi János út 4; adult/concession 1000/750Ft; 10am-4pm mid-Apr–mid-Oct, to noon mid-Oct–mid-Apr, shorter hours Sun) The one-time Pasha Gazi Kassim Mosque is now the **Inner Town Parish Church** (Belvárosi plébánia templom), but it's more commonly referred to as the Mosque Church. It is the largest building from the time of the Turkish occupation still standing in Hungary and the very symbol of Pécs.

Synagogue   SYNAGOGUE
(Zsinagóga; Kossuth tér; adult/concession 750/500Ft; 10am-5pm Sun-Fri May-Oct, 10.30am-12.30pm Sun-Fri Nov-Mar) Pécs' beautifully preserved 1869 Conservative synagogue is south of Széchenyi tér and faces renovated Kossuth tér.

Cella Septichora Visitors Centre   RUIN
(Cella Septichora látogató központ; 72-224 755; www.pecsorokseg.hu; Janus Pannonius utca; adult/concession 1700/900Ft; 10am-6pm Tue-Sun Apr-Oct, 10am-4pm Tue-Thu & Sun, to 5pm Sat & Sun Nov-Mar) This early Christian burial site illuminates a series of early Christian tombs that have been on Unesco's World Heritage list since 2000. The highlight is the so-called **Jug Mausoleum** (Korsós sírkamra; incl in admission to Cella Septichora Visitors Centre; 10am-6pm Tue-Sun Apr-Oct, 10am-4pm Tue-Thu & Sun, to 5pm Sat & Sun Nov-Mar), a 4th-century Roman tomb; its name comes from a painting of a large drinking vessel with vines.

★ Csontváry Museum   MUSEUM
(72-310 544; www.jpm.hu; Janus Pannonius utca 11; adult/child 1500/750Ft; 10am-6pm Tue-Sun) The Csontváry Museum shows the major works of master 19th-century symbolist painter Tivadar Kosztka Csontváry (1853–1919), whose tragic life is sometimes compared with that of his contemporary, Vincent van Gogh. Don't miss *Solitary Cedar* and *Baalbek*.

🛏 Sleeping

Hotel Főnix   HOTEL €€
(72-311 680; www.fonixhotel.com; Hunyadi János út 2; s/d/ste 8000/13,000/14,000Ft; ❋@🛜) The Főnix appears to be a hotel too large for the land it's built on and some of the 13 rooms and suites are not even big enough to swing, well, a phoenix in. Still, the welcome is always warm here and the Mosque Church is within easy reach. The suite has a large open terrace.

Corso Hotel   BUSINESS HOTEL €€€
(📞72-421 900; www.corsohotel.hu; Koller utca 8;
s/d/ste from 19,500/23,200/32,000Ft; ✳@📶)
The Corso is a prime choice if you want the
amenities of a business-class hotel within
a 10-minute walk of the town centre. Its 81
rooms are inviting with plush carpets and
velvet curtains, and all suites have their own
outdoor terrace (one features a private sauna).
There's a restaurant on the ground floor serving solid international and Hungarian fare.

✖ Eating & Drinking

★**Jókai Bisztró**   HUNGARIAN €€
(📞06 20 360 7337; www.jokaibisztro.hu; Jókai tér
6; mains 1690-3390Ft; ⊘11am-midnight) Arguably the best eatery in Pécs, this charming
bistro with its stylish decor and oversized
lamps overlooks charming Jókai tér and a
seat on the terrace in summer is hot property. The menu is short and savoury but
exceptionally well constructed and seasonal; most of the produce and meat is grown
and reared by the restaurant. Only down-
side: cavalier service.

Áfium   HUNGARIAN €€
(📞72-511 434; www.afiumetterem.hu; Irgalmasok
utca 2; mains 1690-3190Ft; ⊘11am-1am Mon-Sat,
to midnight Sun) This homey restaurant with
its delightfully retro decor will fill the needs
(and stomachs) of most diners searching
for Hungarian staples, but it occasionally
slips across the border with such dishes as
csevap (spicy Serbian-style meatballs of beef
or pork; 1690Ft). Don't miss the 'hatted' (actually a swollen bread crust) bean soup with
trotters (1190Ft). Lovely staff here.

Cooltour Café   CAFE
(📞72-310 440; http://cooltourcafe.hu; Király utca
26; ⊘11am-midnight Sun-Tue, to 2am Wed & Thu,
to 3am Fri & Sat) Cooltour embodies so many
cool things it's hard to choose what we love
best. It's a 'ruin pub', yet it's open all day,
making it fine for both coffee and snacks or
cocktails and mellow chit-chat. It's on the
main drag, but its rear garden feels like a
secret spot. Occasional live music and parties in the evening.

ℹ Information

Tourinform (📞72-213 315; www.iranypecs.hu;
Széchenyi tér 7; ⊘9am-5pm Mon-Fri, 10am-
3pm Sat & Sun Jun-Aug, closed Sun May, Sep
& Oct, closed Sat & Sun Nov-Apr) Knowledgeable staff, copious information on Pécs and
surrounds.

ℹ Getting There & Away

BUS
Eight buses a day connect Pécs with Budapest
(3690Ft, 4¼ hours), eight with Szeged (3410Ft,
3¼ hours) and three with Kecskemét (3410Ft,
3½ hours).

TRAIN
Pécs is on a main rail line with Budapest's Déli
train station (3950Ft, four hours, nine daily).
One daily train runs from Pécs to Osijek/Eszék
in Croatia (two hours), with continuing service to
Sarajevo (nine hours) in Bosnia.

GREAT PLAIN

Like the outback for Australians or the Wild
West for Americans, the Nagy Alföld (Great
Plain) holds a romantic appeal for Hungar-
ians. Many of these notions come as much
from the collective imagination, paintings
and poetry as they do from history, but
there's no arguing the spellbinding potential of big-sky country. The Great Plain is
home to cities of graceful architecture and
rich history such as Szeged and Kecskemét.

Szeged
📞 62 / POP 162,000

Szeged (*seh*-ged) is a bustling border town,
with a handful of historic sights that line
the embankment along the Tisza River and
a clutch of sumptuous art nouveau town
palaces. Importantly, it's also a big university town, which means lots of culture, lots
of partying and an active festival scene that
lasts throughout the year.

◎ Sights & Activities

Dóm tér   SQUARE
'Cathedral Square' contains Szeged's most
important buildings and monuments and
is the centre of events during the annual
summer **Szeged Open-Air Festival** (📞62-
541 205; www.szegediszabadteri.hu). Lording
above all else is the twin-towered **Votive
Church** (Fogadalmi templom; 📞62-420 157;
www.szegedidom.hu; Dóm tér; ⊘6.30am-7pm
Mon-Sat, from 7.30am Sun), a disproportion-
ate brick monstrosity that was pledged
after the 1879 flood but built from 1913
to 1930. Running along three sides of the
square is the **National Pantheon** (Nemzeti
Emlékcsarnok; ⊘24hr) FREE, with statues

and reliefs of more than 100 Hungarian notables (almost 100% male).

★New Synagogue
SYNAGOGUE

(Új Zsinagóga; ☑ 62-423 849; www.zsinagoga. szeged.hu; Jósika utca 10; adult/concession 500/250Ft; ☉ 10am-noon & 1-5pm Sun-Fri Apr-Sep, 9am-2pm Sun-Fri Oct-Mar) The art nouveau New Synagogue, which was designed by Lipót Baumhorn in 1903, is the most beautiful Jewish house of worship in Hungary. It is still in use, though the community has dwindled from 8000 before WWII to about 50 people now. Dominating the enormous blue-and-gold interior is the cupola, decorated with stars and flowers (representing infinity and faith) and appearing to float skyward.

Reök Palace
ARCHITECTURE

(Reök Palota; ☑ 62-541 205; www.reok.hu; Tisza Lajos körút 56; ☉ 10am-6pm Tue-Sun) The Reök Palace is a mind-blowing green-and-lilac art nouveau structure built in 1907 that looks like an aquarium decoration. It's been polished up to its original lustre and now hosts regular photography and visual arts exhibitions.

🛌 Sleeping

Família Vendégház
GUESTHOUSE €€

(☑ 62-441 122; www.familiapanzio.hu; Szentháromság utca 71; s €27, d €35-43, tr €50; ✲ 🕏) Families and international travellers often book up this family-run guesthouse with contemporary, if nondescript, furnishings in a great old-town building close to the train station. The two-dozen rooms have high ceilings and loads of light from tall windows. Air-conditioning costs an extra €2.

Dóm Hotel
BOUTIQUE HOTEL €€€

(☑ 62-423 750; www.domhotel.hu; Bajza utca 6; s/d/apt from 19,900/23,900/47,000Ft; ✲ @ 🕏) A welcome addition to Szeged's top-end accomodation scene is this very smart and extremely central 16-room boutique hotel. There's a small wellness centre with Jacuzzi, sauna and massage, a popular in-house restaurant and a 21st-century underground carpark accessed by lift. But the main draw is the extremely helpful multilingual staff for whom no request is too much.

WORTH A TRIP

KECSKEMÉT

A worthwhile destination is the lovely city of Kecskemét (pop 112,000), which lies halfway between Budapest and Szeged along the main rail and road arteries. It's a surprisingly green, pedestrian-friendly place with beautiful art nouveau architecture. **Tourinform** (☑ 76-481 065; www.visitkecskemet.hu; Kossuth tér 1; ☉ 8.30am-5.30pm Mon-Fri, 9am-1pm Sat May-Sep, 8.30-4.30pm Mon-Fri Oct-Apr) is centrally located on the main square. It can advise on sights, places to stay and outings to **Kiskunság National Park** (Kiskunsági Nemzeti Park; www.knp.hu). Kecskemét is served by bus to/from Budapest (1680Ft, 1¼ hours, half-hourly) and Szeged (1680Ft, 1¾ hours, nine daily).

🍴 Eating & Drinking

Boci Tejivó
FAST FOOD €

(☑ 62-423 154; www.bocitejivo.hu; Zrínyi utca 2; dishes 220-890Ft; ☉ 24hr; 🖉) This is a very modern take on an old-fashioned idea – the 'milk bar' so popular during socialist times. Though not vegetarian there are dozens of meatless dishes – cheese and mushroom omelettes, noodles with walnuts or poppyseed and anything with the ever-popular *túró* (curd), especially *túrógombóc* (curd dumplings; 650Ft).

Vendéglő A Régi Hídhoz
HUNGARIAN €€

(☑ 62-420 910; www.regihid.hu; Oskola utca 4; mains 1700-2600Ft; ☉ 11.30am-11pm Sun-Thu, to midnight Fri & Sat) For an authentic meal that won't break the bank, head for 'At the Old Bridge', a traditional Hungarian restaurant with all the favourites and a great terrace just a block in from the river. It's a great place to try *Szögedi halászlé* (1700Ft), Szeged's famous fish soup.

Classic Cafe
SERBIAN €€

(☑ 62-422 065; www.classiccafe.hu; Széchenyi tér 5; mains 2190-2700Ft; ☉ 10am-midnight Mon-Sat, to 10pm Sun) This welcoming Serbian place with its lovely inner courtyard garden (fine for a quiet drink, too) serves up grills like *csevap* (spicy meatballs of beef or pork) and *pljszkavica* (meat patties).

A Cappella CAFE
(☑62-559 966; http://acappella.atw.hu/; Kárász
utca 6; ☺7am-10pm) This two-storey sidewalk
cafe overlooking Klauzál tér has a generous
choice of cakes (485Ft to 650Ft), ice creams
and frothy coffee concoctions.

ℹ Information

Tourinform Branches include the exceptionally helpful main office (☑62-488 690; www.
szegedtourism.hu; Dugonics tér 2; ☺9am-5pm
Mon-Fri, to 1pm Sat), tucked away in a courtyard near the university, and a seasonal kiosk
(Széchenyi tér; ☺8am-8pm Jun-Sep).

ℹ Getting There & Around

BUS
Buses run to Kecskemét (1680Ft, 1¾ hours, nine
daily) and Pécs (3410Ft, 3¼ hours, four daily).
You can also get to the Serbian city of Subotica
(1200Ft, 1½ hours) up to four times a day by bus.

TRAIN
Szeged is on the main rail line to Budapest's
Nyugati train station (3705Ft, 2½ hours,
half-hourly); many trains also stop halfway along
in Kecskemét (2375Ft, 1¼ hours).

NORTHEASTERN HUNGARY

This is the home of Hungary's two most famous
wines – honey-sweet Tokaj and Eger's famed
Bull's Blood – and a region of microclimates
conducive to wine production. The chain of
wooded hills in the northeast constitutes the
foothills of the Carpathian Mountains, which
stretch along the Hungarian border with
Slovakia.

Eger

☑36 / POP 54,500
Filled with wonderfully preserved baroque
buildings, Eger (*egg*-air) is a jewelbox of a
town. Learn about the Turkish conquest and
defeat at its hilltop castle, climb an original
minaret, hear an organ performance at the
massive basilica and, best of all, go from cellar to cellar in the Valley of Beautiful Wom-
en, tasting the celebrated Bull's Blood wine
from the region where it's made.

◉ Sights & Activities

★**Eger Castle** FORTRESS
(Egri Vár; ☑36-312 744; www.egrivar.hu; Vár köz 1;
castle grounds adult/child 800/400Ft, incl museum
1400/700Ft; ☺exhibits 10am-5pm Tue-Sun May-
Oct, 10am-4pm Tue-Sun Nov-Apr, castle grounds
8am-8pm May-Aug, to 7pm Apr & Sep, to 6pm Mar &
Oct, to 5pm Nov-Feb) Climb up cobbled Vár köz
from Dózsa György tér to reach Eger Castle,
erected in the 13th century after the Mongol
invasion. Models and drawings in the István Dobó Museum, housed in the former
Bishop's Palace (1470), painlessly explain the
history of the castle. The Eger Art Gallery
on the northwestern side of the courtyard
has works by Canaletto and Ceruti. Beneath
the castle are casemates (*kazamata*) hewn
from solid rock, which can be visited.

Eger Basilica CHURCH
(Egri Bazilika; ☑36-420 970; www.eger-bazilika.
plebania.hu; Pyrker János tér 1; requested donation adult/conession 300/100Ft; ☺8.30am-6pm
Mon-Sat, 1-6pm Sun) A highlight of the town's
amazing architecture is Eger Basilica. This
neoclassical monolith was designed in 1836
by József Hild, the same architect who later worked on the cathedral at Esztergom.
A good time to see the place is when the
ornate altars and a soaring dome create interesting acoustics for the half-hour organ
concert (adult/child 800/500Ft; ☺11.30am
Mon-Sat, 12.30pm Sun mid-May–mid-Oct).

Minaret ISLAMIC
(☑06 70 202 4353; www.minareteger.hu; Knézich
Károly utca; admission 300Ft; ☺10am-6pm Apr-
Sep, 10am-5pm Oct, 10am-3pm Sat & Sun Nov-Mar)
This 40m-high minaret, topped incongruously with a cross, is one of the few reminders
of the Ottoman occupation of Eger. Nonclaus-
trophobes will brave the 97 narrow spiral
steps to the top for the awesome views.

★**Valley of the Beautiful Women** WINE TASTING
(Szépasszony-völgy) Wine tasting is popular in the wine cellars of this evocatively
named valley. Try ruby-red Bull's Blood or
any of the whites: Leányka, Olaszrizling and
Hárslevelű from nearby Debrő. The choice
of wine cellars can be a bit daunting so walk
around and have a look yourself. The valley
is a little over 1km southwest across Rte 25
and off Király utca.

★ **Turkish Bath** SPA
(Török Fürdő; ☑ 36-510 552; www.egertermal.
hu; Fürdő utca 3-4; 2½hr session adult/child
2200/1500Ft; ⏱ 4.30-9pm Mon & Tue, 3-9pm Wed
& Thu, 1-9pm Fri, 9am-9pm Sat & Sun) Nothing
beats a soak and steam at this historic spa,
which has a bath dating to 1617 at its core.
A multimillion-forint renovation has added
five pools, saunas, steam room and a hamam
(Turkish bath). Various kinds of massage and
treatments are also available.

🛏 Sleeping

Agria Retur Vendégház GUESTHOUSE €
(☑ 36-416 650; www.returvendeghaz.hu; Knézich
Károly utca 18; s/d/tr 3800/6400/9300Ft; 🛜)
You couldn't find sweeter hosts than the
daughter and mother who own this guesthouse near the minaret. Walking up three
flights of stairs, you enter a cheery communal kitchen/eating area central to four
mansard rooms with fridge. Out the back is
a huge garden with tables and a barbecue at
your disposal.

★ Hotel Senator-Ház BOUTIQUE HOTEL €€
(Senator House Hotel; ☑ 36-320 466; www.senator
haz.hu; Dobó István tér 11; s €40-48, d €53-65; ✸)
Eleven warm and cosy rooms with traditional white furnishings fill the upper floors of
this delightful 18th-century inn on Eger's
main square. The ground floor is shared between a quality restaurant and a reception
area stuffed with antiques and curios.

Dobó Vendégház GUESTHOUSE €€
(☑ 36-421 407; www.dobovendeghaz.hu; Dobó István utca 19; s 9000-10,500Ft; d 13,500-15,900Ft;
🛜) Tucked away along one of the old town's
pedestrian streets, just below Eger Castle,
this lovely little hotel has seven spic-and-
span rooms, some with balconies. Check
out the museum-quality Zsolnay porcelain
collection in the breakfast room.

🍴 Eating & Drinking

Palacsintavár CREPERIE €
(Pancake Castle; ☑ 36-413 980; www.palacs
intavar.hu; Dobó István utca 9; mains 1850-2250Ft;
⏱ noon-11pm Tue-Sat, to 10pm Sun) Pop art and
a fascinating collection of antique cigarettes
still in their packets line the walls in this
eclectic eatery. Savoury *palacsinták* – pancakes, for a better word – are served with
an abundance of fresh vegetables and range
in flavour from Asian to Mexican. There's
a large choice of sweet ones (from 1690Ft),
too. Enter from Fazola Henrik utca.

> **WORTH A TRIP**
>
> ## TOKAJ
>
> A worthwhile wine destination is the
> small village of Tokaj (population 4900),
> 43km northeast of Eger, which has long
> been celebrated for its sweet dessert
> wines. **Tourinform** (☑ 06 70 388 8870,
> 47-552 070; www.tokaj-turizmus.hu; Serház
> utca 1; ⏱ 9am-5pm Mon-Sat, 10am-3pm
> Sun Jun-Aug, 9am-4pm Mon-Fri Sep-May) is
> just off Rákóczi út and can help with ac-
> commodation. Travelling to/from Eger
> choose the train (3425Ft, two hours,
> hourly), though you need to change in
> Füzesabony. Up to seven trains a day
> head for Budapest (4605Ft, 2½ hours).

★ **Fő Tér** HUNGARIAN €€
(Main Square; ☑ 36-817 482; http://fotercafe.hu;
Gerl Matyas utca 2; mains 1300-3400Ft; ⏱ 10am-
10pm) This new kid on the block facing
Dobó István tér adds a bit of colour to Eger's
dining scene, with its chartreuse-and-plum
pop-art decor and a glassed-in terrace with
a tented roof. The food is Hungarian with
a contemporary taste; we loved the grilled
smoked-ewe cheese with orange salad
(1950Ft) and pork knuckle braised in dark
beer (2000Ft).

Bikavér Borház WINE BAR
(☑ 36-413 262; http://www.egrikirakat.hu/
tagok-bemutatkozasa/bikaver-borhaz; Dobó István
tér 10; ⏱ 10am-10pm) Try one or two (or three)
of the region's best vintages at this central
wine bar with a choice of 50-plus wines. The
waiters can guide you with the right selection and supply a plate of cheese or grapes to
help you cleanse your palate.

ℹ Information

Tourinform (☑ 36-517 715; http://www.eger.
hu/hu/turizmus/tdm-tourinform; Bajcsy-
Zsilinszky utca 9; ⏱ 8am-6pm Mon-Fri, 9am-
1pm Sat & Sun Jul & Aug, 8am-5pm Mon-Fri,
9am-1pm Sat & Sun May, Jun, Sep & Oct, 8am-
5pm Mon-Fri Nov-Apr) Promotes both the town
and areas surrounding Eger.

ℹ Getting There & Away

BUS

From Eger, buses serve Kecskemét (3130Ft,
4½ hours, three daily) and Szeged (3950Ft, five
hours, two daily). To get to Tokaj by bus, you
have to go to Nyíregyháza (2520Ft, three hours,

HUNGARY EGER

three daily) and catch another bus to Tokaj (650Ft, half-hour, three daily).

TRAIN

Up to eight direct trains a day head to Budapest's Keleti train station (2725Ft, two hours). You can reach Tokaj (3425Ft, two hours, hourly) with a change in Füzesabony.

SURVIVAL GUIDE

Directory A–Z

BUSINESS HOURS

Banks 8am or 9am to 4pm or 5pm Monday to Friday

Bars Usually 11am to midnight Sunday to Thursday, to 1am or 2am on Friday and Saturday

Museums 9am or 10am to 5pm or 6pm Tuesday to Sunday

Restaurants Roughly 11am to midnight

Shops 9am or 10am to 6pm Monday to Friday, 10am to 1pm on Saturday, some to 8pm Thursday

DISCOUNT CARDS

The **Hungary Card** (www.hungarycard.hu; basic/standard/plus 2550/5800/9300Ft) offers free entry to many museums; 50% off on six return train fares and some bus and boat travel; up to 20% off selected accommodation; and 50% off the price of the Budapest Card (p186). It's available at Tourinform offices.

INTERNET RESOURCES

Hungary Museums (www.museum.hu)
Hungarian National Tourist Office (www.gotohungary.com)

COUNTRY FACTS

Area 93,030 sq km

Capital Budapest

Country Code ⏻ 36

Currency Forint (Ft)

Emergency Ambulance ⏻ 104, emergency assistance ⏻ 112, fire ⏻ 105, police ⏻ 107

Language Hungarian

Money ATMs abound

Population 9.96 million

Visas None for EU, USA, Canada, Australia and New Zealand

MEDIA

Budapest has two English-language newspapers: the weekly **Budapest Times** (www.budapesttimes.hu; 750Ft), with interesting reviews and opinion pieces, and the business-oriented biweekly **Budapest Business Journal** (www.bbjonline.hu; 1250Ft). Both are available on newsstands.

MONEY

The unit of currency is the Hungarian forint (Ft). Coins come in denominations of five, 10, 20, 50, 100 and 200Ft, and notes are denominated in 500, 1000, 2000, 5000, 10,000 and 20,000Ft. ATMs are everywhere, even in small villages. Tip waiters, hairdressers and taxi drivers approximately 10% of the total.

PUBLIC HOLIDAYS

New Year's Day 1 January

1848 Revolution Day 15 March

Easter Monday March/April

International Labour Day 1 May

Whit Monday (Pentecost) May/June

St Stephen's/Constitution Day 20 August

1956 Remembrance/Republic Day 23 October

All Saints' Day 1 November

Christmas Holidays 25 & 26 December

TELEPHONE

Hungary's country code is ⏻ 36. To make an outgoing international call, dial ⏻ 00 first. To dial city-to-city within the country, first dial ⏻ 06, wait for the second dial tone and then dial the city code and phone number. You must always dial ⏻ 06 when ringing mobile telephones. All localities in Hungary have a two-digit city code, except for Budapest, where the code is ⏻ 1.

As with the rest of Europe, Hungarian mobile phones operate on the GSM standard network. Compatible handsets will connect automatically with local providers, but watch for high roaming fees, particularly for data downloads. A cheaper alternative is to purchase a pay-as-you-go SIM card (available at mobile-phone shops and newsagents), which will give you a temporary local number with which to make calls and send text messages.

TOURIST INFORMATION

The **Hungarian National Tourist Office** (HNTO; http://gotohungary.com) has a chain of more than 125 **Tourinform** (⏻ from abroad 36 1 438 80 80, within Hungary 800 36 000 000; www.tourinform.hu; ⏱ 8am-8pm Mon-Fri) information offices across the country. These are the best places to ask general questions and pick up brochures across the country. In the capital, you can also visit **Budapest Info** (Map p182; ⏻ 1-438 8080; www.budapestinfo.hu).

VISAS

Citizens of virtually all European countries, as well as Australia, Canada, Israel, Japan, New Zealand and the USA, do not require visas to visit Hungary for stays of up to 90 days. Check current visa requirements on the Consular Services page of the **Ministry for Foreign Affairs** (http://konzuliszolgalat.kormany.hu/en) website.

ℹ Getting There & Away

Hungary's landlocked status ensures plenty of possibilities for onward travel overland. There are direct train connections from Budapest to major cities in all of Hungary's neighbours. International buses head in all directions and in the warmer months you can take a ferry along the Danube to reach Vienna in Austria.

AIR

Ferenc Liszt International Airport (☑1-296 7000; www.bud.hu), 24km southeast of the city, has two modern terminals next to one another. Terminal 2A is served by flights from countries within the Schengen border, while other international flights and budget carriers use 2B. Among the latter serving Hungary are the following:
Air Berlin (AB; ☑06 80 017 110; www.airberlin.com; hub Cologne)
EasyJet (EZY; www.easyjet.com)
Germanwings (www.germanwings.com)
Ryanair (FR; www.ryanair.com; hub London)
Wizz Air (W6; ☑06 90 181 181; www.wizzair.com; hub Katowice, Poland)

LAND
Bus

Most international buses arrive at the Népliget bus station (p186) in Budapest and most services are run by **Eurolines** (www.eurolines.com) in conjunction with its Hungarian affiliate, **Volán** (www.volan.eu). Useful international routes include buses from Budapest to Vienna in Austria, Bratislava in Slovakia, Subotica in Serbia, Rijeka in Croatia, Prague in the Czech Republic and Sofia in Bulgaria.

Car & Motorcycle

Third-party insurance is compulsory for driving in Hungary; if your car is registered in the EU, it's assumed you have it. Other motorists must show a Green Card or buy insurance at the border.

Travel on Hungarian motorways requires pre-purchase of a highway pass *(matrica)* available from petrol stations and post offices. Your licence-plate/registration number will be entered into a computer database where it can be screened by highway-mounted surveillance cameras. Prices per week are 1470/2975Ft for a motorcycle/car.

Train

Magyar Államvasutak (MÁV; ☑06 40 494 949, 1-371 9449; http://elvira.mav-start.hu/), the Hungarian State Railways, links up with international rail networks in all directions, and its schedule is available online.

EuroCity (EC) and Intercity (IC) trains require a seat reservation and payment of a supplement. Most larger train stations in Hungary have left-luggage rooms open from at least 9am to 5pm.

Some direct train connections from Budapest include Austria, Slovakia, Romania, Ukraine, Croatia, Serbia, Germany, Slovenia, Czech Republic, Poland, Switzerland, Italy, Bulgaria and Greece.

RIVER

Hydrofoils on the Danube River bound for Vienna depart Budapest at 9am on Tuesday, Thursday and Saturday, returning from Vienna at the same time on Wednesday, Friday and Sunday. Adult one-way/return fares are €99/125. Transporting a bicycle costs €25.

ℹ Getting Around

Hungary does not have any scheduled domestic flights.

BOAT

In summer there are regular passenger ferries on the Danube from Budapest to Szentendre, Visegrád and Esztergom as well as on Lake Balaton.

BUS

Domestic buses, run by the Volánbusz (p186), an association of coach operators, cover an extensive nationwide network. Timetables are posted at all stations. Some footnotes you could come across include *naponta* (daily), *hétköznap* (weekdays), *munkanapokon* (on work days), *munkaszüneti napok kivételével naponta* (daily except holidays) and *szabad és munkaszüneti*

ESSENTIAL FOOD & DRINK

Hungary enjoys perhaps the most varied and interesting cuisine in Eastern Europe. Inexpensive by Western European standards and served in huge portions, traditional Hungarian food is heavy and rich. Meat, sour cream and fat abound and the omnipresent seasoning is with paprika, which appears on restaurant tables as a condiment beside the salt and pepper. Things are lightening up though, with vegetarian, 'New Hungarian' and ethnic cuisines increasingly available.

➡ **Galuska** Small dumplings not unlike gnocchi that make a good accompaniment to *pörkölt*.

➡ **Gulyás** (goulash) Hungary's signature dish, though here it's more like a soup than a stew and made with beef, onions and tomatoes.

➡ **Halászlé** Highly recommended fish soup made from poached freshwater fish, tomatoes, green peppers and paprika.

➡ **Lángos** Street food; fried dough topped with cheese and/or *tejföl* (sour cream).

➡ **Palacsinta** Thin crêpes that come either *sós* (savoury) and eaten as a main course or *édes* (sweet) filled with jam, sweet cheese or chocolate sauce for dessert.

➡ **Pálinka** A strong brandy distilled from all kinds of fruit but especially plums and apricots.

➡ **Paprika** The omnipresent seasoning in Hungarian cooking, which comes in two varieties: strong *(erős)* and sweet *(édes)*.

➡ **Pörkölt** Paprika-infused stew; closer to what we would call goulash.

➡ **Savanyúság** Literally 'sourness'; anything from mildly sour-sweet cucumbers to almost acidic sauerkraut, eaten with a main course.

➡ **Wine** Two Hungarian wines are known internationally: the sweet dessert wine Tokaji Aszú and Egri Bikavér (Eger Bull's Blood), a full-bodied red.

napokon (on Saturday and holidays). A few large bus stations have luggage rooms, but these generally close by 6pm.

CAR & MOTORCYCLE
In general, you must be at least 21 years old and have had your driving licence for at least a year to rent a car. There is a 100% ban on alcohol when you are driving, and this rule is strictly enforced. Most cities and towns require that you pay for street parking (usually 9am to 6pm workdays) by buying temporary parking passes from machines.

LOCAL TRANSPORT
Public transport is efficient and extensive in Hungary, with bus and, in many towns, trolley-

EATING PRICE RANGES

Price ranges are as follows:

€ less than 2000Ft (Budapest 3000Ft)

€€ 2000Ft to 3500Ft (Budapest 3000Ft to 7500Ft)

€€€ more than 3500Ft (Budapest 7500Ft)

bus services. Budapest, Szeged and Debrecen also have trams, and there's an extensive metro and a suburban commuter railway in Budapest. Purchase tickets at newsstands before travelling and validate them once aboard. Inspectors frequently check tickets.

TRAIN
MÁV (☑ 1-444 4499; www.mav-start.hu) operates reliable train services on more than 7600km of tracks. Schedules are available on-line and computer information kiosks are popping up at train stations around the country.

IC trains are express trains and are the most comfortable and modern. *Gyorsvonat* (fast trains) take longer and use older cars; *személyvonat* (passenger trains) stop at every village along the way. Seat reservations *(helyjegy)* cost extra and are required on IC and some fast trains; these are indicated on the timetable by an 'R' in a box or a circle (a plain 'R' means seat reservations are available but not required).

In all stations a yellow board indicates departures *(indul)* and a white board is for arrivals *(érkezik)*. Express and fast trains are indicated in red, local trains in black.

Both **InterRail** (www.interrail.eu) and **Eurail** (www.eurail.com) passes cover Hungary.

Kosovo

Best Places to Eat

➜ Tiffany (p205)
➜ Renaissance II (p205)
➜ De Rada Brasserie (p205)
➜ Ego (p209)

Best Places to Stay

➜ Swiss Diamond Hotel (p205)
➜ Dukagjini Hotel (p207)
➜ Han Hostel (p203)
➜ Hotel Prizreni (p209)

Why Go?

Kosovo is Europe's newest country and a fascinating land at the heart of the Balkans that rewards visitors with welcoming smiles, charming mountain towns, incredible hiking opportunities and 13th-century domed Serbian monasteries just for starters. It's safe to travel here now, and indeed is one of the last corners of Europe that remains off the beaten track for travellers.

Kosovo declared independence from Serbia in 2008, and while it has been diplomatically recognised by 110 countries, there are still many nations that do not accept Kosovan independence, including Serbia. The country has been the focus of massive aid from the international community, particularly the EU and NATO, who effectively run the entity politically and keep peace between the ethnic Albanian majority and the minority Serbs. Barbs of its past are impossible to miss, however: roads are dotted with memorials to those killed in 1999, while NATO forces still guard Serbian monasteries.

When to Go
Pristina

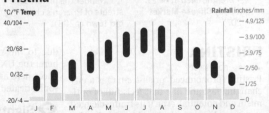

| Apr Pristina International Film Festival (PriFest) brings a touch of glamour to the capital. | May–Sep You don't have to worry about high-season crowds in Kosovo! | Aug The excellent DokuFest in Prizren is Kosovo's best arts event. |

Kosovo Highlights

❶ See the sights in Pristina's charming **bazaar area** and discover this bustling capital.

❷ Breathe deep at Peja's Saturday **Cheese Market** (p207).

❸ Buy local wine and cheese at the serene 14th-century **Visoki Dečani Monastery** (p208).

❹ Wander the picturesque streets of Prizren's charming **old town** (p208).

❺ Trek around the **Rugova Mountains** (p207).

❻ Visit Kosovo's fabulous new **Bear Sanctuary Pristina** and see rescued bears living in excellent conditions (p206).

PRISTINA

☏ 038 / POP 198,000

Pristina (pronounced 'prish-*tee*-na') is a city changing fast and one that feels full of optimism and potential, even if its traffic-clogged streets and mismatched architectural styles don't make it an obviously attractive place. Far more a provincial town than great city, Pristina makes for an unlikely national capital, and yet feels more cosmopolitan than the capitals of many larger Balkan nations

due to the number of foreigners working here: the UN and EU both have large presences here and the city feels rich and more sophisticated as a result.

◉ Sights

◉ Bazaar Area

★**Ethnographic Museum**　HISTORIC BUILDING
(Rr Iliaz Agushi; admission by donation; ⊙10am-5pm) This wonderful annex of the Museum

Two to Three Days
Spend a day in cool little **Pristina** and get to know Kosovo's chaotic but somehow charming capital. The next day, visit **Visoki Dečani Monastery** and then head on to **Prizren**, to see the old town's Ottoman sights and enjoy the view from the castle.

One Week
After a couple of days in the capital, and a visit to **Gračanica Monastery** and the **Bear Sanctuary**, loop to lovely **Prizren** for a night before continuing to **Peja** for monasteries and markets. Then end with a few days of hiking in the beautiful **Rugova Mountains**.

of Kosovo is housed in two beautifully preserved Ottoman houses enclosed in a large walled garden. The clued-up, super-keen English-speaking staff will give you a fascinating tour of both properties and point out the various unique pieces of clothing, weapons, jewellery and household goods on display in each. There's no better introduction to Kosovar culture to be had.

Museum of Kosovo　　　　MUSEUM
(Sheshi Adam Jashari; admission €2; ⊙10am-5pm Tue-Sat) Following a full renovation, Pristina's main museum is now open again and has displays spread over three floors.

On the ground floor you'll find an ethnological exhibit, entirely unlabelled but with some superb examples of wood carving. The 2nd floor contains a poor selection of paintings from various eras, while the top floor is an unbalanced display on the Kosovan War and the birth of the nation.

Mosques　　　　MOSQUES
Fronting the Kosovo Museum is the 15th-century **Carshi Mosque** (Agim Ramadani). Nearby, the **Sultan Mehmet Fatih Mosque** (Big Mosque; Rr Ilir Konushevci) was built by its namesake around 1461, converted to a Catholic church during the Austro-Hungarian era and refurbished again during WWII. **Jashar Pasha Mosque** (Rr Ylfete Humolli) has vibrant interiors that exemplify Turkish baroque style.

Clock Tower　　　　LANDMARK
(Sahat Kulla) This 26m-high tower dates from the 19th century and was central to the bazaar area, as it dictated when stalls should close for prayers. Following damage in the war, it now operates on electricity. The Great Hamam nearby is being renovated.

◉ Centre

The centre of Pristina has been impressively redesigned and is now focused on the new Ibrahim Rugova Sq, the centrepiece of the city at the end of the attractively pedestrianised Bul Nenë Terezë.

National Library　　　　LIBRARY
(www.biblioteka-ks.org; Rr Agim Ramadani; ⊙7am-8pm Mon-Fri, 7am-2pm Sat) FREE Easily one of Pristina's most notable buildings, the National Library, completed in 1982 by Croatian Andrija Mutnjakovic, must be seen to be believed (think gelatinous eggs wearing armour).

National Gallery of Kosovo　　　　GALLERY
(www.galeriakombetare.com; Rr Agim Ramadani 60; ⊙10am-6pm Mon-Fri) FREE This excellent space takes a thoroughly contemporary stance on Kosovan art (don't expect to see paintings from throughout the country's history here) and is always worth a look around.

⌘ Sleeping

★**Han Hostel**　　　　HOSTEL €
(☑044 396 852, 044 760 792; www.hostelhan.com; Rr Fehmi Agani 2/4; dm €10-12, s/d €20/30; @ 🕾) Pristina's best hostel is on the 4th floor of a residential building right in the heart of town. Cobbled together from two apartments that have been joined and converted, this great space has a large communal kitchen, balconies and smart rooms with clean bathrooms. It's well set up for backpackers and run by an extremely friendly local crew.

White Tree Hostel　　　　HOSTEL €
(☑049 166 777; www.whitetreehostel.com; Rr Mujo Ulqinaku 15; dm/r €10/30; ❄🕾) Run by a well-travelled bunch of locals who took a

Pristina

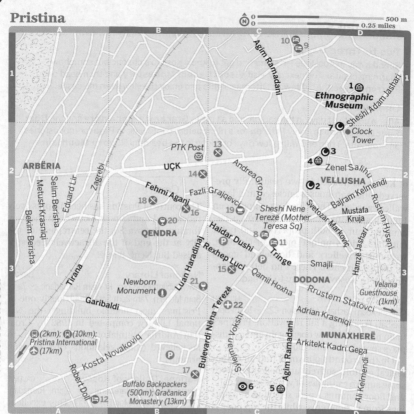

ARBËRIA

VELLUSHA

QENDRA

DODONA

MUNAXHERË

Ethnographic Museum

Clock Tower

PTK Post

Newborn Monument

Buffalo Backpackers (500m); Gračanica Monastery (13km)

Velania Guesthouse (1km)

Pristina International (17km)

derelict house into their care, painted the tree in the courtyard white and gradually began to attract travellers with a cool backpacker vibe, this hostel has more the feel of an Albanian beach resort than a downtown Pristina bolt-hole. The massive 12-bed dorm has its own bathroom, there's a fully equipped kitchen and it adjoins a very chilled lounge bar, which is a perfect place to meet other travellers.

Buffalo Backpackers
HOSTEL €

(☎ 045 643 261; Rr Musine Kokalari 274; dm/ camping incl breakfast €10/6; ☏) This charming dorm-only hostel has some of the cheapest and most chilled-out accommodation in the country, friendly staff and a pleasant location in a self-contained house a little south of Pristina's busy city centre.

Velania Guesthouse
PENSION €

(☎ 038 531 742, 044 167 455; www.guesthouse-ks. net; Velania 4/34; dm €7, s/d/tr from €12/16/24, s/d/tr with shared bathroom from €10/14/21) This

bustling guesthouse is spread over two buildings in an affluent part of town. The jovial professor who runs it loves a chat and could double as your grandfather. The hike up to it is much more fun in a taxi (€1.50) – either way consult the website first and print out the map, as it's hard to find!

Hotel Begolli
HOTEL €€

(☎ 038 244 277; www.hotelbegolli.com; Rr Maliq Pashë Gjinolli 8; s/d incl breakfast €40/50, apt from €50; ❄ @ ☏) While it may have gone overboard with its '90s-style furniture, Begolli is a pleasant, rather sprawling place to stay. The apartment has a Jacuzzi and a kitchen and is good value, while the normal rooms are a little on the small side, but comfy. Staff are friendly and a good breakfast is served in the ground-floor bar.

Hotel Sara
HOTEL €€

(☎ 044 238 765, 038 236 203; www.hotel-sara. com; Rr Maliq Pashë Gjinolli; s/d/tr/apt incl breakfast

Pristina

€30/40/50/70) In a tiny hotel-filled street by the bazaar, this 33-room hotel is rather garishly furnished in a style that suggests aspiration to boutique quality, but sadly rather misses the mark. That said, the rooms are good value at this price, and room 603 has a small balcony with great city views if you can cope with the colour scheme.

★**Swiss Diamond Hotel** LUXURY HOTEL €€€
(☏038 220 000; www.swissdiamondhotelprishtina. com; Sheshi Nëna Terezë; r incl breakfast from €162; ⓟ❄✻@☎🏊) This international standard five-star hotel is the choice of those who can afford it. Opened in 2012 right in the heart of the city, this place is all marble floors, obsequious staff and liveried bell boys. The rooms are lavish and the suites are immense, all decorated with expensive furnishings and many enjoying great city views.

🍴 Eating

Home Bar & Restaurant INTERNATIONAL €
(Rr Luan Haradinaj; mains €5-12; ☺7am-11pm Mon-Sat, 11am-11pm Sun) Having been here since the dark days of 2001, this is the closest Pristina has to an expat institution, and it lives up to its name, being exceptionally cosy and friendly, with scattered curios and antiques. The menu is international and eclectic and offers exactly what most travellers will be dreaming of: spring rolls, hummus, curries, wraps, burgers and even fajitas.

★**Tiffany** TRADITIONAL €€
(☏038 244 040; Rr Fehmi Agani; set meal €12; ☺9am-10pm Mon-Sat, 6-10pm Sun; ☎) The organic oral menu here (delivered by efficient, if somewhat terse, English-speaking staff) is simply dazzling: enjoy the day's grilled special, beautifully cooked seasonal vegetables drenched in olive oil, and freshly baked bread on the sun-dappled terrace. Understandably much prized by the foreign community, this brilliant place is unsigned and somewhat hidden behind a well-tended bush on Fehmi Agani.

★**Renaissance II** KOSOVAN €€
(☏044 118 796; Rr Xhorxh Bush; set meal €15; ☺6pm-midnight) It's hard to imagine a less-expected find down this grotty, dark side street (look for the Green Pharmacy's neon cross and turn down here). Wooden doors open into a traditional kitchen and you'll be brought water, rakia and wine as well as a plate of sublime appetisers to enjoy as the meat course is cooked by the family's matriarch.

★**De Rada Brasserie** INTERNATIONAL €€
(Rr UÇK 50; mains €5-11; ☺8am-midnight Mon-Sat; ☎) A smart and atmospheric place right in the heart of town that serves up breakfasts, lunches and early dinners to an international clientele. The menu leans towards Italian, but there's plenty of choice. Grab a table outside on the street when the weather's good.

Osteria Basilico ITALIAN €€
(Rr Fehmi Agani 29/1; mains €6-13; ☺noon-midnight) This smart place is Pristina's most reliable Italian restaurant. There's a lovely terrace and a stylish interior where you can enjoy the wide-ranging menu, including plenty of regional classics as well as some more inventive dishes.

GRAČANICA MONASTERY & BEAR SANCTUARY PRISTINA

Explore beyond Pristina by heading southeast to two of the country's best sights. Dusty fingers of sunlight pierce the darkness of **Gračanica Monastery** (☉6am-5pm) FREE, completed in 1321 by Serbian King Milutin. It's an oasis in a town that is the cultural centre of Serbs in central Kosovo. Take a Gjilan-bound bus (€0.50, 15 minutes, every 30 minutes); the monastery's on your left. Do dress respectably (that means no shorts or sleeveless tops for anyone, and head scarves for women) and you'll be very welcome to look around this historical complex and to view the gorgeous icons in the main church.

Further along the road to Gjilan is the excellent new **Bear Sanctuary Pristina** (☎045 826 072; www.vier-pfoten.org; Mramor; ☉9am-6pm Apr-Oct, 10am-4pm Nov-Mar) FREE, in the village of Mramor. Here you can visit a number of brown bears that were rescued from cruel captivity by the charity Four Paws. All the bears here were once kept in tiny cages as mascots for restaurants, but when the keeping of bears was outlawed in Kosovo in 2010, Four Paws stepped in to care for these wonderful animals. Sadly, some of them still suffer from trauma and don't socialise well, but their excellent condition is heartening indeed. Ask to be let off any Gjilan-bound bus by the Delfina gas station at the entrance to Mramor, then follow the unsurfaced road back past the lakeside, and then follow the track around to the right.

KOSOVO PRISTINA

NOMNOM INTERNATIONAL €€
(Rr Rexhep Luci 5; mains €7-14; ☉7am-midnight) Just off the main drag, this modern two-floor bar and restaurant caters to a smart local and foreign crowd. It has a huge summer terrace, and plenty of indoor seating too. The menu offers pizza, pasta, salad, grills and burgers. Sadly, the overall style is compromised by terrible muzak.

🍷 Drinking

★ Dit' e Nat' CAFE
(Rr Fazli Grajqevci 5; ☉8am-midnight; 🛜) 'Day and night', a bookshop-cafe-bar-performance space, is one of the best-kept secrets in Pristina. There's a great selection of English-language books, scrubbed wooden floorboards, strong espresso, friendly English-speaking staff and occasional live music in the evenings, including jazz. Sandwiches and a selection of cocktails are also served.

Tingle Tangle BAR
(off Rr Luan Haradinaj; ☉9am-1am; 🛜) Slip into the courtyard of a residential building in the centre of Pristina to find this unsigned boho hang-out. Tingle Tangle is owned by a much-loved local painter and the walls of this cafe-bar proudly display delightful elements of his work. A cold beer on the terrace here is a great way to start the evening amid a cool crowd.

Sabaja Craft Brewery BREWERY
(Stadioni i Prishtinës; ☉noon-midnight) This American-Kosovar venture is Pristina's first microbrewery with several wonderful brews originating in-house, including an IPA and a Session Pale Ale. There are also various seasonal products available. To complement that, there's a relaxed vibe and a good international menu (mains €3 to €8) available.

ⓘ Information

American Hospital (☎038 221 661; www.spitaliamerikan.com; Graçanicë) The best hospital in Kosovo offers American-standard health care, although not always the language skills to match. It's just outside the city in the Serbian-majority town of Graçanicë.

Barnatore Pharmacy (Bul Nëna Terezë; ☉8am-10pm)

PTK Post (Rr UÇK; ☉8am-10pm Mon-Sat) Post and phone services.

ⓘ Getting There & Around

AIR

There is currently no public transport from **Pristina International Airport** (☎958 123; www.airportpristina.com), so you'll have to get a taxi into the city. Taxis charge €25 for the 20-minute, 18km trip to the city centre.

BUS

The **bus station** (Stacioni i Autobusëve; Rr Lidja e Pejes) is 2km southwest of the centre off Bul Bil Klinton. Taxis to the centre should cost €2.

International buses from Pristina include Serbia's Belgrade (€20, 11pm daily, six hours) and Novi Pazar (€5, 10am daily, three hours); Sarajevo (Bosnia and Hercegovina) via Novi Pazar (€23, 4pm daily); Tirana, Albania (€10, daily, five hours); Skopje, Macedonia (€5, every 30 minutes from 5.30am to 5pm, 1½ hours); and Podgorica, Montenegro (€15, three daily at 5.45pm, 7pm and 7.30pm, seven hours).

TRAIN

Trains run from Pristina to Peja (€3, two daily at 8.01am and 4.41pm, two hours) and, internationally, to Skopje in Macedonia (€4, 7.22am daily, three hours).

AROUND PRISTINA

Kosovo is a small country, which can be crossed by car in any direction in around an hour. Not far in distance, but worlds away from the chaotic capital, the smaller towns of Peja and Prizren both offer a different pace and a new perspective on Kosovar life.

Peja (Peć)

☑ 039 / POP 170,000

Peja (known as Peć in Serbian) is Kosovo's third-largest city and one flanked by sites vital to Orthodox Serbians. With a Turkish-style bazaar at its heart and the dramatic but increasingly accessible Rugova Mountains all around it, it's a diverse and progressive place that's fast becoming Kosovo's tourism hub.

◉ Sights

Patriachate of Peć   MONASTERY

(☑ 044 15 07 55; ⊙ 9am-6pm) This church and monastery complex is a slice of Serbian Orthodoxy that has existed here since the late 13th century. Following the war, the buildings are guarded by NATO's Kosovo Force (KFOR) and you will need to hand in your passport for the duration of your visit. From the food stands around the main square, walk along Lekë Dukagjini with the river on your left for 15 minutes until you reach the monastery walls.

Cheese Market   MARKET

(⊙ 8am-4pm Sat) The town's bustling bazaar makes you feel like you've turned left into İstanbul. Farmers gather here on Saturday with wooden barrels of goat's cheese, so follow your nose.

☀ Activities

Peja has established itself as the country's tourism hub and there's an impressive number of activities on offer in the nearby Rugova Mountains, including rock climbing, mountain biking, skiing, hiking and white-water rafting.

★Rugova Experience   ADVENTURE TOUR

(☑ 039 432 352, 044 350 511; www.rugovaexperience.org; Mbretëreshë Teuta) ✐ This excellent, locally run company is championing the Rugova region for hikers and cultural tourists. It organises homestays in mountain villages, runs very good trekking tours, enjoys great local access and works with English-speaking guides.

Outdoor Kosovo   ADVENTURE TOUR

(☑ 049 168 566; fatos64@gmail.com) An adventure tourism company that specialises in rock climbing, caving, skiing, camping, hiking and mountain biking. English is spoken.

⫚ Sleeping & Eating

★Dukagjini Hotel   HOTEL €€

(☑ 038 771 177; www.hoteldukagjini.com; Sheshi I Dëshmorëve 2; s/d incl breakfast €50/70; ⊛❉✿❖) What on earth is a hotel like this doing in Peja, you may well ask yourself as you step into the regal setting of the Dukagjini's lobby. The hotel has been totally remodelled and the entire place displays international standards you probably didn't expect in a small city in Kosovo. Rooms are large, grandly appointed and have supremely comfortable beds.

Hotel Çardak   HOTEL €€

(☑ 049 801 108, 038 731 017; www.hotelcardak.com; Rr Mbretëresha Teuta 101; s/d incl breakfast €40/60; ❖) Run by several supremely friendly brothers, this central, family-oriented place contains both a pleasant hotel with spacious and clean rooms, as well as an expansive restaurant offering up a tasty menu of pizza, pasta, risotto, steak and other meat grills (mains €3 to €8). Rooms at the front can be loud – ask for one at the back if quiet is a priority.

Kulla e Zenel Beut   TRADITIONAL €€

(Rr William Walker; mains €3-9; ❖) A charming option in the centre of town with a pleasant terrace and a cosy dining room to choose from. Excellent pizza, fresh fish, baked mussels, pasta dishes, grills and even a breakfast menu are on offer here, though service isn't particularly quick.

VISOKI DEČANI MONASTERY

This imposing whitewashed **monastery** (☑049 776 254; www.decani.org; ☉11am-1pm & 4-6pm), 15km south of Peja, is one of Kosovo's absolute highlights. Located in an incredibly beautiful spot beneath the mountains and surrounded by a forest of pine and chestnut trees, the monastery has been here since 1327 and is today heavily guarded by KFOR. Despite frequent attacks from locals who'd like to see the Serbs leave – most recently a grenade attack in 2007 – the 25 Serbian monks living here in total isolation from the local community have stayed.

Buses go to the town of Dečani from Peja (€1, 30 minutes, every 15 minutes) on their way to Gjakovë. It's a pleasant 1km walk to the monastery from the bus stop. From the roundabout in the middle of town, take the second exit if you're coming from Peja. You'll need to surrender your passport while visiting.

❶ Getting There & Away

BUS

The town's bus station can be found on Rr Adem Jashari, a short walk from the town centre. Frequent buses run to Pristina (€5, 90 minutes, every 20 minutes) and Prizren (€4, 80 minutes, hourly). International buses link Peja with Ulclinj (€16, 10am and 8.30pm, 10 hours) and Podgorica in Montenegro (€15, 10am, seven hours).

TRAIN

Trains depart Peja for Pristina at 5.30am and 11.10am (two hours) and depart Pristina for Peja at 7.22am and 4.41pm (two hours). The train station is in the centre of town: follow Rr Emrush Miftari away from the Hotel Dukagjini for about five minutes.

Prizren

☑029 / POP 178.000

Picturesque Prizren is Kosovo's second city and it shines with post-independence enthusiasm that's infectious. If you're passing through between Albania and Pristina, the charming mosque- and church-filled old town is well worth setting aside a few hours to wander about in. It's also worth making a special journey here if you're a documentary fan: Prizren's annual Dokufest is Kosovo's leading arts event and attracts documentary makers and fans from all over the world every August.

◉ Sights

Prizren's old town runs along both sides of the Bistrica river, and is awash with mosques and churches. It's been well restored and is a charming place to wander. The town's 15th-century **Ottoman bridge** has been superbly restored. Nearby is **Sinan Pasha Mosque** (1561), which following a full renovation is now a central landmark in

Prizren. On the other side of the river to the mosque, have a peek at the architecturally refined but nonfunctioning **Gazi Mehmed Pasha Baths**.

The town's most important site is the **Orthodox Church of the Virgin of Ljeviš** (Bogorodica Ljeviška; Rr Xhemil Fluku; admission €3), a 14th-century Serbian church that was used as a mosque by the local population until 1911. After a full renovation in the 1950s, it was again largely destroyed in 1999 by the Albanian population, only to be placed back in the hands of the local Serbian community after the war. Given its location, the church is not exactly welcoming; it's surrounded by barbed wire and closed except for when visitors come to see it. You'll need to present yourself first at St George's Church, on the other side of the river, to get approval to visit from one of the few remaining Serbs in the town. This is well worth doing, however, as even though the frescoes in the church are badly damaged (the building was largely destroyed by Albanians during the war), there are some stunning, ancient wall paintings here and the entire experience is a sad and troubling example of how ethnic hatred can fracture previously peaceful societies.

There is not much of interest at the 11th-century **Kalaja** on top of the hill overlooking the old town, but the 180-degree views over Prizren from this fort are worth the walk. On the way, more barbed wire surrounds the heavily guarded **St Savior Church**, hinting at the fragility of Prizren's once-robust multiculturalism.

🛏 Sleeping & Eating

City Hostel   HOSTEL €
(☑049 466 313; www.prizrencityhostel.com; Rr Iljaz Kuka 66; dm incl breakfast €11, d incl breakfast with/without bathroom €28/33; 🛜) Over four

COUNTRY FACTS

Area 10,887 sq km

Capital Pristina

Country Code ☑381

Currency Euro (€)

Emergency Ambulance ☑94, fire ☑93, police ☑92

Language Albanian, Serbian

Money ATMs in larger towns; banks open Monday to Friday

Population 1.82 million

Visas Kosovo is visa-free for most nationalities. All passports are stamped on arrival for a 90-day stay.

floors and a short wander from the heart of the old town, Prizren's first hostel is a great place to stay, with a friendly, international vibe and a chilled-out roof-terrace bar complete with hammocks and awesome city views. To get here follow the left bank of the river and look for Iljaz Kuka on your left.

★**Hotel Prizreni**　　　HOTEL €€
(☑029 225 200; www.hotelprizreni.com; Rr Shën Flori 2; s/d/tr incl breakfast €30/50/60; ❋🛜) With an unbeatable location just behind the Sinan Pasha Mosque (though you may well disagree at dawn), the Prizreni is a pleasant combination of traditional and modern, with 12 stylish and contemporary rooms, great views and enthusiastic staff. There's a good restaurant downstairs (open 8am to 11pm).

★**Ego**　　　INTERNATIONAL €
(Sheshi Shadërvan; mains €2.50-10; ⊙8am-11pm Mon-Fri, 11am-11pm Sat & Sun; 🛜) Right on Prizren's pretty main cobblestone square, this place stands out beyond the many cafes and restaurants here with its sophisticated international menu, smart decor and charming staff. Have lunch on the terrace, drinks inside or a more formal dinner in the upstairs dining room.

Ambient　　　TRADITIONAL €
(Rr Vatrat Shqiptare; mains €3-9; ⊙8am-midnight; 🛜) With by far the most charming location in Prizren beside a waterfall cascading down the cliffside by the river, and with views over the old town, this is a place to come for a romantic dinner or sundowner. The menu includes a Pasha burger, steaks, seafood and a catch of the day cooked to your specification.

❶ Getting There & Away

Prizren is well connected to Pristina (€4, 90 minutes, every 10 to 25 minutes), Peja (€4, 90 minutes, six daily) and Albania's Tirana (€12, four hours). The bus station is on the right bank of the river, a short walk from the old town.

SURVIVAL GUIDE

❶ Directory A–Z

ACCOMMODATION

Accommodation is booming in Kosovo, with most large towns now offering a good range of options.

BUSINESS HOURS

Reviews include opening hours only if they differ significantly from these.

Banks 8am to 5pm Monday to Friday, until 2pm Saturday

Bars 8am to 11pm (on the dot if police are cracking down)

Restaurants 8am to midnight

Shops 8am to 6pm Monday to Friday, until 3pm Saturday

INTERNET RESOURCES

Balkan Insight (www.balkaninsight.com)

Balkanology (www.balkanology.com)

In Your Pocket (www.inyourpocket.com/kosovo)

Kosovo Tourism Center (www.kosovotourismcenter.com)

UN Mission in Kosovo Online (www.unmikonline.org)

MONEY

Kosovo's currency is the euro, despite not being part of the euro zone or the EU. It's best to arrive with small denominations and euro coins are particularly useful. ATMs are common and established businesses accept credit cards.

POST

PTK post and telecommunications offices operate in Kosovo's main towns.

SLEEPING PRICE RANGES

The following price ranges are for a double room with bathroom:

€ less than €40

€€ €40 to €80

€€€ more than €80

EATING PRICE RANGES

The following price categories are for the average cost of a main course:

€ less than €5

€€ €5 to €10

€€€ more than €10

PUBLIC HOLIDAYS

New Year's Day 1 January

Independence Day 17 February

Kosovo Constitution Day 9 April

Labour Day 1 May

Europe Holiday 9 May

SAFE TRAVEL

Check government travel advisories before travelling to Kosovo. Sporadic violence occurs in North Mitrovica. Unexploded ordnance (UXO) has been cleared from roads and paths but you should seek KFOR (www.aco.nato.int/kfor.aspx) advice before venturing off beaten tracks.

VISAS

Visas are only required by some passport holders; check the **Ministry of Foreign Affairs** (www.mfa-ks.net) website for a full list of nationalities enjoying visa-free travel. This includes EU, US, Canadian, Australian and New Zealand passport holders, all of whom may stay for 90 days visa-free.

If you wish to travel between Serbia and Kosovo you'll need to enter Kosovo from Serbia first.

ℹ Getting There & Away

AIR

Pristina International Airport (☑ 038 5958 123; www.airportpristina.com) is 18km from the centre of Pristina. Airlines include:

Adria Airways (www.adria.si)

Air Prishtina (info.airprishtina.com)

Austrian Airlines (www.austrian.com)

Croatia Airways (www.croatiaairlines.com)

Easyjet (www.easyjet.com)

Germania (www.flygermania.de)

Germanwings (www.germanwings.com)

Kosova Airlines (www.kosovaairlines.com)

Swiss (www.swiss.com)

Turkish Airlines (www.turkishairlines.com)

LAND

Kosovo has good bus connections between Albania, Montenegro and Macedonia, with regular services from Pristina, Peja and Prizren to Tirana (Albania), Skopje (Macedonia) and Podgorica (Montenegro). There's also a train line from Pristina to Macedonia's capital, Skopje.

Border Crossings

Albania To get to Albania's Koman Ferry use the Morina border crossing west of Gjakovë. The busiest border is at Vionica, where the excellent new motorway connects to Tirana.

Macedonia Blace from Pristina and Gllobocicë from Prizren.

Montenegro The main crossing is the Kulla/Rožaje crossing on the road between Rožaje and Peja.

Serbia Due to outbreaks of violence, travellers are advised to be extra vigilant if entering Kosovo at Jarinje or Bërnjak/Banja.

ℹ Getting Around

BUS

Buses stop at distinct blue signs, but can be flagged down anywhere. Bus journeys are generally cheap, but the going can be slow on Kosovo's single-lane roads.

CAR

Serbian-plated cars have been attacked in Kosovo, and rental companies do not let cars hired in Kosovo travel to Serbia and vice versa. European Green Card vehicle insurance is not valid in the country, so you'll need to purchase vehicle insurance at the border when you enter with a car; this is a hassle-free and inexpensive procedure.

TRAIN

The train system is something of a novelty, but services connect Pristina to Peja and to Skopje in Macedonia. Locals generally take buses.

ESSENTIAL FOOD & DRINK

'Traditional' food is generally Albanian – most prominently, stewed and grilled meat and fish. *Kos* (goat's-milk yoghurt) is eaten alone or with almost anything. Turkish kebabs and *gjuveç* (baked meat and vegetables) are common.

➜ **Byrek** Pastry with cheese or meat.

➜ **Gjuveç** Baked meat and vegetables.

➜ **Fli** Flaky pastry pie served with honey.

➜ **Kos** Goat's-milk yoghurt.

➜ **Pershut** Dried meat.

➜ **Qofta** Flat or cylindrical minced-meat rissoles.

➜ **Tavë** Meat baked with cheese and egg.

➜ **Vranac** Red wine from the Rahovec region of Kosovo.

Latvia

Best Places to Eat

➡ International (p219)
➡ Istaba (p219)
➡ 36.Line (p222)
➡ Vincents (p219)
➡ Mr Biskvīts (p223)

Best Places to Stay

➡ Dome Hotel (p218)
➡ Neiburgs (p218)
➡ Hotel MaMa (p221)
➡ Ekes Konvents (p217)
➡ Naughty Squirrel (p217)

Why Go?

Tucked between Estonia to the north and Lithuania to the south, Latvia is the meat of the Baltic sandwich. We're not implying that the neighbouring nations are slices of white bread, but Latvia is the savoury middle, loaded with interesting fillings. Rīga is the main ingredient and the country's cosmopolitan nexus; the Gauja Valley pines provide a thick layer of greens; onion-domed cathedrals sprout above regional towns; cheesy Euro-pop blares along coastal beaches; and the whole thing is peppered with Baltic-German, Swedish, Tsarist Russian and Soviet spice.

Travelling here is easy, language difficulties rarely arise and the simple allure of beaches, forests, castles and history-steeped streets holds plenty of appeal. Latvia may not provide the all-you-can-eat feast of other, more high-profile destinations, but it makes a tasty addition to any European menu.

When to Go
Rīga

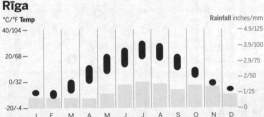

Jun–Aug Summer starts with an all-night solstice romp; then it's off to the beach.

Sep Refusing to let summer go, Rīgans sip lattes under heat lamps at alfresco cafes.

Dec Celebrate the festive season in the birthplace of the Christmas tree.

Latvia Highlights

1 Admire the menagerie of gargoyles, beasts, goddesses and twisting vines that inhabits Riga's **art nouveau architecture** (p217).

2 Clatter along cobblestones, climb church spires and generally enjoy the gingerbread trim that is **Old Rīga** (p218).

3 Explore the castle by candlelight and then stroll the historic streets of **Cēsis** (p223).

4 Trek from castle to castle amid the forested surrounds of **Sigulda** (p222).

5 Indulge in aristocratic decadence as you wander the intricate interiors and gorgeous gardens of **Rundāle Palace** (p21).

6 Case out the castle, then laze on the long and glorious stretch of beach at **Ventspils** (p224).

7 Hobnob with Russian jet-setters in the swanky beachside spa town of **Jūrmala** (p221).

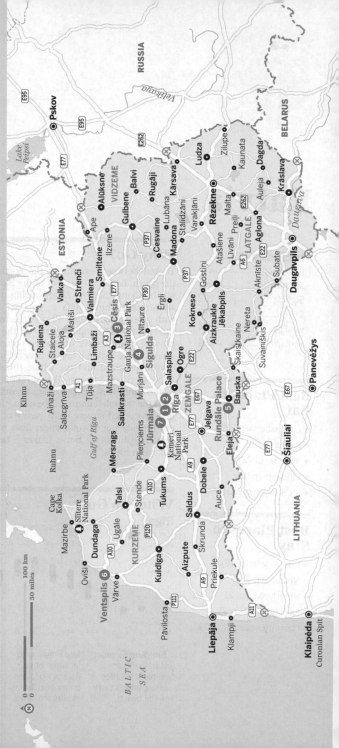

ITINERARIES

Three Days
Fill your first two days with a feast of **Rīga's** architectural eye candy and then take a day trip to opulent **Rundāle Palace**.

One Week
Spend day four lazing on the beach and coveting the gracious wooden houses of **Jūrmala**. The following morning head west to **Kuldīga** before continuing on to **Ventspils**. Spend your last days exploring **Sigulda** and **Cēsis** within the leafy confines of **Gauja National Park**.

RĪGA

POP 700,000

Rīga isn't a 'wallop you over the head with grand sights' kind of city. It's charms are much more subtle than that, coalescing around its laid-back riverside vibe, a compact historic heart and ramshackle suburbs of wooden houses. Most impressively, Rīga has the largest array of art nouveau architecture in Europe. Nightmarish gargoyles and praying goddesses adorn more than 750 buildings along the stately boulevards radiating out from the city's core.

Despite the carnage of wartime bombing, the slaughter of its large Jewish community and the subsequent decades locked behind the Iron Curtain, Rīga has entered the 21st century with a thriving cultural life and a heady cosmopolitan buzz to it.

Sights

Old Rīga (Vecrīga)

Rīga Cathedral   CATHEDRAL
(Rīgas Doms; 6721 3213; www.doms.lv; Doma laukums 1; admission €3; 9am-5pm) Founded in 1211 as the seat of the Rīga diocese, this enormous (once Catholic, now Evangelical Lutheran) cathedral is the largest medieval church in the Baltic. The architecture is an amalgam of styles from the 13th to the 18th centuries: the eastern end, the oldest portion, has Romanesque features; the tower is 18th-century baroque; and much of the rest dates from a 15th-century Gothic rebuilding.

**Rīga History &
Navigation Museum**   MUSEUM
(Rīgas vēstures un kuģniecības muzejs; 6735 6676; www.rigamuz.lv; Palasta iela 4; adult/child €4.27/0.71; 10am-5pm May-Sep, 11am-5pm Wed-Sun Oct-Apr) Founded in 1773, this is the oldest museum in the Baltic, situated in the old cathedral monastery. The permanent collection features artefacts from the Bronze Age all the way to WWII, ranging from lovely pre-Christian jewellery to preserved hands removed from medieval forgers. A highlight is the beautiful neoclassical Column Hall, built when Latvia was part of the Russian Empire and filled with relics from that time.

**Art Museum
Rīga Bourse**   MUSEUM
(Mākslas muzejs Rīgas Birža; www.lnmm.lv; Doma laukums 6; adult/child €6.40/2.85; 10am-6pm Tue-Thu, Sat & Sun, to 8pm Fri) Rīga's lavishly restored stock exchange building is a worthy showcase for the city's art treasures. The elaborate facade features a coterie of deities that dance between the windows, while inside, gilt chandeliers sparkle from ornately moulded ceilings. The Oriental section features beautiful Chinese and Japanese ceramics and an Egyptian mummy, but the main halls are devoted to Western art, including a Monet painting and a scaled-down cast of Rodin's *The Kiss*.

Cat House   HISTORIC BUILDING
(Kaķu māja; Miestaru iela 10/12) The spooked black cats mounted on the turrets of this 1909 art nouveau–influenced building have become a symbol of Rīga. According to local legend, the building's owner was rejected from the Great Guild across the street and exacted revenge by pointing the cats' butts towards the hall. The members of the guild were outraged, and after a lengthy court battle the merchant was admitted into the club on the condition that the cats be turned in the opposite direction.

LATVIA RĪGA

Rīga

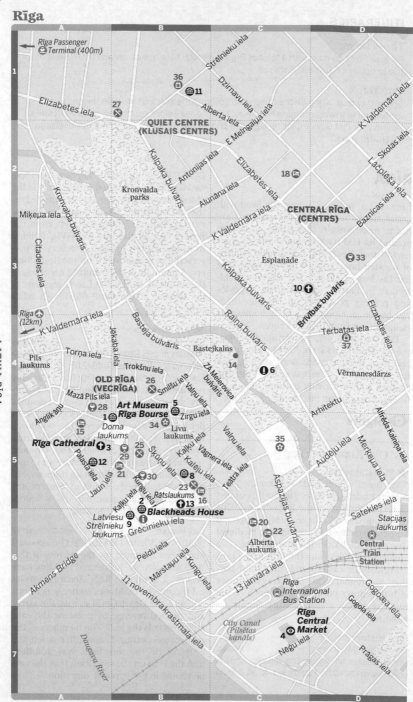

Rīga Passenger
Terminal (400m)

Strēlnieku iela

Dzirnavu iela

36

11

Elizabetes iela

27

Alberta iela

**QUIET CENTRE
(KLUSAIS CENTRS)**

Kalpaka bulvāris

Antonijas iela

E Meingaiļu iela

Elizabetes iela

K Valdemāra iela

Skolas iela

Kronvalda
parks

Alūnana iela

18

**CENTRAL RĪGA
(CENTRS)**

Lāčplēša iela

Baznīcas iela

Miķeļa iela

Kronvalda bulvāris

Citadeles iela

K Valdemāra iela

Kalpaka bulvāris

Esplanāde

33

10

Brīvības bulvāris

Elizabetes iela

Rīga
(12km)

K Valdemāra iela

Basteja bulvāris

Raiņa bulvāris

Tērbatas iela

37

Pils
laukums

Torņa iela

Jēkaba iela

Bastejkalns

ZA Meierovica bulvāris

14

6

Vērmanesdārzs

Trokšņu iela

**OLD RĪGA
(VECRĪGA)**

26

Smilšu iela

Valņu iela

Mazā Pils iela

28

**Art Museum
Rīga Bourse**

5

Zirgu iela

Arhitektu

Anglikāņu

15

1

34

Doma
laukums

Līvu
laukums

Kaļķu iela

35

Vaļņu iela

Alfrēda Kalniņa iela

Rīga Cathedral

3

25

29

Šķūņu iela

Vāgnera iela

Teātra iela

Audēju iela

Merķeļa iela

12

Palasta iela

Jauņ iela

21

30

Kaļķu iela

Kungu iela

8

Kaļēju iela

23

16

Aspazijas bulvāris

Rātslaukums

13

Blackheads House

2

9

Latviešu
Strēlnieku
laukums

Grēcinieku iela

20

22

Alberta
laukums

Satekles iela

Stacijas
laukums

**Central
Train
Station**

Akmens Bridge

Peldu iela

Mārstaļu iela

Kungu iela

13 janvāra iela

Rīga
International
Bus Station

Gogoļa iela

Daugava River

11 novembra krastmala iela

City Canal
(Pilsētas
kanāls)

4

**Rīga
Central
Market**

Ņēģu iela

Gogola iela

Pragas iela

0 ___ 400 m
0 ___ 0.2 miles

Rīga

LATVIA RĪGA

Museum of Decorative Arts & Design

MUSEUM

(Dekoratīvi lietišķās mākslas muzejs; ☎6722 7833; www.lnmm.lv; Skārņu iela 10/20; adult/child

€4.27/2.13; ⊙ 11am-5pm Tue & Thu-Sun, to 7pm Wed) The former St George's Church houses a museum devoted to applied art from the art nouveau period to the present, including an impressive collection of furniture, woodcuts, tapestries and ceramics. The building's foundations date back to 1207 when the Livonian Brothers of the Sword erected their castle here.

St Peter's Church
CHURCH

(Sv Pētera baznīca; www.peterbaznica.riga.lv; Skārņu iela 19; adult/child €2/1, incl steeple €7/3; ⊙ 10am-6pm Tue-Sat, noon-6pm Sun) Forming the centrepiece of Rīga's skyline, this Gothic church is thought to be around 800 years old, making it one of the oldest medieval buildings in the Baltic. Its soaring red-brick interior is relatively unadorned, except for heraldic shields mounted on the columns. A colourful contrast is provided by the art exhibitions staged in the side aisles. At the rear of the church, a lift whisks visitors to a viewing platform 72m up the steeple.

★ Blackheads House
HISTORIC BUILDING

(Melngalvju nams; www.melngalvjunams.lv; Rātslaukums 7) At the time of writing, this fantastically ornate structure was serving as the temporary home of Latvia's president. Built in 1344 as a veritable fraternity house for the Blackheads guild of unmarried German merchants, the original house was decimated in 1941 and flattened by the Soviets seven years later. Somehow the original blueprints survived and an exact replica was completed in 2001 for Rīga's 800th birthday.

OH CHRISTMAS TREE

Rīga's Blackheads House was known for its wild parties; it was, after all, a clubhouse for unmarried merchants. On a cold Christmas Eve in 1510, a squad of bachelors, full of holiday spirit (and other spirits, so to speak), hauled a great pine tree up to their clubhouse and smothered it with flowers. At the end of the evening, they burned the tree to the ground in an impressive blaze. From then on, decorating the 'Christmas Tree' became an annual tradition, which eventually spread across the globe (the burning part never really caught on).

An octagonal commemorative plaque inlaid in cobbled Rātslaukums marks the spot where the original tree once stood.

Museum of the Occupation of Latvia
MUSEUM

(Latvijas Okupācijas muzejs; ☑ 6721 2715; www.omf.lv; Latviešu strēlnieku laukums 1; admission by donation; ⊙ 11am-6pm) Inhabiting an interesting example of Soviet-era architecture on the main square, this museum carefully details Latvia's Soviet and Nazi occupations between 1940 and 1991. Some of the exhibits are extremely disturbing, including first-hand accounts of the murder of Rīga's once-substantial Jewish population, a recreation of a gulag cell and many gruesome photographs. Allow a couple of hours to take it all in.

◉ Central Rīga (Centrs)

Freedom Monument
MONUMENT

(Brīvības bulvāris) Affectionately known as 'Milda', Rīga's Freedom Monument towers above the city between Old and Central Rīga. Paid for by public donations, the monument was designed by Kārlis Zāle and erected in 1935 where a statue of Russian ruler Peter the Great once stood.

Nativity of Christ Cathedral
CATHEDRAL

(Kristus Piedzimšanas katedrāle; Brīvības bulvāris 23) With gilded cupolas peeking through the trees, this sweet little Orthodox cathedral (1883) adds a dazzling dash of Russian bling to the skyline. During the Soviet period the church was converted into a planetarium but it's since been restored to its former use.

Rīga Art Nouveau Museum
MUSEUM

(Rīgas jūgendstila muzejs; www.jugendstils.riga.lv; Alberta iela 12; adult/child May-Sep €5/3.50, Oct-Apr €3.50/2.50; ⊙ 10am-6pm Wed-Sun) If you're curious about what lurks behind Rīga's imaginative art nouveau facades, then it's definitely worth stopping by here. Once the home of Konstantīns Pēkšēns (a local architect responsible for over 250 of the city's buildings), the interiors have been completely restored to resemble a middle-class apartment from the 1920s. Enter from Strēlnieku iela; push No 12 on the doorbell.

◉ Moscow Suburb (Maskavas forštate)

This old part of Rīga takes its name from the main road to Moscow which runs through it.

During the Nazi occupation it was the site of the Rīga Ghetto. In October 1941 the city's entire Jewish population (around 30,000 people) was crammed into the blocks east of Lāčplēša iela and enclosed by barbed wire. Later that year most of them were marched 10km to the Rumbula Forest where they were shot and buried in mass graves.

★ **Rīga Central Market**   MARKET
(Rīgas Centrāltirgus; www.centraltirgus.lv; Nēģu iela 7; ⊙8am-5pm) Haggle for your huckleberries at this vast market, housed in a series of WWI Zeppelin hangars and spilling outdoors as well. It's an essential Rīga experience, providing bountiful opportunities both for people-watching and to stock up for a picnic lunch.

Latvian Academy of Science   HISTORIC BUILDING
(Latvijas Zinātņu Akadēmija; www.panoramariga.lv; Akadēmijas laukums 1; panorama €4; ⊙8am-8pm) Dubbed by local wags 'Stalin's Birthday Cake', this impressive 21-floor, 107m-high confection is Rīga's Russified Empire State Building. Construction commenced in 1951 but wasn't completed until 1961, by which time Stalin had run out of birthdays. Those with an eagle eye will spot hammers and sickles hidden in the convoluted facade. There's a wonderful viewing terrace on the 17th floor.

⟲ Tours

E.A.T. Rīga   WALKING, CYCLING
(☑2246 9888; www.eatriga.lv; tours from €12) Foodies may be initially disappointed to discover that the name stands for 'Experience Alternative Tours' and the focus is on off-the-beaten-track themed walking tours (Old Rīga, Art Nouveau, Alternative Rīga, Retro Rīga). But don't fret – Rīga Food Tasting is an option. It also offers a cycling tour of Jūrmala.

Rīga By Canal   BOATING
(☑2591 1523; www.kmk.lv; adult/child €18/9; ⊙10am-8pm) Enjoy a different perspective of the city aboard the 107-year-old *Darling*, a charming wooden canal cruiser that runs on 15% solar energy (the rest diesel). There are three other boats in the fleet that paddle along the same loop around the city canal and Daugava River.

DON'T MISS

ART NOUVEAU IN RĪGA

If you ask any Rīgan where to find the city's world-famous art nouveau architecture, you will always get the same answer: 'Look up!'

Rīga has the greatest number of art nouveau buildings of any city in Europe. More than 750 buildings boast this flamboyant style of decor which is also known as Jugendstil, meaning 'youth style'. It was named after Munich-based magazine, *Die Jugend*, which popularised it around the turn of the 20th century.

Rīga's art nouveau district (known more formally as the 'Quiet Centre') is anchored around **Alberta iela** (check out 2a, 4 and 13 in particular), but you'll find fine examples throughout the city. Don't miss the renovated facades of **Strēlnieku 4a** and **Elizabetes 10b** and **33**.

🛏 Sleeping

🛏 Old Rīga (Vecrīga)

★ **Naughty Squirrel**   HOSTEL €
(☑2646 1248; www.thenaughtysquirrel.com; Kalēju iela 50; dm/s/d from €16/45/55; ✳@☎) Slashes of bright paint and cartoon graffiti brighten up the city's capital of backpackerdom, which buzzes with travellers rattling the foosball table and chilling out in the TV room. Sign up for regular pub crawls, adrenaline day trips to the countryside and summer BBQs.

Rīga Old Town Hostel   HOSTEL €
(☑6722 3406; www.rigaoldtownhostel.lv; Valņu iela 43; dm €11-14; ✳☎) The Aussie pub on the ground floor doubles as the hostel's hangout space. If you can manage to lug your suitcase past the faux bookshelf door and up the twisting staircase, you'll find spacious dorms with chandeliers and plenty of sunlight.

★ **Ekes Konvents**   HOTEL €€
(☑6735 8393; www.ekeskonvents.lv; Skārņu iela 22; s/d from €60/70; ☎) Not to be confused with Konventa Sēta next door, the 600-year-old Ekes Konvents oozes wobbly medieval

AN ENCHANTING FOREST

If you don't have time to visit the Latvian countryside, a stop at the **Latvian Ethnographic Open-Air Museum** (Latvijas etnogrāfiskais brīvdabas muzejs; www.brivdabasmuzejs.lv; Brīvības gatve 440; adult/child May-Oct €4.27/1.42, Nov-Apr €2.13/0.71; ⏲10am-5pm) is a must. Sitting along the shores of Lake Jugla just northeast of the city limits, this stretch of forest contains more than 100 wooden buildings (churches, windmills, farmhouses etc) from each of Latvia's four cultural regions. Take bus 1 from the corner of Merķeļa iela and Tērbatas iela to the 'Brīvdabas muzejs' stop.

charm from every crooked nook and cranny. Curl up with a book in the adorable stone alcoves on the landing of each storey. Breakfast is served down the block.

★Dome Hotel
HOTEL €€€

(☎6750 9010; www.domehotel.lv; Miesnieku iela 4; r from €249; ☎) It's hard to imagine that this centuries-old structure was once part of a row of butcheries. Today a gorgeous wooden staircase leads guests up to a charming assortment of uniquely decorated rooms that sport eaved ceilings, wooden panelling, upholstered furniture and picture windows with city views.

★Neiburgs
HOTEL €€€

(☎6711 5522; www.neiburgs.com; Jaun iela 25/27; s/d from €152/182; ❋☎) Occupying one of Old Rīga's finest art nouveau buildings, Neiburgs blends preserved details with contemporary touches to achieve its signature boutique-chic style. Try for a room on one of the higher floors – you'll be treated to a view of a colourful clutter of gabled roofs and twisting medieval spires.

🛏 Central Rīga (Centrs)

Hotel Valdemārs
HOTEL €€

(☎6733 4462; www.valdemars.lv; K Valdemāra iela 23; s/d from €56/64; ❋☎) Hidden within an art nouveau block, this Clarion Collection hotel is an excellent choice for those happy to trade fancy decor for reasonable rates. Most surprisingly, the hotel lays on breakfast, afternoon snacks and a simple dinner buffet for all guests.

Krišjānis & Ģertrūde
B&B €€

(☎6750 6604; www.kg.lv; K Barona iela 39; s/d/tr incl breakfast €35/45/55; @☎) Step off the bustling intersection into this quaint, family-run B&B, adorned with still-life paintings of fruit and flowers. It's best to book ahead since there are only six cosy rooms. And pack earplugs for the traffic noise.

Hotel Bergs
HOTEL €€€

(☎6777 0900; www.hotelbergs.lv; Elizabetes iela 83/85; ste from €174; P❋☎) A refurbished 19th-century building embellished with a Scandi-sleek extension, Hotel Bergs embodies the term 'luxury'. The spacious suites are lavished with high-quality monochromatic furnishings and some have kitchens. There's even a 'pillow menu', allowing guests to choose from an array of different bed pillows based on material and texture.

✖ Eating

✖ Old Rīga (Vecrīga)

LIDO Alus Sēta
LATVIAN €

(www.lido.lv; Tirgoņu iela 6; mains around €5; ☎) The pick of the LIDO litter (Rīga's ubiquitous smorgasbord chain), Alus Sēta feels like an old Latvian brew house. It's popular with locals as well as tourists – everyone flocks here for cheap but tasty traditional fare and homemade beer. Seating spills onto the cobbled street during the warmer months.

Domini Canes
EUROPEAN €€

(☎2231 4122; www.dominicanes.lv; Skārpu iela 18/20; mains €7-18; ☎10am-10.30pm) Tables spill out onto the square at this upmarket but relaxed restaurant facing the rear of St Peter's Church. The bistro-style menu includes delicious homemade pasta dishes and plenty of fresh Latvian produce.

Uncle Vanja
RUSSIAN €€

(Tēvocis Vaņa; ☎2788 6963; www.facebook.com/DjadjaVanjaRestorans; Smilšu iela 16; mains €11-21; ☎11am-11pm) The scene opens in what looks like a comfortable 19th-century Russian home (bookshelves, tassled lamps etc). Enter stage left well-dressed serving staff bearing steaming plates of *pelmeņi,* blini (pancakes), and various meat, chicken and fish dishes. Cue a lengthy vodka menu for the final act.

Le Dome Fish Restaurant
SEAFOOD €€€

(☎6755 9884; www.zivjurestorans.lv; Miesnieku iela 4; mains €22-30; ☎8am-11pm) The Dome

Hotel's restaurant quickly reminds diners that Rīga sits near a body of water that's full of delicious fish. Service is impeccable and dishes (including some meat and vegetarian options) are expertly prepared, reflecting the eclectic assortment of recipes in the modern Latvian lexicon.

✗ Central Rīga (Centrs)

★ Istaba
CAFE €€

(✓6728 1141; K Barona iela 31a; mains €17; ⊘noon-11pm) Owned by local chef and TV personality Mārtiņš Sirmais, 'The Room' sits in the rafters above a gallery and occasional performance space. There's no set menu – you're subject to the cook's fancy – but expect lots of free extras (bread, dips, salad, vegies) adding up to a massive serving.

★ Vincents
EUROPEAN €€€

(✓6733 2634; www.restorans.lv; Elizabetes iela 19; mains €24-29; ⊘6-10pm Mon-Sat) 🍴 Rīga's ritziest restaurant has served royalty and rock stars (Emperor Akihito, Prince Charles, Elton John) amid its eye-catching van Gogh–inspired decor. The head chef, Martins Ritins, is a stalwart of the Slow Food movement and crafts his ever-changing menu mainly from produce sourced directly from small-scale Latvian farmers.

✗ Other Neighbourhoods

Although most of Rīga's best eateries are in the centre, a couple of interesting contenders have spilled to the edges.

LIDO Atpūtas Centrs
LATVIAN €

(LIDO Recreation Centre; www.lido.lv; Krasta iela 76; mains around €5; ⊘11am-11pm) If Latvia and Disney World had a love child it would be this enormous log cabin dedicated to the country's coronary-inducing cuisine. Servers dressed like Baltic milkmaids bounce around as patrons hit the rows of buffets. Outside there's a kid's fun park with pony rides and ice-skating.

It's 3.5km southeast of Rīga Central Market; take tram 3, 7 or 9, get off at the 'LIDO' stop and make for the giant windmill.

★ International
INTERNATIONAL €€

(✓6749 1212; www.international.lv; Hospitāļu iela 1; dishes €5-12; ⊘10am-midnight Mon-Fri, noon-midnight Sat & Sun; 🛜) It's well worth a quick tram ride (take tram 11 and get off at Mēness iela) to this wonderful eatery for multiple small plates of yumminess. The name couldn't be more accurate, with a menu containing the likes of 'Tsar's fish soup', sushi, Thai curry and an exceptional beef Wellington.

🍷 Drinking & Nightlife

Skyline Bar
COCKTAIL BAR

(www.skylinebar.lv; Elizabetes iela 55; ⊘5pm-1am Sun-Thu, 3pm-3am Fri & Sat; 🛜) A must for every visitor, glitzy Skyline Bar sits on the 26th floor of the Radisson Blu Hotel Latvija. The sweeping views are the city's best (even from the toilets!), and the mix of glam spirit-sippers makes for great people-watching.

Aptieka
BAR

(Pharmacy Bar; www.krogsaptieka.lv; Mazā Miesnieku iela 1; ⊘4pm-1am Sun-Wed, to 4am Thu-Sat) Antique apothecary bottles confirm the subtle-but-stylish theme at this popular drinking haunt run by a Latvian American. The music's usually excellent and it does a good line in American bar food (burgers and so on).

Egle
BEER GARDEN

(www.spogulegle.lv; Kaļķu iela 1a; ⊘11am-1am) Split between a noisier half with live music most nights (everything from folk to rockabilly), and a quieter half (which generally closes early), this is the best of Old Rīga's open-air beer gardens. It shuts up shop when the weather gets really horrible.

RĪGA CHESS – KNIGHTS TO KING, THEN TSAR

Although some Latvians lament the fact that they are an ethnic minority in their own capital, others are quick to point out that Rīga was never a 'Latvian' city. Founded in 1201 by the German Bishop Albert von Buxhoeveden (say that three times fast) as a bridgehead for the crusade against Europe's last remaining pagan tribes, Rīga was a stronghold for the Knights of the Sword, a member of the Hanseatic League and an important trading junction between Russia and the West. When Sweden snagged the city in 1621, it grew into the largest holding of the Swedish empire (even bigger than Stockholm). By the mid-1860s, with the Russians now as overlords, Rīga was the world's biggest timber port.

Garage

WINE BAR

(www.vinabars.lv; Berga Bazārs, Elizabetes iela 83/85; ⊕10am-midnight) Apart from a semi-industrial fit-out (polished concrete floors, metal chairs) there's nothing even vaguely garagey about this chic little place. It's equal parts wine bar and cafe (the coffee's excellent), serving tapas and a limited selection of mains.

Golden

GAY & LESBIAN

(www.mygoldenclub.com; Ģertrūdes iela 33/35; admission club €10; ⊕4-11pm Tue-Thu, 7pm-5am Fri, 11pm-5am Sat) The golden boy of Rīga's gay scene (admittedly that's not saying much), Golden is a friendly little place with a conservatory-like bar and a weekend-only club.

Cuba Cafe

BAR

(www.cubacafe.lv; Jaun iela 15; ⊕noon-2am Sun-Tue, to 5am Wed-Sat; 🛜) An authentic mojito and a table overlooking Doma laukums is just what the doctor ordered after a long day of sightseeing. On colder days, swig your caipirinha inside amid dangling Cuban flags, wobbly stained-glass lamps and the murmur of trumpet jazz.

☆ Entertainment

Latvian National Opera

OPERA, BALLET

(Latvijas Nacionālajā operā; ☑6707 3777; www. opera.lv; Aspazijas bulvāris 3) With a hefty international reputation as one of the finest opera companies in all of Europe, the national opera is the pride of Latvia. It's also home to the Rīga Ballet; locally born lad Mikhail Baryshnikov got his start here.

Great Guild

CLASSICAL MUSIC

(☑6722 4850; www.lnso.lv; Amatu iela 6) Home to the acclaimed Latvian National Symphony Orchestra.

🛍 Shopping

Art Nouveau Rīga

SOUVENIRS

(www.artnouveauriga.lv; Strēlnieku iela 9; ⊕10am-7pm) Sells a variety of art nouveau–related souvenirs, from guidebooks and postcards to stone gargoyles and bits of stained glass.

Sakta Flower Market

MARKET

(Tērbatas iela 2a; ⊕24hr) Open through the night for those post-midnight *mea culpas*, when you suspect 'Sorry I'm late, honey' just won't do the trick.

ℹ Information

ARS (☑6720 1006; www.ars-med.lv; Skolas iela 5) English-speaking doctors; 24-hour consultation available.

Tourist Information Centre (☑6730 7900; www.liveriga.com; Rātslaukums 6; ⊕10am-6pm) Dispenses tourist maps and walking-tour brochures, helps with accommodation, books day trips and sells concert tickets. It also stocks the **Rīga Card** (www.rigacard.lv; 24-/48-/72-hour card €16/20/26), which offers discounts on sights and restaurants, and free rides on public transport. Satellite offices can be found in Livu laukums (May to September only) and at the bus station.

ℹ Getting There & Away

Rīga is connected by air, bus, train and ferry to various international destinations (p226).

BUS

Buses depart from **Rīga International Bus Station** (Rīgas starptautiskā autoosta; www. autoosta.lv; Prāgas iela 1), located behind the railway embankment just beyond the south-eastern edge of Old Rīga. Destinations include Sigulda (€3, one hour, hourly), Cēsis (€4.15, two hours, hourly), Kuldīga (€6.40, 2½ to 3½ hours, 11 daily) and Ventspils (€7.55, three hours, hourly).

TRAIN

Rīga's **central train station** (Centrālā stacija; ☑6723 2135; www.pv.lv; Stacijas laukums 2) is housed in a conspicuous glass-encased shopping centre near the Central Market. Destinations include Jūrmala (€1.50, 30 minutes, half-hourly), Sigulda (€2.35, 1¼ hours, 10 daily) and Cēsis (€3.50, 1¾ hours, five daily).

ℹ Getting Around

TO/FROM THE AIRPORT

Rīga International Airport (Starptautiskā Lidosta Rīga; ☑1817; www.riga-airport.com; Mārupe District) is in Skulte, 20km west of the city centre.

The cheapest way to get to central Rīga is bus 22 (€1.20, 30 minutes), which runs every 10 to 30 minutes and stops at several points around town.

Taxis cost €12 to €15 and take about 15 minutes.

BICYCLE

Sixt Bicycle Rental (Sixt velo noma; ☑6767 6780; www.sixtbicycle.lv; per 30min/day €0.90/9) Sixt Bicycle Rental has self-hire stands conveniently positioned around Rīga and Jūrmala; simply choose your bike, call the rental service and receive the code to unlock your wheels.

PUBLIC TRANSPORT

Most of Rīga's main tourist attractions are within walking distance of one another, so you might never have to use the city's extensive network of trams, trolleybuses and buses. City transport runs daily from 5.30am to midnight. Some routes have an hourly night service. For Rīga public transport routes and schedules visit www.rigassatiksme.lv.

Tickets can be purchased in advance from the numerous Narvesen convenience stores (per trip €0.60, five-day pass €8). It costs double to buy your ticket directly from the driver (€1.20), but you can get the €0.60 fare from the automated ticket machines on board the newer trams. A trip on the 1901 heritage tram costs €1.50.

TAXI

Taxis charge around €0.70 per kilometre (usually with a surcharge between 10pm and 6am), with a flagfall of around €2.10. Insist on having the meter on before you set off. There are taxi ranks outside the bus and train stations, at the airport, and in front of a few major hotels in central Rīga, such as Radisson Blu Hotel Latvija.

AROUND RĪGA

If you're on a tight schedule, it's easy to get a taste of the Latvian countryside on day trips from Rīga. Within 75km of the capital are two national parks, the country's grandest palace and long stretches of flaxen beach.

Jūrmala

POP 55,600

The Baltic's version of the French Riviera, Jūrmala is a long string of townships with grand wooden beach houses belonging to Russian oil tycoons and their supermodel trophy wives. Even during the height of communism, Jūrmala was a place to see and be seen. On summer weekends, jet-setters and day-tripping Rīgans flock to the resort town for some serious fun in the sun.

If you don't have a car or bicycle, you're best to head straight to the townships of Majori and Dzintari, the heart of the action. A 1km-long pedestrian street, Jomas iela, connects the two and is considered to be Jūrmala's main drag.

WORTH A TRIP

THE BALTIC VERSAILLES

Built as a grand residence for the Duke of Courland, this magnificent palace, **Rundāle Palace** (Rundāles pils; ☑ 6396 2197; www.rundale.net; whole complex/house short route/garden/short route & garden €7.20/5/2.85/5.70; ⊙ 10am-5pm), is a monument to 18th-century aristocratic ostentatiousness, and rural Latvia's architectural highlight. It was designed by Italian baroque genius Bartolomeo Rastrelli, who is best known for the Winter Palace in St Petersburg. About 40 of the palace's 138 rooms are open to visitors, as are the wonderful formal gardens, inspired by those at Versailles.

The highway connecting Rīga to Jūrmala was known as '10 Minutes in America' during Soviet times, because locally produced films set in the USA were always filmed on this busy asphalt strip. Motorists driving the 15km into Jūrmala must pay a €2 toll per day, even if they are just passing through. Keep an eye out for the multilane self-service toll stations sitting at both ends of the resort town.

⊙ Sights

Ķemeri National Park　　　　NATIONAL PARK (Ķemeru nacionālais parks; ☑ 6673 0078; www.kemerunacionalaisparks.lv) Beyond Jūrmala's stretch of celebrity summer homes lies a verdant hinterland of drowsy fishing villages, quaking bogs and thick forests. At the end of the 19th century Ķemeri was known for its curative mud and spring water, attracting visitors from as far away as Moscow.

🛏 Sleeping & Eating

★**Hotel MaMa**　　　BOUTIQUE HOTEL €€€ (☑ 6776 1271; www.hotelmama.lv; Tirgonu iela 22; r from €160; ☎) The bedroom doors have thick, mattress-like padding on the interior (psycho-chic?) and the suites themselves are a veritable blizzard of white drapery. A mix of silver paint and pixie dust accents the ultramodern furnishings and amenities. If heaven had a bordello, it would probably look something like this.

★ **36.Line** MODERN LATVIAN €€€
(☑ 2201 0696; www.lauris-restaurant.lv; Līnija 36; mains €12-30; ⊙ 11am-11pm; ☑) Popular local chef Lauris Alekseyev delivers modern twists on traditional Latvian dishes at this wonderful restaurant, occupying a slice of sand at the eastern end of Jūrmala. Enjoy the beach, then switch to casual attire for lunch or glam up for dinner. In the evening it's not uncommon to find DJs spinning beats.

❶ Information

Tourist Information Centre (☑ 6714 7900; www.jurmala.lv; Lienes iela 5; ⊙ 9am-7pm Mon-Fri, 10am-5pm Sat, 10am-3pm Sun) Located across from Majori train station. Staff can assist with accommodation bookings and bicycle rental.

❶ Getting There & Away

Two to three trains per hour link central Rīga to the sandy shores of Jūrmala. Disembark at Majori station (€1.50, 30 minutes) for the beach or at Ķemeri (€2.05, one hour) for the national park.

If you've got time to kill, the river boat **New Way** (☑ 2923 7123; www.pie-kapteina.lv; adult/child €15/10) departs from the Old Rīga riverfront at 11am daily and takes 2½ hours to reach Majori. It then leaves from Majori pier at 5pm.

Sigulda

POP 11,000

With a name that sounds like a mythical ogress, it's fitting that the gateway to **Gauja National Park** (www.gnp.gov.lv) is an enchanted little spot. Locals proudly call their pine-peppered town the 'Switzerland of Latvia', but if you're expecting a mountainous snow-capped realm, you'll be rather disappointed. Instead, Sigulda is a magical mix of scenic walking and cycling trails, extreme sports and 800-year-old castles steeped in colourful legends.

❂ Sights

Turaida
Museum Reserve CASTLE, MUSEUM
(Turaidas muzejrezervāts; ☑ 6797 1402; www.turaida-muzejs.lv; Turaidas iela 10; adult/child €5/1.14; ⊙ 10am-5pm) Turaida means 'God's Garden' in ancient Livonian, and this green knoll capped with a fairy-tale castle is certainly a heavenly place. The red-brick castle with its tall cylindrical tower was built in 1214

on the site of a Liv stronghold. A museum inside the castle's 15th-century granary offers an interesting account of the Livonian state from 1319 to 1561, and additional exhibitions can be viewed in the 42m-high Donjon Tower, and the castle's western and southern towers.

Sigulda Medieval Castle CASTLE
(Pils iela 18; adult/child €1.50/80; ⊙ 9am-8pm May-Sep, 9am-5pm Mon-Fri, to 8pm Sat & Sun Oct, 9am-5pm Nov-Apr) Constructed between 1207 and 1209 by the Livonian Brothers of the Sword, this castle lies mainly in picturesque ruins after being severely damaged during the Great Northern War (1700-21). Some sections have been restored and you can now walk along the front ramparts and ascend a tower at the rear where there are wonderful views over the forested Gauja Valley. See if you can spy Krimulda Manor and Turaida Castle poking through the trees.

Cable Car CABLE CAR
(☑ 2921 2731; Poruka iela 14; one way adult/child €4/3; ⊙ 10am-6.30pm Jun-Aug, to 4pm Sep-May) Save yourself some hiking time and enjoy terrific views by catching a ride on the cable car over the Gauja River. From the Sigulga side, it departs from a rocky precipice south of the bridge and heads towards Krimulda Manor.

🏃 Activities

Bobsled Track ADVENTURE SPORTS
(Bob trase; ☑ 6797 3813; www.bobtrase.lv; Šveices iela 13; ⊙ noon-5pm Sat & Sun) Sigulda's 1200m bobsled track was built for the Soviet team. In winter you can fly down the 16-bend track at 80km/h in a five-person Vučko **soft bob** (per person €10, from October to mid-March), or book in for the real Olympian experience on the hair-raising **taxi bob** (per person €15, from November to mid-March). Summer speed fiends can ride a wheeled **summer bob** (per person €15, from May to September).

Cable Car
Bungee Jump ADVENTURE SPORTS
(☑ 2644 0660; www.bungee.lv; Poruka iela 14; bungee jump from €30; ⊙ 6.30pm, 8pm & 9.30pm Wed-Sun Apr-Oct) Take your daredevil shenanigans to the next level with a 43m bungee jump from the bright-orange cable car that glides over the Gauja River. For an added thrill, jump naked.

Aerodium
ADVENTURE SPORTS

(🖉 2838 4400; www.aerodium.lv; 2min weekday/weekend €28/32) The one-of-a-kind aerodium is a giant wind tunnel that propels participants up into the sky as though they were flying. Instructors can get about 15m high, while first-timers usually rock out at about 3m. To find the site, look for the sign along the A2 highway, 4km west of Sigulda.

Tarzāns
Adventure Park
ADVENTURE SPORTS

(Piedzīvojumu Parks Tarzāns; 🖉 2700 1187; www.tarzans.lv; Peldu iela 1; combo adult/child €32/22, toboggan €3/1.50, ropes course €17/10; ◷ 10am-8pm May-Oct) Head here to swish down a toboggan track or monkey around on the 'Tarzan' ropes course. There's also a chairlift (€1), tubesliding (€1), reverse bungy (€6), giant swing (€6), climbing wall (€1.50) and archery (€2).

🛏 Sleeping & Eating

Līvkalns
B&B €€

(🖉 2686 4886; Pēterala iela 3; r from €45; P ❋ 🛜) No place is more romantically rustic than this idyllic retreat next to a pond on the forest's edge. The rooms are pine-fresh and sit among a campus of adorable thatch-roof manors.

★ Mr Biskvīts
CAFE, BAKERY €

(www.mr.biskvits.lv; Ausekļa iela 9; mains €3-7; ◷ 8am-9pm Mon-Sat, 9am-7pm Sun) Naughty Mr Biskvīts' candy-striped lair is filled with delicious cakes and pastries, but it's also a good spot for a cooked breakfast, a lunchtime soup or sandwich, and an evening pasta or stir-fry. The coffee's great, too.

ℹ Information

Gauja National Park Visitors Centre (🖉 6780 0388; www.gnp.lv; Turaida iela 2a; ◷ 8.30am-8pm Apr-Oct, 8am-5pm Nov-Mar) Sells maps to the park, town and cycle routes nearby.

Sigulda Tourism Information Centre (🖉 6797 1335; www.tourism.sigulda.lv; Ausekļa iela 6; ◷ 9am-6pm; 🛜) Located within the train station, this extremely helpful centre has stacks of information about activities and accommodation.

ℹ Getting There & Around

Trains run to/from Rīga (€2.35, 1¼ hours, 10 daily) and Cēsis (€2, 45 minutes, five daily).

There are also buses to Rīga (€3, one hour, hourly) and Cēsis (€1.85, 1½ hours, daily).

Cēsis
POP 15,900

Not only is sweet little Cēsis (*tsay*-sis) one of Latvia's prettiest towns, it's also one of its oldest. Nestled within the forested confines of Gauja National Park, its cobbled lanes wend around a sturdy castle, a soaring church spire and a lazy lakeside park.

◉ Sights

Cēsis History &
Art Museum
CASTLE, MUSEUM

(Cēsu Vēstures un mākslas muzejs; Pils laukums 9; whole complex/castle & garden/museum €5/3/3; ◷ 10am-5pm Tue-Sun) Right from the outset when you're handed a lit candle in a glass lantern, it's clear that this isn't an ordinary museum. At its centre is **Cēsis Castle**, founded in 1209 by the Livonian Brothers of the Sword. The candle's to help you negotiate the dark spiral stair in the western tower (the views from the top over Castle Park's picturesque lake are excellent). The museum's extremely interesting displays are in the adjoining 18th-century 'new castle'.

🛏 Sleeping & Eating

Province
B&B €€

(🖉 6412 0849; http://www.province.lv/; Niniera iela 6; r €45; P 🛜) This cute celery-green guesthouse pops out from the dreary Soviet-era housing nearby. The 11 rooms are simple and spotless, and there's a cafe on the ground floor. English isn't its strong point.

Vinetas un
Allas Kārumlādes
CAFE €

(Rīgas iela 12; snacks €3-5; ◷ 9am-7pm) The sign reads 'treats for a good day', which should be enough to entice you through the doors and leave you drooling in front of the cake counter. As well as the delicious sweets on display, it serves salad and soup. It's just a shame that the coffee's not better.

ℹ Information

Cēsis Tourism Information Centre (🖉 6412 1815; www.tourism.cesis.lv; Pils laukums 9; ◷ 10am-5pm daily May-Sep, Tue-Sun Oct-Apr) Within the Cēsis History & Art Museum building.

ⓘ Getting There & Away

Four to five trains a day travel to/from Rīga (€3.50, 1¾ hours) and Sigulda (€2, 45 minutes).

There are also buses to Rīga (€4.15, two hours, hourly) and Sigulda (€1.85, 1½ hours, daily).

WESTERN LATVIA

Latvia's westernmost province, Kurzeme (Courland), offers the simple delights of beautiful beaches and a scattering of historic towns. It's hard to imagine that this low-key region once had imperial aspirations but during the 17th century, while still a semi-independent vassal of the Polish-Lithuanian Commonwealth, the Duchy of Courland had a go at colonising Tobago and the Gambia. The Great Northern War put paid to that, after which the Duchy was subsumed into the Russian Empire.

Kuldīga

POP 11,400

If Kuldīga were a tad closer to Rīga it would be crowded with day-tripping camera-clickers. Fortunately, the town is located deep in the heart of rural Kurzeme, making its quaint historic core the perfect reward for more intrepid travellers.

Kuldīga reached its peak in the 16th and early 17th centuries as one of the most important cities in the Duchy of Courland, but it was badly damaged during the Great Northern War and was never able to regain its former lustre. Today it's a favourite spot to shoot Latvian period-piece films.

There's not a lot to do here except to stroll the streets and the park in the grounds of the old castle (of which nothing much remains), admiring the sculpture garden and gazing down on pretty **Ventas Rumba**, the widest waterfall in Europe. Don't be fooled by the grandness of that title: although it stretches for 249m, it's only a couple of metres high. During spawning season salmon would have little difficulty launching themselves up and over it, giving Kuldīga the curious epithet 'city where salmon fly'.

ⓘ Information

Tourist Information Centre (☑ 6332 2259; www.visit.kuldiga.lv; Baznīcas iela 5; ⊙ 9am-5pm Mon-Sat, 10am-2pm Sun May-Sep, 9am-5pm Mon-Fri Oct-Apr) Tonnes of informative brochures about the town and a souvenir shop on either side. It's located within the old town hall.

ⓘ Getting There & Away

Buses run to/from Rīga (€6.40, three hours, 11 daily) and Ventspils (€6, 1¼ hours, six daily).

Ventspils

POP 36,700

Fabulous amounts of oil and shipping money have given Ventspils an economic edge over Latvia's other small cities, and although locals coddle their Užavas beer and claim that there's not much to do, tourists will find a weekend's worth of fun in the form of brilliant beaches, well-maintained parks and interactive museums.

⦿ Sights

Livionian Order Castle   CASTLE, MUSEUM
(Livonijas ordeņa pils; ☑ 6362 2031; www.ventspilsmuzejs.lv; Jāņa iela 17; adult/child €2.10/1.10; ⊙ 10am-6pm Tue-Sun) This blocky building doesn't look obviously castle-like from the outside, but the 13th-century interior is home to a cutting-edge interactive local history and art museum. During Soviet rule, the castle was used as a prison and an exhibit in the stables recounts its horrors (in Latvian only). An adjacent Zen rock garden will soothe your soul afterwards.

⊨ Sleeping & Eating

Kupfernams   B&B €€
(☑ 6362 6999; www.hotelkupfernams.lv; Kārļa iela 5; s/d €39/59; ☎) Our favourite spot to spend the night, this charming wooden house at the centre of Old Town has a set of cheery upstairs rooms with slanted ceilings, opening onto a communal lounge. Below, there's a cafe and a hair salon (which doubles as the reception).

Melanis Sivēns   LATVIAN €€
(☑ 6362 2396; www.pilskrogs.lv; Jāņa iela 17; mains €6-8; ⊙ noon-10pm Wed-Mon) Located in the castle's dungeon and named after a pig skeleton uncovered by archaeologists, the Black Pig is Ventspils' most atmospheric eatery. Candles flicker on wooden tables, while diners tuck into meaty mains and lashings of ale. Confirmed carnivores should consider the meat platter.

ESSENTIAL FOOD & DRINK

For centuries in Latvia, food equalled fuel, energising peasants as they worked the fields and warming their bellies during bone-chilling Baltic winters. Although it will be a few more years before globetrotters stop qualifying local restaurants as being 'good by Latvia's standards', the cuisine scene has improved by leaps and bounds over the last couple of years.

Pork, herring, boiled potatoes, sauerkraut and black bread are the traditional standbys, pepped up with dill, cottage cheese and sour cream. Other local tastes to look out for include the following:

➡ **Mushrooms** Not a sport but a national obsession, mushroom picking takes the country by storm during the first showers of autumn.

➡ **Smoked fish** Dozens of fish shacks dot the Kurzeme coast – look for the veritable smoke signals rising above the tree line.

➡ **Black Balzām** The jet-black, 45%-proof concoction is a secret recipe of more than a dozen fairy-tale ingredients including oak bark, wormwood and linden blossoms. A shot a day keeps the doctor away, so say most of Latvia's pensioners. To take the edge off, try alternating sips with some blackcurrant juice.

➡ **Alus** For such a tiny nation there's definitely no shortage of *alus* (beer) – each major town has its own brew. You can't go wrong with Užavas or Valmiermuižas.

Skroderkrogs LATVIAN €€
(☏ 6362 7634; Skroderu iela 6; mains €6-13; ⊗ 11am-10pm daily) If you're after big serves of Latvian comfort food in a pleasant local setting (candles and flowers on tables fashioned from old sewing machines), this is the place to come.

ⓘ Information

Tourist Information Centre (☏ 6362 2263; www.visitventspils.com; Dārzu iela 6; ⊗ 8am-6pm Mon-Sat, 10am-4pm Sun) In the ferry terminal.

ⓘ Getting There & Away

Ventspils is served by buses to/from Rīga (€7.55, three hours, hourly) and Kuldīga (€6, 1¼ hours, six daily).

SURVIVAL GUIDE

ⓘ Directory A–Z

FESTIVALS & EVENTS
Check out Kultura (www.culture.lv) for a yearly listing of festivals and events across the country. At midsummer, the cities empty out as locals head to the countryside for traditional celebrations.

GAY & LESBIAN TRAVELLERS
Homosexuality was decriminalised in 1992 and an equal age of consent applies (16 years). However, negative attitudes towards gays and lesbians are the norm and violent attacks occasionally occur. Rīga has a few gay venues and in 2015 it will become the first former-Soviet city to host Europride.

INTERNET RESOURCES
Latvia Travel (www.latvia.travel)
Latvian Institute (www.latinst.lv)
Yellow Pages Directory (www.1188.lv)

PUBLIC HOLIDAYS
New Year's Day 1 January
Good Friday March or April
Easter Sunday & Monday March or April
Labour Day 1 May
Restoration of Independence Day 4 May

COUNTRY FACTS

Area 64,589 sq km

Capital Rīga

Country Code ☏ 371

Currency Euro (€)

Emergency ☏ 112

Language Latvian

Money ATMs are easy to find

Population 2 million

Visas Not required for citizens of the EU, Australia, Canada, New Zealand and the USA, among others. For further information, visit www.mfa.gov.lv.

LATVIA DIRECTORY A–Z

Mothers' Day Second Sunday in May

Pentecost May or June

Līgo (Midsummer's Eve) & Jāņi (Midsummer) 23 and 24 June

National Day 18 November (if it falls on a weekend, the following Monday)

Christmas Holiday 24 to 26 December

New Year's Eve 31 December

TELEPHONE

There are no area codes in Latvia. All telephone numbers have eight digits; landlines start with ⊿ 6 and mobile numbers with ⊿ 2.

ℹ️ Getting There & Away

AIR

Fifteen European airlines fly into Rīga, including the national carrier **airBaltic** (⊿ 9000 1100; www.airbaltic.com).

LAND

In 2007 Latvia acceded to the Schengen Agreement, which removed all border control between it and Estonia and Lithuania. Carry your travel documents with you at all times, as random border checks do occur.

Bus

Ecolines (⊿ 6721 4512; www.ecolines.net) Routes include Rīga–Parnu–Tallinn (€17, four to 4¾ hours, seven daily), Rīga–Tartu (€7, four hours, two daily), Rīga–Vilnius (€17, four hours, seven daily), Rīga–Vilnius–Minsk (€24, eight hours, daily) and Rīga–Moscow (€60, 14 hours, daily).

Kautra/Eurolines (www.eurolines.lt) Operates buses on the Rīga–Vilnius–Warsaw–Berlin–Cologne route (€116, 29 hours).

SLEEPING PRICE RANGES

Prices quoted here are for rooms with a private bathroom unless otherwise stated. We highly advise booking ahead during summer. Rates drop significantly in the colder months. The following price indicators apply for a high-season double room.

€ less than €40

€€ €40 to €80

€€€ more than €80

EATING PRICE RANGES

The following price ranges refer to a standard main course. It's common to tip up to 10% for good service.

€ less than €7

€€ €7 to €17

€€€ more than €17

Lux Express & Simple Express (⊿ 6778 1350; www.luxexpress.eu) Routes include Rīga–Pärnu–Tallinn (from €13, 4½ hours, 11 daily), Rīga–Tartu–St Petersburg (from €23, 12 hours, four daily), Rīga–Vilnius (from €11, four hours, 10 daily) and Rīga–Kaliningrad (€20, eight hours, daily).

Train

International trains head from Rīga to Moscow (16 hours), St Petersburg (15 hours) and Minsk (12 hours) daily. There are no direct trains to Estonia; you'll need to change at Valka.

SEA

Stena Line (⊿ 6362 2999; www.stenaline.nl) Car ferries head from Travemünde, Germany, to Liepāja (26 hours) and Ventspils (26 hours), and from Nynäshamn, Sweden, to Ventspils (12 hours).

Tallink Silja Line (⊿ 6709 9700; www.tallink silja.com; passenger/vehicle from €32/105) Overnight ferries between Rīga and Stockholm (17 hours), departing every other day.

ℹ️ Getting Around

BUS

➤ Buses are generally more frequent than trains and serve more of the country.

➤ Updated timetables are available at www.1188.lv and www.autoosta.lv.

CAR & MOTORCYCLE

➤ Driving is on the right-hand side.

➤ Headlights must be on at all times.

➤ Local car-hire companies usually allow you to drive in all three Baltic countries but not beyond.

TRAIN

➤ There are train services from Rīga to Jūrmala, Sigulda and Cēsis.

➤ Timetables are online at www.1188.lv and www.ldz.lv.

Lithuania

Best Places to Eat
➡ Leičiai (p232)
➡ Pilies kepyklėlė (p232)
➡ Senoji Kibininė (p235)
➡ Moksha (p236)
➡ Momo Grill (p238)

Best Places to Stay
➡ Hotel Euterpė (p237)
➡ Bernardinu B&B (p231)
➡ Miško Namas (p238)
➡ Litinterp Guesthouse (p237)
➡ Jimmy Jumps House (p231)

Why Go?
Compact Lithuania has much to offer. Those with a passion for baroque architecture, ancient castles and archaeological treasures will find plenty in the capital and beyond. There are sculpture parks and interactive museums for travellers wishing to delve into the country's traumatic recent history; modern art spaces and exhibitions to titillate those whose interests are more contemporary; and all-night clubbing in the bigger cities and on the coast for those requiring something less cerebral.

Away from the cities, the pristine beaches and giant sand dunes on the west coast are a must-see. The Hill of Crosses is an unexpected delight. Elsewhere, the country's woods and lakes come alive in summer with cyclists, berry pickers and campers.

When to Go
Vilnius

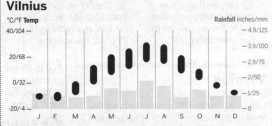

Apr Some of the world's best jazz performers are at the Kaunas International Jazz Festival.

Jun & Jul The loveliest time to explore the forests and sand dunes of the Curonian Spit.

Sep Vilnius Capital Days, a celebration of the capital with street theatre, music and fashion.

Lithuania Highlights

❶ Explore beautiful baroque **Vilnius**, with its cobbled streets, church spires, bars and bistros.

❷ Breathe the pure air amid fragrant pine forests and high sand dunes of the **Curonian Spit** (p238).

❸ Hear the wind whistle between thousands of crosses on eerie **Hill of Crosses** (p236).

❹ Wander wonderful **Trakai** (p234), home of the Karaite people and a stunning island castle.

❺ Experience a taste of Lithuania's communist past at the **Grūtas sculpture park** (p234).

❻ Take in the poignant WWII history of Kaunas' **Ninth Fort** (p235).

Vilnius

📙 5 / POP 523,100

Lithuania's capital, Vilnius, doesn't get the attention it deserves. The city's surprising Old Town is a dazzling assemblage of baroque houses, inviting alleyways and colourful churches built around quiet courtyards. But it's no museum piece: the city's cosmopolitan heritage, enriched by Polish, Jewish and Russian influences, lends a sophisticated vibe, and thousands of students keep the energy level high. Push through big wooden doors to find lively pubs and bars, hidden terraces and romantic restaurants. Tumbledown buildings hide designer boutiques and high-end handicraft shops.

◉ Sights

◉ Cathedral Square & Gediminis Hill

Cathedral Square (Katedros aikštė), dominated by Vilnius Cathedral and its 57m-tall belfry, marks the centre of Vilnius and is home to

ITINERARIES

Three Days
Devote two days to exploring the baroque heart of **Vilnius**, then day trip to **Trakai** for its island castle and the homesteads of the Karaite people, stopping off at **Paneriai** on the way.

One Week
Spend four nights in **Vilnius**, with day trips to both **Trakai** and the **Grūtas Park** sculpture garden near Druskininkai. Travel cross-country to the **Hill of Crosses**, then explore some serious nature on the **Curonian Spit** for two or three days. Head back east via **Klaipėda** and **Kaunas**.

the city's most important sights. The square buzzes with local life, especially at Sunday morning Mass. Amuse yourself by hunting for the secret *stebuklas* (miracle) tile; if found, it can grant you a wish if you stand on it and turn around clockwise. It marks the spot where the 650km Tallinn–Vilnius human chain, protesting against Soviet rule, ended in 1989. The 48m-high **Gediminas Hill** rises just behind the square. The restored ruins of **Gediminas Castle** mark the spot where the city was founded in the 13th century. Scramble up (or take a handy **funicular**) for jaw-dropping views of Old Town.

Vilnius Cathedral CHURCH
(Vilniaus Arkikatedra; ☑5-261 0731; www.katedra.lt; Katedros aikštė 2; ☉7am-7.30pm, Mass Sun 8am, 9am, 10am, 11.15am, 12.30pm, 5.30pm & 6.30pm) This national symbol occupies a spot originally used for the worship of Perkūnas, the Lithuanian thunder god; much later the Soviets turned the cathedral into a gallery. The first wooden cathedral was built here in 1387–88. **St Casimir's Chapel** at the back is the showpiece. It has a baroque cupola, coloured marble and frescoes from St Casimir's life.

⭐ **Palace of the Grand Dukes of Lithuania** MUSEUM
(Valdovų rumai; ☑5-212 7476; www.valdovurumai.lt; Katedros aikštė 4; adult/student €3/1.50, guided tour €20; ☉11am-6pm Tue-Fri, 11am-4pm Sat & Sun) The palace that once marked the seat of the Lithuanian dukes has been painstakingly rebuilt and is a must for understanding Lithuanian history. The visitors' route begins on the ground floor, where traces of the old palace dating from the 16th and 17th centuries, and earlier, can still be seen, and proceeds upward through the centuries. The palace was a modern-day wonder in its day, with a vast courtyard and lively social calendar that included masked balls, banquets and jousting matches. Under the Russian occupation at

the end of the 18th century, the palace was torn down and left a ruin. It reopened in 2013 after a decade-long costly restoration.

National Museum of Lithuania MUSEUM
(Lietuvos Nacionalinis Muziejus; ☑5-262 7774; www.lnm.lt; Arsenalo gatvė 1; adult/child €2/1; ☉10am-6pm Tue-Sat) The National Museum of Lithuania, identified by a proud statue of **Mindaugas** (Arsenalo gatvė 1) – the first and only king of Lithuania – at the front, features exhibits that look at everyday Lithuanian life from the 13th century until WWII. Of particular note are some of the country's earliest coins, dating from the 14th century, as well as folk art and cross-crafting.

Gediminas Castle & Museum MUSEUM
(Gedimino Pilis ir Muziejus; ☑5-261 7453; www.lnm.lt; Gediminas Hill, Arsenalo gatvė 5; adult/child €2/1; ☉10am-7pm May-Sep, 10am-5pm Tue-Sun Oct-Apr) Vilnius was founded on 48m-high Gediminas Hill, topped since the 13th century by the oft-rebuilt tower of ruined Gediminas Castle. For spectacular views of the Old Town, take the spiral staircase to the top of the tower, which houses the Upper Castle Museum. Exhibits include scale models of the castle in the 14th and 18th centuries and medieval arms.

⦿ Old Town

St Anne's Church CHURCH
(Šv Onos Bažnyčia; ☑8-698 17731; www.onos baznycia.lt; Maironio gatvė 8-1; ☉Mass 6pm Mon-Sat, 9am & 11am Sun) Arguably the most beautiful

---

ℹ VILNIUS CITY CARD

If you're planning to do epic amounts of sightseeing within a short period of time, the **Vilnius City Card** (☑5-250 5895; www.vilnius-tourism.lt; per 24/72hr €18/30) provides free or discounted entry to many attractions, and free transport.

Central Vilnius

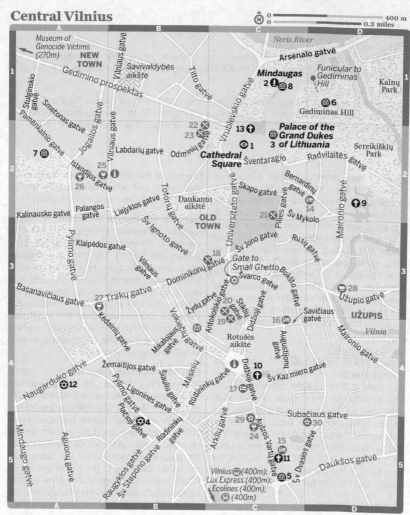

0 ___ 0 ___ **400 m**
0 ___ **0.2 miles**

church in Vilnius is tiny, late-15th-century St Anne's Church (standing in front of the much larger **Bernardine's Church**). A graceful example of Gothic architecture, its sweeping curves and delicate pinnacles frame 33 different types of red brick. It's so fine Napoleon reputedly wanted to take it back to Paris.

St Casimir's Church

CHURCH

(Šv Kazimiero Bažnyčia; ☑5-2121715; www.kazimiero. lt; Didžioji gatvė 34; ⊙7am-7pm) This striking church is the city's oldest baroque place of worship. St Casimir's dome and cross-shaped plan defined a new style for churches when the Jesuits built it between 1604 and 1615. It

was destroyed and rebuilt several times over the centuries and has recently emerged from another bout of renovation.

St Teresa's Church

CHURCH

(Šv Teresės Bažnyčia; ☑5-212 3513; www.ausros vartai.lt; Aušros Vartų gatvė 14; ⊙7am-7pm) This Catholic church is baroque through and through: early baroque outside and ornate late baroque inside. Underneath its entrance is a chamber for the dead, containing examples of baroque tombs, but it is usually locked.

Gates of Dawn

HISTORIC BUILDING

(Aušros Vartai; ☑5-212 3513; www.ausrosvartai. lt; Aušros Vartų 12; ⊙chapel 6am-7pm, Mass 9am,

Central Vilnius

10am, 5.30pm & 6.30pm Mon-Sat, 9.30am Sun)
FREE The southern border of Old Town is
marked by the last standing of 10 portals that
were once built into the Old Town walls. This
16th-century town gate doesn't quite live
up to the breathless 'Gates of Dawn' moni-
ker, though peek inside to see Chapel of the
Blessed Mary and a historic painting of the
Madonna said to work miracles.

◉ New Town & Outside Centre

⭐ **Museum of Genocide Victims** MUSEUM
(Genocido Aukų Muziejus; ☎5-249 8156; www.
genocid.lt/muziejus; Aukų gatvė 2a; adult/child €2/1;
◷10am-6pm Wed-Sat, to 5pm Sun) This former
headquarters of the Soviet KGB houses a museum dedicated to thousands of Lithuanians
who were murdered, imprisoned or deported by the Soviet Union from WWII until the
1960s. Memorial plaques honouring those
who perished tile the outside of the building.
Inside, floors cover the harsh realities of Soviet occupation, including gripping personal
accounts of Lithuanian deportees to Siberia.

TV Tower TOWER
(Televizijos Bokštas; ☎5-252 5333; www.tele
centras.lt; Sausio 13-osios gatvė 10; adult/child
€6/3; ◷observation deck 11am-10pm; 🚌1, 3, 7,
16) It's hard to miss the 326m TV tower on
the city's western horizon. This tall needle
symbolises Lithuania's strength of spirit; on
13 January 1991 Soviet special forces killed
some 14 people here. Lithuanian TV kept
broadcasting until the troops came through

the tower door. From the observation deck
(190m) Vilnius is spread out before you.

🛏 Sleeping

⭐ **Jimmy Jumps House** HOSTEL €
(☎8-607 88435, 5-231 3847; www.jimmyjumps
house.com; Savičiaus gatvė 12-1; dm €11-12, r from
€30; ❀@🛜) This clean, well-run, centrally
located hostel is justifiably popular among
backpackers. The pine-wood bunks are modest in four- to 12-bed rooms, but extras like
free walking tours, themed pub crawls and
a free breakfast add up to money well spent.
Offers discounts if booked directly via email.
No credit cards.

⭐ **Bernardinu B&B** GUESTHOUSE €€
(☎5-261 5134; www.bernardinuhouse.com; Ber-
nardinų gatvė 5; s/d from €54/60; P❀🛜)
Charming family-owned guesthouse located
on one of the most picturesque lanes in the
Old Town. The house dates to the 18th century, but it's been renovated and the owners
have tried hard to preserve elements like old
timber flooring and ceilings. Breakfast is €5
and it's brought to your door on a tray at 9am.

⭐ **Domus Maria** GUESTHOUSE €€
(☎5-264 4880; www.domusmaria.lt; Aušros Vartų
gatvė 12; s/d €60/80; P❀@🛜) The guesthouse of the Vilnius archdiocese is housed in
a former monastery dating to the 17th century and oozes charm. Accommodation is in
the monks' chambers, but they've been given
a thorough, stylish makeover. Two rooms, 207
and 307, have views of the Gates of Dawn and

are usually booked far in advance. Breakfast is served in the vaulted refectory.

Radisson Blu Royal Astorija　　HOTEL €€€
(☑ 5-212 0110; www.radissonblu.com; Didžioji gatvė 35/2; s/d/ste €180/210/360; P 🐾 @ 🗢 ⛫) This excellent splurge or business choice is part of a high-end chain, though the building dates from the early 20th century and exudes character. The central location, overlooking St Casimir's Church, is a plus, as are the popular wintertime Sunday brunches. Mod cons like trouser presses and safes are standard. The Superior-Class rooms got a thorough makeover in 2014.

✗ Eating

★Pilies kepyklėlė　　CREPES €
(☑ 5-260 8992; Pilies gatvė 19; mains €3-6; ⏱ 9am-11pm) A standout from the crowd on Vilnius' busiest tourist street, this relaxed combination creperie-bakery mixes old-world charm with a fresh, upbeat vibe. The 9am omelette here is a must-have as are the savoury pancakes, stuffed with spinach or ham and cheese and topped with sour cream. The poppyseed cake is reputedly the best on this side of town.

★Leičiai　　LITHUANIAN €€
(☑ 5-260 9087; www.bambalyne.lt; Stiklių gatvė 4; mains €4-8; ⏱ 11am-midnight; 🗢) This popular, earthy brew-pub and restaurant serves simple but honest Lithuanian cooking – think potato pancakes and *cepelinai* (meat-stuffed potato dumplings) at everyman prices. The beer is excellent as well, and in warm weather there's a big terrace out the back for relaxing.

Cozy　　INTERNATIONAL €€
(☑ 5-261 1137; www.cozy.lt; Dominikonų gatvė 10; mains €5-8; ⏱ 9am-2am Mon-Wed, to 4am Thu & Fri, 10am-4am Sat, to 2am Sun; 🗢) Cozy defies easy description: is it a bar, cafe or restaurant? The food here, including several inventive salads with duck or turkey meat and more-standard mains like pork and chicken (but often given an Asian twist), is worth the trip alone. By night Cozy morphs into a welcoming drinking den, popular with students from nearby Vilnius University.

Sue's Indian Raja　　INDIAN €€
(☑ 5-266 1887; www.suesindianraja.lt; Odminių gatvė 3; mains €6-10; ✈) OK, it's strange to list an Indian restaurant as a top pick in Vilnius, but the food here is excellent and authentic. *After* you've had your fill of delicious local foods like potato pancakes and *cepelinai*, repair here to have your palate re-energised with

spicy lentils, curries and vindaloo. The three-course 'business lunch', served weekdays, is a steal at €7.50.

Zoe's Bar & Grill　　INTERNATIONAL €€
(☑ 5-212 3331; www.zoesbargrill.com; Odminių gatvė 3; mains €3-8) Zoe's covers many culinary bases and does it well, with the likes of homemade meatballs and sausages, tender steaks, and spicy Thai stir-fries and soups. Dine outdoors with cathedral views or indoors and receive an impromptu cooking lesson.

★Lokys　　LITHUANIAN €€€
(☑ 5-262 9046; www.lokys.lt; Stiklių gatvė 8; mains €8.50-18) Hunt down the big wooden bear outside to find this Vilnius institution, a cellar maze going strong since 1972. Game is its mainstay, with delicacies such as beaver-meat stew with plums or quail with blackberry sauce luring the culinarily curious. Folk musicians play here on summer evenings.

🍷 Drinking & Nightlife

Užupio kavinė　　CAFE
(☑ 5-212 2138; www.uzupiokavine.lt; Užupio gatvė 2; ⏱ 10am-11pm; 🗢) The riverside cafe here in the Bohemian neighbourhood of Užupis is the perfect spot to relax over a coffee, beer or wine. Try booking ahead on warm summer nights, as the place tends to fill up. The cosy interior is equally fun in winter. Some nights bring impromptu live entertainment.

In Vino　　WINE BAR
(☑ 5-212 1210; www.invino.lt; Aušros Vartų gatvė 7; ⏱ 4pm-2am Sun-Thu, to 4am Fri & Sat) Popular drinking spot in the heart of Old Town that's perfect for a girls' (or guys') night out or, if you're single and on the prowl, meeting some friendly locals. In summer sit out in the back courtyard (try to arrive early as the tables fill up fast). Though the names suggests wine, it also serves beer and cocktails.

Jackie　　BAR
(Vilniaus gatvė 31; ⏱ 6pm-2am Sun-Wed, to 3am Thu, to 5am Fri & Sat) This hopping whisky bar, specialising in American whiskeys and bourbon, gets absolutely packed most nights, so if you wish to savour your poison, go early. Or go late on the weekend if you want to catch a DJ set.

Pabo Latino　　CLUB
(☑ 5-262 1045; www.pabolatino.lt; Trakų gatvė 3/2; admission €5-8; ⏱ 8pm-3am Thu-Sat) This sultry-red club specialises in sweet Latino tunes and strong cocktails. Put on your dancing shoes, fortify your liver, and be prepared for a fun night out.

JEWISH VILNIUS

Over the centuries Vilnius developed into one of Europe's leading centres of Jewish life and scholarship until the community was wiped out by the occupying Nazis and their Lithuanian sympathisers during WWII. The former Jewish quarter lay in the streets west of Didžioji gatvė, including present-day Žydų gatvė (Jews St) and Gaono gatvė, named after Vilnius' most famous Jewish resident, Gaon Elijahu ben Shlomo Zalman (1720–97). The **Tolerance Centre** (☑ 5-262 9666; www.jmuseum.lt; Naugarduko gatvė 10/2; adult/child €2.40/1.20; ⊙ 10am-6pm Mon-Fri, 10am-4pm Sun), a beautifully restored former Jewish theatre, houses thought-provoking displays on the history and culture of Jews in Lithuania before the Shoah (Holocaust) and occasional exhibitions. The **Holocaust Museum** (Holokausto Muziejus; ☑ 5-262 0730; www.jmuseum.lt; Pamėnkalnio gatvė 12; adult/child €2.40/1.20; ⊙ 9am-5pm Mon-Thu, 9am-4pm Fri, 10am-4pm Sun), in the so-called Green House, is an unvarnished account detailing the suffering of Lithuanian Jews in an unedited display of horrific images and letters by local survivors. Vilnius' only remaining synagogue, the **Choral Synagogue** (Choralinė Sinagoga; ☑ 5-261 2523; Pylimo gatvė 39; donations welcome; ⊙ 10am-2pm Mon-Fri) **FREE**, was built in a Moorish style in 1903 and survived because it was used as a medical store.

Opium CLUB
(☑ 8-691 41205; www.opiumclub.lt; Islandijos gatvė 4; admission €3-5; ⊙ 10pm-6am Fri, 11pm-5am Sat) This compact venue – playground of the city's best DJs – is for serious clubbers. Come here and there's a good chance you'll get addicted.

☆ Entertainment

Lithuanian
National Philharmonic CLASSICAL MUSIC
(Lietuvos Nacionalinė Filharmonija; ☑ 5-266 5233; www.filharmonija.lt; Aušros Vartų gatvė 5; ⊙ box office 10am-7pm Tue-Sat, to noon Sun) The country's foremost go-to location for classical music, as well as festivals of popular music and other performances.

Tamsta ROCK, JAZZ
(☑ 5-212 4498; www.tamstaclub.lt; Subačiaus gatvė 11a; admission €3-5; ⊙ 7pm-midnight Wed & Thu, to 2am Fri & Sat Sep-Apr) Live music by local musicians – ranging from rock to rock'n'roll to jazz. Inspired jamming some nights and the long bar gets pretty packed most evenings. Note the club shuts down during summer (June to August).

ℹ Information

Baltic-American Medical & Surgical Clinic
(☑ 8-698 52655, 5-234 2020; www.bak.lt; Nemenčinės gatvė 54a; ⊙ 24hr) English-speaking health care inside Vilnius University Antakalnis hospital.

Pharmacy (Gedimino Vaistinė; ☑ 5-261 0135; www.univesitetovaistine.eu; Gedimino prospektas 27; ⊙ 7.30am-8pm Mon-Fri, 10am-5pm Sat, to 4pm Sun)

Vilnius Tourist Information Centre – Old Town (☑ 5-262 9660; www.vilnius-tourism.lt;

Vilniaus gatvė 22; ⊙ 9am-6pm; ⑧) The city's main tourist information office is a helpful repository of maps, brochures and friendly staff willing to sort out transport, accommodation and sightseeing issues.

Vilnius Tourist Information Centre – Town Hall (☑ 5-262 6470; www.vilnius-tourism.lt; Didžioji gatvė 31; ⊙ 9am-12.30pm & 1.15-6pm; ⑧) Convenient branch of the official tourist office, with a wealth of glossy brochures and general information. It also arranges tour guides, books accommodation (hotel reservation fee applies) and rents bicycles.

ℹ Getting There & Away

BUS
The **bus station** (Autobusų Stotis; ☑ information 1661; www.autobusustotis.lt; Sodų gatvė 22) handles both domestic and international coach service and is situated about 1km south of Old Town, across the street from the train station. The main international bus operators include **Ecolines** (☑ information 5-213 3300; www.ecolines.net; Geležinkelio gatvė 15; ⊙ 8am-7pm Mon-Fri, 9am-5pm Sat, 9am-3pm Sun), Lux Express (p240) or one of the affiliated carriers under **Eurolines** (www.eurolines.lt).

Frequent domestic destinations include Kaunas (€6, 1½ hours, hourly), Klaipėda (€20, four to five hours, 15 daily) and Šiauliai (€15, 3¼ to five hours, more than 10 daily).

Sample international connections include Berlin (€32, 15 hours, daily), Rīga (€20, four hours, up to seven daily), Tallinn (€36, nine hours, four daily) and Warsaw (€16, eight hours, two daily).

TRAIN
From the **train station** (Geležinkelio Stotis; ☑ information 5-233 0088; www.litrail.lt; Geležinkelio gatvė 16), Vilnius is linked by rail to various international destinations, including Warsaw,

GRŪTAS PARK – THE GRAVEYARD OF COMMUNISM

Both entertaining and educational, **Grūtas Park** (Grūto Parkas; ☑ 313-55 511; www.gruto parkas.lt; Grūtas; adult/child €6/3; ☺ 9am-10pm summer, to 5pm rest of year; ♨), 125km south of Vilnius, near the spa town of Druskininkai, has been an enormous hit since it opened in 2001. The sprawling grounds, built to resemble a Siberian concentration camp, feature the entire Marxist pantheon and dozens of other statuesque examples of Soviet realism, as well as assorted communist paraphernalia, exhibits on Soviet history (with a focus on the oppression of Lithuania) and loudspeakers bellowing Soviet anthems.

The statues once stood confidently in parks and squares across Lithuania, but now this is all that's left.

There are up to several buses daily between Druskininkai and Vilnius (€10, two hours), and hourly buses to/from Kaunas (€9, 2¼ hours). Ask to be let off at Grūtas village, then walk the final 1km to the park. Catch a bus back to either city from the main road.

Minsk and Moscow, though most trains run through Belarus and require a transit visa.

Frequent domestic destinations include Kaunas (€6, one to 1¾ hours, up to 17 daily), Klaipėda (€15, 4¾ hours, three daily) and Trakai (€1.60, 35 to 45 minutes, up to 10 daily).

Sample international connections include Moscow (from €90, 15 hours, three daily), Minsk (from €10, three to four hours, up to seven daily) and Warsaw (from €25, 15 hours, one daily).

ℹ Getting Around

TO/FROM THE AIRPORT

Bus 1 runs between Vilnius International Airport (p239), 5km south of the city centre, and the train station. A shuttle train service runs from the train station 17 times daily between 5.44am and 9.07pm (around €0.75). A taxi from the airport to the city centre should cost around €15.

BICYCLE

Velo-City (☑ 8-674 12123; www.velovilnius.lt; Aušros Vartų 7; per hr/day €3/12; ☺ 9am-9pm Apr-Sep) Rents bikes and offers daily bike tours of the city. Outside high season you'll find it at Kauna gatvė 5 (open 2pm to 6pm Tuesday to Saturday).

PUBLIC TRANSPORT

Vilnius Transport (☑ 5-210 7050; www.vilnius transport.lt) Vilnius' public transport company operates buses and trolleybuses daily from 5am to 11pm. See the website for a (confusing) time-table. Buy individual journey tickets from the driver for €1. For longer stays, buy an electronic Vilniečio Kortelė (Vilnius Card) from news kiosks for €1.20. Using the card, a 30-minute journey costs about €0.60.

TAXI

Vilnius Veža (☑ 5-233 3337, 1450; www. vilniusveza.lt) Reliable radio-taxi operator. Fares are around €0.72 per kilometre.

Paneriai

During WWII the Nazis – aided by Lithuanian accomplices – murdered 100,000 people, around 70,000 of them Jews, at this site in the forest, 8km southwest of Vilnius.

From the entrance a path leads to the small **Paneriai Museum** (☑ tours 662-89 575; www.jmuseum.lt; Agrastų gatvė 17; ☺ 9am-5pm Sun-Thu May-Sep, by appointment Oct-Apr) FREE, with a graphic display of photographs and personal belongings of those who died here, and the grassed-over pits where the Nazis burnt the exhumed bodies of their victims.

There are hourly trains daily from Vilnius to Paneriai station (€0.60, eight to 11 minutes), from where it's a 1km walk southwest along Agrastų gatvė into the forest.

Trakai

☑ 528 / POP 4930

With its picturesque red-brick castle, Karaite culture, quaint wooden houses and pretty lakeside location, Trakai is a highly recommended day trip, within easy reach of the capital.

The Karaite people are named after the term *kara,* which means 'to study the scriptures' in both Hebrew and Arabic. The sect originated in Baghdad and practises strict adherence to the Torah (rejecting the rabbinic Talmud). In around 1400 the grand duke of Lithuania, Vytautas, brought about 380 Karaite families to Trakai from Crimea to serve as bodyguards. Only a dozen families remain in Trakai today and their numbers are dwindling rapidly.

Trakai's trophy piece is the fairy-tale **Trakai Castle**, occupying a small island in Lake Galvė. A footbridge links the island castle to the shore. The red-brick Gothic castle, painstakingly restored from original blueprints, dates from the late 14th century. Inside the castle, the **Trakai History Museum** (Trakų Istorijos Muziejus; ☑ 528-53 946; www.trakaimuziejus.lt; Trakai Castle; adult/senior/student & child €5.40/3.60/2.40, camera €1.20; ☉ 10am-7pm May-Sep, to 6pm Mar, Apr & Oct, to 5pm Nov-Feb) tells the story of the structure. There's a bewildering variety of objects on show – hoards of coins, weaponry and porcelain, as well as interactive displays.

You can sample *kibinai* (meat-stuffed Karaite pastries similar to empanadas or Cornish pasties) either at **Senoji Kibininė** (☑ 528-55 865; www.kibinas.lt; Karaimų gatvė 65; kibinai €2-3 each, mains €6-9; ☉ 10am-midnight) or at **Kybynlar** (☑ 8-698 06320; www.kybynlar.lt; Karaimų gatvė 29; mains €6-9; ☉ noon-9pm; ☻).

Up to 10 trains daily (€1.60, 35 to 45 minutes) travel between Trakai and Vilnius. There are also frequent buses (€1.80, 40 minutes, twice hourly). From the bus or train station, hike about 15 minutes to find the lakes and castle.

Kaunas

☑ 37 / POP 304,000

Lithuania's second city has a compact Old Town, an entertaining array of museums and plenty of vibrant, youthful energy provided by its large student population. A good time to visit is in late April, during the **Kaunas Jazz Festival** (www.kaunasjazz.lt), when home-grown and international artists perform in venues across the city.

◉ Sights

◉ Old Town

The heart of Kaunas' lovely Old Town is **Rotušės Aikštė**, home of the city's former City Hall, now known as the 'Palace of Weddings', and surrounded by 15th- and 16th-century German merchants' houses.

St Francis Xavier Church & Monastery CHURCH
(☑ 8-614 49310; Rotušės aikštė 7-9; tower €1.50; ☉ tower noon-4.30pm Sat, 2-4pm Sun) The southern side of the main square, Rotušės Aikštė, is dominated by the twin-towered St Francis Xavier Church, college and Jesuit monastery complex, built between 1666 and 1720. Take a peek inside and then climb the tower for the best aerial views of Kaunas.

Sts Peter & Paul Cathedral CHURCH
(Šventų Apaštalų Petro ir Povilo Arkekatedra Bazilika; ☑ 37-324 093; Vilniaus gatvė 1; ☉ 7am-7pm Mon-Sat, 8am-7pm Sun) With its single tower, this church owes much to baroque reconstruction, especially inside, but the original 15th-century Gothic shape of its windows remains. It was probably founded by Vytautas around 1410 and now has nine altars. The **tomb of Maironis** stands outside the south wall.

◉ New Town

Laisvės alėja, a 1.7km-long pedestrian street lined with bars, shops and restaurants, runs east from Old Town to New Town, ending at the white, neo-Byzantine **St Michael the Archangel Church**.

★**MK Čiurlionis National Art Museum** GALLERY
(MK Čiurlionio Valstybinis Dailės Muziejus; ☑ 37-229 475; www.ciurlionis.lt; Putvinskio gatvė 55; adult/child €1.80/0.90; ☉ 11am-5pm Tue-Sun) The Čiurlionis National Art Museum is Kaunas' leading museum. It has extensive collections of the romantic paintings of Mikalojus Konstantinas Čiurlionis (1875–1911), one of Lithuania's greatest artists and composers, as well as Lithuanian folk art and 16th- to 20th-century European applied art.

★**Museum of Devils** MUSEUM
(Velnių Muziejus; ☑ 37-221 587; www.ciurlionis.lt; Putvinskio gatvė 64; adult/child €1.80/0.90; ☉ 11am-5pm Tue-Sun; ☻) Diabolical is the best word

WORTH A TRIP

A DARK CHAPTER IN KAUNAS' HISTORY'

A poignant memorial to the tens of thousands of people, mainly Jews, who were murdered by the Nazis, the excellent **Museum of the Ninth Fort** (IX Forto Muziejus; ☑ 37-377 748; www.9fortomuziejus.lt; Žemaičių plentas 73; adult/child €2.40/1.50, catacombs with guide €6; ☉ 10am-6pm Wed-Mon Apr-Oct, to 4pm Nov-Mar), 7km north of Kaunas, comprises an old WWI-era fort and the bunker-like church of the damned. Displays cover deportations of Lithuanians by the Soviets and graphic photo exhibitions track the demise of Kaunas' Jewish community.

Take bus 23 from Jonavos gatvė to the 9-ojo Forto Muziejus stop and cross under the motorway.

WORTH A TRIP

THE HILL OF CROSSES

One of Lithuania's most awe-inspiring sights is the legendary **Hill of Crosses** (Kryžių kalnas; ☑41-370 860; Jurgaičiai). The sound of the thousands of crosses – which appear to grow on the hillock – tinkling in the breeze is wonderfully eerie.

Planted here since at least the 19th century and probably much older, the crosses were bulldozed by the Soviets, but each night people crept past soldiers and barbed wire to plant more, risking their lives or freedom to express their national and spiritual fervour.

Some of the crosses are devotional, others are memorials (many for people deported to Siberia) and some are finely carved folk-art masterpieces.

The hill is 12km north of the central city of Šiauliai along Hwy A12 near the village of Jurgaičiai. From the highway, it's another 2km east from a well-marked turn-off ('Kryžių kalnas 2'). From Šiauliai, take a Joniškis-bound bus (€1.20, 10 minutes, up to seven daily) to the 'Domantai' stop and walk for 15 minutes, or grab a taxi (around €18).

Šiauliai is reachable by bus from Vilnius, Kaunas and Klaipėda. For accommodation, consult the **Tourism Information Centre** (☑41-523 110; www.siauliai.lt/tic; Vilniaus gatvė 213; ◉9am-1pm & 2-6pm Mon-Fri, 10am-4pm Sat).

to describe the collection of 2000-odd devil statuettes in this museum, collected over the years by landscape artist Antanas Žmuidzinavičius (1876–1966). While the commentary tries to put a pseudo-intellectual sheen on things by linking the devils to Lithuanian folklore, the fun of this museum is all about the spooky masks and stories. Great for kids.

🛏 Sleeping

Apple Economy Hotel HOTEL €
(☑37-321 404; www.applehotel.lt; Valančiaus gatvė 19; s/d from €36/45; P🐕😊@🛜) This simple hotel set on Old Town's edge in a quiet courtyard is a highly commendable no-frills option. The rooms are tiny, but are cheerful and done out in bright colours. The bed in our room was the most comfortable we slept on during our research in Lithuania. Some rooms have shared bathroom, while others are self-contained.

Litinterp GUESTHOUSE €
(☑37-228 718; www.litinterp.lt; Gedimino gatvė 28-7; s/d/tr €30/45/54; ◉office 8.30am-7pm Mon-Fri, 9am-3pm Sat; P🐕😊@🛜) The Litinterp empire boasts quality guesthouses in Vilnius, Klaipėda and Kaunas. There's not a lot of character here, but the rooms are cheap, clean and highly functional. The staff could not be friendlier or more knowledgeable. Call or email in advance if you plan to arrive outside office hours.

Park Inn by Radisson HOTEL €€
(☑37-306 100; www.parkinn.com/hotel-kaunas; Donelaičio gatvė 27; s/d from €80/100; P🐕😊@🛜) This smart business hotel fills eight floors of a renovated building in New Town. Service is slick and professional, and rooms are standard business class, with a few added extras such as heated bathroom floors and free tea and coffee. Count on the restaurant, bar and huge conference centre onsite.

🍴 Eating

★Moksha INDIAN, THAI €€
(☑8-676 71649; www.moksha.lt; Vasario 16-osios gatvė 6; mains €5-8; ◉11am-10pm; 🌿) This tiny place with whitewashed brick walls and fresh flowers everywhere lures you in with exotic smells. You can expect such daily specials as lamb kofta curry or crispy duck with persimmon salad, and there are even vegan options such as lentil soup. On top of that, the service is super-friendly; a rarity in these parts.

Bernelių Užeiga – Old Town LITHUANIAN €€
(☑37-200 913; www.berneliuuzeiga.lt; Valančiaus gatvė 9; mains €5-8; ◉11am-10pm; 🌿) If it's rustic Lithuanian cuisine served by fair maidens in traditional dress that you're after, then this twinset of wooden country inns in the middle of town is for you. Another **branch** (www.berneliuuzeiga.lt; Donelaičio gatvė 11; mains €5-8; 🌿) is in Donelaičio.

🍺 Drinking & Nightlife

Kavinė Kultūra CAFE
(☑8-676 25546; www.facebook.com/kavine.kultura; Donelaičio gatvė 14-16; ◉noon-10pm Sun-Thu, noon-2am Fri & Sat; 🛜) It calls itself a cafe, but this alternative meeting spot covers the bases from pub to cocktail bar to cosy spot to grab a cup of coffee. The clientele is skewed towards students and thinkers, and the space is a bit of fresh air for anyone looking to escape

trendier, commercial bars. Excellent bar food, salads and wings, too.

Whiskey Bar W1640

BAR

(☑ 37-203 984; www.viskiobaras.lt; Kurpių gatvė 29; ☺ 5pm-1am Tue-Thu, 5pm-5am Fri & Sat; ☜) Tucked away down a shabby side street, this bar is a real find. Not only does it have a mind-boggling collection of whiskies (150 types, to be precise) – mostly Scotch, but also some rarer Japanese ones – the bar staff are the friendliest in town. If whisky isn't your poison, then one of its ales just might be.

❶ Information

Tourist Office (☑ 37-323 436; www.visit.kaunas. lt; Laisvės alėja 36; ☺ 9am-6pm Mon-Fri, 10am-3pm Sat & Sun Jun-Aug) Books accommodation, sells maps and guides, and arranges bicycle rental and guided tours of the Old Town from mid-May to September.

❶ Getting There & Away

Kaunas' bus and train stations are located not far from each other, about 2km south of the city centre. From the bus station, frequent domestic buses leave for Klaipėda (€12, three hours, up to 16 daily) and Vilnius (€6, 1¾ hours, up to three per hour). From the train station there are several trains daily to Vilnius (€5.40, 1¼ to 1¾ hours, up to 17 daily).

Klaipėda

☑ 46 / POP 160,400

Klaipėda, Lithuania's main seaport, is known mainly as the gateway to the Curonian Spit, though it has a fascinating history as the East Prussian city of Memel long before it was incorporated into modern Lithuania in the 1920s. It was founded in 1252 by the Teutonic Order, who built the city's first castle, and has served as a key trading port through the centuries to modern times. It was retaken by Nazi Germany in WWII and housed a German submarine base. Though it was heavily bombed in the war, it retains a unique Prussian feel, particularly in the quiet backstreets of the historic Old Town.

◉ Sights

Klaipėda Castle Museum

MUSEUM

(Klaipėda Pilies Muziejus; ☑ 46-410 527; www. mlimuziejus.lt; Pilies gatvė 4; adult/child €1.80/0.90; ☺ 10am-6pm Tue-Sat) This small museum is based inside the remains of Klaipėda's old moat-protected castle, which dates back to the 13th century. It tells the castle's story

through the ages until the 19th century, when most of the structure was pulled down. You'll find fascinating photos from WWII and the immediate postwar years, when the city was rebuilt by Soviet planners.

History Museum of Lithuania Minor

MUSEUM

(Mažosios Lietuvos Istorijos Muziejus; ☑ 46-410 524; www.mlimuziejus.lt; Didžioji Vandens gatvė 6; adult/child €1.50/0.75; ☺ 10am-6pm Tue-Sat) This small museum traces the origins of 'Lithuania Minor' (Kleinlitauen), as much of the Lithuanian coastal region was referred to over the centuries as part of East Prussia. The museum includes fascinating bits of the German legacy, such as Prussian maps, labour-intensive weaving machines and traditional folk art.

🛏 Sleeping

★ Litinterp Guesthouse

B&B €

(☑ 46-410 644; www.litinterp.lt; Puodžių gatvė 17; s/d/tr €30/48/60, without bathroom €24/42/50; ☺ 8.30am-7pm Mon-Fri, 10am-3pm Sat; ⓟ 🖮 @ ☜) This clean, quiet guesthouse gets our nod for value for money. The 19 rooms are spotless and furnished in a light pinewood that creates a fresh, contemporary look. The location is good, north of the river but within walking distance of Old Town. The breakfast (€2.90) is a letdown, just some bread, salami and cheese, but we're not complaining.

★ Hotel Euterpė

HOTEL €€

(☑ 46-474 703; www.euterpe.lt; Daržų gatvė 9; s/d €75/90; ⓟ 🖮 @ ☜) Our bet for the perfect small hotel is this upscale number that sides up to former German merchant houses in Old Town. Expect a warm welcome at reception and snug rooms bathed in earthy colours with a neat, minimalist look. The downstairs restaurant is excellent and there's a small terrace to enjoy your morning coffee in the open air.

✖ Eating & Drinking

Senoji Hansa

LITHUANIAN €€

(☑ 46-400 056; www.senojihansa.lt; Kurpių gatvė 1; mains €6-10; ☺ 10am-midnight; ☜) This combination bar, restaurant and cafe sits wedged on a corner, a block down from the riverside area. It's a popular spot for lunch or dinner, with a menu consisting of meat dishes, pancakes and a very good rendition of cepelinai. The covered terrace is open year-round and draws a fun crowd on weekend evenings.

★ **Momo Grill** STEAKHOUSE €€€
(☑8-693 12355; www.momogrill.lt; Liepų gatvė 20; mains €10-18; ⊙11am-10pm Tue-Sun; ⊜🛜) This tiny, modern, minimalist steakhouse is foodie heaven and the hardest table to book in town. The small menu consists of just three cuts of beef plus grilled fish and leg of duck, and allows the chef to focus on what he does best. The austere interior of white tiles is soothing and the wine list is excellent.

❶ Information

Tourist Office (☑46-412 186; www.klaipeda info.lt; Turgaus gatvė 7; ⊙9am-7pm Mon-Fri, 10am-4pm Sat & Sun) Exceptionally efficient tourist office selling maps and locally published guidebooks. It arranges accommodation and English-speaking guides (around €40 per hour), can help with ferry and bus schedules to the Curonian Spit, and hires out bicycles (per hour/day €2.40/9 plus €100 deposit). It has a couple of computers for surfing (per hour €1.20).

❶ Getting There & Away

The train and bus stations are situated near each other in the modern part of town, about 2km north of Old Town. Three daily trains run to Vilnius (€15, 4¾ hours). There's regular bus service to Vilnius (€18, four to 5½ hours, up to 14 daily) and Kaunas (€12, 2¾ to 4½ hours, up to 15 daily).

Curonian Spit

☑469 / POP 2640
This magical sliver of land, covered by pine forest, hosts some of Europe's most precious sand dunes and a menagerie of elk, deer and avian wildlife. Recognised by Unesco as a World Heritage Site, the fragile spit is divided evenly between Lithuania and Russia's Kaliningrad region, with Lithuania's half protected as **Curonian Spit National Park** (☑46-402 256; www.nerija.lt; Smiltynės gatvė 11, Smiltynė; ⊙visitors centre 9am-noon & 1-4pm Mon-Fri).

Smiltynė, where the ferries from Klaipėda dock, draws weekend crowds with the delightful aquarium and the **Lithuania Sea Museum** (Lietuvos Jūrų Muziejus; ☑46-490 754; www. juru.muziejus.lt; Smiltynė; adult/student €7.50/5; ⊙10.30am-6.30pm Tue-Sun Jun-Aug, Wed-Sun Sep, 10.30am-5.30pm Sat & Sun Oct-Dec; ⛶ inside a 19th-century fort. Further south, the village of **Juodkrantė** is awaft with the tempting smells of smoked fish (žuvis), while picture-perfect **Nida** is home to the unmissable 52m-high **Parnidis Dune**, with its panoramic views of the 'Lithuanian Sahara' – coastline, forest and sand extending towards Kaliningrad.

A flat **cycling trail** runs all the way from Nida to Smiltynė, passing the massive colony of grey herons and cormorants near Juodkrantė, and you stand a good chance of seeing wild boar and other wildlife along the path. Bicycles are easy to hire (around €9/12 per 12/24 hours) in Nida.

The tourist office in Klaipėda can help arrange transport and accommodation; **Miško Namas** (☑469-52 290; www.miskonamas.com; Pamario gatvė 11-2; d €75, 2-/4-person apt from €90/110; P@🛜⛶) and **Naglis** (☑8-699 33682; www.naglis.lt; Naglių gatvė 12; d/apt €75/100; P) are both fine choices.

❶ Getting There & Away

To get to the spit, board a ferry at the **Old Ferry Port** (Senoji perkėla; ☑46-311 117; www.keltas. lt; Danės gatvė 1; per passenger/bicycle €0.90/free) due west of Klaipėda's Old Town (€0.90, 10 minutes, half-hourly). Vehicles must use the **New Ferry Port** (Naujoji perkėla; ☑46-311 117; www. keltas.lt; Nemuno gatvė 8; per passenger/car €0.90/12, bicycle free), 2.5km south of the passenger terminal (per car €12, at least hourly).

Buses (€4.50, one hour, at least seven times daily) run regularly between Smiltynė and Nida via Juodkrantė (€3, 15 to 20 minutes).

SURVIVAL GUIDE

❶ Directory A–Z

ACCOMMODATION
➡ Book ahead in the high season for Vilnius and the Curonian Spit. High-season prices are around 30% higher than low-season prices. Prices are higher in Vilnius.

➡ Vilnius has numerous youth hostels. Budget accommodation is easy to find outside the capital.

BUSINESS HOURS
Banks 8am to 3pm Monday to Friday
Bars 11am to midnight Sunday to Thursday, 11am to 2am Friday and Saturday

---

SLEEPING PRICE RANGES

The following price ranges refer to a double room with bathroom. Breakfast is included in the price unless stated otherwise.

€ less than €45

€€ €45 to €100

€€€ more than €100

COUNTRY FACTS

Area 65,303 sq km

Capital Vilnius

Country Code ☑370

Currency Euro (€)

Emergency ☑112

Language Lithuanian

Money ATMs are everywhere

Population 2.9 million

Visas Not required for citizens of the EU, Australia, Canada, Israel, Japan, New Zealand, Switzerland or the US for stays of 90 days

---

Clubs 10pm to 5am Thursday to Saturday

Post offices 8am to 8pm Monday to Friday, 10am to 9pm Saturday, 10am to 5pm Sunday

Restaurants noon to 11pm; later on weekends

Shops 9am or 10am to 7pm Monday to Saturday; some open Sunday

INTERNET RESOURCES

Bus & Rail Timetable (www.stotis.lt)

In Your Pocket (www.inyourpocket.com)

Lithuania's museums (www.muziejai.lt)

Lithuania's official tourism portal (www.lithuania.travel)

Vilnius Tourism (www.vilnius-tourism.lt)

MONEY

➜ Lithuania adopted the euro (€) on 1 January 2015.

➜ Exchange money with your credit or debit card at ATMs located around the country or at major banks.

➜ Credit cards are widely accepted for purchases.

➜ Some banks still cash travellers cheques, though this is increasingly uncommon.

➜ Tip 10% in restaurants to reward good service.

PUBLIC HOLIDAYS

New Year's Day 1 January

Independence Day 16 February

Lithuanian Independence Restoration Day 11 March

Easter Sunday March/April

Easter Monday March/April

International Labour Day 1 May

Mothers Day First Sunday in May

Feast of St John (Midsummer) 24 June

Statehood Day 6 July

Assumption of Blessed Virgin 15 August

All Saints' Day 1 November

Christmas 25 and 26 December

TELEPHONE

➜ To call a landline within Lithuania, dial ☑8 followed by the city code and phone number.

➜ To call a mobile phone within Lithuania, dial ☑8 followed by the eight-digit number.

➜ To make an international call dial ☑00 before the country code.

➜ Prepaid SIM cards are sold by **Bitė** (www.bite.lt), **Omnitel** (www.omnitel.lt) and **Tele 2** (www.tele2.lt) for around €2.30 to €3.

➜ Payphones – increasingly rare given the widespread use of mobiles – only accept phonecards, sold at newspaper kiosks.

❶ Getting There & Away

Lithuania has frequent transport links to neighbouring countries via bus, train or international ferry, though be sure to route your travel to avoid Belarus or the Russian province of Kaliningrad if you don't have a transit visa for those areas. Latvia and Poland are both members of the EU's common Schengen zone and there are no passport controls at these borders. Vilnius is the country's hub for air travel. There are a handful of direct flights from major European cities, though most routes will require a change in Warsaw or Rīga. Sweden and Germany can be reached by ferry from Klaipėda, Lithuania's international seaport.

Flights, tours and rail tickets can be booked online at www.lonelyplanet.com/travel_services.

AIR

Most international traffic to Lithuania goes through **Vilnius International Airport** (Tarptautinis Vilniaus Oro Uostas; ☑ passenger information 6124 4442; www.vno.lt; Rodūnios kelias 10a; ☎; 🚌1, 2), though only a handful of major European cities, as of this writing, have direct flights.

➜ Many air routes include a stopover in Warsaw, Copenhagen or Rīga.

➜ Major carriers that service Vilnius include airBaltic, Austrian Airlines, Lufthansa, LOT and Scandinavian Airlines.

---

❶ LITHUANIA'S CURRENCY

Lithuania adopted the euro on 1 January 2015. We have done our best in this chapter to convert prices to the new currency, though prices for some attractions may be slightly different than those listed here.

EATING PRICE RANGES

The following price categories refer to the average cost of a main course:

€ less than €5

€€ €5 to €12

€€€ more than €12

➡ Budget carriers include Ryanair, Wizz Air and a relatively new start-up, Air Lituanica, which began flying in 2014.

BOAT

From Klaipėda's **International Ferry Port** (☑ 46-395 051; www.dfdsseaways.lt; Perkėlos gatvė 10), **DFDS Seaways** (☑ 46-395 000; www.dfdsseaways.lt; Šaulių gatvė 19) runs passenger ferries to/from Kiel (from €80, six weekly, 22 hours) in Germany and Karlshamn, Sweden (from €75, 14 hours, daily).

BUS

The main international bus companies operating in Lithuania are **Lux Express** (☑ 5-233 6666; www.luxexpress.eu; Sodų 20b-1; ☺ 8am-7pm Mon-Fri, 9am-7pm Sat & Sun) and **Ecolines** (☑ 5-213 3300; www.ecolines.net; Geležinkelio gatvė 15; ☺ 8am-7pm Mon-Fri, 9am-5pm Sat, 9am-3pm Sun).

CAR & MOTORCYCLE

➡ There are no passport or customs controls if entering from Poland or Latvia.

➡ A valid entry or tranist visa is required to enter or drive through Belarus and the Russian province of Kaliningrad.

TRAIN

➡ Many international train routes, including to Warsaw and Moscow, pass through Belarus and require a transit visa.

➡ Consult the timetable at **Lithuanian Rail** (☑ information 7005 5111; www.litrail.lt) for further information.

ℹ Getting Around

BICYCLE

➡ Lithuania is mostly flat and easily explored by bike.

➡ Large cities and areas popular with visitors have bike-rental and repair shops.

➡ Information about bike touring in Lithuania can be found on **BaltiCCycle** (www.balticcycle.eu).

BUS

➡ The bus network is extensive, efficient and relatively inexpensive.

➡ See **stotis.lt** (www.stotis.lt) for a national bus timetable.

CAR & MOTORCYCLE

Modern four-lane highways link Vilnius with Klaipėda (via Kaunas).

➡ Drivers must be at least 18 years old and have a valid driving licence in their country of residence.

➡ The speed limit is 50km/h in cities, 70km/h to 90km/h on two-lane highways, and 110km/h to 130km/h on motorways.

➡ The blood-alcohol limit is 0.04%.

➡ Headlights must be on day and night.

➡ International and local car-rental agencies are well represented at Vilnius International Airport. Expect to pay around €150 per week for a compact.

LOCAL TRANSPORT

➡ Lithuanian cities generally have good public transport, based on buses, trolleybuses and minibuses.

➡ A ride usually costs around €1.

TRAIN

➡ The country's efficient train network, Lithuanian Rail, links Vilnius to Kaunas, Klaipėda and Trakai, though for some journeys, including Kaunas to Klaipėda, buses are faster.

➡ The Lithuanian Rail website has a handy timetable in English.

ESSENTIAL FOOD & DRINK

➡ **Potato creations** Try the cepelinai (potato-dough 'zeppelin' stuffed with meat, mushrooms or cheese), bulviniai blynai (potato pancakes) or žemaičių blynai (heart-shaped mashed potato stuffed with meat and fried), or the vedarai (baked pig intestines stuffed with mashed potato).

➡ **Beer snacks** No drinking session is complete without a plate of smoked pigs' ears and kepta duona (deep-fried garlicky bread sticks).

➡ **Beetroot delight** Cold, creamy šaltibarščiai (beetroot soup) is a summer speciality, served with a side of fried potatoes.

➡ **Unusual meat** Sample the game, such as beaver stew or bear sausages.

➡ **Smoked fish** The Curonian Spit is famous for its smoked fish, particularly the superb rukytas unguris (smoked eel).

➡ **Beer and mead** Šytutys, Utenos and Kalnapilis are top beers; midus (mead) is a honey-tinged nobleman's drink.

Macedonia

Best Places to Eat

➡ Stara Gradska Kuča (p246)

➡ Restaurant Antiko (p249)

➡ Letna Bavča Kaneo (p249)

➡ Kaj Pero (p245)

➡ Kebapčilnica Destan (p245)

Best Places to Stay

➡ Hotel Radika (p251)

➡ Villa Dihovo (p251)

➡ Sunny Lake Hostel (p249)

➡ Villa Jovan (p249)

➡ Hotel Solun (p245)

Why Go?

Macedonia (Македонија) is a small nation with a complex and fascinating history. Part Balkan, part Mediterranean and rich in Greek, Roman and Ottoman history, it offers impressive ancient sites along with buzzing modernity, managing to pack in more activity and natural beauty than would seem possible for a country its size.

Easygoing Skopje remains one of Europe's more unusual capitals, where constant urban renewal has made the city a bizarre jigsaw puzzle that never fails to surprise.

Elsewhere in the country hiking, mountain biking, wine tasting and climbing beckon, while the remote mountains conceal fascinating medieval monasteries, superb alpine trails and traditional Balkan villages. Ohrid, noted for its beaches, summer festival, sublime Byzantine churches and 34km-long lake, is the centre of the country's tourism industry, while in the winter months skiing at resorts such as Mavrovo become the main draw.

When to Go
Skopje

Jun–Aug Enjoy Ohrid's Summer Festival and dive into its 300m-deep lake.

Sep & Oct Partake in Skopje's Beer Fest, Jazz Festival and harvest celebrations.

Dec–Feb Ski Mavrovo and indulge in Macedonia's holiday carnivals.

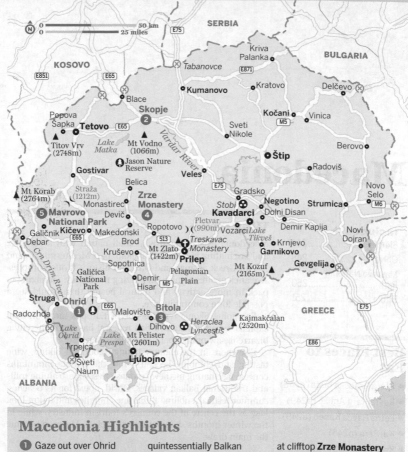

Macedonia Highlights

1 Gaze out over Ohrid from the **Church of Sveti Jovan at Kaneo** (p248), immaculately set on a bluff above the lake.

2 Dive into historic but fast changing **Skopje**, a friendly, quintessentially Balkan capital.

3 Enjoy the old-world ambience of **Bitola** (p251) and hike nearby Pelister National Park.

4 Soak up the serenity at clifftop **Zrze Monastery** (p252), with sweeping views of the Pelagonian Plain and priceless Byzantine artworks.

5 Ski **Mavrovo National Park** (p250), Macedonia's premier winter resort.

SKOPJE   СКОПЈЕ

♫ 02 / POP 670,000

Skopje is among Europe's most entertaining and eclectic small capital cities. While an expensive and rather kitschy government construction spree has sparked controversy in recent years, Skopje's new abundance of statuary, fountains, bridges, museums and other structures built to encourage a national identity has visitors' cameras snapping like never before and has defined the ever-changing city for the 21st century.

Yet plenty survives from earlier times – Skopje's Ottoman- and Byzantine-era wonders include the 15th-century Kameni Most (Stone Bridge), the wonderful Čaršija (old Turkish bazaar) where you can get lost for hours, Sveti Spas Church, with its ornate, hand-carved iconostasis, and Tvrdina Kale Fortress, Skopje's guardian since the 5th century.

ITINERARIES

One Week
Spend two nights in **Skopje**, marvelling at its bold new architecture, and visiting its **Čaršija** (old quarter), with historic churches, mosques, museums and an Ottoman castle. Next head southwest to Macedonia's most charming and historic town, **Ohrid**, and enjoy its spectacular lake, calling at the lush forested mountains of **Mavrovo** on the way. After two days, continue to cultured **Bitola**, the long-famed 'City of Consuls' known for its vibrant cafes and nearby **Pelister National Park**.

Two Weeks
Take your time in and around **Skopje**, **Ohrid** and **Bitola**, then add on a visit to Macedonia's famous **Zrze** monastery. Before returning to Skopje, enjoy winerey-hopping in the **Tikveš wine region**.

◎ Sights

◉ Ploštad Makedonija & the South Bank

Ploštad Makedonija SQUARE
(Macedonia Sq) Fronted by a Triumphal Arch, this square is the centrepiece to Skopje's audacious nation-building-through-architecture project and has massive statues dedicated to national heroes in it. The towering, central 'Warrior on a Horse' is bedecked by fountains that are illuminated at night.

Holocaust Memorial Center for the Jews of Macedonia MUSEUM
(www.holocaustfund.org; Ploštad Makedonija; ◷9am-7pm Tue-Fri, to 3pm Sat & Sun) FREE This moving museum commemorates the all-but-lost Sephardic Jewish culture of Macedonia through a range of photos, English-language wall texts, maps and video. The display documents the Jewish community's history in Macedonia, beginning with their expulsion from Iberia and ending in WWII, when some 98% of Macedonian Jews (7144 individuals in total) perished in the Holocaust.

Museum of the City of Skopje MUSEUM
(Mito Hadživasilev Jasmin bb; ◷9am-5pm Tue-Sat, to 1pm Sun) FREE Occupying the old train station building where the stone fingers of the clock remain frozen in time at 5.17am – the moment Skopje's great earthquake struck on 27 July 1963 – this museum is unsurprisingly focused on that horrific event, and the display includes video footage and photos of the immediate aftermath. It's a moving display about an event that left 1070 people dead.

Memorial House of Mother Teresa MUSEUM
(☑02 3290 674; www.memorialhouseofmotherteresa.org; ul Makedonija bb; ◷9am-8pm Mon-Fri, to 2pm Sat-Sun) FREE This extraordinarily ugly and frankly bizarre, retro-futuristic structure contains a display of memorabilia relating to the famed Catholic nun of Calcutta, born in Skopje in 1910. Look out for the Mother Teresa quotations on plaques around the city centre as well.

◉ North Bank & Čaršija

★**Čaršija** NEIGHBOURHOOD
Čaršija is the hillside Turkish old town of Skopje and evokes the city's Ottoman past with its winding lanes filled with teahouses, mosques, craftsmen's stores, and even good nightlife. It also boasts Skopje's best historic structures and museums, and is the first place any visitor should head. Čaršija runs from the Stone Bridge to the Bit Pazar, a big, busy vegetable market purveying bric-a-brac, household goods and anything random. Expect to get pleasantly lost in its maze of narrow streets.

★**Sveti Spas Church** CHURCH
(Church of the Holy Saviour; Makarije Frčkoski 8; adult/student 120/50MKD; ◷9am-5pm Tue-Fri, to 3pm Sat & Sun) Partially underground (the Turks banned churches from being taller than mosques), this church dates from the 14th century and is the most historically important in the city. Its dark interior boasts a stunning wood-carved iconostasis 10m wide and 6m high, built by early-19th-century master craftsmen Makarije Frčkovski and brothers Petar and Marko Filipovski. It's rather tricky to find as its

Skopje

⦿ Top Sights

⦿ Sights

🛏 Sleeping

✕ Eating

◯ Drinking & Nightlife

✦ Entertainment

ℹ Information

sunken design means it doesn't really look like a church from the outside.

⭐ **Tvrdina Kale Fortress** FORTRESS
(⊙daylight hours) FREE Dominating the skyline of Skopje, this *Game of Thrones*–worthy 6th-century AD Byzantine (and later, Ottoman) fortress is an easy walk up from the Čaršija and its ramparts offer great views over city and river. Inside you'll find various archaeological finds from neolithic to Ottoman times.

Museum of Contemporary Art MUSEUM
(NIMoCA; www.msuskopje.org.mk; Samoilova bb; admission 50MKD; ⊙10am-5pm Tue-Sat, 9am-1pm Sun) Definitely a highlight of Skopje, this excellent museum is housed in an impressive building at the top of a hill with wonderful city views and an extraordinarily good collection for a city of Skopje's size. The museum was formed in the aftermath of the devastating 1963 earthquake, with artists and collections around the world donating works to form a collection that now includes works by Picasso, Léger, Hockney, Alexander Calder, Jasper Johns, Meret Oppenheim, Christo and Bridget Riley.

🛏 Sleeping

⭐ **Urban Hostel** HOSTEL €
(☑02 6142 785; www.urbanhostel.com.mk; Adolf Ciborovski 22; dm/s/d €13/24/35, apt from €46; ❇🛜) A short walk from the centre in the leafy Debar Maalo neighbourhood, this excellent hostel takes excellent care of its guests, with superclean rooms, comfy beds, and even some quirky extras including a fireplace and a piano. The friendly, superhelpful staff members are another highlight. It's about a 15-minute walk from the city centre.

Rekord Hostel HOSTEL €
(☑02 6149 954; Dimitrije Čupovski 7/1-1; dm/s/d €13/25/34; ❇🛜) A brand-new hostel in Skopje's heart, the Rekord is a great addition to the city's budget accommodation. There are three dorms and one private room, all of which have excellent modern beds with curtains for privacy and trunks for security. There's also a common room and a balcony, and though no kitchen, there is a fridge and a sink with plates.

Hotel Pelister BOUTIQUE HOTEL €€
(☑02 3239 584; www.pelisterhotel.com.mk; Ploštad Makedonija; s/d/apt from €59/69/145;

❇@🛜) Located above Restaurant Pelister (and you'll need to go into the restaurant to access the hotel), this place enjoys an unbeatable location on the square, overlooking the city's new architectural wonders. The five rooms are spiffy, with somewhat standard decor. Most come with a computer, while the apartment is spacious and perfect for business travellers.

Hotel Super 8 HOTEL €€
(☑02 3212 225; www.hotelsuper8.com.mk; Bul Krste Misirkov 57/3; s/d/tr €40/60/70; ❇🛜) An excellent midrange choice slap bang in the centre of town between the river and the Čaršija, this 21-room, family-run hotel has comfortable, bright and modern rooms in a modern building. There is also a communal lounge and kitchen for guests to use.

⭐ **Hotel Solun** HOTEL €€€
(☑02 3232 512; www.hotelsolun.com; Nikola Vapcarov 10; s/d from €79/99; ❇@🛜❇) Opening in 2013, the 53-room Solun is easily the best-value top-end hotel in Skopje. In a converted building in a courtyard off a street in the heart of the city, the hotel is a stylish and design-conscious place, with an enormous range of different room categories, the smallest of which are admittedly rather poky.

🍴 Eating

⭐ **Kebapčilnica Destan** KEBAB €
(ul 104 6; set meal 180MKD; ⊙7am-11pm) Skopje's best beef kebabs, accompanied by seasoned grilled bread, are served at this classic Čaršija place. There's no menu; everyone gets the same thing, served gruffly by the non-English-speaking staff. But that's the charm, and the terrace is usually full – that's how good they are. There's a second, more sanitised branch on **Ploštad Makedonija** (kebabs 180MKD; ⊙10am-11pm).

⭐ **Kaj Pero** MACEDONIAN €€
(Orce Nikolov 109; mains 200-600MKD; ⊙8am-midnight; 🅟) This neighbourhood favourite has outside tables that are low lit by the street lights, giving it a great atmosphere for alfresco dining in the summer months. Inside it has a cosy, traditional feel, perfect for winter meals. The menu is focused on *skara* (meat grills), but also has an excellent local wine selection and a range of inventive nongrill dishes.

Pivnica An
MACEDONIAN €€

(Kapan An; mains 300-600MKD; ☺11am-11pm; 🗖) Housed in a *caravansarai* (inn) that is famously tricky to find (it's through an archway off the busy little square in the heart of the Čaršija where the kebab restaurants are concentrated), this place is all about Ottoman tradition in its sumptuous courtyard. The food is very good, and far superior to that served immediately outside its front door.

Skopski Merak
SKARA €€

(☑02 321 2215; Debarca 51; mains 200-800MKD; 🛜🗖) This hugely popular place packs both locals and visitors in with its live music on most evenings and huge menu that reads like an encyclopaedia of everything Macedonian cuisine can throw at you. It's easily one of the best *skara* places in Skopje, and as such it's worth reserving for dinner at the weekend.

Idadija
SKARA €€

(Zhivko Chingo; mains 200-300MKD; ☺noon-midnight) In Debar Maalo's *skara* corner, no-frills Idadija has been serving excellent grills for more than 80 years to punters who crowd its roadside tables. There's a relaxed vibe and great people-watching to be had.

★Stara Gradska Kuča
MACEDONIAN €€€

(www.starakuka.com.mk; Pajko Maalo 14; mains 300-1000MKD; ☺10am-midnight Mon-Fri, noon-11pm Sat & Sun; 🛜🗖) Housed in what the owners claim to be the oldest functioning house in Macedonia, this traditional place has a warm ambience, an excellent assortment of traditional Macedonian dishes and, sometimes, live music. It's a bit touristy, but still a snug and cosy spot with its wooden furnishings and rural village decor in the heart of Skopje.

🍷 Drinking

★Vinoteka Temov
BAR

(Gradište 1a; ☺9am-midnight Mon-Thu, to 1am Fri-Sun) Skopje's best wine bar, in a restored wooden building near Sveti Spas, is refined and atmospheric. A vast wine list presents the cream of Macedonia's vineyards, available by both the glass and bottle, while live traditional and classical guitarists often play. There's also an excellent menu (mains 240MKD to 660MKD) that includes curries, burgers, kebabs and mezze.

Old Town Brewery
BEER HALL

(Gradište 1; ☺9am-1am) This beer bar can be found up a staircase from one of Čaršija's busiest pedestrian streets and is Skopje's only place for a yard of beer. The selection is good, with a range of brews made on the premises.

☆ Entertainment

Multimedia Center Mala Stanica
LIVE MUSIC, ARTS

(www.nationalgallery.mk; Jordan Mijalkov 18; ☺10am-10pm) Featuring arty, ornate decor, the National Art Gallery's cafe hosts temporary exhibitions and live music and is something of a meeting point for the city's more alternative crowd.

ℹ Information

MEDICAL SERVICES

City Hospital (☑02 3130 111; 11 Oktomvri 53; ☺24hr)

MONEY

ATMs and *menuvačnici* (exchange offices) abound.

POST & TELEPHONE

The **main post office** (☑02 3141 141; Orce Nikolov 1; ☺7am-7.30pm Mon-Sat, 7.30am-2.30pm Sun) is 75m northwest of Ploštad Makedonija. Others are opposite the train station, in the Gradski Trgovski Centar and in Ramstore.

TOURIST INFORMATION

Skopje Tourist Information Centre (Vasil Adzilarski bb; ☺8.30am-4.30pm) Skopje's tourist information centre has maps available and can help with excursions and accommodation. Staff speak English.

ℹ Getting There & Away

AIR

Skopje Alexander the Great Airport (☑02 3148 333; www.airports.com.mk; Petrovec) is located 21km east of the city centre. Skopje has direct air services to many cities throughout Europe, Turkey and the Gulf. Airlines include:

Adria Airways (www.adria.si)

airberlin (www.airberlin.com)

Air Serbia (www.airserbia.com)

Austrian Airlines (www.austrian.com)

Croatia Airlines (www.croatiaairlines.hr)

Pegasus Airlines (www.flypgs.com)

Turkish Airlines (www.thy.com)

Wizz Air (www.wizzair.com)

SKOPJE 2014: A GARISH VISION?

The central district of Skopje has undergone monumental change in recent years as the Macedonian government under Prime Minister Nikola Gruevski has implemented the controversial Skopje 2014 project. The project, which began in 2010, has seen the construction of 20 new buildings and 40 new monuments in the area around the river in an attempt simultaneously to give the city a more uniform appearance and to help bolster Macedonian national pride and identity by linking the modern state to its forerunners, many of whose Macedonian credentials are in fact debatable.

Detractors bemoan the tens – if not hundreds – of millions of euros spent on the project to date, while others point out the inherently kitschiness of the plan, with its grotesquely stylised buildings, and blatantly nationalist leanings (the inclusions of Alexander the Great and Philip II of Macedon, for example, being interpreted by many as broad snubs to the Greek government, who object to Macedonia's interpretation of its ancient history).

But Skopje 2014 has at least given visitors lots of fountains, statues and other facades to photograph. Some prominent highlights include the construction of the **Art Bridge** and **Eye Bridge** over the Vadar River, both of which redefine kitschy; and the construction of the new **National Theatre**, a replica of the original building that once stood here on the riverside but was destroyed by the 1963 earthquake. Look out also for the new **Museum of Archeology** and the **Porta Macedonia**, a triumphal arch just off Skopje's main plaza.

BUS

Skopje's **bus station** (02 2466 313; www.sas.com.mk; bul Nikola Karev), with ATM, exchange office and English-language info, adjoins the train station. Bus schedules are online.

Buses to Ohrid go via Kičevo (three hours, 167km) or Bitola (four to five hours, 261km) – book ahead in summer. Most intercity buses are air-conditioned and are generally faster than trains, though more expensive.

International Buses

International services include the following:
Belgrade (1400MKD, 10 hours, eight daily)
Istanbul (1900MKD, 12 hours, three daily)
Ljubljana (3800MKD, 14 hours, one daily)
Pristina (330, two hours, 12 daily)
Sarajevo (3170MKD, 14 hours, Friday and Sunday 8pm)
Sofia (1040MKD, 5½ hours, four daily)
Thessaloniki (1300MKD, four hours, one Monday, Wednesday and Friday)
Zagreb (3200MKD, 12 hours, one daily)

TRAIN

The **train station** (Zhelezníčka Stanica; bul Jane Sandanski) serves local and international destinations. Disagreements with the Greek government have led to periodically suspended train routes with Greece, but the Skopje–Thessaloniki connection (760MKD, 4½ hours, 5.06am daily) was running at the time of research. A train serves Belgrade (1430MKD, eight hours, 8.20am & 8.10pm daily), and

another reaches Pristina (330MKD, 3 hours, 4.10pm daily) in Kosovo.

Domestic Train

Local destinations include the following:
Bitola (315MKD, four hours, four daily)
Gevgelija (270MKD, 2½ hours, three daily)
Kičevo (210MKD, two hours, three daily)
Kumanovo (80MKD, 40 minutes, four daily)
Negotino (200MKD, two hours, three daily)
Prilep (250MKD, three hours, four daily)

Getting Around

TO/FROM THE AIRPORT

An airport shuttle bus, **Vardar Express** (www.vardarexpress.com), runs between the airport and the city. Buy tickets (100MKD) from the marked arrivals terminal booth. The bus leaves half-hourly or hourly, depending on passengers, and stops at several places including the bus/train station and central square. From the airport to centre, taxis cost 1200MKD.

BUS

Skopje's public city buses cost 35MKD. Private ones cost 25MKD. Both follow the same stops and numbered routes. You can buy and validate tickets on board.

TAXI

Skopje's taxis are good value, with the first kilometre costing just 40MKD, and 25MKD for subsequent kilometres. Drivers rarely speak English, but they do use their meters.

DAY TRIPS FROM SKOPJE

A half-hour drive, or slightly longer city bus trip, accesses tranquil **Lake Matka**. Although crowded at weekends, this idyllic spot beneath steep **Treska Canyon** is excellent, offering hiking, rock climbing, caving (€10) and ancient churches in its forested environs. On-site restaurants provide nourishment and lake views. Matka's underwater caverns are as deep, or maybe deeper, than any in Europe, at almost 218m.

Matka's traditional link with the Virgin Mary (Matka means 'womb' in Macedonian) is accentuated by grotto shrines such as **Sveta Bogorodica**. From here a steep path reaches **Sveti Spas**, **Sveta Trojca** and **Sveta Nedela** – the last, a 4km walk (around 1½ hours). These caves once sheltered ascetics and anti-Ottoman revolutionaries.

After the **Church of Sveti Nikola**, beyond the dam and across the bridge, visit the frescoed **Church of Sveti Andrej** (1389). The adjoining mountaineering hut **Matka** (☑02-3052 655) offers guides, climbing gear and accommodation.

From Skopje come by taxi (450MKD) or bus 60 along bul Partizanski Odredi (50MKD, 40 minutes, hourly).

WESTERN MACEDONIA

Ohrid   Охрид

☑ 046 / POP 55,000

Sublime Ohrid is Macedonia's prime destination, with its atmospheric old quarter with beautiful churches along a graceful hill, topped by a medieval castle overlooking serene, 34km-long Lake Ohrid. It's undoubtedly Macedonia's most alluring attraction, especially when you factor in the nearby Galičica National Park and the further secluded beaches that dot the lake's eastern shore.

◉ Sights

★ Church of Sveti Jovan at Kaneo   CHURCH

(admission 100MKD; ⊘9am-6pm) This stunning 13th-century church is set on a cliff over the lake, and is possibly Macedonia's most photographed structure. Peer down into the azure waters and you'll see why medieval monks found spiritual inspiration here. The small church has original frescoes behind the altar.

Church of Sveta Bogorodica Perivlepta   CHURCH

(Gorna Porta; admission 100MKD; ⊘9am-1pm & 4-8pm) Just inside the Gorna Porta, this 13th-century Byzantine church, whose name translates as 'Our Lady the Most Glorious', has vivid biblical frescoes painted by Serbian masters Mihail and Eutihije and superb lake and old town views from its terrace. There's also an **icon gallery** (Gorna Porta; admission 100MKD; ⊘9am-5pm Tue-Sun) highlighting the founders' artistic achievements.

Classical Amphitheatre   AMPHITHEATRE

FREE Ohrid's impressive amphitheatre was built for theatre; the Romans later removed 10 rows to accommodate gladiators.

Car Samoil's Castle   CASTLE

(admission 30MKD; ⊘9am-7pm) The massive, turreted walls of the 10th-century castle indicate the power of the medieval Bulgarian state. Ascend the stairways to the ramparts for fantastic views over the town and lake.

Plaošnik   CHURCH

(⊘9am-6pm) **FREE** Down a wooded path, Plaošnik boasts the Church of Sveti Kliment i Pantelejmon. This 5th-century basilica was restored in 2002 according to its Byzantine design. The multidomed church has glass floor segments revealing the original foundations. It houses St Kliment's relics, with intricate 5th-century mosaics outside.

Sveta Sofia Cathedral   CHURCH

(Car Samoil bb; adult/student 100/30MKD; ⊘10am-7pm) Ohrid's grandest church, 11th-century Sveta Sofia, is supported by columns and decorated with elaborate, if very faded Byzantine frescoes, though they are well preserved and very vivid in the apse, still. Its superb acoustics means it's often used for concerts (300MKD). The exposed beams reveal the very real achievment constructing a church this size would have been in the 11th century.

Robev Family House National Museum
MUSEUM

(Car Samoil 62; adult/student 100/50MKD; ⊙ 9am-2pm & 7-10pm Tue-Sun) In the heart of the old town, the 1827 National Museum is housed over several floors of the remarkably well-preserved Robev Residence. On display is everything from Greek archaeological finds, prehistoric implements and metal work to pottery, jewellery and some wonderful interiors. Across the road the Urania Residence, a further part of the museum, has an ethnographic display.

🛏 Sleeping

⭐ Sunny Lake Hostel
HOSTEL €

(www.sunnylakehostel.mk/; 11 Oktombri 15; dm €10, d €20-24; 🛜) This excellent new hostel is a bustling hub for backpackers stopping off in Ohrid. There are good facilities, including a great terrace with lake views, lockers under each bed and a kitchen to cook in. The bathrooms aren't great though, and hot water isn't always available. That said, it's superbly located and a great deal for the price.

⭐ Villa Jovan
HISTORIC HOTEL €

(📲 076 377 644; vila.jovan@gmail.com; Car Samoli 44; s/d/ste €25/35/49; ❄🛜) There are nine rooms within this 200-year-old mansion in the heart of the Old Town, and they're charmingly rustic and full of old-world furnishings, have wooden beams and feature local art on the walls. While the rooms are definitely on the small side, the friendly English-speaking staff make you feel right at home.

Villa Lucija
GUESTHOUSE €

(📲 046 265 608; www.vilalucija.com.mk; Kosta Abraš 29; s/d/apt €20/30/50; ❄@🛜) Lucija has Old Town ambience and lovingly decorated, breezy rooms with lake views. Breakfast is not included here, and English was nonexistent on our last visit, but it more than makes up for that with its superb location and its enviable balconies over the water.

⭐ Vila Sveta Sofija
HOTEL €€

(📲 046 254 370; www.vilasofija.com.mk; Kosta Abraš 64; s/tw/d/q €29/49/69/99; ❄@) This opulent getaway combines traditional furnishings with chic modern bathrooms in an old Ohrid mansion near Sveta Sofia. The best room is the suite, which sleeps four and has a great balcony with a lake view. Guests enjoy a private sliver of lakeside beach too, with use of umbrellas and deckchairs.

Jovanovic Guest House
GUESTHOUSE €€

(📲 070 589 218; jovanovic.guesthouse@hotmail.com; Boro Sain 5; apt from €40) This property has two apartments, both of which sleep four, set right in the middle of the Old Town. Each apartment is tastefully furnished and stuffed full of antiques. The top-floor apartment has an amazing lake view, and the owner is a professional diver who can organise diving excursions on the lake.

🍴 Eating

Ohrid has some good eating options, but plenty of mediocre places aimed at the summer tour groups as well, so choose carefully. Self-caterers should head to **Tinex supermarket** on Ohrid's main shopping street (bul Makedonski Prosvetiteli) for the best selection of foodstuffs, or buy directly from farmers at the quaint **vegetable market** (Kliment Ohridski).

Ohrid's endemic trout is endangered and (supposedly) protected from fishing – order the equally tasty mavrovska and kaliforniska varieties instead.

⭐ Letna Bavča Kaneo
SEAFOOD €

(Kočo Racin 43; fish 100-200MKD; ⊙ 10am-midnight; 🛜) This simple 'summer terrace' on Kaneo beach is inexpensive and great. A fry-up of diminutive *plasnica* (a small fish commonly eaten fried in the Balkans), plus salad, feeds two, or try other specialities such as eel or carp. Swim in Lake Ohrid directly from the restaurant's dock and then soak up the sun while drinking a local beer – it doesn't come much better than this.

Via Scara
PIZZERIA €

(www.viasacra.mk; Ilindenska 36; mains 150-300MKD; ⊙ 9am-midnight; 🛜📱) Pleasantly fusing the best of Italian and Macedonian fare, Via Scara offers up crisp and tasty pizzas as well as a good selection of Macedonian national cooking and wines. Its location is a big draw too: facing the lovely Sveta Sofia Cathedral on a cobbled street in the middle of the Old Town. Breakfast is also served, a rarity in Ohrid.

⭐ Restaurant Antiko
MACEDONIAN €€

(Car Samoil 30; mains 300-650MKD) In an old Ohrid mansion in the middle of the Old Town, the famous Antiko has great traditional ambience and pricey, but good, traditional dishes. Don't miss the excellent *tavče gravče,* a traditional Macedonian dish of beans cooked in spices and peppers, the

Antiko version of which is widely held to be a classic of the genre.

Restoran Sveta Sofija
MACEDONIAN €€

(Car Samoil 88; mains 300-500MKD; ⊙10am-midnight; 🛜) This upscale restaurant couldn't have a better location, and in the warmer months you can dine alfresco across the road on a little terrace. This is a great spot to try traditional fare and oenophiles will delight in being able to choose from more than 100 Macedonian wines.

🍸 Drinking & Entertainment

★ Cuba Libre
BAR

(www.cubalibreohrid.com; Partizanska 2; ⊙10pm-4am) Perennially popular bar and nightclub. During the summer months it opens nightly and is normally standing-room-only, with DJs from all over the Balkans coming to play for the smart and up-for-it crowd.

Aquarius
CAFE

(Kosta Abraš bb; ⊙10am-1am; 🛜) Ohrid's original lake-terrace cafe, Aquarius remains cool for a midday coffee and is lively at night, with a cocktail menu and lake views.

ℹ️ Information

Sunny Land Tourism (📲070 523 227; www.sunnylandtourism.com; Car Samoil; ⊙9am-7pm) Local expert Zoran Grozdanovski can find accommodation and arrange tours and activities including mountain biking, wine tastings and boat trips on the lake.

Tourist Office (Car Samoil 38; ⊙10am-midnight) Ohrid's friendly, English-speaking tourist office in the middle of the Old Town provides general info including city maps, and can help you find accommodation and outdoor activities.

ℹ️ Getting There & Away

AIR

Ohrid's **St Paul the Apostle Airport** (📲046 252 820; www.airports.com.mk), 10km north, handles summertime charter flights. Take a taxi (400MKD).

BUS

From the **bus station** (7 Noemvri bb), 1.5km east of the centre, buses serve Skopje, either via Kičevo (500MKD, three hours, eight daily) or (the longer route) via Bitola (560MKD); for Bitola itself, eight daily buses run (210MKD, 1¼ hours). Buses to Struga (40MKD, 14km) leave every 15 minutes. In summer, reserve ahead

for Skopje buses, or be prepared to wait. Some *kombi* (minibuses) and taxis wait at the end of Bul Makedonski Prosveiteli.

International buses serve Belgrade (via Kičevo; 1800MKD, 15 hours, one daily at 5.45am). A 7pm bus serves Sofia (1450MKD, eight hours). For Albania, take a bus to Sveti Naum (110MKD, 50 minutes, eight times a day). Cross the border and take a cab (€5, 6km) to Pogradeci. An Ohrid–Sveti Naum taxi costs 1000MKD.

Mavrovo National Park
Маврово
Национален Парк

📞 042

Mavrovo's ski resort is Macedonia's biggest, comprising 730 sq km of birch and pine forest, gorges, karst fields and waterfalls, plus Macedonia's highest peak, **Mt Korab** (2764m). The rarefied air and stunning vistas are great year-round.

👁️ Sights & Activities

Sveti Jovan
Bigorski Monastery
MONASTERY

This revered 1020 Byzantine monastery is off the Debar road. Legend attests an icon of Sveti Jovan Bigorski (St John the Baptist) miraculously appeared, and since then it's been rebuilt often – the icon occasionally reappearing, too. The impressive church also houses what is alleged to be St John's forearm.

Bigorski's awe-inspiring iconostasis was the final of just three carved by local craftsmen Makarije Frčkovski and the brothers Filipovski between 1829 and 1835. This colossal work depicting biblical scenes is enlivened with 700 tiny human and animal figures. Gazing up at this enormous, intricate masterpiece is breathtaking. Upon finishing, the carvers allegedly flung their tools into the nearby Radika River – ensuring that the secret of their artistic genius would be washed away forever.

Galičnik
VILLAGE

Up a winding, tree-lined road ending in a rocky moonscape 17km southwest of Mavrovo, almost depopulated Galičnik features traditional houses along the mountainside. It's placid except for 12 and 13 July, when the **Galičnik Wedding** sees one or two lucky couples wed here. Visit, along with 3000 happy Macedonians, and enjoy eating, drinking, traditional folk dancing and music.

🛏 Sleeping & Eating

Hotel Srna
SKI LODGE €

(☑ 042 388 083; www.hotelsrnamavrovo.com; s/d/apt €25/40/60; ❄ 🐾) The small Srna, 400m from Mavrovo's chairlifts and right on the shore of Lake Mavrovo, has breezy, clean rooms and is good value for this price range.

★ Hotel Radika
SPA HOTEL €€€

(☑ 042 223 300; www.radika.com.mk; s/d/apt €65/90/130; P ❄ 🐾 🏊) Just 5km from Mavrovo, this ultraposh spa hotel is perfect for pampering, with numerous massage treatments and excellent rooms. Prices fall considerably in summer, when the hotel can arrange hiking trips and rents out mountain bikes. Nondrivers should take a taxi from Gostivar (650MKD), on the Skopje–Ohrid road.

ⓘ Getting There & Away

Southbound buses reach Mavrovo Anovi (2km away) en route to Debar (120MKD, seven daily), or while travelling north to Tetovo (140MKD, five daily) and Skopje (180MKD, three daily).

For Sveti Jovan Bigorski Monastery, buses transiting Debar for Ohrid or Struga will be able to drop you off.

CENTRAL MACEDONIA

Bitola
Битола

☑ 047 / POP 95,400

With elegant buildings and beautiful people, elevated Bitola (660m) has a sophistication inherited from its Ottoman days as the 'City of Consuls'. Its 18th- and 19th-century colourful town houses, Turkish mosques and cafe culture make it Macedonia's most intriguing and liveable major town.

◎ Sights & Activities

Širok Sokak
STREET

(ul Maršal Tito) Bitola's Širok Sokak is the city's most representative and stylish street, with its multicoloured facades and European honorary consulates attesting to the city's Ottoman-era sophistication. Enjoying the cafe life here as the beautiful people promenade past is an essential Bitola experience.

VILLA DIHOVO

One of Macedonia's most remarkable guesthouses, **Villa Dihovo** (☑ 070 544 744, 047 293 040; www.villadihovo.com; rates negotiable; 🐾) comprises three traditionally decorated rooms in the 80-year-old home of former professional footballer Petar Cvetkovski and family. Its big flowering lawn is great for kids. The only fixed prices are for the homemade wine, beer and *rakija* (firewater); all else, room price included, is your choice.

Peter himself is a mine of information, deeply involved in the Slow Food movement, and can arrange everything from hikes to Lake Pelisterski, mountain-bike rides and an evening of wine tasting in his cellar. There's also a superb shared kitchen on the premises where guests can cook with the hosts, and a living room with an open fireplace – perfect for colder nights. Booking in advance is essential.

The village of Dihovo is just a short distance outside Bitola, and a taxi will cost between 120 MKD and 150MKD.

Church of Sveti Dimitrija
CHURCH

(11 Oktomvri bb; ⓘ 7am-6pm) This Orthodox church (1830) has rich frescoes, ornate lamps and a huge iconostasis.

Heraclea Lyncestis
ARCHAEOLOGICAL SITE

(admission 100MKD, photos 500MKD; ⓘ 9am-3pm winter, to 5pm summer) Located 1km south of Bitola (70MKD by taxi), Heraclea Lyncestis is among Macedonia's best archaeological sites. Founded by Philip II of Macedon, Heraclea became commercially significant before Romans conquered (168 BC) and its position on the Via Egnatia kept it prosperous. In the 4th century Heraclea became an episcopal seat, but it was sacked by Goths and then Slavs.

See the Roman baths, portico and amphitheatre, and the striking Early Christian basilica and episcopal palace ruins, with beautiful, well-preserved floor mosaics. They're unique in depicting endemic trees and animals. Excavations continue, so you may see newer discoveries.

WORTH A TRIP

ZRZE MONASTERY

Some 26km northwest of Prilep, towards Makedonski Brod, the 14th-century **Zrze Monastery** (Манастир Зрзе; Manastir Sveto Preobrazhenije-Zrze; ☉8am-5pm) **FREE** of the Holy Transfiguration rises like a revelation from a clifftop. The monastery's tranquil position around a spacious lawn, with views over the outstretched Pelagonian Plain, is stunning.

During Ottoman times, Zrze underwent periods of abandonment, rebuilding and plunder but remained an important spiritual centre. Its 17th-century **Church of Sts Peter and Paul** contains important frescoes and icons.

Visitors can enjoy coffee with the kind monks and a tour of the church, with its price-less frescoes and icons. While today the museum in Skopje houses Zrze's most famous icon, the Holy Mother of God Pelagonitsa (1422), a large copy remains in the church. On the adjacent hillside, excavations continue on Zrze's precursor: a 5th-century basilica.

To get to Zrze, take the road towards Makedonski Brod and turn at Ropotovo, following signs for Sv Preobraženie Manastir XIV Vek. You'll pass through three villages as the road worsens, and then you'll have a long drive through tobacco fields along a stretch of unsur-faced road, until you see the monastery on the hillside ahead of you. Near deserted Zrze village, beneath the mountain, is where you should leave your car, unless you have a 4WD vehicle. From here it's a 2km walk uphill to the monastery. There is no public transport.

🛏 Sleeping & Eating

⭐ **Chola Guest House** GUESTHOUSE €
(☑047 224 919; www.chola.mk; Stiv Naumov 80; s/d €12/20; ❄ 🐾 🖥) Overall an excellent-value place to stay, with a quiet location in an atmospheric old mansion that has clean, well-kept rooms and colourful modern bathrooms. It's a short walk from the main drag: there is a useful map on the website, well worth consulting as the guesthouse is hard to find otherwise.

Hotel De Niro HOTEL €
(☑047 229 656; hotel-deniro@t-home.mk; Kiril i Metodij 5; s/d/ste from €17/34/67; ❄🖥) Central yet discreet with lovely old Bitola-style rooms, including a spacious apartment that sleeps four people upstairs. The owner was an art gallery, as you'll quickly see from the paintings that cover almost every cen-timetre of wall space. There's a good pizza-and-pasta restaurant (mains 200MKD to 450MKD) downstairs. Breakfast is €2 extra.

Hotel Milenium HOTEL €€
(☑047 241 001; h.milenium@t-home.mk; Maršal Tito 48; s/d/ste/apt €39/60/80/99; ❄🖥) Atri-ums with stained glass, smooth marble opu-lence and historic relics channel old Bitola, and the location can't be beaten. It's right on the Širok Sokak (you literally have to walk through a bustling cafe terrace to ac-cess the lobby). Rooms are enormous, with high ceilings and sparkling bathrooms, though do request a room at the back if you want peace and quiet.

El Greko PIZZA €
(☑071 279 848; cnr Maršal Tito & Elipda Kara-mandi; mains 150-350MKD; ☉10am-1am) This Sokak taverna and pizzeria has a great beer-hall ambience and is popular with lo-cals. It's one of many decent places along the main street, all of which heave with locals from mid-afternoon until late in the evening.

🍷 Drinking & Entertainment

⭐ **Porta Jazz** BAR
(Kiril i Metodij; ☉8am-1am; 🖥) There's a nota-bly bohemian vibe at this rightly popular, funky place that's packed when live jazz and blues bands play. It's located near the Centar na Kultura, one block back from the Širok Sokak. During the day it's a very pleasant cafe where you can sip espresso on the neatly stencilled terrace.

❶ Getting There & Away

The **bus and train stations** (Nikola Tesla) are adjacent, 1km south of the centre. Buses serve Skopje (480MKD, 3½ hours, 12 daily) via Prilep (140MKD, one hour), Kavadarci (280MKD, two hours, five daily), Strumica (460MKD, four hours, two daily) and Ohrid (210MKD, 1¼ hours, 10 daily).

For Greece, go by taxi to the border (500MKD) and then find a cab to Florina. Some Bitola cab drivers will do the whole trip for about 3000MKD.

Four daily trains serve Skopje (315MKD) via Prilep (85MKD) and Veles (170MKD).

SURVIVAL GUIDE

ℹ️ Directory A–Z

BUSINESS HOURS

Banks 7am to 5pm Monday to Friday
Businesses 8am to 8pm Monday to Friday, to 2pm Saturday
Cafes 10am to midnight
Post offices 6.30am to 8pm

INTERNET RESOURCES

Exploring Macedonia (www.exploring macedonia.com)
Macedonian Information Agency (www.mia.com.mk)
Macedonian Welcome Centre (www.dmwc.org.mk)

MONEY

Macedonian denars (MKD) come in 10-, 50-, 100-, 500-, 1000- and 5000-denar notes, and one-, two-, five-, 10- and 50-denar coins. ATMs are widespread. Credit cards can often be used in larger cities, but you can't really rely on them outside Skopje.

PUBLIC HOLIDAYS

New Year's Day 1 January
Orthodox Christmas 7 January
Orthodox Easter Week March/April
Labour Day 1 May
Saints Cyril and Methodius Day 24 May

COUNTRY FACTS

Area 25,713 sq km

Capital Skopje

Country Code ☎ 389

Currency Macedonian denar (MKD)

Emergency Ambulance ☎ 194, fire ☎ 193, police ☎ 192

Language Macedonian, Albanian

Money ATMs are widespread in major towns

Population 2.1 million

Visas None for EU, US, Australian, Canadian or New Zealand citizens

SLEEPING PRICE RANGES

The following price indicators apply for a high-season double room:

€ less than 3000MKD/€50
€€ 3000MKD/€50 to 5000MKD/€80
€€€ more than 5000MKD/€80

Ilinden Day 2 August
Republic Day 8 September
1941 Partisan Day 11 October

TELEPHONE

Macedonia's country code is ☎ +389. Drop the initial zero in city codes and mobile prefixes (07) when calling from abroad.

VISAS

Citizens of former Yugoslav republics, Australia, Canada, the EU, Iceland, Israel, New Zealand, Norway, Switzerland, Turkey and the USA can stay for three months, visa-free. Otherwise, visa fees average from US$30 for a single-entry visa and US$60 for a multiple-entry visa. Check the Ministry of Foreign Affairs website (www.mfa.gov.mk) if unsure of your status.

ℹ️ Getting There & Away

Skopje's buses serve Sofia, Belgrade, Budapest, Pristina, Tirana, İstanbul, Thessaloniki and more. Trains connect Skopje to Pristina, Belgrade and Thessaloniki. The long-awaited arrival of budget airlines has improved Skopje's modest number of air connections, and it's now connected pretty well to major European cities.

AIR

Alexander the Great Airport (p246), 21km from Skopje, is Macedonia's main airport, with Ohrid's St Paul the Apostle Airport (p250) mostly only for a relatively small number of summer charters.

LAND
Bus

International routes from Macedonia generally arrive and depart from Skopje. Destinations include Belgrade, Pristina, İstanbul, Podgorica and Sofia.

Car & Motorcycle

Bringing your own vehicle into Macedonia is hassle free, though you do need a Green Card (proof of third-party insurance, issued by your insurer), endorsed for Macedonia.

Train

Macedonian Railway (www.mz.com.mk) serves Serbia, Kosovo and Greece.

EATING PRICE RANGES

The following prices are for a main meal:

€ less than 200MKD

€€ 200MKD to 350MKD

€€€ more than 350MKD

ℹ Getting Around

BICYCLE

Cycling is popular in Skopje. Traffic is light in rural areas, though mountains and reckless drivers are common.

BUS

Skopje serves most domestic destinations. Larger buses are new and air-conditioned; *kombi* (minibuses) are usually not. During summer, pre-book for Ohrid.

CAR & MOTORCYCLE

There are occasional police checkpoints; make sure you have the correct documentation. Call ☑196 for roadside assistance.

Driver's Licence

Your national driver's licence is fine, though an International Driving Permit is best.

Hire

Skopje's rental agencies include international biggies and local companies. Ohrid has many, other cities have fewer. Sedans average €60 daily, including insurance. Bring your passport, driver's licence and credit card.

Road Rules

Drive on the right. Seatbelt and headlight use is compulsory. Cars must carry replacement bulbs, two warning triangles and a first-aid kit (available at big petrol stations). Police also fine for drink driving (blood alcohol limit 0.05%). Fines are payable immediately.

TAXI

Taxis are relatively inexpensive. Skopje cabs cost 40MKD for the first kilometre, 20MKD per subsequent kilometre.

TRAIN

Major lines are Tabanovce (on the Serbian border) to Gevgelija (on the Greek border), via Kumanovo, Skopje, Veles, Negotino and Demir Kapija; and Skopje to Bitola, via Veles and Prilep. Smaller Skopje–Kičevo and Skopje–Kočani lines exist.

ESSENTIAL FOOD & DRINK

Macedonian cuisine is typically Balkan, with a combination of Mediterranean and Middle Eastern influences. There's lots of meat grills (*skara*), and plenty of fresh vegetables and herbs used in local dishes.

➡ **Ajvar** Sweet red-pepper sauce; accompanies meats and cheeses.

➡ **Šopska salata** Tomatoes, onions and cucumbers topped with flaky *sirenje* (white cheese).

➡ **Uviač** Rolled chicken or pork wrapped in bacon, filled with melted yellow cheese.

➡ **Tavče gravče** Macedonian speciality of baked beans cooked with spices, onions and herbs and served in earthenware.

Moldova

Best Places to Eat

➡ Vatra Neamului (p259)

➡ Grill House (p259)

➡ Bastion (p259)

➡ Robin Pub (p259)

➡ Kumanyok (p264)

Best Places to Stay

➡ Jazz Hotel (p258)

➡ Hotel Russia (p264)

➡ Art Rustic Hotel (p257)

➡ Hotel Codru (p258)

➡ Agro Pensiunea Butuceni (p261)

Why Go?

Sandwiched between Romania and Ukraine, Moldova is as 'off the beaten track' as you can get in Europe. Attracting just a fraction of the number of visitors of neighbouring countries (12,000 to 20,000 annually in recent years), it's a natural destination for travellers who like to plant the flag and visit lands few others have gone to.

But Moldova's charms run deeper than being merely remote. The country's wines are some of the best in Europe and a fledgling wine-tourism industry, where you can tour wineries and taste the grape, has taken root. The countryside is delightfully unspoiled and the hospitality of villagers is authentic. The capital, Chișinău, is surprisingly lively, with excellent restaurants and bars. Across the Dniestr River lies the separatist Russian-speaking region of Transdniestr. It's a time-warp place, where the Soviet Union still reigns supreme and busts of Lenin line the main boulevards.

When to Go
Chișinău

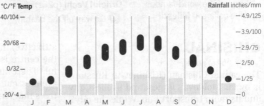

Jun Parks and restaurant terraces fill with students, and the weather is warm.

Jul High season hits its peak with hiking, wine tours and camping in full operation.

Oct The 'National Wine Day' festival takes place during the first weekend in October.

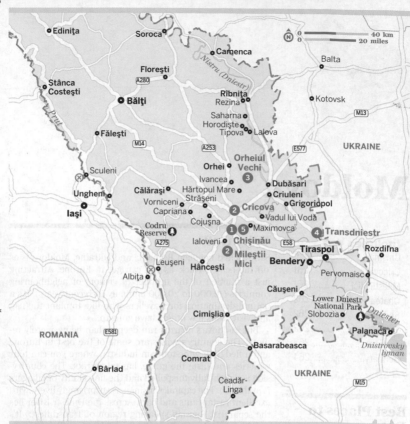

Moldova Highlights

① Stroll the surprisingly pleasant streets and parks of the friendly capital **Chişinău** (p256).

② Designate a driver for tours of the world-famous wine cellars at **Mileştii**

Mici (p261) and **Cricova** (p261).

③ Detox at the fantastic cave monastery, burrowed by 13th-century monks, at **Orheiul Vechi** (p261).

④ Go *way* off the beaten

path in the self-styled 'republic' of **Transdniestr** (p262), a surreal, living homage to the Soviet Union.

⑤ Gorge on the many excellent **dining options** (p259) found in Chişinău.

CHIŞINĂU

♪ 22 / POP 674,000

The capital Chişinău (Kishinev in Russian) is by far Moldova's largest and liveliest city and its main transport hub. While the city's origins date back six centuries to 1420, much of Chişinău (pronounced *kish-i-now*) was levelled in WWII and by a tragic earthquake that struck in 1940. The city was rebuilt in Soviet style from the 1950s onwards, and both the centre and outskirts are dominated by utilitarian (and frankly not very

attractive) high-rise buildings. That said, the centre is surprisingly green and peaceful. There are two large parks, and main avenues cut through groves of old-growth trees that lend a serene element.

◉ Sights

Parcul Catedralei & Grădina Publică Ştefan cel Mare şi Sfînt PARK
(Cathedral Park & Ştefan cel Mare Park; B-dul Ştefan cel Mare; 🏙) These two parks diagonally oppose each other. Both are popular with

ITINERARIES

One Week

Use the capital **Chișinău** as your base and get to know this friendly and fast-changing town. Make day trips out to the stunning cave monastery at **Orheiul Vechi** and to one of the local big-name vineyards for a tour and tasting. Spend a night or two in surreal **Transdniestr** before returning to Chișinău.

Ten Days

Follow the one-week itinerary at a leisurely pace before tacking on a few smaller vineyard tours around **Chișinău**, purchasing your customs limit, and taking an overnight trip to **Soroca** to see the impressive fortress on the mighty Dniestr River.

families and canoodling teenagers on benches. Parcul Catedralei, on the northern side of B-dul Ștefan cel Mare, has two main sights: the Orthodox Cathedral and the Arc de Triomphe. Grădina Publică Ștefan cel Mare și Sfînt is dominated by a **statue of Ștefan cel Mare** at the entrance.

Arc de Triomphe   MONUMENT

(Holy Gates; Parcul Catedralei) **FREE** Chișinău's own Arc de Triomphe dates from the 1840s and marks the centre of the city. It was built to commemorate the victory of the Russian army over the Ottoman Empire. It's often draped with a Moldovan flag in the middle and makes for a stirring photo op.

National Archaeology
& History Museum   MUSEUM

(Muzeul Național de Istorie a Moldovei; ☑ 240 426; www.nationalmuseum.md; Str 31 August 1989, 121a; adult/student 10/5 lei; ☺10am-6pm Sat-Thu; ☏) The granddaddy of Chișinău's museums contains archaeological artefacts from the region of Orheiul Vechi, north of the capital, including Golden Horde coins, Soviet-era weaponry and a huge WWII diorama on the 1st floor.

Pushkin Museum   MUSEUM

(☑ 292 685; Str Anton Pann 19; adult/student 15/5 lei; ☺10am-4pm Tue-Sun) This is where Russia's national poet Alexander Pushkin (1799–1837) spent three years exiled between 1820 and 1823. You can view his tiny cottage, filled with original furnishings and personal items, including a portrait of his beloved Byron on his writing desk. There's also a three-room literary museum in the building facing the cottage, which documents Pushkin's dramatic life.

National Ethnographic
& Nature Museum   MUSEUM

(Muzeul Național de Etnografie și Istorie Naturală; ☑ 240 056; www.muzeu.md; Str M Kogălniceanu 82; adult/child 15/10 lei, English-language tour (arrange in advance) 100 lei; ☺10am-6pm Tue-Sun) The highlight of this massive and wonderful exhibition is a life-sized reconstruction of a dinothere (an elephantlike mammal that lived during the Pliocene epoch – 5.3 million to 1.8 million years ago) skeleton, discovered in the Rezine region in 1966. Allow at least an hour to see the museum's pop art, stuffed animals, and exhibits covering geology, botany and zoology.

🛏 Sleeping

The hotel situation in Chișinău is improving, but most new properties aim for the high end, leaving budget and midrange travellers with less to choose from. An alternative is to rent an apartment. Check out **Marisha. net** (☑06 915 57 53, 488 258; www.marisha.net; apt 500-600 lei) or **Adresa** (☑544 392; www.adresa.md; B-dul Negruzzi 1; apt 500-1800 lei), the former for cheap homestays as well as apartments.

Tapok Hostel   HOSTEL €

(☑068 408 626; www.tapokhostel.com; Str Armeneasca 27a; dm 150-180 lei, r 500 lei; ⓟ☺☏) Friendly, modern youth hostel that offers accommodation in four-, six- and eight-bed dorms in a quiet location near the centre and handy to the city's best bars and restaurants. Free towels, lockers and laundry add to the charms. The four-bed dorm can be booked as a private room. Email in advance for groups or to inquire about availability.

★ Art Rustic Hotel   HOTEL €€

(☑232 593; www.art-rustic.md; Str Alexandru Hajdeu 79/1; s/d/ste 950/1100/1300 lei; ⓟ☺❄☏) This small boutique hotel, about 10 to 15 minutes' walk from the centre, offers excellent value. The 13 rooms are individually and imaginatively furnished (some feature

Central Chişinău

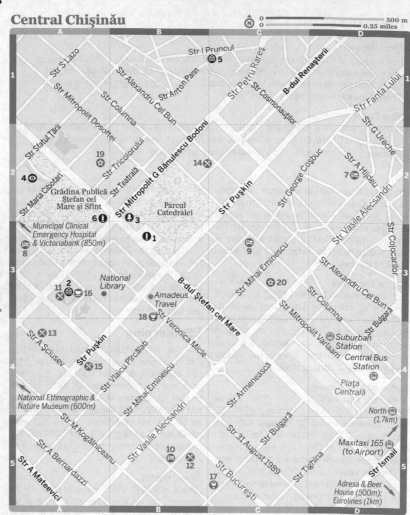

antiques). Rooms come in two classes: 'standart' and cheaper 'econom', with the latter being slightly smaller. Room 11 has a nice big terrace. Note there's no lift.

★ Jazz Hotel
HOTEL €€€

(☎212 626; www.jazz-hotel.md; Str Vlaicu Pârcălab 72; s/d 1250/1800 lei; P✦❋@☎) This well-run, modern hotel makes for an excellent splurge, owing chiefly to the bright, clean rooms and excellent location in the heart of the city. Drivers will enjoy free garage parking at the back. The reception is cheerful and English-speaking. The breakfast buffet of-

fers welcome additions like smoked salmon. There's a small business centre with a computer for checking email.

★ Hotel Codru
HOTEL €€€

(☎208 104; www.codru.md; Str 31 August 1989, 127; s/d incl breakfast from 1600/1800 lei; P❋@☎) Get through the ho-hum lobby and enjoy paradoxically nice rooms that become downright plush (if a bit pricey) when you reach 'luxury' classification. The central location, just across the street from the park, as well as the good balconies and immaculate bathrooms complete the package. There's also a

Central Chişinău

good on-site restaurant and a handy wine shop in the lobby.

✕ Eating

Chişinău has a surprising number of good restaurants. Most are clustered in the centre in the shady neighbourhood along Str Bucureşti and Str 31 August 1989.

Propaganda Cafe INTERNATIONAL €
(☑060 096 666; Str Alexei Şciusev 70; mains 70-130 lei; ☉11am-1am; ☻☎✏) Highly recommended, popular student-oriented cafe that serves very good mains built around chicken, pork and beef, as well as inventive salads and desserts – all at very reasonable prices. The wine list, featuring some of Moldova's best wineries, is terrific. The playfully antique interior, done up like a 19th-century dollhouse, is worth the trip alone.

★Vatra Neamului MOLDOVAN €€
(☑226 839; www.vatraneamului.md; Str Bucureşti 67; mains 90-200 lei; ☉11am-midnight; ☻✏▥) This superb place boasts charming old-world decor and unfailingly genial staff. A long menu of imaginatively dressed-up meats – think stewed pork with polenta, baked rabbit and salmon in pastry, not to mention copious vegetarian options – may prompt repeat visits. Enter via the door on Str Puşkin.

★Robin Pub INTERNATIONAL €€
(☑241 127; Str Alexandru cel Bun 83; mains 90-250 lei; ☉11am-midnight; ☎) A friendly, affordable, local-pub feel reigns in this tastefully decorated hang-out. The menu includes omelettes, pastas and grills, including a professionally

handled rib eye (150 lei), as well as a long list of desserts. Sit on the dark-leather banquettes inside or dine under the trees out front.

★Bastion INTERNATIONAL €€
(☑060 706 070; www.bastion.md; Str Bucureşti 68 (enter at Str 31 August 1989, 117); mains 130-200 lei; ☉11am-midnight; ☻☎) Upscale but relaxed restaurant featuring excellent grilled meats and fish, many with an Asian twist, plus a wide range of sushi dishes. Dine on white linen inside or relax on the terrace. The wine list features some of the best of local wineries such as Purcari, Chateau Vartely and Et'cetera, among others.

Beer House INTERNATIONAL €€
(☑275 627; www.beerhouse.md; B-dul Negruzzi 6/2; mains 75-250 lei; ☉11am-11pm; ☎▥) This brewery-cum-restaurant has four delicious home-brewed beers and a superb menu, warming up with chicken wings and peaking with rabbit or chicken grilled in cognac. The relaxed ambience and good service add to the charm – summer evening meals outside on the terrace are a treat.

★Grill House INTERNATIONAL €€€
(☑224 509; Str Armeneasca 24/2; mains 150-300 lei; ☉11am-midnight; ☻☎▥) It may not look like much from the street, but inside this sleek, low-lit place you'll find the best steaks in town served up by attentive staff from the glassed-in, fire-oven kitchen. Creative pasta dishes complement the array of hearty meat, seafood and fish and there's a great wine list to boot. Go down the atmospheric alley off the street.

🍸 Drinking & Nightlife

Delice d'Ange CAFE
(🕿 245 139; Str 31 August 117/2; 🕙9am-11pm; 📶💷) Popular central cafe offering a dazzling array of great pastries and coffee (25 lei). Sit inside or on the terrace. There's a tree, and a children's play area upstairs.

Dublin Irish Pub PUB
(🕿245 855; Str Bulgară 27; 🕙10am-11pm; 📶) Very comfortable pub and restaurant with big wood-beamed ceilings and brick flooring. The drinks are on the expensive side but it's one of the few places in town where you can get a pint of Guinness and the service is very good.

Tipografia 5 LIVE MUSIC
(🕿079 894 142; http://tipografia5.locals.md; Str Vlaicu Pârcălab 45; 🕙8pm-midnight Sun-Thu, 10pm-4am Fri & Sat) Alternative late-night venue for clubbing and occasional live music. The mood is student-friendly and chilled. The program tends towards indie/trendy, with some nights given over to techno and other nights to disco.

☆ Entertainment

Opera & Ballet Theatre OPERA, BALLET
(🕿box office 245 104; www.nationalopera.md; B-dul Ştefan cel Mare 152; 🕙box office 10am-1pm & 2-6pm Tue-Fri, 11am-4pm Sat & Sun) Home to the esteemed national opera and ballet company, which puts on productions from September to June.

Philharmonic Concert Hall CLASSICAL MUSIC
(🕿237 262, box office 222 734; www.filarmonica. md; Str Mitropolit Varlaam 78) Moldova's National Philharmonic is based here.

ℹ Information

MEDICAL SERVICES
Municipal Clinical Emergency Hospital (🕿emergency 903, info 248 435; Str Toma Ciorba 1; 🕙24hr) Has emergency services and there is a good likelihood of finding English-speaking staff.

MONEY
Victoriabank (Str 31 August 1989, 141; 🕙9am-4pm Mon-Fri)

TRAVEL AGENCIES
Amadeus Travel (Lufthansa City Center; 🕿tours 211 716; www.amadeus.md; Str Puşkin 24; 🕙9am-7pm Mon-Fri) Offers a range of inland tours, including wine tours to the country's best-known vineyards such as Cricova, Cojusna, Mileştii Mici, Chateau Vartely and Purcari.

ℹ Getting There & Away

AIR
Moldova's only international airport is the modern **Chişinău International Airport** (KIV; 🕿525 111; www.airport.md; Str Aeroportului 80/3), 16km southeast of the city centre. There are regular flights to many major European capitals. There are no internal flights within Moldova.

BUS
Chişinău has three bus stations: the **Central Bus Station** (Chişinău Gara; Str Mitropolit Varlaam), the **North Bus Station** (Gara de Nord; www. autogara.md) and the **Southwestern Bus Station** (Autogara Sud-vest or Gara de Sud; www.autogara.md; Şoseaua Hânceşti 143). There's also a small **Suburban Station** (Casele Suburbane). Each bus station serves different destinations (not all of them make sense geographically), so it's important to know in advance which station your bus is using.

Common bus journeys and the stations they use include Bucharest (Central Bus Station; 250 lei, 10 hours, five daily); Kyiv (North Bus Station; 280 lei, 13 hours, two daily); Moscow (North Bus Station; 800 lei, 30 hours, two daily), Orhei/Trebujeni (Suburban Station; 26 lei, 1½ hours, five daily); Soroca (North Bus Station; 70 lei, four hours, frequent); and Tiraspol (Central Bus Station; 35 lei, two hours, frequent). There's a helpful online timetable (in Romanian only) at www.autogara.md.

For long-haul international departures, **Eurolines** (🕿549 813; www.eurolines.md; Aleea Garii 1; 🕙9am-6pm Mon-Fri) operates an office at the train station.

TRAIN
International trains depart from the recently renovated station, at Aleea Gării, southeast of Piaţa Negruzzi.

Common train journeys from Chişinău include Bucharest (500 lei, 14 hours, daily); Tiraspol (80 lei, two hours, daily); Odesa (160 lei, five hours, daily); Moscow (900 lei, 28 to 32 hours, four to five daily); and St Petersburg (1000 lei, 40 hours, daily).

ℹ Getting Around

TO/FROM THE AIRPORT
Maxitaxi 165 departs every 20 minutes from Str Ismail, near the corner of B-dul Ştefan cel Mare for the airport (3 lei). Coming from the airport, this is the last stop. A taxi (call 🕿14 222) to the centre costs from 80 lei to 100 lei.

ORHEIUL VECHI MONASTERY COMPLEX

The archaeological and ecclesiastical complex at **Orheiul Vechi** ('Old Orhei'), about 20km southeast of the modern city of Orhei (60km northeast of Chişinău), is the country's most important historical site and a place of stark natural beauty.

Occupying a remote, rocky ridge over the Răut River, the open-air complex includes ruins, fortifications, baths, caves and monasteries, ranging from the earliest days of the Dacian tribes more than 2000 years ago through the Mongol and Tatar invasions of the early Middle Ages and the time of Ştefan cel Mare, and all the way to the modern period.

Begin your visit to the region at the **Orheiul Vechi Exhibition Centre** (☑235-56 137; http://orhei.dnt.md; Trebujeni; adult/concession 10/5 lei; ☉9am-6pm Tue-Sun), near the village of Trebujeni (along the main road just before the bridge to Butuceni). Here you'll find a small museum filled with objects recovered during archaeological digs and a helpful information centre. Exploration is done on foot; it takes about half a day to see everything.

The most impressive sight is arguably the **Cave Monastery** (Mănăstire în Peşteră; www.orhei.dnt.md; Butuceni, Orheiul Vechi; voluntary donation; ☉8am-6pm) **FREE**, built inside a cliff overlooking the gently meandering river. It's marked by a small bell tower and a cross standing on the rocks. It was dug by Orthodox monks in the 13th century and remained inhabited until the 18th century. In 1996 a handful of monks returned to this secluded place of worship and are slowly restoring it. You can enter the cave via a brick archway, just below the hill from the bell tower.

The Orheiul Vechi Exhibition Centre has six pleasant rooms (600 lei) and a small restaurant, but for something more authentic, try the **Agro Pensiunea Butuceni** (☑235-56 906; www.pensiuneabutuceni.md; Butuceni; r 1000 lei; ⓟ☉✳ⓡ✕ⓗ), a beautifully restored traditional guesthouse in the middle of the village of the same name.

From Chişinău, around five daily buses depart from the Suburban Station for Trebujeni (26 lei, about one hour).

BUS/MAXITAXI

Route 45 runs from Central to Southwestern Bus Station, as does maxitaxi 117 from the train station. Bus 1 goes from the train station to B-dul Ştefan cel Mare. From the city centre, trolleybuses 1, 4, 5, 8, 18 and 22 go to the train station; buses 2, 10 and 16 go to Southwestern Bus Station; and maxitaxis 176 and 191 go to North Bus Station. Tickets are sold on board for buses (2 lei) and trolleybuses (2 lei). Nippy minitaxis (3 lei, pay the driver) serve most routes in town and to many outlying villages. Maxitaxis run regularly between 6am and 10pm, with reduced service until midnight.

AROUND CHIŞINĂU

Cricova

Of Moldova's many vineyards, **Cricova** (☑tours 22-441 204; www.cricova.md; Str Ungureanu 1, Cricova; guided tours per person from 200 lei; ☉10am-5pm Mon-Fri) is arguably the best known. Its underground wine kingdom, 15km north of Chişinău, is one of Europe's biggest.

Some 60km of the 120km-long underground limestone tunnels – dating from the 15th century – are lined wall-to-wall with bottles.

The most interesting part of a tour of the winery is the wineglass-shaped cellar of collectable bottles, including some 19 bottles that once belonged to Nazi party leader Hermann Göring, a 1902 bottle of Becherovka from the Czech Republic, a 1902 bottle of Evreiesc de Paşti from Jerusalem, and pre-WWII French red wines. Legend has it that in 1966 Soviet cosmonaut Yury Gagarin entered the cellars, re-emerging (with assistance) two days later. Russian president Vladimir Putin even celebrated his 50th birthday here.

You must have private transport and advance reservations to get into Cricova or you can arrange for staff to pick you up in Chişinău.

Mileştii Mici

Similar to Cricova but bigger and possibly more impressive, the wine cellars at **Mileştii Mici** (☑tours 22-382 333; www.milestii-mici.md;

Mileştii Mici, Ialoveni; guided 40min tour per person 200 lei; tasting & lunch per person 500-900 lei; ⊙ tours at 10am, 1pm, 3.30pm Mon-Fri), 20km south of Chişinău near the town of Ialoveni, stretch for something like 200km. The cellars here hold more than 2 million bottles, which makes this the world's largest wine collection, according to Guinness World Records.

Guided vehicle tours of the cellars are offered three times daily, though you'll have to book these in advance by phone or email. If you've got your own wheels, the simplest option is to drive your own car through the cellars (with a guide, and it helps to have a small car). Otherwise, you'll have to prearrange a tour through a travel agency or find someone with a car.

Chateau Cojuşna

Just 13km northwest of Chişinău, **Chateau Cojuşna** vineyard (☑ 22-221 630; www.migdal. md; Str Mecanizatorilor 1, Străşeni; tours 220-900 lei) in Cojuşna village in the Străşeni district, offers friendly and affordable tours, though the setting is quieter in comparison to the bigger and more popular wineries at Cricova and Mileştii Mici.

Tours lasting from one to three hours include a gift bottle, tastings and a hot meal, though you must request an English tour in advance.

Drop-ins are possible, but staff aren't always free to open the very worthwhile wine-tasting rooms, decorated in traditional style with wooden furniture carved by a local boy and his father. However, you can always buy wine (30 lei to 300 lei per bottle) from the shop.

It's possible but not easy to reach Cojuşna from Chişinău by public transport. Maxitaxis leave from Calea Eşilor. From where the maxitaxi drops you, the winery is about a 2km walk away.

Soroca

☑ 230 / POP 37,000

The northern city of Soroca occupies a prominent position on the Dniestr River and as such has played an outsized role in the defence of the Moldavian principality through the ages. The main attraction is the **Soroca Fortress**, part of a chain of medieval military bastions built by Moldavian princes from the 14th to the 16th centuries to defend the principality's boundaries. This fortress was founded by Ştefan cel Mare and rebuilt by his son, Petru Rareş, in 1543–45.

◉ Sights

Soroca Fortress   FORTRESS
(Cetatea Soroca; ☑ 30 430; Str Petru Rareş 1) This commanding structure dates from 1499 when Moldavian Prince Ştefan cel Mare built a wooden fortress here. It was given its circular shape, with five stone bastions, in the middle of the 16th century by Petru Rareş. The fortress was closed for reconstruction at the time of research.

Soroca Museum of History & Ethnography   MUSEUM
(☑ 22 264; Str Independenţei 68; adult/student 3/2 lei; ⊙ 10am-1pm & 2-5pm Mon-Fri) This tiny museum is a treat; its exhibits cover archaeological finds, weapons and ethnographic displays.

🛏 Sleeping & Eating

Hotel Central   HOTEL €
(☑ 23 456; www.soroca-hotel.com; Str Kogâlniceanu 20; s/d incl breakfast 500/600 lei; ⊛✳🐾🍴) The best lodging in town is this small, partly renovated hotel in the centre. The ground-level rooms feel damp and uninviting, but the situation improves the next floor up. Room 16 is snug, clean and sports a shiny new bathroom. There's a small sauna and the terrace restaurant is good.

Nistru Hotel   HOTEL €
(☑ 23 783; Str Alecu Russo 15; r without/with bathroom 300/400 lei) Simple, clean rooms that are fairly priced.

ℹ Getting There & Away

There are around a dozen daily buses from Chişinău's North Bus Station (four hours).

By car, Soroca is a straight shot, 150km north of Chişinău, along the M2 highway. Note that at the time of research this road was being extensively rebuilt (north of Orhei). Budget a minimum of three to four hours for the trip.

TRANSDNIESTR

POP 505,000

The self-declared republic of Transdniestr (sometimes called Transnistria, or the Pridnestrovskaya Moldavskaya Respublika, PMR, in Russian), a narrow strip of land on the eastern bank of the Dniestr River, is one of the strangest places in Eastern Europe. It's a ministate that doesn't officially exist in anyone's eyes but its own.

From the Moldovan perspective, Transdniestr is still officially part of its sovereign territory that was illegally grabbed in the early 1990s with Russian support. Officials in Transdniestr see it differently and proudly point to the territory having won its 'independence' in a bloody civil war in 1992. A bitter truce has ensued ever since.

These days, a trip to Transdniestr from Moldova is relatively easy and completely safe. Visitors will be stunned by this idiosyncratic region that still fully embraces the iconography of the Soviet period (lots of photo-worthy busts of Lenin are scattered about) as well as having its own currency, police force, army and borders.

Tiraspol

📞 533 / POP 136,000

The 'capital' of Transdniestr is also, officially at least, the second-largest city in Moldova. But don't expect it to be anything like the chaotic Moldovan capital: here time seems to have stood still since the end of the Soviet Union. Eerily quiet streets, flower beds tended with military precision and old-school Soviet everything from street signs to litter-free parks named after communist grandees, Tiraspol (from the Greek, meaning 'town on the Nistru') will be one of the strangest places you'll ever visit.

◉ Sights

Tiraspol National United Museum   MUSEUM

(📞 90 426; ul 25 Oktober 42; admission 25 roubles; ⊙10am-5pm Sun-Fri) The closest thing to a local history museum, it features an exhibit focusing on poet Nikolai Zelinsky, who founded the first Soviet school of chemistry. Opposite is the **Presidential Palace**, from where President Yevgeny Shevchuk rules the region. Loitering and/or photography here is likely to end in questioning and a guard-escorted trip off the property.

War Memorial   MEMORIAL

(ul 25 Oktober) FREE At the western end of ul 25 Oktober stands a Soviet armoured tank from which the Transdniestran flag flies. Behind is the War Memorial with its **Tomb of the Unknown Soldier**, flanked by an eternal flame in memory of those who died on 3 March 1992 during the first outbreak of fighting. On weekends, it's covered in flowers.

Kvint Factory   BRANDY FACTORY

(📞 96 577; www.kvint.biz; ul Lenina 38; tours 180-900 roubles) Since 1897, Kvint has been making some of Moldova's finest brandies. Purchase a bottle of some of Europe's best-value cognac (starting at under 30 roubles) near the entrance to the plant or at one of several Kvint shops around town. Tasting tours, starting at around 180 roubles per person, must be booked in advance and normally include food.

House of Soviets   NOTABLE BUILDING

(ul 25 Oktober) The House of Soviets, towering over the eastern end of ul 25 Oktober, has Lenin's angry-looking bust peering out from its prime location.

Kirov Park   PARK

(ul Lenina) North along ul Lenina, towards the bus and train stations, is Kirov Park, with a statue of the Leningrad boss who was

MOLDOVA TIRASPOL

ℹ CROSSING INTO TRANSDNIESTR

All visitors to Transdniestr are required to show a valid passport at the 'border'. The formalities are fairly straightforward and take about 15 minutes. Your passport will be scanned and used to generate a slip of paper called a 'migration card', with basic information including your name, nationality and date of birth. The migration card is free of charge and allows for a stay of up to 10 hours. You're required to keep this paper with your passport and surrender it when leaving (so don't lose it!).

The 10-hour time frame should be sufficient for most day trips and to see the main sights (or to transit the country). If you plan on staying the night, you'll have to register at the **OVIR** (📞 533 55 047; ul Kotovskogo 2a (Str Cotovschi 2a); ⊙9am-noon Mon, 9am-noon & 1-4pm Tue & Thu, 1-3pm Fri) immigration office in Tiraspol. Upscale hotels will take care of the registration process for you; if you're staying in a hostel or private home, you'll need to sort this on your own in conjunction with your hosts.

assassinated in 1934, conveniently sparking mass repressions throughout the USSR.

🛌 Sleeping

You must register at OVIR (p263) in central Tiraspol if staying overnight. Marisha.net (p257) can arrange a homestay.

Tiraspol Hostel
HOSTEL €

(Bottle Hotel; ☑ 068 571 472; www.moldova hostels.com; ul Karla Marksa 13, Ternovka (Tîrnauca); dm/r 300/600 roubles; ℗ ➗ 🐾 🌂) Incredible as it seems, Tiraspol has a hostel. Run by an American expat, this converted hotel offers big dorm rooms with bath, as well as rare amenities for a hostel like pool and tennis courts. Prices include a tour. Call or email to arrange pick-up; the hostel is 3km outside of Tiraspol in an area called Ternovka.

★ Hotel Russia
HOTEL €€€

(☑ 38 000; www.hotelrussia.md; ul Sverdlova 69; r incl breakfast 1100 roubles; ℗ ➗ ❄ 🌂) Opening to great fanfare in 2012, this large, luxurious and smartly furnished hotel is definitely the mainstay for business people and anyone wanting comfort. Rooms come with flat-screen TVs, smart bathrooms and comfortable beds. The hotel is located on a side street just by the House of Soviets. Staff can arrange police registration.

🍴 Eating & Drinking

★ Kumanyok
UKRAINIAN €€

(☑ 72 034; www.kumanyok.com; ul Sverdlova 37; mains 60-140 roubles; ⊙ 9am-11pm; 🌂 📶) A second home to Transdniestr's ruling classes (as demonstrated by the rows of black Mercedes outside), this smart, traditional Ukrainian place is set in a kitsch faux-countryside home, where diners are attended to by a fleet of peasant-dressed waitresses. The menu is hearty Ukrainian fare; think dumplings, pancakes, fish, mutton and, above all, excellent, authentic borsch (red-beet soup).

Cafe Larionov
INTERNATIONAL €€

(☑ 47 562; ul Karla Liebknechta 397; mains 70-120 roubles; ⊙ 9am-11pm; 🌂) Named for Tiraspol's own avant-garde modernist painter Mikhail Larionov (1881–1964). The idea is local cuisines drawing from the cultural influences (Russian, Jewish, Moldovan) common in Larionov's time, with an emphasis on soups, stews and grilled meats. The setting is a large atrium, with a cosy terrace at the back.

Baccarat
CLUB

(☑ 94 642; ul 25 Oktober 50; ⊙ 5pm-4am) A stylish hang-out with expensive drinks and indoor/outdoor seating. Frequent karaoke nights pack the joint.

ℹ Information

Transnistria Tour (☑ 069 427 502; www. transnistria-tour.com) Highly recommended company that offers a full range of tours and travel services to foreign visitors. Its excellent English-language website is a great place to start planning your trip. Tours range in theme from Soviet monuments and brandy to football and ecology and start at about 300 roubles per person per day.

ℹ Getting There & Away

BUS

You can only pay for bus tickets with local currency, but there are change facilities at the combined bus and train station. Buy tickets inside the station. From Tiraspol there are eight daily buses to Odesa in Ukraine (50 roubles, three hours). Buses/maxitaxis go to Chişinău (34 roubles) nearly every half-hour from 5am to 6pm. Trolleybus 19 (2.50 roubles) and quicker maxitaxis 19 and 20 (3 roubles) cross the bridge over the Dniestr to Bendery.

TRAIN

There's a useful daily Chişinău to Odesa train, which calls at Tiraspol at 9.20am daily. Tickets to Odesa cost 100 roubles and the journey takes two hours. The train makes the return journey to Chişinău each evening, calling at Tiraspol at 7.20pm.

Bendery

☑ 532 / POP 93,750

Bendery (sometimes called Bender, and previously known as Tighina), on the western banks of the Dniestr River, is the greener, more aesthetically agreeable counterpart to Tiraspol. Despite civil-war bullet holes still decorating several buildings – Bendery was hardest hit by the 1992 military conflict with Moldova – the city centre is a breezy, friendly place.

The highlight is an impressive Ottoman fortress, **Bendery Fortress** (Tighina; ☑ 48 032; www.bendery-fortress.com; ul Kosmodemyanskoi 10; admission 50 roubles; ⊙ 8am-4pm Mon-Fri, 10am-3pm Sat & Sun), located outside the centre near the Bendery–Tiraspol bridge. It was built in the 16th century and saw keen fighting between Turkish and Russian forces before it fell to Tsarist Russia permanently in the early 19th century. Until just a few years ago it was a functioning Russian army base and off limits to the public. Now you're free to amble around.

At the entrance to the city, close to the Bendery–Tiraspol bridge, is a **memorial park** dedicated to local 1992 war victims. An eternal flame burns in front of an armoured tank, from which flies the Transdniestran flag. Haunting memorials to those killed during the civil war are also scattered throughout many streets in the city centre.

SURVIVAL GUIDE

 **Directory A–Z**

ACCOMMODATION

The accommodation situation in Chişinău is improving and the city has a number of very nice top-end hotels. The problem continues to be a lack of decent options at the midrange and budget price points. This may be one city to consider a splurge, since the difference in quality and comfort between the better hotels and cheaper options can be pronounced.

Elsewhere, most towns have small hotels that have survived from communist days and have been somewhat done up. Most hotels these days are totally nonsmoking or at least offer nonsmoking rooms.

On arriving at your hotel, you'll be asked to present your passport and fill in a short identity form.

Camping grounds (*popas turistic*) are rare. The good news is that wild camping is normally allowed unless expressly prohibited.

To supplement a lack of hotels in outlying areas, many municipalities are turning to homestays and privately run pensions. **Moldova Holiday** (www.moldovaholiday.travel) keeps an up-to-date list.

SLEEPING PRICE RANGES

The following price ranges denote one night's accommodation in a double room:

€ less than €50

€€ €50 to €120

€€€ more than €120

MOLDOVA DIRECTORY A–Z

COUNTRY FACTS

Area 33,851 sq km

Capital Chişinău

Country Code ☑373

Currency Moldovan leu (plural lei)

Emergency Ambulance ☑903, fire ☑901, police ☑902

Language Moldovan

Money ATMs are abundant in Chişinău; less common in smaller cities and towns

Population 3.6 million (including Transdniestr)

Visas None for the EU, USA, Canada, Japan, Australia and New Zealand, but required for South Africa and many other countries

BUSINESS HOURS

Banks 9am to 3pm Monday to Friday

Businesses 8am to 7pm Monday to Friday, to 4pm Saturday

Museums 9am to 5pm Tuesday to Sunday

Restaurants 10am to 11pm

Shops 9am or 10am to 6pm or 7pm Monday to Saturday

MONEY

Moldova's currency is the *leu* (plural *lei*). Banknotes are denominated as 1, 5, 10, 20, 50, 100, 200, 500 and 1000 lei notes. One leu is comprised of 100 bani. Little-used coins are denominated as 1, 5, 10, 25 and 50 bani.

The easiest way to get local currency is by using your home debit or credit card through a local ATM. ATMs are scattered throughout the centre in Chişinău, but are harder to find in other towns (stock up on cash when you can). Otherwise, exchange cash at banks.

The only legal tender in Transdniestr is the Transdniestran rouble (TR). Some taxi drivers, shopkeepers and market traders will accept payment in US dollars, euros or even Moldovan lei – but generally you'll need to get your hands on roubles to buy things there. Be sure to spend all your roubles before you leave, as no one honours or exchanges this currency outside Transdniestr.

PUBLIC HOLIDAYS

New Year's Day 1 January

Orthodox Christmas 7 January

International Women's Day 8 March

Orthodox Easter April/May

Victory (1945) Day 9 May
Independence Day 27 August
National Language Day 31 August

VISAS

Citizens of EU member states, USA, Canada, Japan, Australia and New Zealand do not need visas and can stay for up to 90 days within a six-month period. South Africans and some other nationalities require an invitation from a company, organisation or individual to get a visa.

Visas can be acquired on arrival at Chişinău airport or, if arriving by bus or car from Romania, at three border points: Sculeni (north of Iaşi); Leuşeni (main Bucharest–Chişinău border); and Cahul. Visas are not issued at any other border crossings, nor when entering by train.

Check the **Ministry of Foreign Affairs** (www. mfa.gov.md) website and follow the link for Consular Affairs for the latest news on the visa situation.

❶ Getting There & Away

AIR

Moldova's only international airport (p260) is in Chişinău.

LAND

Moldova has decent overland links to neighbouring countries. Daily buses and trains from Chişinău head to Iaşi and Bucharest in Romania, as well as to Odesa in Ukraine. Trains also serve Moscow and St Petersburg. Buses to Odesa often avoid Transdniestr and thus the delays at the border. Trains between Chişinău and Odesa go via Tiraspol, but delays are minimal.

Bus

Moldova is well linked by bus lines to central and western Europe. While not as comfortable as the train, buses tend to be faster, though not always cheaper.

Car & Motorcyle

On arriving at the border, drivers need to show valid vehicle registration, insurance (Green Card), driving licence (US and EU licences OK) and passport. Motorists must purchase a highway sticker (vignette) to drive on Moldovan roads. Buy these at the border crossing. Rates per 7/15/30 days are €2/4/7.

Train

From Chişinău, there are four to five trains to Moscow, as well as daily service to St Petersburg and Odesa, Ukraine (via Tiraspol). There's an overnight service between Bucharest and Chişinău; at 12 to 14 hours.

❶ Getting Around

BUS & MAXITAXI

Moldova has a comprehensive if confusing network of buses running to most towns and villages. Maxitaxis, which follow the same routes as the buses, are usually quicker and more reliable. Public transport costs 2 lei, while city maxitaxis cost 3 lei.

EATING PRICE RANGES

The following price indicators are based on the average cost of a main course:

€ less than €5

€€ €5 to €10

€€€ more than €10

ESSENTIAL FOOD & DRINK

Moldovan cooking bears a strong resemblance to Romanian food across the border. The emphasis is on traditional recipes and farm-fresh ingredients rather than sophisticated preparation techniques.

➜ **Muşchi de vacă/porc/miel** A cutlet of beef/pork/lamb.

➜ **Piept de pui** The ubiquitous chicken breast.

➜ **Mămăligă** Cornmeal mush with a consistency between porridge and bread that accompanies many dishes.

➜ **Brânză** Moldova's most common cheese is a slightly salty-sour sheep's milk product that often comes grated. Put it on *mămăligă*.

➜ **Sarma** Cabbage-wrapped minced meat or pilau rice packages, similar to Turkish dolma or Russian *goluptsy*.

➜ **Wine** Look for bottles from quality local wineries like Cricova, Chateau Vartely and Purcari, among many others.

Montenegro

Best Places to Eat

➡ Konoba Ćatovića Mlini (p274)

➡ Galion (p273)

➡ Restoran Lim (p270)

➡ Taste of Asia (p270)

➡ Juice Bar (p270)

Best Places to Stay

➡ Palazzo Drusko (p273)

➡ Palazzo Radomiri (p273)

➡ Hotel Astoria (p270)

➡ Old Town Hostel (p273)

➡ Hikers Den (p276)

Why Go?

Imagine a place with sapphire beaches as spectacular as Croatia's, rugged peaks as dramatic as Switzerland's, canyons nearly as deep as Colorado's, palazzi as elegant as Venice's and towns as old as Greece's. Then wrap it up in a Mediterranean climate and squish it into an area two-thirds the size of Wales, and you start to get a picture of Montenegro.

More adventurous travellers can easily sidestep the peak-season hordes on the coast by heading to the rugged mountains of the north. This is, after all, a country where wolves and bears still lurk in forgotten corners.

Montenegro, Crna Gora (Црна Гора), Black Mountain: the name itself conjures up romance and drama. There are plenty of both on offer as you explore this perfumed land, bathed in the scent of wild herbs, conifers and Mediterranean blossoms. Yes, it really is as magical as it sounds.

When to Go
Podgorica

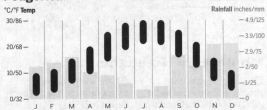

Jun Beat the peak-season rush and prices but enjoy the balmy weather.

Sep Warm water but fewer bods to share it with; shoulder season prices.

Oct The leaves turn golden, making a rich backdrop for walks in the national parks.

BOSNIA &
HERCEGOVINA

Foča

Priboj

Nova
Varoš

SERBIA

Šćepan
Polje

Pljevlja Ranče

Prijepolje

Sjenica

⑤ Tara Canyon

Dobrakovo

Durmitor
National Park   Žabljak
Plužine
Bobotov Kuk   ▲ Savin Kuk
(2523m)   (2313m)
Donja
Brezna

Bijelo
Polje

Dobrilovina

Dračenovac

Rožaje

Mojkovac

Biogradska Gora
National Park

Crna
Glava
(2137m)

Berane

Kulina

Šavnik

Kapa Moračka
(2227m)

Kolašin

Andrijevica

Peć

Morača
Monastery

KOSOVO

Nikšić

Plav

Trebinje   Dolovi

④ Ostrog
Monastery

Surdup
(2182m)

Kolac
(2534m)

Risan   Perast
Debeli   Morinj Ljuta
Brijeg   ③ Kotor Njeguši
Herceg Novi   Tivat
Bay of
Kotor   Mt Lovćen
Luštica Peninsula (1749m) ▲
Lovćen National Park

PODGORICA

② Cetinje   Golubovci
Rijeka Crnojevića
Žabljak Crnojevića
Budva ⑦ Virpazar   Vranjina
Sveti Stefan   Lake Skadar
National Park
Petrovac   Murići

Hani i
Hotit

ALBANIA

ADRIATIC SEA

Bar

Shkodra

0   40 km
0   20 miles

Sukobin

Ulcinj

Velika Plaža

Montenegro Highlights

① Randomly roam the
atmospheric streets of **Kotor**
(p271) until you're at least a
little lost.

② Drive the vertiginous
route from Kotor to the
Njegoš Mausoleum at the
top of **Lovćen National Park**
(p274).

③ Admire the baroque
palaces and churches of pretty
Perast (p273).

④ Seek out the spiritual
at impressive cliff-clinging
Ostrog Monastery (p276).

⑤ Float through paradise,
rafting between the kilometre-
plus walls of the **Tara Canyon**
(p276).

⑥ Dive into Montenegro's
history, art and culture in
the old royal capital, **Cetinje**
(p275).

⑦ Watch the beautiful people
over the rim of a coffee cup in
the cobbled Old Town lanes of
Budva.

Five Days

Basing yourself in **Kotor**, spend an afternoon in Perast and a whole day in Budva. Allow another day to explore **Lovćen National Park** and **Cetinje**.

One Week

For your final two days, head north to **Durmitor National Park**, making sure to stop at **Ostrog Monastery** on the way. Spend your time hiking, rafting and canyoning.

COASTAL MONTENEGRO

Coming from Croatia and entering the mountain-framed folds of the Bay of Kotor (Boka Kotorska), the beauty meter goes off the scale. It doesn't let up when you hit the Adriatic coast, where you'll find a charismatic set of small settlements set against clear waters and sandy beaches.

Budva   Будва

🌙 033 / POP 13,400

The poster child of Montenegrin tourism, Budva – with its atmospheric Old Town and numerous beaches – certainly has a lot to offer. Yet the child has moved into a difficult adolescence, fuelled by rampant development that has leeched much of the charm from the place. Still, it's the buzziest place on the coast so if you're in the mood to party, this is the place to be.

◉ Sights

Budva's best feature and star attraction is the Stari Grad (Old Town) – a mini-Dubrovnik with marbled streets and Venetian walls rising from the clear waters below. Much of it was ruined by two earthquakes in 1979 but it has since been completely rebuilt and now houses more shops, bars and restaurants than residences.

Citadela   FORTRESS

(admission €2.50; ⊘ 9am-midnight May-Oct, to 5pm Nov-Apr) At the Stari Grad's seaward end, the old citadel offers striking views, a small museum and a library full of rare tomes and maps. It's thought to have been built on the site of the Greek acropolis, but the present incarnation dates to the 19th-century Austrian occupation. Its large terrace serves as the main stage of the annual Theatre City Festival.

Town Walls   FORTRESS

(admission €1.50) A walkway about a metre wide leads around the landward walls of the Stari Grad, offering views across the rooftops and down on some beautiful hidden gardens. Admission only seems to be charged in the height of summer; at other times it's either free or locked. The entrance is near the Citadela.

Ploče Beach   BEACH

(www.plazaploce.com) If the sands are getting too crowded in Budva itself, head out to this little pebbly beach at the end of a scrub-covered peninsula, 10km west of town (take the road to Kotor, turn off towards Jaz Beach and keep going). The water is crystal clear but if you prefer fresh water there are little pools set into the sunbathing terraces.

Jaz Beach   BEACH

The blue waters and broad sands of Jaz Beach look spectacular when viewed from high up on the Tivat road. While it's not built up like Budva, the beach is still lined with loungers, sun umbrellas and noisy beach bars. Head down the Budva end of the beach for a little more seclusion.

🛏 Sleeping

Montenegro Freedom Hostel   HOSTEL €

(🌙 067-523 496; montenegrofreedom@gmail.com; Cara Dušana 21; dm/tw/d €14/30/36; ❋ 🛜) In a quieter section of the Old Town, this sociable hostel has tidy little rooms scattered between three buildings. The terraces and small courtyard are popular spots for impromptu guitar-led singalongs.

Montenegro Hostel   HOSTEL €

(🌙 069-039 751; www.montenegrohostel.com; Vuka Karadžića 12; dm/r €12/40; ❋ 🛜) With a right-in-the-thick-of-it Old Town location (pack earplugs), this colourful little hostel provides the perfect base for hitting the bars and beaches. Each floor has its own kitchen and bathroom, and there's a communal space at the top for fraternising.

Hotel Oliva
HOTEL €€

(☏069-551 769; www.hotel-oliva.com; Velji Vinogradi bb; r €50; P※⏾) Don't expect anything flashy, just a warm welcome, clean and comfortable rooms with balconies, and a nice garden studded with the olive trees that give this small hotel its name. The wifi doesn't extend much past the restaurant.

★ Hotel Astoria
HOTEL €€€

(☏033-451 110; www.astoriamontenegro.com; Njegoševa 4; s/d from €115/130; ※⏾) Water shimmers down the corridor wall as you enter this chic boutique hotel hidden in the Old Town's fortifications. The rooms are on the small side but they're beautifully furnished; the sea-view suite is spectacular.

Villa M Palace
APARTMENT €€€

(☏067-402 222; www.mpalacebudva.com; Gospoština 25; apt from €110; P※⏾) There's a seductive glamour to this modern block, hemmed in within a rash of new developments near the Old Town. A chandelier glistens in the lift and the walls sparkle in the darkened corridors – and that's before you even reach the luxurious one- to three-bedroom apartments.

✗ Eating

★ Juice Bar
CAFE €

(www.juicebar.me; Vranjak 13; mains €3-10; ⊙8.30am-late) They may serve delicious juices, smoothies and shakes, but that's only part of the appeal of this cosmopolitan cafe, set on a sunny Old Town square. The crowd-pleasing menu includes light breakfasts, salads, toasted sandwiches, nachos, lasagne, cakes and muffins.

★ Restoran Lim
EUROPEAN €€

(Slovenska Obala; mains €6-19; ⊙8am-1am) Settle into one of the throne-like carved wooden chairs and feast on the likes of grilled meat and fish, homemade sausages, pizza, beef stroganoff, veal Parisienne or Weiner schnitzel. The octopus salad is excellent.

★ Taste of Asia
ASIAN €€

(☏033-455 249; Popa Jola Zeca bb; mains €10-15; ⊙noon-10pm) Spicy food is virtually non-existent in Montenegro, which makes this attractive little eatery such a welcome surprise. The menu ambles through the Orient, with dishes from Indonesia, Malaysia, Singapore and Vietnam, but lingers longest in Thailand and China.

Knez Konoba
MONTENEGRIN, SEAFOOD €€

(Mitrov Ljubiše 5; mains €8-17; ⊙noon-11pm) Hidden within the Old Town's tiny lanes, this atmospheric eatery has only three outdoor tables and a handful inside. The traditional dishes are beautifully presented and often accompanied by free shots of *rakija* (fruit brandy).

Porto
MONTENEGRIN, SEAFOOD €€

(☏033-451 598; www.restoranporto.com; City Marina, Šetalište bb; mains €7-18; ⊙10am-1am) From the waterfront promenade a little bridge arches over a fish pond and into this romantic restaurant where jocular bow-tie-wearing waiters flit about with plates laden with fresh seafood. The food is excellent and the wine list offers plenty of choice from around the region.

▼ Drinking & Nightlife

Casper
CAFE, BAR

(www.facebook.com/casper.budva; Petra I Petrovića bb; ⊙10am-1am Jun-Sep, 5pm-1am Oct-May; ⏾) Chill out under the pine tree in this picturesque Old Town cafe-bar. DJs kick off from July, spinning everything from reggae to house. Casper hosts its own jazz festival in September.

Top Hill
CLUB

(www.tophill.me; Topliški Put; events €10-25; ⊙11pm-5am Jul & Aug) The top cat of Montenegro's summer party scene attracts up to 5000 revellers to its open-air club atop Topliš Hill, offering them top-notch sound and lighting, sea views, big-name touring DJs and performances by local pop stars.

ℹ Information

Tourist Office (☏033-452 750; www.budva.travel; Njegoševa 28; ⊙9am-9pm Mon-Sat, 5-9pm Sun Jun-Aug, 8am-8pm Mon-Sat Sep-May)

ℹ Getting There & Away

The **bus station** (☏033-456 000; Popa Jola Zeca bb) has frequent services to Kotor (€3.50) and Cetinje (€3.50), and a daily bus to Žabljak (€15).

WORTH A TRIP

MORE TO EXPLORE

Herceg Novi A bustling waterfront promenade runs below a small fortified centre, with cafes and churches set on sunny squares.

Sveti Stefan Gazing down on this impossibly picturesque walled island village (now an exclusive luxury resort) provides one of the biggest 'wow' moments on the entire Adriatic coast.

Ulcinj Minarets and a hulking walled town dominate the skyline, providing a dramatic background for the holidaymakers on the beaches.

Podgorica The nation's modern capital has a buzzy cafe scene, lots of green space and some excellent galleries.

Lake Skadar National Park The Balkans' largest lake is dotted with island monasteries and provides an important sanctuary for migrating birds.

Biogradska Gora National Park Virgin forest set around a pretty lake.

Kotor   Котор

☑ 032 / POP 13,500

Wedged between brooding mountains and a moody corner of the bay, this dramatically beautiful town combines historic grace with vibrant street life. From a distance Kotor's sturdy ancient walls are barely discernible from the mountain's grey hide but at night they're spectacularly lit, reflecting in the water to give the town a golden halo. Within those walls lie labyrinthine marbled lanes where churches, shops, bars and restaurants surprise you on hidden piazzas.

◉ Sights & Activities

The best thing to do in Kotor is to get lost and found again in the maze of streets. You'll soon know every corner, as the town is quite small, but there are plenty of churches to pop into and many coffees to be drunk in the shady squares.

Sea Gate   GATE

(Vrata od Mora) The main entrance to the town was constructed in 1555 when the town was under Venetian rule (1420–1797). Look out for the winged lion of St Mark, Venice's symbol, which is displayed prominently on the walls here and in several other spots around the town. Above the gate the date of the city's liberation from the Nazis is remembered with a communist star and a quote from Tito.

As you pass through the gate, look for the 15th-century stone relief of the Madonna and Child flanked by St Tryphon and St Bernard. Stepping through onto **Trg od Oružja** (Weapons Sq) you'll see a strange stone pyramid in front of the **clock tower** (1602); it was once used as a **pillory** to shame wayward citizens.

Town Walls   FORTRESS

(admission €3; ⊗ 24hr, fees apply 8am-8pm May-Sep) Kotor's fortifications started to head up St John's Hill in the 9th century and by the 14th century a protective loop was completed; it was added to right up until the 19th century. The energetic can make a 1200m ascent up the fortifications via 1350 steps to a height of 260m above sea level. There are entry points near the North Gate and behind Trg od Salate; avoid the heat of the day and bring lots of water.

St Nicholas' Church   CHURCH

(Crkva Sv Nikole; Trg Sv Luke) Breathe in the smell of incense and beeswax in this relatively unadorned Orthodox church (1909). The silence, the iconostasis with its silver bas-relief panels, the dark wood against bare grey walls, the filtered light through the dome and the simple stained glass conspire to create a mystical atmosphere.

St Tryphon's Cathedral   CHURCH

(Katedrala Sv Tripuna; Trg Sv Tripuna; admission €2.50; ⊗ 8am-7pm) Kotor's most impressive building, this Catholic cathedral was consecrated in the 12th century but reconstructed after several earthquakes. When the

Kotor

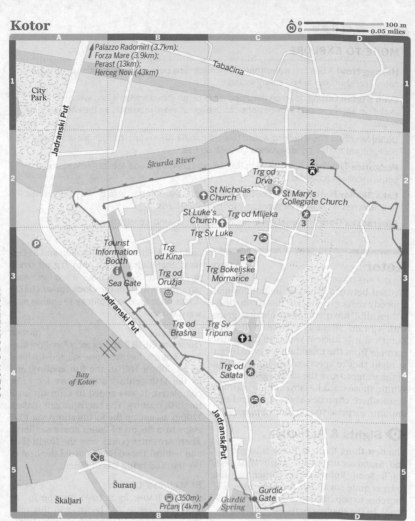

entire frontage was destroyed in 1667, the baroque bell towers were added; the left one remains unfinished. The cathedral's gently hued interior is a masterpiece of Romanesque architecture with slender Corinthian columns alternating with pillars of pink stone, thrusting upwards to support a series of vaulted roofs. Its gilded silver bas-relief altar screen is considered Kotor's most valuable treasure.

Gurdić Gate GATE

(Vrata od Gurdića) Fewer tourists make it to the south end of town, where the houses narrow into a slim corridor leading to this bastion and gate (parts of which date from the 13th century) and the drawbridge over the Gurdić spring. Without the crowds you can easily imagine yourself transported through time here.

A Day Out On
Monty B SAILING

(www.montenegro4sail.com; from €79 per person) If you don't have €1000 to blow on a luxury yacht, join British expats Katie and Tim (and their two little doggies) for a sail on the 44ft ketch which doubles as their home (and kennel).

Kotor

⊚ Sights

⊕ Activities, Courses & Tours

🛏 Sleeping

⊗ Eating

🛏 Sleeping & Eating

Although the Stari Grad is a charming place to stay, you'd better pack earplugs. In summer the bars blast music onto the streets until 1am every night and rubbish collectors clank around at 6am. Some of the best options are just out of Kotor in quieter Dobrota. Inquire about private accommodation at the tourist information booth.

★ Old Town Hostel   HOSTEL €

(☑ 032-325 317; www.hostel-kotor.me; near Trg od Salata; dm €12-15, r without/with bathroom €39/44, apt €49; ❄🛜) If the ghosts of the Bisanti family had any concerns when their 13th-century palazzo (palatial mansion) was converted into a hostel, they must be overjoyed now. Sympathetic renovations have brought the place to life, and the ancient stone walls now echo with the cheerful chatter of happy travellers, mixing and mingling beneath the Bisanti coat of arms.

★ Palazzo Drusko   GUESTHOUSE €€

(☑ 032-325 257; www.palazzodrusko.me; near Trg od Mljeka; s/d from €49/75; ❄🛜) Loaded with character and filled with antiques, this venerable 600-year-old palazzo is a memorable place to stay, right in the heart of the old town. Thoughtful extras include a guest kitchen, 3D TVs and old-fashioned radios rigged to play Montenegrin music.

Hotel Monte Cristo   HOTEL €€

(☑ 032-322 458; www.montecristo.co.me; near Trg Bokeljske Mornarice; r/apt from €90/125; ❄🛜) It's not going to win any hip design awards but this old stone place offers a cheerful welcome and clean, brightly tiled rooms in a supremely central location. There's a restaurant downstairs, so expect some noise.

★ Palazzo Radomiri   HOTEL €€€

(☑ 032-333 172; www.palazzoradomiri.com; Dobrota 220; s/d/ste from €110/140/200; ⊙ Apr-Oct; 🅿❄🛜🏊) This honey-coloured early-18th-century palazzo on the Dobrota waterfront, 4km north of the old town, has been transformed into a first-rate boutique hotel. Some rooms are bigger and grander than others, but all 10 have sea views and luxurious furnishings. Guests can avail themselves of a small workout area, sauna, pool, private jetty, bar and restaurant.

Forza Mare   HOTEL €€€

(☑ 032-333 500; www.forzamare.com; Kriva bb, Dobrota; r from €200; ⊙ Apr-Oct; 🅿❄🛜🏊) A bridge arches over a small tiled pool before you even reach the front door of this hotel, dripping in marble, slate and a general air of over-the-top opulence. Downstairs there's a tiny private beach, an upmarket restaurant and a spa centre.

★ Galion   SEAFOOD €€€

(☑ 032-325 054; Šuranj bb; meals €12-23; ⊙ noon-midnight) With an achingly romantic setting, extremely upmarket Galion gazes directly at the Old Town across the millionaire yachts in the marina. Fresh fish is the focus, but you'll also find steaks and pasta. It usually closes in winter.

ⓘ Information

Tourist Information Booth (☑ 032-325 950; www.tokotor.me; outside Vrata od Mora; ⊙ 8am-8pm Apr-Nov, 8am-5pm Dec-Mar) Stocks free maps and brochures, and can help with contacts for private accommodation.

ⓘ Getting There & Away

The **bus station** (☑ 032-325 809; ⊙ 6am-9pm) is to the south of town, just off the road leading to the Tivat tunnel. Buses head to Budva (€3.50, 40 minutes) at least hourly and to Žabljak (€13, 3½ hours) twice daily.

A taxi to Tivat airport should cost around €10.

Perast   Пераст

☑ 032 / POP 270

Looking like a chunk of Venice that has floated down the Adriatic and anchored itself onto the Bay of Kotor, Perast hums with melancholic memories of the days when it was rich and powerful. Despite its diminutive size it boasts 16 churches and 17 formerly grand palazzi.

WORTH A TRIP

MONTENEGRO'S MOST ATMOSPHERIC EATERY

A crystalline stream flows around and under this rustic former mill, **Konoba Ćatovića Mlini** (☑032-373 030; www.catovicamlini.me; mains €12-25; ☺11am-11pm), which masquerades as a humble family-owned *konoba* but in reality is one of Montenegro's best restaurants. Watch the geese idle by as you sample the magical bread and olive oil, which appears unbidden at the table. Fish is the focus but traditional Njeguši specialities are also offered. You'll find it in the village of Morinj, in the western corner of the inner section of the Bay of Kotor.

◉ Sights

Sveti Đorđe & Gospa od Škrpjela ISLANDS

Just offshore from Perast are two peculiarly picturesque islands. The smaller, **Sveti Đorđe** (St George), rises from a natural reef and houses a Benedictine monastery shaded by cypresses. Boats (€5 return) ferry people to its big sister, **Gospa od Škrpjela** (Our-Lady-of-the-Rocks), which was artificially created in the 15th century around a rock where an image of the Madonna was found. Every year on 22 July the locals row over with stones to continue the task.

St Nicholas' Church CHURCH

(Crkva Sv Nikole; treasury €1; ☺10am-6pm) This large church has never been completed, and given that it was commenced in the 17th century and the bay's Catholic community has declined markedly since then, one suspects it never will be. Its treasury contains beautifully embroidered vestments and the remains of various saints. Climb the imposing 55m bell tower for views over the bay.

Perast Museum MUSEUM

(Muzej grada Perasta; adult/child €2.50/1.50; ☺9am-7pm) The Bujović Palace, dating from 1694, has been lovingly preserved and converted into a museum showcasing the town's proud seafaring history. It's worth visiting for the building alone and for the wondrous photo opportunities afforded by its balcony.

🛏 Sleeping & Eating

Hotel Conte APARTMENTS €€€

(☑032-373 687; www.hotel-conte.com; apt €80-160; ❄☎) Conte is not so much a hotel as a series of deluxe studio, one- and two-bedroom apartments in historic buildings scattered around St Nicholas' Church. The sense of age resonating from the stone walls is palpable, even with the distinctly nontraditional addition of a Jacuzzi and sauna in the flashest apartment. It's worth paying €20 extra for a sea view.

Per Astra HOTEL €€€

(☑032-373 608; www.perastra.me; ste €169-329; ☺Apr-Oct; P❄☎☎) Located right at the top of the town (the stairs will get you fit, but they can be difficult at night), this old stone complex offers 11 suites with glitzy decor, fine views and a small pool.

Restaurant Conte SEAFOOD €€€

(☑032-373 687; mains €9-20; ☺8am-midnight; ☎) Meals come with lashings of romance on the flower-bedecked waterside terrace of the Hotel Conte. You'll be presented with platters of whole fish to select from; the chosen one will return, cooked and silver-served, to your table.

❶ Getting There & Away

Paid parking is available on either approach to town; car access into the town itself is restricted.

Buses stop at least hourly on the main road at the top of town. Expect to pay less than €3 for any journey within the bay between Kotor (25 minutes) and Herceg Novi (40 minutes).

CENTRAL MONTENEGRO

The heart of Montenegro – physically, spiritually and politically – is easily accessed as a day trip from the coast, but it's well deserving of a longer exploration. This really is the full Monte: soaring peaks, hidden monasteries, steep river canyons and historic towns.

Lovćen National Park Ловћен

Directly behind Kotor is Mt Lovćen (1749m), the black mountain that gave Crna Gora (Montenegro) its name (*crna/negro* means 'black' and *gora/monte* means 'mountain' in Montenegrin and Italian respectively). This locale occupies a special place in the hearts of all Montenegrins. For most of its history it represented the entire nation – a rocky island of Slavic resistance in an Ottoman sea. The old capital of Cetinje nestles in its foothills.

The national park's 6220 hectares are criss-crossed with well-marked hiking paths.

◎ Sights & Activities

Njegoš Mausoleum   MONUMENT
(Njegošev Mauzolej; admission €3; ⊙8am-6pm) Lovćen's star attraction, this magnificent mausoleum (built 1970–74) sits at the top of its second-highest peak, Jezerski Vrh (1657m). Take the 461 steps up to the entry where two granite giantesses guard the tomb of Montenegro's greatest hero. Inside under a golden mosaic canopy a 28-tonne Petar II Petrović Njegoš rests in the wings of an eagle, carved from a single block of black granite by Croatian sculptor Ivan Meštrović.

Avanturistički Park   ADVENTURE SPORTS
(☑069-543 156; Ivanova Korita; adult/child €18/12; ⊙10am-6pm Jun-Aug, noon-6pm Sat & Sun May, Sep & Oct) This 2-hectare adventure park has zip lines and ropes courses of varying degrees of difficulty set among the trees near the National Park Visitor Centre.

❶ Information

National Park Visitor Centre (www.nparkovi. me; Ivanova Korita; ⊙9am-5pm) Offers accommodation in four-bed bungalows (€40).

❶ Getting There & Away

If you're driving, the park can be approached from either Kotor or Cetinje (entry fee €2). Tour buses provide the only transport into the park.

Cetinje   Цетиње
☑041 / POP 14,000
Rising from a green vale surrounded by rough, grey mountains, Cetinje is an odd mix of former capital and overgrown village where single-storey cottages and stately mansions share the same street.

◎ Sights

A collection of four Cetinje museums and two galleries are collectively known as the **National Museum of Montenegro**.

A joint ticket will get you into all of them (adult/child €10/5), or you can buy individual tickets.

History Museum   MUSEUM
(Istorijski muzej; ☑041-230 310; www.mnmuseum. org; Novice Cerovića 7; adult/child €3/1.50; ⊙9am-5pm) Housed in Cetinje's most imposing building, the former parliament (1910), this fascinating museum is well laid out, following a timeline from the Stone Age to 1955. There are few English signs but the enthusiastic staff will walk you around and give you an overview before leaving you to your own devices.

Montenegrin Art Gallery   GALLERY
(Crnogorska galerija umjetnosti; www.mnmuseum. org; Novice Cerovića 7; adult/child €4/2; ⊙9am-5pm) The national collection is split between the former parliament and a striking modern building on Cetinje's main street (mainly used for temporary exhibitions). All of Montenegro's great artists are represented, with the most famous (Milunović, Lubarda, Đurić etc) having their own separate spaces.

King Nikola Museum   PALACE
(Muzej kralja Nikole; www.mnmuseum.org; Dvorski Trg; adult/child €5/2.50; ⊙9am-5pm) Entry to this 1871 palace, home to the last sovereign of Montenegro, is by guided tour (you may need to wait for a group to form). Although looted during WWII, enough plush furnishings, stern portraits and taxidermied animals remain to capture the spirit of the court.

Njegoš Museum   PALACE
(Njegošev muzej; www.mnmuseum.org; Dvorski Trg; adult/child €3/1.50; ⊙9am-5pm) This castle-like palace was the residence of Montenegro's favourite son, prince-bishop and poet Petar II Petrović Njegoš. It was built and financed by the Russians in 1838 and housed the nation's first billiard table, hence the museum's alternative name, Biljarda.

Cetinje Monastery   MONASTERY
(Cetinjski Manastir; ⊙8am-6pm) It's a case of four times lucky for the Cetinje Monastery, having been repeatedly destroyed during Ottoman attacks and rebuilt. This sturdy incarnation dates from 1786, with its only exterior ornamentation being the capitals of columns recycled from the original building, founded in 1484.

DON'T MISS

OSTROG MONASTERY ОСТРОГ

Clinging to a cliff 900m above the Zeta valley, this gleaming white Orthodox monastery (1665) is a strangely affecting place that gives the impression that it has grown out of the very rock.

A guesthouse near the Lower Monastery offers tidy single-sex dorm rooms (€5), while in summer sleeping mats are provided for free to pilgrims in front of the Upper Monastery. There's no public transport but numerous tour buses head here from the coast.

🛏 Sleeping & Eating

Pansion 22　　　　　　　　GUESTHOUSE €
(☑ 069-055 473; www.pansion22.com; Ivana Crnojevića 22; s/d €22/40; 🛜) They may not be great at speaking English or answering emails, but the family who run this central guesthouse offer a warm welcome nonetheless. The rooms are simply decorated yet clean and comfortable, with views of the mountains from the top floor.

Kole　　　　　　MONTENEGRIN, EUROPEAN €€
(☑ 041-231 620; www.restaurantkole.me; Bul Crnogorskih Junaka 12; mains €3-12; ⏱ 7am-11pm) They serve omelettes and pasta at this snazzy modern eatery, but it's the local specialities that shine. Try the Njeguški *ražanj*, smoky spit-roasted meat stuffed with *pršut* (prosciutto) and cheese.

ⓘ Information

Tourist Information (☑ 041-230 250; www.cetinje.travel; Novice Cerovića bb; ⏱ 8am-6pm Mar-Oct, to 4pm Nov-Feb)

ⓘ Getting There & Away

Buses stop at Trg Golootočkih Žrtava, two blocks from the main street. There are regular services to Budva (€3.50).

Durmitor National Park Дурмитор

☑ 052

Magnificent scenery ratchets up to stupendous in this national park (entry €3), where ice and water have carved a dramatic landscape from the limestone. The Durmitor range has 48 peaks over 2000m, with the highest, **Bobotov Kuk**, reaching 2523m. Scattered in between are 18 glacial lakes known as *gorske oči* (mountain eyes). The largest, **Black Lake** (Crno jezero), is a pleasant 3km walk from **Žabljak**, the park's principal gateway. Slicing through the mountains at the northern edge of the national park like they were made from the local soft cheese, the **Tara River** forms a **canyon** that at lowest point is 1300m deep.

From December to March Durmitor is a ski resort, while in summer it's popular with hikers and rafters.

🏃 Activities

The two-day raft along the river is the country's premier outdoor attraction (May to October only). Most of the day tours from the coast traverse only the last 18km of the river – this is outside the national park and hence avoids hefty fees. This section also has the most rapids – but don't expect much in the way of white water.

Summit Travel Agency　　　ADVENTURE TOUR
(☑ 052-360 082; www.summit.co.me; Njegoševa 12, Žabljak; half-/1-/2-day rafting trip €50/110/200) As well as rafting trips, this long-standing agency can arrange jeep tours, mountain-bike hire and canyoning expeditions.

🛏 Sleeping

★**Hikers Den**　　　　　　　　　HOSTEL €
(☑ 067-854 433; www.hostelzabljak.com; Božidara Žugića bb, Žabljak; dm €11-13, s/d €22/35; ⏱ Apr-Oct; 🖥🛜) Split between three neighbouring houses, this laid-back and sociable place is by far the best hostel in the north. If you're keen on a rafting or canyoning trip, the charming hosts will happily make the arrangements.

Eko-Oaza
Suza Evrope　　　　　CABINS, CAMPGROUND €
(☑ 069-444 590; ekooazatara@gmail.com; Dobrilovina; campsites per tent/person/campervan €5/1/10, cabins €50; ⏱ Apr-Oct) Consisting of four comfortable wooden cottages (each sleeping five people) and a fine stretch of lawn above the river, this magical family-run 'eco oasis' offers a genuine experience of Montenegrin hospitality. Home-cooked meals are provided on request, and rafting trips and jeep safaris can be arranged.

Hotel Soa　　　　　　　　　　HOTEL €€
(☑ 052-360 110; www.hotelsoa.com; Put Crnog Jezera bb, Žabljak; s/d/ste from €60/75/120; 🛜) Rooms at this snazzy new hotel are kitted out with monsoon shower heads, Etro toiletries,

robes and slippers. Plus there's a playground, bikes for hire (per hour/day €2/10) and a restaurant.

ⓘ Information

Durmitor National Park Visitor Centre
(☑ 052-360 228; www.nparkovi.me; Jovana Cvijića bb; ⊙ 7am-3pm Mon-Fri) On the road to the Black Lake, this centre includes a micromuseum on the park's flora and fauna. Staff sell hiking maps and guidebooks.

ⓘ Getting There & Away

The bus station is at the southern edge of Žabljak, on the Šavnik road. Bus destinations include Kotor (€13, 3½ hours, two daily) and Budva (€15, 4¾ hours, daily).

SURVIVAL GUIDE

ⓘ Directory A–Z

ACCOMMODATION
Private accommodation (rooms and apartments for rent) and hotels form the bulk of the sleeping options, although there are some hostels in the more touristy areas. Camping grounds operate in summer and some of the mountainous areas have cabin accommodation in 'eco villages' or mountain huts.

In the peak summer season, some places require minimum stays (three days to a week). Many establishments on the coast close during winter. An additional tourist tax (usually less than €1 per night) is added to the rate for all accommodation types.

GAY & LESBIAN TRAVELLERS
Although homosexuality was decriminalised in 1977 and discrimination outlawed in 2010, attitudes to homosexuality remain hostile and life for gay people is extremely difficult. Many gay men resort to online connections (try www. gayromeo.com) or take their chances at a hand-

---

> **SLEEPING PRICE RANGES**
>
> The following price indicators apply for a double room in the shoulder season (roughly June and September):
>
> **€** less than €40
>
> **€€** €40 to €100
>
> **€€€** more than €100

> **EATING PRICE RANGES**
>
> Tipping isn't expected, although it's common to round up to the nearest euro. The following price categories refer to a standard main course:
>
> **€** less than €7
>
> **€€** €7 to €12
>
> **€€€** more than €12

---

ful of cruisy beaches. Lesbians will find it even harder to access the local community.

INTERNET RESOURCES
Explore Montenegro (www.explore montenegro.com)
Montenegrin National Tourist Organisation (www.montenegro.travel)
National Parks of Montenegro (www. nparkovi.me)

PUBLIC HOLIDAYS
New Year's Day 1 and 2 January
Orthodox Christmas 6, 7 and 8 January
Orthodox Good Friday & Easter Monday Usually April/May
Labour Day 1 May
Independence Day 21 May
Statehood Day 13 July

TELEPHONE
The international access prefix is ☑ 00 or + from a mobile. Mobile numbers start with ☑ 06. Local SIM cards are easy to find.

ⓘ Getting There & Away

AIR
Montenegro has two international airports – **Tivat** (TIV; ☑ 032-671 337; www.montenegro airports.com) and **Podgorica** (TGD; ☑ 020-444 244; www.montenegroairports.com) – although many visitors use Croatia's Dubrovnik Airport, which is very near the border.

Montenegro Airlines (www.montenegro airlines.com) is the national carrier.

LAND
Bus

There's a well-developed bus network linking Montenegro with major cities in the neighbouring countries, including Dubrovnik, Sarajevo, Belgrade, Priština and Shkodra.

ESSENTIAL FOOD & DRINK

Loosen your belt; you're in for a treat. By default, most Montenegrin food is local, fresh and organic, and hence very seasonal. The food on the coast is virtually indistinguishable from Dalmatian cuisine: lots of grilled seafood, garlic, olive oil and Italian dishes. Inland it's much more meaty and Serbian-influenced. The village of Njeguši in the Montenegrin heartland is famous for its *pršut* (prosciutto, air-dried ham) and cheese. Anything with Njeguški in its name is going to be a true Montenegrin dish and stuffed with these goodies.

Eating in Montenegro can be a trial for vegetarians and almost impossible for vegans. Pasta, pizza and salad are the best fallback options.

Here are some local favourites:

→ **Riblja čorba** Fish soup, a staple of the coast.

→ **Crni rižoto** Black risotto, coloured and flavoured with squid ink.

→ **Lignje na žaru** Grilled squid, sometimes stuffed (*punjene*) with cheese and smoke-dried ham.

→ **Jagnjetina ispod sača** Lamb cooked (often with potatoes) under a metal lid covered with hot coals.

→ **Rakija** Domestic brandy, made from nearly anything. The local favourite is grape-based *loza*.

→ **Vranac & Krstač** The most famous indigenous red and white wine varietals (respectively).

Car & Motorcycle

Vehicles need Green Card insurance or insurance must be bought at the border.

Train

At lease one train heads between Bar and Belgrade daily (€21, 17 hours); see www.zpcg.me for details.

COUNTRY FACTS

Area 13,812 sq km

Capital Podgorica

Country Code ☑382

Currency Euro (€)

Emergency Ambulance ☑124, fire ☑123, police ☑122

Language Montenegrin

Money ATMs in larger towns

Population 779,000

Visas None for citizens of EU, Canada, USA, Australia, New Zealand and many other countries

SEA

Montenegro Lines (☑030-303 469; www.montenegrolines.net) operates car ferries between Bar and the Italian port of Bari.

ⓘ Getting Around

BUS

The bus network is extensive and reliable. Buses are usually comfortable and air-conditioned, and are rarely full.

CAR & MOTORCYCLE

Cars drive on the right-hand side and headlights must be kept on at all times. Drivers are recommended to carry an International Driving Permit (IDP) as well as their home country's driving licence. Traffic police are everywhere, so stick to speed limits. Sadly, requests for bribes do happen (especially around the Durmitor area), so don't give the police any excuse to pull you over.

Allow more time than you'd expect for the distances involved, as the terrain will slow you down.

The major international car-hire companies have a presence in various centres.

Poland

Best Places to Eat

➜ Restauracja Pod Norenami (p290)

➜ Dwie Trzecie (p285)

➜ Szeroka 9 (p307)

➜ Papierówka (p300)

➜ Cafe & Restaurant Steinhaus (p298)

Best Places to Stay

➜ Wielopole (p290)

➜ Castle Inn (p284)

➜ Hostel Mleczarnia (p298)

➜ Hotel Stare Miasto (p300)

➜ Hotel Petite Fleur (p307)

Why Go?

If they were handing out prizes for 'most eventful history', Poland would get a medal. The nation has spent centuries at the pointy end of history, grappling with war and invasion. Nothing, however, has succeeded in suppressing Poles' strong sense of nationhood and cultural identity. As a result, bustling centres like Warsaw and Kraków exude a sophisticated energy that's a heady mix of old and new.

Away from the cities, Poland is surprisingly diverse, from its northern beaches to a long chain of mountains on its southern border. In between, towns and cities are dotted with ruined castles, picturesque market squares and historic churches.

Although prices have steadily risen in the postcommunist era, Poland is still good value. As the Poles continue to reconcile their distinctive national identity with their place in Europe, it's a fascinating time to pay a visit.

When to Go
Warsaw

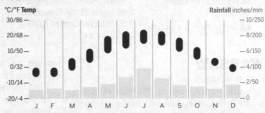

May & Jun Stately Kraków returns to life after a long winter.

Jul & Aug A brief but hot summer is good for swimming in the Baltic Sea or hiking in the mountains.

Sep & Oct Warm and sunny enough for an active city break to Warsaw.

Poland Highlights

1 Experience the beauty and history of **Kraków's** Old Town.

2 Enjoy the student-fuelled party vibe in **Wrocław** (p296).

3 Remember the victims of the Nazi German genocide at **Auschwitz-Birkenau** (p292).

4 Relive Poland's inspirational anticommunist struggle at the **European Solidarity Centre** (p304) in Gdańsk.

5 Ski or hike the Tatry mountains from **Zakopane** (p295).

6 Prepare to be dazzled by the **Museum of the History of Polish Jews** (p284) in Warsaw.

WARSAW

POP 1.73 MILLION

Poland's vibrant capital, Warsaw (Warszawa in Polish, *var-shah-va*), is the country's largest city and epicentre of Polish commerce and culture. It offers an abundance of museums, clubs and concert halls, as well as the widest array of eating options. It's a major transport hub, and even if you're not planning a long stay, chances are you'll change trains here or arrive at/depart from one of the city's airports.

First impressions may not be entirely positive. Warsaw was levelled during World War II by occupying German soldiers and rebuilt in the 1950s and '60s in bleak Soviet style. Modern touches added since communism fell in 1989 have softened the edges, however, and the passing decades have lent that old Soviet architecture a hip, retro gloss.

ITINERARIES

One Week

Spend a day exploring **Warsaw**, with a stroll around the Old Town and a stop at the Museum of the History of Polish Jews. Next day, head to historic **Kraków** for three days, visiting the beautiful Old Town, Wawel Castle and former Jewish district of Kazimierz. Take a day trip to **Auschwitz-Birkenau**, the former Nazi German extermination camp. Afterward, head to **Zakopane** for a day in the mountains.

Two Weeks

Follow the above itinerary, then travel to **Wrocław** for two days, taking in its graceful town square. Head north to Gothic **Toruń** for a day, then onward to **Gdańsk** for two days, exploring the museums and bars of the main town and visiting the magnificent castle at **Malbork**.

◉ Sights

◉ Old Town

Warsaw's Old Town looks old but dates from just around 60 years ago. It was rebuilt from the ground up after being reduced to rubble during WWII. The reconstruction, which took place between 1949 and 1963, aimed at restoring the appearance of the town in the 17th and 18th centuries. The centre is the rebuilt **Old Town Square** (Rynek Starego Miasta).

Royal Castle   CASTLE
(☑ 22 355 5170; www.zamek-krolewski.pl; Plac Zamkowy 4; adult/concession 22/15zł; ◷10am-4pm Tue-Sat, 11am-4pm Sun) This massive brick edifice, a copy of the original blown up by the Germans in WWII, began life as a wooden stronghold of the dukes of Mazovia in the 14th century. Its heyday came in the mid-17th century, when it became one of Europe's most splendid royal residences. It then served the tsars and, in 1918, after Poland regained independence, became the residence of the president. Today it is filled with period furniture and works of art.

Barbican   FORTRESS
(ul Nowomiejska) Heading north out of the Old Town along ul Nowomiejska you'll soon see the red-brick Barbican, a semi-circular defensive tower topped with a decorative Renaissance parapet. It was partially dismantled in the 19th century, but reconstructed after WWII, and is now a popular spot for buskers and art sellers.

◉ Royal Way

This 4km historic route connects the Old Town with the modern city centre, running south from about Plac Zamkowy along elegant ul Krakowskie Przedmieście, and ul Nowy Świat all the way to busy Al Jerozolimskie.

St Anne's Church   CHURCH
(ul Krakowskie Przedmieście 68) Marking the start of the Royal Way, this is arguably the most ornate church in the city. It escaped major damage during WWII, which explains why it sports an original trompe l'œil ceiling, a rococo high altar and a gorgeous organ. The facade is also baroque in style, although there are neoclassical touches here and there.

Church of the Holy Cross   CHURCH
(Kościół św Krzyża; ☑22 826 8910; ul Krakowskie Przedmieście 3; ◷10am-4pm) **FREE** This neighbourhood is chock-a-block with sumptuous churches, but the one most visitors will want to see is the Holy Cross, not so much for the fine baroque altarpieces that miraculously survived fighting during the Warsaw Rising, but to glimpse a small urn by the second pillar on the left side of the nave. The urn, adorned with an epitaph to Frédéric Chopin, contains what remains of the composer's heart, brought here from Paris after Chopin's death.

Chopin Museum   MUSEUM
(☑ booking 22 441 6251; www.chopin.museum/pl; ul Okólnik 1; adult/concession 22/13zł; ◷11am-8pm Tue-Sun) The baroque Ostrogski Palace

POLAND WARSAW

Central Warsaw

0 500 m
0 0.25 miles

Museum of the History
of Polish Jews (500m);
Hotel Maria (1.4km)

Świętojerska

12 ✗ 1

Warsaw Tourist
Information
– Old Town

4

Świętojańska

Długa

Miodowa

Podwale

9

Bugaj

6

Generała Andersa

Al Solidarności

Senatorska

8

Moliera

Bednarska

Furmańska

Dobra

Ratusz-
Arsenał

Długa

Wierzbowa

Trębacka

19

Krakowskie Przedmieście

Browarna

Senatorska

Elektoralna

Saxon
Gardens

7

Plac
Piłsudskiego

Plac
Małachowskiego

Traugutta

3

Oboźna

10

Seweryów

Dynasy

Marszałkowska

Królewska

Kredytowa

Plac
Dąbrowskiego

17

Czackiego

Mazowiecka

Świętokrzyska

Tamka

2

Warsaw Rising
Museum
(1.4km)

Grzybowska

Próżna

Zielna

Plac
Grzybowski

11

Twarda

Świętokrzyska

Marszałkowska

Moniuszki

18

Sienkiewicza

Jasna

Szpitalna

Górskiego

Warecka

Plac
Powstańców
Warszawy

14

16

Nowy Świat

Ordynacka

Okólnik

Kopernika

Foksal

Smolna

Plac
Defilad

Złota

Zgoda

Chmielna

Bracka

5

Warsaw Tourist
Information –
Palace of Culture
& Science

Centrum

Widok

Al Jerozolimskie

Sienna

Emilii Plater

Złota

Warszawa
Śródmieście
Train Station

Warszawa
Centralna
Train Station

Al Jerozolimskie

Nowogrodzka

Żurawia

Plac Trzech
Krzyży

Książęca

Warszawa Zachodnia
Terminal
(2.2km)

Niepodległości

Emilii Plater

Wspólna

Poznańska

Marszałkowska

Hoża

Wspólna

Krucza

Wilcza

Mokotowska

Al Ujazdowskie

Wiejska

Hoża

13

15

Hotel Rialto
(100m)

Charlotte Chleb i
Wino (500m);
Plan B (500m)

Łazienki
Park (1km)

Central Warsaw

◎ **Sights**
1	Barbican	B1
2	Chopin Museum	D4
3	Church of the Holy Cross	C4
4	Old Town Square	C1
5	Palace of Culture & Science	A6
6	Royal Castle	C1
7	Saxon Gardens	B3
8	St Anne's Church	C2

▣ **Sleeping**
9	Castle Inn	C1
10	Hostel Helvetia	D4
11	Oki Doki Hostel	B4

✕ **Eating**
12	Bar Mleczny Pod Barbakanem	B1
13	Beirut Hummus & Music Bar	C7
14	Dawne Smaki	C5
15	Dwie Trzecie	C7

◔ **Drinking & Nightlife**
16	Cafe Blikle	D5
17	Enklawa	C4

✿ **Entertainment**
18	Filharmonia Narodowa	B5
19	Teatr Wielki	B3

is home to a high-tech, multimedia museum showcasing the work of the country's most famous composer. You're encouraged to take your time through four floors of displays, including stopping by the listening booths in the basement where you can explore Chopin's oeuvre to your heart's content. Visitation is limited each hour, so your best bet is to book your visit in advance by phone or email.

Saxon Gardens   GARDENS

FREE Stretching out a couple of blocks west of ul Krakowskie Przedmieście, these magnificent gardens date from the early 18th century and were the city's first public park. Modelled on the French gardens at Versailles, the gardens are filled with chestnut trees and baroque statues (allegories of the Virtues, the Sciences and the Elements), and there's an ornamental lake overlooked by a 19th-century water tower in the form of a circular Greek temple.

◉ **City Centre & Beyond**

Palace of Culture & Science   HISTORIC BUILDING

(PKiN; ☑ 22 656 7600; www.pkin.pl; Plac Defilad 1; ☉ 9am-6pm) Love it or hate it, every visitor to Warsaw should visit the iconic, Socialist-Realist PKiN. This 'gift of friendship' from the Soviet Union was built in the early 1950s, and at 231m high remains the tallest building in Poland. The structure is home to a huge congress hall, theatres, a multiplex and two museums. Take the high-speed lift to the 30th-floor (115m) **viewing terrace** (adult/concession 18/12zł; 9am to 6pm) to take it all in.

★ **Warsaw Rising Museum**   MUSEUM

(Muzeum Powstania Warszawskiego; ☑ 22 539 7905, audioguides 22 539 7941; www.1944.pl; ul Grzybowska 79; adult/concession 14/10zł, audioguide 10zł; ☉ 8am-6pm Mon, Wed & Fri, 8am-8pm Thu, 10am-6pm Sat & Sun) This modern, high-tech wonder traces the history of the city's heroic but doomed uprising against the Nazi occupation in 1944 through three levels of interactive displays, photographs, film archives and personal accounts. The volume of material is overwhelming, but the museum does an excellent job of instilling visitors with a sense of the desperation residents felt in deciding whether to oppose the occupation by force, and the inevitable consequence, including the Nazis' destruction of the city in the aftermath.

Łazienki Park   GARDENS

(☑ 22 506 0028; www.lazienki-krolewskie.pl; ul Agrykola; ☉ dawn-dusk) FREE This park – pronounced wah-zhen-kee – is a beautiful place of manicured greens and wild patches. Its popularity extends to families, peacocks and fans of classical music, who come for the alfresco **Chopin concerts** on Sunday afternoons at noon and 4pm from mid-May through September. Once a hunting ground attached to Ujazdów Castle, Łazienki was acquired by King Stanisław August Poniatowski in 1764 and transformed into a splendid park complete with palace, amphitheatre and various follies and other buildings.

◉ **Former Jewish District**

The suburbs northwest of the Palace of Culture & Science were once predominantly inhabited by Warsaw's Jewish community.

★ **Museum of the
History of Polish Jews** MUSEUM
(Polin; ☑info 22 471 0301; www.polin.pl; ul Mordechaja Anielewicza 6; adult/concession permanent exhibition 25/15zł, incl temporary exhibits 30/20zł; ☺10am-6pm Mon, Wed-Fri & Sun, 10am-8pm Sat) This high-tech marvel of a museum, years in the planning, opened to great fanfare in 2014. The permanent exhibition traces 1000 years of Jewish history in Poland, from accounts of the earliest Jewish traders in the region through the waves of mass migration, progress and pogroms, all the way to WWII and the destruction of Europe's largest Jewish community. Take an audioguide (10zł) to get the most out of the rooms of displays, interactive maps, photos and video.

Jewish Cemetery CEMETERY
(☑22 838 2622; www.beisolam.jewish.org.pl; ul Okopowa 49/51; admission 8zł; ☺10am-dusk Mon-Thu, 9am-1pm Fri, 11am-4pm Sun) Founded in 1806, Warsaw's main Jewish Cemetery incredibly suffered little during WWII and contains more than 150,000 tombstones, the largest collection of its kind in Europe. A notice near the entrance lists the graves of many eminent Polish Jews, including Ludwik Zamenhof, creator of the artificial international language Esperanto.

🛏 **Sleeping**

Apartments Apart (www.apartmentsapart. com) offers short-term apartment rentals in the Old Town and city centre.

Oki Doki Hostel HOSTEL €
(☑22 828 0122; www.okidoki.pl; Plac Dąbrowskiego 3; dm 40-90zł, s/d from 100/154zł; ☞) Oki Doki is arguably Warsaw's most popular hostel and definitely one of the best. Each of its bright, large rooms is individually named and decorated. Accommodation is in three- to eight-bed dorms, with a special three-bed dorm for women only. The owners are well travelled and know the needs of backpackers, providing a self-service laundry and bike rental. Breakfast available (15zł).

Hostel Helvetia HOSTEL €
(☑22 826 7108; www.hostel-helvetia.pl; ul Sewerynów 7; dm/r from 41/180zł; ☞) Helvetia has spick-and-span rooms, painted in warm, bright colours, with wooden floors and a good amount of space. Choose from three- to eight-bed dorms or good-value private singles and doubles. Laundry and kitchen

facilities are in top order, and with a limited number of beds, it's best to book ahead in summer.

★ **Castle Inn** HOTEL €€
(☑22 887 9530; www.castleinn.eu; ul Świętojańska 2; s/d from 220/280zł; @☞) This nicely done-up 'art hotel' is housed in a 17th-century townhouse. All rooms overlook either Castle Sq or St John's Cathedral, and come in a range of playful styles. Our favourite would be No 121, 'Viktor', named for a reclusive street artist, complete with tasteful graffiti and a gorgeous castle view. Breakfast costs an extra 35zł.

Hotel Maria HOTEL €€
(☑22 838 4062; www.hotelmaria.pl; Al Jana Pawła II 71; s/d 320/380zł; P✳☞) The Maria is a rambling old house of a hotel set on three floors (no lifts, just steep wooden stairs), with friendly staff, a delightful restaurant and breakfast nook, and spacious rooms. The location is outside the centre, but convenient to the Jewish sights and just a few tram stops away from the Old Town.

Hotel Rialto BOUTIQUE HOTEL €€€
(☑22 584 8700; www.rialto.pl; ul Wilcza 73; r from 450zł; P✳@☞) This converted townhouse is a monument to early-20th-century design. Each of the 44 rooms is individually decorated in art nouveau or art deco style, with antique and reproduction furniture, period fittings and tiled or marbled baths. There are plenty of modern touches where it counts, such as flat-screen TVs, power showers, and a sauna and steam room.

🍴 **Eating**

**Bar Mleczny
Pod Barbakanem** CAFETERIA €
(☑22 831 4737; ul Mostowa 27; mains 6-10zł; ☺8am-5pm Mon-Sat; ☑) This popular milk bar, very close to the Old Town, looks as though it hasn't changed for decades. It serves cheap, unpretentious Polish standards in a location that would be the envy of many upmarket eateries.

**Beirut Hummus
& Music Bar** MIDDLE EASTERN €
(www.beirut.com.pl; ul Poznańska 12; mains 15-22zł; ☺noon-1am; ☞☑) Hip and informal, this popular place has recently expanded to add seafood (like herring or grilled calamari) to an already nice mix of hummus varieties and Middle Eastern dishes. Choose from the menu above the counter and then find

a table. There's a turntable on hand for later in the evening, when the music part of the name kicks in.

Charlotte Chleb i Wino
FRENCH €€

(☑600 807 880; www.bistrocharlotte.com; Al Wyzwolenia 18, Plac Zbawiciela; mains 15-30zł; ⊙7am-midnight Mon-Thu, to 1am Fri, 9am-1am Sat, to 10pm Sun; 🛜) Dazzling French bakery and bistro, dishing out tantalising croissants and pastries at the break of dawn, and then transitioning to big salads and crusty sandwiches through the lunch and dinner hours, and finally to wine on the terrace in the evening.

Dawne Smaki
POLISH €€

(☑22 465 8320; www.dawnesmaki.pl; ul Nowy Świat 49; mains 25-50zł; ⊙noon-11pm; 🛜) Excellent, easy-to-reach place to try Polish specialties such as herring in cream, stuffed cabbage rolls, *pierogi* (dumplings) and all the rest. The interior is traditional white walls, wood and lace, without being overly hokey. Try the good-value lunch specials.

★ Dwie Trzecie
MEDITERRANEAN €€€

(☑22 623 0290; www.dwietrzecie.waw.pl; ul Wilcza 50/52; mains 30-70zł; ⊙noon-11pm; 🛜) It's worth splurging on well-turned-out dishes such as spicy pumpkin soup, flavoured with beetroot and shrimp, followed by slow-roasted veal cheeks and polenta. The interior is formal without a hint of fussiness, and the warm brick-lined walls and plank flooring lend a calming feel. The wine list is excellent, including a good choice of wine by the glass.

🍸 Drinking & Nightlife

Good places for pub crawls include along ul Mazowiecka in the centre, in Praga across the Vistula River, and the Powiśle district, near the university.

Cafe Blikle
CAFE

(☑22 826 0569; www.blikle.pl; ul Nowy Świat 35; coffee from 10zł, doughnut to go from 3zł; ⊙9am-8pm Mon-Sat, 10am-8pm Sun; 🛜) The mere fact that Blikle has survived two world wars and the pressure of communism makes it a household name. But what makes this legendary cafe truly famous is its doughnuts, for which people have been queuing up for generations. Join the back of the line and find out why.

Plan B
BAR

(☑503 116 154; Al Wyzwolenia 18, Plac Zbawiciela; ⊙11am-late) This phenomenally popular upstairs bar on Plac Zbawiciela draws a mix of students and young office workers. Find some couch space and relax to smooth beats from regular DJs. On warm summer evenings the action spills out onto the street, giving Plac Zbawiciela the feel of a summer block party.

Enklawa
CLUB

(☑22 827 3151; www.enklawa.com; ul Mazowiecka 12; ⊙10pm-4am Tue-Sat) Red and orange dominates this space with comfy plush seating, mirrored ceilings, two bars and plenty of room to dance. Check out the extensive drinks menu, hit the dance floor or observe the action from a stool on the upper balcony. Wednesday night is 'old school' night, with music from the '70s to '90s.

☆ Entertainment

Filharmonia Narodowa
CLASSICAL MUSIC

(National Philharmonic; ☑switchboard 22 551 7103, tickets 22 551 7128; www.filharmonia.pl; ul Jasna 5; ⊙box office 10am-2pm & 3-7pm Mon-Fri) Home of the world-famous National Philharmonic Orchestra and Choir of Poland, founded in 1901, this venue has a concert hall (enter from ul Sienkiewicza 10) and a chamber-music hall (enter from ul Moniuszki 5), both of which stage regular concerts. The box office entrance is on ul Sienkiewicza.

Teatr Wielki
OPERA

(National Opera; ☑reservations 22 826 5019; www.teatrwielki.pl; Plac Teatralny 1; ⊙box office 9am-7pm Mon-Fri, 11am-7pm Sat & Sun) This magnificent neoclassical theatre, dating from 1833 and rebuilt after WWII, is the city's main stage for opera and ballet, with a repertoire of international classics and works by Polish composers, notably Stanisław Moniuszko.

ℹ Information

Warsaw Tourist Information (www.warsawtour.pl) operates three helpful branches at various points around town: **Old Town** (Centrum Informacji Turystycznej; Stary Rynek 19/21/21a; ⊙9am-8pm May-Sep, to 6pm Oct-Apr; 🛜), the **Palace of Culture & Science** (Plac Defilad 1, entrance from ul Emilii Plater; ⊙8am-8pm May-Sep, to 6pm Oct-Apr; 🛜) and **Warsaw-Frédéric Chopin Airport** (Terminal A, Warsaw-Frédéric Chopin Airport, ul Żwirki i Wigury 1; ⊙8am-8pm May-Sep, to 6pm Oct-Apr). They offer free city maps as well as advice on what to see and where to stay.

Lux Med (☑22 332 2888; www.luxmed.pl; Marriott Hotel Bldg, al Jerozolimskie 65/79;

ℹ WANT MORE?

For in-depth information, reviews and recommendations at your fingertips, head to www.lonelyplanet.com/poland/warsaw for planning advice, author recommendations, traveller reviews and insider tips.

⊙7am-8pm Mon-Fri, to 4pm Sat) Private clinic with English-speaking specialist doctors and its own ambulance service; carries out laboratory tests and arranges house calls.

Verso Internet (22 635 9174; ul Freta 17; per hour 5zł; ⊙8am-8pm Mon-Fri, 9am-5pm Sat, 10am-4pm Sun) Copy shop with internet terminals for use. Enter from ul Świętojerska.

ℹ Getting There & Away

AIR

Warsaw's main international airport, **Warsaw-Frédéric Chopin Airport** (WAW – Lotnisko Chopina w Warszawie; ☑ flight information 22 650 4220; www.lotnisko-chopina.pl; ul Żwirki i Wigury 1), 10km from the city centre, handles most flights in and out of the city. The airport's Terminal A has undergone extensive renovation. The terminal has bank ATMs, restaurants and a branch of the Warsaw Tourist Information office.

Some budget flights, including Ryanair services, use outlying **Warsaw Modlin** (☑ 801 801 880, Ryanair 703 303 033; www.modlinairport. pl; ul Generała Wiktora Thommée 1a, Nowy Dwór Mazowiecki), 35km north of the city.

BUS

Warsaw's main bus station is **Warszawa Zachodnia** (☑ 703 403 330, PKS Polonus 22 823 6200; www.pksbilety.pl; Al Jerozolimskie 144; ⊙ information & tickets 6am-9pm), southwest of the centre and adjoining Warszawa Zachodnia train station. This sprawling terminal handles most (but not all) international and domestic routes. To get here from the Warszawa Centralna train station, take bus 127, 158 or 517.

Popular coach services run by **Polski Bus** (☑ 22 417 6227; www.polskibus.com) often depart from a small bus terminal near the Wilanowska metro station. Check the website for further information and give yourself plenty of time to find the bus station. Buy tickets online.

Domestic bus connections include Gdańsk (40zł, five hours, hourly), Kraków (40zł, five hours, hourly), Lublin (15zł, three hours, five daily), Toruń (25zł, three hours, five daily), Poznań (20zł, five hours, five daily) and Wrocław (30zł, five hours, five daily). Warsaw has good bus services to Berlin (80zł, 10 hours, two daily) and Prague (100zł, 11 hours, two daily).

TRAIN

Warsaw has several train stations and is connected directly to a number of international destinations. The station most travellers use is **Warszawa Centralna** (Warsaw Central; 22 391 9757; www.pkp.pl; Al Jerozolimskie 54; ⊙24hr), but it's not always where trains start or finish so be sure to board promptly.

Regular international train services include those to Berlin (six hours, five daily), Bratislava (six hours, one daily), Budapest (10½ hours, two daily), Minsk (9½ to 12 hours, two to three daily), Moscow (18 to 21 hours, two to three daily) and Prague (8½ to 10½ hours, two daily).

ℹ Getting Around

TO/FROM THE AIRPORT

To reach the centre from Warsaw-Frédéric Chopin Airport, take commuter SKM rail service train 52 or 53. Train 52 runs to the Warszawa Zachodnia and Warszawa Śródmieście train stations, while 53 goes to Warszawa Centralna (Central Railway Station). Tickets cost 4.40zł. Bus 175 (4.40zł) terminates at Plac Piłsudskiego, about a 500m walk from the Old Town. A taxi fare between the airport and city centre is around 50zł.

From Warsaw Modlin, the easiest way to the centre is aboard the regular Modlin bus (19zł). A taxi will cost from 100zł to 130zł.

PUBLIC TRANSPORT

Warsaw has a reliable system of trams, buses and metro cars. Trams running east–west across busy Al Jerozolimskie are particularly handy.

Buy tickets from machines (have coins or small bills handy) or from news kiosks near stops. A standard ticket (4.40zł) is valid for one ride by bus, tram or metro. Day passes are available for 15zł. Be sure to validate the ticket on boarding.

TAXI

Super Taxi (☑ 196 22; www.supertaxi.pl) Reliable, inexpensive radio taxi service.

MAŁOPOLSKA

Małopolska (literally 'Lesser Poland') covers southeastern Poland from the former royal capital of Kraków to the eastern Lublin Uplands. The name does not refer to size or relative importance, but rather that Lesser Poland was mentioned in atlases more recently (of the 15th century!) than Wielkopolska ('Greater Poland'). It's a colourful region filled with remnants of traditional life and historic cities.

Kraków

POP 756,500

Many Polish cities are centred on an attractive Old Town, but none compare to Kraków (pronounced *krak-oof*) for effortless beauty. As it was the royal capital of Poland until 1596 and miraculously escaped destruction in WWII, Kraków is packed with appealing historic buildings and streetscapes. One of the most important sights is Wawel Castle, from where the ancient Polish kingdom was once ruled.

South of the castle lies the former Jewish quarter of Kazimierz. Its silent synagogues are a reminder of the tragedy of WWII. These days, the quarter has been injected with new life and is home to some of the city's best bars and clubs.

⊙ Sights

◉ Wawel Hill

South of Old Town, this prominent hilltop is crowned with the former Royal Castle and Cathedral – both enduring symbols of Poland.

★Royal Wawel Castle   CASTLE
(Zamek Królewski na Wawelu; ☑Wawel Visitor Centre 12 422 5155; www.wawel.krakow.pl; Wawel Hill; grounds admission free, attractions priced separately; ⊘grounds 6am-dusk) As the political and cultural heart of Poland through the 16th century, Wawel Castle is a potent symbol of national identity. It's now a museum containing five separate sections: Crown Treasury & Armoury; State Rooms; Royal Private Apartments; Lost Wawel; and Exhibition of Oriental Art. Each requires a separate ticket. Of the five, the State Rooms and Royal Private Apartments are most impressive. There's a limited quota of tickets, so arrive early or book in advance by phone.

Wawel Cathedral   CHURCH
(☑12 429 9515; www.katedra-wawelska.pl; Wawel 3, Wawel Hill; cathedral free, combined entry for crypts, bell tower & museum adult/concession 12/7zł; ⊘9am-5pm Mon-Sat, from 12.30pm Sun) The Royal Cathedral has witnessed many coronations, funerals and entombments of Poland's monarchs and strongmen over the centuries. This is the third church on this site, consecrated in 1364. The original

was founded in the 11th century by King Bolesław I Chrobry and replaced with a Romanesque construction around 1140. When that burned down in 1305, only the Crypt of St Leonard survived. Highlights include the **Holy Cross Chapel, Sigismund Chapel, Sigismund Bell**, the **Crypt of St Leonard** and **Royal Crypts.**

⊙ Old Town

This vast Rynek Główny (main square) is the focus of the Old Town and Europe's largest medieval town square (200m by 200m).

Cloth Hall   HISTORIC BUILDING
(Sukiennice; www.museum.krakow.pl; Rynek Główny 1/3) FREE Dominating the middle of the square, this building was once the centre of Kraków's medieval clothing trade. It was created in the early 14th century when a roof was put over two rows of stalls, then extended into a 108m-long Gothic structure. The hall was rebuilt in Renaissance style after a fire in 1555; the arcades were added in the late 19th century.

Rynek Underground   MUSEUM
(☑12 426 5060; www.podziemiarynku.com; Rynek Główny 1; adult/concession 19/16zł, Tue free; ⊘10am-8pm Mon, to 4pm Tue, to 10pm Wed-Sun) From the northern end of the Cloth Hall, enter this fascinating attraction beneath the market square. It consists of an underground route through medieval market stalls and other long-forgotten chambers. The 'Middle Ages meets 21st century' experience is enhanced by a multitude of holograms and other audiovisual wizardry. There's always a scrum at the door, so prebook an entry time at one of the tourist offices.

St Mary's Basilica   CHURCH
(Basilica of the Assumption of Our Lady; ☑12 422 0737; www.mariacki.com; Plac Mariacki 5, Rynek Główny; adult/concession 10/5zł; ⊘11.30am-5.30pm Mon-Sat, 2-5.30pm Sun) Overlooking the square, this striking brick church, best known simply as St Mary's, is dominated by two towers of different heights. The first church here was built in the 1220s and following its destruction during a Tatar raid, construction of the basilica began. Tour the exquisite interior, with its remarkable Veit Stoss pentaptych, and in summer climb the **tower** for excellent views. Don't miss the hourly *hejnał* (bugle call) from the taller tower.

Kraków – Old Town & Wawel

0 — 200 m
0 — 0.1 miles

Basztowa
Plac Matejki ✕ 16
Zacisze
Worcella
Pawia
Galeria Krakowska (100m)
(100m)
Bosacka

Pijarska
Reformacka
Basztowa
Św Tomasza
Szczepańska
Sławkowska
Św Jana
Florian Gate
Florian
Floriańska
Szpitalna
Plac Św Ducha
Św Marka
Św Krzyża
Zamenhofa
Skłodowskiej-Curie
Radziwiłłowska
Westerplatte
Plac Kolejowy
Kraków Główny Train Station
Lubicz

Restauracja Pod Norenami (200m)
Rynek Główny
🛈
📮 3
12 📮
17
21 📮
Św Tomasza
Jagiellońska
Szewska
18
14
10
✕ 23
⭐
🏛 2
🛈 6
7 ⊕
Plac Mariacki
Mikołajska
Mikołajska
Kopernika
Blich
Kołłątaja
Gen Sołtyka

Wiślna
Gołębia
Bracka
Stolarska
Grodzka
Mały Rynek
Sienna
Planty
Zyblikiewicza
WESOŁA

Filharmonia Krakowska (100m)
Franciszkańska
Dominikańska
Plac Dominikański
Plac Wszystkich Świętych
Poselska
Wielopole
13 🎭
Bonerowska

Plac Św Marii Magdaleny
Kanonicza
Grodzka
Św Gertrudy
Sarego
Św Sebastiana
Bogusławskiego
Starowiślna
Dietla
Dietla
Wrzesińska
Siedleckiego

Podzamcze
Św Idziego
8 ⊕
1 🏰
Royal Wawel Castle
Wawel Hill
Droga do Zamku
Bernardyńska
Stradomska
Św Agnieszki
Dietla
Dietla

Smocza
Koletek
Sukiennicza
Orzeszkowej
Krakowska
Meiselsa
Meiselsa
Paulińska
Józefa
Brzozowa
Podbrzezie
Miodowa
✕ 15
Schindler's Factory (1.2km)
Szeroka
Św Sebastiana
Joselewicza
Jakuba
Starowiślna

Most Grunwaldzki
19 🍴
22 ⊕
Warszauera
20
Plac Nowy
Estery
Izaaka
Nowa
Bożego Ciała
🛈
Józefa
🛍 11
Józefa
Wąska
Bartosza
5 🏛
4 🏛
Dajwór
KAZIMIERZ
Św Wawrzyńca

Kraków – Old Town & Wawel

Czartoryski Museum   MUSEUM
(www.czartoryski.org; ul Św Jana 19) The Czartoryski Museum boasts the city's richest art collection, including Kraków's most valuable painting: Leonardo da Vinci's *Lady with an Ermine*. Among other important works is Rembrandt's *Landscape with the Good Samaritan*. Other exhibitions include Greek, Roman, Egyptian and Etruscan art as well as Turkish weaponry. At the time of research, the museum was closed for renovation but expected to reopen in 2015. During renovation, the *Lady with an Ermine* was being exhibited at Wawel Castle.

◎ Kazimierz & Podgórze

Founded by King Kazimierz III Wielki in 1335, Kazimierz was originally an independent town and then became a Jewish district. During WWII, the Germans relocated Jews south across the Vistula River to a walled ghetto in Podgórze. They were exterminated in the nearby Płaszów Concentration Camp, as portrayed in the Steven Spielberg film *Schindler's List*. In addition to the attractions below, many synagogues are still standing and can be visited individually.

Schindler's Factory   MUSEUM
(Fabryka Schindlera; ☑12 257 1017; www.mhk.pl; ul Lipowa 4; adult/concession 19/16zł, free Mon; ⊙10am-8pm Mon, 10am-4pm Tue-Sun) This impressive interactive museum covers the Nazi occupation of Kraków in WWII. It's housed in the former enamel factory of Oskar Schindler, the Nazi industrialist who famously saved the lives of members of his Jewish labour force during the Holocaust. Well-organised, innovative exhibits tell the moving story of the city from 1939 to 1945, recreating urban elements such as a tram carriage, a train station underpass and a crowded ghetto apartment within the factory walls.

Jewish Museum   MUSEUM
(Old Synagogue; ☑12 422 0962; www.mhk.pl; ul Szeroka 24; adult/concession 9/7zł, free Mon; ⊙10am-2pm Mon, 9am-5pm Tue-Sun) At the southern end of ul Szeroka this museum is housed in the **Old Synagogue**, which dates to the 15th century. The prayer hall, complete with a reconstructed *bimah* (raised platform at the centre of the synagogue where the Torah is read) and the original *aron kodesh* (the niche in the eastern wall where Torah scrolls are kept), houses an exhibition of liturgical objects. Upstairs there's a photographic exhibit focusing on Jewish Kraków and the Holocaust.

Galicia Jewish Museum   MUSEUM
(☑12 421 6842; www.galiciajewishmuseum.org; ul Dajwór 18; adult/concession 15/10zł; ⊙10am-6pm) This museum both commemorates Jewish victims of the Holocaust and celebrates the Jewish culture and history of the former Austro-Hungarian region of Galicia. It features an impressive photographic exhibition depicting modern-day remnants of southeastern Poland's once-thriving Jewish community, called 'Traces of Memory', along with video testimony of survivors and regular temporary exhibits.

🛏 Sleeping

Kraków is unquestionably Poland's major tourist destination, with prices to match. **AAA Kraków Apartments** (www.krakow-apartments.biz) is one of several companies offering good-value, short-term apartment rentals.

Hostel Flamingo   HOSTEL €
(🖂12 422 0000; www.flamingo-hostel.com; ul Szewska 4; dm 47-65zł, d 158zł; 🛜) Highly rated hostel with an excellent central location, just a couple steps from the main square. Pluses – in addition to the expected amenities – include free breakfast, an in-house cafe and a cheeky attitude. Sleeping is in six- to 12-bed dorms plus a few private doubles.

Greg & Tom Hostel   HOSTEL €
(🖂12 422 4100; www.gregtomhostel.com; ul Pawia 12/7; dm 57zł, d from 150zł; 🛜) This well-run hostel is spread over three locations, though all check-in is handled at the main branch on ul Pawia. The staff is friendly, the rooms are clean, and laundry facilities are included. On Tuesday and Saturday evenings, hot Polish meals are served.

★ Wielopole   HOTEL €€
(🖂12 422 1475; www.wielopole.pl; ul Wielopole 3; s/d 260/360zł; 🅰🛜) Wielopole's selection of bright, modern rooms – all of them with spotless bathrooms – is housed in a renovated block with a great courtyard on the eastern edge of the Old Town, within easy walk of Kazimierz. The breakfast spread here is impressive.

Hotel Abel   HOTEL €€
(🖂12 411 8736; www.abelkrakow.pl; ul Józefa 30; s/d 150/190zł; 🛜) Reflecting the character of Kazimierz, this modest, good-value hotel has a distinctive personality, evident in its polished wooden staircase, arched brickwork and age-worn tiles. The rooms are clean but simply furnished. The hotel makes a good base for exploring the historic Jewish neighbourhood.

> ### ⓘ WANT MORE?
> For in-depth information, reviews and recommendations at your fingertips, head to www.lonelyplanet.com/poland/malopolska/krakow for planning advice, author recommendations, traveller reviews and insider tips.

Hotel Pod Różą   HOTEL €€€
(🖂12 424 3300; www.podroza.hotel.com.pl; ul Floriańska 14; s 650zł, d 650-720zł; 🅰@🛜) A hotel that has never closed, even in the dark, dreary days of communism, 'Under the Rose' offers antiques, oriental carpets, a wonderful glassed-in courtyard restaurant and state-of-the-art facilities. Breakfast costs an extra 50zł.

✖ Eating

Glonojad   VEGETARIAN €
(🖂12 346 1677; www.glonojad.com; Plac Matejki 2; mains 10-16zł; ⊘8am-10pm; 🛜🖈) Attractive modern vegetarian restaurant with a great view onto Plac Matejki, just north of the Barbican. The diverse menu has a variety of tasty dishes including samosas, curries, potato pancakes, burritos, gnocchi and soups. There's also an all-day breakfast menu, so there's no need to jump out of that hotel bed too early.

Milkbar Tomasza   POLISH €
(🖂12 422 1706; ul Św Tomasza 24; mains 10-20zł; ⊘8am-10pm) Cleverly modernised version of the traditional *bar mleczny* (milkbar), serving affordable dishes including breakfast in a pleasant dining area. The two-course set menu for 18zł is great value.

★ Restauracja
Pod Norenami   ASIAN, VEGETARIAN €€
(🖂661 219 289; www.podnorenami.pl; ul Krupnicza 6; mains 18-30zł; ⊘10am-10pm; 🛜🖈) This warm and inviting Asian-fusion restaurant is ideal for vegans and vegetarians. The menu pivots from Japanese to Thai and Vietnamese, with lots of spicy noodle and rice dishes, vegetarian sushi and many other excellent choices. Breakfast (served from 10am to noon) has Middle Eastern overtones, with hummus and pita and spicy scrambled eggs. Book in advance.

Dawno Temu
Na Kazimierzu   JEWISH €€
(Once upon a Time in Kazimierz; 🖂12 421 2117; www.dawnotemu.nakazimierzu.pl; ul Szeroka 1; mains 20-35zł; ⊘10am-midnight) Arguably the smallest and most atmospheric of several restaurants in Kazimierz playing on the old-time Jewish theme. The traditional Polish-Jewish cooking (think of hearty variations of lamb and duck) is very good and the warm, candle-lit space, with klezmer music playing in the background, is the perfect spot to enjoy this part of Kraków.

A UNESCO-PROTECTED SALT MINE

Some 14km southeast of Kraków, **Wieliczka** (☑12 278 7302; www.kopalnia.pl; ul Daniłowicza 10; adult/concession 79/64zł; ☉7.30am-7.30pm Apr-Oct, 8am-5pm Nov-Mar), pronounced *vyeh-leech-kah*, is famous for its deep salt mine. It's an eerie world of pits and chambers, and everything within its depths has been carved by hand from salt blocks. A section of the mine, some 22 chambers, is open to the public and it's a fascinating trip.

You visit three upper levels of the mine, from 64m to 135m below ground. Some have been made into chapels, with altarpieces and figures, others are adorned with statues and monuments – and there are even underground lakes.

Guided tours take about two hours. Wear comfortable shoes and dress warmly as the temperature in the mine is 14°C. In summer, English-language tours depart every half-hour. During the rest of the year, tours are less frequent.

Minibuses to Wieliczka (3zł) depart Kraków frequently from ul Pawia near the Galeria Krakowska shopping mall next to Kraków Główny train station.

Chimera　　　　　　　　　POLISH €€€
(☑12 292 1212; www.chimera.com.pl; ul Św Anny 3; mains 35-60zł; ☉10am-10pm) Not to be confused with the salad bar of the same name, this is a Kraków classic. The vaulted cellar is the perfect setting to sample the specialty roasted lamb, goose or game meats.

🍷 Drinking & Nightlife

There are hundreds of pubs and bars in Kraków's Old Town, many housed in ancient vaulted cellars. Kazimierz also has a lively bar scene, centred around Plac Nowy.

Mleczarnia　　　　　　　　CAFE
(☑12 421 8532; www.mle.pl; ul Meiselsa 20; ☉10am-midnight; 🚊3, 6, 8, 10) Wins the prize for best courtyard cafe. Shady trees and blooming roses make this place tops for a sunny-day drink. If it's rainy, never fear, for the cafe is warm and cosy, with crowded bookshelves and portrait-covered walls. Self service.

Miejsce Bar　　　　　　　　BAR
(☑600 960 876; www.miejsce.com.pl; ul Estery 1; ☉10am-2am; 🛜) Trendy bar that draws an eclectic mix of intellectual types, hipsters, students and generally anyone who enjoys good cocktails and a relaxed vibe. Quiet during the day; rowdier and more adventurous by night.

Pauza　　　　　　　　　　　BAR
(☑12 422 4866; www.klubpauza.pl; ul Floriańska 18; ☉10am-2am Mon-Sat, from noon Sun; 🚊2, 3, 4, 12, 13, 14, 15) Beloved for its alternative atmosphere, Pauza offers stiff drinks and heady conversation on the 1st floor (not to mention the occasional art exhibit and great window seats overlooking Floriańska).

Frantic　　　　　　　　　　CLUB
(☑12 423 0483; www.frantic.pl; ul Szewska 5; ☉10pm-4am Wed-Sat) With two dance floors, three bars, a chill-out room and top Polish and international DJs, Frantic is regularly packed out with smart young locals. There's sniffy door selection, so don't be too scruffy.

☆ Entertainment

Baccarat Live　　　　　　LIVE MUSIC
(☑605 057 234; www.baccaratlive.pl; Rynek Główny 28; ☉9pm-late Wed-Sat) Upmarket dance club brings in a mix of students and young professionals for live music as well as DJ and theme nights.

Alchemia　　　　　　　　LIVE MUSIC
(☑12 421 2200; www.alchemia.com.pl; ul Estery 5; ☉9am-late) This Kazimierz venue exudes a shabby-is-the-new-cool look with rough-hewn wooden benches, candlelit tables and a companionable gloom. It hosts regular live-music gigs and theatrical events through the week.

Filharmonia Krakowska　CLASSICAL MUSIC
(Filharmonia im. Karola Szymanowskiego w Krakowie; ☑ www.filharmonia.krakow.pl; ul Zwierzyniecka 1; ☉box office 10am-2pm & 3-7pm Tue-Fri) Home to one of the best orchestras in the country.

❶ Information

The official tourist information office, **Info-Kraków** (www.infokrakow.pl), maintains branches around town, including at the **Cloth Hall** (☑12 433 7310; Rynek Główny

AUSCHWITZ-BIRKENAU

Many visitors pair a trip to Kraków with a visit to the **Auschwitz-Birkenau Museum & Memorial** (☑ guides 33 844 8100; www.auschwitz.org.pl; ul Wieźniów Oświęcimia 20, Oświęcim; admission free, compulsory guided tour adult/concession 25/20zł; ⊘ 8am-7pm Jun-Aug, 8am-6pm May & Sep, 8am-5pm Apr & Oct, 8am-4pm Mar & Nov, 8am-3pm Dec-Feb) FREE – or as it's known officially the 'Auschwitz-Birkenau: German Nazi Concentration & Extermination Camp' – in the town of Oświęcim. More than a million Jews as well large numbers of ethnic Poles and Roma were systematically murdered here by occupying Germans during WWII.

Both the main camp at Auschwitz (Auschwitz I) and a larger outlying camp at Birkenau (Auschwitz II), about 2km away, are open to the public and admission is free (though if arriving between 10am and 3pm from May to October, a guided tour is compulsory). A visit is essential to understanding the Holocaust, though the scope and nature of the crimes are horrifying and may not be suitable for children under 14.

The tour begins at the main camp, Auschwitz I, which began life as a Polish military barracks but was co-opted by the Nazis in 1940 as a death camp. Here is the infamous gate, displaying the grimly cynical message: 'Arbeit Macht Frei' (Through Work Freedom). Some 13 of 30 surviving prison blocks house museum exhibitions.

From here, the tour moves to Birkenau (Auschwitz II), where most of the killings took place. Massive and purpose-built to be efficient, the camp had more than 300 prison barracks. Here you'll find the remnants of gas chambers and crematoria.

Auschwitz-Birkenau is a workable day trip from Kraków. Most convenient are the approximately hourly buses to Oświęcim (12zł, 1½ hours), departing from the bus station in Kraków. There are also numerous minibuses to Oświęcim (10zł, 1½ hours) from the minibus stands off ul Pawia, next to Galeria Krakowska.

1/3; ⊘ 9am-7pm May-Sep, 9am-5pm Oct-Apr), **Kazimierz** (☑ 12 422 0471; ul Józefa 7; ⊘ 9am-5pm), the **Old Town** (☑ 12 421 7787; ul Św Jana 2; ⊘ 9am-7pm) and the **Airport** (☑ 12 285 5341; John Paul II International Airport, Balice; ⊘ 9am-7pm).

Klub Garinet (☑ 12 423 2233; www.garinet.pl; ul Floriańska 18; internet per hour 4zł; ⊘ 9am-10pm) The pick of the crop of internet cafes near the main square.

ⓘ Getting There & Away

AIR

Kraków's **John Paul II International Airport** (KRK; ☑ information 12 295 5800; www.krakowairport.pl; Kapitana Mieczysława Medweckiego 1, Balice) was undergoing massive reconstruction during the time of research. Flights were operating as scheduled, but expect delays. Train service between the aiport and the centre had been temporarily suspended. If the train is not operating, public buses 292 and 208 (tickets 4zł) run to the main bus station. Taxis to the centre cost about 70zł.

The main Polish carrier LOT (p309) flies to Warsaw and other large cities. LOT subsidiary **Eurolot** (www.eurolot.com) services Gdańsk. Budget operators connect Kraków to cities in Europe.

BUS

Kraków's modern **bus station** (☑ 703 403 340; www.mda.malopolska.pl; ul Bosacka 18; ⊘ information 7am-8pm) is conveniently located next to the main train station, Kraków Główny, on the fringe of the Old Town.

Bus travel is the best way to reach Zakopane (16zł, two hours, hourly). Modern **Polski Bus** (www.polskibus.com) coaches depart from here to Warsaw (five hours, several daily) and Wrocław (three hours, several daily); check fares and book tickets online.

TRAIN

Newly remodeled and gleaming **Kraków Główny** (Dworzec Główny; ☑ information 22 391 9757; www.pkp.pl; Plac Dworcowy) train station, on the northeastern outskirts of the Old Town, handles all international trains and most domestic rail services.

Useful domestic destinations include Gdańsk (80zł, eight hours, three daily), Lublin (62zł, four hours, two daily), Poznań (80zł, eight hours, three daily), Toruń (73zł, seven hours, three daily), Warsaw (60zł to 130zł, three hours, at least hourly) and Wrocław (50zł, 5½ hours, hourly).

Popular international connections include Bratislava (7½ hours, one daily), Berlin (10 hours, one daily), Budapest (10½ hours, one daily),

Lviv (7½ to 9½ hours, two daily) and Prague (10 hours, one daily).

Lublin

POP 349,000

Poland's eastern metropolis admittedly lacks the grandeur of Gdańsk or Kraków, but does have an attractive Old Town, with beautiful churches and tiny alleyways. It's a natural jumping off point for exploring southeastern Poland. Thousands of students make for a lively restaurant, bar and club scene.

Lublin plays an important role in Polish and Jewish history. It was here in 1569 that the Lublin Union was signed, uniting Poland and Lithuania to form one of the largest and most powerful entities in Europe in its day. For those interested in Jewish heritage, for centuries Lublin served as a centre of European Jewish culture. The Holocaust ended this vibrant community, and one of the most notorious Nazi extermination camps, Majdanek, lies at Lublin's doorstep.

Sights

Lublin Castle
MUSEUM

(☑ 81 532 5001; www.muzeumlubelskie.pl; ul Zamkowa 9; adult/concession museum 6.50/4.50zł, chapel 6.50/4.50zł; ☺ 10am-5pm Tue-Sun) Lublin's royal castle dates from the 12th and 13th centuries, though it's been rebuilt many times over the years. It was here in 1569 where the union with Lithuania was signed. The castle is home to both the Lublin Museum and the surviving Gothic Chapel of the Holy Trinity, which dates from the 14th century. Each requires a separate entry ticket.

Historical Museum of Lublin
MUSEUM

(www.muzeumlubelskie.pl; Plac Władysława Łokietka 3; adult/concession 5.50/4.50zł; ☺ 9am-4pm Wed-Sat, to 5pm Sun) Inside the Kraków Gate (accessed from its eastern wall), which links the Old Town to the modern city, this small museum displays documents and moving photographs of the town's history.

Cathedral of
St John the Baptist
CHURCH

(www.diecezja.lublin.pl; Plac Katedralny; ☺ dawn-sunset, treasury 10am-2pm & 3-5pm Tue-Sun) FREE This former Jesuit church dates from the 16th century and is the largest in Lublin. There are many impressive details to behold, including the baroque trompe l'œil frescoes (the work of Moravian artist Józef Majer) and the 17th-century altar made from a black Lebanese

pear tree. The acoustic vestry (so called for its ability to project whispers) and the treasury (skarbiec), behind the chapel, also merit attention.

Majdanek
CONCENTRATION CAMP

(Państwowe Muzeum na Majdanku; ☑ 81 710 2833; www.majdanek.pl; Droga Męczenników Majdanka 67; ☺ 9am-6pm Apr-Oct, 9am-4pm Nov-Mar) FREE Four kilometres southeast of the centre is the German Nazi Majdanek extermination camp, where tens of thousands of people were murdered during WWII. Unlike other extermination camps, the Nazis went to no effort to conceal Majdanek. A 5km walk starts at the visitors centre, passes the foreboding Monument of Fight & Martyrdom, through parts of the barracks and finishes at the guarded mausoleum containing the ashes of many victims.

Old Jewish Cemetery
CEMETERY

(Cmentarz żydowski; cnr ul Kalinowszczyzna & ul Sienna; ☺ by appointment) The old Jewish cemetery, established in 1541, has 30-odd readable tombstones, including the oldest Jewish tombstone in Poland in its original location. The graveyard is on a hill between ul Sienna and ul Kalinowszczyzna, about 500 metres to the east and north of the main bus terminal. It is surrounded by a high brick wall and the gate is locked. Contact the tourist office (p295) before you walk over to arrange a visit.

Tours

Underground Route
WALKING TOUR

(☑ tour booking 81 534 6570; Rynek 1; adult/concession 9/7zł; ☺ 10am-4pm Tue-Fri, noon-5pm Sat & Sun) This 280m trail winds its way through connected cellars beneath the Old Town, with historical exhibitions along the way. Entry is from the neoclassical Old Town Hall in the centre of the pleasant Market Sq (Rynek) at approximately two-hourly intervals; check with the tourist office (p295) for exact times.

Sleeping

Hostel Lublin
HOSTEL €

(☑ 792 888 632; www.hostellublin.pl; ul Lubartowska 60; dm/r 40/100zł; ☺) The city's first modern hostel is situated within a former apartment building and contains neat, tidy dorms, a basic kitchenette and a cosy lounge. Take trolleybus 156 or 160 north from the Old Town, crossing busy Al Tysiąclecia for two stops.

Hotel Waksman HOTEL €€
(☎81 532 5454; www.waksman.pl; ul Grodzka 19; s/d 210/230zł, apt from 270zł; P ⊖ @ ≋) Hotel Waksman deserves a blue ribbon for many reasons, not least of which is the atmospheric Old Town location. Each standard room (named 'yellow', 'blue', 'green' or 'red' for its decor) has individual character. The two apartments on top are special; they offer ample space for lounging or working, and views over the Old Town and castle.

Vanilla Hotel HOTEL €€
(☎81 536 6720; www.vanilla-hotel.pl; ul Krakowskie Przedmieście 12; s/d 330/370zł; P ⊖ ≋) The name must be tongue-in-cheek. This beautiful boutique, just off the main pedestrian corso, is anything but vanilla. The rooms are filled with inspired, even bold styling, with vibrant colours, big headboards behind the beds and stylish, retro lamps and furniture. Lots of attention to detail here that continues into the stylish Jazz Age restaurant and coffee bar.

Eating

Magia INTERNATIONAL €€
(☎502 598 418; www.magia.lublin.pl; ul Grodzka 2; mains 20-65zł; ⊙noon-midnight; ≋) Magia's atmosphere is eclectic; there are numerous vibes to choose from throughout the warren of dining rooms and large outdoor courtyard, with each area decorated with a touch of magic. The chef uses only fresh ingredients to create dishes ranging from tiger shrimps and snails to deer and duck, with every sort of pizza, pasta and pancake in between.

Mandragora JEWISH €€
(☎81 536 2020; www.mandragora.lublin.pl; Rynek 9; mains 20-60zł; ⊙noon-10pm; ≋) There's good kitsch and there's bad kitsch, and at Mandragora, it's all good. Sure they're going for the *Fiddler on the Roof* effect with the lace tablecloths, knick-knacks and photos of old Lublin, but in the romantic Rynek locale, it works wonderfully. The food is a hearty mix of Polish and Jewish, with mains like goose and duck featuring.

Drinking & Nightlife

Szklarnia CAFE
(Centrum Kultury w Lublinie; ☎81 466 6140; www.ck.lublin.pl; ul Peowiakow 12; ⊙10am-11pm Mon-Fri, noon-midnight Sat & Sun; ≋) It's not easy finding good coffee in Lublin. This sleek cafe in the recently refurbished Lublin Cultural Centre has great coffee as well as a daily

WORTH A TRIP

ZAMOŚĆ: POLAND'S RENAISSANCE HEART

While most Polish cities' attractions centre on their medieval heart, Zamość (*zah-moshch*) is pure 16th-century Renaissance. It was founded in 1580 by nobleman Jan Zamoyski and designed by an Italian architect. The splendid architecture of Zamość's Old Town escaped serious destruction in WWII and was added to Unesco's World Heritage List in 1992.

The **Rynek Wielki** (Great Market Square) is the heart of Zamość's attractive Old Town. This impressive Italianate Renaissance square (exactly 100m by 100m) is dominated by a lofty, pink town hall and surrounded by colourful, arcaded burghers' houses.

The **Museum of Zamość** (Muzeum Zamojskie; ☎84 638 6494; www.muzeum-zamojskie.pl; ul Ormiańska 30; adult/concession 10/5zł; ⊙9am-5pm Tue-Sun) is based in two of the loveliest buildings on the square and houses interesting exhibits, including paintings, folk costumes and a scale model of the 16th-century town.

The city's **synagogue** (☎84 639 0054; www.zamosc.fodz.pl; ul Pereca 14; admission 7zł; ⊙10am-6pm Tue-Sun) was recently reopened to the public after a long renovation. It was built around 1620 and served as the Jewish community's main house of worship until WWII, when it was shuttered by the Germans. The highlight of the exhibition is a gripping computer presentation on the history of the town's Jewish community, including its roots in Sephardic Judaism.

The helpful **tourist office** (☎84 639 2292; www.travel.zamosc.pl; Rynek Wielki 13; ⊙8am-6pm Mon-Fri, 10am-5pm Sat & Sun May-Sep, 8am-5pm Mon-Fri, 9am-3pm Sat & Sun Oct-Apr) in the town hall has maps, brochures and souvenirs. Zamość makes for an easy day trip from Lublin. Buses and minibuses make the 80km trip (15zł) in around 90 minutes.

selection of cakes. There's live entertainment some nights, and a nice terrace at the back in warm weather.

Złoty Osioł

PUB

(☑81 532 9042; ul Grodzka 5a; ⊙3pm-midnight; ☜) Złoty Osioł offers traditional ambience and extraordinarily good-value traditional meals. There are delicious fish dishes, slightly bizarre drink selections (like hot dry wine with jelly), and daily meal sets for the indecisive. The restaurant is set in a candlelit cellar with an annexed cosy green courtyard. Folk music concerts are occasionally held here.

ⓘ Information

Tourist Information Centre in Lublin

(LOITiK; ☑81 532 4412; www.lublin.eu; ul Jezuicka 1/3; ⊙9am-7pm Mon-Fri, from 10am Sat & Sun May-Oct, 9am-5pm Mon-Fri, from 10am Sat & Sun Nov-Apr) Extremely helpful English-speaking staff, souvenirs for sale and lots of brochures, including handy maps of the most popular walking tours in Lublin. There's a computer on hand for short-term web-surfing.

ⓘ Getting There & Away

BUS

PKS buses run from the **bus station** (☑703 402 622; ul Hutnicza 1 , cross Al Tysiąclecia), opposite the castle. From here, **Polski Bus** (www.polskibus.com) heads to Warsaw (three hours, five daily). Private minibuses run to various destinations, including Zamość (15zł, 1½ hours, hourly), from a minibus station north of the bus terminal.

TRAIN

The **train station** (Dworzec Kolejowy Lublin Główny; ☑info 19 757; www.pkp.pl; Plac Dworcowy 1) is 1.8km south of the Old Town. Useful direct train connections included to Kraków (62zł, four hours, two daily) and Warsaw (37zł, 2¾ hours, five daily).

CARPATHIAN MOUNTAINS

The Carpathians (Karpaty) stretch from the southern border with Slovakia into Ukraine, and their wooded hills and snowy mountains are a beacon for hikers, skiers and cyclists. The most popular destination here is the resort of Zakopane.

Zakopane

POP 27,485

Zakopane, 100km south of Kraków, is Poland's main alpine resort, situated at the foot of the Tatra Mountains. It's a popular jumping-off spot for trekking and mountain hikes, as well as Poland's best ski resort. The busy high street, ul Krupówki, is a jumble of tacky souvenir shops, bars and restaurants, but away from the centre, the pace slows down. This was an artists' colony in the early 20th century, and the graceful timbered villas from those days – built in what's known as the 'Zakopane style' of architecture – are still scattered around town.

◉ Sights & Activities

Museum of Zakopane Style

MUSEUM

(Willa Koliba; ☑18 201 3602; www.muzeum tatrzanskie.pl; ul Kościeliska 18; adult/concession 7/5.50zł; ⊙9am-5pm Wed-Sat, to 3pm Sun) Housed in the Villa Koliba, this was the first of several grand wooden villas designed by the noted Polish painter and architect Stanisław Witkiewicz in his 'Zakopane Style' (similar to the Arts and Crafts movement that swept the US and Britain at the turn of the 20th century). The interior has been restored to its original state, complete with the highlander furnishings and textiles, all designed for the villa.

Old Church & Cemetery

CHURCH

(Stary Kościół, Pęksowy Brzyzek National Cemetery; ul Kościeliska) FREE This small, wooden church and adjoining atmospheric cemetery date from the mid-19th century. The Old Church has charming carved wooden decorations and pews, and Stations of the Cross painted on glass on the windows. Just behind, the old cemetery is certainly one of the country's most beautiful, with a number of amazing wood-carved headstones, some resembling giant chess pieces. The noted Polish painter and creator of the Zakopane Style, Stanisław Witkiewicz, is buried here beneath a modest wooden grave marker.

Morskie Oko

LAKE

(admission 9zł) The most popular outing near Zakopane is to this emerald-green mountain lake, about 12km from the centre. Buses regularly depart from ul Kościuszki, across from the main bus station, for Polana Palenica (30 minutes), from where a 9km-long road continues uphill to the lake. Cars, bikes and buses are not allowed, so you'll have to walk (allow about two hours each way) or take a horse-drawn carriage to within 2km of the lake. Travel agencies organise day trips.

Mt Kasprowy Wierch Cable Car   CABLE CAR

(☑18 201 5356; www.pkl.pl; Kuźnice; adult/concession return 58/48zł; ☉7.30am-4pm Jan-Mar, 7.30am-6pm Apr-Jun & Sep-Oct, 7am-9pm Jul & Aug, 9am-4pm Nov-Dec) The cable-car trip from Kuźnice (2km south of Zakopane) to the Mt Kasprowy Wierch summit (1985m) is a classic tourist experience. At the end of the ascent (20 minutes, climbing 936m), you can get off and stand with one foot in Poland and the other in Slovakia. The view from the top is spectacular (clouds permitting). The cable car normally closes for two weeks in May, and won't operate if the snow or wind conditions are dangerous.

🛏 Sleeping

Travel agencies in Zakopane can usually arrange private rooms. Expect a double to cost about 80zł in the high season in the town centre, and about 60zł for somewhere further out.

Youth Hostel Szarotka   HOSTEL €

(☑18 201 3618; www.schroniskomlodziezowe.zakopane.org.pl; ul Nowotarska 45; dm/d 41/102zł; ☻) This cheerful and homely place with 62 beds gets packed in the high season and is on a busy road. But it's friendly and has a kitchen and washing machine on site.

★ Hotel Sabała   HOTEL €€€

(☑18 201 5092; www.sabala.zakopane.pl; ul Krupówki 11; s/d from 300/400zł; ☻📶🏊) Built in 1894 but thoroughly up to date, this striking timber hotel has a superb location overlooking the picturesque pedestrian thoroughfare. The hotel offers 51 cosy, attic-style rooms, and there's a sauna, solarium and swimming pool. The restaurant here serves both local specialties and international favourites.

✗ Eating

Pstrąg Górski   SEAFOOD €€

(☑512 351 746; ul Krupówki 6a; mains 20-40zł; ☉10am-10pm; ☻📶) This fish restaurant, done up in traditional style and overlooking a narrow stream, serves some of the freshest trout, salmon and sea fish in town. Trout

is priced at 5zł and up per 100g (whole fish), bringing the price of a standard fish dinner to around 30zł, not including sides.

Stek Chałupa   POLISH €€

(☑18 201 5918; www.stekchalupa.pl; ul Krupówki 33; mains 20-40zł; ☉8am-midnight; ☻) One of the better choices on ul Krupówki. This atmospheric highlander outfit is good for grilled sausages and steaks in all their guises.

ℹ Information

Tourist Information Centre (☑18 201 2211; www.zakopane.pl; ul Kościuszki 17; ☉9am-5pm Mar-Aug, 9am-5pm Mon-Fri Sep-Feb) Small but helpful tourist office not far from the bus station has city maps and sells hiking maps. Can advise on accommodation, mountain guides and day trips.

Tatra National Park Headquarters (Tatrzański Park Narodowy; ☑18 202 3300; www.tpn.pl; ul Chałubińskiego 44; ☉9am-4pm Mon-Fri) The information office of the Tatra National Park is located in a small building near the Rondo Kuźnickie on the southern outskirts of the city. It's a good place for maps, guides and local weather and hiking information.

ℹ Getting There & Away

Though Zakopane has a small train station, the majority of visitors arrive by bus from Kraków. Coaches make the journey (16zł, two hours) every 30 to 60 minutes during the day. The leading bus company is **Szwagropol** (www.szwagropol.pl). Buy tickets bound for Kraków at Zakopane **bus station** (ul Chramcówki).

SILESIA

Silesia (Śląsk in Polish; pronounced *shlonsk*), in the far southwest of the country, is a traditional industrial and mining region with a fascinating mix of landscapes. The historic capital, Wrocław, has an enormous and beautiful town square as well as epic, student-fuelled nightlife.

Wrocław

POP 632,065

When citizens of beautiful Kraków enthusiastically encourage you to visit Wrocław (vrots-wahf), you know you're onto something good. The city's gracious Old Town is a mix of Gothic and baroque styles, and its large student population ensures a healthy number of restaurants, bars and nightclubs.

Wrocław has been traded back and forth between various domains over the centuries, but began life around 1000 AD. History buffs may know the city better as Breslau, the name it had as part of Germany until the end of WWII. When the city went over to Polish hands after the war, Wrocław was a shell of its former self. Sensitive restoration has returned the historic centre to its old beauty.

◎ Sights

The main draw is the city's magnificent market square, the **Rynek**, dotted at the centre by the old **Town Hall** (Stary Ratusz). Note the dignified red-brick Gothic churches that are sprinkled around the centre in all directions. These statuesque beauties survived the bombardment during WWII and wear their blackened, chipped facades with pride.

◎ Old Town

Museum of Bourgeois Art   MUSEUM
(Muzeum Sztuki Mieszczańskiej; ☑71 347 1690; www.muzeum.miejskie.wroclaw.pl; Stary Ratusz; permanent exhibitions free, temporary exhibitions adult/concession 10/7zł; ☉10am-5pm Wed-Sat, to 6pm Sun) FREE The unusual name here hides the main attraction: the Gothic interiors of the Old Town Hall. Look for the **Great Hall** (Sala Wielka) on the 1st floor, with carved decorations from the second half of the 15th century. Adjoining it is the **Princes' Room** (Sala Książęca), which was built as a chapel in the mid-14th century.

Church of St Elizabeth   CHURCH
(www.kosciolgarnizon.wroclaw.pl; ul Św Elżbiety 1; tower admission 5zł; ☉10am-7pm Mon-Sat, noon-7pm Sun, tower 9am-7pm Mon-Fri, 11am-5pm Sat, 1-5pm Sun) Just north of the Hansel and Gretel houses is this monumental Gothic brick church, with an 83m-high **tower**. You can climb the narrow stairwell with 300-plus steps to the top for a great view of Wrocław.

Church of St Mary Magdalene   CHURCH
(ul Łaciarska; tower adult/concession 4/3zł; ☉10am-6pm Mon-Sat, tower 10am-6pm Apr-Oct) One block east of the Rynek is this mighty Gothic red-brick building dating from the 14th century. Its showpiece is a copy of a Romanesque portal from around 1280 on the south wall, which originally adorned the Benedictine Abbey in Ołbin, but was moved here in 1546 after the abbey was demolished. You can climb the 72m-high **tower** and cross the so-called **Penance Footbridge**.

The original tympanum is on display in Wrocław's National Museum.

◎ Outside the Old Town

★ Panorama of Racławice   MUSEUM
(☑71 344 1661; www.panoramaraclawicka.pl; ul Purkyniego 11; adult/concession 25/18zł; ☉9am-5pm May-Sept, to 4pm Tue-Sun Oct-Apr) Wrocław's pride and joy is this giant painting of the battle for Polish independence fought at Racławice on 4 April 1794 between the Polish army led by Tadeusz Kościuszko and Russian troops under General Alexander Tormasov. The Poles won but it was all for naught: months later the nationwide insurrection was crushed by the tsarist army. The canvas measures 15m by 114m, and is wrapped around the internal walls of a rotunda.

National Museum   MUSEUM
(☑71 372 5150; www.mnwr.art.pl; Plac Powstańców Warszawy 5; adult/concession 15/10zł; ☉10am-5pm Tue-Sun) This treasure trove of fine art is 200m east of the Panorama of Racławice. Medieval stone sculpture is displayed on the ground floor; exhibits include the Romanesque tympanum from the portal of the Church of St Mary Magdalene, depicting the Assumption of the Virgin Mary, and 14th-century sarcophagi from the Church of SS Vincent and James. There are also collections of Silesian paintings, ceramics, silverware and furnishings from the 16th to 19th centuries.

Cathedral of St John the Baptist   CHURCH
(☑71 322 2574; www.katedra.archidiecezja.wroc.pl; Plac Katedralny 18; tower adult/concession 5/4zł; ☉10am-4pm Mon-Sat, 2-4pm Sun, tower 10am-6pm Mon-Sat) The centrepiece of Cathedral Island, this three-aisled Gothic basilica was built between 1244 and 1590. Seriously damaged during WWII, it was reconstructed in its previous Gothic form, complete with dragon guttering. For once you don't need strong legs to climb the 91m-high **tower** as there is a lift (elevator).

⌂ Sleeping

★ Hostel Mleczarnia
HOSTEL €

(🖉 71 787 7570; www.mleczarniahostel.pl; ul Włodkowica 5; dm from 40zł, d 220zł; 🕾) This hostel on a quiet road not far from the Rynek has bags of charm, having been decorated in a deliberately old-fashioned style within a former residential building. There's a women-only dorm available, along with a kitchen and free laundry facilities. Downstairs is the excellent Mleczarnia cafe-bar.

Hostel Babel
HOSTEL €

(🖉 71 342 0250; www.babelhostel.pl; ul Kołłątaja 16/3; dm from 45zł, d 140zł; 🕾) A tatty old staircase leads up to pleasant budget accommodation just 100m from the train station. Dorms are set in renovated apartment rooms with ornate lamps and decorative ceilings. Bathrooms are shiny clean, and guests have access to a kitchen. There's a DVD player for rainy days.

B&B Hotel Wrocław Centrum
HOTEL €

(🖉 71 324 0980; www.hotelbb.pl; ul Ks Piotra Skargi 24-28; r 149zł; 🅿 ✱ 🕾) This thrifty budget option offers plain but spotlessly clean rooms, big comfortable beds and an excellent central location, about 500m from the Rynek. Drivers will appreciate the large, protected parking lot (25zł) at the rear of the hotel. It's just under 1km from the train and bus stations.

Art Hotel
HOTEL €€

(🖉 71 787 7400; www.arthotel.pl; ul Kiełbaśnicza 20; s/d from 280/300zł; ✱ 🕾) Elegant splurge candidate in a renovated apartment building, with tastefully restrained decor, quality fittings and gleaming bathrooms. There's a top-notch Polish-French restaurant, and a fitness room for working off any extra weight gained therein. Breakfast is an additional 50zł per person.

✗ Eating

Bar Bazylia
CAFETERIA €

(🖉 71 375 2065; www.bazyliabar.pl; ul Kuźnicza 42; mains 2.49zł per 100g; ⊘ 8am-7pm Mon-Fri, from 7.30am Sat & Sun; 🖊) Inexpensive, bustling modern take on the classic *bar mleczny* in a curved space with huge plate-glass windows overlooking the university. The menu has Polish standards such as *bigos* (sauerkraut and meat stew) and *gołąbki* (stuffed cabbage rolls), and a decent range of salads and other vegetable dishes. Everything is priced by weight; order and pay at the till before receiving your food.

Bernard Pub-Restaurant
CZECH, INTERNATIONAL €€

(🖉 71 344 1054; www.bernard.wroclaw.pl; Rynek 35; mains 30-60zł; ⊘ 10.30am-11pm; 🕾) This lively split-level bar-restaurant was inspired by the highly respected Czech beer of the same name, and the restaurant features some Czech dishes such as rabbit and pork knee. There's also upmarket comfort food including burgers, steak and fish dishes, as well as plenty of Bernard beer. The stylish interior is conducive to a quiet evening or group outing.

★ Cafe & Restaurant Steinhaus
POLISH €€€

(🖉 512 931 071; www.steinhaus.pl; ul Włodkowica 11; mains 40-70zł; ⊘ 11am-11pm; 🕾) Old-fashioned Polish and Jewish cooking in an elegant but unfussy setting. The goose in cranberry sauce can't be topped but the grilled duck-breast comes close. Be sure to reserve on weekends as this place is justifiably popular.

🍷 Drinking & Nightlife

Mleczarnia
CAFE, BAR

(🖉 71 788 2448; www.mle.pl; ul Włodkowica 5; ⊘ 8am-4am; 🕾) Hidden away in a backstreet that was once the city's main Jewish neighbourhood, this atmospheric place is stuffed with chipped old wooden tables bearing lace doilies and candlesticks. It turns out good coffee and light meals, including breakfast. At night the cellar opens, adding another moody dimension. There's a beautiful back garden in summer.

Pub Guinness
PUB

(🖉 71 344 6015; www.pubguinness.pl; Plac Solny 5; ⊘ noon-2am; 🕾) No prizes for guessing what this pub serves. A lively, fairly authentic Irish pub, spread over three levels on a busy corner. The ground-floor bar buzzes with student and traveller groups getting together, and there's a restaurant and beer cellar as well. A good place to wind down after a hard day's sightseeing.

Jazzda
CLUB

(☑607 429 602; www.jazzda.pl; Rynek 60; ⊙5pm-late Mon-Fri, noon-late Sat & Sun) Looking for a John Travolta kind of evening? This central bar and club with a lit-up, multicoloured dance floor and strobe lights will fit the bill.

Bezsenność
CLUB

(☑570 669 570; www.bezsennoscklub.com; ul Ruska 51, Pasaż Niepolda; ⊙7pm-late) With its alternative/rock/dance line-up and distressed decor, 'Insomnia' attracts a high-end clientele and is one of the most popular clubs in town. It's located in the Pasaż Niepolda, a group of bars, clubs and restaurants situated just off Ruska.

☆ Entertainment

Filharmonia
CLASSICAL MUSIC

(☑tickets 71 792 1000; www.filharmonia.wroclaw.pl; ul Piłsudskiego 19) If you're interested in hearing classical sounds, Friday and Saturday evenings are your best bets. It's located 800m southwest of the Rynek.

ℹ Information

Intermax (☑71 794 0573; www.imx.pl; ul Psie Budy 10/11; per hour 4zł; ⊙9am-11pm) Enter from ul Kazimierza Wielkiego.

Tourist Office (☑71 344 3111; www.wroclaw-info.pl; Rynek 14; ⊙9am-9pm)

ℹ Getting There & Away

BUS

The **bus station** (Dworzec Centralny PKS; ☑71 333 0530; ul Sucha 1/11) is south of the train station and offers several daily PKS buses to Warsaw (60zł, seven hours). For most other destinations the train is a better choice, though handy **Polski Bus** (www.polskibus.com) services run from here to Warsaw (seven hours, twice daily) and Prague (five hours, twice daily).

TRAIN

Wrocław Main Train Station (Wrocław Główny; ☑71 717 3333; www.rozklad.pkp.pl; ul Piłsudskiego 105) was opened in 1857 as a lavish architectural confection. It's easily Poland's most attractive railway station and worth visiting even if you're not travelling by train. Sample destinations include Warsaw (61zł, 6½ hours, hourly), Kraków (50zł, 5½ hours, several daily), Poznań (46zł, 3½ hours, hourly) and Toruń (56zł, five hours, several daily).

WIELKOPOLSKA

Wielkopolska (Greater Poland) is the region where Poland came to life in the Middle Ages. As a result of this ancient eminence, its cities and towns are full of historic and cultural attractions. The battles of WWII later caused widespread destruction in the area, though Poznań has been since restored to its prominent economic role.

Poznań
POP 551,600

Poznań is the cultural, economic and transport hub of Wielkopolska. It's strongly associated with the early formation of the Polish kingdom at the turn of the first millennium, and Poland's first ruler, Mieszko I, is buried at Poznań Cathedral.

After the partitions of the late-18th century, Poznań fell under Prussian domination and until the re-establishment of independent Poland at the end of WWI was the German city of Posen. Much of Poznań, including the main square (Stary Rynek), was destroyed in fighting in WWII and painstakingly rebuilt in the decades after.

These days, Poznań is a vibrant university city. There's a beautiful Old Town, with a number of interesting museums and a range of lively bars, clubs and restaurants.

◉ Sights

◉ Old Town

Town Hall
HISTORIC BUILDING

(Ratusz; ☑61 856 8193; www.mnp.art.pl; Stary Rynek 1) Poznań's Renaissance Town Hall, topped with a 61m-high tower, instantly captures attention. Its graceful form replaced a 13th-century Gothic structure, which burned down in the early-16th century. Every day at noon two metal goats appear through a pair of small doors above the clock and butt their horns together 12 times, in deference to an old legend. These days, the Town Hall is home to the Historical Museum of Poznań.

Historical Museum of Poznań
MUSEUM

(Muzeum Historii Miasta Poznania; ☑61 856 8000; www.mnp.art.pl; Stary Rynek 1; adult/concession 7/5zł, Sat free; ⊙9am-3pm Tue-Thu, noon-9pm Fri, 11am-6pm Sat & Sun) This museum inside the town hall displays an interesting and well-presented exhibition on the town's history, and the building's original interiors are worth the entry price on their own. The Gothic vaulted **cellars** are the only remains of the first town hall. They were initially used for trade but later became a jail.

◉ Ostrów Tumski

The island of Ostrów Tumski, east of the main square and across the Warta River, is the place where Poznań was founded, and with it the Polish state.

Poznań Cathedral   CHURCH
(Cathedral Basilica of Sts Peter & Paul; ☑ 61 852 9642; www.katedra.archpoznan.pl; ul Ostrów Tumski 17; crypt adult/concession 3.50/2.50zł; ⊙ 9am-4pm) Ostrów Tumski is dominated by this monumental, double-towered cathedral. Basically Gothic with additions from later periods, most notably the baroque tops of the towers, the cathedral was damaged in 1945 and took 11 years to rebuild. The aisles and the ambulatory are ringed by a dozen chapels containing numerous tombstones. The most famous is the Golden Chapel behind the high altar, which houses the remains of the first two Polish rulers: Mieszko I and Bolesław Chrobry.

Porta Posnania
Interactive Heritage Centre   MUSEUM
(☑ 61 647 7634; www.bramapoznania.pl; ul Gdańska 2; adult/concession 15/9zł, audioguide 5/3zł; ⊙ 9am-6pm Tue-Fri, 10am-7pm Sat & Sun; 🛜) This cutting-edge multimedia museum opened in 2014 to tell the tale of the island's eventful history and the birth of the Polish nation via interactive displays and other technological gadgetry. It's located on the island's eastern shore and is linked to the cathedral area by footbridge. The exhibitions are multilingual, but opt for an audioguide to help put everything together.

🛏 Sleeping

Poco Loco Hostel   HOSTEL €
(☑ 61 883 3470; www.hostel.poco-loco.pl; ul Taczaka 23; dm 39-55zł, r 140-160zł; @🛜) Clean, well-run and central, this is one of the city's most popular hostels and for a good reason. There's dorm accommodation in four- to 10-bunk rooms plus private rooms for two to four people. There's a shared kitchen plus laundry facilities and computers. The man-

agers are adventure travellers and pride themselves on offering good-value lodging.

Fusion Hostel   HOSTEL €
(☑ 61 852 1230; www.fusionhostel.pl; ul Św Marcin 66/72; dm 50-69zł, s 119-130zł, d 195-210zł; 🛜) Hostel with a view, perched on the 7th floor of a scuffed commercial building. The decor is modern and bright, and guests have access to a lounge, a kitchen and bicycle hire. There's dorm accommodation in four- and six-bunk rooms, as well as private singles and doubles. The lift is hidden behind the security booth in the foyer.

★ Hotel Stare Miasto   HOTEL €€
(☑ 61 663 6242; www.hotelstaremiasto.pl; ul Rybaki 36; s/d from 224/340zł; P🌸🛜) Stylish value-for-money hotel with a tastefully chandeliered foyer and spacious breakfast room. Rooms can be small but are clean and bright with lovely starched white sheets. Some upper rooms have skylights in place of windows.

Brovaria   HOTEL €€
(☑ 61 858 6868; www.brovaria.pl; Stary Rynek 73/74; s/d from 250/290zł; 🛜) This multitalented hotel also operates as a restaurant and bar, but most impressive is its in-house boutique brewery, whose operations you can view within the building. The elegant rooms have tasteful dark timber tones, and some have views onto the Rynek.

✕ Eating

Apetyt   CAFETERIA €
(☑ 61 852 0742; ul Szkolna 4; mains 5-12zł; ⊙ 9am-8pm Mon-Fri, 10am-7pm Sat, 11am-7pm Sun; 🥄) The latest-closing *bar mleczny* in town enjoys a good, central location. The Polish steam-table food is exactly what you'd expect, and none the worse for that, with *naleśniki* (crêpes) choices galore.

★ Papierówka   POLISH €€
(☑ 797 471 388; www.restauracjapapierowka.pl; ul Zielona 8; mains 20-40zł; ⊙ 9am-10pm; 🛜) This no-frills, slow-food restaurant offers some of the best cooking in town. Order at the counter and watch a team of chefs prepare your meal in the open kitchen. There are a half-dozen daily options, reflecting what's in season. The specialty is duck, though expect a couple of pork and fish choices. The winelist is tiny but impeccable.

Ludwiku do Rondla   JEWISH €€
(☑ 61 851 6638; ul Woźna 2/3; mains 26-38zł; ⊙ 1-10pm) This small, cosy place, two blocks

east of the main square, specialises in both Jewish and Polish cooking – particularly where the two intertwine. Menu items are helpfully marked if an item is Polish or Jewish in origin. We started with herring in oil (Polish/Jewish) and stuffed meat roulade with buckwheat (Polish), but everything looks good.

Wiejskie Jadło   POLISH €€

(☑ 61 853 6600; www.wiejskie-jadlo.pl; Stary Rynek 77; mains 18-51zł; ⊗ 10am-11pm) Compact Polish restaurant hidden a short distance back from the Rynek along ul Franciszkańska. It offers a range of filling dishes including *pierogi* (dumplings), soups, and pork in all its varied possibilities, served in a homely rustic space with flowers on the table.

🍷 Drinking & Nightlife

Proletaryat   BAR

(☑ 61 852 4858; www.proletaryat.pl; ul Wrocławska 9; ⊗ 1pm-late Mon-Sat, 3pm-late Sun; 🛜) Bright red communist-nostalgia bar with an array of socialist-era gear on the walls, including military insignia, portraits of Brezhnev and Marx, and the obligatory bust of Lenin in the window. Play 'spot the communist leader' while sipping a boutique beer from the Czarnków Brewery.

Atmosfera   CLUB

(☑ 61 853 3434; www.atmosfera-klub.pl; Stary Rynek 67; ⊗ 6pm-late Mon-Sat; 🛜) Arguably the best of several music and dance clubs located on the main square. Descend the stairs to find a large bar and dance floor. Dependable place for a very late drink, as some weekends the club stays open until 11am the next morning.

Van Diesel Music Club   CLUB

(☑ 515 065 459; www.vandiesel.pl; Stary Rynek 88; ⊗ 9pm-5am Fri & Sat) Happening venue on the main square, with DJs varying their offerings between pop, house, R&B, soul and dance. Given the variety, you're sure to find a night that will get you on the dancefloor.

☆ Entertainment

Johnny Rocker   LIVE MUSIC

(☑ 61 850 1499; www.johnnyrocker.pl; ul Wielka 9; ⊗ 6pm-late) This super-smooth basement venue with a curvy bar is crammed with happy drinkers sitting cabaret-style in front of a stage that features live blues, jazz or rock acts every weekend. If the sounds are overwhelming, you can always retreat to the stylish 'red room'.

Filharmonia   CLASSICAL MUSIC

(☑ box office 61 853 6935; www.filharmoniapoznanska.pl; ul Św Marcin 81; ⊗ box office 1-6pm) This musical institution holds concerts at least weekly by the house symphony orchestra. Poznań also has Poland's best boys' choir, the Poznańskie Słowiki (Poznań Nightingales), which can be heard here. Buy tickets at the box office or one hour before performances.

ℹ Information

Adax (☑ 61 850 1100; www.adaxland.poznan.pl; ul Półwiejska 28; per hr 4zł; ⊗ 10am-10pm Mon-Sat, from noon Sun) Near the Stary Browar shopping mall.

City Information Centre – Main Square (☑ 61 852 6156; www.poznan.travel; Stary Rynek 59/60; ⊗ 9am-8pm Mon-Sat, 10am-6pm Sun May-Sep, 10am-5pm Mon-Fri Oct-Apr) Poznań's helpful tourist information office is located conveniently on the main square. They have a wealth of information on the city and can advise on finding rooms and booking transport.

City Information Centre – Train Station (☑ 61 633 1016; www.poznan.travel; ul Dworcowa 2, Poznań Główny; ⊗ 8am-9pm Mon-Fri, 10am-5pm Sat & Sun) Branch of the Poznań tourist office located in the main train station.

ℹ Getting There & Away

BUS

The **bus station** (Dworzec PKS; ☑ timetable 703 303 330; www.pks.poznan.pl; ul Stanisława Matyi 2; ⊗ information 8am-7pm Mon-Sat, 10am-7pm Sun; 🚋 5, 8, 11, 12, 14 to Most Dworcowy) is located near the train station and part of the Poznań City Centre transport and shopping complex. It's 1.5km southwest of the Old Town and can be reached on foot in 15 minutes, or by tram to stop 'Most Dworcowy'.

Polski Bus (www.polskibus.com) runs services to Warsaw (four hours, five daily) and Wrocław (three hours, five daily). Polski Bus coaches arrive and depart at one of two stations: the main bus station or a smaller station, Dworzec Górczyn, 3km southwest of the main station. Check the website to use the right station. Buy tickets online.

ℹ POZNAŃ CITY CARD

Poznań City Card (1 day/35 zł), available from the city information centres, provides free entry to major museums, sizable discounts at restaurants and recreational activities, and free public transport.

TRAIN

Busy **Poznań Main Train Station** (Poznań Główny; ☑ 61 633 1659; www.pkp.pl; ul Dworcowa 2; ☑ 5, 8, 11, 12, 14 to Most Dworcowy) is 1.5km southwest of the Old Town and can be reached on foot in 15 minutes, or by tram to stop 'Most Dworcowy'.

Useful domestic train connections include to Gdańsk (60zł, 3½ hours, three daily), Kraków (80zł, eight hours, three daily), Toruń (30zł, two hours, two daily), Wrocław (60zł, 2¾ hours, five daily) and Warsaw (80zł, three hours, six daily). Poznań is a natural jumping-off spot for Berlin (150zł, three hours, six daily).

POMERANIA

Pomerania (Pomorze in Polish) is an attractive region with diverse drawcards, from beautiful beaches to architecturally pleasing cities. The historic port city of Gdańsk is situated at the region's eastern extreme, while the attractive Gothic city of Toruń lies inland.

Gdańsk

POP 460,400

The Hanseatic port of Gdańsk grew wealthy during the Middle Ages, linking inland cities with seaports around the world. That wealth is on display in the form of a bustling riverbank, mammoth red-brick churches and a gleaming central square.

Gdańsk has played an outsized role in history. The creation of the 'Free City of Danzig', at the conclusion of World War I, served as a pretext for Hitler to invade Poland at the start of WWII. The Germans fired the first shots of the war here on 1 September 1939 at the Polish garrison at Westerplatte.

In August 1980, the city became the centre of Poland's anticommunist movement with the establishment of the Solidarity trade union, led by its charismatic leader (and future Polish president), Lech Wałęsa.

◉ Sights

Gdańsk's major sights are situated in the **Main Town** (Główne Miasto). Much of what you see, including the dazzling palaces that line the central promenade, **Long St** (ul Długa), was rebuilt from rubble after the bombardment of WWII.

A sensible approach is to walk the former **Royal Route**, starting at the **Upland Gate** (Brama Wyżynna), at the western end of Long St and the nearby **Golden Gate** (Złota Brama), a triumphal arch built in 1612. Then follow the street as it widens into Long Market (Długi Targ) to end at the majestic **Green Gate** (Brama Zielona). From here, pick up the city's evocative river walk along the embankment of the **River Motława**.

◉ Main Town

Historical Museum of Gdańsk
MUSEUM

(Town Hall; ☑ 58 767 9100; www.mhmg.pl; Długa 46/47; adult/concession 12/6zł; ☺ 10am-1pm Tue, 10am-4pm Wed-Sat, 11am-4pm Sun) The museum is located in the historic town hall, which boasts Gdańsk's highest tower at 81.5m. The showpiece is the **Red Room** (Sala Czerwona), done up in Dutch Mannerist style from the end of the 16th century. The 2nd floor houses exhibitions related to Gdańsk's history, including photos of the destruction of 1945. From here you can enter the **tower** for great views across the city.

Amber Museum
MUSEUM

(☑ 58 301 4733; www.mhmg.pl; Targ Węglowy 26; adult/concession 10/5zł; ☺ 10am-1pm Mon, 10am-4pm Tue-Sat, 11am-4pm Sun) This museum is dedicated to all things amber and the craft of designing and creating amber jewellery. The musuem is located in the **Foregate**, a former prison and torture chamber, so in addition to amber displays, there's also some startlingly realistic displays of torture chambers. Two for one!

St Mary's Church
CHURCH

(☑ 58 301 3982; www.bazylikamariacka.pl; ul Podkramarska 5; tower adult/concession 5/3zł; ☺ 8.30am-6pm, except during services) Dominating the heart of the Main Town, St Mary's is often cited as the largest brick church in the world. Some 105m long and 66m wide at the transept, its massive squat tower climbs 78m high into the Gdańsk cityscape. Begun in 1343, St Mary's didn't reach its present proportions until 1502. Don't miss the 15th-century astronomical clock, placed in the northern transept, and the church tower (405 steps above the city).

National Maritime Museum
MUSEUM

(Narodowe Muzeum Morskie w Gdańsku; ☑ Maritime Cultural Centre 58 329 8700, information 58 301 8611; www.nmm.pl; ul Tokarska 21-25, entry from Motława River side; Maritime Cultural Center adult/child 8/5zł, other exhibitions priced separately; ☺ 10am-4pm Tue-Sun) This is a sprawling exhibition of maritime history

Gdańsk

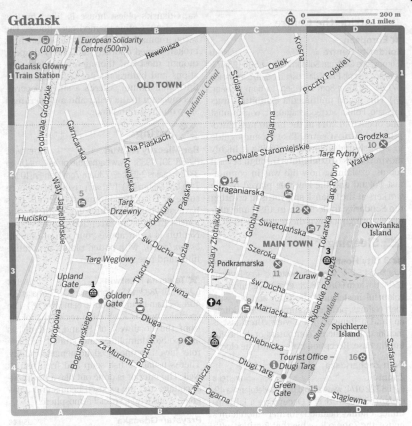

Gdańsk

Sights
1	Amber Museum	A3
2	Historical Museum of Gdańsk	C4
3	National Maritime Museum	D3
4	St Mary's Church	C3

Sleeping
5	3 City Hostel	A2
6	Dom Aktora	C2
7	Dom Zachariasza Zappio	D3
8	Kamienica Gotyk	C3

Eating
9	Bar Mleczny Neptun	B4
10	Przystań Gdańska	D2
11	Restauracja Pod Łososiem	C3
12	Tawerna Mestwin	C2

Drinking & Nightlife
13	Cafe Ferber	B3
14	Cafe Lamus	C2
15	Miasto Aniołów	D4

Entertainment
16	Klub Morza Zejman	D4

and Gdańsk's role through the centuries as a Baltic seaport. Headquarters is the multi-million-euro **Maritime Cultural Centre**, with a permanent interactive exhibition 'People-Ships-Ports'. Other exhibitions include the **MS Sołdek**, the first vessel to be built at the Gdańsk shipyard in the postwar years and the **Żuraw** (ul Szeroka 67/68), a 15th-century loading crane that was the biggest in its day. More displays are housed in **granaries** (ul Ołowianka 9-13) across the river.

Outside the Centre

★ European Solidarity Centre
MUSEUM

(Europejskie Centrum Solidarności; ☑ 506 195 673; www.ecs.gda.pl; Pl Solidarności 1; adult/concession 17/13zł; ⊙ 10am-8pm May-Sep, to 6pm Oct-Apr; 🛜) This grand multimedia exhibition tracing the Polish struggle against communist rule opened in 2014 in the brand new European Solidarity Centre. Take an audioguide in English and follow a confusing if highly moving series of exhibitions through several rooms, explaining how life was in communist Poland and the key role played by the workers at the Gdańsk shipyards in creating the Solidarity trade union in 1980 and ultimately bringing down the regime in 1989.

🛏 Sleeping

★ 3 City Hostel
HOSTEL €

(☑ 58 354 5454; www.3city-hostel.pl; Targ Drzewny 12/14; dm from 60zł, r 180zł; @🛜) Big, modern, colourful hostel near the train station, with high ceilings, pleasant common areas, a kitchen, and a lounge with a view. Breakfast is included, plus there's computers on-hand for internet use. Reception runs round the clock.

Dom Zachariasza Zappio
HOSTEL €

(☑ 58 322 0174; www.zappio.pl; ul Świętojańska 49; dm/s/d 60/95/170zł; 🛜) Occupying a labyrinthine, chunky-beamed former merchant's house, the Zappio is so big that families with kiddies and party animals won't get in each other's way. In addition to high-ceilinged dorms sleeping up to 14, and 13 rooms of various medieval shapes and sizes, this remarkable hostel also has its own pub, bike rental, guest kitchen and 24-hour reception.

Dom Aktora
HOTEL €€

(☑ 58 301 5901; www.domaktora.pl; ul Straganiarska 55/56; s/d 250/330zł, apt 360-570zł; P🛜) The no-nonsense apartments at this former thespians' dorm are affordable and have simply equipped kitchens, making this a prime target for self-caterers. Bathrooms throughout are 21st-century conceptions but otherwise not much has changed here decor-wise since the mid-1990s. The homemade breakfast buffet is the best in town.

Kamienica Gotyk
HOTEL €€

(☑ 58 301 8567; www.gotykhouse.eu; ul Mariacka 1; s/d 280/310zł; 🛜) Wonderfully located at the St Mary's Church end of ul Mariacka, Gdańsk's oldest house is filled by this neat, clean, Gothic-themed guesthouse. The seven rooms have Gothic touches such as broken-arched doorways and hefty drapery, though most are thoroughly modern creations and bathrooms are definitely of the third millennium. There's a small Copernicus museum in the cellar and a gingerbread shop on the ground floor.

🍴 Eating

Bar Mleczny Neptun
CAFETERIA €

(☑ 58 301 4988; www.barneptun.pl/en/; ul Długa 33/34; mains 2-16zł; ⊙ 7.30am-7pm Mon-Fri, 10am-7pm Sat & Sun; 🛜) It's surprising just where some of Poland's communist-era milk bars have survived and this one, right on the tourist drag, is no exception. However, the Neptun is a cut above your run-of-the-mill *bar mleczny*, with potted plants, decorative tiling and free wi-fi.

★ Tawerna Mestwin
POLISH €€

(☑ 58 301 7882; ul Straganiarska 20/23; mains 20-40zł; ⊙ 11am-10pm Tue-Sun, to 6pm Mon; 🛜) The specialty here is Kashubian regional cooking from the northwest of Poland, and dishes like potato dumplings and stuffed cabbage rolls have a pronounced homemade quality. There's usually a fish soup and fried fish as well. The interior is done out like a traditional cottage and the exposed beams and dark-green walls lend a special atmosphere.

Przystań Gdańska
POLISH €€

(☑ 58 301 1922; ul Wartka 5; mains 17-43zł; ⊙ 11am-10pm) An atmospheric place to enjoy outdoor dining, with a view along the river to the Gdańsk crane. Serves Polish classics and a range of fish dishes, plus a few pizzas tossed in. The food's above average but the view from the terrace is arguably the best in the Old Town.

Restauracja Pod Łososiem
POLISH €€€

(☑ 58 301 7652; www.podlososiem.com.pl; ul Szeroka 52/54; mains 60-85zł; ⊙ noon-11pm) Founded in 1598 and famous for salmon, this is one of Gdańsk's most highly regarded restaurants. Red leather seats, brass chandeliers and a gathering of gas lamps fill out the rather sober interior, illuminated by the specialty drink here – Goldwasser. This gooey, sweet liqueur with flakes of gold was produced in its cellars from the 16th century until WWII.

POLAND GDAŃSK

🍸 Drinking & Nightlife

Cafe Lamus BAR
(📱531 194 277; ul Lawendowa 8; ⊘noon-2am;
📶) Achingly cool retro-themed bar serving
a broad range of bottled beers from small
local breweries. Enter from ul Straganiarska.

Cafe Ferber CAFE, BAR
(📱791 010 005; www.ferber.pl; ul Długa 77/78;
⊘9am-late; 📶) It's startling to step straight
from Gdańsk's historic main street into this
very modern café-bar, dominated by bright
red panels, a suspended ceiling and boxy
lighting. The scarlet decor contrasts with
its comfy armchairs, from which you can
sip coffee and cocktail creations such as the
szary kot (grey cat). On weekends, DJs spin
tunes into the wee small hours.

Miasto Aniołów CLUB
(📱58 768 5831; www.miastoaniolow.com.pl; ul
Chmielna 26) The City of Angels covers all
the bases – late-night revellers can hit the
spacious dance floor, crash in the chill-out
area, or hang around the atmospheric deck
overlooking the Motława River. Nightly DJs
play disco and other dance-oriented sounds.

☆ Entertainment

State Baltic Opera Theatre OPERA
(📱58 763 4906; www.operabaltycka.pl; Al Zwy-
cięstwa 15) Founded in 1950, Gdańsk's premier opera company resides in this opera
house in the Wrzeszcz district, next to the
Gdańsk Politechnika train station. Alongside the usual operatic repertoire, it stages
regular ballets. Symphonic concerts are also
held here.

Klub Morza Zejman LIVE MUSIC
(📱669 070 557; www.bractwozeglarzy.home.pl;
Chmielna 111/113; admission 2zł; ⊘6-10pm Wed,
Fri & Sat, 8pm-midnight Thu) This salty warren
of crusty old sea hands on Spichlerze Island
has a delightfully tumble-down feel. Most
nights sailors and their wives just meet up
for beers around the bar, but Thursday evenings (and occasionally other nights) bring
live performances of old sea shanties (sailor
songs) that simply can't be missed.

ℹ Information

Jazz 'n' Java (📱58 305 3616; ul Tkacka 17/18;
per hour 6zł; ⊘10am-10pm) Internet access.
Tourist Office – Długi Targ (📱58 301 4355;
www.gdansk4u.pl; Długi Targ 28/29; ⊘9am-
7pm Jun-Aug, to 5pm Sep-May) Helpful,
centrally located tourist information office has

MALBORK

Magnificent **Malbork Castle** (📱tickets
55 647 0978; www.zamek.malbork.pl; ul
Starościńska 1; adult/concession 40/30zł;
⊘9am-7pm 15 Apr–15 Sep, 10am-3pm 16
Sep–14 Apr) makes a great day trip from
Gdańsk. It's the largest Gothic castle
in Europe and was once headquarters
for the medieval Teutonic Knights. Its
sinister form looms over the relatively
small town and Nogat River. Trains run
regularly from Gdańsk Głowny station
(45 minutes). Once you get to Malbork
station, turn right, cross the highway
and follow ul Kościuszki to the castle.
Compulsory tours come with an audio
tour in English. There are places to eat
at the castle and in the town.

---

a free city map and loads of information on
sightseeing, accommodation and transport.

ℹ Getting There & Away

BUS
The **bus station** (PKS Gdańsk; 📱58 302 1532;
www.pks.gdansk.pl; ul 3 Maja 12) is behind the
main train station. PKS buses head to Warsaw
hourly (55zł, 5¾ hours), as do services of **Polski
Bus** (www.polskibus.com).

TRAIN
The city's train station, **Gdańsk Głowny** (Gdańsk
Głowny; www.pkp.pl; ul Podwale Grodzkie 1),
is located on the western outskirts of the Old
Town. Most long-distance trains actually start
or finish at Gdynia, so make sure you get on/off
quickly here.

Useful direct train connections include to
Toruń (50zł, three hours, three daily), Kraków
(80zł, eight hours, three daily), Poznań (30zł,
3¾ hours, three daily) and Warsaw (90zł, six
hours, five daily). International destinations
include Berlin (seven hours, two daily).

Toruń
POP 205,000

Toruń escaped major damage in WWII and
is widely considered the best-preserved
Gothic town in Poland. The city is known
around the country for the quality of its gingerbread and, indeed, with its handsome,
red-brick churches and elegant, intricate
facades, Toruń resembles nothing more than
a beautifully crafted gingerbread cookie.

GREAT MASURIAN LAKES

The northeastern corner of Poland features a beautiful postglacial landscape dominated by thousands of lakes. About 200km of canals connect these bodies of water, making the area a prime destination for canoeists, as well as those who love to hike, fish and mountain bike.

The towns of **Giżycko** and **Mikołajki** make good bases. Both the Giżycko **tourist office** (☑87 428 5265; www.gizycko.turystyka.pl; ul Wyzwolenia 2; ☉9am-5pm Mon-Fri, 10am-2pm Sat & Sun Apr-Oct, 9am-4pm Mon-Fri, 10am-2pm Sat Nov-Mar) and the Mikołajki **tourist office** (☑87 421 6850; www.mikolajki.pl; Plac Wolności 3; ☉10am-6pm Jun-Aug, 10am-6pm Mon-Sat May & Sep) supply useful maps for sailing and hiking, provide excursion boat schedules, and assist in finding accommodation.

Nature aside, there are some interesting fragments of history in this region. A grim reminder of the past is the **Wolf's Lair** (Wilczy Szaniec; ☑89 752 4429; www.wolfsschanze. pl; adult/concession 15/10zł; ☉8am-dusk). Located at **Gierłoż**, 8km east of Kętrzyn, this ruined complex was Hitler's wartime headquarters for his invasion of the Soviet Union. In 1944, a group of high-ranking German officers tried to assassinate Hitler here. These dramatic events were reprised in the 2008 Tom Cruise movie *Valkyrie*.

Toruń is famous as the birthplace of Nicolaus Copernicus, who revolutionised the field of astronomy in 1543 by asserting the earth travelled around the sun. He's a figure you will not be able to escape – you can even buy gingerbread men in his likeness.

◉ Sights

The usual starting point on Toruń's Gothic trail is the Old Town Market Square (Rynek Staromiejski), dominated by a massive red-brick **Town Hall** and lined with finely restored houses. At the southeast corner, look for a **Statue of Copernicus**, a regular feature in holiday snaps.

Old Town Hall MUSEUM

(Ratusz Staromiejski; www.muzeum.torun.pl; Rynek Staromiejski 1; adult/concession museum 11/7zł, tower 11/7zł; ☉museum 10am-6pm Tue-Sun May-Sep, to 4pm Tue-Sun Oct-Apr, tower 10am-8pm May-Sep, 10am-5pm Oct-Apr) The Old Town Hall dates from the 14th century and hasn't changed much since, though some Renaissance additions lent an ornamental touch to the sober Gothic structure. Today, it houses the main branch of the Toruń Regional Museum. Displays include a collection of Gothic art (painting and stained glass), a display of local 17th- and 18th-century crafts, and a gallery of Polish paintings from 1800 to the present. Climb the **tower** for a fine panoramic view of Toruń's Gothic townscape.

House of Copernicus MUSEUM

(☑56 660 5613; www.muzeum.torun.pl; ul Kopernika 15/17; museum adult/concession 11/8zł, audiovisual presentation 13/8zł, gingerbread exhibition 11/8zł, combined entry 22/17zł; ☉10am-6pm Tue-Sun May-Sep, to 4pm Tue-Sun Oct-Apr) While it's not clear if Copernicus was actually born here, this branch of the regional museum is dedicated to the famed astronomer's life and works. More engaging than the exhibitions of period furniture and writing is a short audiovisual presentation regarding Copernicus' times in Toruń, with a model of the town. A third element of the museum, titled **World of Toruń's Gingerbread**, offers insights into the arcane art of gingerbread creation.

Cathedral of SS John the Baptist & John the Evangelist CHURCH

(☑56 657 1480; www.katedra.diecezja.torun.pl; ul Żeglarska 16; adult/concession 3/2zł; ☉9am-5.30pm Mon-Sat, 2-5.30pm Sun Apr-Oct) Toruń's mammoth Gothic cathedral was begun around 1260 but only completed at the end of the 15th century. Its massive tower houses Poland's second-largest historic bell, the **Tuba Dei** (God's Trumpet). On the southern side of the tower, facing the Vistula, is a large 15th-century clock; its original face and single hand are still in working order. Check out the dent above the VIII – it's from a cannonball that struck the clock during the Swedish siege of 1703.

Gingerbread Museum MUSEUM

(Muzeum Piernika; ☑56 663 6617; www.muzeumpiernika.pl; ul Rabiańska 9; adult/concession 12/9.50zł; ☉9am-6pm) Learn about gingerbread's history and create a spicy concoction of your own under the enlightened instruction of a mock-medieval gingerbread master. All of it takes place in a renovated 16th-century gingerbread factory.

🛏 Sleeping

Green Hostel
HOSTEL €

(☑56 561 4000; www.greenhostel.eu; ul Małe Garbary 10; r from 100zł; 🕙) Located up a 14th-century set of steep stairs opposite Hotel Heban, this dorm-less hostel offers 34 beds over four floors, bathrooms on each floor and 24-hour reception. Rates are not per person – you pay for the whole room and there are no singles, so this is definitely a better deal if you're travelling in a two- or moresome.

★ Hotel Petite Fleur
HOTEL €€

(☑56 621 5100; www.petitefleur.pl; ul Piekary 25; s/d 210/270zł; 🕙) One of the better midrange options in Toruń has understated rooms containing slickly polished timber furnishings and elegant prints, though the singles can be a touch space-poor. The French brick cellar restaurant is one of Toruń's better hotel eateries and the buffet breakfast is the best we had in Poland.

Hotel Pod Czarną Różą
HOTEL €€

(☑56 621 9637; www.hotelczarnaroza.pl; ul Rabiańska 11; s/d 170/210zł; 🕙) 'Under the Black Rose' fills out both a historic inn and a newer wing facing the river, though its interiors present a uniformly clean, up-to-date look with the odd antique reproduction. Buffet breakfast included.

Hotel Karczma Spichrz
HOTEL €€

(☑56 657 1140; www.spichrz.pl; ul Mostowa 1; s/d 250/310zł, apt from 290zł; ✼🕙) Wonderfully situated within a historic waterfront granary, this hotel's 19 rooms are laden with personality, featuring massive exposed beams above characterful timber furniture and contemporary bathrooms. The location by the river is within walking distance of the sights but away from the crowds. Good restaurant next door.

🍴 Eating

Bar Mleczny Pod Arkadami
CAFETERIA €

(☑56 622 2428; ul Różana 1; mains 4-12zł; ⊙9am-7pm Mon-Fri, to 4pm Sat & Sun) The city centre's last remaining *bar mleczny* offers substantial Polish stodge for a fistful of złoty. The outdoor window serves up waffles, ice cream and perhaps northern Poland's best *zapiekanki* (Polish pizza).

Luizjana
CAJUN €€

(☑56 692 6678; www.restauracjaluizjana.pl; ul Mostowa 10/1; mains 22-50zł; ⊙noon-10pm; 🕙) Cajun or creole food is a novel concept in these parts, but one that works exceedingly well here. Enjoy mains like spicy grilled chicken served in sweet coconut sauce with rice or blackened salmon with spinach pesto in a charming, low-key cafe-like setting. Portions (especially soups) are huge and suitable for sharing. The vibe is hip without being pretentious.

★ Szeroka 9
POLISH €€€

(☑56 622 8424; www.szeroka9.pl; ul Szeroka 9; mains 35-50zł; ⊙9am-11pm; 🕙) Elegant, refined (with being fussy) dining, a short walk from the main square. The chef dabbles in traditional Polish main courses like rabbit, goose and duck, but with a contemporary flair (for example, stuffed leek and plum sauce with the goose). The service is attentive and the wine list is excellent. A perfect choice for a special meal.

🍷 Drinking & Nightlife

Kona Coast Cafe
CAFE

(☑56 664 0049; www.konacoastcafe.pl; ul Chełmińska 18; ⊙9am-9pm Mon-Sat, 11am-6pm Sun; 🕙) Claims to be the only cafe in town that roasts their own beans. The coffee is decent as is the homemade lemonade, chai and various cold drinks. There's also a light-meal menu.

☆ Entertainment

Lizard King
LIVE MUSIC

(☑56 621 0234; www.lizardking-torun.pl; ul Kopernika 3; ⊙7pm-late; 🕙) Live-music venue with gigs ranging from local tribute bands to quite big rock acts from around Eastern and Central Europe.

Teatr Baj Pomorski
PUPPETRY

(☑56 652 2424, 56 652 2029; www.bajpomorski.art.pl; ul Piernikarska 9) Puppet theatre shaped like a huge wooden cabinet, staging a variety of entertaining shows.

ℹ Information

Tourist Office (☑56 621 0930; www.torun.pl; Rynek Staromiejski 25; ⊙9am-4pm Mon & Sat, to 6pm Tue-Fri, 11am-3pm Sun; 🕙) Free internet access, heaps of info and very professional staff who know their city.

POLAND TORUŃ

❶ Getting There & Away

BUS

The **bus station** (Dworzec Autobusowy Arriva; www.rozklady.com.pl; ul Dąbrowskiego 8-24) is a 10-minute walk north of the Old Town; from here, **Polski Bus** (www.polskibus.com) connects to Warsaw (3¾ hours, four daily) and Gdańsk (two hours, four daily). For other places, it's usually better to take the train.

TRAIN

Toruń's **main train station** (Toruń Główny; www.pkp.pl; Kujawska 1; ☐ 22, 27) is located on the opposite side of the Vistula River and linked to the Old Town by bus 22 or 27 (or a 2km walk). Useful direct train connections include those to Gdańsk (50zł, three hours, three daily), Kraków (73zł, seven hours, three daily), Poznań (30zł, two hours, two daily), Warsaw (52zł, 2¾ hours, five daily).

SURVIVAL GUIDE

❶ Directory A–Z

ACCOMMODATION

Polish accommodation runs the gamut from youth hostels, bungalows and mountain cabins to modest hotels and pensions all the way to up-market boutiques and business-oriented chains.

➜ Youth hostels are divided into 'older-style', where accommodation is offered in university dorms, and modern hostels, geared toward international backpackers. A dorm bed can cost anything from 40zł to 60zł per person per night.

COUNTRY FACTS

Area 312,679 sq km

Capital Warsaw

Country Code ☑ 48

Currency Złoty (zł)

Emergency Ambulance ☑ 999, fire ☑ 998, police ☑ 997

Language Polish

Money ATMs are all over; banks open Monday to Friday

Population 38.5 million

Visas Not required for citizens of the EU, US, Canada, New Zealand and Australia

---

SLEEPING PRICE RANGES

In this chapter, our price breakdown is based on a double room in season. Unless otherwise noted, rooms have private bathrooms and the rate includes breakfast.

€ less than 150zł

€€ 150zł to 400zł

€€€ more than 400zł

➜ A handy campsite resource is the website of the **Polish Federation of Camping and Caravanning** (www.pfcc.eu).

➜ Hotel prices vary substantially depending on the day of the week or season. In cities, expect higher rates during the week and weekend discounts. In heavily touristed areas, rates may rise over the weekend.

➜ Two reliable websites for arranging hotel accommodation over the internet are www.poland4u.com and www.hotelspoland.com.

➜ In big cities like Warsaw, Kraków and Gdańsk, private apartments are available for short-term rentals. These can offer an affordable alternative to hotels.

BUSINESS HOURS

Banks 8am to 5pm Monday to Friday, sometimes 8am to 2pm Saturday

Cafes & restaurants 11am to 11pm

Shops 10am to 6pm Monday to Friday, 10am to 2pm Saturday

Nightclubs 9pm to late

GAY & LESBIAN TRAVELLERS

➜ Homosexual activity is legal in Poland and overt discrimination is banned, though public attitudes are generally not supportive.

➜ Warsaw and Kraków are the best places to find gay-friendly bars and clubs.

➜ A decent, though somewhat dated, source of online information: www.gayguide.net.

INTERNET ACCESS

➜ Nearly all hotels and hostels offer internet, usually wi-fi.

➜ Many cafes, restaurants and bars offer free wi-fi for customers.

➜ Internet cafes are not as abundant as they once were, but normally charge around 5zł per hour.

INTERNET RESOURCES

In Your Pocket (www.inyourpocket.com)

Online train timetable (http://rozklad-pkp.pl)

Poland's official travel website (www.poland. travel)

Useful promotional website (www.polska.pl)

MONEY

➡ Poland's currency is the złoty (*zwo*-ti), abbreviated as zł (international currency code PLN). It's divided into 100 groszy (gr).

➡ *Bankomats* (ATMs) accept most international credit cards and are easily found. Private *kantors* (foreign-exchange offices) are also everywhere.

➡ Tipping isn't common in Poland, but feel free to leave 10% extra for waitstaff or taxi drivers if you've had good service.

PUBLIC HOLIDAYS

New Year's Day 1 January
Epiphany 6 January
Easter Sunday March/April
Easter Monday March/April
State Holiday 1 May
Constitution Day 3 May
Pentecost Sunday Seventh Sunday after Easter
Corpus Christi Ninth Thursday after Easter
Assumption Day 15 August
All Saints' Day 1 November
Independence Day 11 November
Christmas 25 and 26 December

TELEPHONE

➡ Polish landlines have nine digits, consisting of a two-digit area code and a seven-digit number. Mobile phone numbers have nine digits, normally starting with a 5, 6 or 7.

➡ To call a landline from another landline, dial 🔲 0 plus the area code and the seven-digit number. To call a mobile phone from a landline, dial 🔲 0 plus the nine-digit number.

➡ To call a mobile from a mobile, simply dial the number.

➡ To call Poland from abroad, dial the country code 🔲 48, then the area code plus seven-digit landline number, or the nine-digit mobile-phone number.

➡ The main mobile operators are Plus, Orange, T-Mobile and Play; all offer inexpensive prepaid SIM cards that come with call and data allowances.

➡ The cheapest way to make international calls from public telephones is via prepaid international cards, available at post offices and kiosks.

VISAS

➡ EU citizens do not need visas to visit Poland and can stay indefinitely.

ESSENTIAL FOOD & DRINK

➡ **Żurek** Hearty, sour rye soup includes sausage and hard-boiled egg.

➡ **Barszcz** Famous beetroot soup comes in two varieties: red (made from beetroot) and white (with wheat flour and sausage).

➡ **Bigos** Thick stew with sauerkraut and meat.

➡ **Pierogi** Flour dumplings, usually stuffed with cheese, mushrooms or meat.

➡ **Szarlotka** Apple cake with cream; a Polish classic.

➡ **Wódka** Vodka: try it plain, or ask for *myśliwska* (flavoured with juniper berries).

➡ Citizens of Australia, Canada, Israel, New Zealand, Switzerland and the USA can stay in Poland up to 90 days without a visa.

➡ Other nationals should check the website of the **Ministry of Foreign Affairs** (www.msz. gov.pl).

ⓘ Getting There & Away

AIR

Warsaw-Frédéric Chopin Airport (p286) is the nation's main international gateway, while other important airports include Kraków, Gdańsk, Poznań and Wrocław.

➡ The national carrier **LOT** (☑ call centre 801 703 703; www.lot.com) flies to major European cities and select destinations further afield.

➡ A vast array of budget carriers, including **Ryanair** (☑ 703 303 033; www.ryanair.com) and **Wizz Air** (☑ 703 603 993; www.wizzair. com), fly into Poland from airports across Europe, including regional airports in Britain and Ireland.

LAND

Poland is well connected to both Western and Eastern Europe by rail and bus networks.

Border Crossings

➡ As Poland is a member of the EU's Schengen Zone, there are no passport or customs controls if arriving from Germany, the Czech Republic, Slovakia or Lithuania.

➡ Expect border delays if arriving from Ukraine, Belarus or Russia's Kaliningrad province.

POLAND GETTING THERE & AWAY

Bus

International buses head in all directions, including eastward to the Baltic States. From Zakopane, it's easy to hop to Slovakia via bus or minibus.

Several companies operate long-haul coach service. Two reliable operators include **Eurolines Polska** (☑146 571 777; www.eurolines.pl) and **Polski Bus** (www.polskibus.com).

Car & Motorcycle

➡ The minimum legal driving age is 18.

➡ The maximum blood-alcohol limit is 0.02%.

➡ All drivers are required to carry their home driving licence, along with identity card, vehicle registration and liability insurance.

Train

There are direct rail services to Berlin from Warsaw (via Poznań) and to Prague from Warsaw and Kraków. Trains also link Warsaw to Minsk in Belarus and Moscow in Russia.

SEA

Ferry services operated by **Polferries** (☑801 003 171; www.polferries.pl), **Stena Line** (☑58 660 9200; www.stenaline.pl) and **Unity Line** (www.unityline.pl) connect Poland's Baltic coast ports of Gdańsk, Gydnia and Świnoujscie to destinations in Scandinavia, including Denmark and Sweden.

ⓘ Getting Around

AIR

LOT (p309) and/or its cheaper **Eurolot** (☑22 275 8740; www.eurolot.com) subsidiary fly between Warsaw, Gdańsk, Kraków, Poznań, Wrocław and Lublin.

BUS

Most buses are operated by the state bus company, PKS. It operates both ordinary buses (marked in black on timetables) and fast buses (marked in red).

➡ Buy tickets at bus terminals or directly from the driver.

➡ Polski Bus (p310) offers modern, comfortable long-haul coach service to select large Polish cities and beyond; buy tickets from its website.

CAR

Major international car-rental companies are represented in larger cities and airports.

Avis (☑22 572 6565; www.avis.pl)

Europcar (☑22 255 5600; www.europcar.com.pl)

Hertz (☑22 500 1620; www.hertz.pl)

TRAIN

Polish State Railways (PKP; ☑information 19 757; www.pkp.pl) operates trains to nearly every tourist destination; its online timetable is helpful, providing routes, fares and intermediate stations in English.

➡ **EIC** (Express InterCity) and **EC** (EuroCity) trains link large cities and offer the best and fastest connections. Reservations are obligatory.

➡ **TLK** (Tanie Linie Kolejowe) trains tend to be as fast as EC, but are cheaper. Trains are often crowded and no reservations are taken for second class on some trains.

➡ **IR** (InterRegio) and **R** (Regio) are cheap and slow local trains.

➡ Buy tickets at station ticket windows or at special PKP passenger-service centres, located in major stations. Also buy online at the Polish State Railways (PKP) website.

Romania

Best Places to Eat

➡ Central Park (p322)
➡ Casa Bunicii (p329)
➡ Caru' cu Bere (p316)
➡ Crama Sibiul Vechi (p323)
➡ Bistro de l'Arte (p320)

Best Places to Stay

➡ Casa Georgius Krauss (p322)
➡ Casa Reims (p319)
➡ The Guest House (p320)
➡ Hotel Central (p325)
➡ Hostel Costel (p328)

Why Go?

Beautiful and beguiling, Romania's rural landscape remains relatively untouched by the country's urban evolution. It's a land of aesthetically stirring hand-ploughed fields, sheep-instigated traffic jams, and lots of homemade plum brandy.

Most visitors focus their attention on Transylvania, with its legacy of fortified Saxon towns like Braşov and Sighişoara, plus tons of stirring natural beauty. Similar in character but even more remote, the region of Maramureş offers authentic folkways and villages marked by memorable wooden churches. Across the Carpathians, the Unesco-listed painted monasteries dot southern Bucovina. The Danube Delta has more than 300 species of birds, including many rare varieties, and is an ideal spot for birdwatching.

Energetic cities such as Timişoara, Cluj-Napoca and, especially, Bucharest offer culture – both high- and low-brow – and showcase Romania as a rapidly evolving modern European country.

When to Go
Bucharest

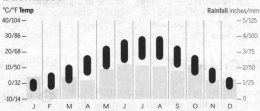

May Good for festivals, including the ever-popular Sibiu Jazz Festival.

Jun Mountain hiking starts in mid-June, while birding season gets rolling in the Danube Delta.

Sep The summer heat is gone, but sunny days are perfect for exploring big cities.

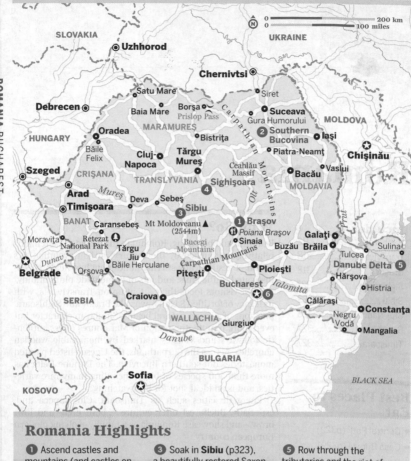

0   200 km
0   100 miles

SLOVAKIA
UKRAINE
● Uzhhorod
Chernivtsi ◉
● Satu Mare
◉ Siret
Debrecen ◉
Baia Mare
Borşa ◉
Prislop Pass
◉ Suceava
Gura Humorului
MOLDOVA
● Oradea
MARAMUREŞ
◉ Southern
Bucovina
◉ Iaşi
HUNGARY
Băile
Felix
● Bistriţa
Piatra-Neamţ
◉ Chişinău
Cluj-
Napoca
Târgu
Mureş
Ceahlău
Massif
Szeged ◉
CRIŞANA
TRANSLYVANIA
Sighişoara
● Bacău
Vaslui
Arad
Mureş
Deva
Sebeş
Sibiu
MOLDAVIA
Timişoara
BANAT
Caransebeş
Mt Moldoveanu ▲
(2544m)
Braşov
Poiana Braşov
Galaţi
Moraviţa
Retezat
National Park
Târgu
Jiu
Bucegi
Mountains
Sinaia
Buzău
Brăila
Tulcea
Sulina
Dunav
Băile Herculane
Carpathian Mountains
Danube Delta
Belgrade
Orşova
Piteşti
Ploieşti
Hârşova
Bucharest
Ialomiţa
Histria
SERBIA
Craiova
Călăraşi
Negru
Vodă
Constanţa
WALLACHIA
Giurgiu
Mangalia
Danube
BULGARIA
Sofia
BLACK SEA
KOSOVO

Romania Highlights

① Ascend castles and mountains (and castles on top of mountains), using **Braşov** (p318) as a base.

② Follow the Unesco World Heritage line of painted monasteries in **southern Bucovina** (p327).

③ Soak in **Sibiu** (p323), a beautifully restored Saxon town.

④ Explore the medieval citadel of **Sighişoara** (p321), Dracula's birthplace.

⑤ Row through the tributaries and the riot of nature in the **Danube Delta** (p328).

⑥ Enjoy the museums and cacophonous nightlife of the capital **Bucharest**.

BUCHAREST

🎵 021 / POP 1.9 MILLION

Romania's capital gets a bad rap, but in fact it's dynamic, energetic and more than a little bit funky. It's where unreconstructed communism meets unbridled capitalism; where the soporific forces of the EU meet the passions of the Balkans and Middle East. Many travellers give the city just a night or two before heading off to Transylvania but, frankly, that's not enough. Budget at least a few days to take in the museums, stroll the parks and hang out at trendy cafes.

◉ Sights

◉ South of the Centre

Palace of Parliament   HISTORIC BUILDING
(Palatul Parlamentului/Casa Poporului; 🎵 tour bookings 021-311 3611; www.cdep.ro; B-dul Naţiunile Unite; complete tour adults/students 45/23 lei,

One Week
Spend a day ambling around the **capital**, then take a train to **Braşov** – Transylvania's main event – for castles, activities and beer at streetside cafes. Spend a day in **Sighişoara**'s medieval citadel, then catch a train back to Bucharest or on to Budapest.

Two Weeks
Arrive in Bucharest by plane or **Timişoara** by train, then head into **Transylvania**, devoting a day or two each to Braşov, Sighişoara and **Sibiu**. Tour southern **Bucovina's** painted monasteries, then continue on to **Bucharest**.

standard adult/students 25/13 lei; ☺10am-4pm; Ⓜlzvor) The Palace of Parliament is the world's second-largest building (after the Pentagon) and former dictator Nicolae Ceauşescu's most infamous creation. Started in 1984 (and still unfinished), the building has more than 3000 rooms and covers 330,000 sq metres. Entry is by guided tour only (book in advance). Bring your passport since they check IDs. Today it houses the parliament.

👁 Old Town & Piaţa Revoluţiei

The Old Town and Piaţa Revoluţiei mark the heart of the centre. The Old Town was the seat of power in the 15th century, but today it's a pedestrianised warren of clubs and cafes.

Piaţa Revoluţiei, just to the north, saw the heaviest fighting in the 1989 overthrow of dictator Nicolae Ceauşescu. Those days are commemorated by the **Rebirth Memorial** in the middle of the square. Nearby, the balcony of the **Central Committee of the Communist Party Building** was where he made his infamous last speech before escaping (briefly) by helicopter.

Old Princely Court RUINS
(Palatul Voievodal, Curtea Veche; Str Franceză 21-23; admission 3 lei; ☺10am-6pm) The Old Princely Court dates to the 15th century, when Bucharest was the capital of the Wallachian principality. The ruins are being slowly excavated but for now you can wander around some of the rooms of the former court. The **Vlad Ţepeş statue** out the front makes a good photo.

Stavropoleos Church CHURCH
(☎021-313 4747; www.stavropoleos.ro; Str Stavropoleos 4; ☺7am-8pm) The tiny and lovely Stavropoleos Church, which dates from 1724, perches a bit oddly a block over from some of Bucharest's craziest Old Town carousing. It's one church, though, that will make a last-

ing impression, with its courtyard filled with tombstones and an ornate wooden interior and carved wooden doors.

National History Museum MUSEUM
(Muzeul Naţional de Istorie a Romaniei; ☎021-315 8207; www.mnir.ro; Calea Victoriei 12; adult/student 27/7 lei; ☺10am-6pm Wed-Sun) Houses an excellent collection of maps, statues and ancient jewels, and is particularly strong on the country's ties to ancient Rome, including a replica of the 2nd-century Trajan's Column. Our favourite piece, though, is not inside the museum at all, but rather on the steps outside: a controversial (and funny) **Statue of Emperor Trajan** standing naked holding a Dacian wolf.

National Art Museum MUSEUM
(Muzeul Naţional de Artă; ☎021-313 3030; www.mnar.arts.ro; Calea Victoriei 49-53; admission 15 lei; ☺11am-7pm Wed-Sun) Housed in the 19th-century Royal Palace, this massive museum – all signed in English – houses two permanent galleries: one for National Art and the other for European Masters. The national gallery is particularly strong on ancient and medieval art, while the European gallery includes some 12,000 pieces laid out by nationality.

👁 North of the Centre

Luxurious villas and parks line grand Şos Kiseleff, which begins at Piaţa Victoriei. The major landmark is the **Triumphal Arch** (Arcul de Triumf; Piaţa Arcul de Triumf), which stands halfway up Şos Kiseleff.

★ Grigore Antipa
Natural History Museum MUSEUM
(Muzeul de Istorie Naturală Grigore Antipa; ☎021-312 8826; www.antipa.ro; Şos Kiseleff 1; adult/student 20/5 lei ; ☺10am-8pm Wed-Sun; 👪) One of the few attractions in Bucharest squarely aimed at kids, this natural history museum

Central Bucharest

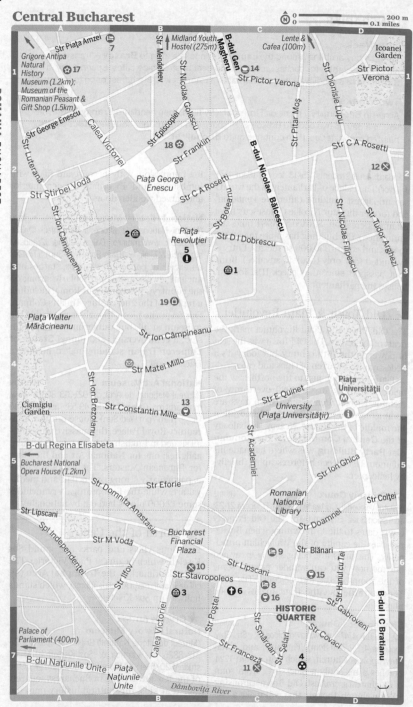

Central Bucharest

has been thoroughly renovated and now features modern bells and whistles such as video displays, games and interactive exhibits. Much of it is signed in English.

Museum of the Romanian Peasant
MUSEUM

(Muzeul Țăranului Român; ☎ 021-317 9661; www.muzeultaranuluiroman.ro; Șos Kiseleff 3; adult/child 8/2 lei; ☺10am-6pm Tue-Sun) The collection of peasant bric-a-brac, costumes, icons and partially restored houses makes this one of the most popular museums in the city. There's not much English signage, but little cards in English posted in each room give a flavour of what's on offer. An 18th-century church stands in the back lot, as does a great gift shop and restaurant.

National Village Museum
MUSEUM

(Muzeul Național al Satului; ☎ 021-317 9103; www.muzeul-satului.ro; Șos Kiseleff 28-30; adult/child 10/5 lei; ☺9am-7pm Tue-Sun, to 5pm Mon; 🖐) On the shores of Herăstrău Lake, this museum is a terrific open-air collection of several dozen homesteads, churches, mills and

windmills relocated from rural Romania. Built in 1936 by royal decree, it is one of Europe's oldest open-air museums and a good choice for kids to boot.

🛌 Sleeping

Hotels in Bucharest are typically aimed at businesspeople, and prices are higher here than the rest of the country. **Cert Accommodation** (☎0720-772 772; www.cert-accommodation.ro) offers good-value private apartment stays, starting at around 200 lei per night.

★ Little Bucharest Old Town Hostel
HOSTEL €

(☎0786-055 287; www.littlebucharest.ro; Str Smârdan 15; dm 45-60 lei, r 225 lei; ☻@🛜) Bucharest's most central hostel is super clean, white walled and well run. Accommodation is over two floors, with dorms ranging from 6 to 12 beds. Private doubles are also available. The staff is travel-friendly and youth oriented and can advise on sightseeing and fun. The location is in the middle of Bucharest's lively Old Town.

Midland Youth Hostel
HOSTEL €

(☎021-314 5323; www.themidlandhostel.com; Str Biserica Amzei 22; dm 40-60 lei; ☻❄@🛜) A happening hostel, with an excellent central location not far from Piața Romană. Accommodation is in six-, 10- or 14-bed dorms. There's a common kitchen and free breakfast.

Rembrandt Hotel
HOTEL €€

(☎021-313 9315; www.rembrandt.ro; Str Smârdan 11; tourist s/d 180/230 lei, standard s/d 260/300 lei, business s/d 350/380 lei; ☻❄@🛜) It's hard to say enough good things about this place. Stylish beyond its three-star rating, this 16-room, Dutch-run hotel faces the landmark National Bank in the historic centre. Rooms come in three categories: tourist, standard and business, with the chief difference being size. All rooms have polished wooden floors, timber headboards, and DVD players. Book well in advance.

Hotel Amzei
HOTEL €€€

(☎021-313 9400; www.hotelamzei.ro; Piața Amzei 8; s/d 450/550 lei; ☻❄🛜) This tastefully reconstructed villa just off Calea Victoriei has 22 rooms on four floors. The wrought-iron atrium in the lobby lends a refined feel. The rooms are in a more restrained contemporary style, but everything about the place says quality.

✕ Eating

★ Caru' cu Bere
ROMANIAN €€

(☏ 021-313 7560; www.carucubere.ro; Str Stavropoleos 3-5; mains 20-45 lei; ⊙8am-midnight Sun-Thu, 8am-2am Fri & Sat; 🛜) Despite a decidedly tourist-leaning atmosphere, with peasant-girl hostesses and sporadic traditional song-and-dance numbers, Bucharest's oldest beer house continues to draw in a strong local crowd. The colourful belle epoque interior and stained-glass windows dazzle, as does the classic Romanian food. Dinner reservations recommended.

Divan
MIDDLE EASTERN €€

(☏ 021-312 3034; www.thedivan.ro; Str Franceză 46-48; mains 20-30 lei; ⊙10am-2am; 🛜) Deservedly popular Turkish and Middle Eastern place, where snagging a prized terrace table will take a mix of patience and good fortune. The waiter will first bring around a tantalising selection of starters, such as hummus and babaganoush. Select a few of these and then settle back for the enormous platters of grilled meats and kebabs.

Lente & Cafea
INTERNATIONAL €€

(☏ 021-310 7424; www.lente.ro; Str Gen Praporgescu 31; mains 25-40 lei; ⊙11.30am-1am; 🛜) The *tomatina*, tomato soup served with croutons and yellow cheese, is a classic, but all the entrees are creative, filling and good value. We especially like the 'Anthos' main, which is strips of beef tenderloin flavoured with celery soy sauce and served with basmati rice. The garden terrace is a respite on a hot day.

♀ Drinking & Nightlife

★ Grădina Verona
CAFE

(☏ 0732-003 060; Str Pictor Verona 13-15; ⊙9am-1am; 🛜) A garden oasis hidden behind the Cărturești bookshop, serving standard-issue but excellent espresso drinks and some of the wackiest iced-tea infusions ever concocted in Romania, such as peony flower, mango and lime (it's not bad).

St Patrick
PUB

(☏ 021-313 0336; www.stpatrick.ro; Str Smârdan 25; 🛜) This popular pub gets the authentic Irish bar look down with dark woods and a green ceiling. Grab a table on busy Str Smârdan and settle back with a pint of Guinness or cider. They also do good renditions of standards such as steak and kidney pie (25 lei) and Irish breakfast (25 lei).

Control
CLUB

(☏ 0733-927 861; www.control-club.ro; Str Constantin Mille 4; ⊙6pm-4am; 🛜) This is a favourite among club-goers who like alternative, indie and garage sounds. Hosts both live acts and DJs, depending on the night.

La Muse
CLUB

(☏ 0734-000 236; www.lamuse.ro; Str Lipscani 53; ⊙9am-3am Sun-Wed, to 6am Thu-Sat; 🛜) Just about anything goes at this popular Old Town dance club. Try to arrive early, around 11pm, since it can get crowded later. La Muse draws everyone from university students to young professionals in their 20s and 30s. Everyone looks great.

☆ Entertainment

Bucharest National Opera House
OPERA

(Opera Națională București; ☏ box office 021-310 2661; www.operanb.ro; B-dul Mihail Kogălniceanu 70-72; tickets 10-70 lei; ⊙box office 9am-1pm & 3-7pm) The city's premier venue for classical opera and ballet. Buy tickets online or at the venue box office.

Romanian Athenaeum
CLASSICAL MUSIC

(Ateneul Roman; ☏ box office 021-315 6875; www.fge.org.ro; Str Franklin 1-3; tickets 15-65 lei; ⊙box office noon-7pm Tue-Fri, 4-7pm Sat, 10-11am Sun) The historic Athenaeum is home to the respected George Enescu Philharmonic and offers a wide array of classical music concerts from September to May as well as a number of one-off musical shows and spectacles throughout the year. Buy tickets at the venue box office.

Green Hours 22 Jazz Club
JAZZ

(☏ concerts 0788-452 485; www.greenhours.ro; Calea Victoriei 120; ⊙6pm-2am) This old-school basement jazz club runs a lively program of jazz nights through the week and hosts an international jazz fest in May/June. Check the website for the schedule during your trip and try to book in advance.

🔒 Shopping

★ Anthony Frost
BOOKS

(☏ 021-311 5136; www.anthonyfrost.ro; Calea Victoriei 45; ⊙10am-8pm Mon-Fri, to 7pm Sat, to 2pm Sun) Serious readers will want to make time for arguably the best English-language bookshop in Eastern Europe. Located in a small passage next to the Crețulescu Church, this shop has a carefully chosen selection of highbrow contemporary fiction and nonfiction.

Museum of the
Romanian Peasant Gift Shop   FOLK CRAFTS
(www.muzeultaranuluiroman.ro;   Şos Kiseleff 3;
⊙10am-6pm Tue-Sun) For beautifully made woven rugs, table runners, national Romanian costumes, ceramics and other local crafts, don't miss the excellent folk-art shop at the Museum of the Romanian Peasant; access to the shop is from the back of the museum.

ℹ️ Information

You'll find hundreds of bank branches and ATMs in the centre. Most banks have a currency-exchange office and can provide cash advances against credit or debit cards. Always bring your passport, since you will have to show it to change money.

Best Cafe (✐021-312 4816; www.best-cafe.ro; B-dul Mihail Kogălniceanu 19; per hr 5 lei; ⊙24hr; 🕾) Internet cafe.

Bucharest Tourist Information Center (✐021-305 5500, ext 1003; http://en.see bucharest.ro; Piaţa Universităţii; ⊙10am-6pm Mon-Fri, to 2pm Sat & Sun) This small, poorly stocked tourist office is the best the city can offer visitors. While there's not much information on hand, the English-speaking staff can field basic questions, make suggestions and help locate things on a map.

Central Post Office (✐021-315 9030; www.posta-romana.ro; Str Matei Millo 10; ⊙7.30am-8pm Mon-Fri)

Emergency Clinic Hospital (✐021-599 2300, 021-9622; www.scub.ro; Calea Floreasca 8; ⊙24hr) The first port of call in any serious emergency. Arguably the city's (and country's) best emergency hospital.

ℹ️ Getting There & Away

AIR

All international and domestic flights use Henri Coandă International Airport (p331; often referred to by its previous name, Otopeni). Henri Coandă is 17km north of Bucharest on the road to Braşov. The airport is a modern facility, with restaurants, newsagents, currency exchange offices and ATMs.

It's also the hub for national carrier **Tarom** (✐call centre 021-204 6464, office 021-316 0220; www.tarom.ro; Spl Independenţei 17, City Centre; ⊙8.30am-7.30pm Mon-Fri, 9am-1.30pm Sat) Tarom has a comprehensive network of internal flights to major Romanian cities as well as to capitals and big cities around Europe and the Middle East.

BUS

It's possible to get just about anywhere in the country by bus from Bucharest, but figuring out where your bus or maxitaxi departs from can be tricky. Bucharest has several bus stations and they don't seem to follow any discernible logic.

The best bet is to consult the websites www.autogari.ro and www.cdy.ro. Both keep up-to-date timetables and are fairly easy to manage. Another option is to ask your hotel to help with arrangements or book through a travel agency.

CAR & MOTORCYCLE

Driving in Bucharest is lunacy and you won't want to do it for more than a few minutes before you stow the car and use the metro. If you're travelling around by car and want to visit Bucharest for the day, park at a metro station on the outskirts and take the metro in.

Autonom (✐airport 0742-215 361, call centre 0721-442 266; www.autonom.com; Henri Coandă International Airport; rates per day start at around 150 lei) Reputable, locally owned car rental company offers a range of Romanian and European makes.

TRAIN

Domestic and international trains use the main station, **Gara de Nord** (✐phone reservations 021-9522; www.cfrcalatori.ro; Piaţa Gara de Nord 1; Ⓜ Gara de Nord). It's around 2km from the centre and best reached by metro. The station has restaurants, ATMs and left-luggage facilities.

Buy tickets at ticket windows. For international tickets, the private travel agency **Wasteels** (✐021-300 2730; www.triptkts.ro; Gara de Nord; ⊙10am-5pm Mon-Fri), located inside the station, can sort out complicated connections.

Sample destinations and fares from Bucharest on fast IC trains include Braşov (50 lei, three hours, several daily), Cluj-Napoca (94 lei, 10 hours, two daily), Sibiu (75 lei, six hours, two daily), Timişoara (105 lei, nine hours, two daily) and Suceava (94 lei, seven hours, one daily).

ℹ️ Getting Around

TO/FROM THE AIRPORT
Bus

Express bus 783 leaves every 30 to 40 minutes from the airport arrivals hall to various points in the centre, including Piaţa Victoriei and Piaţa Unirii. Buy a ticket for 7 lei from the RATB ticket booth near the stop.

Taxi

Order a taxi by touchscreen at the airport arrivals terminal. Simply choose a company and rate (all are about the same), and you'll get a ticket and number. Pay the driver. A reputable taxi to the centre should cost no more than 70 lei.

PUBLIC TRANSPORT

Bucharest's public transport system of metros, buses, trams and trolleybuses is operated by the transport authority **RATB** (Regia Autonomă de Transport Bucureşti; ✆ info 021-9391; www. ratb.ro). The system runs from 5am to approximately 11.30pm.

For buses, trams and trolleybuses, buy tickets at any RATB street kiosk, marked *'casa de bilete'*. Tickets for standard buses cost 1.30 lei per trip and are sold in two-ticket increments for 2.60 lei. Tickets for a small number of express buses, such as bus 783 which goes to the airport, cost 7 lei (good for two journeys). Punch your ticket on board or risk a spot fine.

Metro stations are identified by a large 'M'. To use the metro, buy a magnetic-strip ticket available at ticketing machines inside station entrances (have small bills handy). Tickets valid for two journeys cost 4 lei. A 10-trip ticket costs 15 lei.

TRANSYLVANIA

After a century of being name-checked in literature and cinema, the word 'Transylvania' enjoys worldwide recognition. The mere mention conjures a vivid landscape of mountains, castles, spooky moonlight and at least one well-known count with a wicked overbite. Unexplained puncture wounds notwithstanding, Transylvania is all those things and more. A melange of architecture and chic sidewalk cafes punctuate the towns of Braşov, Sighişoara and Sibiu, while the vibrant student town Cluj-Napoca has some vigorous nightlife. Bran Castle, too, is well worth the trip – even if 'Dracula' never did spend much time there.

Braşov

POP 253,200

Legend has it the Pied Piper re-emerged from Hamelin in Braşov, and indeed there's something whimsical about the city, with its fairy-tale turrets and cobbled streets. Dramatically overlooked by Mt Tâmpa, the trees sporting a russet-gold coat (and cocky Hollywood-style sign), this is a remarkably relaxed city. Wander its maze of streets, stopping for caffeine injections at bohemian cafes, and lose yourself in a beguiling coalescence of Austro-Hungarian gingerbread roofs, baroque statues, medieval spires and Soviet flat-tops.

◎ Sights

In addition to the sights below, explore the Old Town walls and bastions that line the centre on the eastern and western flanks. Many have been restored.

Piaţa Sfatului   PUBLIC SQUARE

This wide square, chock-full with cafes, was once the heart of medieval Braşov. In the centre stands the 1420 **Council House** (Casa Sfatului), topped by the **Trumpeter's Tower**, in which town councillors, known as centurions, would meet. These days at midday, traditionally costumed musicians appear from the top of the tower like figures in a Swiss clock.

Black Church   CHURCH

(Biserica Neagră; ✆ 0268-511 824; www.honter usgemeinde.ro; Curtea Johannes Honterus 2; adult/child 8/5 lei; ◎ 10am-7pm Tue-Sat, noon-7pm Sun) Braşov's main landmark, the Black Church is the largest Gothic church between Vienna and İstanbul, and is still used by German Lutherans today. Built between 1383 and 1480, it was named for its appearance after a fire in 1689. The original statues from the exterior of the apse are now inside.

Mt Tâmpa   MOUNTAIN

(Telecabina Tampa; ✆ 0268-478 657; Aleea Tiberiu Brediceanu; cable car one way/return 10/16 lei; ◎ Tue-Sun 9.30am-5pm) Towering over the city from the east, 940m Mt Tâmpa – with its Hollywood-style sign – was Braşov's original defensive wall. You can hike up (about an hour) or take a cable car to reach a small viewing platform offering stunning views over the city and the possibility of a light bite or drink at a communist-era dining room.

⊨ Sleeping

Centrum House Hostel   HOSTEL €

(✆ 0727-793 169; www.hostelbrasov.eu; Str Republicii 58; dm 45 lei; r 135-360 lei; ❀ ⊛) This clean and airy modern hostel, located dead centre down a passageway off Str Republicii, opened its doors in 2013 and is a great choice. The white walls, with a splash of colour here and there, give it a fresh feel. Most rooms offer various combinations of bunks and dorms (check the website). The White Room is a comfy private triple.

Braşov

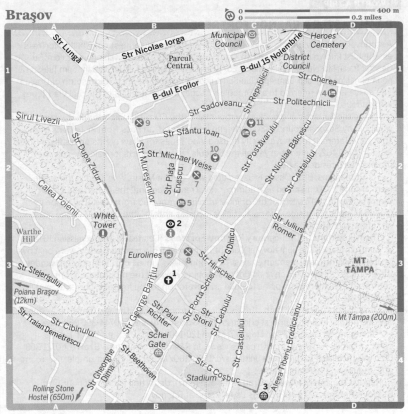

Rolling Stone Hostel HOSTEL €
(☎0268-513 965; www.rollingstone.ro; Str Piatra Mare 2a; dm 40 lei, r from 120 lei; ⊜@☎) Run by helpful sisters with unlimited reserves of energy, super-friendly Stone attracts a cosmo stew of travellers. Dorms are a little crowded, save for the smaller one downstairs. The private double room (without bathroom) has couches and armoire. You'll be given a map and bags of info on arrival. Personal lockers, organised tours and basic breakfast.

★**Casa Reims** BOUTIQUE HOTEL €€
(☎0368-467 325; www.casareims.ro; Str Castelului 85; s/d 200/250 lei; P⊜❄☎) High-end mum and dad boutique with glamourous touches like quality linens, flower-print spreads and hardwood floors. You'll get an enthusiastic welcome at the reception desk and a hearty home-cooked breakfast. There's a big enclosed parking lot for drivers and the pedestrian centre is five minutes away on foot. Recommended.

Braşov

★**Casa Wagner** HOTEL € €€
(☎0268-411 253; www.casa-wagner.com; Piaţa Sfatului 5; s/d incl breakfast 260/320 lei; ⊜❄@☎)

BRAN CASTLE & RÂȘNOV FORTRESS

A stopover in Brașov affords an excellent chance to take in some spooky hilltop fortresses; the best known is certainly **Bran Castle** (✆0268-237 700; www.bran-castle.com; Str General Traian Moșoiu 24; adult/student 25/10 lei, camera or video 20 lei; ⊙9am-6pm Tue-Sun & noon-6pm Mon May-Sep, 9am-4pm Tue-Sun & noon-4pm Mon Oct-Apr), 30km south of Brașov. The castle is often referred to as 'Dracula's Castle', though its links to the real Vlad Țepeș are tenuous.

Facing the flatlands and backed by mountains, the 60m-tall castle is spectacular. It was built by Saxons around 1380 to defend important Bran pass from incursions from Turks and Tatars. It may have briefly housed Vlad Țepeș for a few nights on his flight from the Turks in 1462, but contrary to all the Dracula tat and T-shirts for sale, the ruler never maintained a residence here.

For Romanians, Bran Castle is associated with Queen Marie, who lived in the castle from around 1920. It served as a summer royal residence until the forced abdication of King Michael in 1947. Much of the original furniture imported from Western Europe by Queen Marie is still inside. The castle ticket includes entry to the open-air village museum at the foot of the castle.

The hilltop ruins of 13th-century **Râșnov Fortress** (Cetatea Râșnov; admission 10 lei; ⊙9am-7pm May-Oct, to 5pm Nov-Apr), about 12km from Bran toward Brașov, were built by Teutonic Knights as protection against Tatar and Turkish invasions. Visitors can wander the grounds to see a church and admire sweeping views of the mountains. From the central square, there were plans to build an elevator up to the fortress; currently, you'll have to hike it.

Most visitors do one or both sites as a day trip from Brașov, though there are a couple of good hotels. In Bran, our first choice is **The Guest House** (✆0744-306 062; www.guesthouse.ro; Str General Traian Moșoiu 7; r from 120-140 lei, tr 150 lei; P ❉ 🛜 🛉), a welcoming, family-run pension with castle views. In Râșnov, **Pensiunea Stefi** (✆0721-303 009; www.hotelstefi-ro.com; Piața Unirii 5; s/d/tr 90/100/130 lei; ❉🛜) is a simple, five-room guesthouse on the main square.

Regular minibuses leave for Bran (7 lei, one hour), departing every half hour from Brașov's Autogara 2 (p321). Buses usually stop at Râșnov.

This former 15th-century German bank has been converted to a luxury boutique hotel, with 24 well-appointed rooms. Right in the heart of the city, its exposed-brick walls, tasteful furnishings, modern en suites, welcoming breakfast area and pleasant management make this an excellent choice.

✖ Eating

★ Bistro de l'Arte
BISTRO €€

(✆0720-535 566; www.bistrodelarte.ro; Str Piața Enescu 11; mains 15-35 lei; ⊙9am-1am Mon-Sat, noon-1am Sun; 🛜) Tucked down a cobbled street straight out of a folk tale, this joint has decidedly boho genes with walls dotted with local artists' work. Gazpacho soup, shrimps and tomato gratin, snails...or just a croque monsieur. Perfect for nursing a cappuccino and working on your laptop.

Sergiana
ROMANIAN €€

(✆0268-419 775; http://sergianagrup.ro; Str Mureșenilor 28; mains 25-40 lei; ⊙11am-11pm)

Authentically Saxon, this subterranean carnivore's heaven has two sections: the white room for 'pure' nonsmokers, and the exposed brick vaults for *fumeurs*. Choose from a menu of venison, stag, boar, pork ribs, sirloin steak, and Transylvanian sour soup with smoked gammon and tarragon (11.50 lei). A hunter's dream.

Keller Steak House
STEAK €€€

(✆0268-472 278; www.kellersteakhouse.ro; Str Apollonia Hirscher 2; mains 60-90 lei; ⊙11am-11pm) One of Brașov's premier steakhouses, you can eat inside its ochre interior or tackle your sirloin outside on the terrace. Steak and Roquefort cheese, salad and boar...one thing is for certain: you won't leave here with an empty stomach.

♟ Drinking & Nightlife

Festival 39
BAR

(✆0743-339 909; www.festival39.com; Str Republicii 62; ⊙7am-midnight) This romantic watering hole is an art-deco dream of stained-glass ceilings, wrought-iron finery, candelabra and leather banquettes, and has a bar long enough to keep an army of barflies content. Sheer elan.

Deane's Irish Pub & Grill   PUB

(☑0268-474 542; www.deanes.ro; Str Republicii 19; ⊘10am-1am Mon-Thu, 10am-3am Fri & Sat, noon-1am Sun) As if transplanted from Donegal, this subterranean Irish pub with its early-20th-century cloudy mirrored bar, shadowy booths and old-world soundtracks, is a haven for the Guinness-thirsty. Live music some nights.

ⓘ Information

You'll find numerous ATMs and banks on and around Str Republicii and B-dul Eroilor.

County Hospital (☑0268-320 022; www.hospbv.ro; Calea Bucureşti 25-27; ⊘24hr) Northeast of the centre.

Internet Cafe (Str Michael Weiss 11; per hr 3 lei; ⊘24 hr)

Tourist Information Centre (☑0268-419 078; www.brasovcity.ro; Piaţa Sfatului 30; ⊘10am-6pm Mon-Fri) Easily spotted in the gold city council building in the centre of the square, the English-speaking staff offer free maps and brochures and track down hotel vacancies and train and bus times. The centre shares space with the history museum.

ⓘ Getting There & Around

BUS

Maxitaxis leave every half-hour for Bucharest (30 lei, 2½ hours); about four or five maxitaxis leave for Sibiu (25 lei, 2½ hours); nine or 10 go daily to Sighişoara (25 lei, two hours). The most accessible station is **Autogara 1** (Bus Station 1; ☑0268-427 267; www.autogara.ro; B-dul Gării 1), next to the train station. Some buses, including several to Bran (7 lei, one hour), leave from **Autogara 2** (Bus Station 2; ☑0268-426 332; www.autogari.ro; Str Avram Iancu 114), 3km north of the centre.

European routes are handled by **Eurolines** (☑0268-474 008; www.eurolines.ro; Piaţa Sfatului 18; ⊘9am-8pm Mon-Fri, 10am-2pm Sat).

TRAIN

The **train station** (Gara Braşov; ☑0268-421 700; www.cfrcalatori.ro; B-dul Gării 5) is 2km northeast of the centre. Buy tickets at the station. There are ATMs and a left-luggage office. Bus 4 runs from the station to Piaţa Unirii in the centre (or walk 20 minutes).

Braşov is an important train junction and connections are good to cities around the country. Trains to Budapest also pass through here. Daily domestic train service includes hourly to Bucharest (50 lei, three hours), several to Sighişoara (41 lei, 2½ hours), two to Sibiu (50 lei, four hours) and several to Cluj-Napoca (75 lei, six hours).

Sighişoara

POP 26,400

From the moment you enter Sighişoara's fortified walls, wending your way along cobblestones to its central square, the town burns itself into your memory. It's like stepping into a kid's fairy tale, the narrow streets aglow with lustrously coloured 16th-century houses, their gingerbread roofs tumbling down to pretty cafes. Horror fans won't be disappointed either, for this Unesco-protected citadel was reputedly the birthplace of one of history's great 'monsters' – Vlad Ţepeş (The Impaler).

⊙ Sights

Most sights are clustered in the magical, medieval **Citadel** perched on a hillock and fortified with a 14th-century wall (to which 14 towers and five artillery bastions were later added).

Clock Tower   MUSEUM

(Turnul cu Ceas; ☑0265-771 108; Piaţa Muzeului 1; adult/child 12/3 lei; ⊘9am-6.30pm Tue-Fri, 10am-5.30pm Sat & Sun) The symbol of the town is this magnificent medieval clock tower, built in the 14th century and expanded 200 years later. It originally housed the town council, but these days it's purely decorative. The clock and figurines were added in the 17th century. The figurines represent different medieval characters, including Peace, Justice and Law, as well as those representing Day and Night.

The tower houses a **history museum**, which affords access to the viewing platform on the upper floor. The museum is hard to follow (English signage is spotty), but there's a small exhibition on local hero and physicist Hermann Oberth. A couple floors up you can see the clock's famed figures, as well as the clanking innards of the clock behind them.

Casa Dracula   HISTORIC BUILDING

(☑0265-771 596; www.casavladdracul.ro; Str Cositorarilor 5; admission 5 lei; ⊘10am-10pm) Vlad Ţepeş (aka Dracula) was reputedly born in this house in 1431 and lived here until the age of four. It's now a decent restaurant, but for a small admission, the staff will show you Vlad's old room (and give you a little scare). Bubble-burster: the building is indeed centuries old, but has been completely rebuilt since Vlad's days.

Church on the Hill
CHURCH

(Biserica din Deal; admission 3 lei; ⊙10am-6pm) A powerfully evocative late-Gothic church is situated high atop 'School Hill' (420m) and is well worth the hike to see the restored interior, with remains of frescoes dating back to the 15th century. The period altarpiece dates from 1520. Entry is via a *scara acoperită* (covered wooden stairway). Opposite the church is a historic German cemetery (open daily from 8am to 8pm).

🛏 Sleeping

Pensiune Cristina & Pavel
PENSION €

(☑0744-119 211, 0744-159 667; www.pensiuneafaur.ro; Str Cojocarilor 1; dm/s/d 48/90/132 lei; P 🐾) The floors are so clean at this four-room, one-dorm guesthouse, you could eat your lunch off them. En suite rooms are painted in a soothing off-white, plus there's an idyllic garden bursting with flowers. The dining/self-catering area is welcoming and, should you need it, there's a laundry service.

Burg Hostel
HOSTEL €

(☑0265-778 489; www.burghostel.ro; Str Bastionului 4-6; dm 40 lei, s/d without bathroom 70/90 lei, with bathroom 80/95 lei; 🐾🛜) Basic Burg is ubiquitously wood-walled with a number of cosy rooms – the triples have the most space. Single rooms are adequate. There's a bar downstairs, plus a pleasant courtyard to read in.

Casa Wagner
HOTEL €€

(☑0265-506 014; www.casa-wagner.com; Piața Cetății 7; s/d/ste 220/260/350 lei; 🐾🛜) This appealing 16th-century hotel has 32 rooms spread across three buildings. Think peach walls, candelabra, dark-wood furniture and tasteful rugs. The rooms in the eaves are smaller but wood-floored, cosy and very romantic for writing those Harker-esque diary entries. The ground-floor restaurant occasionally has live music in the evenings.

★ Casa Georgius Krauss
BOUTIQUE HOTEL €€€

(☑0365-730 840; www.casakrauss.com; Str Bastionului 11; d/ste 300/450 lei; 🐾🌐@🛜) Dazzling boutique hotel hived out of an old burgher's house at the northern end of the citadel. The lavish restoration left period details like wood-beamed ceilings, wooden floors and, in some rooms, medieval frescoes intact. The Krauss suite, no 2, with wood beams and wall paintings, is a harmonious synthesis of ancient and modern. Good in-house restaurant.

🍴 Eating

★ Central Park
INTERNATIONAL €€

(☑0365-730 006; www.hotelcentralpark.ro; Piața Hermann Oberth 25; mains 25-40 lei; ⊙11am-11pm; 🛜) Even if you're not staying at the Central Park hotel, plan a meal here. Sighișoara is short on good restaurants and this is the best around. The food is a mix of Romanian and international dishes, and the carefully selected wine list offers the best domestic labels. Dress up for the lavish dining room or relax on the terrace.

Casa Dracula
ROMANIAN €€

(☑0265-771 596; www.casavladdracul.ro; Str Cositorarilor 5; mains 30 lei; ⊙11am-11pm; 🛜📶) Despite the ghoulish Dracula bust mounted to the wall, the house where Vlad was born could have been dealt a worse blow than this atmospheric, wood-panelled restaurant. The menu scuttles from tomato soup to salmon fillet – all with Dracula-related references. With a little embellishment from you, your kids will love it.

ℹ Information

Cultural Heritage Info Centre (☑0788-115 511; www.dordeduca.ro; Piața Muzeului 6; ⊙10am-6pm Tue-Sun) Rents out bikes (10 lei per two hours) and offers guided tours of Sighișoara and the fortified churches as well as DVDs on the same subject. It also has maps of the city and region.

Tourist Information (☑0265-770 415; www.infosighisoara.ro; Str O Goga 8; ⊙10am-6pm Tue-Sat) Private accommodation service masquerading as a tourist information office. Can help find rooms but don't expect anything else.

ℹ Getting There & Away

BUS

Next to the train station on Str Libertății, the **bus station** (Autogari Sighisoara; ☑0265-771 260; www.autogari.ro; Str Libertății 53) sends buses around the country, including to Cluj-Napoca (30 lei, three hours) and Brașov (25 lei, two hours).

TRAIN

Sighișoara is on a main international line and has good train connections. Popular destinations include Brașov (41 lei, two hours), Bucharest (69 lei, five hours) and Cluj-Napoca (62 lei, four hours). You'll need to change trains in Mediaş to reach Sibiu (26 lei, four hours). Three daily trains go to Budapest (150 lei, 11 hours). Buy tickets at the **train station** (⏺0265-771130; www.cfr calatori.ro; Str Libertăţii 51).

Sibiu

POP 137,020

Instantly charming, with a maze of cobbled streets and baroque squares, Romania's cultural first lady has a magic all its own. Composers Franz Liszt and Johann Strauss were drawn here in the 19th century, and in 2007 Sibiu became the first Romanian city to be named an EU Capital of Culture. Most months have myriad things going on, from festivals and exhibitions to theatre and opera. There are plenty of cafes for people-watching in the three main squares.

◉ Sights

Brukenthal Museum MUSEUM
(⏺0269-217 691; www.brukenthalmuseum.ro; Piaţa Mare 5; adult/student 20/5 lei; ☉Tue-Sun 10am-6pm) The most important art museum in this part of the country features separate galleries dedicated to European (1st floor) and Romanian (2nd floor) art. The European collection is heavy on Dutch and German painters, and features at least one masterpiece: Pieter Brueghel the Younger's *The Massacre of Innocents*. The Romanian collection is rich in portraits and landscapes.

Biserica Evanghelică CHURCH
(Evangelical Church; Piaţa Huet; closed for reconstruction) The Gothic church, built from 1300 to 1520, was closed and covered in scaffolding during our research due to long-term renovation. The work should be complete by 2016. Once the church reopens, visitors will again be able to admire the 1772 organ, featuring a staggering 6002 pipes, or climb the **church tower**.

Pharmaceutical Museum MUSEUM
(⏺0269-218 191; www.brukenthalmuseum.ro; Piaţa Mică 26; adult/child 10/2.50 lei; ☉10am-6pm Tue-Sun Apr-Oct, 10am-6pm Wed-Sun Nov-Mar) Housed in the Piaţa Mică pharmacy (opened in 1600), the Pharmaceutical Museum is a three-room collection packed with pills and powders, old microscopes and scary medical instruments. Some exhibits highlight Samuel Hahnemann, a founder of homeopathy in the 1770s.

Astra Museum of Traditional Folk Civilisation MUSEUM
(Muzeul Civilizaţiei Populare Tradiţionale Astra; ⏺0269-202 447, reservations 0269-216 453; www.muzeulastra.ro; Str Pădurea Dumbrava 16-20; adult/student 15/7.50 lei; ☉museum 10am-6pm Tue-Sun, gift shop 9am-5pm Tue-Sun) Five kilometres from the centre, this sprawling open-air museum has a dazzling 120 traditional dwellings, mills and churches brought from around the country and set among two small lakes and a tiny zoological garden. Many are signed in English, with maps showing where the structures came from. There's also a nice gift shop and restaurant with creekside bench seats.

🛏 Sleeping

Welt Hostel HOSTEL
(⏺0269-700 704; www.weltkultur.ro; Str Nicolea Bălcescu 13; dm 48-53 lei; ☒@☎) Centrally located hostel offers Teutonically clean accommodation in four-, six- and eight-bed dorms. The choicest rooms are those toward the street; they are brighter and offer views out toward Piaţa Mare. There's a kitchen for self-caterers, as well as lockers and a friendly chill-out room. Have coffee or wine at the trendy ground-floor cafe.

The Council BOUTIQUE HOTEL €€
(⏺0369-452 524; www.thecouncil.ro; Piaţa Mică 31; r standard/deluxe 220/280 lei; ☒@☎) Posh boutique hotel occupies a historic 14th-century townhouse that once served as the town hall. Rooms are priced as standard or deluxe, with the latter being larger and usually offering split levels, wood rafters, and better views. All of the rooms are decorated differently, so you might want to look at a few. It's dead central.

Casa Luxemburg HOTEL €€
(⏺0269-216 854; www.kultours.ro; Piaţa Mică 16; s/d/tr from 260/290/350 lei; ☒☎) Super rooms with parquet flooring, minimal but tasteful furnishings, and well-chosen artwork. There are flat-screen TVs, armoires, bureaus and fresh-looking en suites. Overlooking the Evangelical Church and Piaţa Mică.

✗ Eating

★**Crama Sibiul Vechi** ROMANIAN €€
(⏺0269-210 461; www.sibiulvechi.ro; Str A. Papiu Ilarian 3; mains 25-30 lei; ☉11am-10pm) Hidden in an old wine cellar with its staff dressed in traditional garb, this is the most rustically evocative restaurant in Sibiu. It's certainly the most authentic place to explore Romanian fare such as cheese croquettes, minced

THE WOODEN CHURCHES OF MARAMUREŞ

North of Transylvania, Maramureş is regarded as Romania's most traditional area, scattered with steepled wooden churches and villagers' homes fronted by ornately carved wooden gates.

Some of the churches date back as far as the 14th century and reflect a time when Orthodox Romanians were forbidden by their Hungarian rulers to build churches in stone. Several of the structures are now Unesco-listed heritage sites.

A good base for exploring this rural charm is the Valea Izei (Izei Valley), accessible by car or bus from **Sighetu Marmaţiei**. The valley follows the Iza River eastward from the city to the village of Ieud and beyond.

The first village, **Vadu Izei**, lies at the confluence of the Iza and Mara Rivers, 6km south of Sighetu Marmaţiei. Its museum is in the oldest house in the village (1750). From Vadu Izei, continue for 12km to **Bârsana**, dating from 1326. In 1720 it built its first church, the interior paintings of which were created by local artists Hodor Toador and Ion Plohod. The famous Orthodox **Bârsana Monastery** (Mănăstirea Bârsana) is a popular pilgrimage spot; however, the church was built only in the 1990s.

Continue south to **Rozavlea**. Its church, dedicated to the archangels Michael and Gabriel, was constructed between 1717 and 1720 in another village and moved to Rozavlea to the site of an ancient church destroyed by Tatars.

From Rozavlea, continue south to the sleepy village of **Botiza**, one of the prettiest in all of Maramureş and site of the some of the region's best homestays. Botiza's old church, built in 1694, is overshadowed by the giant new church, constructed in 1974 to serve devout Orthodox families.

Packed with wooden houses and pensioners in traditional garb, the nearby village of **Ieud** has two beautiful churches, including possibly the region's oldest wooden church.

---

meatballs and peasant's stew with polenta. Dimly lit, brick walled...welcome to a local treasure.

Weinkeller　　　　　　　　　ROMANIAN €€
(☑ 0269-210 319; www.weinkeller.ro; Str Turnului 2; mains 18-30 lei; ⊙ noon-midnight; 🛜) Simple menu of just half-a-dozen main dishes, mixing traditional Romanian cuisine, like stuffed cabbage leaves, with Austro-Hungarian fare like *Tafelspitz* (boiled beef) and goulash. Excellent Nachbil wines pair well with the food. The snug cellar location feels just right on a cool evening.

🍸 Drinking & Nightlife

Cafe Wien　　　　　　　　　　　CAFE
(☑ 0269-223 223; www.cafewien.ro; Piaţa Huet 4; ⊙ 10am-2am Mon, 9am-2am Tue-Sun; 🛜) After you've strolled the lovely squares, repair here for your *kaffee und kuchen* (coffee and cake). True to its name, the Wien specialises in Old World sweets, and the view off the terrace to the lower town below is arguably the best in town.

Bohemian Flow Art & Pub　　　　　　BAR
(☑ 0269-218 388; www.bohemianflow.ro; Piaţa Mică 26; ⊙ Mon-Sun 4pm-5am) Lively backstreet cellar club beneath Old Town Hostel, piping out reggae and good vibes for a young crowd.

☆ Entertainment

Philharmonic　　　　　　　　CLASSICAL MUSIC
(☑ tickets 0735-566 486; www.filarmonicasibiu.ro; Str Cetăţii 3-5; tickets 16-20 lei; ⊙ box office noon-4pm Mon-Thu) Founded in 1949, this has played a key role in maintaining Sibiu's prestige as a main cultural centre of Transylvania.

Radu Stancu National Theatre　　　THEATRE
(☑ tickets 0369-101 578; www.tnrs.ro; B-dul Corneliu Coposu 2; tickets 20 lei) Plays here are usually in Romanian, with occasional productions in German through the week (check the website). It hosts the International Theatre Festival in June. Buy tickets online or at the theatre 30 minutes before performances start.

ℹ Information

ATMs are located all over the centre.

Kultours (☑ 0269-216 854; www.kultours.ro; Piaţa Mică 16; ⊙ 9am-9pm) Travel agent offering loads of city tours starting at around 40 lei as well as creative day trips and cycling tours, starting at around 90 lei. Helpful staff can hand out maps and advise on what to see and do.

Tourist Information Centre (☑ 0269-208 913; www.turism.sibiu.ro; Piaţa Mare 2; ⊙ 9am-5pm Mon-Sat, to 1pm Sun) Based at the City Hall, staff here are fantastically helpful at guiding you to make the best of the city, and cultural events, finding accommodation, and booking train and bus tickets. They also give away an excellent city map.

❶ Getting There & Around

BUS

The **bus station** (Autogara Sibiu; www.autogari. ro; Piaţa 1 Decembrie 1918) is opposite the train station. Bus and maxitaxi services include Braşov (28 lei, 2½ hours, two daily), Bucharest (42 lei, 5½ hours, six daily), Cluj-Napoca (32 lei, 3½ hours, several daily) and Timişoara (55 lei, six hours, three daily).

TRAIN

There are five daily direct trains to Braşov (46 lei, 2½ hours), and two trains to Bucharest (75 lei, six hours) and Timişoara (75 lei, six hours). To get to/from Cluj-Napoca (54 lei, four hours), you'll usually change at Copşa Mică or Mediaş (about nine or 10 trains daily).

The **train station** (Gara Sibiu; ☑ 0269-211 139; www.cfrcalatori.ro; Piaţa 1 Decembrie 1918, 6) is 2km east of the centre, about 20 minutes on foot.

Cluj-Napoca

POP 305,600

Cluj-Napoca, shortened to 'Cluj' in conversation, isn't as picturesque as its Saxon neighbours, but it's famed for cafes, clubs and student life. Even outside the clubs, Cluj is one of Romania's most energised and welcoming cities.

◉ Sights

St Michael's Church CHURCH
(Biserica Sfantul Mihail; ☑ 0264-592 089; Piaţa Unirii; ⊙ 9am-6pm) The vast 14th-century St Michael's Church dominates Piaţa Unirii. The neo-Gothic tower (1859) topping the Gothic hall church creates a great landmark and the church is considered to be one of the finest examples of Gothic architecture in Romania. Daily services are in Hungarian and Romanian, and evening organ concerts are often held.

The Pharmacy
History Collection MUSEUM
(☑ 0264-595 677; Piaţa Unirii 28; adult/child 5.20/3.10 lei; ⊙ 10am-4pm Tue-Sun) This tiny museum near the main square can be hit

or miss, depending on whether there's an English-speaking guide on hand. Tours are led by a 'pharmacist' in a white lab coat, who points like a game-show model towards (seemingly ho-hum) glass cases of ground mummy dust, medieval alchemist symbols and 18th-century aphrodisiacs.

National Art Museum MUSEUM
(☑ 0264-596 952; www.macluj.ro; Piaţa Unirii 30; adult/student 8/4 lei; ⊙ 10am-5pm Wed-Sun) Admittedly a sleepy affair, the museum houses mainly Romanian works from the 19th and 20th centuries – though there are several excellent pieces by Romanian impressionist and war painter Nicolae Grigorescu. The highlight is the setting: the baroque town palace of the noble Bánffy family, which hosted Habsburg Emperor Franz Joseph I on two occasions, in 1852 and 1887.

Fabrica de Pensule ART GALLERY
(Paintbrush Factory; ☑ tours 0724-274 040; www. fabricadepensule.ro; Str Henri Barbusse 59-61; ⊙ tours 4pm-8pm Mon-Fri) Cluj takes contemporary art seriously and the centre of the action is Fabrica de Pensule, a rehabilitated former paintbrush factory on the outskirts of town (4km east of Piaţa Unirii). The factory house six art galleries, including renowned painter Adrian Ghenie's Plan B. There are stages for concerts, theatre performances and happenings; check the website. Arrange free guided tours in advance by phone or email.

⨳ Sleeping

Retro Hostel HOSTEL €
(☑ 0264-450 452; www.retro.ro; Str Potaissa 13; dm/s/d incl breakfast from 55/100/150 lei; ⊛ @ 🛜) Well-organised, central and with helpful staff, Retro has clean dorms and decent doubles (with TVs and shared baths). There's a pleasant cafe downstairs. Retro also lends out its bikes for free and offers a great choice of guided tours to Maramureş, the nearby Turda Salt Mine and hiking in the Apuseni Mountains.

★**Hotel Central** HOTEL €€
(☑ 0264-439 959; www.hotelcentralcluj.ro; Str Victor Babeş 13; s/d/apt 260/300/390 lei; P ⊛ ❄ 🛜) Midrange travellers will appreciate the value-for-money here at this modern, centrally located hotel, about 10 minutes on foot from Piaţa Unirii. On offer are sleek, air-conditioned rooms (many with separate bedroom and sitting areas). Those on the fifth floor come with roof-top terraces. Decent

ROMANIA CLUJ-NAPOCA

breakfast and a few parking spaces out front (call ahead to reserve).

Fullton
HOTEL **€€**

(☑ 0264-597 898; www.fullton.ro; Str Sextil Puş-cariu 10; s 175-215 lei, d 200-240 lei; ❸❋🌐) This boutique hotel with a pea-green facade has a great location in the old town and a couple of places to park. Rooms are fragrant and fresh and have individual colour schemes, bureaus and en suites. Some, such as room 101, have four-poster beds. There's also a welcoming patio bar.

✖ Eating

Camino
INTERNATIONAL **€€**

(☑ 0749-200 117; Piaţa Muzeului 4; mains 20-30 lei; ⊙ 9am-midnight; 🌐) With jazz piping through its peeling arched interior decked in candelabra and threadbare rugs, this boho restaurant is perfect for solo book-reading jaunts or romantic dinner alfresco. Its homemade pasta is delicious, the salads and tapas full of zing. Breakfasts, too.

★ Bricks – (M)eating Point Restaurant
STEAKHOUSE **€€€**

(☑ 0364-730 615; www.bricksrestaurant.ro; Str Horea 2; mains 40-60 lei; ⊙ 11am-11pm; 🌐) Bricks has risen from the ashes of a men's drinking den to become a chi chi urban bistro. Shaded rattan chairs look out across the river, while the menu excels with plenty of grilled dishes, some vegie numbers, oriental cuisine, salads, and the best grilled rib-eye we've ever had in Romania. Excellent wine list.

🍷 Drinking & Nightlife

Cluj excels at cafes and clubs. Many of the best are clustered around a quiet square north of Piaţa Unirii called Piaţa Muzeului.

Casa Jazz
BAR, LIVE MUSIC

(☑ 0720-944 251; Str Vasile Goldiş 2; ⊙ noon-2am) With its oxblood walls ornamented with Rat Pack prints and antique trumpets, and Armstrong and Gillespie jumping on the speakers, this smoky joint is a slice of New Orleans. There are piano evenings and exhibitions, too.

Joben Bistro
CAFE

(☑ 0720-222 800; http://joben.ro; Str Avram Iancu 29; ⊙ 8am-2am Mon-Thu, noon-2am Fri-Sun; 🌐) Joben Bistro is another themed cafe. This time the idea is 'steampunk'. The brick walls are artfully decorated with the flotsam of heavy industry, including cogs, levers, pulleys

and clocks. The ginger-infused lemonade is a summertime winner, as is the coffee. Very good light bites, like soups and salads, on hand as well.

☆ Entertainment

National Theatre
THEATRE

(Teatrul Naţional Cluj-Napoca; ☑ tickets 0264-595 363; www.teatrulnationalcluj.ro; Piaţa Ştefan cel Mare 2-4; tickets from 15 lei; ⊙ box office 11am-2pm & 3pm-5pm Tue-Sun) The National Theatre was designed in the 19th century by the famed Habsburg architects Fellner and Hellmer; performances are well attended. The **opera** is in the same building. Buy tickets at the nearby **box office** (Piaţa Ştefan cel Mare 14).

Flying Circus Pub
CLUB

(☑ 0758-022 924; www.flyingcircus.ro; Str Iuliu Maniu 2; ⊙ 5pm-dawn; 🌐) The best of a number of student-oriented dance clubs scattered around the centre. They open at 5pm, but don't expect anything to happen until after 11pm.

❶ Information

There are many banks and ATMs scattered around the centre.

Tourist Information Office (☑ 0264-452 244; www.visitcluj.ro; B-dul Eroilor 6-8; ⊙ 8.30am-6pm Mon-Fri, 10am-6pm Sat) Run by two proactive guys named Marius, this super-friendly office has bags of info on trekking, train and bus times, eating, accommodation and cultural sights and events.

❶ Getting There & Around

BUS

Buses generally leave from **Autogara 2** (Autogara Beta; ☑ 0264-455 249; www.autogari.ro; Str Giordano Bruno 1-3), 300m northwest of the train station. Popular destinations include Braşov (60 lei, five hours, two daily), Bucharest (90 lei, eight hours, three daily) and Sibiu (34 lei, 3½ hours, eight daily).

TRAIN

Cluj has decent train connections around the country. Sample destinations include two daily direct trains to Bucharest (94 lei, 10 hours), three to Braşov (76 lei, seven hours) and two to Sighişoara (62 lei, four hours). Change at Teiuş or Mediaş for Sibiu (53 lei, five hours).

The **train station** (☑ 0264-592 952; www.cfrcalatori.ro; Piaţa Gării 2-3) is 1km north of the centre, a straight shot along Str Horea (10-minute walk). Buy tickets at the station or in town at the **Agenţia de Voiaj CFR** (☑ 0264-432 001; www.cfrcalatori.ro; Piaţa Mihai Viteazul 20;

PAINTED MONASTERIES OF SOUTHERN BUCOVINA

The painted monasteries of southern Bucovina are among the greatest artistic monuments of eastern Europe. In 1993 they were collectively designated a Unesco World Heritage Site.

Erected in the 15th and 16th centuries, when Moldavia was threatened by Turkish invaders, the monasteries were surrounded by strong defensive walls. Biblical stories were portrayed on the church walls in colourful pictures so that illiterate worshippers could better understand them.

The most impressive collection of monasteries is located west of Suceava. It includes the Humor, Voroneţ and Moldoviţa Monasteries.

The **Humor Monastery** (Mănăstirea Humorului; Gura Humorului; adult/student 5/2 lei; 8am-7pm summer, to 4pm winter), built in 1530 and situated near the town of Gura Humorului, boasts arguably the most impressive interior frescoes.

Also not far from Gura Humorului, the **Voroneţ Monastery** (Mănăstirea Voroneţ; 0741-612 529; Voroneţ, Gura Humorului; adult/child 5/2 lei; 8am-7pm summer, to 4pm winter) is the only one to have a specific colour associated with it. 'Voroneţ Blue', a vibrant cerulean colour created from lapis lazuli and other ingredients, is prominent in its frescoes. The monastery was built in just three months and three weeks by Ştefan cel Mare following a key 1488 victory over the Turks.

Moldoviţa Monastery (Mânăstirea Moldoviţa; Vatra Moldoviţei; adult/student 5/2 lei; 8am-7pm summer, to 4pm winter) 35km northwest of the Voroneţ Monastery, occupies a fortified quadrangular enclosure with tower, gates and flowery lawns. The central painted church has been partly restored, and features impressive frescoes from 1537, although the monastery dates from 1532.

The main gateway to the monasteries is **Suceava**, which is reachable by direct train from both Bucharest (94 lei, seven hours, one daily) and Cluj-Napoca (75 lei, seven hours, four daily). By car, it's possible to see all the monasteries in a long day trip; alternatively, there are guesthouses along the way in which to stay the night.

domestic tickets 8am-8pm Mon-Fri, international 8.30am-3.30pm Mon, Wed & Fri, 1-8pm Tue & Thu).

BANAT

Western Romania, with its geographic and cultural ties to neighbouring Hungary and Serbia, and historical links to the Austro-Hungarian Empire, enjoys an ethnic diversity that much of the country lacks. Timişoara, the regional hub, has a nationwide reputation as a beautiful and lively metropolis, and for a series of 'firsts'. It was the world's first city to adopt electric street lights (in 1884) and, more importantly, the first city to rise up against dictator Nicolae Ceauşescu in 1989.

Timişoara

POP 312,000

Romania's third- or fourth-largest city (depending on the source) is also one of the country's most attractive urban areas, built around a series of beautiful public squares and lavish parks and gardens. It's known as Primul Oraş Liber (First Free Town), for it was here that anti-Ceauşescu protests first exceeded the Securitate's capacity for violent suppression in 1989, eventually sending Ceauşescu and his wife to their demise.

Sights

Piaţa Unirii

Piaţa Unirii is Timişoara's most picturesque square, featuring the imposing sight of the Catholic and Serbian Orthodox **churches** facing each other.

★ Permanent Exhibition of the 1989 Revolution   MUSEUM

(0256-294 936; www.memorialulrevolutiei.ro; Str Popa Şapcă 3-5; admission by donation; 8am-4pm Mon-Fri, 9am-1pm Sat) This work in progress is an ideal venue to brush up on the December 1989 anticommunist revolution that began in Timişoara. Displays include documentation, posters and photography from those fateful days, capped by a graphic 20-minute video

WORTH A TRIP

DANUBE DELTA

After passing through several countries and absorbing countless waterways, the Danube River empties into the Black Sea just south of the Ukrainian border.

The Danube Delta (Delta Dunării), included on Unesco's World Heritage list, is one of Romania's leading attractions. At the inland port of Tulcea, the river splits into three separate channels: the Chilia, Sulina and Sfântu Gheorghe, creating a constantly evolving 4187-sq-km wetland of marshes, floating reed islets and sandbars. There are beautiful, secluded beaches at Sulina and Sfântu Gheorghe, and the seafood, particularly the fish soup served in restaurants and pension kitchens throughout the region, is the best in Romania.

For many visitors, the main drawcard is **birdwatching**. The delta is a major migration hub for tens of thousands of birds, with the best viewing times being spring and late autumn.

Much of the delta is under the protection of the **Danube Delta Biosphere Reserve Authority** (DDBRA; ☑0240-518 924; www.ddbra.ro; Str Portului 34a; permits per day 5 lei; ☉9am-4pm Mon-Fri), headquartered in Tulcea. All visitors to protected areas are required to purchase an entry permit at the Danube Delta Biosphere Reserve Authority office. Permits are available for a day or a week.

There is no rail service in the delta and few paved roads, meaning the primary mode of transport is by ferry. The main ferry operator is state-owned **Navrom** (☑0240-511 553; www.navromdelta.ro; Str Portului 26; ☉ticket office 11.30am-1.30pm). It runs both traditional 'slow' ferries and faster hydrofoils from Tulcea's main port to major points in the delta.

The ferry schedule can be confusing. The helpful staff at the **Tourism Information Centre** (☑0240-519 130; www.primariatulcea.ro; Str Gării 26; ☉8am-4pm Mon-Fri) can help piece together a journey, depending on your time and budget.

(not suitable for young children) with English subtitles. Enter from Str Oituz.

Art Museum   MUSEUM
(Muzeul de Artă; ☑0256-491 592; www.muzeul deartatm.ro; Piaţa Unirii 1; admission 10 lei; ☉10am-6pm Tue-Sun) The museum displays a representative sample of paintings and visual arts over the centuries as well as regular, high-quality temporary exhibitions. It's housed in the baroque **Old Prefecture Palace**, built in 1754, which is worth a look inside for the graceful interiors alone.

◉ Piaţa Victoriei

Piaţa Victoriei is a beautifully green pedestrian mall dotted with fountains and lined on both sides with shops and cafes. The square's northern end is marked by the 18th-century National Theatre & Opera House, where thousands of demonstrators gathered on 16 December 1989.

Banat History Museum   MUSEUM
(Muzeul Banatului; Piaţa Huniades 1) Housed in the historic Huniades Palace, the museum was closed at the time of research for renovations expected to last until 2016. The exterior of the palace, though, is still worth a look.

The origins of the building date to the 14th century and to Hungarian king Charles Robert, Prince of Anjou.

Metropolitan Cathedral   CHURCH
(Catedrala Ortodoxă; www.mitropolia-banatului.ro; B-dul Regele Ferdinand I; ☉10am-6pm) The Orthodox cathedral was built between 1936 and 1946. It's unique for its Byzantine-influenced architecture, which recalls the style of the Bucovina monasteries.

🛏 Sleeping

★**Hostel Costel**   HOSTEL €
(☑0356-262 487; www.hostel-costel.ro; Str Petru Sfetca 1; dm 40-45 lei, d 135 lei; ☉@☎) Run by affable staff, this charming 1920s art nouveau villa is the city's best hostel. The vibe is relaxed and congenial. There are three dorm rooms and one private double, plus ample chill rooms and a big garden. The hostel is 1km east of the centre, across the Bega Canal near the Decebal Bridge; take tram 1.

Pension Casa Leone   PENSION €
(☑0256-292 621; www.casaleone.ro; B-dul Eroilor la Tisa 67; s/d/tr 125/150/200 lei; P☉❄☎) This lovely seven-room pension offers exceptional service and individually decorated rooms. To

find it, take tram 8 from the train station, alight at Deliblata station and walk one block northeast to B-dul Eroilor (or call ahead to arrange transport).

★**Pensiunea Park**   PENSION €€
(☎0356-264 039; www.pensiuneapark.ro; Str Remus 17; s/d/ste 170/220/250 lei; P🅿😊❄🌐) Small, family-owned hotel in an old villa on a leafy side street, about 10 minutes' walk from Piaţa Victoriei. Lots of period touches, including beautiful chandeliers and fixtures in the hallways, though the rooms themselves are modestly furnished. There's a small terrace in the back for morning coffee and bikes to ride for free during your stay.

✕ Eating

★**Casa Bunicii**   ROMANIAN €€
(☎0356-100 870; www.casa-bunicii.ro; Str Virgil Onitiu 3; mains 20-35 lei; 🍴) The names translates to 'Granny's House' and indeed this casual, family-friendly restaurant specialises in home cooking and regional specialities from the Banat. The duck soup and grilled chicken breast served in sour cherry sauce come recommended.

Casa cu Flori   ROMANIAN €€
(☎0256-435 080; www.casacuflori.ro; Str Alba Iulia 1; mains 18-28 lei) One of the best-known restaurants in the city and for good reason. Excellent high-end Romanian cooking with refined service at moderate prices. In nice weather, climb three flights to the flower-lined rooftop terrace.

🍺 Drinking & Nightlife

Scârţ loc lejer   CAFE
(☎0751-892 340; Str Zoe 1; ⊙10am-11pm Mon-Fri, 11am-11pm Sat, 2-11pm Sun; 🌐) Old villa that's been retrofitted into a funky coffeehouse with albums pinned to the wall and chill tunes on the turntable. There are several cosy rooms in which to read and relax, but our favourite is the garden out back, with shady nooks and even hammocks for stretching out. Located about 1km south of the city centre.

La Căpiţe   BEER GARDEN
(☎0720-400 333; www.lacapite.ro; B-dul Vasile Pârvan; ⊙10am-midnight Sun-Thu & 10am-4am Fri & Sat May-Oct; 🌐) Shaggy riverside beer garden and alternative hangout is strategically located across the street from the university, ensuring lively crowds on warm summer evenings. Most nights bring live music or DJs. The name translates as 'haystack', and

bales of hay strewn everywhere make for comfy places to sit and chill.

Aethernativ   CAFE
(☎0724-012 324; Str Mărăşeşti 14; ⊙10am-1am Mon-Fri, noon-1am Sat, 5pm-1am Sun; 🌐) This trendy art club, cafe and bar occupies a courtyard of a run-down building two blocks west of Piaţa Unirii and has eclectic furnishings and an alternative, student vibe. There are no signs to let you know you're here; simply find the address, push open the door and walk up a flight of stairs.

☆ Entertainment

State Philharmonic Theatre   CLASSICAL MUSIC
(Filharmonica de Stat Banatul; ☎0256-492 521; www.filarmonicabanatul.ro; B-dul CD Loga 2; ⊙box office 2-7pm Tue & Thu, 10am-2pm Mon, Wed & Fri) Classical concerts are held most evenings here. Tickets (from 40 lei) can be bought at the box office inside the theatre and one hour before performances.

National Theatre & Opera House   THEATRE, OPERA
(Teatrul Naţional şi Opera Română; ☎opera 0256-201 286, theatre 0256-499 908; www.tntimisoara. com; Str Mărăşeşti 2; ⊙box office 10am-1pm, 5pm-7pm) The National Theatre & Opera House features both dramatic works and classical opera, and is highly regarded. Buy tickets (from around 40 lei) at the box office, but note that most of the dramatic works will be in Romanian.

ℹ Information

Internet Cafe (B-dul Mihai Eminescu 5; per hr 6 lei; ⊙24hr; 🌐)

Timişoara County Hospital (Spitalul Clinic Judeţean de Urgenţă Timişoara; ☎0356-433 111; www.hosptm.ro; B-dul Iosif Bulbuca 10) Modern hospital, located 2km south of the centre, with 24-hour emergency service.

Tourist Information Centre (Info Centru Turistic; ☎0256-437 973; www.timisoara-info. ro; Str Alba Iulia 2) This great tourism office can assist with accommodation and trains, and provide maps and Banat regional info.

ℹ Getting There & Away

BUS
Buses and minibuses are privately operated and depart from several points around the city. Consult the website www.autogari.ro for departure points. Bus service is extensive. Sample fares include Cluj-Napoca (65 lei) and Sibiu (45 lei).

International buses leave from the **East bus station**. Main international operators include **Atlassib** (☑ call centre 0269-229 224, local office 0256-226 485; www.atlassib.ro; Str Gheorghe Lazăr 27) and **Eurolines** (☑ 0256-288 132; www.eurolines.ro; Str M Kogălniceanu 20). Belgrade-based **Gea Tours** (☑ 0316-300 257; www.geatours.rs) offers daily minibus service between Timişoara and Belgrade for one way/ return 90/180 lei. Book over the website.

TRAIN

Trains depart from **Gara Timişoara-Nord** (Gara Timişoara-Nord; ☑ 0256-200 457; www. cfrcalatori.ro; Str Gării 2), the 'northern' station, west of the centre. Daily express trains include two to Bucharest (105 lei, nine hours) and two to Cluj-Napoca (75 lei, six hours).

SURVIVAL GUIDE

ℹ Directory A–Z

ACCOMMODATION

Romania has a wide choice of accommodation to suit most budgets, including hotels, pensions and private rooms, hostels and camping grounds. Prices are generally lower than in Western Europe.

Budget properties include hostels, camping grounds and cheaper guesthouses. Midrange accommodation includes three-star hotels and pensions. Top-end means fancy hotels, corporate chains and boutiques.

BUSINESS HOURS

Banks 9am to noon and 1pm to 5pm Monday to Friday

Clubs 8pm to 3am

Restaurants 10am to 11pm

Shops 10am to 6pm Monday to Friday, 10am to 5pm Saturday

GAY & LESBIAN TRAVELLERS

Public attitudes towards homosexuality remain relatively negative. In spite of this, Romania has made significant progress in decriminalising homosexual acts and adopting antidiscrimination laws.

COUNTRY FACTS

Area 237,500 sq km

Capital Bucharest

Country code ☑ 40

Currency Romanian leu

Emergency ☑ 112

Language Romanian

Money ATMs are abundant

Population 20 million

Visas Not required for citizens of the EU, USA, Canada, Australia, and New Zealand

---

➡ Bucharest remains the most tolerant city, though here too gay couples should refrain from open displays of affection.

➡ Bucharest-based **Accept Romania** (☑ 021-252 9000; www.accept-romania.ro) organises a six-day Bucharest Pride Festival in early summer.

INTERNET RESOURCES

Romanian National Tourist Office (www.romaniatourism.com)

Bucharest Life (www.bucharestlife.net)

Bus Timetable (www.autogari.ro)

Train Timetable (www.cfrcalatori.ro)

MONEY

The currency is the leu (plural: lei), noted in this guide as 'lei'. One leu is divided into 100 bani. Banknotes come in denominations of 1, 5, 10, 50, 100, 200 and 500 lei. Coins come in 50 and 10 bani.

➡ Romania is a member of the European Union, but the euro is not used here.

➡ ATMs are nearly everywhere and give 24-hour withdrawals in lei on a variety of international bank cards. Romanian ATMs require a four-digit PIN.

➡ The best place to exchange money is at a bank. You can also change money at a private exchange booth (*casa de schimb*), but be wary of commission charges.

➡ International credit and debit cards are widely accepted at hotels, restaurants and shops in cities. In rural areas, you'll need cash.

PUBLIC HOLIDAYS

New Year 1 and 2 January

Orthodox Easter Monday April/May

Labour Day 1 May

Pentecost May/June, 50 days after Easter Sunday

SLEEPING PRICE RANGES

The following price categories are for the cost of a double room:

€ less than 150 lei

€€ 150 lei to 300 lei

€€€ more than 300 lei

Assumption of Mary 15 August
Feast of St Andrew 30 November
Romanian National Day 1 December
Christmas 25 and 26 December

TELEPHONE

Romania has a modern telephone network of landlines and mobile phones. The country code is ☑ 40.

→ All Romanian numbers have 10 digits, consisting of a ☑ 0, plus a city code and number. Mobile phone numbers are identified by a three-digit prefix starting with ☑ 7.

→ Romanian mobiles use the GSM 900/1800 network, the standard throughout Europe as well as in Australia and New Zealand, but not compatible with mobile phones in North America or Japan.

→ To reduce expensive roaming fees, buy a prepaid local SIM card from one of Romania's three main carriers: **Vodafone** (www.vodafone. ro), **Cosmote** (www.cosmote.ro) and **Orange** (www.orange.ro).

→ Public phones require a magnetic-stripe phonecard bought at post offices and newspaper kiosks. Phonecard rates start at about 10 lei.

VISAS

Citizens of EU countries do not need visas to visit Romania and can stay indefinitely. Citizens of the USA, Canada, Australia, New Zealand, Israel, Japan and some other countries can stay for 90 days without a visa. Other nationalities check with the **Ministry of Foreign Affairs** (www.mae.ro).

ⓘ Getting There & Away

AIR

Romania has good air connections to Europe and the Middle East. At the time of research there were no direct flights to Romania from North America or Southeast Asia.

Airports

The majority of international flights to Romania arrive at Bucharest's **Henri Coandă International Airport** (OTP/Otopeni; ☑ 021-204 1000; www.bucharestairports.ro; Şos Bucureşti-Ploieşti).

Other cities with international airports:
Cluj Avram Iancu International Airport (CLJ; ☑ 0264-307 500, 0264-416 702; www.airport cluj.ro; Str Traian Vuia 149-151)

Sibiu International Airport (SBZ; ☑ 0269-253 135; www.sibiuairport.ro; Şos Alba Iulia 73)

Timişoara Traian Vuia International Airport (TSR; ☑ 0256-386 089; www.aerotim.ro; Str Aeroport 2, Ghiroda)

LAND

The main train corridor to Romania from Western Europe passes through Budapest, and three trains daily make the slog down to Bucharest, via Braşov, and back. The western city of Timişoara has excellent train, bus and air connections throughout Europe. By road, the main entry points from the west are at Arad and Oradea.

Romania shares borders with five countries: Bulgaria, Hungary, Moldova, Serbia and Ukraine. It has four car-ferry crossings with Bulgaria. Highway border posts are normally open 24 hours, though smaller crossings may only be open from 8am to 8pm.

Romania is not a member of the EU's common border and customs Schengen Zone, meaning you'll have to show valid passport (and visa, if required) at the border.

Bus

Long-haul bus service remains a popular way of travelling from Romania to Western Europe, as well as to parts of southeastern Europe and Turkey. Bus travel is comparable in price to train travel, but can be faster.

Bus services to and from Western Europe are dominated by **Eurolines** (www.eurolines.ro) and **Atlassib** (☑ 0740-104 446, 021-420 3665; www.atlassib.ro; Soseaua Alexandriei 164). Both maintain vast networks from cities throughout Europe to destinations all around Romania. Check the websites for latest schedules and prices.

Car & Motorcycle

Ensure your documents (personal ID, car insurance and car registration) are in order before crossing into Romania.

Train

Romania is integrated into the European rail grid with decent connections to Western Europe and neighbouring countries. Trains arrive at and depart from Bucharest's main station, Gara de Nord (p317).

Budapest is the main rail gateway from Western Europe. There are three daily direct trains between Budapest and Bucharest (13 hours), with regular onward direct connections from Budapest to Prague, Munich and Vienna.

EATING PRICE RANGES

The following price categories are for the cost of a main course:

€ less than 15 lei

€€ 15 lei to 30 lei

€€€ more than 30 lei

ESSENTIAL FOOD & DRINK

Romanian food borrows heavily from its neighbours, including Turkey, Hungary and the Balkans, and is centred on pork and other meats. Farm-fresh, organically grown fruits and vegetables are in abundance, lending flavour and colour to a long list of soups and salads. Condiments typically include sour cream, garlic sauce and grated sheep's cheese, used to flavour everything from soup to the most common side dish: polenta.

➡ **Mămăligă** Cornmeal mush, sometimes topped with sour cream or cheese.

➡ **Ciorbă** Sour soup that's a mainstay of the Romanian diet.

➡ **Sarmale** Spiced meat wrapped in cabbage or grape leaves.

➡ **Covrigi** Oven-baked pretzels served warm from windows around town.

➡ **Ţuică** Fiery plum brandy sold in water bottles at roadside rest stops.

 Getting Around

AIR

Given the poor state of the roads, flying between cities is feasible if time is a concern. The Romanian national carrier **Tarom** (☑ 021-204 6464; www.tarom.ro) operates a comprehensive network of domestic routes. The airline flies regularly between Bucharest and Cluj-Napoca, Iaşi, Oradea, and Timişoara.

BUS

A mix of buses and maxitaxis form the backbone of the national transport system. If you understand how the system works, you can move around easily and cheaply, but finding updated information without local help can be tough. The website www.autogari.ro is a helpful online timetable.

CAR & MOTORCYCLE

Roads are crowded and in poor condition. There are only a few stretches of motorway (autostrada), meaning most travel is along two-lane national highways (drum naţional) or secondary roads. When calculating travel times, figure on 50km per hour.

Western-style petrol stations are plentiful. A litre of unleaded 95 octane costs about 6.20 lei. Most stations accept credit cards.

Road Rules

➡ Blood-alcohol limit: 0.00

➡ Seatbelts: compulsory

➡ Headlights: on day and night

➡ Speed limits: 90km/h on major roads, 50km/h in town

LOCAL TRANSPORT

Romanian cities have good public transportation systems. Bucharest is the only city with a metro. The method for accessing the systems is broadly similar. Purchase tickets at street kiosks marked bilete or casă de bilete before boarding and validate the ticket once aboard. For maxitaxis, buy the ticket from the driver.

Taxis

Taxis are cheap and a useful supplement to the public transport systems. Drivers are required by law to post rates on windscreens. The going rate varies but runs from 1.39 to 1.89 lei per kilometre. Any driver posting a higher fare is likely a rip-off.

TRAIN

The extensive network covers much of the country, including most of the main tourist sights. The national rail system is run by **Căile Ferate Române** (CFR | Romanian State Railways; www.cfr.ro). Romania has three types of trains that travel at different speeds. InterCity, listed as 'IC' on timetables, are the most expensive and most comfortable.

Buy tickets at station windows, specialised Agenţia de Voiaj CFR ticket offices or online at www.cfrcalatori.ro.

Russia

Best Places to Eat

➡ Delicatessen (p341)

➡ Varenichnaya No 1 (p341)

➡ Duo Gastrobar (p351)

➡ Yat (p351)

Best Places to Stay

➡ Hotel Metropol (p341)

➡ Blues Hotel (p341)

➡ Soul Kitchen Hostel (p351)

➡ Rachmaninov Antique Hotel (p351)

Why Go?

Could there be a more iconic image of eastern Europe than the awe-inspiring architectural ensemble of Moscow's Red Square? The brash, exciting and oil-rich capital of Russia (Россия) is a must on any trip to the region.

St Petersburg, on the Baltic coast, is another stunner. The former imperial capital is still Russia's most beautiful and alluring city, with its grand Italianate mansions, wending canals and enormous Neva River. Also make time for Veliky Novgorod, home to an ancient stone fortress and many fresco-decorated churches. Emulating the tourist-friendly nature of its Baltic neighbours is little Kaliningrad, wedged between Poland and Lithuania on the Baltic Sea. It's a fascinating destination, combining all the best elements of its enormous mother.

Visa red tape deters many travellers from visiting – don't let it keep you from experiencing the incredible things to see and do in the European part of the world's largest country.

When to Go
Moscow

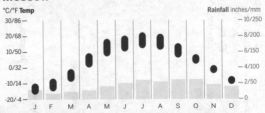

May Big military parades and a public holiday mark the end of WWII.

Jun & Jul Party during St Petersburg's White Nights, and bask on the beaches of Kaliningrad.

Dec & Jan Snow makes Moscow and St Petersburg look magical, while hotel rates drop.

Russia Highlights

1 Be awe-inspired by the massive scale and riches of **Moscow**, Russia's brash, energetic capital.

2 Take a walking, bike or boat tour of **St Petersburg**

(p346), an Italianate slice of Old Europe incongruously placed in Russia.

3 Ogle the seemingly endless collection of masterpieces in St

Petersburg's unrivalled **State Hermitage Museum** (p347).

4 Take a day trip out of St Petersburg to see the imperial country estates at

Petrodvorets and **Tsarskoe Selo** (p352).

5 Trace Russia's roots back to **Veliky Novgorod** (p344) with its well-preserved kremlin and many picturesque churches.

6 Explore **Kaliningrad** (p354), once part of the Prussian empire, and home to the pristine beaches of the Kurshskaya Kosa National Park.

ITINERARIES

One Week

In **Moscow**, touring the Kremlin and Red Square will take up one day, viewing the spectacular collections at the Tretyakov, New Tretyakov and Pushkin art museums another. On day three size up the magnificent Novodevichy Convent, and the revamped Gorky Park. Take the night train to **Veliky Novgorod** and spend a day exploring its ancient kremlin and churches. The rest of the week is reserved for splendid **St Petersburg**. Wander up Nevsky pr, see Dvortsovaya pl, and spend a half-day at the Hermitage. Tour the canals and the mighty Neva River by boat. Visit Peter & Paul Fortress, the Church of the Saviour on Spilled Blood and the wonderful Russian Museum.

Two Weeks

With two extra days in Moscow, sweat it out in the luxurious Sanduny Baths or do a metro tour. In St Petersburg, spend more time in the Hermitage and other museums, and tack on an excursion to **Petrodvorets** or **Tsarskoe Selo**. Then fly to **Kaliningrad**. Admire the capital's reconstructed Gothic Cathedral and wander along the river to the excellent World Ocean Museum. Enjoy either the old Prussian charm of the spa town of **Svetlogorsk** or the sand dunes and forests of the **Kurshskaya Kosa National Park**.

Moscow   МОСКВА

📱 495 & 📱 499 / POP 11.5 MILLION

Intimidating in its scale, but also exciting and unforgettable, Moscow is a place that inspires extreme passion or loathing. History, power and wild capitalism hang in the air alongside an explosion of creative energy throwing up edgy art galleries and a dynamic restaurant, bar and nightlife scene.

The sturdy stone walls of the Kremlin, the apex of Russian political power and once the centre of the Orthodox Church, occupy the city's founding site on the northern bank of the Moscow River. Remains of the Soviet state, such as Lenin's Tomb, are nearby in Red Square and elsewhere in the city which radiates from the Kremlin in a series of ring roads.

⊙ Sights

⊙ The Kremlin & Red Square

Covering Borovitsky Hill on the north bank of the Moscow River, the **Kremlin** (Кремль; www.kreml.ru; adult/student R350/100; ⊙10am-5pm Fri-Wed, ticket office 9.30am-4.30pm Fri-Wed; Ⓜ Aleksandrovsky Sad) is enclosed by high walls 2.25km long, with Red Square outside the east wall. The best views of the complex are from Sofiyskaya nab across the river.

Before entering the Kremlin, deposit bags at the **left-luggage office** (per bag R60; ⊙9am-6.30pm Fri-Wed), beneath the Kutafya Tower. The main ticket office is in the Alexandrovsky Garden. The entrance ticket covers admission to all five of the church-museums, and the Patriarch's Palace. It does not include the Armoury, the Diamond Fund Exhibition or special exhibits, which are priced separately.

From the Kutafya Tower, walk up the ramp and pass through the Kremlin walls beneath the **Trinity Gate Tower** (Троицкая надвратная башня). The lane to the right (south) passes the 17th-century **Poteshny Palace** (Потешный дворец), where Stalin lived. The horribly out of place glass-and-concrete **State Kremlin Palace** (Государственный Кремлевский Дворец) houses a concert and ballet auditorium, where many Western pop stars play when they are in Moscow.

Photography is not permitted inside the Armoury or any of the buildings on Sobornaya pl (Cathedral Sq).

★ Armoury   MUSEUM

(Оружейная палата; adult/student R700/250; ⊙10am, noon, 2.30pm & 4.30pm; Ⓜ Aleksandrovsky Sad) The Armoury dates back to 1511, when it was founded under Vasily III to manufacture and store weapons, imperial arms and regalia for the royal court. Later it also produced jewellery, icon frames and embroidery. To this day, the Armoury still contains plenty of treasures for ogling, and remains a highlight of any visit to the Kremlin. If possible, buy your time-specific ticket to the Armoury when you buy your ticket to the Kremlin.

Central Moscow

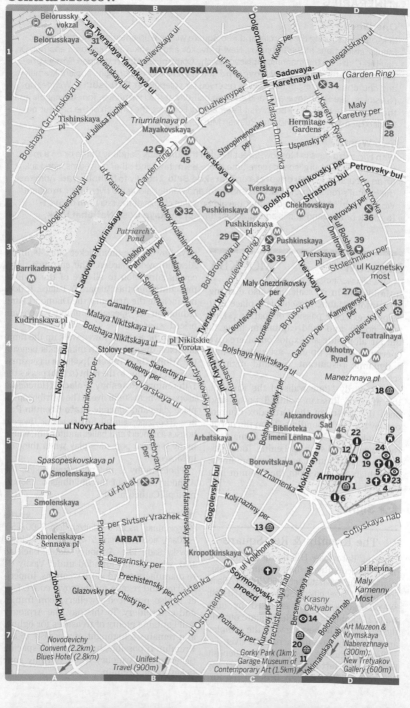

RUSSIA MOSCOW

A | **B** | **C** | **D**

Belorussky vokzal
Belorusskaya
1-ya Tverskaya-Yamskaya ul
31
Vasilevskaya ul
1-ya Brestskaya ul
ul Fadeeva
Dolgorukovskaya ul
Kosoy per
Delegatskaya ul

MAYAKOVSKAYA

Sadovaya-Karetnaya ul
(Garden Ring)
34
ul Karetny Ryad

Bolshaya Gruzinskaya ul
Tishinskaya pl
ul Juliusa Fuchika
Oruzheyny per
ul Malaya Dmitrovka
Staropimenovsky per
Maly Karetny per

Triumfalnaya pl
Mayakovskaya
Hermitage Gardens
38
Uspensky per
28

42
45
Tverskaya ul
Petrovsky bul

ul Krasina
(Garden Ring)
40
Tverskaya
Bolshoy Putinkovsky per
Strastnoy bul
ul Petrovka

Zoologicheskaya ul
Bolshoy Kozikhinsky per
32
Pushkinskaya
Chekhovskaya
Petrovsky per
36

Patriarch's Pond
Pushkinskaya pl
29
33
Pushkinskaya
35
ul Bolshaya Dmitrovka
39

Barrikadnaya
Bolshoy Patriarshy per
Malaya Bronnaya ul
Bol Bronnaya ul (Boulevard Ring)
Tverskaya pl
Stoleshnikov per
ul Kuznetsky most

ul Spiridonovka
Maly Gnezdnikovsky per
Tverskoy bul

Granatny per
Leontevsky per
Voznesensky per
Bryusov per
Gazetny per
Kamergersky per
Georgievsky per
43

Malaya Nikitskaya ul
Bolshaya Nikitskaya ul
27
Teatralnaya

Kudrinskaya pl
Stolovy per
Skatertny pr
pl Nikitskie Vorota
Bolshaya Nikitskaya ul
Nikitsky bul
Kalashny per
Okhotny Ryad

Novinsky bul
Trubnikovsky per
Khlebny per
Povarskaya ul
Merzlyakovsky per
Manezhnaya pl
18

ul Novy Arbat
Bolshoy Kislovsky per
Alexandrovsky Sad
46
22
9

Spasopeskovskaya pl
Serebryany per
Arbatskaya
Biblioteka imeni Lenina
12
24

Smolenskaya
Bolshoy Afanasyevsky per
Gogolevsky bul
Borovitskaya
19
8
5
23

ul Arbat
37
ul Znamenka
Armoury
1
3
4

Smolenskaya
Kolymazhny per
6

Smolenskaya-Sennaya pl
ARBAT
Plotnikov per
per Sivtsev Vrazhek
13
Sofiyskaya nab

Gagarinsky per
Kropotkinskaya
ul Volkhonka
pl Repina
Maly Kamenny Most

Zubovsky bul
Glazovsky per
Chisty per
Prechistensky per
ul Prechistenka
7
Soymonovsky proezd

Bersenevskaya nab
Bolotnaya nab

Novodevichy Convent (2.2km);
Blues Hotel (2.8km)
Unifest Travel (900m)
ul Ostozhenka
Pozharsky per
Kursovoy per
Prechistenskaya nab
Krasny Oktyabr
14
Yakimanskaya nab
Art Muzeon & Krymskaya Naberezhnaya (300m);
New Tretyakov Gallery (600m)

Gorky Park (1km);
Garage Museum of Contemporary Art (1.5km)
20
11

A | **B** | **C** | **D**

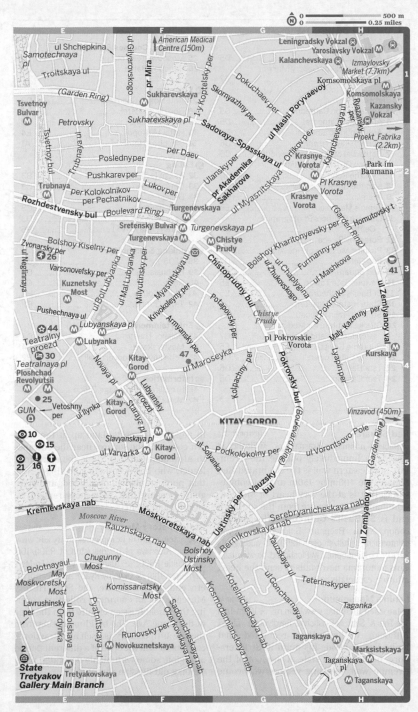

0 500 m
0 0.25 miles

ul Shchepkina

Samotechnaya pl

Troitskaya ul

ul Gilyarovskogo

American Medical Centre (150m)

Dokuchaev per

Leningradsky Vokzal

Yaroslavsky Vokzal

Kalanchevskaya

Izmaylovsky Market (7.7km)

(Garden Ring)

Sukharevskaya

pr Mira

Skornyazhny per

Komsomolskaya pl

Komsomolskaya

Tsvetnoy Bulvar

Petrovsky

Sukharevskaya pl

Sadovaya-Spasskaya ul

ul Mashi Poryvaevoy

Ryazansky per

Kazansky Vokzal

Tsvetnoy bul

Trubnaya

Poslednyper

per Daev

Ulansky per

pr Akademika Sakharova

Orlikov per

Krasnye Vorota

Proekt_Fabrika (2.2km)

Park im Baumana

Pushkarevper

Lukov per

ul Myasnitskaya

Pl Krasnye Vorota

per Kolokolnikov

per Pechatnikov

Turgenevskaya

Krasnye Vorota

(Garden Ring)

Homutovsky t

Rozhdestvensky bul

(Boulevard Ring)

Sretensky Bulvar

Turgenevskaya pl

Bolshoy Kharitonyevsky per

Furmanny per

ul Mashkova

Zvonarsky per

ul Neglinnaya

Bolshoy Kiselny per

Turgenevskaya

Chistye Prudy

ul Chaplygina

ul Zhukovskogo

41

Varsonovefsky per

ul Bol Lubyanka

ul Mal Lubyanka

Milyutinsky per

Myasnitskaya ul

Chistoprudny bul

ul Pokrovka

ul Zemlyanoy val

Kuznetsky Most

Krivokoleyny per

Potapovsky per

Chistye Prudy

Maly Kazenny per

Pushechnaya ul

Lubyanskaya pl

Armyansky per

pl Pokrovskie Vorota

Kurskaya

44

Teatralny proezd

Lubyanka

47

ul Maroseyka

Pokrovsky bul

Lyapin per

30

Kitay-Gorod

Novaya ul

Kolpachny per

(Boulevard Ring)

Teatralnaya pl

Ploshchad Revolyutsii

25

Vetoshny per

ul Ilynka

Lubyansky proezd

Kitay-Gorod

KITAY GOROD

Vinzavod (450m)

ul Vorontsovo Pole

(Garden Ring)

GUM

10

15

Slavyanskaya pl

Kitay-Gorod

ul Solyanka

21 16 17

ul Varvarka

Podkolokolny per

Kremlevskaya nab

Moscow River

Moskvoretskaya nab

Ustinsky per

Yauzsky bul

Serebryanicheskaya naboy

ul Zemlyanoy val

Rauzhskaya nab

Bernikovskaya nab

Chugunny Most

Bolshoy Ustinsky Most

Yauzskaya ul

Teterinskyper

Bolotnayaul

May Moskvoretsky Most

Komissariatsky Most

Kosmodamianskaya nab

ul Goncharnaya

Taganka

Lavrushinsky per

ul Bolshaya Ordynka

Pyatnitskaya ul

Sadovnicheskaya nab

Ozetkovskaya nab

Taganskaya

Marksistskaya

2

Runovsky per

Novokuznetskaya

Taganskaya pl

State Tretyakov Gallery Main Branch

Tretyakovskaya

Taganskaya

Central Moscow

Red Square   HISTORIC SITE

(Красная площадь; Krasnaya pl; Ⓜ Ploshchad Revolyutsii) Immediately outside the Kremlin's northeastern wall is the celebrated Red Square, the 400m by 150m area of cobblestones that is at the very heart of Moscow. Commanding the square from the southern end is **St Basil's Cathedral** (Покровский собор, Храм Василия Блаженного; www.saintbasil.ru; adult/student R250/50, audioguide R200; ⊙11am-5pm; Ⓜ Ploshchad Revolyutsii). This panorama never fails to send the heart aflutter, especially at night.

Lenin's Mausoleum   MEMORIAL

(Мавзолей Ленина; www.lenin.ru; ⊙10am-1pm Tue-Thu & Sat; Ⓜ Ploshchad Revolyutsii) **FREE** Although Vladimir Ilych requested that he be buried beside his mum in St Petersburg, he still lies in state at the foot of the Kremlin wall, receiving visitors who come to pay their respects. Line up at the western corner of the square (near the entrance to Alexander Garden) to see the embalmed leader, who has been here since 1924. Note that photography is not allowed; and stern guards ensure that all visitors remain respectful and silent.

State History Museum   MUSEUM

(Государственный исторический музей; www.shm.ru; Krasnaya pl 1; adult/student R300/100, audioguide R300; ⊙10am-6pm Wed & Fri-Mon, 11am-9pm Thu; Ⓜ Okhotny Ryad) At the northern end of Red Square, the State History Museum has an enormous collection covering the whole Russian empire from the time of the Stone Age. The building, dating from the late 19th century, is itself an attraction – each room is in the style of a different period or region, some with highly decorated walls echoing old Russian churches.

◉ South of the Moscow River

★ **State Tretyakov Gallery Main Branch**   GALLERY
(Главный отдел Государственной Третьяковской галереи; www.tretyakovgallery.ru/en; Lavrushinsky per 10; adult/student R400/250; ⏱10am-6pm Tue, Wed, Sat & Sun, to 9pm Thu & Fri, last tickets 1hr before closing; ⓜTretyakovskaya) The exotic *boyar* castle on a little lane in Zamoskvorechie contains the main branch of the State Tretyakov Gallery, housing the world's best collection of Russian icons and an outstanding collection of other pre-revolutionary Russian art. Show up early to beat the queues.

New Tretyakov Gallery   GALLERY
(Новая Третьяковская галерея; www.tretyakovgallery.ru/en/; ul Krymsky val 10; adult/student R400/250; ⏱10am-6pm Tue, Wed, Sat & Sun, 10am-9pm Thu & Fri, last tickets 1hr before closing; ⓜPark Kultury) The premier venue for 20th-century Russian art is this branch of the State Tretyakov Gallery, better known as the New Tretyakov. This place has much more than the typical socialist realist images of muscle-bound men wielding scythes, and busty women milking cows (although there's that too). The exhibits showcase avant-garde artists such as Malevich, Kandinsky, Chagall, Goncharova and Popova.

Art Muzeon & Krymskaya Naberezhnaya   SCULPTURE PARK
(ul Krymsky val 10; ⓜPark Kultury) `FREE` Now fully revamped and merged with the wonderfully reconstructed Krymskaya Naberezhnaya embankment, is this motley collection of (mostly kitschy) sculpture and monuments to Soviet idols (Stalin, Sverdlov, a selection of Lenins and Brezhnevs) that were ripped from their pedestals in the post-1991 wave of anti-Soviet feeling. All of these stand in lovely gardens with boardwalks and many inviting benches.

★ **Gorky Park**   PARK
(Парк Горького; ⏱24hr; 🛜♿; ⓜOktyabrskaya) `FREE` Moscow's main escape from the city within the city is not your conventional expanse of nature preserved deep inside an urban jungle. It is not a fun fair either, though it used to be one. Its official name says it all – Maxim Gorky's Central Park of Culture

---

SOBORNAYA PLOSHCHAD

On the northern side of Sobornaya pl, with five golden helmet domes and four semi-circular gables facing the square, is the **Assumption Cathedral** (Успенский собор), built between 1475 and 1479. As the focal church of prerevolutionary Russia, it's the burial place of most heads of the Russian Orthodox Church from the 1320s to 1700. The iconostasis dates from 1652, but its lowest level contains some older icons, including the Virgin of Vladimir (Vladimirskaya Bogomater), an early-15th-century Rublyov-school copy of Russia's most revered image, the Vladimir Icon of the Mother of God (Ikona Vladimirskoy Bogomateri).

The delicate little single-domed church beside the west door of the Assumption Cathedral is the **Church of the Deposition of the Robe** (ерковь Ризоположения), built between 1484 and 1486 by masons from Pskov.

With its two golden domes rising above the eastern side of Sobornaya pl, the 16th-century **Ivan the Great Bell Tower** (Колокольня Ивана Великого) is the Kremlin's tallest structure. Beside the bell tower stands the **Tsar Bell** (Царь-колокол), a 202-tonne monster that cracked before it ever rang. North of the bell tower is the mammoth **Tsar Cannon** (Царь-пушка), cast in 1586 but never shot.

The 1508 **Archangel Cathedral** (Архангельский собор), at the square's southeastern corner, was for centuries the coronation, wedding and burial church of tsars. The tombs of all of Russia's rulers from the 1320s to the 1690s are here bar one (Boris Godunov, who was buried at Sergiev Posad).

Finally, the **Annunciation Cathedral** (Благовещенский собор; Blagoveshchensky sobor), at the southwest corner of Sobornaya pl and dating from 1489, contains the celebrated icons of master painter Theophanes the Greek. He probably painted the six icons at the right-hand end of the diesis row, the biggest of the six tiers of the iconostasis. Archangel Michael (the third icon from the left on the diesis row) and the adjacent St Peter are ascribed to Russian master Andrei Rublyov.

& Leisure. That's exactly what it provides: culture and leisure in all shapes and forms. Designed by avant-garde architect Konstantin Melnikov as a piece of communist utopia in the 1920s, these days it showcases the enlightened transformation Moscow has undergone in the recent past.

West of the Kremlin

Pushkin Museum of
Fine Arts   MUSEUM
(Музей изобразительных искусств им Пушкина; www.arts-museum.ru; ul Volkhonka 12; admission each branch R200-300; ⊙10am-7pm Tue-Sun, to 9pm Thu; Ⓜ Kropotkinskaya) Moscow's premier foreign-art museum is split over three branches and shows a broad selection of European works, including masterpieces from ancient civilisations, the Italian Renaissance and the Dutch Golden Age.

Novodevichy Convent   CONVENT
(Новодевичий монастырь; adult/student R300/100, photos R100; ⊙grounds 8am-8pm, museums 9am-5pm Wed-Mon; Ⓜ Sportivnaya) The Novodevichy Convent was founded in 1524 to celebrate the taking of Smolensk from Lithuania, an important step in Moscow's conquest of the old Kyivan Rus lands. The oldest and most dominant building in the grounds is the white Smolensk Cathedral, with a sumptuous interior covered in 16th-century frescoes. Novodevichy is a functioning monastery. Women are advised to cover their heads and shoulders when

---

THE BANYA

Taking a traditional Russian banya is a must. These wet saunas are a social hub and a fantastic experience for any visitor to Russia. Leave your inhibitions at home and be prepared for a beating with birch twigs (far more pleasant than it sounds). Ask at your accommodation for the nearest public banya. In Moscow, try the luxurious **Sanduny Baths** (☑495-628 4633; www.sanduny.ru; Neglinnaya ul 14; per person R1500-2300; ⊙8am-10pm; Ⓜ Kuznetsky Most) and in St Petersburg the traditional **Mytninskiye Bani** (Мытнинские бани; www.mybanya.spb.ru; Mytninskaya ul 17-19; per hr R100-200; ⊙8am-10pm Fri-Tue; Ⓜ Ploshchad Vosstaniya).

---

entering the churches, while men should wear long pants.

Cathedral of
Christ the Saviour   CHURCH
(Храм Христа Спасителя; ul Volkhonka 15; ⊙1-5pm Mon, 10am-5pm Tue-Sun; Ⓜ Kropotkinskaya) FREE This gargantuan cathedral was completed in 1997 – just in time to celebrate Moscow's 850th birthday. It is amazingly opulent, garishly grandiose and truly historic. The cathedral's sheer size and splendour guarantee its role as a love-it-or-hate-it landmark. Considering Stalin's plan for this site (a Palace of Soviets topped with a 100m statue of Lenin), Muscovites should at least be grateful they can admire the shiny domes of a church instead of the shiny dome of Ilyich's head.

Tours

Moscow Free Tour   WALKING TOUR
(☑495-222 3466; http://moscowfreetour.com; Nikolskaya ul 4/5; paid tours R950-1550) Every day, these enthusiastic ladies offer an informative, inspired two-hour guided walk around Red Square and Kitay Gorod – and it's completely free. It's so good, that (they think) you'll sign up for one of their excellent paid tours, covering the Kremlin, the Arbat and the Metro, or more thematic tours like communist Moscow or mystical Moscow.

Moscow 360   WALKING TOUR
(☑8-915-205 8360; www.moscow360.org) FREE This ambitious company offers four – count 'em, four! – different walking tours, all of which are free. They include tours of Red Square, the Cathedral of Christ the Saviour and the Metro, as well as – the most unusual – an AK-47 Tour (the tour and transport are free, but you'll pay to shoot). Tips are gratefully accepted, obviously.

Sleeping

Affordable alternatives to generally expensive hotels are the city's many hostels and rental apartments.

Godzillas Hostel   HOSTEL €
(☑495-699 4223; www.godzillashostel.com; Bolshoy Karetny per 6; dm from R760, s/d R2400/2600; ✳@⍈; Ⓜ Tsvetnoy Bulvar) Tried and true, Godzillas is Moscow's best-known hostel, with dozens of beds spread out over four floors. The rooms come in various sizes, but they are all spacious and light-filled and

painted in different colours. To cater to the many guests, there are bathroom facilities on each floor, three kitchens and a big living room with satellite TV.

Anti-Hostel Cosmic
HOSTEL €

(☑ 499-390 8132; http://anti-hostel.ru; ul Bolshaya Dmitrovka 7/5 str 3; capsules from R1350; 🖥; Ⓜ Teatralnaya) Occupying a converted apartment, this place marries the idea of hostel with that of capsule hotel. The location is hard to beat – Red Square is just a five-minute walk away. Capsules create a tiny, though comfortable, universe for guests to enjoy on their own. There is also a nice common area to mingle with fellow capsule-dwellers.

★ Blues Hotel
BOUTIQUE HOTEL €€

(☑ 495-961 1161; www.blues-hotel.ru; ul Dovatora 8; s/d from R5800/6300; ⊜🌐🖥; Ⓜ Sportivnaya) The location is not exactly central, but is not a disadvantage. It is steps from the red-line metro (five stops to Red Square) and a few blocks from Novodevichy, with several worthwhile restaurants in the vicinity. Considering that, this friendly, affordable boutique hotel is a gem, offering stylish, spotless rooms with king-size beds and flat-screen TVs.

Sleepbox Hotel
HOTEL €€

(☑ 495-989 4104; www.sleepbox-hotel.ru; ul 1-ya Tverskaya-Yamskaya 27; s without bathroom from R3200, d from R4700, q from R5500; 🌐🖥; Ⓜ Belorusskaya) It might draw comparisons with capsule hotels, but it is actually better. Think a comfortable train compartment – it's close to what you get in this immaculately clean and unusual hotel, conveniently located for those arriving by train from Sheremetyevo airport. Common showers and toilets are very modern and clean; queues are unusual.

★ Hotel Metropol
HISTORIC HOTEL €€€

(☑ 499-501 7800; www.metropol-moscow.ru; Teatralny proezd 1/4; d R9930-11,400; ⊜🌐@🖥; Ⓜ Teatralnaya) Nothing short of an art nouveau masterpiece, the 1907 Metropol brings an artistic, historic touch to every nook and cranny, from the spectacular exterior to the grand lobby, to the individually decorated (but small) rooms. The breakfast buffet (R2000) is ridiculously priced, but it's served under the restaurant's gorgeous stained-glass ceiling.

Hotel de Paris
BOUTIQUE HOTEL €€€

(☑ 495-777 0052; www.hotel-deparis.ru; Bolshaya Bronnaya ul 23, bldg 3; s/d from R9000/9450; 🅿⊜🌐🖥; Ⓜ Pushkinskaya) Steps from the madness of Tverskaya, this is a delightfully stylish hotel tucked into a quiet courtyard off the Boulevard Ring. Situated on the lower floors, the rooms do not get much natural light, but they feature king-size beds, Jacuzzi tubs and elegant design. Service is consistently friendly. Prices drop by 40% on weekends, offering terrific value.

🍴 Eating

★ Varenichnaya No 1
RUSSIAN €

(www.varenichnaya.ru; ul Arbat 29; mains R200-400; ⊙ 10am-midnight; ⊜🌐@🖥; Ⓜ Arbatskaya) Retro Soviet is all the rage in Moscow, but this old-style Varenichnaya does it right, with books lining the walls, old movies on the black-and-white TV, and Cold War-era prices. The menu features tasty, filling *vareniki* and *pelmeni* (different kinds of dumplings), with sweet and savoury fillings. Bonus: an excellent housemade pickled vegie plate to make you pucker.

★ Delicatessen
INTERNATIONAL €€

(Деликатесы; www.newdeli.ru; Savodvaya-Karetnaya ul 20; mains R450-700; ⊙ noon-midnight Tue-Sat; 🖥@; Ⓜ Tsvetnoy Bulvar) The affable (and chatty) owners of this place travel the world and experiment with the menu a lot, turning burgers, pizzas and pasta into artfully constructed objects of modern culinary art. The other source of joy is a cabinet filled with bottles of ripening fruity liquors, which may destroy your budget if consumed uncontrollably (a pointless warning, we know).

Khachapuri
GEORGIAN €€

(☑ 8-985-764 3118; http://hacha.ru; Bolshoy Gnezdnikovsky per 10; khachapuri R200-350, mains R400-600; ⊜🖥@; Ⓜ Pushkinskaya) Unassuming, affordable and appetising, this urban cafe exemplifies what people love about Georgian culture: the warm hospitality and the freshly baked *khachapuri* (cheese bread). Aside from seven types of delicious *khachapuri,* there's also an array of soups, *shashlyki* (kebabs), *khinkali* (dumplings) and other Georgian favourites.

As Eat Is
INTERNATIONAL €€

(Как Есть; ☑ 495-699 5313; www.aseatis.ru; Tryokhprudny per 11/13; mains R500-900; ⊙ noon-11pm; ⊜🌐@; Ⓜ Mayakovskaya) We love the understated, eclectic interior, with its mismatched textures, appealingly packed bookshelves and vintage detailing. Even more, we love the contemporary seasonal fare, which is delightful to look at and divine to eat. It's

MOSCOW'S WHITE-HOT ART SCENE

Revamped old industrial buildings and other spaces in Moscow are where you'll find gems of Russia's super creative contemporary art scene. Apart from the following recommended spots, also see www.artguide.ru.

Garage Museum of Contemporary Art (www.garageccc.com; ul Krymsky val 9; adult/student R300/150; ⊘11am-9pm Mon-Thu; Ⓜ Oktyabrskaya) In a temporary pavilion constructed of cardboard in Gorky Park, Garage hosts exciting exhibitions by top artists.

Proekt_Fabrika (www.proektfabrika.ru; 18 Perevedenovsky per; ⊘10am-8pm Tue-Sun; Ⓜ Baumanskaya) **FREE** A still-functioning paper factory is the location for this nonprofit set of gallery and performance spaces enlivened by arty graffiti and creative-industry offices.

Red October (Завод Красный Октябрь; Bersenevskaya nab; Ⓜ Kropotkinskaya) **FREE** The red-brick buildings of this former chocolate factory now host the **Lumiere Brothers Photography Centre** (www.lumiere.ru; Bolotnaya nab 3, Bldg 1; ⊘noon-9pm Tue-Fri, to 10pm Sat & Sun) plus other galleries, cool bars and restaurants. In an adjacent building the **Strelka Institute for Media, Architecture and Design** (www.strelkainstitute.ru; bldg 5a, Bersenevskaya nab 14/5; Ⓜ Novokuznetskaya) is worth checking out for its events, bookshop and bar.

Vinzavod (Винзавод; www.winzavod.ru; 4 Syromyatnichesky per 1; Ⓜ Chkalovskaya) **FREE** A former wine factory has morphed into this postindustrial complex of prestigious galleries, shops, a cinema and trendy cafe.

---

the kind of food that would normally cost big bucks, but prices are reasonable. Extra love for the bilingual pun of a name.

Lavka-Lavka INTERNATIONAL €€
(Лавка-Лавка; ☑903-115 5033; http://restoran.lavkalavka.com/?lang=en; ul Petrovka 21 str 2; dishes R400-600; ⊘10am-midnight Sun-Thu, 10am-1am Fri-Sat; ⚐; Ⓜ Teatralnaya) ⚐ Welcome to the Russian Portlandia – all the food here is organic and hails from little farms where you may rest assured all the lambs and chickens lived a very happy life before being served to you on a plate. Irony aside, this is a great place to sample local food cooked in a funky improvisational style.

Café Pushkin RUSSIAN €€€
(Кафе Пушкинь; ☑495-739 0033; www.cafe-pushkin.ru; Tverskoy bul 26a; business lunch R750, mains R1000-2200; ⊘24hr; ⚐⚐⚐; Ⓜ Pushkinskaya) The tsarina of *haute-russe* dining, with an exquisite blend of Russian and French cuisines – service and food are done to perfection. The lovely 19th-century building has a different atmosphere on each floor, including a richly decorated library and a pleasant rooftop cafe.

 Drinking & Nightlife

★**3205** CAFE
(☑905-703 3205; www.veranda3205.ru; ul Karetny Ryad 3; ⊘11am-3am; Ⓜ Pushkinskaya) The biggest drinking/eating establishment in Hermitage Gardens, this verandah positioned at the back of the main building looks a bit like a greenhouse. In summer, tables (and patrons) spill out into the park, making it one of the city's best places for outdoor drinking. With its long bar and joyful atmosphere, the place also heaves in winter.

Enthusiast BAR
(Энтузиаст; per Stoleshnikov str 5; ⊘noon-11pm; Ⓜ Teatralnaya) Scooter enthusiast, that is. But you don't have to be one in order to enjoy this superbly laid-back bar hidden at the far end of a fancifully shaped courtyard and disguised as a spare-parts shop. On a warm day, grab a beer or cider, settle into a beach chair and let harmony descend on you.

Noor BAR
(☑499-130 6030; www.noorbar.com; ul Tverskaya 23; ⊘3pm-3am Mon-Wed, noon-6am Thu-Sun; Ⓜ Pushkinskaya) There is little to say about this misleadingly unassuming bar, apart from the fact that everything in it is close to

perfection. It has it all – prime location, convivial atmosphere, eclectic DJ music, friendly bartenders and superb drinks. Though declared 'the best' by various magazines on several occasions, it doesn't feel like they care.

Time-Out Bar   COCKTAIL BAR
(www.timeoutbar.ru; 12th fl, Bolshaya Sadovaya ul 5; ⊙noon-2am Sun-Thu, noon-6am Fri & Sat; ⓂMayakovskaya) On the upper floors of the throwback Pekin Hotel, this trendy bar is nothing but 'now'. That includes the bartenders sporting plaid and their delicious concoctions, especially created for different times of day. The decor is pretty impressive – particularly the spectacular city skyline. Perfect place for sundowners (or sun-ups, if you last that long).

OMG! Coffee   CAFE
(☑495-722 6954; www.omgcoffee.net; ul Staray Basmannaya 6 str 3; ⊙8.30am-11pm Mon-Fri, 11am-11pm Sat & Sun; ⓂKrasnye Vorota) The more Russia falls out with the US, the more Brooklyn-esque the Moscow cafe scene becomes. This smallish local is very scientific (or in their own words – psychotic) about coffee, which they buy from trusted roasting specialists and brew using seven different methods. They also serve delightful gourmet burgers and sandwiches.

☆ Entertainment

To find out what's on, see the entertainment section in Thursday's *Moscow Times*. Most theatres, including the Bolshoi, are closed between late June and early September.

★Bolshoi Theatre   BALLET, OPERA
(Большой театр; www.bolshoi.ru; Teatralnaya pl 1; tickets R200-4000; ⊙closed Jul & Aug; ⓂTeatralnaya) An evening at the Bolshoi is still one of Moscow's most romantic and entertaining options for a night on the town. The glittering six-tier auditorium has an electric atmosphere, evoking over 235 years of premier music and dance. Both the ballet and opera companies perform a range of Russian and foreign works here. After the collapse of the Soviet Union, the Bolshoi was marred by politics, scandal and frequent turnover. Yet the show must go on – and it will.

Tchaikovsky Concert Hall   CLASSICAL MUSIC
(Концертный зал имени Чайковского; ☑495-232 0400; www.meloman.ru; Triumfalnaya pl 4/31; tickets R300-3000; ⊙closed Jul & Aug; ⓂMayak-

CAFES, CLUBS & ANTI-CAFES
There's a hazy distinction between cafe, bar and nightclub in Russia's cities, with many places serving all three functions. As such, we list them all in one place.

Top clubs have strict *feis kontrol* (face control); beat by arriving early before the bouncers are posted, or by speaking English, as being a foreigner helps.

Currently popular are 'anti-cafes': 'creative spaces' where you pay by the minute and enjoy coffee, snacks and access to everything from wi-fi to computer games and musical instruments. They are great places to meet locals.

ovskaya) Home to the famous Moscow State Philharmonic (Moskovskaya Filharmonia), the capital's oldest symphony orchestra, Tchaikovsky Concert Hall was established in 1921. It's a huge auditorium, with seating for 1600 people. This is where you can expect to hear the Russian classics such as Stravinsky, Rachmaninov and Shostakovich, as well as other European favourites. Look out for special children's concerts.

Masterskaya   LIVE MUSIC
(Мастерская; www.mstrsk.ru; Teatralny proezd 3 str 3; ⊙noon-6am; ☎; ⓂLubyanka) All the best places in Moscow are tucked into far corners of courtyards, and they often have unmarked doors. Such is the case with this super-funky music venue. The eclectic, arty interior makes a cool place to chill out during the day. Evening hours give way to a diverse array of live-music acts or the occasional dance or theatre performance.

🔒 Shopping

Ul Arbat has always been a tourist attraction and is littered with souvenir shops and stalls.

GUM   MALL
(ГУМ; www.gum.ru; Krasnaya pl 3; ⊙10am-10pm; ⓂPloshchad Revolyutsii) The elaborate 240m facade on the northeastern side of Red Square, GUM is a bright, bustling shopping mall with hundreds of fancy stores and restaurants. With a skylight roof and three-level arcades, the spectacular interior was a revolutionary design when it was built

in the 1890s, replacing the Upper Trading Rows that previously occupied this site.

Izmaylovsky Market
MARKET

(www.kremlin-izmailovo.com; Izmaylovskoye shosse 73; ◷10am-8pm; Ⓜ Partizanskaya) This sprawling area, also known as Vernisazh market, is packed with art, handmade crafts, antiques, Soviet paraphernalia and just about anything you might want for a souvenir. You'll find Moscow's biggest original range of *matryoshki, palekh* and *khokhloma* ware, as well as less traditional woodworking crafts. There are also rugs from the Caucasus and Central Asia, pottery, linens, jewellery, fur hats, chess sets, toys, Soviet posters and much more.

ⓘ Information

Wireless access is ubiquitous and almost always free.

36.6 (Аптека 36.6; ☑ 495-797 6366; www.366.ru) A chain of 24-hour pharmacies with many branches all around the city.

American Medical Centre (☑ 495-933 7700; www.amcenter.ru; Grokholsky per 1; ◷24hr; Ⓜ Pr Mira) Offers 24-hour emergency service, consultations and a full range of medical specialists.

Main Post Office (Myasnitskaya ul 26; ◷24hr; Ⓜ Chistye Prudy)

Maria Travel Agency (☑ 495-777 8226; www.maria-travel.com; ul Maroseyka 13; Ⓜ Kitay-Gorod) Offers visa support, apartment rental and some local tours, including the Golden Ring.

Moscow Times (www.themoscowtimes.com) Best locally published English-language newspaper, widely distributed free of charge.

Unifest Travel (☑ 495-234 6555; http://unifest.ru/en.html; Komsomolsky prospekt 16/2) On-the-ball travel company offers rail and air tickets, visa support and more.

ⓘ Getting Around

TO/FROM THE AIRPORT

All three Moscow airports (Domodedovo, Sheremetyevo or Vnukovo) are accessible by the convenient **Aeroexpress Train** (☑ 8-800-700 3377; www.aeroexpress.ru; R340-400; ◷6am-midnight) from the city centre; reduced rate is available for online purchase.

Alternatively, order an official airport taxi from the dispatcher's desk in the terminal (R2000 to R2200 to the city centre). You can save some cash by booking in advance to take advantage of the fixed rates offered by most companies (usually from R1500 to R1800 to/

METRO TOUR

For just R40 you can spend the day touring Moscow's magnificent metro stations. Many of these are marble-faced, frescoed, gilded works of art. Among our favourites are **Komsomolskaya**, a huge stuccoed hall, its ceiling covered with mosaics depicting military heroes; **Novokuznetskaya**, featuring military bas-reliefs done in sober khaki, and colourful ceiling mosaics depicting pictures of the happy life; and **Mayakovskaya**, Grand Prize winner at the 1939 World's Fair in New York.

---

from any airport). Driving times vary wildly depending on traffic.

PUBLIC TRANSPORT

The **Moscow Metro** (www.mosmetro.ru) is by far the easiest, quickest and cheapest way of getting around the city. Stations are marked outside by 'M' signs. Magnetic tickets (R40) are sold at ticket booths. Save time by buying a multiple-ride ticket (five rides for R160, 11 rides for R320, 20 rides for R540). The ticket is a contactless smart card, which you must tap on the reader before going through the turnstile.

Buses, trolleybuses and trams are useful along a few radial or cross-town routes that the metro misses, and are necessary for reaching sights away from the city centre. Tickets (R40) are sold on the vehicle by a conductor.

TAXI

Unofficial taxis are still common in Moscow. Expect to pay R200 to R400 for a ride around the city centre, depending on your haggling skills.

Detskoe Taxi (Детское такси; ☑ 495-765 1180; www.detskoetaxi.ru; 8km for R500) 'Children's Taxi' has smoke-free cars and car seats for your children.

Taxi Blues (☑ 495-105 5115; www.taxi-blues.ru)

Veliky Novgorod
Великий Новгород

☑ 8162 / POP 219,925

Veliky Novgorod (usually shortened to Novgorod) is a proud and beautiful city, billed as the 'Birthplace of Russia'. It was here, in 862, that Prince Rurik proclaimed the modern Russian state – the Rurik dynasty went on to rule Russia for more than 750 years. Its glorious Cathedral of St Sophia is the oldest church in Russia. Straddling the

Volkhov River, this attractive, tourist-friendly destination is a popular weekend getaway for St Petersburg residents – to avoid the crowds, come during the week.

⊙ Sights

Kremlin
FORTRESS

(⊙ 6am-midnight) FREE On the west bank of the Volkhov River, and surrounded by a pleasant wooded park, the kremlin is one of Russia's oldest. Originally called the Detinets (and still often referred to as such), the fortification dates back to the 9th century, though it was later rebuilt with brick in the 14th century; this still stands today. The complex is worth seeing with a guide; arrange one through the tourist office. Boat tours run hourly (May to October, R300) from the Kremlin's pier and Yaroslav's Court towards Lake Ilmen: contact the tourist office to book.

★ Cathedral of St Sophia
CHURCH

(Софийский собор; www.saintsofianovg.ortox. ru; ⊙ 8am-8pm, services 10am-noon daily & 6-8pm Wed-Sun) This is the oldest church in Russia (finished in 1050) and one of the country's oldest stone buildings. It's the kremlin's focal point and you couldn't miss it if you tried – its golden dome positively *glows*. St Sophia houses many icons dating from the 14th century, but none are as important as that of Novgorod's patron saint, Our Lady of the Sign, which, the story goes, miraculously saved the city from destruction in 1170 after being struck by an arrow.

★ Novgorod State United Museum
MUSEUM

(Новгородский государственный объединенный музей-заповедник; www.novgorodmuseum.ru; adult/student R150/100; ⊙ 10am-6pm Wed-Mon, closed last Thu of the month) This must-see museum houses three strikingly comprehensive exhibitions covering the history of Veliky Novgorod, Russian woodcarving and Russian icons. The latter contains one of the world's largest collections of icons, with around 260 pieces placed in chronological order, allowing you to appreciate the progression of skills and techniques through the centuries.

Yaroslav's Court
HISTORIC SITE

Across a footbridge from the kremlin are the remnants of an 18th-century market arcade. Beyond that is the market gatehouse, an array of churches sponsored by 13th- to 16th-century merchant guilds, and a 'road palace' built in the 18th century as a rest stop for Catherine the Great.

The 12th-century **Court Cathedral of St Nicholas** (Храм Николая Чудотворца; adult/student R100/60; ⊙ 10am-noon & 1-6pm Wed-Sun, closed last Fri of month) is all that remains of the early palace complex of the Novgorod princes, from which Yaroslav's Court (Yaroslavovo dvorishche) gets its name. The cathedral holds church artefacts and temporary exhibitions of local interest. Downstairs you can see fragments from the church's original frescoes.

🛏 Sleeping & Eating

★ Hotel Volkhov
HOTEL €€

(Гостиница Волхов; ☎ 8162-225 500; www.hotel-volkhov.ru; ul Predtechenskaya 24; s/d from R2150/3100; @ 🕏) This centrally located, modern hotel runs like a well-oiled machine, with nicely furnished rooms, pleasant English-speaking staff, laundry service and free wi-fi. A sauna (extra fee) is available to guests. The included breakfasts (choice of Continental, Russian or 'American') are actually very good.

★ Nice People
INTERNATIONAL €€

(Хорошие люди; ☎ 8162-730 879; www.gonicepeople.ru; ul Meretskova-Volosova 1/1; meals R380-620; ⊙ 8am-midnight; 🕏 📱) By far the most appealing choice in Novgorod, this cafe-bar lives up to its name – you'll get a warm welcome from English-speaking staff, and the clientele is pretty easygoing, too. The menu includes speciality DIY salads, with a huge range of ingredients from which to choose. Other tasty treats and daily specials are written on the walls.

❶ Getting There & Away

The train station (Новгород-на-Волхове on RZD timetables) and bus station (Автовокзал) are next to each other on Oktyabryskaya ul, 1.5km northwest of the kremlin.

Lastochka high speed trains connect with St Petersburg's Moscow Station (R400, three hours, two daily). Moscow can be reached in 4½ hours on a combination of *Lastochka* and *Sapsan* high speed trains or via a handy overnight train (*platskart/kupe* R1250/2400, eight hours) leaving at 9.20pm.

Bus services include St Petersburg (R330, four hours, 13 daily).

St Petersburg
Санкт-Петербург

📋 812 / POP 4.8 MILLION

Affectionately known as Piter to locals, St Petersburg is a visual delight. The Neva River and surrounding canals reflect unbroken facades of handsome 18th- and 19th-century buildings that house a spellbinding collection of cultural storehouses, culminating in the incomparable Hermitage. Home to many of Russia's greatest creative talents (Pushkin, Dostoevsky, Tchaikovsky), Piter still inspires a contemporary generation of Russians making it a liberal, hedonistic and exciting place to visit as well as a giant warehouse of culture.

The city covers many islands, some real, some created through the construction of canals. The central street is Nevsky pr, which extends some 4km from the Alexander Nevsky Monastery to the Hermitage.

⊙ Sights

General Staff Building   MUSEUM
(Здание Главного штаба; www.hermitage museum.org; Dvortsovaya pl 6-8; admission R100; ☺10.30am-6pm Tue & Thu-Sun, 10.30am-9pm Wed; Ⓜ Admiralteyskaya) The east wing of this magnificent building, wrapping around the south of Dvortsovaya pl and designed by Carlo Rossi in the 1820s, marries restored interiors with contemporary architecture to create a series of galleries displaying the Hermitage's amazing collection of Impressionist and post-Impressionist works. Contemporary art is here, too, often in temporary exhibitions by major artists.

Russian Museum   MUSEUM
(Русский музей; www.rusmuseum.ru; Inzhenernaya ul 4; adult/student R350/150, 4-palace ticket adult/child R600/300; ☺10am-6pm Wed & Fri-Sun, 10am-5pm Mon, 1-9pm Thu; Ⓜ Nevsky Prospekt) The handsome Mikhailovsky Palace is home to the country's biggest collection of Russian art. After the Hermitage you may feel you have had your fill of art, but try your utmost to make some time for this gem of a museum. There's also a lovely garden behind the palace.

Church on the Spilled Blood   CHURCH
(Храм Спаса-на-Крови; http://cathedral. ru; Konyushennaya pl; adult/student R250/150; ☺10.30am-6pm Thu-Tue; Ⓜ Nevsky Prospekt) This five-domed dazzler is St Petersburg's most elaborate church with a classic Russian Orthodox exterior and interior decorated with some 7000 sq metres of mosaics. Officially called the Church of the Resurrection of Christ, its far more striking colloquial name references the assassination attempt on Tsar Alexander II here in 1881.

St Isaac's Cathedral   MUSEUM
(Isaakievsky Sobor; www.cathedral.ru; Isaakievskaya pl; cathedral adult/student R250/150, colonnade R150; ☺10.30am-6pm Thu-Tue, cathedral closed Wed, colonnade 1st & 3rd Wed; Ⓜ Admiralteyskaya)

RUSSIA'S MOST FAMOUS STREET

Walking **Nevsky Prospekt** is an essential St Petersburg experience. Highlights along it incude the **Kazan Cathedral** (Казанский собор; http://kazansky-spb.ru; Kazanskaya pl 2; ☺8.30am-7.30pm; Ⓜ Nevsky Prospekt) FREE with its curved arms reaching out towards the avenue.

Opposite is the **Singer Building** (Nevsky pr 28; Ⓜ Nevsky Prospekt), a Style Moderne (art deco) beauty restored to all its splendour when it was the headquarters of the sewing-machine company; inside is the bookshop **Dom Knigi** (www.spbdk.ru; Nevsky pr 28; ☺9am-1am; 🖥; Ⓜ Nevsky Prospekt) and **Café Singer** (Nevsky pr 28; ☺9am-11pm; 🖥; Ⓜ Nevsky Prospekt), serving good food and drinks with a great view over the street.

Further along are the covered arcades of Rastrelli's historic **Bolshoy Gostiny Dvor** (Большой Гостиный Двор; http://bgd.ru; Nevsky pr 35; ☺10am-10pm; Ⓜ Gostiny Dvor) department store, while on the corner of Sadovaya ul is the Style Moderne classic **Kupetz Eliseevs** (http://kupetzeliseevs.ru; Nevsky pr 56; ☺10am-10pm; 🖥; Ⓜ Gostiny Dvor) reincarnated as a luxury grocery and cafe.

An enormous **statue of Catherine the Great** stands at the centre of **Ploshchad Ostrovskogo** (Площадь Островского; Ⓜ Gostiny Dvor), commonly referred to as the Catherine Gardens; at the southern end of the gardens is **Alexandrinsky Theatre** (📋 812-710 4103; www.alexandrinsky.ru; pl Ostrovskogo 2; Ⓜ Gostiny Dvor), where Chekhov's *The Seagull* premiered (to tepid reviews) in 1896.

DON'T MISS

STATE HERMITAGE MUSEUM

Mainly set in the magnificent Winter Palace and adjoining buildings, the **Hermitage** (Государственный Эрмитаж; www.hermitagemuseum.org; Dvortsovaya pl 2; adult/student R400/free, 1st Thu of month free, camera R200; ⊙ 10.30am-6pm Tue & Thu-Sun, to 9pm Wed; Ⓜ Admiralteyskaya) fully lives up to its sterling reputation. You can be absorbed by its treasures for days and still come out wanting more.

The enormous collection (over three million items, only a fraction of which are on display in around 360 rooms) almost amounts to a comprehensive history of Western European art. Viewing it demands a little planning, so choose the areas you'd like to concentrate on before you arrive. The museum consists of five connected buildings. From west to east they are:

Winter Palace Designed by Bartolomeo Rastrelli, its opulent state rooms, Great Church, Pavilion Hall and Treasure Rooms shouldn't be missed.

Small Hermitage and Old Hermitage Both were built for Catherine the Great, partly to house the art collection started by Peter the Great, which she significantly expanded. Here you'll find works by Rembrant, Da Vinci and Caravaggio.

New Hermitage Built for Nicholas II, to hold the still-growing art collection. The Old and New Hermitages are sometimes grouped together and labelled the Large Hermitage.

State Hermitage Theatre Built in the 1780s by the Giacomo Quarenghi. Concerts and ballets are still performed here.

The golden dome of St Isaac's Cathedral dominates the St Petersburg skyline. Its obscenely lavish interior is open as a museum, although services are held in the cathedral on major religious holidays. Most people bypass the museum to climb the 262 steps to the *kolonnada* (colonnade) around the drum of the dome, providing superb city views.

Peter & Paul Fortress   FORTRESS

(Петропавловская крепость; www.spbmuseum. ru; grounds free, exhibitions adult R60-150, student R40-80; ⊙ grounds 8.30am-8pm, exhibitions 11am-6pm Mon & Thu-Sun, 10am-5pm Tue; Ⓜ Gorkovskaya) Housing a cathedral where the Romanovs are buried, a former prison and various exhibitions, this large defensive fortress on Zayachy Island is the kernel from which St Petersburg grew into the city it is today. History buffs will love it and everyone will swoon at the panoramic views from atop the fortress walls, at the foot of which lies a sandy riverside beach, a prime spot for sunbathing.

Kunstkamera   MUSEUM

(Кунсткамера; www.kunstkamera.ru; Tamozhenny per; adult/child R250/50; ⊙ 11am-7pm Tue-Sun; Ⓜ Admiralteyskaya) Also known as the Museum of Ethnology and Anthropology, the Kunstkamera is the city's first museum and was founded in 1714 by Peter himself. It is famous largely for its ghoulish collection of monstrosities, preserved 'freaks', two-headed mutant foetuses, deformed animals and odd body parts, all collected by Peter with the aim of educating the notoriously superstitious Russian people. While most rush to see these sad specimens, there are also very interesting exhibitions on native peoples from around the world.

Strelka   LANDMARK

Among the oldest parts of Vasilyevsky Island, this eastern tip is where Peter the Great wanted his new city's administrative and intellectual centre to be. In fact, the Strelka became the focus of St Petersburg's maritime trade, symbolised by the colonnaded Customs House (now the Pushkin House). The two Rostral Columns, archetypal St Petersburg landmarks, are studded with ships' prows and four seated sculptures representing four of Russia's great rivers: the Neva, the Volga, the Dnieper and the Volkhov.

🏃 Activities

Especially during White Nights, cycling is a brilliant and economical way to get around St Petersburg's spread-out sights, restaurants and bars. Off main drags like Nevsky pr

Central St Petersburg

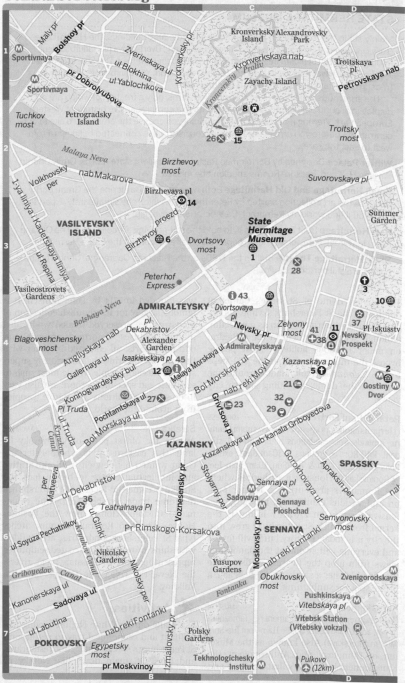

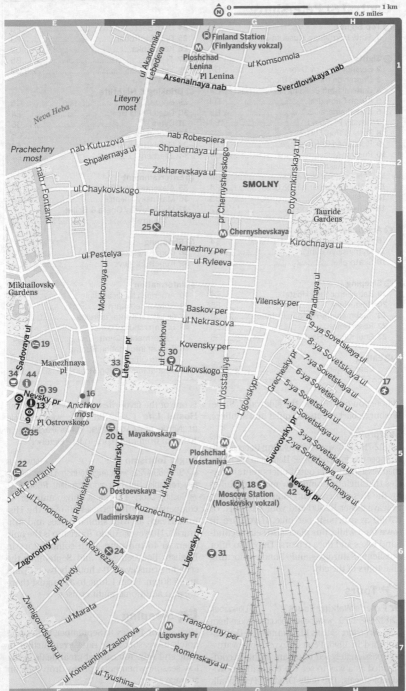

RUSSIA ST PETERSBURG

Central St Petersburg

(where you can ride on the sidewalk), St Petersburg's backstreets are quiet and sublime.

Skatprokat CYCLING
(☑812-717 6838; www.skatprokat.ru; Goncharnaya ul 7; per day from R400; ☺11am-8pm; Ⓜ Ploshchad Vosstaniya) This outfit offers rental bicycles that include brand-new mountain bikes by the Russian company Stark. You'll need to leave either R2000 and your passport, or R7000 as a deposit per bike. If you are in town for a while, this place also sells secondhand bikes and does repairs. They also offer excellent Saturday- and Sunday-morning bike tours of the city.

⌖ Tours

★ **Peter's Walking Tours** WALKING TOUR
(☑812-943 1229; www.peterswalk.com; tours from R750 per person; ☺tours 10.30am mid-Apr–Oct) Established in 1996, Peter Kozyrev's innovative and passionately led tours are highly recommended as a way to see the city with knowledgable locals. The daily Original Peterswalk

is one of the favourites and leaves daily from **Hostel Life** (☑812-318 1808; www.hostel-life.ru; Nevsky pr 47, Vosstaniya; Ⓜ Mayakovskaya) at 10.30am from mid-April to late October.

Anglo Tourismo BOAT TOUR
(☑921-989 4722; www.anglotourismo.com; 27 nab reki Fontanki; 1hr tour adult/student R650/550; Ⓜ Gostiny Dvor) There's a huge number of companies offering cruises all over the Historic Heart, all with similar prices and itineraries. However, Anglo Tourismo is the only operator to run tours with commentary in English. Between May and September the schedule runs every 1½ hours between 11am and 6.30pm. From 1 June to 31 August there are also additional night cruises.

⌸ Sleeping

High season is May to September, with some hotels increasing their rates even further in June and July. You can get great deals in the low season, when hotel prices drop 30% on average.

★**Soul Kitchen Hostel** HOSTEL €

(☎8-965-816 3470; www.soulkitchenhostel.com; nab reki Moyki 62/2, apt 9, Sennaya; dm/d from R900/3600; ☻@☎; ⓂAdmiralteyskaya) Soul Kitchen blends boho hipness and boutique-hotel comfort, scoring perfect 10s in many key categories: private rooms (chic), dorm beds (double-wide with privacy-protecting curtains), common areas (vast), kitchen (vast *and* beautiful) and bathrooms (down-right inviting). There is also bike hire, table football, free Macs to use, free international phone calls and stunning Moyka views from a communal balcony.

Baby Lemonade Hostel HOSTEL €

(☎812-570 7943; www.facebook.com/pages/Baby-Lemonade-Hostel; Inzhernernaya ul 7; dm/d with shared bathroom from R790/2590, d from R3250; @☎; ⓂGostiny Dvor) The owner of Baby Lemonade is crazy about the 1960s and it shows in the pop-art, psychedelic design of this friendly, fun hostel with two pleasant, large dorms and a great kitchen and living room. However, it's worth splashing out for the boutique, hotel-worthy private rooms that are in a separate flat with great rooftop views. Breakfast included.

★**Rachmaninov Antique Hotel** BOUTIQUE HOTEL €€

(☎812-327 7466; www.hotelrachmaninov.com; Kazanskaya ul 5; s/d incl breakfast from R6300/7100; @☎; ⓂNevsky Prospekt) The long-established Rachmaninov still feels like a secret place for those in the know. Perfectly located and run by friendly staff, it's pleasantly old world with hardwood floors and attractive Russian furnishings, particularly in the breakfast salon which has a grand piano.

Rossi Hotel BOUTIQUE HOTEL €€€

(☎812-635 6333; www.rossihotels.com; nab reki Fontanki 55; s/d/ste incl breakfast from R12,000/12,900/18,000; ⊛@☎; ⓂGostiny Dvor) Occupying a beautifully restored building on one of St Petersburg's prettiest squares, the Rossi's 53 rooms are all designed differently, but their brightness and moulded ceilings are uniform. Antique beds, super-sleek bathrooms, exposed brick walls and lots of cool designer touches create a great blend of old and new.

✕ **Eating**

★**Duo Gastrobar** FUSION €

(☎812-994 5443; www.duobar.ru; ul Kirochnaya 8a; mains R200-500; ⊙1pm-midnight, to 2am Fri & Sat; ⊖; ⓂChernyshevskaya) This light-bathed place, done out in wood and gorgeous glass lampshades, has really helped put this otherwise quiet area on the culinary map. Its short fusion menu excels, featuring such unlikely delights as passionfruit and gorgonzola mousse and salmon with quinoa and marscarpone. There are also more conventional choices such as risottos, pastas and salads.

★**Yat** RUSSIAN €€

(Ять; ☎812-957 0023; http://eatinyat.com; nab reki Moyki 16; mains R500; ⊙11am-11pm; ☎⅏; ⓂAdmiralteyskaya) Perfectly placed for eating near to the Hermitage, this country-cottage-style restaurant has a very appealing menu of traditional dishes, which are presented with aplomb. The *shchi* (cabbage-based) soup is excellent and they offer a tempting range of flavoured vodkas. There's also a fab kids area with pet rabbits for them to feed.

Dom Beat INTERNATIONAL €€

(Дом Быта; www.dombeat.ru; ul Razyezzhaya 12; mains R300-500; ☎⅏⌀; ⓂLigovsky Prospekt) As if naming St Petersburg's coolest bar, lounge and restaurant after a Soviet all-purpose store and then dressing the model-gorgeous staff in tailored pastiches of factory uniforms wasn't a solid enough start, the sleek, retro-humorous interior, sumptuous menu and great atmosphere add up to make this one of the best eating choices in town.

Teplo MODERN EUROPEAN €€

(☎812-570 1974; www.v-teple.ru; Bolshaya Morskaya ul 45; mains R250-650; ⊙9am-midnight; ☻☎⅏⌀; ⓂAdmiralteyskaya)This much-feted, eclectic and original restaurant has got it all just right. The venue itself is a lot of fun to nose around, with multiple small rooms, nooks and crannies. Service is friendly and fast (when it's not too busy) and the peppy, inventive Italian-leaning menu has something for everyone. Reservations are usually needed, so call ahead.

Koryushka RUSSIAN, GEORGIAN €€

(Корюшка; ☎812-917 9010; http://ginzaproject.ru/SPB/Restaurants/Korushka/About; Petropavlovskaya krepost 3, Zayachy Island; mains R500; ⊙noon-midnight; ☎⌀⅏; ⓂGorkovskaya) Lightly battered and fried *koryushka* (smelt) is a St Petersburg speciality every April, but you can eat the small fish year-round at this relaxed, sophisticated restaurant beside the Peter and Paul Fortress. There are plenty of other very appealing Georgian dishes on the

WORTH A TRIP

PETERHOF & TSARSKOE SELO

Several palace estates around St Petersburg, country retreats for the tsars, are now among the most spectacular sights in Russia.

Peterhof (Петергоф; also known as Petrodvorets), 29km west of the city and built for Peter the Great, is best visited for its **Grand Cascade** (ul Razvodnaya 2; ◷10am-6pm Mon-Fri, to 8.30pm Sat, to 7pm Sun, May-early Oct) and Water Avenue, a symphony of over 140 fountains and canals located in the **Lower Park** (Нижний парк; adult/student R500/250, free Nov-Apr; ◷9am-8pm). There are several additional palaces, villas and parks here, each of which charges its own hefty admission price.

Tsarskoe Selo (Царское Село), 25km south of the city in the town of Pushkin, is home to the baroque **Catherine Palace** (Екатерининский дворец; http://eng.tzar.ru; adult/student R400/200, audioguide R150; ◷10am-6pm Wed-Sun, to 9pm Mon), expertly restored following its near destruction in WWII. From May to September individual visits to Catherine's Palace are limited to noon to 2pm and 4pm to 5pm, other times being reserved for tour groups.

Buses and *marshrutky* to Petrodvorets (R55, 30 minutes) run frequently from outside metro stations Avtovo and Leninsky Prospekt. From May to September, the **Peterhof Express** (adult single/return R650/1100, student single/return R450/800; ◷10am-6pm) hydrofoil leaves from jetties behind the Hermitage and behind the Admiralty.

The easiest way to get to Tsarskoe Selo is by *marshrutka* (R35) from Moskovskaya metro station.

---

menu to supplement the stunning views across the Neva.

🍷 Drinking & Nightlife

★**Borodabar** COCKTAIL BAR
(Kazanskaya ul 11; ◷6pm-6am; 🛜; Ⓜ Nevsky Prospekt) Boroda means beard in Russian, and sure enough you'll see plenty of facial hair and tattoos in this hipster cocktail hang-out. Never mind, as the mixologists really know their stuff – we can particularly recommend their smoked old fashioned, which is infused with tobacco smoke, and their colourful (and potent) range of shots.

★**Ziferberg** ANTI-CAFE
(http://ziferburg.ziferblat.net; 3rd fl, Passage, Nevsky pr 48; 1st hr/thereafter per min charge R2/1, max charge R360; ◷11am-midnight Sun-Thu, 11am-7am Fri & Sat; 🛜; Ⓜ Gostiny Dvor) Occupying much of the 3rd-floor gallery of Passage is this anti-cafe with a range of quirky, boho-hipster decorated spaces, some intimate, others very social. There's an excellent range of activities to enjoy with your coffee or tea, from board games and movies to concerts by classical music students, particularly on the weekends.

Dead Poets Bar COCKTAIL BAR
(ul Zhukovskogo 12; ◷2pm-2am; 🛜; Ⓜ Mayakovskaya) This very cool place is an adult cocktail bar, with a sophisticated drinks menu

and an almost unbelievable range of spirits stacked along the long bar and served up by a committed staff of mixologists. It's more of a quiet place, with low lighting, a jazz soundtrack and plenty of space to sit down.

Union Bar & Grill BAR
(Liteyny pr 55; ◷6pm-4am Sun-Thu, until 6am Fri & Sat; 🛜; Ⓜ Mayakovskaya) The Union is a glamorous and fun place, characterised by one enormous long wooden bar, low lighting and a New York feel. It's all rather adult, with a serious cocktail list and designer beers on tap. It's crazy at the weekends, but quiet during the week, and always draws a cool twenty- and thirty-something crowd.

Dyuni BAR
(Дюны; Ligovsky pr 50; ◷4pm-midnight, to 6am Fri & Sat; 🛜; Ⓜ Ploshchad Vosstaniya) What looks like a small suburban house sits rather incongruously here amid repurposed warehouses in this vast courtyard. There's a cosy indoor bar and a sand-covered outside area with table football and ping pong, which keeps the cool kids happy all night in the summer months. To find it, simply continue in a straight line from the courtyard entrance.

Radiobaby BAR, CLUB
(www.radiobaby.com; Kazanskaya ul 7; ◷6pm-6am; Ⓜ Nevsky Prospekt) Go through the arch at Kazanskaya 5 (not 7 – that's just the street

address), turn left through a second arch and you'll find this super-cool barnlike bar on your right. It's divided into several different rooms, there's a 'no techno, no house' music policy, table football, a relaxed crowd and an atmosphere of eternal hedonism. After 10pm each night the place becomes more a club than a bar.

☆ Entertainment

From July to mid-September the big theatres like the Mariinsky and the Mikhailovsky close but plenty of performances are still staged. Check the *St Petersburg Times* for comprehensive listings.

Mariinsky Theatre OPERA, BALLET
(Мариинский театр; ☎ 812-326 4141; www.mariinsky.ru; Teatralnaya pl 1; tickets R1000-6000; Ⓜ Sadovaya) Petersburg's most spectacular venue for ballet and opera, the Mariinsky Theatre is an attraction in its own right. Tickets can be bought online or in person, but they should be bought in advance during the summer months. The magnificent interior is the epitome of imperial grandeur, and any evening here will be an impressive experience.

Mikhailovsky Opera & Ballet Theatre OPERA, BALLET
(☎ 812-595 4305; www.mikhailovsky.ru; pl Iskusstv 1; tickets R300-4000; Ⓜ Nevsky Prospekt) While not quite as grand as the Mariinsky, this illustrious stage still delivers the Russian ballet or operatic experience, complete with multitiered theatre, frescoed ceiling and elaborate concerts. Pl Iskusstv (Arts Sq) is a lovely setting for this respected venue, which is home to the State Academic Opera & Ballet Company.

ℹ Information

Free wi-fi access is common across the city.
American Medical Clinic (☎ 812-740 2090; www.amclinic.ru; nab reki Moyki 78; ⊙24hr; Ⓜ Admiralteyskaya) One of the city's largest private clinics.
Apteka Petrofarm (Nevsky pr 22; ⊙24hr) An excellent, all-night pharmacy.
Express to Russia (☎ 812-570 6342; www.expresstorussia.com; Muchnoi per 2) Visas, tours, hotel bookings, tickets.
Main Post Office (Pochtamtskaya ul 9; ⊙24hr; Ⓜ Admiralteyskaya) Worth visiting for its elegant Style Moderne interior.
Ost-West Kontaktservice (☎ 812-327 3416; www.ostwest.com; Nevsky pr 100; ⊙10am-

6pm Mon-Fri; Ⓜ Ploshchad Vosstaniya) Can find you an apartment to rent and organise tours and tickets.
St Petersburg Times (www.sptimes.ru) Published every Tuesday and Friday, when it has an indispensable listings and arts review section.
Tourist Information Bureau (☎ 812-310 2822; http://eng.ispb.info; Sadovaya ul 14/52; ⊙10am-7pm Mon-Fri, noon-6pm Sat; Ⓜ Gostiny Dvor) There are also branches outside the **Hermitage** (Dvortsovaya pl 12; ⊙10am-7pm; Ⓜ Admiralteyskaya), **St Isaac's Cathedral** (Isaakievskaya pl) and **Pulkovo Airport** (⊙10am-7pm Mon-Fri).

ℹ Getting Around

TO/FROM THE AIRPORT
From St Petersburg's superb new Pulkovo International Airport (p357), an official taxi to the centre should cost around R900, or you can take the bus to Moskovskaya metro station for R30, then take the metro from Moskovskaya (Line 2) all over the city for R28 – a journey of about 50 minutes all told.

PUBLIC TRANSPORT
The metro is usually the quickest way around the city. *Zhetony* (tokens) and credit-loaded cards can be bought from booths in the stations (R28).

If you are staying more than a day or two, it's worth buying a smart card (R55), which is good for multiple journeys to be used over the course of a fixed time period.

Buses, trolleybuses and *marshrutky* (fares R22 to R30) often get you closer to the sights and are especially handy to cover long distances along main avenues like Nevsky pr.

TAXI
Unofficial taxis are common. Official taxis (four-door Volga sedans with a chequerboard strip down the side and a green light in the front

---

MOSCOW TO ST PETERSBURG

The fastest **trains** between Moscow and St Petersburg are the *Sapsan* services (from R2600; three to four hours; six daily). There are also around 10 overnight services which can take anywhere from seven to 11 hours (*platskart/kupe* from R1000/2200). Tickets often sell out in the high months, but keep your plans flexible and you should be able to find something, even at the last minute. Many **flights** (from R2300) also connect the two cities and they rarely sell out.

WORTH A TRIP

KALININGRAD REGION КАЛИНИНГРАДСКАЯ ОБЛАСТЬ

Sandwiched by Poland and Lithuania, the Kaliningrad Region is a Russian exclave that's intimately attached to the Motherland yet also a world apart. In this 'Little Russia' – only 15,100 sq km with a population of 941,873 – you'll also find beautiful countryside, charming old Prussian seaside resorts and splendid beaches. Citizens of Japan and many European countries can visit Kaliningrad on a 72-hour visa.

The capital, **Kaliningrad** (Калининград; formely Königsberg), was once a Middle European architectural gem equal to Prague or Kraków. Precious little of this built heritage remains but there are attractive residential suburbs and remnants of the city's old fortifications that evoke the Prussian past. The most impressive building is the Gothic **Kaliningrad Cathedral** (Кафедральный собор Кёнигсберга; ☑4012-631 705; www.sobor-kaliningrad.ru; Kant Island; adult/student R150/130, photos R50, concerts R250-300; ☺10am-5pm), founded in 1333 and restored after almost being destroyed during WWII. West of the Cathedral along the river also make time for the fascinating **Museum of the World Ocean** (Музей Мирового Океана; www.world-ocean.ru/en; nab Petra Velikogo 1; adult/student R300/200, individual vessels adult/student R100/80; ☺10am-6pm Wed-Sun).

The best places to stay are the budget **Amigos Hostel** (Амигос Хостел; ☑8-911-485 2157; www.amigoshostel.ru; ul Yablonevaya Alleya 34; dm R500-550, d R1200; ☎) and the midrange **Skipper Hotel** (Гостиница Шкипер; ☑4012-307 237; www.skipperhotel.ru; ul Oktyabrskaya 4a; r from R2800; ✳☎) in the attractive, slightly kitsch Fish Village riverside development. There are plenty of good places to eat and drink including **Fish Club** (Рыбный клуб; ul Oktyabrskaya 4a; meals R500-1500; ☺noon-midnight), **Zarya** (Заря; ☑4012-300 388; pr Mira 43; meals R200-540; ☺10am-3am; ☎) and the hip apartment-cum-cafe **Kvartira** (Apartment; ☑4012-216 736; ul Serzhanta Koloskova 13; ☎).

It's easy to access the region's other key sights on day trips from Kaliningrad, but if you did want to spend time away from the city, base yourself in the seaside resort of **Svetlogorsk** (Светлогорск) which is only a few hours' drive down the Baltic coast from the pine forests and Sahara-style dunes of the **Kurshskaya Kosa National Park** (Национальный парк Курьшская коса; www.park-kosa.ru; admission per person/car R40/300), a Unesco World Heritage Site.

window) have meters that drivers sometimes use, though you most often pay a negotiated price.

Peterburgskoe Taksi 068 (☑812-324 7777, within St Petersburg just dial 068; http://taxi068.spb.ru)

Taxi Blues (☑812-321 8888; www.taxiblues.ru)

SURVIVAL GUIDE

ℹ Directory A–Z

ACCOMMODATION

There has been a boom in budget-friendly hostels in both Moscow and St Petersburg, and if you're on a budget you'll want to consider these – even if you typically don't 'do' hostels, most offer a few private rooms.

In hostels you're looking at R600 to R1000 for a dorm bed, and R2500 for a private room with a shared bathroom. Elsewhere hotel rooms with a bathroom start at about R3000. At the other end of the spectrum the sky is the limit, but figure on at least R10,000 for top-end accommodation in Moscow and St Petersburg (quite a bit less elsewhere).

Apartment Rental

Booking an apartment is a good way to save money on accommodation, especially for small groups. They typically cost around R4300 to R8600 per night. The following agencies can make bookings in Moscow and/or St Petersburg.

Enjoy Moscow (www.enjoymoscow.com; per night from US$155; ☎)

HOFA (www.hofa.ru; apartments from per night €44; ☎)

Moscow Suites (www.moscowsuites.ru; studio per night from US$199; ☎)

Ost-West Kontaktservice (p353)

BUSINESS HOURS

Restaurants and bars often stay open later than their stated hours if the establishment is full. In fact, many simply say that they work *do poslednnogo klienta* (until the last customer leaves).

Note that most museums close their ticket offices one hour (in some cases 30 minutes) before the official closing time.

Banks 9am to 6pm Monday to Friday, some open 9am to 5pm Saturday

Bars & Restaurants noon to midnight

Shops 10am to 9pm Monday to Friday, to 7pm Saturday and Sunday

INTERNET RESOURCES

Russia Made Easy (www.redtape.ru)
The Moscow Expat Site (www.expat.ru)
Visit Russia (www.visitrussia.org.uk)
Way to Russia (www.waytorussia.net)

MONEY

The Russian currency is the rouble, written as 'рубль' and abbreviated as 'руб' or 'р'. Roubles are divided into 100 almost worthless *kopeki* (kopecks). Coins come in amounts of R1, R2, R5 and R10 roubles, with banknotes in values of R10, R50, R100, R500, R1000 and R5000.

ATMs that accept all major credit and debit cards are everywhere, and most restaurants, shops and hotels in major cities gladly accept plastic. You can exchange dollars and euros (and some other currencies) at most banks; when they're closed, try the exchange counters at top-end hotels. You may need your passport. Note that crumpled or old banknotes are often refused. Many banks cash travellers cheques for a small commission.

POST

The Russian post service is **Pochta Rossia** (www.russianpost.ru). The main offices are open from 8am to 8pm or 9pm Monday to Friday, with shorter hours on Saturday and Sunday. To send a postcard or letter up to 20g anywhere in the world by air costs R26.

PUBLIC HOLIDAYS

Many businesses are closed from 1 to 7 January. Russia's main public holidays:

New Year's Day 1 January
Russian Orthodox Christmas Day 7 January
Defender of the Fatherland Day 23 February
International Women's Day 8 March
Easter Monday April
International Labour Day/Spring Festival 1 May
Victory Day 9 May
Russian Independence Day 12 June
Unity Day 4 November

SAFE TRAVEL

Travellers have nothing to fear from Russia's 'mafia' – the increasingly respectable gangster classes are not interested in such small fry. However, petty theft and pickpockets are prevalent in both Moscow and St Petersburg, so be vigilant with your belongings.

Some police officers can be bothersome, especially to dark-skinned or foreign-looking people. Other members of the police force target tourists, though reports of tourists being hassled about their documents and registration have declined. Still, you should always carry a photocopy of your passport, visa and registration stamp. If you are stopped for any reason – legitimate or illegitimate – you will surely be hassled if you don't have these.

Sadly, racism is a problem in Russia. Be vigilant on the streets around Hitler's birthday (20 April), when bands of right-wing thugs have been known to roam around spoiling for a fight with anyone who doesn't look Russian.

TELEPHONE

The international code for Russia is ☏ 7. The international access code from landline phones in Russia is ☏ 8, followed by ☏ 10 after the second tone, followed by the country code.

The three main mobile-phone companies, all with prepaid and 4G internet options, are **Beeline** (www.beeline.ru), **Megafon** (www.megafon.ru) and **MTS** (www.mts.ru). Company offices are everywhere. It costs almost nothing to purchase a SIM card, but bring your passport.

Local telecom rules mean mobile calls or texts from your 'home' city or region to another city or region are more expensive – essentially long-distance calls/texts. So active callers should consider purchasing a Moscow SIM while in Moscow, and a St Petersburg SIM while in St Petersburg.

To dial another area code (mobile or land line), dial ☏ 8 plus 10 digits. Mobile numbers have 10 digits, always starting with ☏ 9 – often ☏ 915, ☏ 916 or ☏ 926. Mobile numbers are written in the following format: ☏ 8-9xx-xxx xxxx.

RUSSIA DIRECTORY A–Z

SLEEPING PRICE RANGES

The following price categories are for the cost of a double room:

€ Moscow and St Petersburg less than R3000 (rest of country less than R1500)

€€ Moscow and St Petersburg R3000 to R8000 (rest of country R1500 to R4000)

€€€ Moscow and St Petersburg more than R8000 (rest of country more than R4000)

ESSENTIAL FOOD & DRINK

Russia's rich black soil provides an abundance of grains and vegetables used in a wonderful range of breads, salads, appetisers and soups. Its waterways yield a unique range of fish and, as with any cold-climate country, there's a great love of fat-loaded dishes – Russia is no place to go on a diet!

➡ **Soups** For example, the lemony, meat *solyanka* or the hearty fish *ukha*.

➡ **Bliny** (pancakes) Served with *ikra* (caviar) or *tvorog* (cottage cheese).

➡ **Salads** A wide variety usually slathered in mayonnaise, including the chopped potato Olivier.

➡ **Pelmeni** (dumplings) Stuffed with meat and eaten with sour cream and vinegar.

➡ **Central Asian dishes** Try *plov* (Uzbek pilaf), *shashlyk* (kebab) or *lagman* (noodles).

➡ **Vodka** The quintessential Russian tipple.

➡ **Kvas** A refreshing, beerlike drink, or the red berry juice mix *mors*.

VISAS

Everyone needs a visa to visit Russia. For most travellers a tourist visa (single- or double-entry, valid for a maximum of 30 days) will be sufficient. If you plan to stay longer than a month, you can apply for a business visa or – if you are a US citizen – a three-year multi-entry visa.

Applying for a visa is undeniably a headache, but the process is actually quite straightforward. There are three stages: invitation, application and registration.

Invitation

To obtain a visa, everyone needs an invitation, also known as 'visa support'. Hotels and hostels will usually issue anyone staying with them an invitation voucher free or for a small fee (typically around €20 to €30). If you are not staying in a hotel or hostel, you will need to buy an invitation – this can be done through most travel agents or via specialist visa agencies, also for around €20.

Application

Invitation voucher in hand, you can then apply for a visa. Wherever in the world you are applying you can start by entering details in the online form of the Consular Department of the Russian Ministry of Foreign Affairs (https://visa.kdmid. ru/PetitionChoice.aspx).

Take care in answering the questions accurately on this form, including listing all the countries you have visited in the last 10 years and the dates of the visits – stamps in your passport will be checked against this information and if there are anomalies you will likely have to restart the process. Keep a note of the unique identity number provided for your submitted form – if you have to make changes later, you will need this to access it without having to fill in the form again from scratch.

Russian embassies in the UK and US have contracted separate agencies to process the submission of visa applications; these companies use online interfaces that direct the relevant information into the standard visa application form. In the UK, the agency is **VFS.Global** (http://ru.vfsglobal.co.uk) with offices in London and Edinburgh; in the US it's **Invisa Logistic Services** (http://ils-usa.com) with offices in Washington DC, New York, San Francisco, Houston and Seattle.

Consular offices apply different fees and slightly different application rules country by country. Avoid potential hassles by checking well in advance what these rules might be. Among the things that you will need:

➡ a printout of the invitation/visa support document

➡ a passport-sized photograph for the application form

➡ if you're self-employed, bank statements for the previous three months showing you have sufficient funds to cover your time in Russia.

➡ details of your travel insurance.

The charge for the visa will depend on the type of visa applied for and how quickly you need it.

We highly recommend applying for your visa in your home country rather than on the road.

Registration

Every visitor to Russia must have their visa registered *within seven days of arrival,* excluding weekends and public holidays. Registration is handled by your accommodating party. If staying in a homestay or rental apartment, you'll need to make arrangements with either the landlord or a friend to register you through the post office. See http://waytorussia.net/RussianVisa/Registration.html for how this can be done.

Once registered, you'll receive a registration slip. Keep this safe – that's the document that any police who stop you will ask to see. You do not need to register more than once unless you stay in additional cities for more than seven days, in which case you'll need additional registration slips.

72-Hour Visa-Free Travel

To qualify for this visa for St Petersburg, you need to enter and exit the city on a cruise or ferry such as that offered by **St Peter Line** (☑ 812-386 1147; www.stpeterline.com). For Kaliningrad, make arrangements in advance with locally based tour agencies.

Immigration Form

Immigration forms are produced electronically by passport control at airports. Take good care of your half of the completed form as you'll need it for registration and could face problems while travelling in Russia – and certainly will on leaving – if you can't produce it.

ⓘ Getting There & Away

AIR

International flights land and take off from Moscow's three airports – **Domodedovo** (Домодедово; www.domodedovo.ru), **Sheremetyevo** (Шереметьево, SVO; ☑ 495-578 6565; www.svo.aero) and **Vnukovo** (Внуково; www.vnukovo.ru) – and St Petersburg's **Pulkovo** (LED; www.pulkovoairport.ru) airport. International flights to Kaliningrad's

Khrabrovo (☑ 4012-610 620; www.kgd.aero) airport are rarer.

LAND

Russia has excellent train and bus connections with the rest of Europe. However, many routes connecting St Petersburg and Moscow with points east – including Kaliningrad – go through Belarus, for which you'll need a transit visa. Buses are the best way to get from St Petersburg to Tallinn. St Petersburg to Helsinki can be done by bus or train, as well as by boat.

Adjoining 13 countries, the Russian Federation has a huge number of border crossings. From Eastern Europe you are most likely to enter from Finland near Vyborg; from Estonia at Narva; from Latvia at Rēzekne; from Belarus at Krasnoye or Ezjaryshcha; and from Ukraine at Chernihiv. You can enter Kaliningrad from Lithuania and Poland at any of seven border posts.

SEA

Between early April and late September, international passenger ferries connect Stockholm, Helsinki and Tallinn with St Petersburg's **Morskoy Vokzal** (Морской вокзал; pl Morskoy Slavy 1).

ⓘ Getting Around

AIR

Flying in Russia is not for the faint-hearted. Safety aside, flights can be delayed, often for hours and with little or no explanation.

That said, booking flights within Russia online is easier than ever, and domestic flights are relatively cheap. Major Russian airlines, including **Aeroflot** (www.aeroflot.com), **Rossiya** (www.rossiya-airlines.com), **S7** (www.s7.ru), **Sky Express** (www.skyexpress.ru/en), **Transaero** (www.transaero.com) and **UTAir** (www.utair.ru) have online booking, with the usual discounts for advance purchases. Otherwise, it's no problem buying a ticket at ubiquitous *aviakassa* (ticket offices) which may be able to tell you about flights that you can't easily find out about online overseas. Online agencies specialising in Russian air tickets with English interfaces include

Anywayanyday (☎ 495-363 6164; www.any-wayanyday.com) and **Pososhok.ru** (☎ 495-234 8000; www.pososhok.ru).

BUS

Buses and *marshrutky* (fixed-route vans or minibuses) are often more frequent, more convenient and faster than trains, especially on short-distance routes. There's almost no need to reserve a seat – just arrive a good 30 minutes before the scheduled departure and buy a ticket. Prices are comparable to 3rd-class train fares.

Marshrutky are quicker than the rusty old buses and often leave when full, rather than according to a schedule. Where roads are good and villages frequent, *marshrutky* can be twice as fast as buses, and are well worth the double fare.

CAR & MOTORCYCLE

You can bring your own vehicle into Russia, but expect delays, bureaucracy and the attention of the roundly hated GAI (traffic police), who take particular delight in stopping foreign cars for document checks.

To enter Russia with a vehicle you will need a valid International Driving Permit as well as the insurance and ownership documents for your car.

As you don't really need a car to get around big cities, hiring a car comes into its own for making trips out of town where public transport may not be so good. All the major agencies have offices in Moscow and St Petersburg.

Driving is on the right-hand side, and at an intersection traffic coming from the right generally (but not always) has the right of way. The maximum legal blood-alcohol content is 0.03%, a rule that is strictly enforced.

TAXI

Russian cities have plenty of official taxis, but few people think twice about flagging down any car to request a ride. A fare is negotiated for the journey – simply state your destination and ask *'skolko?'* (how much?), and off you go. Proceed with caution if you are alone and/or it's late at night, especially if you are a woman. While exceedingly rare, violent attacks on passengers have occurred.

TRAIN

Russia's extensive train network is efficiently run by **Russian Railways** (www.eng.rzd.ru). *Prigorodny* (suburban) or short-distance trains – also known as *elektrichky* – do not require advance booking: you can buy your ticket at the *prigorodny poezd kassa* (suburban train ticket offices) at train stations.

There are a number of options on where to buy, including online from RZD. Bookings open 45 days before the date of departure. You'd be wise to buy well in advance over the busy summer months and holiday periods such as New Year and early May, when securing berths at short notice on certain trains can be difficult.

For long-distance trains, unless otherwise specified we quote 2nd-class sleeper *(kupe)* fares. Expect 1st-class (SV) fares to be double this, and 3rd class *(platskartny)* to be about 40% less. Children under five travel free if they share a berth with an adult; otherwise, children under 10 pay a reduced fare for their own berth.

You'll need your passport (or a photocopy) to buy tickets. You can buy tickets for others if you bring their passports or photocopies. Queues can be very long and move with interminable slowness. At train ticket offices (*'Zh/D kassa'*, short for *'zheleznodorozhnaya kassa'*), which are all over most cities, you can pay a surcharge of around R200 and avoid the queues. Alternatively, most travel agencies will organise the reservation and delivery of train tickets for a substantial mark-up.

Serbia

Includes ➜

Best Places to Eat

➜ Šešir Moj (p365)

➜ To Je To (p364)

➜ Radost Fina Kuhinjica (p365)

➜ Fish i Zeleniš (p370)

Best Places to Stay

➜ Hotel Moskva (p364)

➜ Hostel Bongo (p364)

➜ Green Studio Hostel (p363)

➜ Hotel Veliki (p370)

Why Go?

Warm, welcoming and a hell of a lot of fun – everything you never heard about Serbia (Србија) is true. Exuding a feisty mix of élan and *inat* (classic Serbian rebellious defiance), this country doesn't do 'mild': Belgrade is one of the world's wildest party destinations, the northern town of Novi Sad hosts the rocking EXIT festival, and even its hospitality is emphatic – expect to be greeted with *rakija* (fruit brandy) and a hearty three-kiss hello.

While political correctness is about as commonplace as a nonsmoking bar, Serbia is nevertheless a cultural crucible: the art nouveau town of Subotica revels in its proximity to Hungary, bohemian Niš echoes to the clip-clop of Roma horse carts, and minaret-studded Novi Pazar nudges some of the most sacred sites in Serbian Orthodoxy. And in the mountainous Kopaonik and Zlatibor regions, ancient traditions coexist with après-ski bling. Forget what you think you know: come and say *zdravo* (hello)...or better yet, *živeli* (cheers)!

When to Go
Belgrade

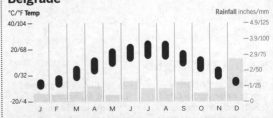

Apr Watch winter melt away with a scenic ride on the nostalgic Šargan 8 railway.

Jul & Aug Rock out at Novi Sad's EXIT, go wild at Guča and get jazzy at Nišville.

Dec–Mar Head to Zlatibor for alpine adventure.

Serbia Highlights

1 Marvel at Belgrade's mighty **Kalemegdan Citadel** (p361) and party the night away on a *splav* (river barge nightclub).

2 Witness the laid-back town of **Novi Sad** (p369) as it morphs into the state of EXIT every July.

3 Steel your eardrums (and liver) at Guča's **Dragačevo Trumpet Assembly** (p367), one of the world's most frenetic music festivals.

4 Escape reality in the fantastic village of **Drvengrad** (p369), built by director Emir Kusturica for indie drama *Life is a Miracle*.

5 Goggle at splendid surprises bursting from the Vojvodinian plains, including the art nouveau treasures of **Subotica** (p371).

6 Ponder the creepy, cryptic rock towers of **Djavolja Varoš** (p372).

7 Ski, hike or just take the mountain air in the magical villages of **Zlatibor** (p369).

One Week

Revel in three days of cultural and culinary exploration in **Belgrade**, allowing for at least one night of hitting the capital's legendary night spots. Carry on to **Novi Sad** for trips to the vineyards and monasteries of **Fruška Gora** and **Sremski Karlovci**.

Two Weeks

Follow the above itinerary then head north for the art nouveau architecture of **Subotica**, before slicing south to **Zlatibor** en route to traditional Serbian villages, the eerie **Djavolja Varoš** and the lively city of **Niš**.

BELGRADE БЕОГРАД

📋 011 / POP 1.6 MILLION

Outspoken, adventurous, proud and audacious: Belgrade is by no means a 'pretty' capital, but its gritty exuberance makes it one of the most happening cities in Europe. It is here where the Sava River meets the Danube (Dunav), and old-world culture gives way to new-world nightlife. Grandiose coffee houses, quirky sidewalk ice-creameries and smoky dens all find rightful place along Knez Mihailova, a lively pedestrian boulevard flanked by historical buildings all the way to the ancient Kalemegdan Citadel, crown of the city. 'Belgrade' literally translates as 'White City', but Serbia's colourful capital is red hot.

⊙ Sights & Activities

★**Kalemegdan Citadel** FORTRESS

(Kalemegdanska tvrđava) FREE Some 115 battles have been fought over imposing, impressive Kalemegdan, and the citadel was destroyed more than 40 times throughout the centuries. Fortifications began in Celtic times, and the Romans extended it onto the flood plains during the settlement of 'Singidunum', Belgrade's Roman name. The fort's bloody history, discernible despite today's plethora of jolly cafes and funfairs, only makes Kalemegdan all the more fascinating.

Military Museum MUSEUM

(www.muzej.mod.gov.rs; Kalemegdan Citadel; adult/child 150/70DIN; ⊙10am-5pm Tue-Sun) Tucked away in Belgrade's sprawling Kalemegdan Citadel, this museum presents the complete military history of the former Yugoslavia. Gripping displays include captured Kosovo Liberation Army weapons, bombs and missiles (courtesy of NATO), rare guns and bits of the American stealth fighter shot down in 1999. You'll find the museum through the Stambol Gate, built by the Turks in the mid-1700s and used for public executions.

National Museum MUSEUM

(Narodni Muzej; www.narodnimuzej.rs; Trg Republike 1a; adult/child 200/100DIN; ⊙10am-5pm Tue-Wed & Fri, noon-8pm Thur & Sat, 10am-2pm Sun) Trg Republike (Republic Sq), a meeting point and outdoor exhibition space, is home to the National Museum. Lack of funding for renovations has kept it mostly shuttered for the last decade, though some exhibitions are again open to the public.

Ethnographic Museum MUSEUM

(Etnografski Muzej; www.etnografskimuzej.rs; Studentski Trg 13; adult/student 150/60DIN; ⊙10am-5pm Tue-Sat, 9am-2pm Sun) This museum features traditional costumes, working utensils and folksy mountain-village interiors.

SERBIA BELGRADE

DON'T MISS

BELGRADE'S HISTORIC 'HOODS

Skadarska or 'Skadarlija' is Belgrade's Montmartre. This cobblestoned strip east of Trg Republike was the bohemian heartland at the turn of the 20th century; local artistes and dapper types still gather in its legion of cute restaurants and cafes.

Savamala, cool-Belgrade's destination du jour, stretches along the Sava down ul Karadjordjeva. Constructed in the 1830s for Belgrade's smart set, the neighbourhood (p366) now houses cultural centres, ramshackle, photogenic architecture, nightspots galore and a buzzing vibe.

Central Belgrade

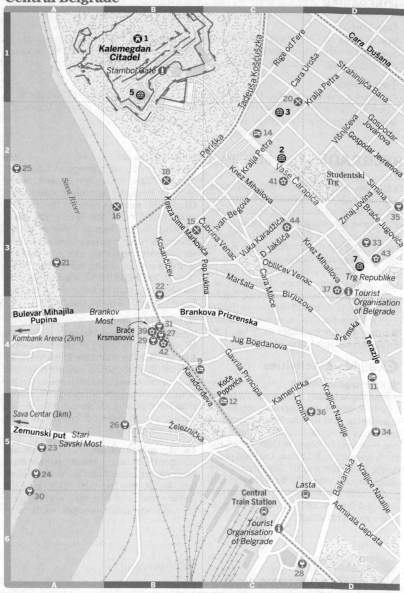

Gallery of Frescos
GALLERY

(www.narodnimuzej.rs; Cara Uroša 20; admission 100DIN; ☺10am-5pm Tue, Wed, Fri & Sat, noon-8pm Thu, 10am-2pm Sun) The gallery features replicas (and the odd original) of Byzantine Serbian church art, down to the last scratch.

Unlike the sensitive originals, these frescoes can be photographed to your heart's content.

Nikola Tesla Museum
MUSEUM

(www.tesla-museum.org; Krunska 51; admission incl guided tour in English 500DIN; ☺10am-6pm Tue-Sun) Meet the man on the 100DIN note at one

Museum of Automobiles MUSEUM
(www.automuseumbgd.com; Majke Jevrosime 30; adult/child 200/80DIN; ⊙9am-7pm) A compelling collection of cars and motorcycles located in Belgrade's first public garage. Check out the '57 Caddy convertible: only 25,000km and one careful owner – President Tito.

Historical Museum of Serbia MUSEUM
(Istorijski Muzej Srbije; www.imus.org.rs; Trg Nikole Pašića 11; adult/child 200/100DIN; ⊙noon-7pm Tue-Sun) Home to an absorbing wealth of archaeological, ethnographic and military collections. It's your best bet until the National Museum reopens entirely.

Sveti Sava CHURCH
(www.hramsvetogsave.com; Svetog Save) Sveti Sava is the world's biggest Orthodox church, a fact made entirely obvious when looking at the city skyline from a distance or standing under its dome. The church is built on the site where the Turks apparently burnt relics of St Sava. Work on the church interior (frequently interrupted by wars) continues today.

Maršal Tito's Grave MONUMENT
(House of Flowers; www.mij.rs; Botićeva 6; admission incl entry to Museum of Yugoslav History 200DIN; ⊙10am-8pm Tue-Sun May-Oct, to 6pm Tue-Sun Nov-April) A visit to Tito's mausoleum is obligatory. Also on display are thousands of elaborate relay batons presented to him by young 'Pioneers', plus gifts from political leaders and the voguish set of the era. It's attached to the fascinating **Museum of Yugoslav History**. Take trolleybus 40 or 41 at the south end of Parliament on Kneza Miloša. It's the second stop after turning into Bul Mira: ask the driver to let you out at Kuća Cveća.

Ada Ciganlija BEACH
(www.adaciganlija.rs) In summertime, join the hordes of sea-starved locals (up to 250,000 a day) for sun and fun at this artificial island on the Sava. Cool down with a swim, kayak or windsurf after a leap from the 55m bungee tower. Take bus 52 or 53 from Zeleni Venac.

🛏 Sleeping

⭐ **Green Studio Hostel** HOSTEL €
(☏011-218 5943; www.greenstudiohostel.com; Karađorđeva 61, 6th floor, Savamala; dm from €9, r €9-40, apt €40; ✺ 🛜) Clean, airy and staffed by your new best friends, this sunny spot has a handy location near the bus and train stations, as well as Belgrade's main attractions. Nightly happy hours, daily activities, tons of local advice, and free *rakija*!

of Belgrade's best museums. Tesla's ashes are kept here in a glowing, golden orb: at the time of writing, debate was raging between the museum and its supporters and the church as to whether they should be moved to hallowed ground.

Central Belgrade

Hostel Bongo ★ HOSTEL €
(☎011-268 5515; www.hostelbongo.com; ul Terazije 36; dm/d from €11/38; ❄🛜) Guests at the modern, brightly painted Bongo can take their pick: plunge into the attractions, bars and restaurants nearby, or hide in the hostel's sweet garden terrace. Fantastic staff has oodles of hostelling experience.

YOLOstel HOSTEL €
(☎064 141 9339; www.yolostel.rs; ul Uzun Mirkova 6, Apt 6, 3rd floor; dm/d from €11/35; ❄🛜) This new designer hostel enjoys an awesome location just a short stumble from Savamala. With custom-made furniture, quirky, gorgeous decor and a hip, refined air, this is not your usual backpacker flophouse.

Soul House Apartments APARTMENTS €€
(☎064 135 2255; www.soul-house.net; ul Makedonska 15; one person/two people stays from €25/35; ❄🛜) These three themed apartments are located within the same building a quick amble from Trg Republike. The 'hippie suite' (€25/35) is yellow and bright, the 'modernistic studio' (€30/40) has trippy, fun furnishings, and the 'retro apartment' (€40/50) is done up Tito-era style. All have good kitchens. There's a minimum two-night stay on weekends.

Jump Inn HOTEL €€
(☎011-404 9650; www.jumpinnhotelbelgrade.com; ul Koče Popovića 2a; s/d from €60/70; 🅿❄🛜) This new design hotel, aptly located in the trendy Savamala district, has spacious, stylish rooms, all with Smart TVs, and many with Sava River and Ada Bridge views.

Hotel Moskva ★ HISTORIC HOTEL €€€
(Hotel Moscow; ☎011-364 2069; www.hotelmoskva.rs; Balkanska 1; s/d/ste from €90/110/130; ❄🛜) Art nouveau icon and proud symbol of the best of Belgrade, the majestic Moskva has been wowing guests, including Albert Einstein, Indira Gandhi and Alfred Hitchcock, since 1906. Laden with ye olde glamour, this is the place to write your memoirs at a big old desk.

✖ Eating

To Je To ★ BALKAN €
(bul Despota Stefana 21; mains 220-750DIN; ☺8am-midnight) 'To je to' means 'that's it', and in this case, they're talking about meat. Piles of the stuff, grilled in all its juicy glory, make up the menu here in the forms of Sarajevo-style *ćevapi* (spicy skinless sausages), turkey kebab, sweetbreads and more. It

BETON HALA

Belgrade's bastion of banqueting is undoubtedly Beton Hala. The unglamorous name – it means 'Concrete Hall' – belies the wealth of astonishingly hip restaurants, cafes, bars and clubs that make themselves at home in the once-derelict warehouse. Beton Hall is the place to hit if you're after classy-cool nosh. We recommend:

Comunale (www.comunale.rs; Beton Hala; mains 650-1700DIN; ⊘10am-1pm) For fancy homemade pastas and a classy take on the Serbian grill.

Cantina de Frida (www.cantinadefrida.com; Beton Hala; mains 270-1300DIN; ⊘10am-3am) Tasty tapas in cool, colourful surrounds.

Iguana (www.iguana.rs; Beton Hala; mains 900-1750DIN; ⊘10am-2am) Peruse the small but smart menu to a soundtrack of live jazz.

Toro Latin Gastro Bar (www.richardsandoval.com/torobelgrade; Beton Hala; mains 400-1500DIN; ⊘10am-2am) Toro offers posh sharing plates, grilled meats galore and vegetarian and gluten-free options.

serves home-made *sarma* (stuffed cabbage rolls) on the weekends. Cheap, scrumptious and highly recommended by locals.

★**Šešir Moj** SERBIAN €€
(My Hat; www.restoransesirmoj.co.rs; Skadarska 21; meals 420-1300DIN; ⊘9am-1am) Roma bands tug the heartstrings while traditional dishes such as *punjena bela vešalica* (pork stuffed with *kajmak* – clotted cream) buoy the belly.

★**Radost Fina Kuhinjica** VEGETARIAN €€
(⊘060 603 0023; Pariska 3; mains 450-1300DIN; ⊘2pm-midnight Tue-Sat, 1pm-9pm Sun; ⊘) Barbecue-obsessed Serbia isn't the easiest place for vegetarians, but thanks to this cheery eatery, you'll never have to settle for eating garnish and chips again. Its ever-changing menu features curries, veg burgers, innovative pastas and meat substitutes galore, some of which are vegan. The healthy cupcakes are a delight.

? SERBIAN €€
(Znak Pitanja; www.varoskapija.rs; Kralja Petra 6; mains 550-1100DIN; ⊘9am-1am) Belgrade's oldest *kafana* has been attracting the bohemian set since 1823 with dishes such as stuffed chicken and 'lamb under the iron pan'. Its quizzical name follows a dispute with the adjacent church, which objected to the boozy tavern – originally called 'By the Cathedral' – referring to a house of god.

Smokvica CAFE €€
(www.smokvica.rs; Kralja Petra 73; meals 250-1200DIN; ⊘9am-1am; ⊛) With its winsome courtyard terrace, arty crowd and with-it gourmet menu, to stumble across Smokvica ('little fig') is to forget you're in hustling, bustling Belgrade. Nibble innovative salads, gourmet tasting plates and sandwiches or just sip good coffee in an atmosphere both rare and rarified.

Little Bay EUROPEAN €€
(www.littlebay.rs; Dositejeva 9a; meals 595-1390DIN; ⊘11am-1am) Little wonder locals and visitors have long been singing the praises of this gem: it's one of the best dining experiences in Belgrade. Tuck yourself into a private opera box and let the spinach-and-feta-stuffed chicken or a traditional English roast lunch (795DIN, Sundays only) melt in your mouth.

🍷 Drinking & Nightlife

Bars

★**Kafana Pavle Korčagin** TAVERNA
(⊘011-240 1980; Ćirila i Metodija 2a; ⊘8pm-1am) Raise a glass to Tito at this frantic, festive *kafana*. Lined with communist memorabilia and packed to the rafters with revellers this table-thumping throwback fills up nightly; reserve a table in advance.

Rakia Bar BAR
(www.rakiabar.com; Dobračina 5, Dorćol; ⊘9am-midnight Sun-Thu, to 1am Fri & Sat) An ideal spot for *rakija* rookies to get their first taste of the spirit of Serbia. English-speaking staff will guide you through the extensive drinks menu. Beware: this stuff is strong.

WATS BAR
(We Are The Shit; Lomina 5-9; ⊘6pm-1am Thur & Sat, to 2am Fri-Sat) This cheeky pre-Savamala-clubbing bar is akin to a club itself – albeit a small one – with DJs spinning and a cool crowd jostling for dancing, drinking and ogling space.

THE SAVAMALA SCENE

The once-derelict, now-dapper Savamala creative district is Belgrade's hip HQ, with bars, clubs and cultural centres that morph into achingly cool music/dance venues come sundown. Dress codes and attitudes are far more relaxed here than in other parts of the city, and in most places there appears to be an unwritten ban on turbofolk; indie, electro, funk, rock and '90s disco are the go in this part of town. And don't let the bedraggled buildings fool you; there's magic going down inside. Give these happening haunts a go:

Mikser House (www.house.mikser.rs; Karadjordjeva 46; ⊘10am-2am) Mikser House is the symbol of Savamala. Hidden in an old warehouse, it has a shop, creative workspaces, a cafe and galleries showcasing the talents of local designers; come nighttime, it morphs into a bar, restaurant and music venue hosting live acts and DJs from Serbia and around the world. Check the website for upcoming events.

KC Grad (www.gradbeograd.eu; Braće Krsmanović 4; ⊘noon-midnight Mon-Fri, 2pm-midnight Sat-Sun) Like Mikser House, this wonderful warehouse space promotes local creativity with workshops, exhibitions, a restaurant and nightly avant-garde music events.

Peron (Braće Krsmanović 12; ⊘10pm-late) Eclectic hotspot where crowds go bonkers to everything from string quartets to pounding electro.

Lasta (Hercegovačka bb, Savamalski kej; ⊘midnight-6am Thur-Sun) Belgrade's first city-side *splav* pulls in a happy crowd of hip-hop, funk, electro and disco lovers.

Mladost i Ludost (Karadjordjeva 44; ⊘9pm-5am) These two bars are within the same building; punters hepped up on old-school DJ tunes criss-cross between them at their leisure. The names mean 'youth' and 'crazy': no false advertising here!

Prohibicija   BAR
(ul Karadjordjeva 36, Savamala; ⊘9am-1am) This stylish spot is perfectly located for pre-Savamala clubbing drinks. Sip craft beers and cocktails while watching the street action out the huge windows.

Idiott   BAR
(Dalmatinska 13; ⊘noon-2am) This fun little bar has long been alternative HQ in Belgrade, much loved for its '80s, punk and electro tunes, pinball machines and brilliant summer garden terrace. It's beside the Botanic Gardens.

Bašta   BAR
(www.jazzbasta.com; Karadjordjeva 43, Savamala; ⊘5pm-2am) Located in an old building with a whimsical courtyard, creative cocktails and frequent live jazz, Bašta is very Savamala. Find it by clambering up the steps near Brankov Most.

Radionica Bar   BAR
(Dobračina 59, Dorćol; ⊘8pm-3am weeknights, 9pm-4am Fri-Sat) 'Radionica' means 'workshop', and that's exactly what this place once was. Traces of its blue-collar past remain in its industrial-cool decor, but there's nothing rough about its hipster clientele or swish cocktail menu.

Samo Pivo   BAR
(ul Balkanska 13; ⊘noon-1am) The name means 'just beer', and with seven draught beers and 50 brands of bottled beers available, it's not kidding. A great choice for when you're sick of Lav or Jelen (though of course, it has those too).

Nightclubs

Belgrade has a reputation as one of the world's top party cities, with a wild club scene limited only by imagination and hours in the day. Many clubs move to river barges in summertime.

Klub Beton   NIGHTCLUB
(Beton Hala; ⊘10pm-4am) Frock up and shake your well-clad thang to sophisticated electro at this new Beton Hala nightspot.

Mr Stefan Braun   NIGHTCLUB
(www.mrstefanbraun.rs; Nemanjina 4) Those who want to party like (and with) Serbian superstars will find their bliss at this 9th-storey den of decadence. Get your finest threads – and most model-like pout – on and get there before 1am to beat the queues.

Plastic   NIGHTCLUB
(www.clubplastic.rs; cnr Dalmatinska & Takovska; ⊘Wed-Sat 10pm-6am Oct-May) A perennial favourite among electro-heads and booty

shakers, this slick venue is frequented by top local and international DJs. The more intimate Mint Club is within Plastic. Between May and October, head to Plastic Light, the floating version of the club on the Sava River.

Tube
NIGHTCLUB

(www.thetube.rs; Simina 21; ☺11pm-6am Thu-Sat) Lovers of all music electronic will have a blast in this beautifully designed former nuclear bunker. It's a big club, but does get packed: get in early to stake yourself some space.

River Barges

According to Michael Palin, Belgrade has so many nightclubs 'they can't fit them all on land'. Indeed: the city is famous for its Sava and Danube river barge clubs, known collectively as *splavovi*. Most are open only in summer. The Sava boasts a 1.5km strip of *splavovi* on its west bank: these are the true wild-and-crazy party boats. Walk over Brankov Most or catch tram 7, 9 or 11 from the city.

Adjacent to Hotel Jugoslavija in Novi Belgrade, the 1km strip of Danube barges are a bit more sophisticated; many are restaurants that get their dancing shoes on later in the evening. Take bus 704 or 706 from Zeleni Venac and get out by Hotel Jugoslavija.

Hot Mess
RIVER BARGE

(Ušće bb, Sava River; ☺9am-3am) Hot Mess epitomises the sybaritic *splav*, with selfie-snappers posing by the on-board pool, blinding neon lights and a young, uninhibited crowd going wild to disco, house and R&B. They also do great hangover breakfasts.

Blaywatch
RIVER BARGE

(www.blaywatch.com; Brodarska bb, Sava River; ☺midnight-late) This throbbing place gets crowded and dress codes may be enforced (scruffy bad on boys, skimpy good on girls). The crowd is a mix of local 'beautiful people'

and foreigners, all occupied with each other and the turbo tunes.

20/44
RIVER BARGE

(Savski kej bb, Sava River; ☺6pm-4am) Retro, run-down and loads of fun, this alternative *splav* is named for Belgrade's map coordinates. Open year-round.

Freestyler
RIVER BARGE

(www.freestyler.rs; Brodarska bb, Sava River; ☺11pm-5am Tue-Sun) The gigantic Freestyler has been a symbol of *splav* saturnalia for years, not least for its infamous foam parties.

Povetarac
RIVER BARGE

(Brodarska bb, Sava River; ☺11pm-late, 8pm-late winter) This rusting cargo ship attracts an indie crowd. Open year-round.

Amsterdam
RIVER BARGE

(www.amsterdam.rs; Kej Oslobodjenja bb, Danube River; ☺10am-1am, until 2am Sat) Restaurant by day (and evening), polished party boat by night, with interesting cocktails, DJs and occasional live pop and folk music. It's right by the Hotel Jugoslavija.

Acapulco
RIVER BARGE

(Danube River; ☺noon-late) Blinged-up boys come here to flaunt their (new) money and she-accessories. Got a low turbofolk threshold? Start swimming.

☆ Entertainment

For concert and theatre tickets, go to **Bilet Servis** (☎0900 110 011; www.eventim.rs; Trg Republike 5; ☺10am-8pm Mon-Fri, noon-8pm Sat). Large venues for visiting acts include **Sava Centar** (☎011-220 6060; www.savacentar.net; Milentija Popovića 9; ☺box office 10am-8pm Mon-Fri, to 3pm Sat) and **Kombank Arena** (☎011-220 2222; www.kombankarena.rs; Bul Arsenija Čarnojevića 58; ☺box office 10am-8pm Mon-Fri, to 3pm Sat).

SERBIA BELGRADE

MADNESS, MADE IN SERBIA

On the surface, the **Dragačevo Trumpet Assembly** (an annual gathering of brass musicians) sounds harmless; nerdily endearing, even. But band camp this ain't: it *is*, however, the most boisterous music festival in all of Europe, if not the world.

Known simply as 'Guča', after the western Serbian village that has hosted it each August since 1961, the four-day debauch is hedonism at its most rambunctious: tens of thousands of beer-and-brass-addled visitors dance wild *kola* (fast-paced circle dances) through the streets, gorging on spit-meat and slapping dinar on the sweaty foreheads of the (mostly Roma) *trubači* performers. The music itself is relentless and frenzy-fast; even Miles Davis confessed, 'I didn't know you could play trumpet that way.'

Sleep is a dubious proposition, but bring a tent or book ahead anyway: www.guca.rs has information on accommodation and transport.

Bitef Art Cafe
LIVE MUSIC

(www.bitefartcafe.rs; Skver Mire Trailović 1; ⊙ 7pm-4am) There's something for everyone at this delightful hotchpotch of a cafe-club. Funk, soul and jazz get a good airing, as do rock, world music and classical. In summer, Bitef moves their stage to Kalemegdan Fortress.

Čorba Kafe
LIVE MUSIC

(Braće Krsmanović 3; ⊙ 9am-2am Sun-Thur, til 3am Fri-Sat) This rockin' little joint has live music, from rock and metal to pop and '70s hits, almost every night of the week; it's smoky, sweaty and loud, and that's the fun of it. It's under Brankov Most.

National Theatre
THEATRE

(☑ 011-262 0946; www.narodnopozoriste.co.rs; Trg Republike; ⊙ box office 11am-3pm, 5pm until start of performance) Stages operas, dramas and ballets during winter.

Kolarčev University Concert Hall
LIVE MUSIC

(☑ 011-263 0550; www.kolarac.rs; Studentski Trg 5; ⊙ box office 10am-7.30pm) Home to the Belgrade Philharmonica.

Dom Omladine
CULTURAL CENTRE

(Youth Centre; www.domomladine.org; Makedonska 22; ⊙ box office 10am-10pm Mon-Sat) Hosts a range of cultural events from underground concerts to pop culture panels.

Serbian Academy of Arts & Sciences
LIVE MUSIC

(☑ 011-234 2400; www.sanu.ac.rs; Knez Mihailova 35) Stages free concerts and exhibitions.

ℹ Information

TOURIST INFORMATION

Tourist Organisation of Belgrade (☑ freecall 0800 110 011; www.tob.rs) Trg Republike 5 (☑ 011-263 5622; ⊙ 9am-7pm); Train Station (☑ 011-361 2732; Savski Trg 2; ⊙ 7am-1.30pm Mon-Sat); Nikola Tesla Airport (☑ 011-209 7828; ⊙ 9am-9.30pm) Helpful folk with a raft of brochures, city maps and all the info you could need.

WEBSITES

Belgraded (www.belgraded.com)

Belgradian (www.belgradian.com)

Lonely Planet (www.lonelyplanet.com/serbia/belgrade)

ℹ Getting There & Away

BUS

Belgrade has two adjacent bus stations, near the eastern banks of the Sava River: **BAS** (☑ 011-263 6299; www.bas.rs; Železnička 4) and **Lasta** (☑ 011-334 8555; www.lasta.rs; Železnička 2). Buses run from both to international and Serbian destinations. Sample daily routes include Belgrade to Sarajevo (2340DIN, eight hours), Ljubljana (4000DIN, 7½ hours) and Vienna

---

WORTH A TRIP

SREM DISTRICT
СРЕМ

Fruška Gora is an 80km stretch of rolling hills where monastic life has continued since 35 monasteries were built between the 15th and 18th centuries to safeguard Serbian culture and religion from the Turks. With your own vehicle you can flit freely between the 16 remaining monasteries; otherwise, ask about tours at tourist offices in Novi Sad and Sremski Karlovci. Public transport gets you from Novi Sad to villages within the park, from where you can walk between sights. An easy outing is done with a bus from Novi Sad bound for Irig (170DIN, 40 minutes); ask to be let out at the **Novo Hopovo Monastery**. From here, walk or catch local buses to other points such as Vrdnik and Venac. Visit www. npfruskagora.co.rs for a rundown on the region; www.psdzeleznicarns.org.rs has detailed information on individual monasteries (click on 'Фрушкогорски манастири'). At the edge of Fruška Gora on the banks of the Danube is the photogenic village of **Sremski Karlovci**. Lined with stunning structures like the Orthodox cathedral (1758–62), the baroque Four Lions fountain and the Chapel of Peace at the southern end of town (where the Turks and Austrians signed the 1699 Peace Treaty), Sremski Karlovci is also at the heart of a famed wine region. Visit the **Museum of Beekeeping & Wine Cellar** (☑ 021-881071; www. muzejzivanovic.com; Mitropolita Stratimirovića 86) to try famous *bermet* wine, or drop in at any of the family-owned cellars around town. Buzzing during summer weekends with lively wedding parties, Sremski Karlovci also hosts a grape-harvesting festival in late September. Take frequent buses 60, 61 or 62 from Novi Sad (140DIN, 30 minutes) and visit the **tourist organisation** (☑ 021-882 127; www.karlovci.org.rs; Patrijarha Rajačića 1; ⊙ 8am-6pm Mon-Fri, 10am-6pm Sat) just off the main square.

ZLATIBOR

Zlatibor is a romantic region of gentle mountains, traditions and hospitality.

Quirky adventures await in the village of Mokra Gora. **Drvengrad** (Küstendorf; www. mecavnik.info; Mećavnik hill, Mokra Gora; adult/child 200/120DIN; ⊙9am-9pm) was built by Serbian director Emir Kusturica in 2002 for his film *Life is a Miracle*, and offers surreal fun and prime panoramas.

The fun of a 2½-hour journey on the twisty-turny **Šargan 8 railway** (☑bookings 031-800 125; www.serbianrailways.com; adult/child 600/300DIN; ⊙daily April-Oct, by appointment Nov-March) tourist train is its disorienting twists, turns and tunnels (all 22 of them).

Reach these sights via bus from Užice or through **Zlatibor Tours** (☑031-845 957; www. zlatibortours.com; Tržni centar, bus station; ⊙8am-10pm).

(4400DIN, 9½ hours); frequent domestic services include Subotica (800DIN, three hours), Novi Sad (520DIN, one hour), Niš (1380DIN, three hours) and Novi Pazar (1400DIN, three hours).

CAR & MOTORCYCLE

Most major car-hire companies have offices at Nikola Tesla Airport. See www.beg.aero/en for a full list.

TRAIN

The **central train station** (Savski Trg 2) has an information office on Platform 1, tourist information office, **exchange bureau** (⊙6am-10pm) and **sales counter** (⊙24hrs).

Frequent trains go to Novi Sad (288DIN, 1½ hours), Subotica (560DIN, three hours) and Niš (784DIN, four hours). See www.serbianrailways. com for timetables and fares.

ℹ Getting Around

TO/FROM THE AIRPORT

Nikola Tesla airport is 18km from Belgrade. Local bus 72 (73DIN to 150DIN, half-hourly, 5.20am to midnight from airport, 4.40am to 11.40pm from town) connects the airport with Zeleni Venac; the cheapest tickets must be purchased from news stands. A minibus also runs between the airport and the central Trg Slavija (250DIN, 5am to 3.50am from airport, 4.20am to 3.20am from the square).

Don't get swallowed up by the airport taxi shark pit: ask the tourist office in the arrivals hall to call one for you. A taxi from the airport to Knez Mihailova should be around 1800DIN.

CAR & MOTORCYCLE

Parking in Belgrade is regulated by three parking zones – red (one hour, 56DIN), yellow (two hours, 48DIN per hour) and green (three hours, 41DIN per hour). Tickets must be bought from kiosks or via SMS (in Serbian).

PUBLIC TRANSPORT

Trams and trolleybuses ply limited routes but buses chug all over town. Rechargeable BusPlus cards can be bought and topped up (73DIN per ticket) at kiosks across the city; they're 140DIN if you buy from the driver.

Tram 2 connects Kalemegdan Citadel with Trg Slavija, bus stations and the central train station.

TAXI

Move away from obvious taxi traps and flag down a distinctly labelled cruising cab, or get a local to call you one. Flagfall is 170DIN; reputable cabs should charge about 70DIN per kilometre.

VOJVODINA ВОЈВОДИНА

Home to more than 25 ethnic groups, six languages and the best of Hungarian and Serbian traditions, Vojvodina's pancake plains mask a diversity unheard of in the rest of the country. Affable capital Novi Sad hosts the eclectic EXIT festival – the largest in southeast Europe – while the hilly region of Fruška Gora keeps the noise down in hushed monasteries and ancestral vineyards. Charming Subotica, 10km from Hungary, is an oasis of art nouveau delights.

Novi Sad Нови Сад

☑021 / POP 366,860

As convivial as a *rakija* toast – and at times just as carousing – Novi Sad is a chipper town with all the spoils and none of the stress of the big smoke. Locals sprawl in pretty parks and outdoor cafes, and laneway bars along pedestrian thoroughfare Zmaj Jovina, which stretches from the town square (Trg Slobode) to Dunavska street, pack out nightly.

⊙ Sights

★**Petrovaradin Citadel** FORTRESS (museum admission 200DIN; ⊙museum 9am-5pm Tue-Sun) Towering over the river on a

40m-high volcanic slab, this mighty citadel (*tvrđava*) is aptly nicknamed 'Gibraltar on the Danube'. Constructed with slave labour between 1692 and 1780, its dungeons have held notable prisoners including Karađorđe (leader of the first uprising against the Turks and founder of a dynasty) and Tito. Have a good gawk at the iconic clock tower: the size of the minute and hour hands are reversed so far-flung fishermen can tell the time. Within the citadel walls, a **museum** (021-643 3145; Petrovaradin Citadel; admission 150DIN; 9am-5pm Tue-Sun) offers insight (sans English explanations) into the site's history. The museum can also arrange tours (300DIN) of Petrovaradin's creepy – but cool – underground passageways.

Museum of Vojvodina   MUSEUM
(Muzej Vojvodine; www.muzejvojvodine.org.rs; Dunavska 35-7; admission 200DIN, free on Sundays; 9am-7pm Tue-Fri, 10am-6pm Sat & Sun) This museum houses historical, archaeological and ethnological exhibits. Building 35 covers Vojvodinian history from Palaeolithic times to the late 19th century. Building 37 takes the story to 1945 with a harrowing emphasis on WWI and WWII.

Štrand   BEACH
One of Europe's best by-the-Danube beaches.

✦ Festivals & Events

The Petrovaradin Citadel is stormed by thousands of revellers each July during the epic **EXIT Festival** (www.exitfest.org). The first festival in 2000 lasted 100 days and galvanised a generation of younger Serbs against the Milošević regime. The has been attended by the likes of the Chemical Brothers, Gogol Bordello and Patti Smith...and an annual tally of about 200,000 merrymakers.

⛏ Sleeping

★ Hostel Sova   HOSTEL €
(021-527 556; www.hostelsova.com; Ilije Ognjanovića 26; dm from €10, d €15 pp; P 🛜) This cute spot is akin to a mini Novi Sad: super-friendly, attractive and given to laid-back socialising (not to mention the odd *rakija* or two). It's perched above a deceptively quiet street that's just around the corner from buzzy Zmaj Jovina and a couple of minutes' stagger from the best bars in town.

Downtown   HOSTEL €
(021-524 818; www.hostelnovisad.com; Njegoševa 2; dm from €12, s/d €21/30; @) Super-

friendly staff and an 'in the thick of it' location off Trg Slobode make this rambunctious, slightly ramshackle hostel a classic Novi Sad experience in itself.

★ Hotel Veliki   HOTEL €€
(021-472 3840; www.hotelvelikinovisad.com; Pašića 24; s/d €33/46, apt from €65; P ✳ 🛜) Sitting atop an absolutely stupendous Vojvodinian restaurant of the same name, the Veliki ('Big') lives up to its name: some of the rooms are truly huge. Staff are delightful and the location around the corner from Zmaj Jovina is top-notch. Extra bonus: free breakfast downstairs!

✕ Eating

Kukuriku   FAST FOOD €
(Despota Stefana 5; mains 160-280DIN; 8am-11pm Mon-Fri, until 1am Sat) Without a skerrick of a doubt, this hole-in-the-wall joint in the cool Chinatown district makes the freshest, tastiest *pljeskavica* in town: you will salivate over the memory of these burgers for months to come. Their homemade pizzas and other fast-food offerings are also worth loosening your belt for. They're on the right-hand corner of the unmissable cartoon-coloured building.

★ Fish i Zeleniš   MEDITERRANEAN €€
(Fish and Greens; 021-452 000; www.fishizelenis.com; Skerlićeva 2; mains from 680DIN; noon-midnight;) This bright, snug little nook serves up the finest vegetarian/pescatarian meals in northern Serbia. Organic, locally sourced ingredients? Ambient? Ineffably delicious? Tick, tick, tick. A three-minute walk from Zmaj Jovina.

Restoran Lipa   SERBIAN €€
(www.restoranlipa.com; Svetozara Miletića 7; meals from 700DIN; 9am-11pm Mon-Thur & Sun, 9am-1am Fri-Sat) This down-home eatery has been dishing up old-school ambience alongside traditional Vojvodinian fare since the 19th century. Live *tamburaši* (string-instrument serenaders) on Fridays and Saturdays.

♟ Drinking & Nightlife

Novi Sad nightlife is far more laid-back than Belgrade's frenzy of clubs and hedonistic *splavovi*. **Laze Telečkog** (pedestrian sidestreet running off Zmaj Jovina) is lined with bars to suit every whim.

★ Martha's Pub   BAR
(Laze Telečkog 3; 8am-3am) One of the best in a street of top bars, Martha's is a small,

smokey and stupendously sociable den famous for its divine *medovača* (honey *rakija*). Crowbar yourself inside, or get there early to nab a table outside to watch the party people of Laze Telečkog romp by.

Culture Exchange   CAFE
(☑ 064 432 9197; www.cultureexchangeserbia.org; Jovana Subotića 21; ☺9am-11pm; 🛜) Run by a well-travelled staff of volunteers, Culture Exchange offers coffees, cakes and pretty much everything else you can imagine: free bike repairs, Serbian language classes, live music gigs, film screenings and art exhibitions. It's a top spot for pre-big-night-out drinks. There's nowhere quite like it in town (or indeed, Serbia!).

Crni Bik   PUB
(Trg Mladenaca 8; ☺10am-late) Boisterous dive bar a short stagger south of Zmaj Jovina. Friendly local eccentrics prop up the bar while eclectic bands and DJs do their thing on a small stage.

ℹ Information

Tourist Information Centre (www.turizamns.rs; Jevrejska 10; ☺7.30am-6pm Mon-Fri, 10am-3pm Sat) Ultra-helpful with maps and English info.

ℹ Getting There & Away

The **bus station** (Bul Jaše Tomića; ☺information counter 6am-11pm) has regular departures to Belgrade (520DIN, one hour, every 10 minutes) and Subotica (600DIN, 1½ hours), plus services to Užice (1120DIN, five hours) and Zlatibor (1300DIN, six hours). From here, four stops on bus 4 will take you to the town centre: nip down the underpass and you'll see Trg Slobode on emerging.

Frequent trains leave the **train station** (Bul Jaše Tomića 4), next door to the bus station, for Belgrade (288DIN, 1½ hours) and Subotica (384DIN, 1½ hours).

Subotica   Суботица
☑ 024 / POP 148,000
Sugar-spun art nouveau marvels, a laid-back populace and a delicious sprinkling of Serbian and Hungarian flavours make this quaint town a worthy day trip or stopover.

◉ Sights

Town Hall   HISTORIC BUILDING
(Trg Slobode) Built in 1910, this behemoth is a curious mix of art nouveau and something Gaudí may have had a playful dab at. The council chambers – with its exquisite stained-glass windows and elaborate decor – are not to be missed.

Modern Art Gallery   HISTORIC BUILDING
(www.likovnisusret.rs; Park Ferenca Rajhla 5; admission 50DIN; ☺8am-7pm Mon-Fri, 9am-1pm Sat) This mansion was built in 1904 as an architect's design studio, and it shows. One of the most sumptuous buildings in Serbia, it's a vibrant flourish of mosaics, ceramic tiles, floral patterns and stained glass.

🛏 Sleeping

Hostel Incognito   HOSTEL €
(☑ 062 666 674; www.hostel-subotica.com; Hugo Badalića 3; s/d/tr/apt 1000/1800/2400/7000DIN; 🅿🛜) This basic but clean, friendly hostel is a couple of minutes' walk from all the Subotica sights. Reception is in the restaurant downstairs: call before lobbing up.

SERBIA SUBOTICA

DON'T MISS

NOVI PAZAR & STUDENICA MONASTERY   НОВИ ПАЗАР

Novi Pazar is the cultural centre of the Raška/Sandžak region, with a large Muslim population. Turkish coffee, cuisine and customs abound, yet some idyllic Orthodox sights are in the vicinity: this was the heartland of the Serbian medieval state.

One of the most sacred sites in Serbia, Unesco-listed **Studenica** was established in the 1190s by founder of the Serbian empire (and future saint) Stefan Nemanja and developed by his sons Vukan, Stefan and Rastko (St Sava). Active monastic life was cultivated by Sava and continues today, though this thriving little community doesn't mind visitors.

Two well-preserved churches lie within impressive white-marble walls. **Bogorodičina Crkva** (Church of Our Lady), a royal funeral church, contains Stefan's tomb. Smaller **Kraljeva Crkva** (King's Church) houses the acclaimed *Birth of the Virgin* fresco and other masterpieces.

From Novi Pazar, catch a Kraljevo-bound bus to the village of Ušće (about one hour) and hop a local bus from there, or negotiate a return taxi journey.

WORTH A TRIP

DJAVOLJA VAROŠ

Djavolja Varoš (Devil's Town) in Serbia's deep south, is a trippy cluster of 202 natural stone pyramids looming eerily over bright red, highly acidic mineral streams. According to local whispers, the towers – which teeter between 2m and 15m in height and are topped with creepy volcanic 'heads' – were formed after guests at an incestuous wedding were petrified by an offended god.

Djavolja Varoš is easily reached by car; otherwise catch a bus to Kuršumlija, and grab a taxi from there. Camping at the park isn't allowed, but there are plenty of villagers willing to take in strays. You could camp nearby, but snakes and wolves abound. It's not called Devil's Town for nothing!

Hotel Galleria
HOTEL €€

(☑024-647 111; www.galleria-center.com; Matije Korvina 17; s/d €45/57, apt/ste from €76/135; ❋❢) These four-star rooms come over all 'gentleman's den', with warm mahogany-look fittings and beds lined with bookshelves. The hotel also houses a gigantic 'wellness centre' and several eateries. It's inside the Atrium shopping plaza.

✖️ Eating

Ravel
CAFE €

(Nušićeva 2; cakes 60-200DIN; ☻9am-10pm Mon-Sat, 11am-10pm Sun) Dainty nibbles at *gateaux* and twee tea-taking is the name of the game at this adorable art nouveau classic.

Boss Caffe
INTERNATIONAL €€

(www.bosscaffe.com; Matije Korvina 7-8; mains 450-1000DIN; ☻7am-midnight Mon-Thu, until 1am Fri-Sat, 9am-midnight Sun) The best restaurant in town has a huge menu spanning Chinese, Italian, Mexican and Serbian cuisines; somehow it pulls it off with aplomb. It's directly behind the Modern Art Gallery.

ℹ️ Information

Tourist Information Office (☑024-670 350; www.visitsubotica.rs; Town Hall; ☻8am-6pm Mon-Fri, 9am-1pm Sat) Tons of friendly, English-speaking advice and info. It's also home to the Subotica Greeters, local volunteers only too thrilled to show you around their hometown (bookings essential).

ℹ️ Getting There & Away

From the **bus station** (www.sutrans.rs; Senćanski put 3) there are hourly services to Novi Sad (600DIN, two hours) and Belgrade (800DIN, 3½ hours). See the website for other destinations. Subotica's **train station** (Bose Milećević bb) has two trains to Szeged, Hungary (320DIN, 1¾ hours). Trains to Belgrade (560DIN, 3½ hours) stop at Novi Sad (384DIN, 1½ hours).

SOUTH SERBIA

Niš
Ниш

☑018 / POP 183,000

Niš is a lively city of curious contrasts, where Roma in horse-drawn carriages trot alongside new cars, and posh cocktails are sipped in antiquated alleyways. Niš was settled in pre-Roman times and flourished during the time of local-boy-made-good Emperor Constantine (AD 280–337).

◉ Sights

Niš Fortress
FORTRESS

(Niška tvrđava; Jadranska; ☻24hr) While its current incarnation was built by the Turks in the 18th century, there have been forts on this site since ancient Roman times. Today it's a sprawling recreational area with restaurants, cafes and market stalls. It hosts the **Nišville International Jazz Festival** (www.nisville.com) each August and **Nišomnia** (www.facebook.com/festivalnisomnia), featuring rock and electro acts, in September. The city's main pedestrian boulevard, Obrenovićeva, stretches before the citadel.

Tower of Skulls
MONUMENT

(Ćele Kula; Bul Zoran Đinđić; adult/child 150/130DIN; ☻9am-7pm Tue-Fri, to 3pm Sat-Sun) With Serbian defeat imminent at the 1809 Battle of Čegar, the Duke of Resava kamikazeed towards the Turkish defences, firing at their gunpowder stores, killing himself, 4000 of his men, and 10,000 Turks. The Turks triumphed regardless, and to deter future acts of rebellion, they beheaded, scalped and embedded in this tower the skulls of the dead Serbs. Only 58 of the initial 952 skulls remain. Contrary to Turkish intention, the tower serves as a proud monument to Serbian resistance.

Get there on any bus marked 'Niška Banja' from the stop opposite the Ambassador Hotel: ask to be let out at Ćele Kula.

Red Cross Concentration Camp MUSEUM
(Crveni Krst; Bul 12 Februar; adult/child 150/130DIN; ⊗9am-4pm Tue-Fri, 10am-3pm Sat-Sun) One of the best-preserved Nazi camps in Europe, the deceptively named Red Cross held about 30,000 Serbs, Roma, Jews and Partisans during the German occupation of Serbia (1941–45). Harrowing displays tell their stories, and those of the prisoners who attempted to flee in the biggest ever breakout from a concentration camp. A short walk north of the Niš bus station.

🛏 Sleeping

Day 'n' Night Hostel HOSTEL €
(☑064 481 5869; www.daynnighthostel.com; Božidarčeva 9; dm/s/d from €9/15/20; ⓟ❅🤶) This spanking new hostel is clean, bright and has a kitchen and common room on each of its two floors. Friendly English-speaking staff do their utmost to ensure you have a good stay, and can organise excursions. It's a ten-minute walk to downtown Niš.

★Hotel Sole HOTEL €€
(☑018-292 432; www.hotelsole.rs; Kralja Stefana Prvovenčanog 11; s/d from €45/55 incl breakfast; ⓟ❅🤶) Sitting pretty right in the heart of Niš, this totally refurbished hotel has modern, super-spacious rooms and one of the best free breakfasts you'll find anywhere. Staff is top-notch.

🍴 Eating & Drinking

The cobblestoned Kopitareva (Tinkers' Alley) is chock-full of fast-paced eating and drinking options.

Stara Srbija SERBIAN €€
(Old Serbia; ☑018-521 902; Trg Republike 12; mains 220-1500DIN; ⊗8am-midnight) Right at home in a restored 1876 house in the centre of Niš, this atmospheric spot serves up filling, fantastic traditional southern Serbian cuisine, including baked beans with smoked meat and the divine chicken stuffed with prosciutto and *kajmak* (clotted cream).

Crazy Horse BAR
(Davidova 8; ⊗8am-2am Sat-Thu, to 4am Fri; 🤶) Guinness, darts, live Irish music, Champions League on TV...in the birthplace of Constantine the Great? Crazy – like the name says – but somehow, this bar works.

ℹ Information

Tourist Organisation of Niš (☑018-250 222; www.visitnis.com; Tvrđava; ⊗7.30am-7pm

SERBIA NIŠ

Mon-Fri, 9am-1pm Sat) Helpful info within the citadel gates.

❶ Getting There & Away

The **bus station** (Bul 12 Februar) behind the fortress has frequent services to Belgrade (1380DIN, three hours) and Brus (710DIN, 1½ hours) for Kopaonik, and three daily to Novi Pazar (1120DIN, four hours).

From the **train station** (Dimitrija Tucovića), there are seven trains to Belgrade (784DIN, 4½ hours) and two to Sofia, Budapest (730DIN, five hours).

SURVIVAL GUIDE

❶ Directory A–Z

ACCOMMODATION
Private rooms and apartments offer superb value and can be organised through tourist offices. 'Wild' camping is possible outside national parks.

MONEY
Serbia retains the dinar (DIN); though accommodation prices are often quoted in euro, you must pay in dinar.

TELEPHONE
Local and international phonecards can be bought in post offices and tobacco kiosks. Mobile-phone SIM cards (around 200DIN) and recharge cards can be purchased at supermarkets and kiosks.

VISAS
Tourist visas for stays of less than 90 days aren't required by citizens of EU countries, most other European countries, Australia, New Zealand, Canada and the USA. **The Ministry of Foreign Affairs** (www.mfa.gov.rs/en) has full details.

Officially, all visitors must register with the police. Hotels and hostels will do this for you but if you're camping or staying in a private home, you are expected to register within 24 hours of arrival. Unofficially? This is rarely enforced, but

EATING PRICE RANGES

The following price categories for the cost of a main course are used in the listings in this chapter:

€ less than €6 (600DIN)

€€ €6 to €10 (600DIN to 1000DIN)

€€€ more than €10 (1000DIN)

SLEEPING PRICE RANGES

The following price categories for the cost of a high-season double room are used in the listings in this chapter:

€ less than €30 (3000DIN)

€€ €30 to €75 (3000DIN to 7000DIN)

€€€ more than €75 (7000DIN)

being unable to produce registration documents upon leaving Serbia could result in a fine.

❶ Getting There & Away

AIR
Belgrade's **Nikola Tesla Beograd Airport** (☎ 011-209 4444; www.beg.aero) handles most international flights. Serbia's national carrier is **Air Serbia** (www.airserbia.com). The airport website has a full list of Serbia-bound airlines.

LAND
Because Serbia does not acknowledge crossing points into Kosovo as international border crossings, it may not be possible to enter Serbia from Kosovo unless you first entered from Serbia. Driving Serbian-plated cars into Kosovo isn't advised, and is often not permitted by rental agencies or insurers.

Drivers need International Driving Permits. Drivers from EU countries don't need Green Card or border insurance to drive in Serbia; otherwise, border insurance costs about €107 for a car, €67 for a motorbike.

Bus services to both Western Europe and Turkey are well developed.

International rail connections leaving Serbia originate in Belgrade. For more information, visit **Serbian Railways** (www.serbianrailways.com).

❶ Getting Around

Bus services are extensive, though outside major hubs connections can be sporadic. Reservations are only worthwhile for international buses and during festivals.

Major car-hire companies are ubiquitous. The **Automobile & Motorcycle Association of Serbia** (Auto-Moto Savez Srbije; ☎ 011-333 1100, roadside assist 1987; www.amss.org.rs; Ruzveltova 18) provides roadside assistance and extensive information on its website.

Serbian Railways serves Novi Sad, Subotica and Niš from Belgrade.

Bicycle paths are improving in larger cities.

Slovakia

Best Places to Eat

➡ Traja Mušketieri (p381)

➡ Koliba Patria (p386)

➡ Republika Východu (p391)

Best Places to Stay

➡ Hotel Marrol's (p380)

➡ Grand Hotel Kempinski (p386)

➡ Hotel Bankov (p391)

Why Go?

Going strong over two decades as an independent state after the breakup of Czechoslovakia, Slovakia, Europe's most castellated country, is a bastion of untrammelled wildernesses, where some of the continent's densest forest coverage gives way to dramatic fortresses and craggy mountains harbouring outstanding hiking. It savours wine over beer and, in its tradition-steeped hinterland, cradles an entrancing folk culture most European nations have lost.

Slovakia's small size is possibly its biggest attraction. You can traipse woodsy waterfall-filled gorges one day and yodel from 2500m-plus peaks the next.

Dinky capital Bratislava is awash with quirky museums and backed by thick forests, but don't leave without heading east, where fortresses tower over tradition-rich medieval towns such as Levoča or Bardejov and hiking trails lace the hills. Down a *slivovica* (firewater-like plum brandy) and drink a toast for us – *nazdravie*!

When to Go
Bratislava

Jun & Jul Festivals abound across the country, High Tatras hiking trails are all open.

Jan & Feb Peak ski season in the mountains, but many other sights are closed.

Sep Fewer crowds but wine season means it's ripe time for alcohol-themed festivities.

Slovakia Highlights

1 Linger over drinks at one of myriad sidewalk or riverfront cafes in old town **Bratislava.**

2 Hike between mountain huts in one of Europe's smallest alpine mountain ranges, the **High Tatras (p384).**

3 Wander the ruins of **Spiš Castle** (p388), among the biggest in Europe.

4 Climb creaking ladders past crashing waterfalls in the dramatic gorges of **Slovenský Raj National Park** (p389).

Three Days

Two nights in **Bratislava** is enough to wander the old town streets and see some museums. The following day is best spent on a castle excursion, either to **Devín** or **Trenčín**. Or, better yet, spend all three days hiking in the rocky **High Tatras mountains**, staying central in the resort town of **Starý Smokovec** or in more off-beat **Ždiar** in the **Belá Tatras**.

One Week

After a day or two in **Bratislava**, venture east. Spend at least four nights around the **Tatras** so you have time to hike to a mountain hut as well as take day trips to the must-see **Spiš Castle** ruins, medieval **Levoča**, or to **Slovenský Raj National Park** for its highly rated Suchá Belá Gorge hike. For the last night or two, continue to Bardejov to marvel at its complete Renaissance town square and nearby wooden churches.

BRATISLAVA

📱 02 / POP 430,000

Proximity to nature gives Slovakia's capital its strongest flavouring. The Danube wends through town, and cycle paths through its verdant flood plain begin just outside the centre. Meanwhile, erupting a 30-minute walk from the train station are the densely forested Small Carpathians; the trailer to a mountainous extent that runs countrywide, virtually unimpeded by civilisation. Then there's ski runs and vineyards to amble among.

The charming – if tiny – old town (*starý mesto*) is the place to start appreciating Bratislava. Stroll narrow pedestrian streets of pastel 18th-century buildings or sample the myriad sidewalk cafes under the watchful gaze of the city castle, harking back to medieval times. Done with the old? In with the new(er): the city boasts intriguing socialist-era architecture worth checking out and one of Eastern Europe's most spectacular modern art spaces. Contrasts like this are all part of Bratislava's allure.

History

Founded in AD 907, by the 12th century Bratislava (then called Poszony in Hungarian or Pressburg in German) was a large city in greater Hungary. King Matthias Corvinus founded a university here, Academia Istropolitana. Many of the imposing baroque palaces you see date to the reign of Austro-Hungarian empress Maria Theresa (1740–80), when the city flourished. From the 16th-century Turkish occupation of Budapest to the mid-1800s, Hungarian parliament met locally and monarchs were crowned in St Martin's Cathedral.

'Bratislava' was officially born as the second city of a Czechoslovakian state after WWI and became capital of the new nation of Slovakia in 1993.

◉ Sights

In addition to those we recommend, there are several small museums and increasingly well-regarded galleries scattered about the old town: ask at the Bratislava Culture & Information Centre for the *Art Plan* leaflet.

★ **Bratislava Castle** CASTLE
(www.snm.sk; grounds free, admission all exhibits adult/senior €7/4; ⊙ grounds 9am-9pm, museum 10am-6pm Tue-Sun) Dominating the southwest of the old town on a hill above the Danube, the castle today is largely a 1950s reconstruction; an 1811 fire left the fortress ruined for more than a century and renovations continue. Most buildings contain administrative offices, but there is a museum of Slovakia through the ages, and lawns and ramparts provide great vantage points for city viewing.

★ **Museum of Jewish Culture** MUSEUM
(www.snm.sk; Židovská 17; adult/child €7/2; ⊙11am-5pm Sun-Fri) The most moving of the three floors of exhibits here focuses on the large Jewish community and buildings lost during and after WWII. Black-and-white photos show the neighbourhood and synagogue before it was ploughed under.

★ **St Martin's Cathedral** CHURCH
(Dóm sv Martina; cnr Kapitulská & Staromestská; admission €2; ⊙9-11.30am & 1-6pm Mon-Sat, 1.30-4pm Sun May-Sep, until 4pm Mon-Sat Oct-Apr) A relatively modest interior belies the elaborate history of St Martin's Cathedral: 11

Central Bratislava

N 0 ———— 200 m
0 ———— 0.1 miles

Slavín War Memorial (1km)

Moyzesova

Tolstého
18

Sládkovičova

Štefánikova

Grassalkovich Palace (Presidential Palace)

Nám 1 mája

Palisády

Hodžovo nám

Mýtna

Tatra centrum

Vysoká

Hotel-Penzión Arcus (850m); Hlava XXII (1.2km)

Panenská
19

11

13

Konventná

Crowne Plaza

Drevená
14

Obchodná
27

21

Kozia

Pilárikova ulica

Staromestská

Poštová

Zochova

Hurbanovo nám

Nám SNP

Monument of the Slovak National Uprising

Svoradova

Michael's Gate & Tower

Nám SNP

Zámocká

Kapucínska

Baštová

Zámočnícka

Františkánska

Nedbalova
23

Bistro St Germain (450m)

Skalná

Klariská

Michalská

Biela

Františkánske nám

7

Primaciálne nám

Uršulínska

Klobučnícka

Bratislava Culture & Information Centre

Farská

Sedlárska

Klobučnícka

9

Radničná

8

Laurinská

Museum of Jewish Culture
3

Židovská

Staromestská

Úzka

Kapitulská

Prepoštská

Ventúrska

Zelená

5

Hlavné nám

Rybárska brána

Tulip House Hotel (250m); Nu Spirit Club (400m); Main (1.2km); Bratislava (10km)

1
Bratislava Castle

Panská

25

Jesenského

St Martin's Cathedral

4

Rudnayovo nám

17

15

Gorkého

Eugena Suchoň nám

Žámocké schody

Hviezdoslavovo nám

6

Mostová

Palackého

Hotel Marrol's (200m); New SND (1km)

24

26

Medená

20

22

Nový Most Bus Stop

Rybné nám

16

12

Paulínyho

10

Nám L Štúra

Židovská

Nábr arm gen L Svobodu

Rázusovo nábr

Hydrofoil Terminal (90m); Slovak Shipping & Ports (100m)

Propeller Terminal

2
Most SNP

Danube River

Viewing Platform (100m); Petržalka (750m)

Central Bratislava

Austro-Hungarian monarchs (10 kings and one queen, Maria Theresa) were crowned in this large 14th-century church. The busy motorway almost touching St Martin's follows the moat of the former city walls.

Hviezdoslavovo Námestie   SQUARE
Embassies, restaurants and bars are the mainstay of the long, tree-lined plaza that anchors the pedestrian zone's southern extremity. At Hviezdoslavovo's east end, the ornate 1886 Slovak National Theatre (p381), one of the city's opera houses, steals the show. The theatre is not open for tours, but ticket prices are not prohibitive. The nearby neo-baroque 1914 Reduta Palace (Eugena

Suchoň nám; ⊘ 9am-2pm Mon, 1-7pm Tue-Fri & 1hr before concerts) houses the Slovak Philharmonic.

Hlavné Námestie   SQUARE
Cafe tables outline pretty Hlavné nám (Main Sq), the site of numerous festival performances. Roland's Fountain, at the square's heart, is thought to have been built in 1572 as a fire hydrant of sorts. Flanking the northeast side of the square is the 1421 Old Town Hall (www.muzeum.bratislava.sk; adult/child €5/2; ⊘ 10am-5pm Tue-Fri, 11am-6pm Sat & Sun), home to the city museum. You'll often find a musician in traditional costume playing a *fujara* on the steps of the Jesuit Church, on the edge of adjoining Františkánske nám.

Slovak National Gallery   MUSEUM
(Slovenská Národná Galéria; ☑ 2049 6243; www.sng.sk; Rázusovo nábr 2; ⊘ 10am-6pm Tue & Wed & Fri-Sun, noon-8pm Thu, closed Mon) FREE A socialist modernist building and an 18th-century palace make interesting co-hosts for the Slovak National Gallery. The nation's eclectic art collection contained here ranges from Gothic to graphic design. In 2014 the gallery experimented with free admission; they are hopeful this will still be possible in subsequent years.

🏃 Activities

Slovak Shipping & Ports   BOAT TOUR
(☑ 5293 2226; www.lod.sk; Fajnorovo nábr 2) From April through September, Slovak Shipping & Ports runs 45-minute Bratislava return boat trips (adult/child €6/4.50) on the Danube. Its Devín sightseeing cruise (adult/child return €8/6) plies the waters to the castle, stops for about an hour and returns to Bratislava in 30 minutes.

☞ Tours

Authentic Slovakia   CULTURAL TOUR
(☑ 0908 308 234; www.authenticslovakia.com; per 2/4hr tour €27/43) Want to know about the Slovakia the other tours don't let on? Sign up with these guys for forays to weird socialist-era buildings and typical *krčmy* (Slovak pubs): authentic (uncensored) Slovakia.

✦ Festivals & Events

Fjúžn   CULTURAL
(www.fjuzn.sk; ⊘ Apr) Dunaj (p381), an important venue for world music year-round, hosts this annual celebration of Slovak minorities and their cultures.

SLOVAKIA BRATISLAVA

Cultural Summer Festival   CULTURAL
(www.visit.bratislava.sk; ☉ Jun-Sep) A smorgasbord of plays and performances comes to the streets and venues around town in summer.

Bratislava Music Festival   MUSIC
(www.bhsfestival.sk; ☉ Oct) One of Slovakia's best music festivals; international classical music performances take place in October.

Christmas Market   SHOPPING
(☉ Nov-Dec) From late November, Hlavné and Hviezdoslavo nám fills with food and drink, crafts for sale and staged performances: very atmospheric.

🛏 Sleeping

Getting a short-term rental flat in the old town (€60 to €120 per night) is also a great way to stay central without paying hotel prices, plus you can self-cater. Family-run and friendly, the modern units of **Apartments Bratislava** (www.apartmentsbratislava.com) are our top choice. Many hostels also have kitchens.

Downtown Backpackers   HOSTEL €
(☑ 5464 1191; www.backpackers.sk; Panenská 31; dm €17-18, tw €54; ☺ @ ☎) The first hostel in Bratislava, Backpackers is still a boozy (you enter through a bar) bohemian classic. Red-brick walls and tapestries add character. Serves good food in the cosy downstairs restaurant.

Penzión Portus   GUESTHOUSE €
(☑ 0911 978 026; www.portus.sk; Paulínyho 10; r incl breakfast from €40) Above an atmospheric old cellar restaurant, the modern, less-characterful rooms still represent the old town's best deal on private rooms.

Penzión Virgo   GUESTHOUSE €€
(☑ 2092 1400; www.penzionvirgo.sk; Panenská 14; s/d/apt €61/74/85; ☺ @ ☎) Exterior-access rooms are arranged around a courtyard; light and airy despite dark-wood floors and baroque-accent wallpaper. Sip an espresso with the breakfast buffet (€5).

Hotel-Penzión Arcus   GUESTHOUSE €€
(☑ 5557 2522; www.hotelarcus.sk; Moskovská 5; s €54-66, d €80-100, all incl breakfast; ☺ ☎) Family-run place with varied rooms (some with balcony, some with courtyard views). It's 500m northeast of Tesco, via Špitalska.

★ Hotel Marrol's   BOUTIQUE HOTEL €€€
(☑ 5778 4600; www.hotelmarrols.sk; Tobrucká 4; d/ste incl breakfast from €152/290; ☎ ❄) You could imagine Kaiser Wilhelm puffing contentedly on a cigar here: no member of the aristocracy would feel out of place in these 54 sumptuous rooms and suites, or in the Jasmine spa. Considering it's a regular in 'world's best luxury hotel' lists, prices are very proletariat-friendly.

Tulip House Hotel   BOUTIQUE HOTEL €€€
(☑ 3217 1819; www.tuliphouse.sk; Štúrova 10; ste incl breakfast €150-390; P ☺ ❄ @ ☎) Exquisite art nouveau property with a cafe-restaurant at street level: penthouses available, too.

✕ Eating

The pedestrian centre is packed with overpriced samey dining options. Scour between the cracks, however, and you'll find great cafes and a few decent restaurants. Decent Slovak food isn't easy to find, but that Slovak fave, the set-lunch menu, can be a real steal.

Shtoor   CAFE €
(Panská 23; light lunches €3-6; ☎ ☑) With its tasty, cheap, healthy lunches, Shtoor has three locations in Bratislava, but this one has the best (coffee- and cake-fuelled) atmosphere. Check out the menus: written in old-fashioned Slovak as set down by Ľudovít Štúr, pioneer of Slovak literary language.

Bistro St Germain   BISTRO €
(Rajská 7; mains €3-8; ☉ 10am-11pm Mon-Fri, noon-11pm Sat & Sun; ☎ ☑) Relocated to a much bigger premise, St Germain remains a wonderfully decorated, relaxed place to gossip over homemade lemonade, cupcakes or light lunches (salads, baguettes and the like).

★ Café Verne   INTERNATIONAL €€
(Hviezdoslavovo nám 18; mains €4-11; ☉ 9am-midnight) Lively, friendly, good-value dining in the old town: the Czech beers flow and everyone from expats to students wolfs down hearty no-nonsense grub, including Slovak staples and decent English breakfasts.

Hradná Hviezda   FUSION €€
(☑ 0944 142 718; http://hradnahviezda.sk; Bratislava Castle; starters €4-7, mains €10-22; ☉ 11am-11pm) Being right under Bratislava Castle, you'd think the location would signify an over-touristy low-quality joint, but this beautiful restaurant is quiet, dignified, and high end. It specialises in taking typical Slovak food and making it that little bit sexier.

Bratislavský Meštiansky Pivovar   SLOVAK €€
(☑ 0944 512 265; www.mestianskypivovar.sk; Drevená 8; mains €5.50-19; ☉ 11am-midnight Mon-Thu & Sat, to 1am Fri, to 11pm Sun; ☎) This stylish

microbrewery serves Bratislava's freshest beer and offers creative Slovak cooking beneath vaulted ceilings and stylised old town artwork.

Lemon Tree
THAI €€€

(☑ 0948 109 400; www.lemontree.sk; Hviezdoslavovo nám 7; mains €7-18) Top-end Thai-Mediterranean restaurant with a 7th-floor upscale bar, Skybar, with great views. Reservations are a good idea. An €8 set menu is also offered daily.

★ Traja Mušketieri
PUB FOOD €€€

(☑ 5443 0019; Sládkovičova 7; mains €10-20) This way-upmarket version of a medieval tavern comes with a poetic menu. 'Treacherous Lady de Winter' is a skewered chicken stuffed with Parma ham. Courteous service; reservations recommended.

🍷 Drinking & Nightlife

From mid-April to October, sidewalk cafe tables sprout up in every corner of the pedestrian old town. Hviezdoslavovo námestie has good options. Admission prices for Bratislava's bars and clubs are usually quite low (free to €5).

Slovak Pub
PUB

(Obchodná 62; ☺ 10am-midnight Mon-Thu, 10am-2am Fri & Sat, noon-midnight Sun; ☜) It's touristy, but most beers are available and it serves every traditional national dish (mains €3.50 to €11) you can think of, albeit far from top quality.

Nu Spirit Bar
BAR

(Medená 16; ☺ 10am-2am Mon-Fri, 5pm-4am Sat & Sun) Deservedly popular cellar bar with regular live music as underground as its location: jazz, electronica, soul etc.

Nu Spirit Club
CLUB

(Šáfarikovo nám 7; ☺ 10pm-late, closed Sun & Mon) Under the Nu Spirit umbrella, Nu Spirit Club continues the theme with big, danceable environs.

Apollon Club
GAY & LESBIAN

(www.apollon-gay-club.sk; Panenská 24; ☺ 6pm-3am Mon, Tue & Thu, 6pm-5am Wed, 8pm-5am Fri & Sat, 8pm-1am Sun) The gay disco in town. Tuesday is karaoke night.

Subclub
CLUB

(Nábrežie arm gen L Svobodu; ☺ 10pm-4am Thu-Sat) An institution in the subterranean passages under Bratislava Castle. Techno, indy, hardcore dance etc pounds out to a young crowd.

☆ Entertainment

Check **Slovak Spectator** (http://spectator.sme.sk), the **Bratislava Culture & Information Centre** (www.bkis.sk) and **Kam do Mesta** (www.kamdomesta.sk) for the latest.

Live Music

Hlava XXII
LIVE MUSIC

(Bazová 9; ☺ 6pm-midnight Tue-Thu, 6pm-3am Fri & Sat) Jam sessions, blues and world beat – live. It's 1km northeast of the center, off Záhradnicka.

Performing Arts

Slovak National Theatre
THEATRE

(Slovenské Národné Divadlo; SND; www.snd.sk; Hviezdoslavovo nám) The national theatre company stages quality operas (Slavic and international), ballets and dramas in two venues: the gilt decoration of the landmark **Historic SND** (www.snd.sk; Hviezdoslavovo nám, booking office cnr Jesenského & Komenského; ☺ 8am-noon & 12.30-7pm Mon-Fri, 9am-1pm Sat & 1hr before shows) is a show in itself; the modern **New SND** (☑ 2047 2296; www.snd.sk; Pribinova 17; ☺ 9am-5pm Mon- Fri) has a cafe and guaranteed English-speaking reservation line.

Slovak Philharmonic
THEATRE

(www.filharm.sk; Eugena Suchoň nám; tickets €5-20; ☺ 9am-2pm Mon, 1-6pm Tue-Fri & before performances) Neo-baroque 1914 Reduta Palace houses the Slovak Philharmonic: refurbishment to this grand building included adding the impressive €1.5 million organ, and there are regular acclaimed classical music concerts here.

Dunaj
PERFORMING ARTS

(www.kcdunaj.sk; Nedbalova 3; ☺ 4pm-late; ☜) Cultural centre hosting some of Slovakia's most interesting drama and music performances. Something is on almost nightly. Also has a bar with old town panoramas from the terrace.

🛍 Shopping

There are several crystal, craft and jewellery stores, as well as souvenir booths, around Hlavné nám. Artisan galleries and antique shops inhabit alleyways off old town streets.

Úľuv
HANDICRAFTS

(www.uluv.sk; Obchodná 64) For serious folk-art shopping head to the main outlet of Úľuv, the national handicraft cooperative, where a courtyard is filled with artisans' studios. Look for *šupolienky*: expressive figures sculpted from corn husks.

SOCIALIST BRATISLAVA

The stint under socialism left its mark around town in bizarre and monumental ways.

Most SNP (New Bridge; Viedenská cesta; observation deck adult/child €6.50/3.50; ⊙10am-11pm) Colloquially called the UFO (pronounced ew-fo), this Danube-spanning bridge is a modernist marvel from 1972 with a cool viewing platform (Most SNP; admission €6.50) (sky-high admission!) and, just below, a restaurant (out-of-this-world prices!). The viewing platform is free if you eat in the restaurant.

Slavín War Memorial Huge memorial to the Soviets who fell in WWII, in a park of the same name which also yields great city views.

ℹ️ Information

Most cafes have wi-fi access; Hlavné nám and Hviezdoslavovo nám are free wi-fi zones. Bratislava has numerous banks and ATMs in the old town, with several branches on Poštova. There are also ATMs/exchange booths in the train and bus stations, and at the airport.

Bratislava Culture & Information Centre (BKIS; ☑ 16 186, 5441 9410; http://visit. bratislava.sk; Klobučnícka 2; ⊙9am-7pm Apr-Oct, 9am-6pm Nov-Mar) Amicable official tourist office. Brochures galore, including a small Bratislava guide.

Lonely Planet (www.lonelyplanet.com/slovakia/bratislava)

Main Police Station (☑158; Hrobákova 44) Main police station for foreigners, in Petržalka, about 3.75km south of Most SNP.

Main Post Office (Nám SNP 34-35) In a beautiful building.

Poliklinika Ruzinov (☑4827 9111; www.ruzinovskapoliklinika.sk; Ružinovská 10) Hospital with emergency services and 24-hour pharmacy.

Slovak Spectator (www.spectator.sme.sk) English-language weekly newspaper with current affairs and event listings.

Tatra Banka (Dunajská 4) English-speaking staff.

ℹ️ Getting There & Away

Bratislava is the main hub for trains, buses and the few planes that head in and out of the country.

AIR

Keep in mind that Vienna's much busier international airport is only 60km west.

Bratislava Airport (BTS; ☑02-3303-3353; www.bts.aero) Nine kilometres northeast of the centre. Connections to Italy, Spain, UK cities and more.

BOAT

From April to October, plying the Danube is a cruisey way to get between Bratislava and Vienna.

Slovak Shipping & Ports (☑5293 2226; www.lod.sk; Hydrofoil Terminal, Fajnorova nábr 2) Several weekly hydrofoils to Vienna and back between April and October (€18 one way, 1¾ hours). Daily runs are July and August only.

Twin City Liner (☑0903 610 716; www.twincityliner.com; Propeller Terminal, Rázusovo nábr) Up to four boats daily to Vienna (one way €20 to €35, 1½ hours) from the Hydrofoil Terminal on Fajnorova nábr 2. You can also book through the office of Flora Tours (☑5443 1023; www.floratour.sk; Kúpelná 6) on Kúpelná.

BUS

Direct destinations include cities throughout Slovakia and Europe, but the train is usually comparably priced and more convenient. The **Bratislava bus station** (Mlynské Nivy; 🚌 Autobusová stanica, AS) is 1km east of the old town; locals call it 'Mlynské Nivy' (the street name). For schedules, see www.cp.atlas.sk.

International bus routes include those to Vienna (€7.70, 1¼ hours, 12 daily), Prague (€14, 4¾ hours, eight daily), Budapest (€10, three hours, two daily) and London (€76, 23 to 24 hours, one daily).

Eurolines (☑in Bratislava 5556 2195; www.slovaklines.sk; Bratislava bus station, Mlynské Nívy 31) Contact for most international buses.

Eurobus (☑in Košice 680 7306; www.eurobus.sk; Bratislava bus station)

Slovak Lines (www.slovaklines.sk; Bratislava bus station) Services throughout the country; outside Bratislava under the name of Slovenská Autobusová Doprava (thankfully SAD for short).

TRAIN

Rail is the main way to get around Slovakia and to neighbouring countries. Intercity (IC) and Eurocity (EC) trains are quickest. *Rýchlik* (R; 'fast' trains) take slightly longer, but run more frequently and cost less. For schedules see www.cp.atlas.sk. Prices listed here are for the cheapest direct services.

Domestic trains run to Trenčín (€9.50, 1½ hours, 12 daily), Žilina (€12.50, 2½ hours, 12 daily), Poprad (€15, four hours, 12 daily) and Košice (€19, 5½ hours, 12 daily).

International trains run to Vienna (return €17.50; includes Vienna city transport, one hour, hourly), Prague (from €15 when booked through Slovak Rail website, 4¼ hours, six daily) and Budapest (€15, 2¾ hours, seven daily).

Main Train Station (Hlavná Stanica; www.slovakrail.sk; Predštanicné nám)

ⓘ Getting Around

TO/FROM THE AIRPORT
➡ City bus 61 links Bratislava Airport with the main train station (20 minutes).

➡ Standing taxis (over)charge about €20 to town; ask the price before you get in.

➡ A regular bus (€7.70) connects Vienna, Vienna Airport, Bratislava bus station and Bratislava Airport.

CAR
Numerous international car-hire companies such as Hertz and Sixt have offices at Bratislava Airport. **Buchbinder** (✆ 4363 7821; www.buchbinder.sk) In-town pick-up possible for a fee.

PUBLIC TRANSPORT
Bratislava has an extensive tram, bus and trolleybus network; though the old town is small, so you won't often need it. **Dopravný Podnik Bratislava** (DPB; www.dpb.sk; Hodžovo nám; ☺ 6am-7pm Mon-Fri) is the public transport company; you'll find a route map online. The office is in the underground passage beneath Hodžovo nám. Check www.imhd.zoznam.sk for city-wide schedules.

Tickets cost €0.70/0.90 for 15/60 minutes. Buy at newsstands and validate on board (or risk a legally enforceable €50 fine). Passes cost €4.50/8.30/10 for one/two/three days; buy at the DPB office, validate on board.

Important lines:

Bus 93 Main train station to Hodžovo nám then Petržalka train station.

Trolleybus 206 Bratislava bus station to Hodžovo nám.

Trolleybus 210 Bratislava bus station to Main train station.

TAXI
Standing cabs compulsively overcharge foreigners; an around-town trip should never cost above €10. To save money ask someone to help you order a taxi (not all operators speak English). **AA Euro Taxi** (✆ 16 022)

Around Bratislava

Some of the best sights in Bratislava are actually way out of the city centre. The ruins of poignant **Devín Castle** (www.muzeum.bratislava.sk; adult/child €4/2; ☺ 10am-5pm Tue-Fri, to 7pm Sat & Sun May-Sep), 9km west, was once the military plaything of 9th-century warlord Prince Ratislav, with a stunning location at the confluence of the Danube and Morava rivers. Bus 29 links Devín with Bratislava's Nový Most (New Bridge) bus stop, under Most SNP. Austria is just across the river from the castle.

Heading east out of the city you'll reach **Danubiana Meulensteen Art Museum** (www.danubiana.sk; Via Danubia, Čunovo; adult/child €8/4), Slovakia's most daring contemporary art museum. Boat trips run here down the Danube from the city centre from June to October (€10/6 return, see website for details); otherwise take bus 91 from Nový Most bus stop to Čunovo and walk from the terminus (2.5km), or drive.

TATRAS MOUNTAINS

Poprad

Poprad will likely be your first experience of mountain country, being the nearest sizeable city to the High Tatras and a major regional transport hub. The delightful 16th-century neighbourhood of Spišska Sobota and a popular thermal water park may make you linger. From the adjacent train and bus stations, the central pedestrian square, Nám sv Egídia, is a five-minute walk south on Alžbetina.

⊙ Sights & Activities

Spišská Sobota   NEIGHBOURHOOD
Sixteenth-century Spiš-style merchants' and artisans' houses line Spišska Sobota town square. The suburb is 1.2km northeast of Poprad's train station.

Aqua City   SPA
(✆ 785 1111; www.aquacity.sk; Športová 1397; treatments €10-30; ☺ 8am-9pm) ✦ Sauna, swim, bubble and slide zones are all part of Poprad's thermal water park. The park employs admirable green initiatives; the heat and electricity derive from geothermal and solar sources.

Adventoura   ADVENTURE SPORTS
(✆ 0903 641 549; www.adventoura.eu; Uherova 33) Dog sledding, hut-to-hut hikes, snowboarding...this company can organise the works. Day prices for trips around the Tatras start at about €30 per person.

🛏 Sleeping & Eating

★ Penzión Sabato   B&B €€
(🖉 776 9580; www.sabato.sk; Sobotské nám 6; r incl breakfast €50-100; 🛜) Exposed stone arches, a cobblestone courtyard and open-hearth restaurant reveal this inn's 17th-century age – as do romantically decorated rooms.

★ Vino & Tapas   INTERNATIONAL €€€
(🖉 0918 969 101; Sobotské nám 18; 2 courses €19; ⊘ evenings Mon-Sat) It's worth splashing out on Poprad's most atmospheric restaurant. The guys here have cooked for the Queen of England, and the food's a cut above. Best phone ahead if you're set on eating here.

ℹ Information

City Information Centre   TOURIST INFORMATION
(🖉 436 1192; www.poprad.sk; Dom Kultúry Štefániková 72, Poprad; ⊘ 9am-5pm Mon-Fri, 9am-noon Sat) Town info only; lists private rooms.

ℹ Getting There & Away

AIR
Poprad-Tatry International Airport (p393) is 5km west of the town centre and has a brand-new route to London four times weekly with Wizz Air.

BUS
Buses serve Levoča (€1.70, 45 minutes, hourly), Bardejov (€4.50, 2½ hours, one to two hourly) and Zakopane in Poland (€5.50, two hours, two to four daily June to October).

CAR
Pick-up around town is available by pre-arrangement from Car Rental Tatran (🖉 775 8157; www.autopozicovnatatry.sk).

TRAIN
Electric trains traverse the 14km or so to the High Tatras resorts. Mainline trains run directly to Bratislava (€15, four hours, hourly, four IC trains daily) and Košice (€5, 1¼ hours, hourly).

High Tatras
🖉 052

The High Tatras (Vysoké Tatry), the tallest range in the Carpathian Mountains, tower over most of Eastern Europe. Some 25 peaks measure above 2500m. The massif is only 25km wide and 78km long, but photo opportunities are enough to get you fantasising about a *National Geographic* career – pristine snowfields, ultramarine mountain lakes, thundering waterfalls, undulating pine forests and shimmering alpine meadows. Most of this jagged range is part of the Tatra National Park (Tanap): not that this fact has arrested considerable development on the Slovakian ski slopes.

Midmountain, three main resort towns string west to east. Štrbské Pleso is the traditional ski centre and is most crowded, with construction galore. Smokovec, 11km east, is an amalgam of the Nový (New), Starý (Old), Dolný (Lower) and Horný (Upper) settlements. Here there's still a bit of a turn-of-the-20th-century heyday feel, plus the most services. Tatranská Lomnica, 5km further, is the quaintest, quietest village. All have mountain access by cable car, funicular or chairlift. Poprad is the closest city (with mainline train station and airport), 14km south of central Starý Smokovec.

When planning your trip, keep in mind that the highest trails are closed because of snow from November to mid-June. July and August are the warmest (and most crowded) months. Hotel prices and crowds are at their lowest from October to April.

⊙ Sights & Activities

A 600km network of trails covers the alpine valleys and some peaks, with full-service mountain huts where hikers can stop for a meal or a rest along the way. Routes are colour-coded and easy to follow.

The red 65km **Tatranská Magistrála Trail** transects the High Tatras from west to east, running beneath the peaks at average elevations of 1300m to 1800m. It's connected at several points by cable car to the resort towns. Our favourite section is Skalnaté pleso to Chata pri Zelenom plese (2¼ hours).

Pick up one of the numerous detailed maps and hiking guides available at bookstores and information offices. Park regulations require you to keep to trails and refrain from picking flowers. Be aware that many trails are rocky and uneven, watch for sudden thunderstorms on ridges where there's no protection, and know that the assistance of the Mountain Rescue Service is not free.

Distances for hikes in Slovak national parks are officially given in hours rather than kilometres, so we have done the same, as per official trail estimates. Depending on the gradient and terrain in the High Tatras a reasonably fit person can expect to hike between 2km and 5km per hour.

Note that ski resorts in peak season (Christmas through January and February) command higher prices for passes. If in doubt check www.vt.sk for further information.

Smokovec Resort Towns

From Starý Smokovec a **funicular railway** (www.vt.sk; adult/child return €8/5.50; ☺7am-7pm Jul & Aug, 8am-5pm Sep-Jun) takes you up to **Hrebienok** (1280m) where you have a great view of the **Velká Studená Valley**. From here the red **Tatranská Magistrála Trail** heads west to the lakeside **Sliezsky dom** hotel (two hours). From here, make the hike a loop by following a small green connector trail to the yellow-marked trail back to Starý Smokovec (four hours total). Following the Magistrála east for one hour brings you up to atmospheric **Zamkovského chata** hut.

Mountain climbers scale to the top of **Slavkovský štít** (2452m) via the blue trail from Starý Smokovec (seven to eight hours return). To ascend the peaks without marked hiking trails (**Gerlachovský štít** included), you must hire a guide. Contact the **Mountain Guides Society Office** (☎4422 066; www.tatraguide.sk; Starý Smokovec 38; ☺10am-6pm Mon-Fri, noon-6pm Sat & Sun, closed weekends Oct-May).

At **Funtools** (☎0902 932 657; www.vt.sk; Hrebienok; per hour rides €5; ☺8:30am-4:30pm Jun-Sep) you can take a fast ride down the mountain on a two-wheeled scooter, a luge-like three-wheel cart or on a four-wheel modified skateboard.

Rent mountain bikes at **Tatrasport** (www.tatry.net/tatrasport; Starý Smokovec 38; per day €12; ☺8am-6pm), above the bus-station parking lot; www.vt.sk keeps a great list of adventurous routes (some for pros only).

Tatranská Lomnica & Around

While in the Tatras, you shouldn't miss the ride to the precipitous 2634m summit of **Lomnický štít** (bring a jacket!). From Lomnica, a large **gondola** (www.vt.sk; return adult/senior/child €14/11/1; ☺8.30am-7pm Jul & Aug, to 4pm Sep-Jun) pauses midstation at **Štart** before it takes you to the winter-sports area, restaurant and lake at **Skalnaté pleso**. From there you can take a smaller **cable car** (www.vt.sk; return adult/child €26/19; ☺8.30am-5.30pm Jul & Aug, to 3.30pm Sep-Jun) right up to the giddy summit. The latter requires a time-reserved ticket. You're given 50 minutes at the top to admire the views and snack in the cafe before your return time.

Štrbské Pleso & Around

Condo and hotel development continue unabated in the village but the namesake clear-blue glacial lake *(pleso)* remains beautiful, surrounded by dark pine forest and rocky peaks. **Row boats** (per 45min €15-20; ☺10am-6pm May-Sep) can be rented from the dock by Grand Hotel Kempinski.

One of the mountains' most popular day hikes departs from here. Follow the red-marked **Magistrála Trail** uphill from the train station on a rocky forest trail for about 1¼ hours to **Popradské pleso**, an even more idyllic lake at 1494m. The busy mountain hut there has a large, self-service restaurant. From here the Magistrála zig-zags dramatically up the mountainside, then traverses east towards Sliezsky dom

There is also a year-round **chairlift** (www.parksnow.sk; return adult/child €12/9; ☺8am-3.30pm) up to **Chata pod Soliskom**, from where it's a one-hour walk north along a red trail to the 2093m summit of **Predné Solisko**.

Park Snow (www.parksnow.sk; day-lift ticket adult/child €26/18), Štrbské Pleso's popular ski and snowboard resort, has two chairlifts, four tow lines, 12km of easy-to-moderate runs, one jump and a snow-tubing area.

🛏 Sleeping

For a full listing of Tatra lodgings, check www.tatryinfo.eu. No wild/backcountry camping is permitted: there is a camping ground near Tatranská Lomnica. For the quintessential Slovak mountain experience, you can't beat hiking from one *chata* (mountain hut; could be anything from a shack to a chalet) to the next, high up among the peaks. Food (optional meal service or restaurant) is always available. Beds fill up, so book ahead.

Smokovec Resort Towns

Look for reasonable, been-there-forever boarding houses with one-word names like 'Delta' just west of the Nový Smokovec electric train stop on the several no-name streets that run to the south.

Penzión Tatra GUESTHOUSE €
(☎0903 650 802; www.tatraski.sk; Starý Smokovec 66; s/d incl breakfast €35/50; @📶) Colourful modern rooms fill this classic 1900 alpinesque

SLOVAKIA HIGH TATRAS

building above the train station. It's super central. Billiard table and ski storage available.

Bilíkova Chata
MOUNTAIN HUT €

(☑0949 579 777, 0903 691 712; www.bilikova chata.sk; s & d from €40, without bathroom €25, apt €70) Basic but beautifully located log-cabin hotel with full-service restaurant among the clouds; near Hrebienok funicular station. Big low-season discounts. Breakfast (€5) and dinner (€6) available.

Villa Siesta
HOTEL €€

(☑478 0931; www.villasiesta.sk; Nový Smokovec 88; s/d/ste €57/87/109; ☎) Light fills this airy, contemporary mountain villa furnished in natural hues. The full restaurant, sauna and Jacuzzi are a bonus.

Grand Hotel Starý Smokovec
HOTEL €€

(☑290 1339; www.grandhotel.sk; Starý Smokovec 38; d €82; ☎☒) More than a century of history is tied up in Starý Smokovec's *grande dame*. Rooms could use an update to the 21st century.

▦ Tatranská Lomnica & Around

Look for private rooms (*privat* or *zimmer frei*), from €15 per person, on the back streets south and east of the train station.

★ Zamkovského Chata
MOUNTAIN HUT €

(☑0905 554 471, 442 2636; www.zamka.sk; per person €15) Atmospheric wood chalet with four-bed bunk rooms and restaurant; great hike stop midway between Skalnaté Pleso and Hrebienok.

Grandhotel Praha
HOTEL €€

(☑290 1338; www.ghpraha.sk; Tatranská Lomnica; d incl breakfast from €70; @☒) Remember when travel was elegant and you dressed for dinner? Well, the 1899 Grandhotel's sweeping marble staircase and crystal chandeliers do. Rooms are appropriately classic and there's a snazzy spa here, high above the village.

▦ Štrbské Pleso & Around

Horský Hotel Popradské Pleso
MOUNTAIN HUT €

(☑0910 948 160, 0908 761 403; www.popradske pleso.com; Popradské pleso; dm €16, s/d €28/56, without bathroom €18/36) Sizeable mountain hotel with restaurant and bar. It's a one-hour rugged hike up from the village or a paved hike (same time) up from Popradské pleso train stop.

★ Grand Hotel Kempinski
HOTEL €€€

(☑326 2222; www.kempinski.com/hightatras; Kupelna 6, Štrbské Pleso; d from €180-210, ste from €320; ❄@☒) The swankiest Tatra accommodation is the classic, villa-like Kempinski, enticing high-end travellers with evening turndown service, heated marble bathroom floors and incredible lake views. See the mountains stretch before you through two-storey glass from the luxury spa.

Eating

The resort towns are close enough that it's easy to sleep in one and eat in another. There's at least one grocery store per town.

Smokovec Resort Towns

Pizzeria La Montanara
ITALIAN €

(Starý Smokovec 22; mains €4-8; ☉10am-9pm Mon-Sat, 2-10pm Sun) A local favourite, La Montanara serves good pizzas, pastas, soups and vegetables. It's above a grocery store on the eastern edge of town.

Reštaurácia Svišť
SLOVAK €€

(Nový Smokovec 30; mains €5-16; ☉6-11pm) From hearty dumplings to beef fillet with wine reduction, this stylish Slovak restaurant does it all well – and it's surprisingly reasonable. Want to know what a typical 'Tatas plate' entails? Now's your chance! (Clue: meat).

Koliba Smokovec
SLOVAK €€

(Starý Smokovec 5; mains €4-14; ☉3-10pm) A traditional rustic grill restaurant; some evening folk music. There's a pension, too (singles/doubles €25/40).

Štrbské Pleso & Around

★ Koliba Patria
SLOVAK €€

(Southern lake shore, Štrbské Pleso; mains €6-15) Come here for the lovely lakeside terrace and complex meat dishes. It's certainly more refined than a typical *koliba* (rustic mountain restaurant serving Slovak sheepherder specialities).

Drinking

Tatry Pub
PUB

(Tatra Komplex, Starý Smokovec; ☉3pm-late; ☎) The official watering hole of the Mountain Guide Club is the liveliest place to drink, with a full schedule of dart tournaments, concerts etc.

ℹ Information

All three main resort towns have ATMs on the main street.

EMERGENCY
Mountain Rescue Service (☑ 787 7711, emergency ☑ 18 300; www.hzs.sk; Horný Smokovec 52) The main office of Slovakia.

TOURIST INFORMATION
Note that information offices do not book rooms; they hand out a brochure that lists some – not all – accommodation.

Tatra Information Office Starý Smokovec (TIK; ☑ 442 3440; www.tatry.sk/infocentrum; Starý Smokovec 23; ⊘ 8am-8pm May-Sep, 8am-4pm or 6pm Oct-Apr) Largest area info office, with the most brochures.

ℹ Getting There & Around

To reach the Tatras by public transport, you first have to make it to Poprad, on the main west–east railway line between Bratislava and Košice.

From Poprad train station, a narrow-gauge electric train runs up to the resort town of Starý Smokovec. It then makes numerous stops heading west to Štrbské Pleso and east to Tatranská Lomnica; buses also run from Poprad to all three resort towns. Check schedules at www.cp.atlas.sk.

BUS
Buses run from Poprad to Starý Smokovec (€0.90, 15 minutes, half-hourly), Tatranská Lomnica (€1.30, 35 minutes, hourly) and Štrbské Pleso (€1.70, one hour, every 45 minutes).

TRAIN
From 6am until 10pm, electric trains (TEZ) run more or less hourly. Buy individual TEZ tickets at stations and block tickets (one to three) at tourist offices. Validate all on board.

The High Tatras Electric Railway has trains from Poprad up to Starý Smokovec (€1.50, 25 minutes), Tatranská Lomnica (€1.50, 40 minutes) and Štrbské Pleso (€2, 70 minutes). Other routes on this line include Štrbské Pleso–Starý Smokovec (€1.50, 40 minutes) and Štrbské Pleso–Tatranská Lomnica (€2, 70 minutes).

EAST SLOVAKIA

Life gets, well, more laid-back the further east you venture. Somehow picturesque towns such as Levoča and Bardejov have avoided modern bustle and unfortunate 20th-century architectural decisions, while lingering over a streetfront cafe in delightful Košice is nigh-on obligatory. Meanwhile national parks beckon with untrammelled wildernesses free from those Tatras-bound tourists.

ℹ MULTIRESORT SKI PASSES

Park Snow and Vysoký Tatry resorts, the ski concessions in Štrbské Pleso and Tatranská Lomnica have all joined forces to offer multiday, multiresort lift passes (three-day adult/child €72/50). The **Super Slovak Ski Pass** (www.vt.sk; 10-day adult €290) covers some of the main resorts as well as other smaller ski areas around Slovakia.

Levoča
☑ 053 / POP 14,900

So this is what Slovakia looked like in the 13th century... Unesco-listed Levoča still has its high medieval walls, surrounding old town buildings and cobblestone alleyways. At the centre of it all stands the pride of the country's religious architectural collection, the Gothic Church of St Jacob. Levoča is one of Slovakia's most important pilgrimage centres.

⊙ Sights

Church of St Jacob   CHURCH
(Chrám sv Jakuba; www.chramsvjakuba.sk; Nám Majstra Pavla; adult/child €2/1; ⊘ by hourly tour 11am-4pm Mon, 8.30am-4pm Tue-Sat, 1-4pm Sun) The spindles-and-spires Church of St Jacob, built in the 14th and 15th centuries, elevates your spirit with its soaring arches, precious art and rare furnishings, where the main attraction is Slovakia's tallest altar, an impressive 18m high.

Buy tickets from the cashier inside the Municipal Weights House across the street from the north door. Entry is generally on the hour. The adjacent 16th-century **cage of shame** was built to punish naughty boys and girls.

Nám Majstra Pavla   SQUARE
Gothic and Renaissance eye candy abound on the main square, Nám Majstra Pavla. The private **Thurzov House** (1517), at No 7, has a characteristically frenetic Spiš Renaissance roofline. No 20 is the **Master Pavol Museum**, dedicated to the works of the city's most celebrated son. The 15th-century **Historic Town Hall** (Radnica) building, centre square, is really more interesting than the limited exhibits within.

One ticket gets you into both of the latter, as they are branches of the **Spiš Museum** (www.spisskemuzeum.com; adult/child €3.50/2.50; ⊘ 9.30am-3pm Tue-Fri).

🛏 Sleeping & Eating

Hotel U Leva
HOTEL €€

(☑ 450 2311; www.uleva.sk; Nám Majstra Pavla 24; s/d/apt €33/43/79; ➌☎) Spread across two old town buildings, each of the 23 cleanly contemporary rooms is unique, and apartments come with kitchens. The fine restaurant (mains €6 to €12) combines atypical ingredients (brie, spinach) with time-honored Slovak techniques.

ℹ Information

Everything you're likely to need, banks and post office included, is on the main square. Most accommodation and restaurants have wi-fi.

Tourist Information Office (☑ 451 3763; http://eng.levoca.sk; Nám Majstra Pavla 58; ⊙ 9am-4pm Mon-Fri year-round, plus 9am-4pm Sat & Sun May-Sep)

ℹ Getting There & Away

Levoča is on the main E50 motorway between Poprad (28km) and Košice (94km). Bus travel is the most feasible option here.

The local bus stop at Nám Štefana Kluberta is much closer to town than the bus station, which is 1km southeast of the town centre. From the bus stop, follow Košicka west two blocks and you'll hit the main square.

Frequent bus services take you to the following destinations:

Košice (€5, two hours, 12 to 14 daily)

Poprad (€1.70, 45 minutes, at least hourly) Most convenient onward mainline train connections.

Spišská Nová Ves (€0.90, 20 minutes, half-hourly) For Slovenský Raj National Park.

Spišské Podhradie (€0.90, 20 minutes, half-hourly) For Spiš Castle.

Spišské Podhradie

☑ 053 / POP 4000

Sprawling for four hectares above the village of Spišské Podhradie, ruined Spiš Castle is undoubtedly one of the largest in Europe. Even if you've never been, you may have seen pictures: the fortress is Slovakia's most-photographed sight. Two kilometres west, the medieval Spiš Chapter ecclesiastical settlement is also a Unesco World Heritage Site. In between, the village itself has basic services.

◉ Sights

Spiš Castle
CASTLE

(Spišský hrad; www.snm.sk; adult/child €5/3; ⊙ 9am-7pm May-Sep, Oct & Nov by request) Heralding from at least as early as the 13th century, Spiš Castle and its vast complex of ruins crown a ridge above Spišské Podhradie. Its claim to fame as one of Europe's largest castle complexes will seem accurate as you explore. Be sure to ascend the central tower for spectacular panoramic views across the Spiš region, and imagine yourself as a patrolling medieval guard whilst traipsing this colossal fortress's outer walls.

Chronicles first mention the castle in 1209; it was from here that defenders allegedly repulsed the Tatars in 1241. Rulers and noble families kept adding fortifications and palaces during the 15th and 16th centuries, but by 1780 the site had already lost military significance and much was destroyed by fire. It wasn't until the 1970s that efforts were made to restore what remained. A Romanesque palace contains the very small **museum**, and the chapel adjacent to it. Night tours and medieval festivals take place some summer weekends. Get the English audio tour that brings the past into focus through story and legend.

Spiš Castle is 1km east of Spišské Podhradie, a healthy, uphill hike above the spur rail station. The easiest way to the castle by car is off the E50 highway on the east (Prešov) side.

Spiš Chapter
MONASTERY

(Spišská Kapitula; adult/child €2/1) On the west side of Spišské Podhradie, you'll find still-active Spiš Chapter, a 13th-century Catholic complex encircled by a 16th-century wall. The pièce de résistance is **St Martin's Cathedral** (1273), towering above the community of quirky Gothic houses and containing some arresting 15th-century altars.

Buy tickets for the cathedral and pick up a guide from the (often-closed) information office at Spišská Kapitula 4. If you're travelling to Spiš Chapter by bus from Levoča, get off one stop (and 1km) before Spišské Podhradie, at Kapitula.

🛏 Sleeping & Eating

This is a day trip from the High Tatras or Košice.

★ Spišsky Salaš
SLOVAK €

(☑ 454 1202; Levočská cesta 11; mains from €4; ⊙ 10am-9pm; ⏍) Dig into lamb stew in the folksy dining room or on the covered deck, and watch the kids romp on rough-hewn play sets. The rustic log complex also has three simple rooms for rent (per person €13). It's 3km west of Spiš Chapter, on the road towards Levoča. It's a great hike from here to Spiš Chapter and Spiš Castle.

ⓘ Getting There & Away

Spišské Podhradie is 15km east of Levoča and 78km northeast of Košice.

BUS

Frequent buses connect with Levoča (€0.90, 20 minutes), Poprad (€2.20, 50 minutes) and Košice (€4.25, 1½ hours).

TRAIN

An inconvenient spur railway line heads to Spišské Podhradie from Spišské Vlachy (€0.75, 15 minutes, five daily), a station on the Bratislava–Košice main line; only during summer. Check schedules at www.cp.atlas.sk.

Slovenský Raj & Around

☑ 053

With rumbling waterfalls, sheer gorges and dense forests, Slovenský Raj lives up to the name of 'Slovak Paradise'. A few easier trails exist, but the one-way ladder-and-chain ascents make this a national park for the passionately outdoorsy. You cling to metal rungs headed up a precipice while an icy waterfall sprays you from a metre away: pure exhilaration.

The nearest major town is uninspiring Spišská Nová Ves, 23km southeast of Poprad. Of the three trailhead resort villages, pretty Čingov, 5km west of Spišská Nová Ves, is our favourite. Podlesok (16km southwest of Poprad), has good accommodation. About 50km south, Dedinky is more of a regular village with a pub and supermarket fronting a lake.

⊙ Sights & Activities

Before you trek, pick up VKÚ's 1:25,000 Slovenský Raj hiking map (No 4) or 1:50,000 regional map (No 124). There are several good biking trails criss-crossing the national park.

Slovenský Raj National Park   PARK

(www.slovenskyraj.sk; admission Jul & Aug €1, Sep-Jun free) The national park has numerous trails that include one-way *roklina* (gorge) sections and take at least half a day. Slovenský Raj is most famous for its sometimes hair-raising ladder-and-chain ascents – paths where you're clinging to a waterfall-splashed rock face on creaky metal supports.

From Čingov a green trail leads up Hornád River Gorge an hour to **Tomašovský výhľad**, a rocky outcropping and overlook that is a good short-hike destination. Or continue to the green, one-way, technically aided **Kláštorisko Gorge** trail, allowing at least eight hours for the circuit. You can also

reach the Kláštorisko Gorge ascent from Podlesok (six hours). There is accommodation available at **Kláštorisko Chata**.

Another excellent alternative from Podlesok is to hike on the six- to seven-hour circuit up the dramatic, ladder and technical-assist **Suchá Belá Gorge**, then east to Kláštorisko Chata, where you'll find a reconstructed 13th-century monastery, on yellow then red trails. From there, take the blue trail down to the Hornád River, then follow the river gorge upstream to return to Podlesok.

One of the shortest, dramatic, technical-assist hikes starts at Biele Vody (15 minutes northeast of Dedinky via the red trail) and follows the green trail up **Zejmarská Gorge**. The physically fit can clamber up in 50 minutes. To get back, you can follow the green trail down to Dedinky, or there's a chairlift that works sporadically.

The best viewpoint is at Medvedia Hlava in the east of the park. Slovenský Raj's forested gorges lie in one direction, the jagged teeth of the High Tatras in the other. Access it via a 4½ hour hike from Spišská Nová Ves tourist information centre.

Dobšinská Ice Cave   CAVE

(www.ssj.sk; adult/child €7/3.50; ⊙ 9am-4pm Tue-Sun by hourly tour, closed Oct–mid-May) The fanciful frozen formations in this Unesco-noted ice cave are more dazzling in early June than September. A 15-minute hike leads up from the settlement of Dobšinská ľadová jaskyňa to where tours begin every hour or so.

🛏 Sleeping & Eating

Many lodgings have restaurants. Several eateries and a small grocery store are available in Podlesok. The biggest supermarket is next to the bus station in Spišská Nová Ves.

Penzión Lesnica   GUESTHOUSE €

(☑ 449 1518; www.stefani.sk; Čingov 113; s/d/ apt incl breakfast €30/40/50; 🕲) Nine simple, sunny-coloured rooms close to the trail fill up fast, so book ahead. The attached restaurant is one of the best local places for a Slovak repast (mains €5.50 to €15).

Grand Hotel Spiš   HOTEL €

(☑ 449 1129; www.grandhotelspis.com; Spišské Tomášovce; s/d €26/41; 🅿🕲) Grand is a grandiose word, but services here are above par, with an agreeable mountain rusticity spreading from the public areas into the rooms. This is our favourite hotel in the park: 1km outside Čingov with good hike access.

Ranč Podlesok GUESTHOUSE €
(☑ 0918 407 077; www.rancpodlesok.sk; Podlesok 5; r per person from €17; 🕿 🛏) A blue park trail runs behind this stone-and-log lodge and restaurant at the park's edge. There's sand volleyball too, if you fancy it. It's 1km past the Podlesok village area.

❶ Information

Outside Spišská Nová Ves, lodgings are the best source of information; park info booths are open July through August. Get cash before you arrive in the park; there is an ATM and exchange at Spišská Nová Ves train station. Helpful websites include www.slovenskyraj.sk.

Mountain Rescue Service (☑ emergency 183 00; http://his.hzs.sk)

Tourist Information Centre (☑ 442 8292; en.spisskanovaves.eu; Letná 49, Spišská Nová Ves; ⊙ 8am-6pm Mon-Fri, 9am-1pm Sat, 2-6pm Sun) Helps with accommodation.

❶ Getting There & Around

During low season especially, you may consider hiring a car in Košice; connections to the park can be a chore. You'll have to transfer at least once, usually in Spišská Nová Ves.

BUS

Buses travel more infrequently on weekends, most often in July and August. No buses run directly between trailhead villages. Carefully check schedules at www.cp.atlas.sk.

Buses run from Slovenský Raj's transport hub of Spisška Nová Ves to Poprad (€1.70, 40 minutes, every one to two hours). Other buses run to Levoča (€0.90, 20 minutes, hourly), Čingov (€0.60, 15 minutes, two to four direct Monday to Friday, one direct Saturday), Hrabušice (for Podlesok; €1.10, 30 minutes, nine daily Monday to Friday, four Saturday) and Dedinky (€2.50, 80 minutes, four direct Monday to Saturday).

TRAIN

Trains run from Spisška Nová Ves to Poprad (€1.50, 20 minutes, at least hourly) and Košice (€4, one hour, at least hourly). The train station is 1½ blocks east of the bus station.

Košice

☑ 055 / POP 240,000

East Slovakia's industrial powerhouse has cosmopolitan clout and a buoyant cultural scene plonking it firmly on Europe's citybreak map, fiercely independent of Bratislava. As 2013's European Capital of Culture, Košice has accordingly initiated a new string of attractions including major arts installations in a combination of impressively revamped buildings, and eclectic events to enliven city streets.

Košice, for centuries the eastern stronghold of the Hungarian Kingdom, was always a medieval gem. New enhancements build on an arts scene already home to the paintings of Andy Warhol and one of Europe's loveliest theatres. Its vast oval-shaped *námestie* (central square) contains the largest collection of historical monuments in Slovakia, enlivened by myriad buzzing cafes and restaurants.

It's base-of-choice, too, for forays deeper into the tradition-seeped east. From here, top trips include Unesco-listed medieval Bardejov, with Slovakia's most beautiful town square, and the surrounding area's stunning wooden churches, reflecting a Carpatho-Rusyn heritage shared with neighbouring parts of Ukraine and Poland.

◉ Sights

Hlavné Nám SQUARE
Almost all of the sights are in or around the town's long plaza-like main square, Hlavná. Landscaped flowerbeds surround the central **musical fountain**, across from the 1899 State Theatre (p391). Look for the turn-of-the-20th-century, art nouveau **Hotel Slávia** at No 63. **Shire Hall** (1779), at No 27, is where the Košice Government Program was proclaimed in 1945; today there's a minor art gallery inside.

Cathedral of St Elizabeth CHURCH
(Dóm sv Alžbety; Hlavné nám; church admission adult/child €1.50/1; ⊙ 1-9pm Mon, 9am-9pm Tue-Thu, 9am-8pm Fri & Sat, 1-7pm Sun) Dark, brooding 14th-century Cathedral of St Elizabeth wins the prize for the sight most likely to grace your Košice postcard home. You can't miss Europe's easternmost (and perhaps mightiest) Gothic cathedral, which dominates the square. Below the church, the **crypt** contains the tomb of Duke Ferenc Rákóczi, who was exiled to Turkey after the failed 18th-century Hungarian revolt against Austria.

Don't forget to ascend the 160 narrow, circular stone steps up the church's vertigo-inducing tower for city views. Climbing the royal staircase as the monarchs once did provides an interior perspective: note the rare interlocking flights of steps. Just to the south, the 14th-century **St Michael's Chapel** (Kaplinka sv Michala) has sporadic entry hours.

Lower Gate Underground Museum MUSEUM
(Hlavné Nám; adult/child €0.90/0.50; ⊙ 10am-6pm Tue-Sun May-Sep) The underground remains of

medieval Košice – lower gate, defence chambers, fortifications and waterways dating from the 13th to 15th centuries – were uncovered during construction work in 1996. Get lost in the maze-like passages of the archaeological excavations at the south end of the square.

East Slovak Museum
MUSEUM
(Východoslovenské múzeum; ☑ 622 0309; www.vsmuzeum.sk; Hviezdoslavova 3; per exhibition €1-3; ☺9am-5pm Tue-Sat, 9am-1pm Sun) Hidden treasure can be found at the East Slovak Museum. Workers found the secret stash of 2920 gold coins, dating from the 15th to 18th centuries, while renovating a house on Hlavná in 1935. There's a romp through various aspects of regional history, too, showcased through a former prison and a metal foundry. In the museum yard there's a relocated 1741 wooden church.

🛌 Sleeping

Penzión Slovakia
GUESTHOUSE €
(☑728 9820; www.penzionslovakia.sk; Orlia 6; s/d/ste incl breakfast €45/55/65; ❇🛜) Charming guesthouse with grill restaurant downstairs.

K2
HOSTEL €
(☑625 5948; Štúrova 32; r without bathroom from €16.50) These dowdy singles and doubles are the most centrally located budget option. Ask for a room away from the road.

★ Hotel Bankov
HISTORIC HOTEL €€
(☑632 4522 ext 4; www.hotelbankov.sk; Dolný Bankov 2; s/d from €59/74; P@🛜❇) Going strong since 1869, Slovakia's oldest hotel lies 4km northwest of central Košice in a verdant location overlooking woodland. Rooms are surprisingly good value, oozing old-world charm (beams, period furniture). There's an elegant restaurant and a wellness centre, plus there's complimentary taxi service for guests.

Golden Royal Hotel & Spa
BOUTIQUE HOTEL €€
(☑720 1011; www.goldenroyal.sk; Vodná 8; s/d €75/90; 🛜) Rooms are more modern than that classic old facade would suggest, but we love the slick furnishings. The spa goes down a treat, too. The best central option.

🍴 Eating

★ Republika Východu
INTERNATIONAL €
(Hlavné nám 3; mains €3-7; ☺7am-10pm Mon-Thu, 7/8am-midnight Fri & Sat, 8am-10pm Sun) Proudly proclaiming independence from Western Slovakia and indeed anywhere else, Republika Východu (Republic of the East) baits you with cakes and good coffee then becalms

you with its salads, pancakes and exclusively eastern takes on some of the Slovak classics. Menus are in special eastern dialect.

★ Villa Regia
INTERNATIONAL €€
(www.villaregia.sk; Dominikánske nám 3; mains €7-14; 🍴) Steaks, seafood and vegetarian dishes get artistic treatment amid a rustic old-world atmosphere. The vaulted ceilings and stone walls extend to the upstairs pension rooms.

Le Colonial
INTERNATIONAL €€
(Hlavná 8; mains €8-17; ☺11am-11pm) Get a hit of colonial plushness at this top-of-the-top-end place. The menu is rather less of an adventure, but the cooking is good.

🍷 Drinking & Entertainment

For a city this small, options are plentiful. Any sidewalk cafe on the main square is great for a drink. Check free monthly publication *Kam do Mesta* (www.kamdomesta.sk) for entertainment listings.

Caffe Trieste
CAFE
(Uršulínska 2; ☺7.30am-7.30pm) Original of the mini-chain now found in Bratislava. Knock-out espresso, in slurp-it-and-go Italian fashion.

Jazz Club
CLUB
(http://jazzclub-ke.sk; Kováčska 39) DJs spin here most nights, but there are also occasional live concerts.

State Theatre
THEATRE
(Štátne Divadlo Košice; ☑245 2269; www.sdke.sk; Hlavné nám 58; ☺box office 9am-5.30pm Mon-Fri, 10am-1pm Sat) Local opera and ballet companies stage performances in this 1899 neobaroque theatre.

State Philharmonic Košice
CLASSICAL MUSIC
(Štátna Filharmónia Košice, House of the Arts; ☑622 4509, 622 0763; www.sfk.sk; Moyzesova 66) Concerts take place year-round but the spring musical festival is a good time to catch performances of the city's philharmonic.

ℹ️ Information

Most hotels, cafes and restaurants have free wi-fi; plus catch a regularly updated list of free wi-fi spots at www.kosice.info/wifi. Lots of banks with ATMs are scattered around Hlavné nám.

City Information Centre (☑625 8888; www.visitkosice.eu; Hlavná 59; ☺10am-6pm Mon-Fri, 10am-3pm Sat & Sun) Ask for both the free annual town guide and the colour brochure of historic sites. Guided city tours can be arranged.

Nemocnica Košice-Šaca (☎723 4313; www. nemocnicasaca.sk; Lúčna 9) Good private healthcare; 12km southwest of central Košice.

Police Station (☎158; Pribinova 6)

ⓘ Getting There & Away

Check bus and train schedules at www.cp.atlas.sk.

AIR

Košice International Airport (p393) is 6km southwest of the city centre. **Czech Airlines** (www.csa.cz) has two daily flights to Bratislava (weekdays only) as well as Prague.

BUS

You can book ahead on some Ukraine-bound buses through Eurobus (p382). Getting to Poland is easier from Poprad. Destinations include Bardejov (€3.80, 1¾ hours, half-hourly), Levoča (€5, two hours, 12 to 14 daily) and Uzhhorod (Ukraine; €7, three to four hours, three daily).

CAR

Several international car-hire companies have representatives at the airport.

Buchbinder (☎683 2397; www.buchbinder.sk; Košice International Airport) Small company with good rates and gratis pick-up in the city.

TRAIN

Trains from Košice run to Bratislava (€19, five to six hours, every 1½ hours), Poprad in the High Tatras (€5, 1¼ hours, hourly) and Spišská Nová Ves for Slovenský Raj (€4, one hour, hourly). There are also trains over the border to Miskolc, Hungary (€7, 11 hours, one to two daily) and Lviv, Ukraine (€13, 11 hours, one to two daily).

ⓘ Getting Around

The old town is small, so you probably can walk everywhere. Bus 23 between the airport and the train station requires a two-zone ticket (€1): buy at newsstands and validate onboard.

SURVIVAL GUIDE

ⓘ Directory A–Z

ACCOMMODATION

Bratislava has more hostels and five-star hotels than midrange accommodation. Outside the capital, you'll find plenty of reasonable *penzióny* (guesthouses). Breakfast is usually available (often included) at all lodgings and wi-fi is near ubiquitous. Many lodgings offer nonsmoking rooms. Parking is only a problem in Bratislava. A recommended booking resource in the capital city is **Bratislava Hotels** (www.bratislavahotels.com).

BUSINESS HOURS

Sight and attraction hours vary throughout the year; standard opening times for the tourist season (May through September) are listed below. Schedules in remoter tourist destinations vary from October to April; check ahead. Museums and other sights are usually closed on Mondays.

Banks 8am to 5pm Monday to Friday

Bars 11am to midnight Monday to Thursday, 11am to 2am Friday and Saturday, 4pm to midnight Sunday

Grocery stores 6.30am to 6pm Monday to Friday, 7am to noon Saturday

Post offices 8am to 5pm Monday to Friday, 8am to 11am Saturday

Nightclubs 4pm to 4am Wednesday to Sunday

Restaurants 10.30am to 10pm

Shops 9am to 6pm Monday to Friday, 9am to noon Saturday

INTERNET ACCESS

Wi-fi is widely available at lodgings and cafes across the country; so much so that internet cafes are becoming scarce. For the laptopless, lodgings also often have computers you can use.

INTERNET RESOURCES

Slovakia Document Store (www.panorama.sk)

Visit Bratislava (www.visit.bratislava.sk/EN/)

MONEY

➞ In January 2009 Slovakia's legal tender became the euro. Previously, it was the Slovak crown, or Slovenská koruna (Sk).

➞ Slovaks almost never tip; still, for foreigners, a 5% to 10% tip is a polite gesture for a nice meal out.

POST

Post office service is reliable (outgoing) but waits are far longer when you're expecting incoming mail from abroad. For outgoing mail, bank on five working days to other parts of Europe and seven for the US/Australia.

PUBLIC HOLIDAYS

New Year's and Independence Day 1 January

Three Kings Day 6 January

Good Friday and Easter Monday March/April
Labour Day 1 May
Victory over Fascism Day 8 May
Cyril and Methodius Day 5 July
SNP Day 29 August
Constitution Day 1 September
Our Lady of Sorrows Day 15 September
All Saint's Day 1 November
Christmas 24 to 26 December

TELEPHONE
Landline numbers can have either seven or eight digits. Mobile phone numbers (10 digits) are often used for businesses; they start with 09. When dialling from abroad, you need to drop the zero from both city area codes and mobile phone numbers. Purchase local and international phone cards at newsagents. Dial 🗹 00 to call out of Slovakia.

Mobile Phones
The country has GSM (900/1800MHz) and 3G UMTS networks operated by providers Orange, T-Mobile and O2.

TOURIST INFORMATION
Association of Information Centres of Slovakia (AICES; 🗹 44-551 4541, in Liptovský Mikuláš; www.aices.sk) Runs an extensive network of city information centres.
Slovak Tourist Board (http://slovakia.travel/en) No Slovakia-wide information office exists; it's best to go online.

VISAS
For a full list of visa requirements, see www.mzv.sk (under 'Consular Info').
➡ No visa is required for EU citizens.
➡ Visitors from Australia, New Zealand, Canada, Japan and the US do not need a visa for up to 90 days.
➡ Visas are required for South African nationals, among others. For the full list see www.slovak-republic.org/visa-embassies.

COUNTRY FACTS
Area 49,035 sq km
Capital Bratislava
Country Code 🗹 00421
Currency Euro (€)
Emergency General 🗹 112, fire 🗹 150, ambulance 🗹 155, police 🗹 158
Language Slovak
Money ATMs widely available in cities
Population 5.4 million
Visas Not required for most visitors staying less than 90 days

EATING PRICE RANGES
Restaurant review price indicators are based on the cost of a main course.
€ less than €7
€€ €7 to €12
€€€ more than €12

❶ Getting There & Away
Bratislava and Košice are the country's main entry/exit points – Poprad would be in distant third place. Flights, tours and rail tickets can be booked online at www.lonelyplanet.com/travel_services.

Entering Slovakia from the EU, indeed from most of Europe, is a breeze. Lengthy custom checks make arriving from Ukraine more tedious.

Though few airlines fly into Slovakia itself, Bratislava is just 60km from well-connected Vienna International Airport. By train from Bratislava, Budapest (three hours) and Prague (five hours) are easily reachable, as well as Vienna (one hour). Buses connect to Zakopane in Poland (two hours) from Poprad, and to Uzhhorod in Ukraine (2½ hours) via Košice.

AIR
Bratislava's intra-European airport (p382), 9km northeast of the city centre, is small. Unless you're coming from the UK, which has several direct flights, your arrival is likely to be by train. Vienna in Austria has the nearest international air hub.

Airports
Vienna International Airport (VIE; www.viennaairport.com) Austrian airport with regular buses that head the 60km east to Bratislava. Worldwide connections.
Košice International Airport (KSC; www.airportkosice.sk)
Poprad-Tatry International Airport (www.airport-poprad.sk; Na Letisko 100)

Airlines
The main airlines operating in Slovakia:
Austrian Airlines (www.aua.com) Connects Košice with Vienna.
Czech Airlines (www.csa.cz) Flies between Košice, Bratislava and Prague.
Ryanair (www.ryanair.com) Connects Bratislava with numerous destinations across the UK and Italy, coastal Spain, Dublin, Paris and Brussels.
Wizz Air (http://wizzair.com) Connects Košice and Poprad to London Luton.

LAND
Border posts between Slovakia and fellow EU Schengen member states – Czech Republic, Hungary, Poland and Austria – are nonexistent. You can come and go at will. This makes checks

ESSENTIAL FOOD & DRINK

➡ **Sheep's cheese** *Bryndza* – sharp, soft and spreadable; *oštiepok* – solid and ball-shaped; *žinčina* – a traditional sheep's-whey drink (like sour milk).

➡ **Meaty moments** *Vývar* (chicken/beef broth served with *slížiky*, thin pasta strips, or liver dumplings); *kapustnica* (thick sauerkraut and meat soup, often with chorizo or mushrooms); baked duck/goose served in *lokše* (potato pancakes) and stewed cabbage.

➡ **Dumplings** Potato-based goodies in varieties such as *halušky* (mini-dumplings in cabbage or *bryndza* sauce topped with bacon) or *pirohy* (pocket-shaped dumplings stuffed with *bryndza* or smoked meat). For sweets, try *šulance* (walnut- or poppy seed–topped dumplings).

➡ **Fruit firewater** Homemade or store-bought liquor, made from berries and pitted fruits, such as *borovička* (from juniper) and *slivovica* (from plums).

at the Ukrainian border all the more strident, as you will be entering the EU. By bus or car, expect at least one to two hours' wait.

Bus

Local buses connect Poprad and Ždiar with Poland during the summer season. Eurolines (p382) and Košice-based Eurobus (p382) handle international routes across Europe from Bratislava and heading east to Ukraine from Košice.

Car & Motorcycle

Private vehicle requirements for driving in Slovakia are registration papers, a 'green card' (proof of third-party liability insurance), nationality sticker, first-aid kit and warning triangle.

Train

See www.cp.atlas.sk for domestic and international train schedules. Direct trains connect Bratislava to Austria, the Czech Republic, Poland, Hungary and Russia; from Košice, trains connect to the Czech Republic, Poland, Ukraine and Russia. The fastest domestic trains are Intercity (IC) or Eurocity (EC). *Ryclík* (R; 'fast' trains) take slightly longer, but run more frequently and cost less. *Osobný* (Ob) trains are slowest (and cheapest).

RIVER

Danube riverboats offer an alternative way to get between Bratislava and Vienna. Vienna–Budapest boats don't stop in Bratislava.

ℹ Getting Around

AIR

Czech Airlines (p393) offers the only domestic air service: weekdays only, between Bratislava and Košice.

BICYCLE

Roads are often narrow and potholed, and in towns cobblestones and tram tracks can prove dangerous for bike riders. Bike rental is uncommon outside mountain resorts. The cost of transporting a bike by rail is usually 10% of the train ticket.

BUS

Read timetables carefully; different schedules apply for weekends and holidays (although these are still well serviced). You can find up-to-date schedules online at www.cp.atlas.sk. The main national bus companies in Slovakia are Slovenská Autobusová Doprava (SAD) and **Slovak Lines** (www.slovaklines.sk).

CAR & MOTORCYCLE

➡ Foreign driving licences with photo ID are valid in Slovakia.

➡ *Nálepka* (toll stickers) are required on *all* green-signed motorways. Fines for not having them can be hefty. Buy at petrol stations (rental cars usually have them).

➡ City streetside parking restrictions are eagerly enforced. Always buy a ticket from a machine, attendant or newsagent in old town centres.

➡ Car hire is available in Bratislava and Košice primarily.

LOCAL TRANSPORT

Towns all have efficient bus systems; most villages have surprisingly good services. Bratislava and Košice have trams and trolleybuses; the High Tatras also has an efficient electric railway.

➡ Public transport generally operates from 4.30am to 11.30pm daily.

➡ City transport tickets are good for all local buses, trams and trolleybuses. Buy at newsstands and validate on board or risk serious fines (this is not a scam).

TRAIN

Train is the way to travel in Slovakia; most tourist destinations are off the main Bratislava–Košice line. No online reservations: ticket machines are also rare. Reserve at train station offices. Visit www.cp.atlas.sk for up-to-date schedules.

Slovak Republic Railways (ŽSR; ☑ 18 188; www.slovakrail.sk) Far-reaching, efficient national rail service.

Slovenia

Includes ➡

Best Places to Eat

➡ Špajza (p400)
➡ Casa Nostromo (p408)
➡ Ostarija Peglez'n (p403)
➡ Skuhna (p400)

Best Places to Stay

➡ Antiq Palace Hotel & Spa (p400)
➡ Penzion Mayer (p403)
➡ Dobra Vila (p405)
➡ Max Piran (p407)
➡ Hostel Tresor (p399)

Why Go?

It's a pint-sized place, with a surface area of just over 20,000 sq km, and two million people. But 'good things come in small packages', and never was that old chestnut more appropriate than in describing Slovenia. The country has everything – from beaches, snowcapped mountains, hills awash in grape vines and wide plains blanketed in sunflowers to Gothic churches, baroque palaces and art nouveau buildings. Its incredible mixture of climates brings warm Mediterranean breezes up to the foothills of the Alps, where it can snow in summer.

The capital, Ljubljana, is a culturally rich city that values liveability and sustainability over unfettered growth. This sensitivity toward the environment also extends to rural and lesser-developed parts of the country. With more than half of its total area covered in forest, Slovenia really is one of the 'greenest' countries in the world.

When to Go
Ljubljana

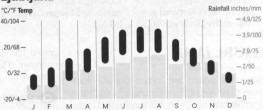

Apr–Jun Spring is a great time to be in the lowlands and the flower-carpeted valleys of the Julian Alps.

Sep This is the month for everything – still warm enough to swim and made for hiking.

Dec–Mar Everyone (and their grandma) dons their skis in this winter-sport-mad country.

Slovenia Highlights

1 Enjoy a 'flight' on the funicular up to **Ljubljana Castle**.

2 Consider the genius of architect Jože Plečnik at Ljubljana's **National & University Library** (p397).

3 Gaze on the natural perfection that is **Lake Bled** (p403).

4 Gawk in awe at the 100m-high walls of the incredible **Škocjan Caves** (p406).

5 Climb to the top of the country's tallest mountain, **Mt Triglav** (p402).

6 Get lost wandering the narrow Venetian-style alleyways of **Piran** (p407).

LJUBLJANA

☑ 01 / POP 283,000

Slovenia's capital and largest city also happens to be one of Europe's greenest and most liveable capitals. Car traffic is restricted in the centre, leaving the leafy banks of the emerald-green Ljubljanica River, flowing through the city's heart, free for pedestrians and cyclists. In summer, cafes set up terrace seating along the river, lending the feel of a perpetual street party. Slovenia's master of early-modern, minimalist design, Jože Plečnik,

graced Ljubljana with beautiful bridges and buildings. The museums, hotels and restaurants are among the best in the country.

◉ Sights

The easiest way to see Ljubljana is on foot. The oldest part of town, with the most important historical buildings and sights (including Ljubljana Castle), lies on the right (east) bank of the Ljubljanica River. Center, which has the lion's share of the city's museums and galleries, is on the left (west) side of the river.

ITINERARIES

Three Days
Spend a couple of days in **Ljubljana**, then head north to unwind in romantic **Bled** or **Bohinj** beside idyllic mountain lakes. Alternatively, head south to visit the caves at **Škocjan** or **Postojna**.

One Week
A full week will allow you to see all the country's top highlights. After two days in the capital head for Bled and Bohinj. Depending on the season, take a bus or drive over the hair-raising **Vršič Pass** into the valley of the vivid blue **Soča River** and take part in some adventure sports in **Bovec**. Continue south to the caves at Škocjan and Postojna and then to the sparkling Venetian port of **Piran** on the Adriatic.

★**Ljubljana Castle**   CASTLE
(Ljubljanski Grad; ☑01-306 42 93; www.ljubljanski grad.si; Grajska Planota 1; adult/child incl funicular & castle attractions €8/5, castle attractions only €6/3, with guided tour €10/7; ☉9am-11pm Jun-Sep, 9am-9pm Apr, May & Oct, 10am-8pm Jan-Mar & Nov, 10am-10pm Dec) There's been a human settlement on the site of this hilltop castle since at least Celtic times, but the oldest structures these days date back 500 years and were built following an earthquake in 1511. It's free to ramble around the castle precincts, but you'll have to pay to enter the Watchtower, the Chapel of St George, to see the Slovenian history exhibition and join the costumed Time Machine tour. The fastest way to reach the castle is via the funicular from Krekov trg, which keeps the same hours as the castle.

Prešernov Trg   SQUARE
The centrepiece of Ljubljana's wonderful architectural aesthetic is this marvellous square, a public space of understated elegance that not only serves as the link between the Center district and the Old Town, but as the city's favourite meeting point. The square itself is dominated by a monument to the national poet France Prešeren (1905). Immediately south of the statue is the city's architectural poster-child, the small but much celebrated Triple Bridge (Tromostovje), designed by prolific architect Jože Plečnik.

★**National & University Library**   HISTORIC BUILDING
(Narodna in Univerzitetna Knjižnica; NUK; ☑01-200 11 10; Turjaška ulica 1; ☉8m-8pm Mon-Fri, 9am-2pm Sat) This library is Plečnik's masterpiece, completed in 1941. To appreciate this great man's philosophy, enter through the main door (note the horse-head doorknobs) on Turjaška ulica – you'll find yourself in near darkness, entombed in black marble. As you

ascend the steps, you'll emerge into a colonnade suffused with light – the light of knowledge, according to the architect's plans.

City Museum Ljubljana   MUSEUM
(Mestni Muzej Ljubljana; ☑01-241 25 00; www. mgml.si; Gosposka ulica 15; adult/child €4/2.50, with special exhibits €6/4; ☉10am-6pm Tue, Wed & Fri-Sun, to 9pm Thu) The excellent city museum focuses on Ljubljana's history, culture and politics via imaginative multimedia and interactive displays. The reconstructed Roman street that linked the eastern gates of Emona to the Ljubljanica, and the collection of well-preserved classical finds in the basement, are both worth a visit in themselves.

National Museum of Slovenia   MUSEUM
(Narodni Muzej Slovenije; ☑01-241 44 00; www. nms.si; Prešernova cesta 20; adult/child €6/4, 1st Sun of month free; ☉10am-6pm Fri-Wed, to 8pm Thu) Highlights here include the highly embossed Vače *situla*, a Celtic pail from the late 6th century BC unearthed in a town east of Ljubljana, and a Stone Age bone flute discovered near Cerkno in western Slovenia in 1995. There are also examples of Roman glass and jewellery found in 6th-century Slavic graves, along with many other historical finds. Check out the statues of the Muses and Fates relaxing on the stairway banisters.

Museum of Modern Art   MUSEUM
(Moderna Galerija; ☑01-241 68 00; www.mg-lj. si; Tomšičeva ulica 14; adult/student €5/2.50; ☉10am-6pm Tue-Sun) This museum houses the very best in Slovenian art – modern or otherwise. Keep an eye out for works by painters Tone Kralj *(Peasant Wedding)*, the expressionist France Mihelič *(The Quintet)* and the surrealist Štefan Planinc *(Primeval World series)* as well as sculptors including

Ljubljana

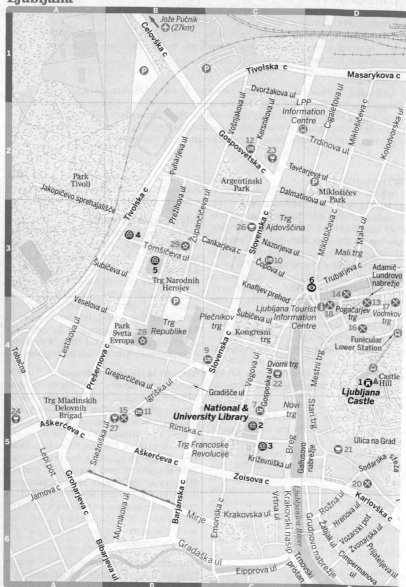

Jakob Savinšek (*Protest*). The museum also owns works by the influential 1980s and 1990s multimedia group Neue Slowenische Kunst (NSK; *Suitcase for Spiritual Use: Baptism under Triglav*) and the artists' co-operative Irwin (*Kapital*).

🛏 Sleeping

The Ljubljana Tourist Information Centre (TIC) has details of private rooms (single/double from €30/50) and apartments (double/quad from €55/80), though only a handful are central.

SLOVENIA LJUBLJANA

currencies. Dorms have between four and 12 beds but are spacious, and beds are curtained off. The communal areas (we love the atrium) are stunning; breakfast is in the vaults.

Celica Hostel HOSTEL €€
(📞 01-230 97 00; www.hostelcelica.com; Metelkova ulica 8; dm €19-27, s/d cell €58/62; @ 🛜) This revamped former prison (1882) in Metelkova has 20 'cells', designed by different artists and architects and with original bars. There are nine rooms and apartments with three to seven beds and a packed, popular 12-bed dorm. The Celica even has its own gallery where everyone can show their work.

Slamič B&B PENSION €€
(📞 01-433 82 33; www.slamic.si; Kersnikova ulica 1; s €65-75, d €95-110, ste from €135; ✳ 🛜) It's slightly

★ **Hostel Tresor** HOSTEL €€
(📞 01-200 90 60; www.hostel-tresor.si; Čopova ulica 38; dm €15-24, s/d €40/70; ✳ @ 🛜) This new 28-room hostel in the heart of Center is housed in a Secessionist-style former bank. The money theme continues into rooms named after

away from the action but Slamič, a B&B above a famous cafe and teahouse, offers 17 bright rooms, some with vintage furnishings and parquet floors. Choice rooms include the ones looking on to a back garden and the one just off an enormous terrace used by the cafe.

Penzion Pod Lipo
PENSION €€

(☑ 01-031 809 893; www.penzion-podlipo.com; Borštnikov trg 3; d/tr/q €59/75/100, ste from €125; ❈ @ 🛜) Sitting atop a famous *gostilna* (inn-like restaurant) with a 400-year-old linden tree in front, this 10-room inn offers straightforward but excellent-value accommodation in a neighbourhood filling up with bars and restaurants. We love the communal kitchen, the original hardwood floors and the east-facing terrace with deck chairs to catch the morning sun.

★ Antiq Palace Hotel & Spa
BOUTIQUE HOTEL €€€

(☑ 083 896 700, mobile 040 638 163; www.antiqpalace.com; Gosposka ulica 10 & Vegova ul 5a; s/d €180/210; ❈ @ 🛜) Among the capital's most luxurious sleeping options, the Antiq Palace occupies a 16th-century townhouse a block from the river. Accommodation is in 21 individually designed suites, some with multiple rooms and stretching to 250 sq metre in size. The list of amenities is a mile long and includes a luxurious spa and fitness centre.

Cubo
BOUTIQUE HOTEL €€€

(☑ 01-425 60 00; www.hotelcubo.com; Slovenska cesta 15; s/d €120/140; ❈ @ 🛜) This sleek boutique hotel with 26 rooms in the centre of town boasts high-end, minimalist design. The owners have placed great emphasis on using the best construction materials – lamps formed from silkworm cocoons (would you believe?) and silver thread in the drapes. High-quality bedding and double-glazing ensure a good night's sleep.

🍴 Eating

Klobasarna
FAST FOOD €

(☑ 051 605 017; www.klobasarna.si; Ciril-Metodov trg 15; dishes €3.50-6; ⊙ 10am-11pm Mon-Sat, to 3pm Sun) This hole-in-the-wall eatery in the Old Town specialising in that most Slovenian of dishes, *Kranjska klobasa*, an EU-protected fatty sausage from the city of Kranj, is almost a one-trick pony but can occasionally rustle up *jota* and *ričet*, two hearty stews, as well.

Ribca
SEAFOOD €

(☑ 01-425 15 44; www.ribca.si; Adamič-Lundrovo nabrežje 1; dishes €4-8.50; ⊙ 8am-4pm Mon, 8am-

9pm Tue-Sat, 11am-6pm Sun) One of the culinary joys of a visit to Ljubljana is the chance to sample inexpensive and well-prepared fish dishes. This basement seafood bar below the Plečnik Colonnade in Pogačarjev trg is one of the best for tasty fried squid, sardines and herrings. The setting is informal, though the cuisine is top notch.

★ Skuhna
INTERNATIONAL €

(☑ 041 339 978; www.skuhna.si; Trubarjeva cesta 15; mains €5-7, menu €11; ⊙ 11.30am-9pm Mon-Fri, noon-9pm Sat) This unique eatery is the work of two Slovenian nonprofit organisations that are helping the city's migrant community to integrate. A half-dozen chefs from countries as diverse as Egypt, Kenya and Colombia take turns cooking everyday, and the result is a cornucopia of authentic world cuisine. The choicest tables are in the kitchen.

Gostilna Rimska XXI
SLOVENIAN €€

(☑ 01-256 56 54; http://www.r-g.si/xxi; Rimska cesta 21; mains €8.5-16; ⊙ 11am-11pm Mon-Fri, noon-5pm Sat) This reliable old favourite specialises in traditional Slovenian cuisine, using locally sourced ingredients and lots of home-made extras, including its own homemade beer and brandy. There's no English menu, so ask the server what looks good in the kitchen. Try the *žlikrofi* (ravioli of cheese, bacon and chives) with game sauce.

★ Špajza
SLOVENIAN €€€

(☑ 01-425 30 94; www.spajza-restaurant.si; Gornji trg 28; mains €18-24; ⊙ noon-11pm Mon-Sat, noon-10pm Sun) The popular 'Pantry' restaurant in the Old Town is the perfect spot for a romantic meal. The interior is decorated with rough-hewn tables and chairs, wooden floors, painted ceilings and vintage bits and pieces. The terrace in summer is a delight. The cooking is high-end Slovenian, with an emphasis on less common mains like rabbit, lamb and colt, a Slovenian speciality.

Open-Air Market
MARKET

(Vodnikov trg; ⊙ 6am-6pm Mon-Fri, 6am-4pm Sat summer, 6am-4pm Mon-Sat winter) Self-caterers will want to head directly to Ljubljana's vast open-air market on Pogačarjev trg and Vodnikov trg, across the Triple Bridge to the southeast of Prešernov trg. Come here on Friday from 8am to 8pm from mid-March to October for **Open Kitchen** (Odprta Kuhna), a weekly food fair with home-cooked local and international specialities.

Covered Market MARKET
(Pogačarjev trg 1; ☺7am-4pm Mon-Fri, 7am-2pm Sat) Sells meats and cheeses.

Fish Market MARKET
(Adamič-Lundrovo nabrežje 1; ☺7am-4pm Mon-Fri, 7am-2pm Sat) In addition to fresh fish at the covered fish market, you'll find open-air fish stands in Vodnikov trg selling plates of fried calamari for as little as €7.

🍷 Drinking & Nightlife

Cafe Kolaž CAFE
(☑059 142 824; www.facebook.com/kafe.kolaz; Gornji trg 15; ☺9am-1am Mon-Sat, 10am-midnight Sun) One of the most chilled places to drink (and eat) in the Old Town, the gay-friendly 'Collage' picks up where the much-missed Open Cafe left off. Exhibitions, literary nights and DJ evenings, with sandwiches and canapés (€2.80 to €4.50), too.

★Žmavc BAR
(☑01-251 03 24; Rimska cesta 21; ☺7.30am-1am Mon-Fri, from 10am Sat, from 6pm Sun; 🛜) Everyone's favourite louche bar in Ljubljana, this popular hang-out west of Slovenska cesta has *manga* comic-strip scenes and figures running halfway up the walls. There's a great garden terrace for summer evening drinking, but try to arrive early to snag a table. Also excellent for morning coffee.

★Nebotičnik CAFE
(☑040 601 787; www.neboticnik.si; 12th fl, Štefanova ulica 1; ☺9am-1am Sun-Wed, to 3am Thu-Sat) After more than a decade in hibernation, this elegant cafe with its breathtaking terrace atop Ljubljana's famed art deco Skyscraper (1933) has reopened, and the 360-degree views are spectacular.

Dvorni Bar WINE BAR
(☑01-251 12 57; www.dvornibar.net; Dvorni trg 2; ☺8am-1am Mon-Sat, 9am-midnight Sun) This wine bar is an excellent place to taste Slovenian vintages; it stocks more than 100 varieties and has wine tastings every month (usually the 2nd Wednesday). Tapas cost €4 to €10.

KMŠ Hangover CLUB
(☑01-425 74 80; www.klubkms.si; Tržaška cesta 2; ☺pub 24hr, club 10pm-6am Fri & Sat) Located in the deep recesses of a former tobacco factory complex, this studenty place stays comatose round the clock till the weekend when it turns into a raucous place with music (jungle, reggae, drum 'n' bass) and dancers all over the shop.

METELKOVA MESTO

For a scruffy antidote to trendy clubs in Ljubljana, head for **Metelkova Mesto** (Metelkova Town; www.metelkovamesto. org; Masarykova cesta 24), an ex–army garrison taken over by squatters in the 1990s and converted into a free-living commune. In this two-courtyard block, a dozen idiosyncratic bars and clubs hide behind brightly tagged doorways, coming to life generally about 7pm during the week and at 11pm at the weekend.

Klub K4 CLUB
(☑040 212 292; www.klubk4.org; Kersnikova ulica 4; ☺11pm-4am Wed, 9pm-1am Thu, 11pm-6am Fri & Sat) This evergreen venue in the basement of the Student Organisation of Ljubljana University (ŠOU) headquarters features rave-electronic music Friday and Saturday, with other styles of music on weeknights, and a popular gay and lesbian night called Klub Roza (Pink Club) usually on Sunday.

☆ Entertainment

Ljubljana in Your Pocket (www.inyourpocket. com), which comes out every two months, is a good English-language source for what's on in the capital. Buy tickets for shows and events at the venue box office, online through Eventim (www.eventim.si), or at the Ljubljana Tourist Information Centre (p402).

Cankarjev Dom CLASSICAL MUSIC
(☑01-241 71 00, box office 01-241 72 99; www. cd-cc.si; Prešernova cesta 10; ☺box office 11am-1pm & 3-8pm Mon-Fri, 11am-1pm Sat, 1hr before performance) Ljubljana's premier cultural and conference centre has two large auditoriums (the Gallus Hall is said to have perfect acoustics) and a dozen smaller performance spaces offering a remarkable cornucopia of performance arts.

Opera Ballet Ljubljana OPERA, DANCE
(☑01-241 59 00, box office 01-241 59 59; www. opera.si; Župančičeva ulica 1; ☺box office 10am-1pm & 2-6pm Mon-Fri, 10am-1pm Sat, 1hr before performance) Home to the Slovenian National Opera and Ballet companies, this historic neo-Renaissance theatre has been restored to its former glory in recent years. Enter from Cankarjeva cesta.

ℹ Information

There are ATMs at every turn, including a row of them outside the main Ljubljana Tourist Information Centre (TIC) office. At the train station you'll find a **bureau de change** (train station; ⊙ 8am-8pm) changing cash for no commission, but not travellers cheques.

Health Centre Ljubljana (Zdravstveni Dom Ljubljana; ☑ 01-472 37 00; www.zd-lj.si; Metelkova ulica 9; ⊙ 7.30am-7pm Mon-Fri, 8am-4pm Sat) For non-emergencies.

Ljubljana Tourist Information Centre (TIC; ☑ 01-306 12 15; www.visitljubljana.si; Adamič-Lundrovo nabrežje 2; ⊙ 8am-9pm Jun-Sep, 8am-7pm Oct-May) Knowledgeable and enthusiastic staff dispense information, maps and useful literature and help with accommodation. Maintains an excellent website.

Slovenian Tourist Information Centre (STIC; ☑ 01-306 45 76; www.slovenia.info; Krekov trg 10; ⊙ 8am-9pm Jun-Sep, 8am-7pm Mon-Fri & 9am-5pm Sat & Sun Oct-May) Good source of information for the rest of Slovenia, with free internet.

University Medical Centre Ljubljana (Univerzitetni Klinični Center Ljubljana; ☑ 01-522 50 50, 01-522 23 61; www.kclj.si; Zaloška cesta 2; ⊙ 24hr) University medical clinic with 24-hour accident and emergency service.

ℹ Getting There & Away

BUS

Buses to destinations both within Slovenia and abroad leave from the **bus station** (Avtobusna Postaja Ljubljana; ☑ 01-234 46 00; www.ap-ljubljana.si; Trg Osvobodilne Fronte 4; ⊙ 5am-11pm Mon-Sat, from 5.30am Sun) in front of the train station. Next to the ticket windows are multilingual information phones and a touch-screen computer; there's a **left luggage** (Trg OF 4; per day €2; ⊙ 5.30am-10.30pm Sun-Fri, 5am-10pm Sat) area at window 3. Frequent buses serve Bohinj (€8.30, two hours, hourly) via Bled (€6.50, 1¼ hours), Divača (€7.90, 1½ hours, eight daily), Piran (€12, 2½ hours, up to seven daily) and Postojna (€6, one hour, half-hourly).

TRAIN

Domestic and international trains arrive at and depart from central Ljubljana's **train station** (Železniška Postaja; ☑ 01-291 33 32; www.slo-zeleznice.si; Trg Osvobodilne Fronte 6; ⊙ 6am-10pm). Buy domestic tickets from window Nos 1 to 8, international ones from window No 9. There are **coin lockers** (Trg OF 6; per day €2-3; ⊙ 24hr) for left luggage on platform 1. Useful domestic destinations include Bled (€5.10, one hour, half-hourly) and Bohinjska Bistrica (€7.20, two hours, six daily) via Jesenice.

ℹ Getting Around

TO/FROM THE AIRPORT

You can reach Ljubljana's **Jože Pučnik Airport** (LJU/Aerodrom Ljubljana; ☑ 04-206 19 81; www.lju-airport.si/eng; Zgornji Brnik 130a, Brnik) by public bus (€4.10, 45 minutes) from stop No 28 at the bus station. These run at 5.20am and hourly from 6.10am to 8.10pm Monday to Friday; at the weekend there's a bus at 6.10am and then one every two hours from 9.10am to 7.10pm. Buy tickets from the driver.

The best of several airport-shuttle services is **GoOpti** (☑ 01-320 45 30; www.goopti.com), which can also transfer you to Jože Pučnik Airport (from €9, half-hour) along with some 20 other airports in the region including Venice, Vienna and Klagenfurt. Book by phone or online; rates depend on pick-up time and whether you are sharing or prefer a private transfer.

A taxi from the airport to Ljubljana will cost from €30.

BICYCLE

Ljubljana is a pleasure for cyclists, and there are bike lanes and special traffic lights everywhere. The **Bicike(lj)** (www.bicikelj.si; subscription weekly/yearly €1/€3 plus hourly rate; ⊙ 24hr) cycle-sharing scheme is generally geared towards residents and short rides. Instead, rent two-wheelers by the hour or day from **Ljubljana Bike** (☑ 01-306 45 76; www.visitljubljana.si; Krekov trg 10; per 2hr/4hr/day €2/4/8; ⊙ 8am-7pm Apr, May & Oct, 8am-9pm Jun-Sep) at the Slovenian Tourist Information Centre.

PUBLIC TRANSPORT

Ljubljana's city buses operate every five to 15 minutes from 5am (6am on Sunday) to around 10.30pm. A flat fare of €1.20 (good for 90 minutes of unlimited travel, including transfers) is paid with a stored-value magnetic **Urbana** (☑ 01-430 51 74; www.jhl.si/en/single-city-card-urbana) card, which can be purchased at newsstands, tourist offices and the **LPP Information Centre** (☑ 01-430 51 75; www.lpp.si; Slovenska cesta 56; ⊙ 7am-7pm Mon-Fri) for €2; credit can then be added (from €1 to €50).

JULIAN ALPS

The Julian Alps – named in honour of Caesar himself – form Slovenia's dramatic northwest frontier with Italy. Triglav National Park, established in 1924, includes almost all of the Alps lying within Slovenia, including triple-peaked **Mt Triglav**, at 2864m Slovenia's highest mountain. Along with an abundance of fauna and flora, the area offers a wide range of adventure sports.

SLOVENIA JULIAN ALPS

Bled

☑ 04 / POP 8100

With its emerald-green lake, picture-postcard church on a tiny island, medieval castle clinging to a rocky cliff and some of the country's highest peaks as backdrops, Bled seems to have been designed by the very god of tourism. It's a small and convenient base from which to explore the mountains.

⊙ Sights

Lake Bled
LAKE

(Blejsko jezero) Bled's greatest attraction is its crystal green lake, measuring just 2km by about 1.5km. Mild thermal springs warm the water to a swimmable 26°C from June through August. From the shore tiny, tear-shaped **Bled Island** (Blejski Otok; www.blejski otok.si) beckons. There's a church and small museum on it, but the real thrill is the ride out by **gondola** (pletna; ☑ 041 427 155; per person return €12). The boat sets you down on the south side at the monumental South Staircase (Južno Stopnišče).

Bled Castle
CASTLE, MUSEUM

(Blejski Grad; www.blejski-grad.si; Grajska cesta 25; adult/child €9/4.50; ☺8am-8pm Apr-Oct, 8am-6pm Nov-Mar) Perched atop a steep cliff more than 100m above the lake, Bled Castle is how most people imagine a medieval fortress to be, with towers, ramparts, moats and a terrace offering magnificent views. The castle houses a museum collection that traces the lake's history from earliest times, a chapel, a printing works and a restaurant.

Vintgar Gorge
CANYON

(www.vintgar.si; adult/child €4/2; ☺8am-7pm late Apr-Oct) The highlight of visiting the gorge, an easy walk 4km to the northwest of the centre, is the 1600m-long wooden walkway (1893) that criss-crosses the swirling Radovna River.

🏃 Activities

Several local outfits organise a wide range of outdoor activities in and around Bled, including trekking, mountaineering, rock climbing, ski touring, cross-country skiing, mountain biking, rafting, kayaking, canyoning, caving, horse riding and paragliding.

3glav Adventures
ADVENTURE SPORTS

(☑041 683 184; www.3glav-adventures.com; Ljubljanska cesta 1; ☺9am-7pm Apr-Oct) The number-one adventure-sport specialists in Bled for warm-weather activities from 15

April to 15 October. The most popular trip is the Emerald River Adventure (€65), an 11-hour hiking and swimming foray into Triglav National Park and along the Soča River. It also rents bikes for €15 a day.

🛏 Sleeping

Kompas has a list of private rooms and farmhouses, with prices starting at €21 per person.

Traveller's Haven
HOSTEL €

(☑059 044 226, mobile 041 396 545; www.travel lers-haven.si; Riklijeva cesta 1; dm/d from €19/48; @🛜) This is arguably the nicest of several hostels clustered on a hillside on the eastern shore of the lake, about 500m north of the centre. The setting is a renovated villa, with six rooms (including one private double), a great kitchen and free laundry.

★Penzion Mayer
PENSION €€

(☑04-576 57 40; www.mayer-sp.si; Želeška cesta 7; s/d €57/82, apt from €120; @🛜) This flower-bedecked 12-room inn in a renovated 19th-century house is located above the lake. The larger apartment is in a lovely wooden cabin and the in-house restaurant is excellent.

Hotel Triglav Bled
BOUTIQUE HOTEL €€€

(☑04-575 26 10; www.hoteltriglavbled.si; Kolodvorska cesta 33; s €89-159, d €109-179, ste from €199; ❋@🛜☀) The 22 rooms in this painstakingly restored *caravanserai* that opened in 1906 have hardwood floors and Oriental carpets and are furnished with antiques. There's an enormous sloped garden that grows the vegetables served in the terrace restaurant. It's just up from Bled Jezero train station.

🍴 Eating & Drinking

Pizzeria Rustika
PIZZA €

(☑04-576 89 00; www.pizzeria-rustika.com; Riklijeva cesta 13; pizza €6-10; ☺noon-11pm; 🛜) Conveniently located on the same hill as much of Bled's budget accommodation, Rustika serves the best pizza in town.

Slaščičarna Šmon
CAFE €

(☑04-574 16 16; www.smon.si; Grajska cesta 3; ☺7.30am-9pm) Bled's culinary speciality is *kremna rezina* (€2.70), a layer of vanilla custard topped with whipped cream and sandwiched between two layers of flaky pastry. Šmon may not be its place of birth, but it remains the best place in which to try it.

★Ostarija Peglez'n
SEAFOOD €€

(☑04-574 42 18; Cesta Svobode 19a; mains €9-16; ☺noon-10.30pm) One of the better restaurants in Bled, the 'Iron Inn' has fascinating retro decor with lots of old household antiques and curios (including the eponymous iron) and serves some of the best fish dishes in town.

Pub Bled PUB

(Cesta Svobode 19a; ⊙9am-1am Sun-Thu, 9am-3am Fri & Sat) This ultra-friendly pub above the Oštarija Peglez'n restaurant has great cocktails. There's a DJ most nights.

ℹ Information

Kompas (🖉 04-572 75 01; www.kompas-bled.si; Bled Shopping Centre, Ljubljanska cesta 4; ⊙8am-7pm Mon-Sat, to 3pm Sun) Full-service travel agency.

Tourist Information Centre Bled (🖉 04-574 11 22; www.bled.si; Cesta Svobode 10; ⊙8am-9pm Mon-Sat, 9am-6pm Sun Jul & Aug, 8am-6pm Mon-Sat, 10am-4pm Sun Sep-Jun) Occupies a small office behind the lakeside Casino; rents bikes (half-/full day €8/11), does laundry (€20/16 same/next day) and has a computer for checking email.

ℹ Getting There & Around

BUS

Hourly buses run from Bled to Lake Bohinj (€3.60, 45 minutes) via Bohinjska Bistrica, with the first bus leaving around 7am and the last about 10pm. Buses depart at least hourly for Ljubljana (€6.50, 1¼ hours).

TRAIN

Bled has two train stations, though neither is close to the centre. Mainline trains to/from Ljubljana (€5.10, one hour, up to 21 daily) and Austria use Lesce-Bled station, 4km to the east of town. Trains to/from Bohinjska Bistrica (€1.85, 20 minutes, eight daily), from where you can catch a bus to Lake Bohinj, and Italy use the smaller Bled Jezero station, which is 2km west of central Bled.

Bohinj

🖉 04 / POP 5300

Bohinj, a larger and much less developed glacial lake 26km to the southwest of Bled, is a world apart. Triglav itself is visible from Bohinj and there are activities galore – from kayaking and mountain biking to trekking up Triglav via one of the southern approaches. **Ribčev Laz** is the main tourist hub at the lake; **Bohinjska Bistrica** (pop 1890), the area's largest centre, is 6km east of the lake and useful for its train station.

◉ Sights & Activities

Church of St John the Baptist CHURCH
(Cerkev sv Janeza Krstnika; Ribčev Laz; ⊙10am-5pm daily Jul & Aug, 10am-5pm Sat & Sun Sep-Jun) The walls and ceilings of this picturesque church, on the northern side of the Sava Bohinjka river across the stone bridge, is covered with frescoes dating from the 14th to 16th centuries.

Savica Waterfall WATERFALL
(Slap Savica; Ukanc; adult/child €2.50/1.25; ⊙9am-6pm Jul & Aug, to 5pm Apr-Jun, Sep & Oct) This magnificent waterfall, which cuts deep into a gorge almost 80m below, is 4km from the settlement of Ukanc and can be reached by footpath from there.

Alpinsport ADVENTURE SPORTS
(🖉 04-572 34 86, mobile 041 596 079; www.alpinsport.si; Ribčev Laz 53; ⊙9am-8pm Jul-Sep, to 7pm Oct-Jun) Rents sporting equipment, canoes/kayaks (per hour €7/3) and bikes (per hour/day €4/13.50) and organises guided rafting, canyoning and caving trips from a kiosk near the stone bridge.

🛏 Sleeping

The tourist office can help arrange accommodation in private rooms and apartments (double €38 to €50).

Hostel Pod Voglom HOSTEL €
(🖉 04-572 34 61; www.hostel-podvoglom.com; Ribčev Laz 60; dm €16-18, r per person €23-27, without bath €19-22; @🖃🛜) This premier hostel, some 3km west of Ribčev Laz on the road to Ukanc, has 119 beds in 46 rooms in two buildings.

★ Penzion Gasperin PENSION €€
(🖉 041 540 805; www.bohinj.si/gasperin; Ribčev Laz 36a; d €54-92, apt €70-120; ⊛@🛜) This spotless chalet-style guesthouse with 24 rooms is just 350m southeast of the TIC and run by a friendly British-Slovenian couple. Most rooms have balconies.

Hotel Jezero HOTEL €€€
(🖉 04-572 91 00; www.bohinj.si/alpinum/jezero; Ribčev Laz 51; s €57-78, d €94-136; @🛜🏊) This 76-room place just opposite the lake has a lovely indoor swimming pool, two saunas and a fitness centre.

✗ Eating

Strud'l SLOVENIAN €
(🖉 041 541 877; www.strudl.si; Triglavska cesta 23; mains €6-11; ⊙8am-9pm; 🛜) This take on traditional farmhouse cooking is incongruously

located in the centre of Bohinska Bistrica. Try local treats such as *ričet s klobaso* (barley stew served with sausage and beans). The *hišni krožnik* (house plate) is a sampling of everything, including ham, sausage, mashed beans, sauerkraut and cooked buckwheat.

Gostilna Mihovc SLOVENIAN €
(☑051 899 111; www.gostilna-mihovc.si; Stara Fužina 118; mains €7-15; ⊘9am-11pm) This place in Stara Fužina, the next village over from Ribčev Laz, is popular for its home cooking and its home-made brandy. Try the *pasulj* (bean soup) with sausage (€6) or the grilled trout (€10). Live music at the weekend.

❶ Information

Tourist Information Centre Ribčev Laz (TIC; ☑04-574 60 10; www.bohinj-info.com; Ribčev Laz 48; ⊘8am-8pm Mon-Sat, 8am-6pm Sun Jul & Aug, 8am-6pm Mon-Sat, 9am-3pm Sun Sep-Jun) Ask for the comprehensive new *Cycling Routes* (Kolesarske Poti) map.

❶ Getting There & Away

BUS
Buses run regularly from Ljubljana (€8.30, two hours, hourly) to Bohinj Jezero and Ukanc – marked 'Bohinj Zlatorog' – via Bled and Bohinjska Bistrica. Around 20 buses daily go from Bled (€3.60, 45 minutes) to Bohinj Jezero (via Bohinjska Bistrica) and return, with the first bus leaving around 5am and the last about 9pm.

TRAIN
A half-dozen daily trains daily make the run to Bohinjska Bistrica from Ljubljana (€7.20, two hours), though this route requires a change in Jesenice. There are also frequent trains between Bled's small Bled Jezero station (€1.85, 20 minutes, eight daily) and Bohinjska Bistrica.

SOČA VALLEY

The Soča Valley region (Posočje) is defined by the 96km-long Soča River, coloured a deep, almost artificial cobalt blue. The valley has more than its share of historical sights, most of them related to WWI, but most visitors are here for rafting, hiking, skiing and other active sports.

Bovec

☑05 / POP 1700
Soča Valley's de facto capital, Bovec, offers plenty to adventure-sports enthusiasts.

With the Julian Alps – including Mt Kanin (2587m) – above, the Soča River below and Triglav National Park all around, you could spend a week here hiking, kayaking, canyoning and mountain biking without ever doing the same thing twice.

🏃 Activities

You'll find everything you need on the compact village square, **Trg Golobarskih Žrtev**, including a half-dozen adrenaline-raising adventure-sports companies. Among the best are **Aktivni Planet** (☑031 653 417; www.aktivniplanet.si; Trg Golobarskih Žrtev 19; ⊘9am-7pm) and **Soča Rafting** (☑05-389 62 00, mobile 041 724 472; www.socarafting.si; Trg Golobarskih Žrtev 14; ⊘9am-7pm).

Rafting, kayaking and **canoeing** on the beautiful Soča River are major draws. The season lasts from April to October. Rafting trips of two to eight people over a distance of 8km to 10km (1½ hours) and cost from €37. Canoes for two are €45 for the day; single kayaks €30. A 3km **canyoning** trip, in which you descend through gorges and jump over falls near the Soča attached to a rope, costs €45.

🛏 Sleeping & Eating

Hostel Soča Rocks HOSTEL €
(☑041 317 777; http://hostelsocarocks.com; Mala Vas 120; dm €13-15, d €34-36; @🛜) This new 14-room arrival sleeping 68 people is a new breed of hostel: colourful, bathed in light, spotlessly clean and with a bar that never seems to quit. Dorms sleep six people maximum and some rooms have balconies and views of Mt Kanin. Discounted activities on offer.

Martinov Hram GUESTHOUSE €€
(☑05-388 62 14; www.martinov-hram.si; Trg Golobarskih Žrtev 27; s €33-41, d €56-71; 🛜) This lovely and very friendly *gostišče* (inn) near the centre has a dozen plain but adequate rooms and an excellent restaurant with an emphasis on specialities from the Bovec region.

★ Dobra Vila BOUTIQUE HOTEL €€€
(☑05-389 64 00; www.dobra-vila-bovec.si; Mala Vas 112; d €125-165, tr €170-195; ❄@🛜) This absolute stunner of an 11-room boutique hotel is housed in a one-time telephone-exchange building dating to 1932. Peppered with interesting artefacts and objets d'art, it has its own library and wine cellar, and a fabulous restaurant with set menus, a winter garden and an outdoor terrace.

ℹ️ Information

Tourist Information Centre Bovec (☑ 05-388 19 19; www.bovec.si; Trg Golobarskih Žrtev 8; ⏲ 8.30am-8.30pm Jul & Aug, 9am-4pm Mon-Sat Sep-Jun)

ℹ️ Getting There & Away

There are a couple of daily buses to Ljubljana (€13.60, 3½ hours) via Kobarid and Idrija. From late June to August a service to Kranjska Gora (€6.80, 1¾ hours) via the Vršič Pass departs several times a day, continuing on to Ljubljana.

KARST & COAST

Slovenia's short coast (47km) is an area for both recreation and history; the town of Piran, famed for its Venetian Gothic architecture and picturesque narrow streets, is among the main drawcards here. En route from Ljubljana or the Soča Valley, you'll cross the Karst, a huge limestone plateau and a land of olives, ruby-red Teran wine, *pršut* (air-dried ham), old stone churches and deep subterranean caves, including those at Postojna and Škocjan.

Postojna & Škocjan Caves

☑ 05

As much of a draw as the mountains and the sea in Slovenia are two world-class but very different cave systems in the Karst area.

👁️ Sights

Postojna Cave CAVE
(Postojnska Jama; ☑ 05-700 01 00; www.postojnska-jama.eu; Jamska cesta 30; adult/child €22.90/13.70, with Predjama Castle €28.90/17.40; ⏲ tours hourly 9am-5pm or 6pm May-Sep, 3 or 4 times 10am-4pm Oct-Apr) Just under 2km northwest of the town of Postojna (population 7900), Postojna Cave is one of the largest caverns in the world, and its stalagmite and stalactite formations are unequalled anywhere. It's a busy destination – visited by as many as a third of all tourists coming to Slovenia – but it's amazing how the large crowds at the entrance seem to get swallowed whole by the size of the cave.

Postojna is home to the endemic Proteus anguinus – a cute, eyeless salamander nicknamed 'the human fish' because of its skin colour. Visits of 1½ hours involve a 4km underground train ride as well as a 1.7km walk with some gradients but no steps. Dress warmly or rent a shawl as it's 8°C to 10°C down there.

Škocjan Caves CAVE
(☑ 05-708 21 10; www.park-skocjanske-jame.si; Škocjan 2; adult/child €16/7.50; ⏲ tours hourly 10am-5pm Jun-Sep, 2 or 3 times 10am-3pm Oct-Apr) The quieter and more remote Škocjan Caves are 4km southeast of Divača (population 1300). A World Heritage site, this immense system is more captivating than the one at Postojna – a page right out of Jules Verne's *A Journey to the Centre of the Earth* – and for many travellers this will be the highlight of their trip to Slovenia. The temperature in the caves is constant at 12°C so bring along a light jacket or sweater. Good walking shoes, for the sometimes slippery paths, are also recommended.

You can walk to the caves from Divača in about 40 minutes; the trail is signposted. Alternatively, a van meets incoming trains (when running) or replacement buses, and ferries ticket holders to the caves up to four times a day.

🛏️ Sleeping & Eating

Hotel Kras HOTEL €€
(☑ 05-700 23 00; www.hotel-kras.si; Tržaška cesta 1; s/d €71/89, apt €121; ❄️ 🛜) In the heart of Postojna town a couple of kilometres southeast of the cave, this rather flash hotel offers 27 comfortable rooms with all the mod cons. If you're feeling flush, choose one of the three apartments on the top (5th) floor with enormous terraces.

Hotel Malovec HOTEL €€
(☑ 05-763 33 33; www.hotel-malovec.si; Kraška cesta 30a; s/d hotel €54/80, pension €43/54; ❄️ @ 🛜) This new build in the centre of Divača, some 4km northwest of the caves, has 20 modern rooms, including a large family one with balcony. There's an equal number of rooms in the Malovec's original pension right next to its popular restaurant, which serves Slovenian favourites to an appreciative local crowd.

ℹ️ Information

Kompas Postojna (☑ 05-721 14 80; www.kompas-postojna.si; Titov trg 2a; ⏲ 8am-7pm Mon-Fri, 9am-1pm Sat Jun-Oct, 8am-6pm Mon-Fri, 9am-1pm Sat Nov-May) The best source of information in Postojna; has private rooms and changes money.

ℹ️ Getting There & Away

Buses from Ljubljana en route to Piran stop in Postojna (€6, one hour, half-hourly) and Divača

PREDJAMA CASTLE

The tiny village of Predjama (population 80), 10km northwest of Postojna, is home to the remarkable **Predjama Castle** (☑ 05-700 01 03; www.postojnska-jama.eu; Predjama 1; adult/child €9/5.40, with Postojna Cave €28.90/17.40; ⊘ tours hourly 9am-7pm Jul & Aug, 9am-6pm May, Jun & Sep, 10am-5pm Apr & Oct, 10am-4pm Nov-Mar), an all-but-impregnable redoubt in the gaping mouth of a cavern halfway up a 123m cliff. Its four storeys were built piece-meal over the years since 1202, but most of what you see today is 16th century. It looks simply unconquerable.

The castle holds great features for kids of any age – a drawbridge over a raging river, holes in the ceiling of the entrance tower for pouring boiling oil on intruders, a very dank dungeon, a 16th-century chest full of treasure (unearthed in the cellar in 1991), and a hiding place at the top called Erazem's Nook. And in mid-July, the castle hosts the Erasmus Tournament, a day of medieval duelling, jousting and archery.

In summer a shuttle bus ferries joint ticket-holders from Postojna Cave to the castle hourly between 1pm and 6pm.

(€7.90, 1½ hours, eight daily). Severe ice storms in 2014 destroyed much of the track in Notranjska province; train traffic to Postojna (€5.80, one hour) and Divača (€7.70, 1¾ hours) was suspended indefinitely at the time of research, though replacement buses were in operation.

Piran

☑ 05 / POP 4700

Little Piran (Pirano in Italian) sits on the tip of a narrow peninsula, the westernmost point of Slovenian Istria. Piran Bay and Portorož (population 3000), Slovenia's largest beach resort, lie to the south. The centre of Piran's Old Town is **Tartinijev trg**, an oval-shaped, marble-paved square that was the inner harbour until it was filled in 1894.

◉ Sights

Sergej Mašera
Maritime Museum
MUSEUM

(☑ 05-671 00 40; www.pomorskimuzej.si; Cankarjevo nabrežje 3; adult/child €3.50/2.10; ⊘ 9am-noon & 5-9pm Tue-Sun Jul & Aug, 9am-5pm Tue-Sun Sep-Jun) Just southeast of Tartinijev trg in the lovely 19th-century Gabrielli Palace on the waterfront, this museum's focus is the sea, sailing and salt-making – three things that have been crucial to Piran's development over the centuries. The antique model ships upstairs are very fine; other rooms are filled with old figureheads and weapons, including some lethal-looking blunderbusses.

Aquarium Piran
AQUARIUM

(☑ 05-673 25 72, mobile 051 602 554; www.aquariumpiran.com; Kidričevo nabrežje 4; adult/child €7/5; ⊘ 9am-10pm Jun-Aug, to 9pm Apr & May, to 7pm Sep & Oct, to 5pm Nov-Mar) About

100m southwest of Tartinijev trg along the harbour, Piran's aquarium might be small, but there's a tremendous variety of sea life packed into its more than two dozen tanks.

Cathedral of St George
CATHEDRAL

(Stolna Cerkev sv Jurija; Adamičeva ul 2) Piran is watched over by the hilltop Cathedral of St George, mostly dating from the 17th century. If time allows, visit the attached **Parish Museum of St George** (☑ 05-673 34 40; Adamičeva ul 2; admission €1; ⊘ 9am-1pm & 5-7.30pm Tue-Fri, 9am-2pm & 5-8pm Sat, 11am-2pm & 5-8pm Sun), which contains a church plate, paintings and a lapidary in the crypt. The cathedral's free-standing **bell tower** (Zvonik; admission €2; ⊘ 10am-2pm & 5-8pm) dates back to 1609 and can be climbed. The octagonal **baptistery** (1650) has imaginatively reused a 2nd-century Roman sarcophagus as a baptismal font. To the east is a reconstucted stretch of the 15th-century **town wall** complete with loopholes.

⎸ Sleeping

★ Max Piran
B&B €€

(☑ 05-673 34 36, mobile 041 692 928; www.maxpiran.com; Ul IX Korpusa 26; d €60-70; ❄@🛰) Piran's most romantic accommodation has just six rooms, each bearing a woman's name rather than a number, in a delightful coral-coloured, early-18th-century townhouse.

Miracolo di Mare
B&B €€

(☑ 05-921 76 60, mobile 051 445 511; www.miracolodimare.si; Tomšičeva ul 23; s €50-55, d €60-70; @🛰) A cosy B&B near the waterfront, the 'Wonder of the Sea' has a dozen charming (though smallish) rooms, some of which (like No 3 and the breakfast room) give on to the most charming raised back garden in Piran. Floors and stairs are wooden (and original) and beds metal framed.

Hotel Tartini
HOTEL €€€

(☑05-671 10 00; www.hotel-tartini-piran.com; Tartinijev trg 15; s €76-92, d €102-128, ste from €140; ❋) This attractive, 45-room property faces Tartinijev trg and manages to catch a few sea views from the upper floors. The staff are especially friendly and helpful. For a real treat, splash out on suite No 40a; we're suckers for eyrie-like round rooms with million-euro views.

✗ Eating

Restaurant Neptune
SEAFOOD €

(☑05-673 41 11, 041 715 890; Župančičeva ul 7; mains €8-20; ⊘12pm-4pm, 6pm-10pm) It's no bad thing to be more popular with locals than tourists, and this family-run place hits all the buttons – a friendly welcome, big seafood platters and a choice of meat dishes, too.

Riva Piran
SEAFOOD €€

(☑05-673 22 25; Gregorčičeva ul 46; mains €8-28; ⊘11.30am-midnight) Riva is the best waterfront seafood restaurant and is worth patronising. It has the strip's best decor, unparalleled sea views and friendly service.

★ Casa Nostromo
SEAFOOD €€

(☑030 200 000; www.piranisin.com; Tomšičeva ul 24; mains €8-22; ⊘noon-11pm) Making a big splash (as it were) on the Piran culinary scene these days is decorated chef Gradimir Dimitrić's new waterfront eatery, serving seafood and Istrian specialities.

❶ Information

Tourist Information Centre Piran (☑05-673 44 40; www.portoroz.si; Tartinijev trg 2; ⊘9am-8pm Jul & Aug, 9am-noon & 12.30-5pm Mon-Sat, 10am-2pm Sun Sep-Jun) In the impressive Municipal Hall.

❶ Getting There & Away

BUS

Up to seven buses a day make the run to/from Ljubljana (€12, 2½ hours, via Divača and Postojna). Some five buses go daily to Trieste (€10, 1¾ hours) in Italy, except Sundays. One bus a day heads south for Croatian Istria from late June to September, stopping at the coastal towns of Umag, Poreč and Rovinj (€10.30, 2¾ hours).

SURVIVAL GUIDE

❶ Directory A–Z

BUSINESS HOURS

Bars Usually 11am to midnight Sunday to Thursday, to 1am or 2am on Friday and Saturday.

Banks 9am to 5pm weekdays, and (rarely) 8am to noon on Saturday.

Grocery stores 8am to 7pm weekdays, to 1pm on Saturday.

Museums 10am to 6pm Tuesday to Sunday (winter hours may be shorter).

Restaurants Generally 11am to 10pm daily.

MONEY

The official currency is the euro. Exchanging cash is simple at banks, major post offices, travel agencies and a *menjalnica* (bureau de change), although many don't accept travellers cheques. Major credit and debit cards are accepted almost everywhere, and ATMs are ubiquitous.

PUBLIC HOLIDAYS

If a holiday falls on a Sunday, then the following Monday becomes the holiday.

New Year's holidays 1 and 2 January

Prešeren Day (Slovenian Culture Day) 8 February

Easter & Easter Monday March/April

Insurrection Day 27 April

Labour Day holidays 1 and 2 May

National Day 25 June

Assumption Day 15 August

Reformation Day 31 October

All Saints Day 1 November

Christmas Day 25 December

Independence Day 26 December

COUNTRY FACTS

Area 20,273 sq km

Capital Ljubljana

Country code ☑386

Currency Euro (€)

Emergency Ambulance ☑112, fire ☑112, police ☑113

Language Slovene

Money ATMs are everywhere; banks open Monday to Friday and (rarely) Saturday morning

Population 2.06 million

Visas Not required for citizens of the EU, Australia, USA, Canada or New Zealand

ESSENTIAL FOOD & DRINK

Little Slovenia can boast an incredibly diverse cuisine, with as many as two dozen different regional styles of cooking. Here are some of the highlights:

➡ **Brinjevec** A very strong brandy made from fermented juniper berries (a decidedly acquired taste).

➡ **Gibanica** Layer cake stuffed with nuts, cheese and apple.

➡ **Jota** A hearty bean-and-cabbage soup.

➡ **Postrv** Trout, particularly the variety from the Soča River, is a real treat.

➡ **Potica** A kind of nut roll eaten at teatime or as a dessert.

➡ **Prekmurska gibanica** A rich concoction of pastry filled with poppy seeds, walnuts, apples and cheese and topped with cream.

➡ **Pršut** Air-dried, thinly sliced ham from the Karst region, not unlike Italian prosciutto.

➡ **Ričet** A rich stew of barley and beef.

➡ **Štruklji** Scrumptious dumplings made with curd cheese and served either savoury as a main course or sweet as a dessert.

➡ **Wine** Distinctively Slovenian tipples include peppery red Teran from the Karst region and Malvazija, a straw-colour white wine from the coast.

➡ **Žganci** The Slovenian stodge of choice – groats made from barley or corn but usually *ajda* (buckwheat).

➡ **Žlikrofi** Ravioli-like parcels filled with cheese, bacon and chives.

TELEPHONE

To call Slovenia from abroad, dial the international access code ☑ 386 (the country code for Slovenia), the area code (minus the initial zero) and the number. There are six area codes in Slovenia (☑ 01 to ☑ 05 and ☑ 07). To call abroad from Slovenia, dial ☑ 00 (the international access code) followed by the country and area codes and then the number. Numbers beginning with ☑ 80 in Slovenia are toll-free.

Mobile Phones

Network coverage amounts to more than 95% of the country. Mobile numbers carry the prefix ☑ 030 and ☑ 040 (SiMobil), ☑ 031, ☑ 041, ☑ 051 and ☑ 071 (Mobitel) and ☑ 070 (Tušmobil).

SIM cards with €5 credit are available for around €15 from SiMobil (www.simobil.si), Mobitel (www.mobitel.si) and Tušmobil

(www.tusmobil.sil). A basic hand unit with SIM is available from vending machines at the airport and bus station for €30. Top-up scratch cards are available at post offices, newsstands and petrol stations.

All three networks have outlets throughout Slovenia, including in Ljubljana.

TOURIST INFORMATION

The **Slovenian Tourist Board** (Slovenska Turistična Organizacija | STO; ☑ 01-589 18 40; www.slovenia.info; Dunajska cesta 156), based in Ljubljana, is the umbrella organisation for tourist promotion in Slovenia, and produces a number of excellent brochures, pamphlets and booklets in English. In addition, the organisation oversees dozens of tourist information centres (TICs) across the country.

VISAS

Citizens of nearly all European countries, as well as Australia, Canada, Israel, Japan, New Zealand and the USA, do not require visas to visit Slovenia for stays of up to 90 days. Holders of EU and Swiss passports can enter using a national identity card.

Those who do require visas (including South Africans) can get them for up to 90 days at any Slovenian embassy or consulate – see the website of the Ministry of Foreign Affairs (www.mzz.gov.si) for a full listing. Visas cost €35 regardless of the type of visa or length of validity.

SLEEPING PRICE RANGES

The following price ranges refer to a double room, with ensuite toilet and bath or shower, and breakfast, unless otherwise indicated:

€ less than €50

€€ €50 to €100

€€€ more than €100

ℹ Getting There & Away

AIR

Slovenia's only international airport is Ljubljana's Jože Pučnik Airport (p402) at Brnik, 27km north of Ljubljana. Apart from the Slovenian flag-carrier, **Adria Airways** (JP; ☑ 01-369 10 10, 080 13 00; www.adria-airways.com), several other airlines offer regular flights to and from Ljubljana, including budget carriers **easyJet** (☑ 04-206 16 77; www.easyjet.com) and **Wizz Air** (www.wizzair.com).

LAND
Bus

International bus destinations from Ljubljana include Serbia, Germany, Croatia, Bosnia & Hercegovina, Macedonia, Italy and Scandinavia. You can also catch buses to Italy and Croatia from coastal towns, including Piran.

Train

It is possible to travel to Italy, Austria, Germany, Croatia and Hungary by train; Ljubljana is the main hub, although you can hop on international trains in certain other cities. International train travel can be expensive. It is sometimes cheaper to travel as far as you can on domestic routes before crossing borders.

SEA

Piran sends catamarans to Trieste daily and to Venice at least twice a week in season.

ℹ Getting Around

BICYCLE

Cycling is a popular way of getting around. Bikes can be transported for €3.50 in the baggage compartments of some IC and regional trains. Larger buses can also carry bikes as luggage. Most towns and cities have dedicated bicycle lanes and traffic lights.

BUS

Buy your ticket at the *avtobusna postaja* (bus station) or simply pay the driver as you board. In Ljubljana you should book your seat at least a day in advance (fees: domestic €1.50, inter-

---

THE GREAT OUTDOORS

Slovenes have a strong attachment to nature, and most lead active, outdoor lives from an early age. As a result the choice of activities and range of facilities on offer are endless. From skiing and climbing to canyoning and cycling, Slovenia has it all and it's always affordable. The major centres are Bovec, Lake Bled and Lake Bohinj. The Slovenian Tourist Board publishes specialist brochures on skiing, hiking, cycling, golfing and horse riding, as well as one on the nation's top spas and heath resorts.

---

national €2.20) if you're travelling on Friday, or to destinations in the mountains or on the coast on a public holiday. Bus services are restricted on Sundays and holidays. A range of bus companies serve the country, but prices are uniform: €3.10/5.60/9.20/12.80/16.80 for 25/50/100/150/200km of travel.

CAR & MOTORCYCLE

Roads in Slovenia are generally good. Tolls are not paid separately on the motorways; instead all cars must display a *vinjeta* (road-toll sticker) on the windscreen. They cost €15/30/110 for a week/month/year for cars and €7.50/30/55 for motorbikes, and are available at petrol stations, post offices and certain newsstands and tourist information centres. These stickers will already be in place on a rental car; failure to display such a sticker risks a fine of up to €300.

Renting a car in Slovenia allows access to cheaper out-of-centre hotels and farm or village homestays. Rentals from international firms such as Avis, Budget, Europcar and Hertz vary in price; expect to pay from €40/210 a day/week, including unlimited mileage, collision damage waiver (CDW), theft protection (TP), Personal Accident Insurance (PAI) and taxes. Some smaller agencies have somewhat more competitive rates; booking on the internet is always cheaper.

Dial ☑ 1987 for roadside assistance.

TRAIN

Much of the country is accessible by rail, run by the national operator, **Slovenian Railways** (Slovenske Železnice, SŽ; ☑ 01-291 33 32; www.slo-zeleznice.si). The website has an easy-to-use timetable.

Figure on travelling at about 60km/h except on the fastest InterCity Slovenia (ICS) express trains that run at an average speed of 90km/h.

Purchase your ticket before travelling at the *železniška postaja* (train station); buying it from the conductor onboard costs an additional €2.50.

EATING PRICE RANGES

The following price ranges are an approximation for a two-course, sit-down meal for one person, with a drink. Many restaurants offer an excellent-value set menu of two or even three courses at lunch. These typically run from €5 to €10:

€ less than €15

€€ €15 to €30

€€€ more than €30

Ukraine

Best Places to Eat

➡ Spotykach (p415)

➡ Masonic Restaurant (p420)

➡ Arbequina (p415)

➡ Dim Lehend (p419)

➡ Kupol (p419)

Best Places to Stay

➡ Sunflower B&B (p415)

➡ Astoria (p419)

➡ Hotel 7 Days (p419)

➡ Dream House Hostel (p414)

Why Go?

Big, diverse and largely undiscovered, Ukraine (Україна) is one of Europe's last genuine travel frontiers, a poor nation rich in colour-splashed tradition, off-the-map travel experiences and warm-hearted people. And with the country hitting the headlines recently for all the wrong reasons, those locals are perhaps happier than ever to see foreign visitors.

'Ukraine' means 'land on the edge', an apt title for this slab of Eurasia in many ways. This is the Slavic hinterland on Europe's periphery, just over two decades into a very troubled independence and dogged by conflict with neighbouring Russia. But it's a country whose peoples can pull together when need arises, as the recent Maidan Revolution and nationwide war effort has shown.

Most visitors head for the eclectic capital Kyiv, but architecturally rich Lviv is Ukraine's true big hope for tourism and both are well away from the conflict zones. However, while Russia continues to occupy Crimea, beach fun is off for the foreseeable future.

When to Go
Kyiv

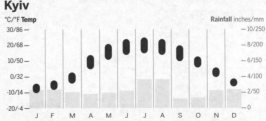

Jan Party on New Year's Eve then repent at an Orthodox Christmas service a week later.

May A great time to visit Kyiv when its countless horse chestnut trees are in blossom.

Aug Sip Ukraine's best coffee in one of Lviv's many outdoor cafes.

Ukraine Highlights

❶ Inspect Kyiv's collection of mummified monks by candlelight at **Kyevo-Pecherska Lavra** (p414).

❷ Make an ascent of **Andriyivsky Uzviz** (p414), Kyiv's most atmospheric street.

❸ Do a spot of cobble-surfing in **Lviv's** (p418) historical centre, packed with churches, museums and eccentric restaurants.

❹ Take a stroll through the island town of **Kamyanets-Podilsky** (p419) to its photogenic fortress.

ITINERARIES

Two Days

A couple of days are just enough to 'do' **Kyiv**, starting at its stellar attraction, the Kyevo-Pecherska Lavra (aka the Caves Monastery). Follow this with a hike up artsy Andriyivsky Uzviz for a taste of prewar Ukraine, before plunging into the beeswax-perfumed Byzantine interior of Unesco-listed St Sophia's Cathedral.

Five Days

Having seen the sights in Kyiv, hop aboard a slow night train to **Lviv**, Ukraine's most central European city – complete with bean-scented coffee houses, Gothic and baroque churches, and quaintly rattling trams.

Kyiv   Київ

📇 044 / POP 2.8 MILLION

Sometimes chaotic central Asia, other times quaint central Europe, Kyiv (many agree) is the former USSR's most pleasant city. A pretty spot amid the wooded hills hemming the wide River Dnipro, this eclectic capital has preserved the legacy of its former possessors, from Viking chieftains to post-Soviet dictators. Despite its starring role in the 2014 Maidan Revolution which toppled the last of those rulers, only the very centre around Maidan Nezalezhnosti bears any scars, the rest of the city untouched by the tumultuous events that put the geopolitical spotlight firmly on Ukraine.

◉ Sights

★ Kyevo-Pecherska Lavra   MONASTERY

(Києво-Печерська Лавра | Caves Monastery; 📇 044 280 3071; www.kplavra.ua; vul Lavrska 9; grounds 15uah, caves & exhibitions adult/child 50/25uah; ⏱ 8am-7pm Apr-Oct, 9am-6pm Nov-Mar; Ⓜ Arsenalna) Tourists and Orthodox pilgrims alike flock to the Lavra. It's easy to see why the tourists come. Set on 28 hectares of grassy hills above the Dnipro River, the monastery's tight cluster of gold-domed churches is a feast for the eyes, the hoard of Scythian gold rivals that of the Hermitage in St Petersburg, and the underground labyrinths lined with mummified monks are exotic and intriguing.

★ St Sophia's Cathedral   CHURCH

(pl Sofiyska; admission grounds/cathedral/bell tower 10/55/20uah; ⏱ grounds 9am-7pm, cathedral 10am-6pm Thu-Tue, to 5pm Wed; Ⓜ Maydan Nezalezhnosti) The interior is the most astounding aspect of Kyiv's oldest standing church, St Sophia's Cathedral. Many of the mosaics and frescoes are original, dating back to 1017–31, when the cathedral was built to celebrate Prince Yaroslav's victory in protecting Kyiv from the Pechenegs (Tribal Raiders). While equally attractive, the building's gold domes and 76m-tall wedding-cake bell tower are 18th-century baroque additions.

Andriyivsky Uzviz   STREET

(Ⓜ Kontraktova Pl) According to legend a man walked up the hill, erected a cross and prophesied: 'A great city will stand on this spot'. That man was the Apostle Andrew, hence the name of Kyiv's quaintest thoroughfare, a steep cobbled street that winds its way up from Kontraktova pl to vul Volodymyrska. Its vague Montparnasse feel has attracted Ukraine's wealthy, but despite gentrification it still retains an atmosphere unique for Kyiv, as well as its multiple stalls selling junk souvenirs and dubious art.

🛏 Sleeping

★ Dream House Hostel   HOSTEL €

(📇 044 580 2169; www.dream-family.com; Andriyivsky uzviz 2D; dm/d from 110/390uah; ✳@🛜; Ⓜ Kontraktova pl) Kyiv's most happening hostel is a gleaming 100-bed affair superbly located at the bottom of Andriyivsky uzviz. An attached cafe-bar, basement kitchen, laundry room, key cards, bike hire, tours and daily events make this a comfortable and engaging base from which to explore the capital.

Oselya   BOUTIQUE HOTEL €€

(Оселя; 📇 044 258 8281; www.oselya.in.ua; vul Kamenyariv 11; s 614uah, d from 790uah; ✳@🛜; Ⓜ Lybidska) Inconveniently located around 5km south of the city centre, just to the east of Zhulyany airport, this superb seven-room family-run hotel has immaculately kept rooms in period style and receives encouraging reviews from travellers for its friendly welcome. The location feels almost rural, but you'll need to arrange a pickup from Lybidska metro station to find it, or grab a cab.

★ Sunflower B&B Hotel
B&B €€€

(☑ 044 279 3846; www.sunflowerhotel.kiev.ua; vul Kostyolna 9/41; s/d from 850/1000uah; ✳@⊙; Ⓜ Maydan Nezalezhnosti) The name is an oxymoron – it's more B&B than hotel – but we're not complaining. The highlight is the continental breakfast delivered to your room, on request, by English-speaking staff. It's centrally located but nearly impossible to find – calling for a pickup is not a bad idea.

✗ Eating

Kyivska Perepichka
FAST FOOD €

(Київська перепічка; vul Bohdana Khmelnytskoho 3; pastry 6uah; ⊙8.30am-9pm Mon-Sat, 10am-9pm Sun; Ⓜ Teatralna) A perpetually long queue moves with lightning speed towards a window where two women hand out pieces of fried dough enclosing a mouthwatering sausage. The place became a local institution long before the first 'hot dog' hit town. An essential Kyiv experience.

★ Spotykach
UKRAINIAN €€

(Спотикач; ☑ 044 586 4095; vul Volodymyrska 16; mains 50-190uah; ⊙11am-midnight; ⊙; Ⓜ Zoloti Vorota) A tribute to the 1960s, this discreetly stylish retro-Soviet cellar will make even a hardened dissident shed a nostalgic tear. The menu is Kremlin banquet, but with a definite Ukrainian twist. *Spotykach* is vodka-based liquor made with different flavours, from blackcurrant to horseradish, and takes its name from the Russian for 'stumble' – an effect it might cause on the uninitiated.

★ Arbequina
SPANISH, SEAFOOD €€

(☑ 044 223 9618; vul Borysa Hrinchenka; mains 80-150uah; ⊙9am-11pm; ⊙; Ⓜ Maydan Nezalezhnosti) Barcelona meets Odesa in this miniature restaurant a few steps away from Maidan. Food is mostly Spanish, but the chef successfully experiments with Black Sea fish and East European staples, which results in most unusual combinations. From Wednesday to Friday there's live Cuban or Spanish music in the evenings.

♟ Drinking & Nightlife

Kupidon
PUB

(Купідон | Cupid; vul Pushkinska 1-3/5; ⊙10am-10pm; ⊙; Ⓜ Kreshchatyk) Perhaps no longer the hotbed of nationalism it once was, Cupid is still a great Lviv-styled cellar knaypa (pub) abutting a second-hand bookshop. Well-crafted coffees and Ukrainian food are enjoyed at the jumble of table and chairs and there's plenty

of reading and drawing material lying around to keep you occupied afterwards.

Kaffa
COFFEE

(Каффа; prov Tarasa Shevchenka 3; ⊙11am-10.30pm Mon, from 9am Tue-Fri, 10am-10pm Sat & Sun; Ⓜ Maydan Nezalezhnosti) Around for years, Kaffa still serves the most heart-pumping, rich-tasting brew in town. Coffees and teas from all over the world are served in a pot sufficient for two or three punters, in a white-washed African-inspired interior – all ethnic masks, beads and leather.

☆ Entertainment

Art Club 44
LIVE MUSIC

(www.club44.com.ua; vul Khreshchatyk 44B; Ⓜ Teatralna) Some of the best gigs and DJ nights in the city centre with everything from west Ukrainian ethno-rock to German disc spinners packing them in.

Taras Shevchenko National Opera Theatre
OPERA

(☑ 044 235 2606; www.opera.com.ua; vul Volodymyrska 50; Ⓜ Zoloti Vorota) Performances at this lavish theatre (opened 1901) are grandiose affairs but tickets are cheap. True disciples of Ukrainian culture should not miss a performance of Zaporozhets za Dunaem (Zaporizhzhyans Beyond the Danube), a sort of operatic, purely Ukrainian version of Fiddler on the Roof.

ⓘ Information

Almost every cafe and restaurant offers free wi-fi and there are hotspots throughout the city centre. Kyiv has no tourist office.

Central Post Office (www.ukrposhta.com; vul Khreshchatyk 22; ⊙8am-9pm Mon-Sat, 9am-7pm Sun; Ⓜ Maydan Nezalezhnosti)

Lonely Planet (www.lonelyplanet.com/ukraine/kyiv)

ⓘ Getting There & Away

AIR

Most international flights use Boryspil International Airport (p422), 35km east of the city. Some domestic airlines and Wizzair use **Zhulyany airport** (☑ 044 585 7254; www.airport.kiev.ua), 7km southwest of the centre. There's at least one flight a day to all regional capitals and international flights serve many European cities.

Plane tickets are sold at **Kiy Avia** (www.kiyavia.com; pr Peremohy 2; ⊙8am-9pm Mon-Fri, 8am-8pm Sat, 9am-6pm Sun; Ⓜ Vokzalna).

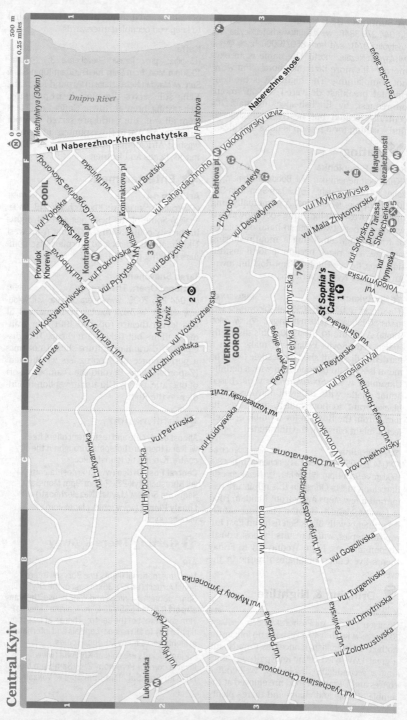

Central Kyiv

500 m
0.25 miles

Dnipro River

Mezhyhirya (30km)

PODIL

Provulok Khoreviy

VERKHNIY GOROD

St Sophia's Cathedral

Maydan Nezalezhnosti

vul Naberezhno-Khreshchatytska

Naberezhne shose

pl Poshtova

Volodymyrsky uzviz

Poshtova pl

vul Volodymyrska

vul Grygoriya Skovorody

vul Spaska

vul Illjinska

Kontraktova pl

vul Bratska

vul Sahaydachnoho

Z hyvopysna aleya

vul Desyatynna

vul Mykhaylivska

vul Mala Zhytomyrska

prov Tarasa Shevchenka

vul Sofiyska

vul Voloska

Kontraktova pl

vul Khoryva

vul Pokrovska

vul Prybytsko Mykilska

vul Borychiv Tik

vul Velyka Zhytomyrska

vul Striletska

Andriyivsky Uzviz

vul Vozdvyzhenska

vul Reytarska

vul YaroslaviVal

vul Kostyantynivska

vul Verkhniy Val

vul Kozhumyatska

Peyzazhna aleya

vul Yuriya Kotsyubynskoho

vul Honcharab Olesya

vul Frunze

vul Vosnesensky uzviz

vul Petrivska

vul Kudryavska

vul Observatorna

prov Chekhovsky

vul Hlybochytska

vul Lukyanivska

vul Artyoma

vul Vorovskoho

vul Gogolivska

vul Mykoly Pymonenka

vul Turgenivska

vul Hlybochytska

vul Poltavska

vul Pavlivska

vul Dmytrivska

Lukyanivska

vul Vyacheslava Chornovola

vul Zolotoustivska

Petrivska aleya

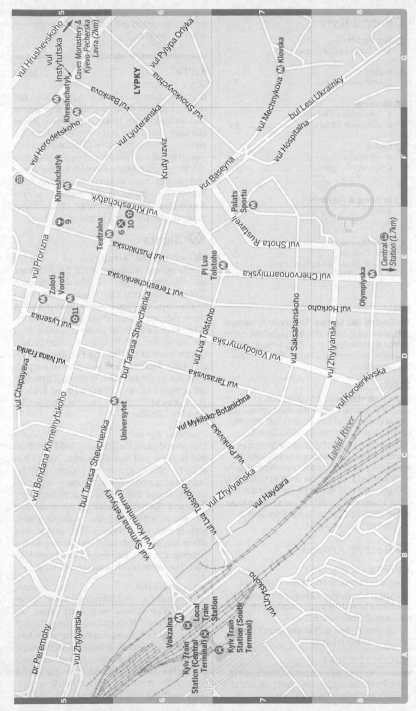

Central Kyiv

BUS

The **Central Bus Station** (Tsentralny Avtovokzal; pl Moskovska 3) is one stop from Lybidska metro station on trolleybus 1 or 12. Only a couple of overnight coaches (eight hours, 250uah) make the Lviv run.

TRAIN

Kyiv's **train station** (☎ 044 503 7005; pl Vokzalna 2; Ⓢ Vokzalna) handles domestic services as well as international trains to Moscow, Warsaw, Berlin, Chişinău (Moldova) and Bucharest.

The quickest way to Lviv is on the Intercity+ express (260uah, five hours, one daily) which leaves early evening. Cheaper overnight passenger trains and a few daytime services (200uah to 250uah, eight to 10 hours) are more popular.

Buy tickets at the station or the **advance train ticket office** (bul Tarasa Shevchenka 38/40; ⊗7am-9pm; Ⓢ Universytet).

ℹ Getting Around

TO/FROM THE AIRPORT
A taxi to the city centre costs around 250uah.

SkyBus (50uah, 45 minutes) departs round the clock from behind the train station's South Terminal every 20 to 40 minutes.

Trolleybus 22 runs to Zhulyany airport from Shulyavska metro station.

PUBLIC TRANSPORT
Kyiv's metro runs between around 6am and midnight. Plastic tokens (*zhetony*; 2uah) are sold at windows and dispensers at stations.

Buy tickets (1.50uah to 2.50uah) for buses, trolleybuses, trams and *marshrutky* from the driver or conductor.

Lviv   Львів

☎ 032 / POP 725,350

If you've done time in any other Ukrainian region, Lviv will come as a shock. Mysterious and architecturally lovely, this Unesco World Heritage-listed city is the country's least Soviet and exudes the same Central European charm as pre-tourism Prague or Kraków once did. Its quaint cobbles, aromatic coffeehouses and rattling trams feel a continent away from the war-torn badlands of Ukraine's east. It's also a place where the candle of Ukrainian national identity burns brightest.

◉ Sights

★**Lychakivske Cemetery**   CEMETERY
(Личаківське кладовище; ☎ 032-275 5415; www.lviv-lychakiv.ukrain.travel; vul Pekarska; admission 20uah; ⊗9am-6pm) Don't leave town until you've seen this amazing cemetery, only a short ride on tram 7 from the centre. This is the Père Lachaise of Eastern Europe, with the same sort of overgrown grounds and Gothic aura as the famous Parisian necropolis (but containing less-well-known people). Laid out in the late 18th century, it's packed full of west Ukraine's great and good. Pride of place goes to the grave of revered nationalist poet Ivan Franko.

Ploshcha Rynok   SQUARE
Lviv was declared a Unesco World Heritage Site in 1998, and this old market square lies at its heart. The square was progressively rebuilt after a major fire in the early 16th century destroyed the original. The 19th-century **Ratusha** (Town Hall) stands in the middle of the plaza, with fountains featuring Greek gods at each of its corners. Vista junkies can climb the 65m-high neo-Renaissance **tower** (admission 10uah; ⊗9am-9pm Apr-Oct, to 6pm Nov-Mar). The ticket booth is on the 4th floor.

Latin Cathedral   CATHEDRAL
(pl Katedralna 1; ⊗7.30am-7pm, closed 2-3pm Mon-Fri) With various parts dating from between 1370 and 1480, this working cathedral is one of Lviv's most impressive churches. The exterior is most definitely Gothic while the heavily gilded interior, one of the city's highlights, has a more baroque feel, with colourfully wreathed pillars hoisting frescoed vaulting and mysterious side chapels

KAMYANETS-PODILSKY КАМ'ЯНЕЦЬ-ПОДІЛЬСЬКИЙ

The unique town of Kamyanets-Podilsky (K-P) stands out for its gorgeous castle backed by dramatic natural beauty. The name Kamyanets refers to the massive stone island created by a sharp bend in the river Smotrych, and the resulting verdant canyon rings a charming old town, Ukraine's best preserved.

Top billing goes to the **fortress** (adult/child 20/10uah; ⊙9am-8pm Tue-Sun, 9am-7pm Mon), one of the country's finest. The large structure is a mishmash of styles, but the overall impression is breathtaking. Scramble round the walls, turrets and dungeons then visit the fantastic museum, a nostalgic romp through the history of K-P and Ukraine over the last century.

The town's other must-see is the **Cathedral of Sts Peter & Paul** (vul Starobulvarna) in the Polish Market Sq. It features a 42m-high minaret topped by a golden statue of the Virgin Mary – K-P was where the Polish and Turkish empires collided.

As transport links are poor, you'll probably want to sleep over in K-P. The **Hotel 7 Days** (☑03849 690 69; http://7dniv.ua; vul Soborna 4; s/d from 290/480uah; ❋🅿🏊) between the Old Town and the bus station has a swimming pool and 218 comfortable rooms. The most characterful place to eat is the folksy **Kafe Pid Bramoyu** (Кафе під брамою; vul Zamkova 1A; mains 15-45uah; ⊙9am-midnight), located in the 17th-century casemates, where mostly Ukrainian favourites populate the menu.

There are two or three buses per day from Lviv (130uah, seven hours) and three day buses plus several overnighters from Kyiv (200uah, seven to 11 hours). The express train from Kyiv is the quickest way to reach Kamyanets-Podilsky. It departs Kyiv at 4.48pm (108uah, seven hours) and arrives just before midnight. There's also at least one overnight sleeper service to and from Kyiv (166uah, 8½ hours).

---

glowing in candlelit half light. Services are in four languages including English.

🛏 Sleeping

★ Old City Hostel HOSTEL €
(☑032 294 9644; www.oldcityhostel.lviv.ua; vul Beryndy 3; dm/d from 120/450uah; @🛜) Occupying two floors of an elegantly fading tenement just steps from pl Rynok, this expertly run hostel with period features and views of the Shevchenko statue from the wrap-around balcony has long since established itself as the city's best. Frill-free dorms hold four to 16 beds, shower queues are unheard of, sturdy lockers keep your stuff safe and there's a well-endowed kitchen.

NTON HOTEL €€
(НТОН; ☑032 242 4959; www.hotelnton.lviv.ua; vul Shevchenka 154B; s/d from 300/420uah; ❋🛜) Near the terminus of tram 7 in Lviv's western suburbs, this far-flung hotel on the road out to the Polish border may not seem too promising, but this fully renovated place is possibly Lviv's best deal. Rooms are spacious and well furnished, and contain little extras like kettles, sewing kits and hairdryers (yes, these *are* extras in Ukraine!).

★ Astoria BOUTIQUE HOTEL €€€
(☑032 242 2701; www.astoriahotel.ua; vul Horodotska 15; r from 1250uah) A hotel since 1914, the Astoria was given a stylishly moody retrofit in 2013, sending it reeling back to the monochrome world of the 1930s. The seven floors are all marble and cast iron, weighty lacquered doors and hangar-style lighting. Rooms are art-deco studies in black and white and every shade in between. Breakfast is served in the superb restaurant.

🍴 Eating

★ Dim Lehend UKRAINIAN €€
(Дім легенд; vul Staroyevreyska 48; mains 30-70uah; ⊙11am-2am) Dedicated to the city of Lviv, there's nothing dim about the 'House of Legends'. The five floors contain a library stuffed with Lviv-themed volumes, a room showing live webcam footage of Lviv's underground river, rooms dedicated to lions and cobblestones, and another featuring the city in sounds. The menu is limited to Ukrainian staples but coffee and desserts are excellent.

★ Kupol CENTRAL EUROPEAN €€
(Купол; vul Chaykovskoho 37; mains 100-150uah; ⊙11am-9pm) One of the pretourism 'originals', this place is designed to feel like stepping

back in time – to 1938 in particular, 'the year before civilisation ended' (ie before the Soviets rolled in). The olde-worlde interior is lined with framed letters, ocean-liner ads, antique cutlery, hampers and other memorabilia, and the Polish/Austrian/Ukrainian food is tasty and served with style.

★**Masonic Restaurant** EUROPEAN €€€
(pl Rynok 14; mains before discount 300-500uah; ☺11am-2am) Ascend to the 2nd floor and open the door of apartment 8. You'll be accosted by an unshaven bachelor type, who eventually opens the door to reveal a fancy beamed restaurant full of Masonic symbols and portraits. Advertised as Galicia's most expensive restaurant, prices are 10 times higher than normal...so make sure you pick up a 90% discount card at Dim Lehend or Livy Bereh beforehand.

The food, by the way, is great and the beer and *kvas* (gingery, beer-like soft drink) come in crystal vases. The toilet is a candlelit Masonic throne. Ukraine's weirdest restaurant experience? Probably.

🍷 Drinking & Nightlife

Lvivska Kopalnya Kavy CAFE
(pl Rynok 10; ☺8am-11pm; 🛜) Lviv is Ukraine's undisputed coffee capital and the 'Lviv Coffee Mine' is where the stratum of arabica is excavated by the local colliers from deep beneath pl Rynok. You can tour the mine or just sample the heart-pumping end product at tables as dark as the brews inside, or out on the courtyard beneath old timber balconies.

ℹ Information

Tourist Information Centre (☏ 032 254 6079; www.touristinfo.lviv.ua; pl Rynok 1, Ratusha; ☺10am-8pm Mon-Fri, to 7pm Sat, to 6pm Sun May-Sep, shorter hours Oct-Apr) Ukraine's best tourist information centre. Branches at the airport (☏ 067 673 9194; ☺10am-8pm Mon-Fri, to 7pm Sat, to 6pm Sun May-Sep, shorter hours Oct-Apr) and the train station (☏ 032 226 2005; Ticket Hall; ☺10am-8pm Mon-Fri, to 7pm Sat, to 6pm Sun May-Sep, shorter hours Oct-Apr).

ℹ Getting There & Away

AIR

Around 7km southwest of the centre, Lviv's **airport** (LWO; www.airport.lviv.ua) has flights to Kyiv (two daily). Book through **Kiy Avia** (☏ 032 255 3263; www.kiyavia.com; vul Hnyatuka 20; ☺8am-8pm Mon-Fri, 9am-5pm Sat, 10am-3pm Sun).

There are international flights to/from Vienna, Munich, Warsaw, İstanbul, Venice, Naples, Milan and Moscow.

BUS

Take trolleybus 25 to the **main bus station** (Holovny Avtovokzal; vul Stryska) 8km south of the centre.

There are overnight services to Kyiv (210uah, nine hours, four daily) and daytime buses to Kamyanets-Podilsky (130uah, seven hours, two or three daily).

TRAIN

The quickest way to Kyiv is on the Intercity+ express (260uah, five hours, one daily) departing early morning. There are also cheaper overnight and daytime passenger trains (200uah to 250uah, eight to 10 hours).

Buy tickets from the station or city centre **train ticket office** (Залізничні квиткові каси; vul Hnatyuka 20; ☺8am-2pm & 3-8pm Mon-Sat, to 6pm Sun).

ℹ Getting Around

From the train station, take tram 1, 6 or 9 to the centre. Trolleybus 9 goes to/from the university to the airport. Bus 48 also runs to the airport from pr Shevchenko.

SURVIVAL GUIDE

ℹ Directory A–Z

ACCOMMODATION

Ukraine has hundreds of hostels with, Lviv and Kyiv boasting tens each. There's also a bewildering array of hotel and room types from Soviet-era budget crash pads to 'six-star' overpriced luxury.

COUNTRY FACTS

Area 603,628 sq km

Capital Kyiv

Country Code ☏ 380

Currency Hryvnia (uah)

Emergency ☏ 112

Language Ukrainian, Russian

Money ATMs are common; credit cards widely accepted

Population 44.6 million

Visas Not required for EU, UK, US and Canadian citizens for stays up to 90 days

Everything in between can be hit and miss, and there are no national standards to follow.

Booking ahead isn't normally essential except around New Year. Accommodation is the single biggest expense in Ukraine, but with the virtual collapse of the hryvnya rooms are very affordable.

BUSINESS HOURS

Banks 9am to 5pm
Restaurants noon to 11pm
Shops 9am to 6pm, to 8pm or 9pm in cities
Sights 9am to 5pm or 6pm, closed at least one day a week

CUSTOMS REGULATIONS

You are allowed to bring in up to US$10,000, 1L of spirits, 2L of wine, 5L of beer, 200 cigarettes or 250g of tobacco, and gifts up to the value of €200.

GAY & LESBIAN TRAVELLERS

Ukraine is generally more tolerant of homosexuality than Russia. Homosexuality is legal, but attitudes vary across the country. Useful gay websites include www.gayua.com, www.gay.org.ua and www.gaylvov.at.ua.

INTERNET ACCESS

Most hotels offer free wi-fi and free hotspots are much more common than in Western Europe. Many restaurants and cafes have wi-fi. Internet cafes are not as common as they once were.

INTERNET RESOURCES

Brama (www.brama.com)
Infoukes (www.infoukes.com)
Ukraine.com (www.ukraine.com)

MONEY

US dollars, the euro and Russian roubles are the easiest currencies to exchange. Damaged or marked notes may not be accepted. Credit cards are increasingly accepted everywhere, however, Ukraine remains primarily a cash economy.

➟ Coins: one, five, 10, 25 and 50 kopecks and one hryvnia.
➟ Notes: one, two, five, 10, 20, 50, 100, 200 and 500 hryvnia.
➟ Hryvnya are virtually impossible to buy pre-departure.
➟ The currency saw huge devaluation in 2014.
➟ ATMs are common.

EATING PRICE RANGES

The following price indicators are for a main meal:

€ less than 50uah

€€ 50uah to 150uah

€€€ more than 150uah

SLEEPING PRICE RANGES

The following price indicators apply for a high-season double room:

€ less than 400uah

€€ 400uah to 800uah

€€€ more than 800uah

POST

Ukrposhta (www.ukrposhta.com) runs Ukraine's postal system. Sending a postcard or a letter up to 20g costs the equivalent of a US dollar to anywhere abroad. Mail takes about a week to Europe and around two weeks to the USA or Australia.

PUBLIC HOLIDAYS

New Year's Day 1 January
Orthodox Christmas 7 January
International Women's Day 8 March
Orthodox Easter April
Labour Day 1–2 May
Victory Day (1945) 9 May
Orthodox Pentecost June
Constitution Day 28 June
Independence Day (1991) 24 August

SAFE TRAVEL

Despite the recent conflict, western Ukraine and Kyiv remain safe. Donetsk, Luhansk and Crimea should be avoided, and care should be taken when visiting Kharkiv and Odesa.

TELEPHONE

All numbers in Ukraine start with ☎ 0 and there are no pre-dialling codes.

Ukraine's country code is ☎ 0038. To call Kyiv from overseas, dial ☎ 00 38 044 and the subscriber number.

To call internationally from Ukraine, dial ☎ 0, wait for a second tone, then dial ☎ 0 again, followed by the country code, city code and number.

European GSM phones work in Ukraine. Local SIM cards work out much cheaper if making several calls.

VISAS

Tourist visas for stays of less than 90 days aren't required by citizens of the EU/EEA, Canada, the USA and Japan. Australians and New Zealanders need a visa.

❶ Getting There & Away

The majority of visitors to Ukraine fly – generally to Kyiv. Flights, tours and rail tickets can be booked online through Lonely Planet (www.lonelyplanet.com/bookings).

ESSENTIAL FOOD & DRINK

'Borshch and bread – that's our food.' With this national saying, Ukrainians admit that theirs is a cuisine of comfort, full of hearty, mild dishes designed for fierce winters rather than one of gastronomic zing. Here are some of the Ukrainian staples you are certain to find on restaurant menus:

➡ **Borshch** The national soup made with beetroot, pork fat and herbs.

➡ **Salo** Basically raw pig fat, cut into slices and eaten with bread.

➡ **Varenyky** Pasta pockets filled with everything from mashed potato to sour cherries.

➡ **Kasha** Buckwheat swimming in milk and served for breakfast.

➡ **Vodka** Also known as *horilka*, it accompanies every celebration and get-together – in copious amounts.

AIR

Only a couple of low-cost airlines fly to Ukraine.

Most international flights use Kyiv's main airport, **Boryspil International Airport** (☑ 044 393 4371; www.kbp.aero). **Lviv International Airport** (LWO; ☑ 032 229 8112; www.lwo.aero) also has a few international connections.

Ukraine International Airlines (PS; www.flyuia.com) is Ukraine's flag carrier.

LAND

Ukraine is well linked to its neighbours, particularly Russia and Belarus, with whom it shares the former Soviet rail system. Kyiv is connected by bus or train to Moscow, St Petersburg, Minsk, Warsaw and Budapest, as well as other Eastern European capitals. Lviv is the biggest city servicing the Polish border – it's possible to take a budget flight to Poland then cross the border to Lviv by bus or train.

Border Crossings

The Poland–Ukraine and Romania–Ukraine borders are popular smuggling routes, hence the thorough customs checks. Expect customs personnel to scrutinise your papers and search your vehicle.

Bus

Buses are slower, less frequent and less comfortable than trains for long-distance travel.

Car & Motorcycle

To bring your own vehicle into the country, you'll need your original registration papers and a 'Green Card' International Motor Insurance Certificate.

ⓘ Getting Around

AIR

Flying is an expensive way of getting around. Overnight train is cheaper and more reliable.

Kiy Avia (www.kiyavia.com) has branches across the country.

BUS

Buses serve every city and small town, but are best for short trips (three hours or less). Tickets resembling shop-till receipts are sold at bus stations up to departure.

Marshrutky are minibuses that ply bus routes but stop anywhere on request. They're most common in big cities but also serve intercity routes. Fares are usually slightly higher; journey times shorter.

LOCAL TRANSPORT

Trolleybus, tram, bus and metro run in Kyiv. A ticket for one ride by bus, tram or trolleybus costs 1.50uah to 2uah. There are no return, transfer, timed or day tickets available. Tickets must be punched on board (or ripped by the conductor).

Metro barriers take plastic tokens (*zhetony*), sold at counters inside stations.

TRAIN

For long journeys, overnight train is best. **Ukrainian Railways** (www.uz.gov.ua) features timetables and an online booking facility.

All seating classes have assigned places. Carriage (*vahon*) and bunk (*mesto*) numbers are printed on tickets.

Lyuks or SV *Spalny vahon* (SV) – 1st-class (sleeper) compartment for two people.

Kupe 2nd-class sleeper compartment for four people. Train prices quoted here are for *kupe*.

Platskart 50-bunk 3rd-class open-carriage sleeper.

C1 and C2 First/second-class on fast Intercity+ services.

Few Ukrainian Railways employees speak English; have a local write down your destination, date, time, train number etc in Cyrillic. At Kyiv train station there are dedicated windows (8 and 9) for foreigners.

Survival Guide

Directory A–Z

Accommodation

There's accommodation to match every budget in Eastern Europe, from Soviet-era concrete behemoths, five-star luxury palaces and international hotel groups to rural campsites and homely grandmother-run private rooms.

Price Ranges

Price categories are broken down differently for individual countries – see each country for full details.

Reservations

➡ Generally a good idea in high season and can usually be made by phone or online.

➡ Hostels and cheap hotels fill up very quickly, especially in popular backpacker destinations such as Prague, Budapest and Kraków. Note that across the region there is also a shortage of good-value midrange accommodation options.

➡ Tourist offices, where they exist, may be able to make reservations on your behalf (some charge a small fee for this service) but, in general, do not expect a Western European standard of service from tourist offices in Eastern Europe.

Seasons

➡ High season is typically in July and August.

➡ Rates often drop outside the high season – in some cases by as much as 50%.

➡ In business-oriented hotels in cities, rooms are most expensive from Monday to Friday and cheaper over the weekend.

Camping

There are many camping grounds throughout the region and they are all generally inexpensive. That said, a large proportion of the region's attractions are found in cities, where there are often no camping grounds. Most camping grounds near urban areas are large sites, intended mainly for motorists, though they're usually accessible by public transport and there's almost always space for backpackers with tents.

Many camping grounds in Eastern Europe rent small on-site cabins, bungalows or caravans for double or triple the regular camping fee; in the most popular resorts all the bungalows are usually full in July and August. Generally, camping grounds charge per tent, plus an extra fee per person.

The standard of camping grounds in Eastern Europe varies from country to country. They're unreliable in Romania, crowded in Slovenia and Hungary (especially on Lake Balaton), and variable in the Czech Republic, Poland, Slovakia and Bulgaria. Some countries, including Moldova and Belarus, have very few official camping grounds, but you can usually find somewhere to pitch your tent. Croatia's coast has nudist camping grounds galore (signposted FKK, the German acronym for 'naturist'); they're excellent places to stay because of their secluded locations, although they can be a bit far from other attractions.

➡ Camping grounds may be open from April to October, May to September, or perhaps only June to August, depending on the category of the facility, the location and demand.

➡ A few private camping grounds are open year-round.

➡ Camping in the wild is usually illegal; ask local

people about the situation before you pitch your tent on a beach or in an open field.

➡ In Eastern Europe you are sometimes allowed to build a campfire; ask first, however.

Farmhouses

'Village tourism', which means staying at a farmhouse, is highly developed in Estonia, Latvia, Lithuania and Slovenia, and popular in Hungary. It's like staying in a private room or pension, except that the participating farms are in picturesque rural areas and may have activities nearby such as horse riding, kayaking, skiing and cycling. See **World Wide Opportunities on Organic Farms** (www.wwoof.net) for information about working on organic farms in exchange for room and board.

Guesthouses & Pensions

Small private pensions are common in parts of Eastern Europe. Priced somewhere between hotels and private rooms, pensions typically have fewer than a dozen rooms and may sometimes have a small restaurant or bar on the premises. You'll get much more personal service at a pension than you would at a hotel, though there's a bit less privacy. Pensions can be a lifesaver if you arrive at night or on a weekend, when the travel agencies assigning private rooms are closed. Call ahead to check prices and ask about reservations – someone will usually speak some halting English, German or Russian.

Homestays, Private Rooms & Couchsurfing

Homestays are often the best and most authentic way to see daily life in Eastern Europe. If you want to take advantage of Eastern European hospitality, consider the following:

➡ In most Eastern European countries, travel agencies can arrange accommodation in private rooms in local homes. In Hungary you can get a private room almost anywhere, but in other countries only the main tourist centres have them. Some rooms are like mini-apartments, with cooking facilities and private bathrooms for the sole use of guests. Prices are low but there's often a 30% to 50% surcharge if you stay fewer than three nights. In Hungary, the Czech Republic and Croatia, higher taxation has added to the cost of a private room, but it's still good value and cheaper than a hotel.

➡ People may approach you at train or bus stations in Eastern Europe offering a private room or a hostel bed. This can be good or bad – it's impossible to generalise. Just make sure it's not in some cardboard-quality housing project in the outer suburbs and that you negotiate a clear price. Obviously, if you are staying with strangers, you don't leave your money, credit cards, passport or other essential valuables behind when you go out.

➡ You don't have to go through an agency or an intermediary on the street for a private room. Any house, cottage or farmhouse with *Zimmer Frei* (German), Сниму Комнату (Russian), *sobe* (Slovak) or *szoba kiadó* (Hungarian) displayed outside is advertising the availability of private rooms; just knock on the door and ask if any are available. However, in countries such as Russia or Belarus where visa registration is necessary, you may have to pay a travel agency to register your visa with a hotel.

➡ Online hospitality clubs, linking travellers with thousands of global

residents who'll let you occupy their couch or spare room – and sometimes show you around town – all cost free, include: **Couchsurfing** (www.couchsurfing.com); **Global Freeloaders** (www.globalfreeloaders.com); **Hospitality Club** (www.hospitalityclub.org); and **5W** (www.womenwelcomewomen.org.uk). Check the rules of each organisation.

➡ If you're staying for free with friends or strangers, make sure you bring some small gifts for your hosts – it's a deeply ingrained cultural tradition throughout the region. Flowers, chocolates or nicely packaged biscuits and cakes will work.

➡ Always let friends and family know where you're staying and carry your mobile phone with you. Single women should be especially careful of homestay situations – as well as following the general safety rules, if you get weird vibes from your host on arrival don't risk staying on.

Hostels

Hostels offer the cheapest roof over your head in Eastern Europe and you don't have to be young to take advantage of them. Most hostels are part of the national Youth Hostel Association (YHA), which is affiliated with the **Hostelling International** (HI; www.hihostels.com) umbrella organisation.

➡ Hostels affiliated with HI can be found in most Eastern European countries. A hostel card is seldom required, though you sometimes get a small discount if you have one.

➡ At a hostel, you get a bed for the night plus use of communal facilities; there's often a kitchen where you can prepare your own meals. You may be required to have a bed sheet or a sleeping bag; if you don't have one, you can usually hire one for a small fee.

➡ Hostels vary widely in their character and quality.

➡ A number of privately run hostels in Prague, Budapest, Moscow and St Petersburg are serious party venues, while many Hungarian hostels outside Budapest are student dormitories that are open to travellers for six or seven weeks in summer only.

➡ There are many hostel guides and websites with listings, including HI's *Europe*, the hostel bible. Many hostels accept reservations by phone or email, but not always during peak periods (though they might hold a bed for you for a couple of hours if you call from the train or bus station). You can also book beds through national hostel offices.

Hotels

At the bottom end of the scale, cheap hotels may be no more expensive than private rooms or guesthouses, while at the other extreme you'll find beautifully designed boutique hotels and five-star hotels with price tags to match.

➡ Single rooms can be hard to find in Eastern Europe, as you are generally charged by the room and not by the number of people in it.

➡ The cheapest rooms sometimes have a washbasin but no bathroom, which means you'll have to go down the corridor to use the toilet and shower.

➡ Breakfast may be included in the price of a room, or it may be extra.

Rental Accommodation

In larger cities sometimes a good option is to rent an apartment from a local agency. These can often be better value than a hotel, and you can self-cater and be far more independent, but they can also be of varying quality and some accommodation can be far flung. The agencies operate independently and sometimes quasi-legally, so you will have no recourse if you have a disagreement with them. The agencies we list have good reputations and we have generally used them ourselves.

➡ Cities where renting accommodation is a good idea include Prague, Budapest, Bratislava, Chişinău, Minsk, Kraków and Moscow.

➡ When dealing with agencies you've found online, never send money in advance unless you're sure they are genuine.

University Accommodation

Some universities rent out space in student halls in July and August. This is quite popular in the Baltic countries, Croatia, the Czech Republic, Hungary, Macedonia, Poland, Slovakia and Slovenia.

➡ Accommodation will sometimes be in single rooms (but is more commonly in doubles or triples) and will come with

shared bathrooms. Basic cooking facilities may be available.

➡ Enquire at the college or university, at student-information services or at local tourist offices.

Business Hours

➡ Saturday and Sunday are official days off, although only banks and offices are shut; most shops, restaurants and cafes are open every day of the week.

➡ Banks and offices are usually open from 9am to 5pm Monday to Friday, often with an hour or two off for lunch. They may also be open on Saturday mornings. Shops usually stay open until 7pm or later.

➡ During the hot summer months, some enterprises will shut for two or three hours in the early afternoon, reopening at 3pm or 4pm and working into the evening.

Children

Travelling with your children in Eastern Europe will be a treat and a challenge for the whole family. A couple of tips: avoid packing too much activity into the available time; and allow your children to help plan the trip so they will know what to look forward to and will be more engaged upon arrival.

A good resource is Lonely Planet's *Travel with Children*.

Practicalities

➡ In Eastern Europe most car-rental firms have children's safety seats for hire at a small cost, but it is essential that you book them in advance.

➡ High chairs and cots are standard in many restaurants and hotels, but numbers are limited.

➡ The choice of baby food, infant formulas, soy and cows' milk, disposable

---

EU COUNTRIES IN EASTERN EUROPE

The expansion of the European Union (EU) into Eastern Europe has continued in recent years with Croatia joining in 2013 and Albania, Macedonia, Montenegro and Serbia all set for future membership. Other current EU member countries are Bulgaria, the Czech Republic, Estonia, Hungary, Latvia, Lithuania, Poland, Romania, Slovakia and Slovenia.

nappies and the like is often as great in the Eastern European supermarkets as it is back home.

Discount Cards

Camping Card International

The **Camping Card International** (CCI; www.camping cardinternational.com) is an ID that can be used instead of a passport when checking into a camping ground. Many camping grounds offer a small discount if you sign in with one and it includes third-party insurance.

Hostel Cards

Hostels may charge you less if you have a **Hostelling International** (HI; www.hi hostels.com) card. Some hostels will issue one on the spot or after a few days' stay, though this might cost a bit more than getting it at home.

Rail Passes

The RailPlus card, entitling the holder to train fare reductions of 25% on purchase of standard train tickets for conventional international trains, if at least one border is crossed during the journey, can be used in many Eastern European countries. It costs €25 for those aged 12 to 26 and over 60 and €50 for those over 26 and up to 60.

If you plan to visit more than a few countries, or one or two countries in-depth, you might also save money with a rail pass.

Senior Cards

Many attractions offer reduced-price admission for people over 60 or 65 (or sometimes 55 for women). EU residents, especially, are eligible for discounts in many EU countries. Make sure you bring proof of age.

Before leaving home, check with an agency that caters to senior travel – such as **Elderhostel** (www.roadscholar.org) – for age-

related travel packages and discounts.

Student, Youth & Teacher Cards

The **International Student Identity Card** (www.isic.org), available for students, teachers and under-26s, offers thousands of worldwide discounts on transport, museum entry, youth hostels and even some restaurants. Apply for the cards online or via issuing offices, which include **STA Travel** (www.statravel.com).

For under-26s, there's also the **European Youth Card** (EURO<26; www.euro26.org). Many countries have raised the age limit for this card to under 30.

Electricity

Plugs in Eastern Europe are the standard round two-pin variety, sometimes called the europlug. If your plugs are of a different design, you'll need an adapter.

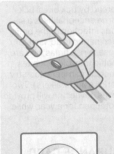

220V/50Hz

Embassies & Consulates

It's important to realise what your embassy can and

cannot do to help if you get into trouble while travelling abroad. Remember that you are bound by the laws of the country you are visiting. Generally speaking, your embassy cannot help much if your emergency is of your own making. It will not post bail or otherwise act to get you out of jail.

If your documents are lost or stolen, your embassy can assist you in obtaining a new passport; this is greatly simplified if you have a photocopy or scan of your passport. Your embassy may refer you to a lawyer or a doctor, but it is highly unlikely to provide any financial assistance, no matter what your emergency.

Gay & Lesbian Travellers

Consensual homosexual sex is legal across Eastern Europe. The laws do not signal an open-minded approach to sexual minorities, however.

➡ You are unlikely to raise any eyebrows by sharing a room (or a bed) with your same-sex partner. But in many countries, society frowns on overt displays of affection in any case – and even more so when it's between members of the same gender.

➡ Many countries have online forums and gay advocacy groups.

➡ Many Eastern European capitals have small, lively gay scenes, usually centred on one or two bars and clubs.

➡ Outside large towns, gay and lesbian life is invisible and the internet is the only realistic way to make contact with other gay people.

Health

Eastern Europe poses no big health risks to travellers, though as with anywhere else in the world there are several things you should be aware of.

Availability & Cost of Health Care

Good basic health care is readily available and pharmacists can give valuable advice and sell over-the-counter medication for minor illnesses. They can also advise when more specialised help is required and point you in the right direction.

The standard of dental care is usually good.

Medical care is not always readily available outside of major cities, but embassies, consulates and five-star hotels can usually recommend doctors or clinics. In some cases, medical supplies required in hospital may need to be bought from a pharmacy and nursing care may be limited. The usual precautions apply to help prevent transmission of hepatitis B and HIV/AIDS.

In general health-care costs are still relatively low in Eastern Europe and tend to be more expensive in EU member states than in non-EU member states; bear in mind, however, that in most non-EU states you'll probably want to go to a private clinic for anything more than a doctor's consultation and therefore comprehensive health insurance is essential.

Potential Illnesses or Conditions

INSECT BITES & STINGS

Mosquitoes are found in most parts of Europe. They may not carry malaria but can cause irritation and infected bites. Use insect repellent, plug in antimosquito devices and cover up your arms and legs in the evening.

RABIES

Spread through bites or licks from an infected animal on broken skin, rabies is always fatal unless treated promptly and is present throughout Eastern Europe. To be vaccinated, three injections are needed over a month. If you are bitten and have not been vaccinated, you will need a course of five injections starting 24 hours, or as soon as possible, after the injury. If you have been vaccinated, you will need fewer injections and have more time to seek medical help.

TICK-BORNE ENCEPHALITIS

Spread by tick bites, tick-borne encephalitis is a serious infection of the brain. Vaccination is advised for those in risk areas who are unable to avoid tick bites (such as campers, forestry workers and walkers). Two doses of vaccine will provide protection for a year, while three doses provide up to three years' protection. Anyone hiking in the Baltics and Russia for any length of time should consider vaccination, as reported cases have been steadily rising.

TRAVELLER'S DIARRHOEA

If you develop diarrhoea, be sure to drink plenty of fluids, preferably in the form of an oral rehydration solution (eg Dioralyte). A few loose stools don't require treatment, but if you start having more than four or five stools a day, you should start taking an antibiotic (usually a quinolone drug) and an antidiarrhoeal agent (such as loperamide). If diarrhoea is bloody, persists for more than 72 hours or is accompanied by fever, shaking, chills or severe abdominal pain, you should seek medical attention.

Water

Tap water may not be safe to drink, so it is best to stick to bottled water or boil water for 10 minutes, use water-purification tablets or a filter. Do not drink water from rivers or lakes, as it may contain bacteria or viruses that can cause diarrhoea or vomiting. Brushing your teeth with tap water is very unlikely to lead to problems, but use bottled water if you want to be very safe.

EUROPEAN HEALTH INSURANCE CARD

Citizens of the EU, Switzerland, Iceland, Norway and Liechtenstein receive free or reduced-cost state-provided health-care cover with the European Health Insurance Card (EHIC) for medical treatment that becomes necessary while in other EU countries. Every EU individual needs their own card. In the UK, you can apply online (www.ehic.org.uk/Internet/startApplication.do).

The EHIC does not cover private health care, so make sure that you are treated by a state health care provider. In EU countries where state-provided health care isn't free, you will need to pay yourself and fill in a treatment form; keep the form to claim any refunds. In general, you can claim back around 70% of the standard treatment cost.

Insurance

A travel-insurance policy to cover theft, loss and medical problems is always a good idea. The policies written by STA Travel and other student-travel organisations are usually good value.

➡ Some insurance policies will specifically exclude 'dangerous activities', which can include scuba diving, motorcycling and even hiking.

➡ Some policies even exclude certain countries, so read the fine print.

➡ Check that your policy covers ambulances and an emergency flight home.

➡ You may prefer a policy that pays doctors or hospitals directly rather than reimbursing your claims after the fact.

➡ Some policies ask you to call back (reverse charges) to a centre in your home country, where an immediate assessment of your problem is made.

➡ If you have to file a claim, make sure you keep all documentation.

➡ Worldwide travel insurance is available at http://www. lonelyplanet.com/travel-insurance. You can buy, extend and claim online at any time – even if you're already on the road.

Internet Access

With few exceptions, any decent-sized town in Eastern Europe has internet access in some shape or form.

Connections may be slow, there might not be coffee and you might be sitting in a smelly room full of teenage boys playing war games – but one way or another you'll never be far from the web, even in less-developed nations such as Albania and Moldova. Indeed, in some cities, internet cafes can be a social hub and a great way to meet locals as well as other travellers.

In general, however, the internet cafe is a thing of the past as wi-fi has become ubiquitous. Laptops and smartphones can easily connect in many cafes, bars, libraries, hotels, hostels and even public places.

It's now practically universal for hotels to have wi-fi in the rooms. A few still charge for this service (five-star international chains are the worst offenders), but nearly all boutique, midrange and budget hotels are more likely to offer it for free.

Legal Matters

➡ Cigarette-smoking bans in bars and restaurants and other public places are increasingly common across the region, so ask before lighting up.

➡ Drugs are available in the region, but that doesn't mean they are legal. They're generally to be avoided as getting caught with drugs can lead to imprisonment in places such as Russia.

Money

The main problem you'll face is constant currency changes as you flit between the crown, złoty, rouble, lei, lev, lek, dinar and various other national currencies.

There is no longer any particular desire for 'hard' currency (the days when hoteliers would slash the rates if you paid in US dollars are long gone), and the convertibility of almost all Eastern European currencies makes them a stable and reliable way to carry cash.

The euro remains the easiest currency to change throughout the region. It's the national currency in Estonia, Latvia, Lithuania, Kosovo, Montenegro, Slovakia and Slovenia.

Many other countries in Eastern Europe are hoping to adopt the euro in the future, though the global financial downturn has tempered enthusiasm in many quarters. That said, it's often possible to pay for services such as hotels and tours in euro in countries where it's not the currency: Albania, Belarus, Moldova and Russia are all very euro friendly, for example.

ATMs

Nearly all Eastern European countries have plenty of ATMs in their capitals and sizeable towns. Check the specific situation in your destination before setting

out from the big city – and never rely entirely on being able to find an ATM.

➡ Cash or debit cards can be used throughout Eastern Europe at ATMs linked to international networks such as Cirrus and Maestro.

➡ Check any bank fees you may pay for using an ATM before leaving home. The exchange rate is usually at a better rate than that offered for travellers cheques or cash exchanges.

➡ If you choose to rely on plastic, go for two different cards – this allows one to be used as backup in the case of loss or, more commonly, if a bank does not accept one card.

➡ A combination of cards and travellers cheques, so you have something to fall back on if there are no ATMs in the area or they accept local cards only, is better still.

Cash

➡ The two most favoured foreign currencies throughout Eastern Europe are the euro and the US dollar.

➡ Although it's not difficult to exchange other major world currencies in big cities, you are at the mercy of the exchange office and its rates.

➡ A far better option is to change your money into euros or US dollars before you leave home. Do note that in some places banks will not change damaged or worn notes. This is especially true in the former Soviet Union, so bring clean and newish notes from home, whenever possible.

Credit Cards

➡ Credit cards are becoming more commonly accepted. You'll be able to use them at upmarket restaurants, shops, hotels, car-rental firms, travel agencies and many petrol stations.

➡ Bear in mind that if you use a credit card for purchases,

exchange rates may have changed by the time your bill is processed, which can work out to your advantage or disadvantage.

→ Charge-card companies such as Amex have offices in most countries in Eastern Europe and, because they treat you as a customer of the company rather than of the bank that issued the card, they can generally replace a lost card within 24 hours.

→ Credit cards such as Visa and MasterCard are more widely accepted because they tend to charge merchants lower commissions.

Money Changers

Never exchange your hard-earned cash without first shopping around for a decent rate. If you happen to be in a tourist area, you will be offered crappy rates everywhere; for example around the Charles Bridge in Prague. In this case, don't bother shopping around – just leave for a less-touristy neighbourhood.

Border crossings, airports and train stations are typically places where rates aren't great, but many people change money here out of necessity.

Tipping

Tipping practices vary from country to country and often from place to place. In general, you can't go wrong if you add 10% onto your bill at a restaurant.

→ Porters at upmarket hotels will appreciate a few euros for their efforts.

→ In fashionable venues in urban centres, the wait staff will expect a tip; in rural locations you might astonish your server.

Travellers Cheques

It's become more difficult to find places that cash travellers cheques. In parts of Eastern Europe only a few

banks handle them, and the process can be quite bureaucratic and costly.

That said, having a few cheques is a good back up. If they're stolen you can claim a refund, provided you have a separate record of cheque numbers.

Amex and Thomas Cook are reliable brands of travellers cheques, while cheques in US dollars, euros or British pounds are the easiest to cash. When changing them ask about fees and commissions as well as the exchange rate.

Western Union

If everything goes horribly wrong – your money, travellers cheques and credit cards are all stolen – don't despair. While it's a terrible (and highly unusual) situation, a friend or relative back home will be able to wire money to you anywhere in Eastern Europe via Western Union (WU). There are literally thousands of WU representatives; just look for the distinctive yellow and black sign. The sender is given a code that they communicate to you, then you take the code to the nearest office, along with your passport, to receive your cash.

Photography & Video

→ Photographing military installations is never a good idea.

→ Ask permission before taking close-up photos of people.

→ Museums often demand that you buy permission to photograph or video their displays.

→ Digital memory, film and camera equipment are available everywhere in Eastern Europe, though you'll have a better selection in larger towns. It's generally possible to download photos to dongles or CDs in internet cafes or any photo shop in Eastern Europe.

→ Lonely Planet's guide to Travel Photography covers all aspects of travel photography.

Post

Both the efficiency and cost of the national postal systems in Eastern Europe vary enormously. There seems to be no set rules, but EU countries are likely to be faster, more reliable and more expensive than the non-EU states.

→ Postal service from Belarus, Moldova, Montenegro, Russia and Ukraine is slow, but the mail usually reaches its destination eventually. For added assurance and speed, most of these countries offer an express service.

→ To send a parcel from Eastern Europe you usually have to take it unwrapped to a main post office; parcels weighing more than 2kg often must be taken to a special customs post office. The post-office staff will usually wrap the parcels for you. The staff may ask to see your passport and note the number on the form; if you don't have a return address within the country put the address of any large tourist hotel.

→ If you desperately need something posted to you, do your research: find a friend of a friend who could receive the mail at their address, or ask nicely at a hotel you plan to stay at. You can also have mail sent to you at Amex offices if you have an Amex card or are carrying its travellers cheques.

Public Holidays

Throughout Eastern Europe, children get the summer months (usually much of July and all of August) off from school, which is one reason why this is the busiest time to go to the beach and other resorts.

There are also usually breaks for Easter and Christmas; keep in mind that dates for Orthodox Christmas and Easter are different to those of their Catholic and Protestant counterparts (though Easter sometimes falls on the same date by both calendars).

Even in countries with a large Muslim population, such as Bosnia & Hercegovina, and Albania, school holidays generally follow these guidelines.

Safe Travel

Eastern Europe is as safe – or unsafe – as any other part of the developed world. Handle yourself as you would in big cities back home – look purposeful, keep alert and you'll be OK.

Some locals will regale you with tales of how dangerous their city is and recount various cases of muggings, break-ins, kidnappings etc, often involving Roma or other popular scapegoats (other Eastern Europeans will tell you horror stories about the Romanians and Albanians). Most of these stories are exaggerated and you are unlikely to have any threatening encounters.

Corruption

➡ Low-level corruption is disappearing fast and is now rare for travellers to encounter. Do not pay bribes to people in official positions, such as police, border guards, train conductors and ticket inspectors.

➡ Be aware, however, that these anachronistic systems still exist in Belarus, Moldova, Russia and Transdniestr. If corrupt cops want to hold you up because some obscure stamp is missing from your documentation or on some other pretext, just let them and consider the experience an integral part of your trip. Insisting on calling

your embassy is always a good move; officers are likely to receive some grief if their superiors learn they are harassing tourists.

➡ If you're taken to the police station for questioning, you'll have the opportunity to observe the quality of justice in that country from the inside. In most cases, the more senior officers will eventually let you go (assuming, of course, you haven't committed a real crime).

➡ If you do have to pay a fine or supplementary charge, insist on a proper receipt before turning over any money; this is now law in Hungary, for example, where traffic police were once notorious for demanding 'gifts' from motorists guilty of some alleged infraction. In all of this, try to maintain your cool, as any threats from you will only make matters worse.

Landmines

Bosnia & Hercegovina, and Kosovo still have landmines in remote areas. Ask locals for the latest situation and stick to established roads and paths in places where mines are still a problem.

Scams

➡ Fraudulent shopkeepers have been known to make several charge-slip imprints with your credit card when you're not looking and then simply copy your signature from the authorised slip.

➡ There have also been reports of people making duplicates of credit- or debit-card information with high-tech machines. If your card leaves your sight for longer than you think necessary, consider cancelling it.

➡ There is no longer a black market for currency exchange in this region. The days of getting five times the official rate for cash on the streets of Warsaw and Bucharest are well

and truly over. Anyone who approaches you offering such a deal (an uncommon occurrence these days) is an outright thief.

Theft

Definitely a problem in Eastern Europe and the threat comes from both local thieves and fellow travellers. The most important things to guard are your passport, other documents (such as a driving licence), tickets and money – in that order.

➡ It's always best to carry these items in a sturdy pouch on your belt or under your shirt. Train-station lockers or luggage-storage counters are useful to store your luggage (but not valuables) while you get your bearings in a new town. Be very suspicious of people who offer to help you operate your locker.

➡ A small daypack is more secure than a camera or shoulder bag, but watch your rear and don't keep valuables in the outside pockets. Loop the strap around your leg while seated at bars or cafes.

➡ Pickpockets are most active in dense crowds, especially in busy train stations and on public transport during peak hours.

➡ Don't leave valuables lying around in your hotel room. Carry your own padlock for hostel lockers and always use them.

➡ Parked cars containing luggage or other bags are prime targets for petty criminals, and cars with foreign number plates and/or rental-agency stickers attract particular attention. While driving in cities, beware of snatch thieves when you pull up at the lights – keep doors locked and windows rolled up.

➡ In the case of theft or loss, always report the incident to the police and ask for a statement; otherwise your travel-insurance company won't pay up.

Violence

It's unlikely that travellers will encounter any violence while in Eastern Europe. Be aware, however, that many countries in the region have thriving neo-Nazi movements, which tend to target local Roma populations as well as non-Caucasian travellers.

Russian neo-Nazis have been known to seek out fights with nonwhite people on Hitler's birthday (20 April); St Petersburg in particular has seen an extraordinary amount of violence against ethnic minorities – and not only on this date.

Telephone

Telephone services in Eastern Europe are generally excellent. The mobile phone is king across the region; most cities have call centres too, although they're used less and less. Call centres tend to be the domain of entrepreneurs who offer discounted rates, although there are also state-run call centres, which are often in the same building as the main post office. Here you can usually make your call from one of the booths inside an enclosed area, paying the cashier as you leave. Public telephones are almost always found at post offices.

Mobile Phones

→ Mobile phones operate on the GSM standard.

Compatible handsets will connect automatically with local providers, but watch for high roaming fees, particularly for data downloads.

→ If you plan to spend more than a week or so in any one country, consider buying a SIM card to slip into your phone, although you'll need to check with your provider at home that your handset has been unlocked.

→ SIM cards can cost as little as €5 and can be topped up with cards available at supermarkets, kiosks, newsagents and mobile-phone dealers. With a smartphone, you can use a local SIM card for data as well.

→ Alternatively, if you have roaming, your phone will usually switch automatically over to a local network. This can be expensive if you use the phone a great deal, but can be very useful for ad hoc and emergency use.

Phone Codes

→ To call abroad from a landline you simply dial the international access code for the country you are calling from (most commonly ☑00 in Eastern Europe, but ☑8-10 in Belarus and Russia).

→ From a mobile phone simply dial + followed by the country code, the city code and the local number.

→ To make a domestic call to another city in the same country, you generally need to dial the area code (with the initial zero) and the number; however, in some countries the area code is an integral part of the phone number and must be dialled every time – even if you're just calling next door.

Phonecards

Local telephone cards are available from post offices, telephone centres, newsstands or retail outlets. In any given country, there's a wide range of local and international phonecards available. For local calls you're usually better off with a local phonecard.

Time

→ Eastern Europe spans three time zones: Central European Time (GMT+ one hour), Eastern European Time (GMT+ two hours) and Moscow Time (GMT+ three hours). At noon in New York, it's 6pm in Warsaw, 7pm in Minsk and 8pm in Moscow.

→ All countries, except Russia, employ daylight savings. Clocks are put forward an hour at the start of daylight savings, usually on the last Sunday in March. They are set back one hour on the last Sunday in October.

Toilets

→ The vast majority of toilets you use will be modern, sit-down, flushing toilets.

→ In Russia, Belarus, Ukraine and Moldova, however, you can expect to find smelly and rather unpleasant squat toilets in bus and train stations, though they are very rare in restaurants or hotels.

→ You'll need to pay a small fee to use most public toilets in Eastern Europe.

→ Using hotel or restaurant facilities is nearly always free and one way to ensure you'll be using a clean bathroom.

Tourist Information

Countries that have successfully realised their potential as holiday destinations have developed a network of excellent tourist information centres (TICs). However, there are still many countries that take little or no interest in the economic benefits tourism can bring.

➡ Countries in the latter category are Ukraine, Belarus and Moldova. Russia is similarly badly organised, though there are TICs in St Petersburg.

➡ Among the best prepared are Slovakia, Slovenia, Croatia, the Czech Republic, Hungary, Poland and Bulgaria, many of which have tourist offices abroad as well as throughout the country.

Travellers with Disabilities

Eastern Europe is a mixed bag for less able travellers. While individual museums and hotels are slowly being brought up to Western European standards of accessibility, there is little coordinated effort to improve things regionally.

➡ In general, wheelchair-accessible rooms are available only at top-end hotels (and are limited, so be sure to book in advance). Rental cars and taxis may be accessible, but public transport rarely is. Most major museums and sites have disabled access, although there are many exceptions.

➡ If you have a physical disability, get in touch with your national support organisation (preferably the travel officer if there is one) and ask about the countries you plan to visit. The organisations often have libraries devoted to travel, including access guides, and staff can put you in touch with travel agencies who specialise in tours for the disabled.

➡ **Disibility Rights UK** (www.radar.org.uk) is a very helpful association and sells a number of publications for people with disabilities.

Visas

Visas are only necessary for anyone wanting to explore the region's eastern extremities – all visitors to Russia and Belarus still require a visa, while several nationalities still require visas for Moldova and Ukraine.

➡ In line with the Schengen Agreement, there are no longer passport controls at the borders between most EU countries, but procedures between EU and non-EU countries can still be fairly thorough.

➡ If you do need to get a visa, note it has an expiration date and you'll be refused entry after that period has elapsed. Consulates sometimes issue visas on the spot, although some levy a 50% to 100% surcharge for 'express service'. If there's a choice, get a visa in advance; they're often cheaper in your home country and this can save on bureaucratic procedure.

➡ Decide in advance if you want a tourist or transit visa; transit visas, usually valid for just 48 or 72 hours, are often cheaper and issued faster, but it's usually not possible to extend a transit visa or change it to a tourist visa.

➡ Some countries require visitors to register with the local authorities within 48 hours of arrival, supposedly so they know where you are staying. If you're staying at a hotel or other official accommodation, the administration will take care of this registration for you.

➡ If you're staying with friends, relatives or in a private room, you're supposed to register with the police yourself. In some cases, this is a formality that is never enforced, so you can skip it. In other cases (such as Russia), you can be fined if you do not go through the motions.

➡ Obtaining registration through the proper channels is a major hassle, often requiring fluent language skills, a pile of documents and several hours of negotiation. You are better off paying a local travel agency for the registration instead of trying to do it yourself.

➡ The hassles created by losing your passport and visa can be considerably reduced if you have a record of its number and issue date or, even better, photocopies of the relevant data pages.

EASTERN EUROPE TIME ZONES

TIME ZONE	LOCATIONS
Central Europe (GMT+ 1hr)	Albania, Bosnia & Hercegovina, Croatia, Czech Republic, Hungary, Kosovo, Macedonia, Montenegro, Poland, Serbia, Slovakia and Slovenia
Eastern Europe (GMT+ 2hrs)	Belarus, Bulgaria, Estonia, Kaliningrad, Latvia, Lithuania, Moldova, Romania and Ukraine
Moscow (GMT+ 3hrs)	Moscow and St Petersburg

A photocopy of your birth certificate can also be useful.

Women Travellers

Women travellers will find that Eastern Europe is a safe and welcoming place to travel, whether you're with company or on your own.

However, it is not unusual for women to be propositioned by strangers on the street, which can be annoying and even feel threatening, but rarely anything more. As a rule, foreigners are still a little exotic and therefore attract more attention, but this attention is rarely dangerous and is easily deflected with a shake of the head and a firm 'no'. Do remember that in much of the Balkans a nod of the head means no, not yes, though! Use the local language if you can, but English usually works fine, too.

In Muslim countries, women travelling solo will certainly be of interest or curiosity to both local men and women. In Albania, and Bosnia & Hercegovina, women may feel self-conscious in bars and cafes outside larger cities, which are usually populated only by men. Unmarried men rarely have contact with women outside their family unit and so may shower travelling women with too much attention. (In such areas, women travelling with a male companion will often experience the opposite and may need to pinch themselves as a reminder that yes, they actually exist.)

Work

EU citizens have free rein to work in many countries in the region. However, with unemployment still a problem, Eastern European countries aren't always keen on handing out jobs to foreigners.

If you're not an EU citizen, the paperwork involved in arranging a work permit can be almost impossible, especially for temporary work. That doesn't prevent enterprising travellers from topping up their funds occasionally – and they don't always have to do this illegally. If you do find a temporary job in Eastern Europe, though, the pay is likely to be low. Do it for the experience, not to earn your fortune.

➡ Teaching English is the easiest way to make some extra cash, but the market is saturated in places such as Prague and Budapest. You'll probably be much more successful in less popular places such as Sofia and Bucharest.

➡ If you play an instrument or have other artistic talents, you could try working the streets. Some countries may require municipal permits for this sort of thing, so talk to other street artists before you start.

➡ *Work Your Way Around the World* by Susan Griffith gives good, practical advice on a wide range of issues.

➡ Volunteer work is another great way to gain a deeper insight into local culture. In some instances volunteers are paid a living allowance, sometimes they work for their keep and sometimes they are required to pay to undertake the program. Lonely Planet's *Volunteer* is filled with practical information.

➡ Several websites can help you search for volunteer work opportunities in Eastern Europe. The **Coordinating Committee for International Voluntary Service** (www.ccivs.org) is an umbrella organisation, with more than 140 member organisations worldwide. It's useful if you want to find out about your country's national volunteer-placement agency. Also check **Transitions Abroad** (www.transitionsabroad.com) to search for vacancies and other volunteering opportunities in Eastern Europe.

Transport

GETTING THERE & AWAY

Flights, cars and tours can be booked online at www.lonelyplanet.com/bookings.

Entering Eastern Europe

All Eastern European countries require travellers to have a valid passport, preferably with at least six months between the time of departure and the passport's expiration date.

EU travellers from countries that issue national identity cards are increasingly using them to travel within the EU, although it's impossible to use them as sole travel documents outside the EU.

Some countries require certain nationalities to buy certain visas allowing entry between certain dates. Specifically, Belarus and Russia require nearly all nationalities to obtain visas, while Aussie and Kiwi travellers also need visas to enter Moldova and Ukraine. Other nationalities may have additional requirements.

Air

Airports

Moscow (Russia), Prague (Czech Republic), Budapest (Hungary) and Warsaw (Poland) are the region's best-connected air hubs. They all have transatlantic flights as well as plenty of flights from Western Europe; they are also well served by budget airlines. Other smaller hubs are St Petersburg (Russia), Rīga (Latvia), Timişoara (Romania), Zagreb (Croatia), Kyiv (Ukraine) and Bratislava (Slovakia), all of which have daily flights to many major European cities. Most of the small hubs also have budget-airline connections, although as a rule the further east you go the fewer there are.

Land

Bus

Buses are always a useful fallback if there are no trains or flights to your destination. As a means for travelling from Western Europe they are also reliably cheap.

Eurolines (www.eurolines.com) Has a vast network with member companies in many Eastern European countries and offers innumerable routes across the continent.

Ecolines (http://ecolines.net/en) Also runs buses between Eastern and Western Europe.

Car & Motorcycle

Travelling by car or motorcycle into Eastern Europe gives travellers an immense amount of freedom and is generally worry free.

If you're driving a car into Eastern Europe, keep in mind

CLIMATE CHANGE & TRAVEL

Every form of transport that relies on carbon-based fuel generates CO_2, the main cause of human-induced climate change. Modern travel is dependent on aeroplanes, which might use less fuel per kilometre per person than most cars but travel much greater distances. The altitude at which aircraft emit gases (including CO_2) and particles also contributes to their climate change impact. Many websites offer 'carbon calculators' that allow people to estimate the carbon emissions generated by their journey and, for those who wish to do so, to offset the impact of the greenhouse gases emitted with contributions to portfolios of climate-friendly initiatives throughout the world. Lonely Planet offsets the carbon footprint of all staff and author travel.

that some insurance packages, especially those covering rental cars, do not include all European countries. Be sure to ask the agency to insure the car in all the countries where you plan to travel. It's outright forbidden to take rental cars into certain countries.

Train

There are numerous routes into the region by train. Major railway hubs are Prague (Czech Republic), Budapest (Hungary), Bucharest (Romania), Belgrade (Serbia) and Moscow (Russia).

Albania, however, has no international train services at all.

From Asia, the Trans-Siberian, Trans-Mongolian and Trans-Manchurian Railways connect Moscow to the Russian Far East, China, North Korea and Mongolia. Central Asian cities such as Tashkent (Uzbekistan) and Almaty (Kazakhstan) are regularly connected by long-distance trains to

Moscow. Overnight trains also connect Belgrade, Bucharest, Budapest, Sofia (Bulgaria) and Zagreb with İstanbul (Turkey).

Sea

Boats from several companies regularly connect Italy with Croatia, Slovenia, Montenegro and Albania; there are also services between Corfu (Greece) and Albania.

Ferries also ply the Gulf of Finland and Baltic Sea, connecting Helsinki (Finland) and Stockholm (Sweden) with Tallinn (Estonia), St Petersburg (Russia) and Rīga (Latvia). In Poland, Gdańsk and Gdynia are linked to Sweden and Denmark.

GETTING AROUND

The Schengen Agreement, which allows for passport-free travel within a large chunk of Europe, includes Czech Republic, Slovakia,

Hungary, Slovenia, Poland, Estonia, Latvia and Lithuania. Bulgaria, Croatia and Romania are also prospective Schengen-area members; for up to date details see www.schengenvisainfo.com.

Air

The major Eastern European cities are connected by a full schedule of regular flights within the region. Budget airline prices are competitive with trains and even buses.

Many countries offer domestic flights, although there is rarely a need to fly internally unless you are in a particular rush. Russia is the exception; flying from either Moscow or St Petersburg to Kaliningrad saves the trouble of getting a double-entry Russian visa. If you travel to Kaliningrad by boat or land, you are given an exit stamp, making your single-entry visa invalid.

AT YOUR OWN RISK

Russia–Belarus Border

There is effectively no border between Russia and Belarus. In theory, it's possible to enter Belarus by train and leave it for Russia – or go to Russia and back from Belarus – without going through passport control, and therefore without needing a visa for the country you're entering. However, a hotel won't take you without a visa, so you'd have to stay with friends or rent an apartment, and if your visa-less documents are checked on the street, you will be deported.

If you do not receive a migration card when entering Russia, contact your embassy immediately upon arrival to find out how to get one. If you do not receive an entry stamp, go to the local OVIR (Visa and Registration) office in Russia – but bring a full supply of patience.

A much better option if you plan to travel from Belarus into Russia is to ensure you have a valid visa for Russia as well. This will be stamped by Belarusian control on entry to Belarus and, under the terms of the Russian–Belarusian 'one state' agreement, is valid as an entry stamp for Russia. Keep your immigration card from Belarus and use it when you leave Russia, as they are valid in both countries.

Russia–Ukraine Border

At the time of writing, because of the dangerous situation with regard to separatists in the east of the country, and the annexation of Crimea in 2014, scores of border posts between Russia and Ukraine were closed. There are, however, still 39 open borders posts between the two countries and trains regularly connect Kyiv with Moscow.

Bicycle

Eastern Europe is compact enough to make it ideal for a cycling trip and mountainous enough to ensure that it will be challenging.

If you are planning a tour of the region by bike, contact one of the following helpful cycling clubs:

Cyclists' Touring Club (CTC; www.ctc.org.uk) Offers members an information service on all matters associated with cycling, including maps, cycling conditions, itineraries and detailed routes.

European Cyclists' Federation (www.ecf.com) Advocates bike-friendly policies and organises tours. Also manages EuroVelo, a project to create bike routes across the continent.

Hire

Except in a few of the more visited regions, it can be difficult to hire bikes. The best spots are often camping grounds and resort hotels during the summer months, or hostels in the major cities.

Transporting a Bicycle

When flying with your own bike, either take it apart and pack all the pieces in a bike bag or box, or simply wheel it to the check-in desk, where it should be treated as a piece of check-in luggage.

Bikes can usually be transported on trains as luggage, subject to a fairly small supplementary fee. If it's possible, book tickets in advance. Alternatively you can look into sending your bike on to your desired destination on a cargo train.

Tours

Plenty of companies offer organised cycling tours of Eastern Europe. These specialist companies generally plan the itinerary, organise accommodation and transport luggage, making life a lot simpler for cyclists:

BaltiCCycle.eu (http://velo vilnius.lt/balticcycle/?q=1st page2011x.html) Promotes cycling in the Baltic countries and provides information on routes, maps and bike rental.

Experience Plus (www. experienceplus.com) Runs tours throughout the region, including Croatia, along the Danube from Budapest to the Black Sea, and cycling through the heart of the Balkans.

Top Bicycle (www.topbicycle. com) This Czech company offers cycling tours of the Czech Republic and Slovakia, as well as more extensive tours around the region.

Velo Touring (www.velo-touring.hu) Based in Budapest, this company offers tours of Hungary, as well as bike rentals for those who want to go it alone.

Boat

Eastern Europe's rivers, canals, lakes and seas provide rich opportunities for boat travel, although in almost all cases these are very much pleasure cruises rather than particularly practical ways to get around. Boat travel is usually far more expensive than the equivalent bus or train journey, but that's not necessarily the point.

Bus

Buses are a viable alternative to the rail network in most Eastern European countries. Generally they tend to complement the rail system rather than duplicate it, though in some countries – notably Hungary, the Czech Republic and Slovakia – you'll almost always have a choice between the two options.

➡ Buses tend to be best for shorter hops, getting around cities and reaching remote rural villages. They are often the only option in mountainous regions.

➡ In general, buses are slightly cheaper and slower than trains. The ticketing system varies in each country, but advance reservations are rarely necessary. On long-distance buses you can usually pay upon boarding, although it's safest to buy your ticket in advance at the station.

➡ The only company covering the majority of the region is **Eurolines** (www. eurolines.com).

Car & Motorcycle

Travelling with your own vehicle allows you increased flexibility and the option to get off the beaten track. However, cars can be inconvenient in city centres when you have to negotiate strange one-way systems or find somewhere to park in the narrow streets of old towns.

➡ Theft from vehicles is a problem in many parts of the region – never leave valuables in your car.

➡ Russia, Belarus and Ukraine still remain tediously difficult places to drive into – border controls can take a long time and bribes are often the order of the day.

➡ It is definitely not recommended to drive a rental car from Serbia into Kosovo, and vice versa.

Driving Licence & Documentation

Proof of ownership of a private vehicle should always be carried when driving in Eastern Europe.

➡ An EU driving licence may be used throughout most of Eastern Europe, as may North American and Australian ones. If you want to be extra cautious – or if you have any other type of licence – you should obtain an International Driving Permit (IDP).

➔ Always double-check which type of licence is required in your chosen destination before departure.

Fuel & Spare Parts

Fuel prices vary considerably from country to country.

➔ Russia is the cheapest spot, followed by Romania, which has prices half those of neighbouring Hungary.

➔ Unleaded petrol of 95 or 98 octane is widely available throughout the region and it's slightly cheaper than super (premium grade). Diesel is usually significantly cheaper than petrol in Eastern Europe.

➔ Spare parts are widely available from garages and dealerships around the region, although this is less the case in Belarus, Moldova and Ukraine, and of course in more rural areas.

Hire

➔ The big international companies will give you reliable service and a good standard of vehicle. Prebooked rates are generally lower than walk-in rates at rental offices, but either way you'll pay about 20% to 40% more than in Western Europe.

➔ Local companies will usually offer lower prices than the multinationals, but it's best to use ones with good reputations; try asking at your hotel.

➔ Bear in mind that many companies will not allow you to take cars into certain countries. Russia, Belarus, Moldova and Kosovo all regularly feature on forbidden lists; check in advance with the car-hire company you're planning to use.

Insurance

Third-party motor insurance is compulsory throughout the EU. For non-EU countries make sure you check the requirements with your insurer.

For more information contact the **Association of British Insurers** (www.abi.org.uk).

➔ Get your insurer to issue a Green Card (which may cost extra), an internationally recognised proof of insurance, and check that it lists all the countries you intend to visit.

➔ If the Green Card doesn't list one of the countries you're visiting and your insurer cannot (or will not) add it, you will have to take out separate third-party cover at the border of the country in question. This may be the case for Bulgaria, Macedonia, Russia and the Baltic states. Allow extra time at borders to purchase insurance.

➔ The European Accident Statement is available from your insurance company and allows each party at an accident to record information for insurance purposes. The Association of British Insurers has more details. Never sign an accident statement you cannot understand – insist on a translation and sign only if it's acceptable.

➔ Taking out a European breakdown-assistance policy, such as those offered by the **AA** (www.theaa.com) and **RAC** (www.rac.co.uk), is a good investment.

➔ Non-Europeans might find it cheaper to arrange for international coverage with their own national motoring organisation before leaving home. Ask about reciprocal services offered by affiliated organisations around Europe.

Road Rules

Motoring organisations can supply members with country-by-country information on motoring regulations, or they may produce motoring guidebooks for general sale.

Driving in Eastern Europe can be much more dangerous than in Western Europe.

Driving at night can be particularly hazardous in rural areas as the roads are often narrow and winding, and you may encounter horse-drawn vehicles, cyclists, pedestrians and domestic animals. In the event of an accident, you're supposed to notify the police and file an insurance claim.

If your car has significant body damage from a previous accident, point this out to customs upon arrival in the country and have it noted somewhere. Damaged vehicles may only be allowed to leave the country with police permission.

Standard international road signs are used in Eastern Europe. When driving in the region, keep the following rules in mind:

➔ Drive on the right-hand side of the road and overtake on the left.

➔ Don't overtake more than one car at a time.

➔ Seatbelts are mandatory for the driver and all passengers.

➔ Motorcyclists (and their passengers) must wear a helmet.

➔ Children under 12 and intoxicated passengers are not allowed to sit in the front seat in most countries.

➔ Drink-driving is a serious offence – most Eastern European countries have a 0% blood-alcohol concentration (BAC) limit.

➔ When two roads of equal importance intersect, the vehicle coming from the right has right of way unless signs indicate otherwise; in many countries this rule also applies to cyclists, so take care.

➔ Trams have priority at crossroads and when they are turning right.

➔ Don't pass a tram that's stopping to let off passengers until everyone is out and the doors have closed again.

→ Never pass a tram on the left or stop within 1m of tram tracks. A police officer who sees you blocking a tram route by waiting to turn left will flag you over.

→ It's usually illegal to stop or park at the top of slopes, in front of pedestrian crossings, at bus or tram stops, on bridges or at level crossings.

→ Speed limits are posted, and are generally 110km/h or 120km/h on motorways; 100km/h on highways; 80km/h on secondary and tertiary roads; 50km/h or 60km/h in built-up areas.

→ Motorcycles are usually limited to 90km/h on motorways, and vehicles with trailers to 80km/h.

→ Traffic police usually administer fines on the spot; always ask for a receipt.

→ Almost everywhere in Europe it is compulsory to carry a red warning triangle, which you must use when parking on a highway in an emergency. If you don't use the triangle and another vehicle hits you from behind, you will be held responsible.

→ A first-aid kit and a fire extinguisher are also required in most Eastern European countries, while a spare-bulb kit and headlamp converters are recommended.

Hitching

Hitching is never entirely safe in any country and we don't recommend it. Travellers who decide to hitch should understand they are taking a small but potentially serious risk.

Because public transport remains relatively cheap in Eastern Europe, hitching is more for the adventure than for the transport. In the former Soviet Union, Albania and Romania, drivers expect riders to pay the equivalent of a bus fare. In Romania, traffic is light, motorists are probably not going far and you'll often face small vehicles overloaded with passengers.

If you want to give it a try, remember the following key points:

→ Hitch in pairs; it will be safer.

→ Solo women should never hitch.

→ Don't hitch from city centres; take public transport to suburban exit routes.

→ Make a clearly written cardboard sign indicating your intended destination, remembering to use the local name for the town or city (Praha not Prague, or Warszawa not Warsaw).

→ Don't let your luggage be put in the boot, only sit next to a door you can open and ask drivers where they are going before you say where you're going.

→ Always let someone know where you're going before heading off.

Local Transport

Eastern Europe has generally good public transport. There are excellent metro networks in Moscow and St Petersburg (Russia), Warsaw (Poland), Prague (Czech Republic), Kyiv (Ukraine), Minsk (Belarus), Budapest (Hungary), Bucharest (Romania) and Sofia (Bulgaria).

Throughout the region, you'll also come across shared minibuses (*marshrutka* in the former Soviet Union, *furgon* in the Balkans) used as both inter- and intra-city transport. It's the most likely way you'll travel between mountain towns in Albania, for example.

Trolleybuses are another phenomenon of Eastern Europe. Although slow, they are environmentally friendly (being powered by electricity) and can be found throughout the former Soviet Union.

Trams are also popular, though they vary greatly in speed and modernity. Those in Russia are often borderline antiques, while Prague's fleet of sleek trams have electronic destination displays and automated announcements.

Tours

A package tour is generally worth considering only if your time is limited or you have a special interest such as skiing, canoeing, sailing, horse riding, cycling or spa treatments.

Cruises on the Danube are an exciting and romantic way to see Europe's most famous river, but they are not cheap.

Most tour prices are for double occupancy, which means singles have to share a double room with someone of the same sex or pay a supplement to have the room to themselves.

Regent Holidays (www.regent-holidays.co.uk) UK-based company offering comprehensive individual and group tours, covering all points from the Baltic to Albania.

Baltic Holidays (www.balticholidays.com) British-Lithuanian company running tours of the Baltic region and northwest Russia, including weekend city breaks, family holidays, spa breaks and activity tours.

Eastern Europe Russian Travel Centre (www.eetbtravel.com) Australia-based company offering dozens of upmarket tours to the whole region, but particularly Russia; it also offers river cruises.

Road Scholar (www.roadscholar.org) Offers educational tours for people over 50 throughout Russia, the Baltic countries, the Balkans and Central Europe.

Train

Trains are the most atmospheric, comfortable and fun way to make long overland journeys in Eastern Europe. All major cities are on the rail network and it's perfectly feasible for train travel to be your only form of intercity transport. In general, trains run like clockwork and you can expect to arrive pretty much to the timetabled minute.

➡ If you're travelling overnight (which is often the case when you're going between countries), you'll get a bed reservation included in the price of your ticket, although you may have to pay a few euros extra for the bedding once on board.

➡ Each carriage is administered by a steward, who will look after your ticket and – crucially, if you arrive during the small hours – make sure that you get off at the correct stop.

➡ Each carriage has a toilet and washbasin at either end – the state of cleanliness varies. Be aware that toilets may be closed while the train is at a station and for a good 30 minutes before you arrive in a big city.

➡ Overnight trains also have the benefit of saving you a night's accommodation. It's a great way to meet locals – and it's not unusual to be invited for dinner or even to stay for a night or two with people who shared your cabin.

Reservations

It's always advisable to buy a ticket in advance. Seat reservations are also recommended, but are only necessary if the timetable specifies one is required. On busy routes and during the summer, however, always try to reserve a seat several days in advance.

➡ You can book most routes in the region from any main station in Eastern Europe.

➡ For peace of mind, you may prefer to book tickets via travel agencies before you leave home, although this will be more expensive than booking on arrival.

Resources

If you plan to travel extensively by train, it might be worth checking the following resources:

DB Bahn (www.reiseauskunft. bahn.de) A particularly useful resource of timetables and fares for trains all across Eastern Europe; the website is available in many languages, including English.

European Rail Timetable (www.europeanrailtimetable. co.uk) Buy complete listing of train schedules, updated monthly, that indicates where supplements apply or where reservations are necessary.

Voyages-sncf.com (http://uk.voyages-sncf.com/en) Provides information on fares and passes as well as schedules for across Europe.

Safety

Trains, while generally safe, can attract petty criminals. Carry your valuables on you at all times – don't even go to the bathroom without taking your cash, wallet and passport.

➡ If you are sharing a compartment with others, you'll have to decide whether or not you trust them. If there's any doubt, be very cautious about leaving the compartment. At night, make sure your door is locked from the inside and your valuables are in your money belt or hidden in your luggage under the bed (which usually can't be accessed when someone is lying down).

➡ If you have a compartment to yourself, you can ask the steward to lock it while you go to the dining car or go for a wander outside when the train is stopped. However, be aware that most criminals strike when they can easily disembark from the train and on occasions the stewards are complicit.

➡ In the former Soviet Union, opinions vary on open-plan 3rd-class

accommodation – with so many people observing the carriage's goings-on it can be argued these are actually safer than the 2nd- and 1st-class compartments.

Train Classes

The system of train classes in Eastern Europe is similar to that in Western Europe. Short trips, or longer ones that don't involve sleeping on the train, are usually seated like a normal train: benches (on suburban trains) or aeroplane-style seats (on smarter intercity services).

There are generally three classes of sleeping accommodation on trains: each country has a different name for them, but for the sake of simplicity we'll call them 3rd, 2nd and 1st class. While it's reasonably priced, train travel costs more than bus travel in some countries. First-class tickets are double the price of 2nd-class tickets, which are in turn approximately twice the price of 3rd-class tickets.

Third class Generally consists of six berths in each compartment and is the cheapest option; you may feel your privacy has been slightly invaded. In the former Soviet Union, 3rd class is called *platskartny* and does not have compartments; instead, there's just one open-plan carriage with beds everywhere. Third-class is not widely available.

Second class Known as *kupe* in the former Soviet Union, 2nd class has four berths in a closed compartment. If there are two of you, you will share your accommodation with two others. However, if there are three of you, you'll often have the compartment to yourselves.

First class SV or *myagky* in the former Soviet Union is a treat, although generally you are paying for space rather than decor. Here you'll find two berths in a compartment plus, possibly, other amenities such as TV.

Train Passes

Not all countries in Eastern Europe are covered by rail passes, but passes do include a number of destinations and so can be worthwhile if you are concentrating your travels on a particular part of the region. These are available online or through most travel agents. Check out the excellent summary of available passes, and their pros and cons, at **Man In Seat 61** (www.seat61.com).

Keep in mind that all passes offer discounted 'youth' prices for travellers who are under 26 years of age on the first day of travel. Those aged four to 11 are eligible for a child rate. Discounted fares are also available if you are travelling in a group of two to five people (although you must always travel together).

In the USA and Australia, you can buy passes through **Rail Europe** (www.raileurope.com and www.raileurope.com.au); in Australia you can also use **Rail Plus** (www.railplus.com.au) or **International Rail** (www.internationalrail.com.au).

BALKAN FLEXIPASS

The Balkan Flexipass covers Bosnia and Herzegovina, Bulgaria, Greece, Macedonia, Montenegro, Romania, Serbia and Turkey. It is not available to anyone who is a resident of Europe, Morocco, Turkey or any of the countries of the former Soviet Union. It's valid for 1st-class travel only. In the USA, Rail Europe charges US$219/175/131/110 per adult/senior (60 plus)/youth/child for five days of 1st-class travel within one month; passes for 10 or 15 days of travel are also available.

EURAIL GLOBAL

The famous **Eurail pass** (www.eurail.com) allows the greatest flexibility for 'overseas' visitors only; if you are a resident of Europe, check out the InterRail Pass. The Eurail Global pass allows unlimited travel in up to 28 countries, including Croatia, the Czech Republic, Hungary, Romania and Slovenia. The pass is valid for a set number of consecutive days or a set number of days within a period of time.

EURAIL SELECT

Again, only non-European residents can purchase this pass, which covers travel in four neighbouring countries, which you choose from the 26 available. Your Eastern European options include Bulgaria, Croatia, the Czech Republic, Hungary, Montenegro, Romania, Serbia and Slovenia. Note that Serbia and Montenegro count as one country for Eurail pass purposes, as do Croatia and Slovenia, so the clever traveller can get five countries for the price of four.

From Rail Europe this would be US$195/157 per adult/youth for five days of 1st-class travel over two months; there is also a youth fare of $129 for 2nd class. Additional days of travel are available for a higher cost.

INTERRAIL GLOBAL

These passes are available to European residents of more than six months' standing (passport identification is required), although residents of Turkey and parts of North Africa can also buy them. Terms and conditions vary slightly from country to country, but the InterRail pass is not valid for travel within your country of residence. For complete information, go online to **InterRail** (www.interrail.eu).

InterRail Global allows unlimited travel in 30 European countries, including Bosnia and Hercegovina, Bulgaria, Croatia, the Czech Republic, Hungary, Macedonia, Montenegro, Poland, Romania, Serbia, Slovakia and Slovenia. The consecutive pass is valid for unlimited travel within a period of 15 or 22 continuous days (from €276/306) or one month (from €392). There is also a pass that allows for five days (from €163) or 10 days of (€339) rail travel within 10 or 22 days, respectively.

INTERRAIL & EURAIL COUNTRY PASSES

If you are intending to travel extensively within any one country, you might consider purchasing a Country Pass (InterRail if you are an EU resident, Eurail if not). The Eurail Country Pass is available for Bulgaria, Croatia, the Czech Republic, Hungary, Poland, Romania and Slovenia. The InterRail Country Pass is available for all of those countries, plus Serbia and Slovakia. The passes and prices vary for each country, so check out the websites for more information. You'll need to travel extensively to recoup your money, but the passes will save you the time and hassle of buying individual tickets that don't require reservations. Some of these countries also offer national rail passes.

Language

This chapter offers basic vocabulary to help you get around Eastern Europe. Read our coloured pronunciation guides as if they were English and you'll be understood. The stressed syllables are indicated with italics.

Some phrases in this chapter have both polite and informal forms (indicated by the abbreviations 'pol' and 'inf' respectively). The abbreviations 'm' and 'f' indicate masculine and feminine gender respectively.

ALBANIAN

In Albanian – also understood in Kosovo – ew is pronounced as 'ee' with rounded lips, uh as the 'a' in 'ago', dh as the 'th' in 'that', dz as the 'ds' in 'adds', and zh as the 's' in 'pleasure'. Also, ll and rr are pronounced stronger than when they are written as single letters.

Basics

Hello.	Tungjatjeta.	toon-dya-tye-ta
Goodbye.	Mirupafshim.	mee-roo-paf-sheem
Excuse me.	Më falni.	muh fal-nee
Sorry.	Më vjen keq.	muh vyen kech
Please.	Ju lutem.	yoo loo-tem
Thank you.	Faleminderit.	fa-le-meen-de-reet
Yes.	Po.	po
No.	Jo.	yo

What's your name?
Si quheni? — see choo-he-nee

My name is ...
Unë quhem ... — oo-nuh choo-hem ...

Do you speak English?
A flisni anglisht? — a flees-nee ang-leesht

I don't understand.
Unë nuk kuptoj. — oo-nuh nook koop-toy

Accommodation

campsite	vend kampimi	vend kam-pee-mee
guesthouse	bujtinë	booy-tee-nuh
hotel	hotel	ho-tel
youth hostel	fjetore për të rinj	fye-to-re puhr tuh reeny

Do you have a single/double room?
A keni një dhomë teke/dopjo? — a ke-nee nyuh dho-muh te-ke/dop-yo

How much is it per night/person?
Sa kushton për një natë/njeri? — sa koosh-ton puhr nyuh na-tuh/nye-ree

Eating & Drinking

Is there a vegetarian restaurant near here?
A ka ndonjë restorant vegjetarian këtu afër? — a ka ndo-nyuh res-to-rant ve-dye-ta-ree-an kuh-too a-fuhr

What would you recommend?
Çfarë më rekomandoni? — chfa-ruh muh re-ko-man-do-nee

I'd like the bill/menu, please.
Më sillni faturën/ menunë, ju lutem. — muh seell-nee fa-too-ruhn/ me-noo-nuh yoo loo-tem

I'll have ...	Dua ...	doo-a ...
Cheers!	Gëzuar!	guh-zoo-ar

Emergencies

Help!	Ndihmë!	ndeeh-muh
Go away!	Ik!	eek

Numbers – Albanian		
1	një	nyuh
2	dy	dew
3	tre	tre
4	katër	ka-tuhr
5	pesë	pe-suh
6	gjashtë	dyash-tuh
7	shtatë	shta-tuh
8	tetë	te-tuh
9	nëntë	nuhn-tuh
10	dhjetë	dhye-tuh

Call the doctor/police!
Thirrni doktorin/
policinë!
theerr·nee dok·to·reen/
po·lee·tsee·nuh

I'm lost.
Kam humbur rrugën.   kam hoom·boor rroo·guhn

I'm ill.
Jam i/e sëmurë. (m/f)   yam ee/e suh·moo·ruh

Where are the toilets?
Ku janë banjat?   koo ya·nuh ba·nyat

Shopping & Services

I'm looking for ...
Po kërkoj për ...   po kuhr·koy puhr ...

How much is it?
Sa kushton?   sa koosh·ton

That's too expensive.
Është shumë
shtrenjtë.
uhsh·tuh shoo·muh
shtreny·tuh

market	*treg*	treg
post office	*posta*	pos·ta
tourist office	*zyrë*	zew·ra
	turistike	too·rees·tee·ke

Transport

boat	*anija*	a·nee·ya
bus	*autobusi*	a·oo·to·boo·see
plane	*aeroplani*	a·e·ro·pla·nee
train	*treni*	tre·nee
One ... ticket (to Shkodër), please.	*Një biletë ... (për në Shkodër), ju lutem.*	nyuh bee·le·tuh ... (puhr nuh shko·duhr), yoo loo·tem
one-way	*për vajtje*	puhr vai·tye
return	*kthimi*	kthee·mee

BULGARIAN

In Bulgarian, vowels in unstressed syllables are generally pronounced shorter and weaker than they are in stressed syllables. Note that uh is pronounced as the 'a' in 'ago' and zh as the 's' in 'pleasure'.

Basics

Hello.	Здравейте.	zdra·vey·te
Goodbye.	Довиждане.	do·veezh·da·ne
Excuse me.	Извинете.	iz·vee·ne·te
Sorry.	Съжалявам.	suh·zhal·ya·vam
Please.	Моля.	mol·ya
Thank you.	Благодаря.	bla·go·dar·ya

Numbers – Bulgarian

1	един	ed·een
2	два	dva
3	три	tree
4	четири	che·tee·ree
5	пет	pet
6	шест	shest
7	седем	se·dem
8	осем	o·sem
9	девет	de·vet
10	десет	de·set

Yes.	Да.	da
No.	Не.	ne

What's your name?
Как се казвате/
казваш? (pol/inf)
kak se kaz·va·te/
kaz·vash

My name is ...
Казвам се ...   kaz·vam se ...

Do you speak English?
Говорите ли
английски?
go·vo·ree·te lee
ang·lees·kee

I don't understand.
Не разбирам.   ne raz·bee·ram

Accommodation

campsite	къмпинг	kuhm·peeng
guesthouse	пансион	pan·see·on
hotel	хотел	ho·tel
youth hostel	общежитие	ob·shte·zhee·tee·ye
Do you have a ... room?	Имате ли стая с ...?	ee·ma·te lee sta·ya s ...
single	едно легло	ed·no leg·lo
double	едно голямо легло	ed·no go·lya·mo leg·lo

How much is it per night/person?
Колко е на вечер/
човек?
kol·ko e na ve·cher/
cho·vek

Eating & Drinking

Do you have vegetarian food?
Имате ли
вегетерианска
храна?
ee·ma·te lee
ve·ge·te·ree·an·ska
hra·na

What would you recommend?
Какво ще   kak·vo shte

препоръчате? pre·po·*ruh*·cha·te

I'd like the bill/menu, please.
Дайте ми сметката/ *dai*·te mee *smet*·ka·ta/
менюто, моля. men·*yoo*·to *mol*·ya

I'll have ... Ще взема ... shte *vze*·ma ...
Cheers! Наздраве! na·*zdra*·ve

Emergencies

Help! Помощ! po·mosht
Go away! Махайте се! *ma*·hai·te se

Call the doctor/police!
Повикайте лекар/ po·*vee*·kai·te le·kar/
полицията! po·*lee*·tsee·ya·ta
I'm lost.
Загубих се. za·*goo*·beeh se
I'm ill.
Болен/Болна bo·len/*bol*·na
съм. (m/f) suhm
Where are the toilets?
Къде има тоалетни? kuh·*de* ee·ma to·a·*let*·nee

Shopping & Services

I'm looking for ...
Търся ... *tuhr*·sya ...
How much is it?
Колко струва? *kol*·ko *stroo*·va
That's too expensive.
Скъпо е. *skuh*·po e

bank банка *ban*·ka
post office поща po·shta
tourist office бюро за *byoo*·ro za
туристическа too·*ree*·stee·
информация ches·ka een·for·
ma·tsee·ya

Transport

boat корабът ko·*ra*·buht
bus автобусът av·to·*boo*·suht
plane самолетът sa·mo·*le*·tuht
train влакът *vla*·kuht
One ... ticket Един билет e·*deen* bee·*let*
(to Varna), ... (за Варна), ... (za *var*·na)
please. моля. *mol*·ya
  one-way в едната v ed·*na*·ta
посока po·*so*·ka
  return за отиване za o·*tee*·va·ne
и връщане ee *vruhsh*·
ta·ne

CROATIAN & SERBIAN

Croatian and Serbian are very similar and mutually intelligible. Using them, you will also be fully understood in Bosnia & Hercegovina, and Montenegro, and in parts of Kosovo.

In this section, significant differences between Croatian and Serbian are indicated with (C) and (S) respectively. Note that r is rolled and that zh is pronounced as the 's' in 'pleasure'.

Basics

Hello. Zdravo. *zdra*·vo
Goodbye. Zbogom. *zbo*·gom
Excuse me. Oprostite. o·*pro*·sti·te
Sorry. Žao mi je. zha·o mi ye
Please. Molim. *mo*·lim
Thank you. Hvala. *hva*·la
Yes. Da. da
No. Ne. ne

What's your name?
Kako se zovete/ *ka*·ko se zo·ve·te/
zoveš? (pol/inf) *zo*·vesh
My name is ...
Zovem se ... *zo*·vem se ...
Do you speak English?
Govorite/Govoriš li go·vo·ri·te/go·vo·rish
engleski? (pol/inf) li en·*gle*·ski
I don't understand.
Ja ne razumijem. ya ne ra·*zu*·mi·yem

Accommodation

campsite kamp kamp
guesthouse privatni *pri*·vat·ni
smještaj *smyesh*·tai
hotel hotel *ho*·tel
youth prenoćište *pre*·no·chish·te

Numbers – Croatian & Serbian		
1	jedan	*ye*·dan
2	dva	dva
3	tri	tri
4	četiri	*che*·ti·ri
5	pet	pet
6	šest	shest
7	sedam	*se*·dam
8	osam	*o*·sam
9	devet	*de*·vet
10	deset	*de*·set

hostel	za mladež	za mla·dezh

Do you have a single/double room?
Imate li jednokrevetnu/ i·ma·te li yed·no·kre·vet·nu/
dvokrevetnu sobu? dvo·kre·vet·nu so·bu

How much is it per night/person?
Koliko stoji po ko·li·ko sto·yi po
noći/osobi? no·chi/o·so·bi

Eating & Drinking

What would you recommend?
Što biste preporučili? shto bi·ste pre·po·ru·chi·li

Do you have vegetarian food?
Da li imate da li i·ma·te
vegetarijanski obrok? ve·ge·ta·ri·yan·ski o·brok

I'd like the bill/menu, please.
Mogu li dobiti račun/ mo·gu li do·bi·ti ra·chun/
jelovnik, molim? ye·lov·nik mo·lim

I'll have ...	Želim ...	zhe·lim ...
Cheers!	Živjeli!	zhi·vye·li

Emergencies

Help!	Upomoć!	u·po·moch
Go away!	Maknite se!	mak·ni·te se

Call the ...!	Zovite ...!	zo·vi·te ...
doctor	liječnika (C)	li·yech·ni·ka
	lekara (S)	le·ka·ra
police	policiju	po·li·tsi·yu

I'm lost.
Izgubio/Izgubila iz·gu·bi·o/iz·gu·bi·la
sam se. (m/f) sam se

I'm ill.
Ja sam bolestan/ ya sam bo·le·stan/
bolesna. (m/f) bo·le·sna

Where are the toilets?
Gdje se nalaze gdye se na·la·ze
zahodi/toaleti? (C/S) za·ho·di/to·a·le·ti

Shopping & Services

I'm looking for ...
Tražim ... tra·zhim

How much is it?
Koliko stoji/ ko·li·ko sto·yi/
košta? (C/S) kosh·ta

That's too expensive.
To je preskupo. to ye pre·sku·po

bank	banka	ban·ka
post office	poštanski ured	po·shtan·skee oo·red
tourist office	turistička agencija	tu·ris·tich·ka a·gen·tsi·ya

Transport

boat	brod	brod
bus	autobus	a·u·to·bus
plane	zrakoplov (C)	zra·ko·plov
	avion (S)	a·vi·on
train	vlak/voz (C/S)	vlak/voz

One ... ticket (to Sarajevo), please.	Jednu ... kartu (do Sarajeva), molim.	yed·nu ... kar·tu (do sa·ra·ye·va) mo·lim
one-way	jedno-smjernu	yed·no-smyer·nu
return	povratnu	po·vrat·nu

CZECH

An accent mark over a vowel in written Czech indicates it's pronounced as a long sound. Note that air is pronounced as in 'hair', aw as in 'law', oh as the 'o' in 'note', ow as in 'how', uh as the 'a' in 'ago', kh as the 'ch' in the Scottish *loch*, and zh as the 's' in 'pleasure'. Also, r is rolled in Czech and the apostrophe (') indicates a slight y sound.

Basics

Hello.	Ahoj.	uh·hoy
Goodbye.	Na shledanou.	nuh·skhle·duh·noh
Excuse me.	Promiňte.	pro·min'·te
Sorry.	Promiňte.	pro·min'·te
Please.	Prosím.	pro·seem
Thank you.	Děkuji.	dye·ku·yi
Yes.	Ano.	uh·no
No.	Ne.	ne

What's your name?
Jak se jmenujete/ yuhk se yme·nu·ye·te/
jmenuješ? (pol/inf) yme·nu·yesh

My name is ...
Jmenuji se ... yme·nu·yi se ...

Do you speak English?
Mluvíte anglicky? mlu·vee·te uhn·glits·ki

I don't understand.
Nerozumím. ne·ro·zu·meem

Accommodation

campsite	tábořiště	ta·bo·rzhish·tye
guesthouse	penzion	pen·zi·on
hotel	hotel	ho·tel
youth hostel	mládežnická ubytovna	mla·dezh·nyits·ka u·bi·tov·nuh

Do you have a ... room?
Máte jednolůžkový/ · ma·te yed·no·loozh·ko·vee
dvoulůžkový pokoj? · dvoh·loozh·ko·vee po·koy

How much is it per ...?	Kolik to stojí ...?	ko·lik to sto·yee ...
night	na noc	nuh nots
person	za osobu	zuh o·so·bu

Eating & Drinking

What would you recommend?
Co byste doporučil/ · tso bis·te do·po·ru·chil/
doporučila? (m/f) · do·po·ru·chi·luh

Do you have vegetarian food?
Máte vegetariánská · ma·te ve·ge·tuh·ri·ans·ka
jídla? · yeed·luh

I'd like the bill/menu, please.
Chtěl/Chtěla bych · khtyel/khtye·luh bikh
účet/jídelníček, · oo·chet/yee·del·nyee·chek
prosím. (m/f) · ... pro·seem

I'll have ...	Dám si ...	dam si ...
Cheers!	Na zdraví!	nuh zdruh·vee

Emergencies

Help!	Pomoc!	po·mots
Go away!	Běžte pryč!	byezh·te prich

Call the doctor/police!
Zavolejte lékaře/ · zuh·vo·ley·te lair·kuh·rzhe/

Numbers – Czech		
1	jeden	ye·den
2	dva	dvuh
3	tři	trzhi
4	čtyři	chti·rzhi
5	pět	pyet
6	šest	shest
7	sedm	se·dm
8	osm	o·sm
9	devět	de·vyet
10	deset	de·set

policii! · po·li·tsi·yi

I'm lost.
Zabloudil/ · zuh·bloh·dyil/
Zabloudila jsem. (m/f) · zuh·bloh·dyi·luh ysem

I'm ill.
Jsem nemocný/ · ysem ne·mots·nee/
nemocná. (m/f) · ne·mots·na

Where are the toilets?
Kde jsou toalety? · gde ysoh to·uh·le·ti

Shopping & Services

I'm looking for ...
Hledám ... · hle·dam ...

How much is it?
Kolik to stojí? · ko·lik to sto·yee

That's too expensive.
To je moc drahé. · to ye mots druh·hair

bank	banka	buhn·kuh
post office	pošta	posh·tuh
tourist office	turistická informační kancelář	tu·ris·tits·ka in·for·muhch·nyee kuhn·tse·larzh

Transport

bus	autobus	ow·to·bus
plane	letadlo	le·tuhd·lo
train	vlak	vluhk

One ... ticket to (Telč), please.	... jízdenku do (Telče), prosim.	... yeez·den·ku do (tel·che) pro·seem
one-way	Jedno-směrnou	yed·no-smyer·noh
return	Zpátečni	zpa·tech·nyee

ESTONIAN

Double vowels in written Estonian indicate they are pronounced as long sounds. Note that air is pronounced as in 'hair', aw as in 'law', ea as in 'ear', eu as the 'u' in 'nurse', ew as 'ee' with rounded lips, oh as the 'o' in 'note', ow as in 'how', uh as the 'a' in 'ago', kh as in the Scottish loch, and zh as the 's' in 'pleasure'.

Basics

Hello.	Tere.	te·re
Goodbye.	Nägemist.	nair·ge·mist
Excuse me.	Vabandage. (pol)	va·ban·da·ge
	Vabanda. (inf)	va·ban·da

Sorry.	Vabandust.	va·ban·dust
Please.	Palun.	pa·lun
Thank you.	Tänan.	tair·nan
Yes.	Jaa.	yaa
No.	Ei.	ay

What's your name?
Mis on teie nimi?   mis on tay·e ni·mi

My name is ...
Minu nimi on ...   mi·nu ni·mi on ...

Do you speak English?
Kas te räägite   kas te rair·git·te
inglise keelt?   ing·kli·se keylt

I don't understand.
Ma ei saa aru.   ma ay saa a·ru

Eating & Drinking

What would you recommend?
Mida te soovitate?   mi·da te saw·vit·tat·te

Do you have vegetarian food?
Kas teil on taimetoitu?   kas tayl on tai·met·toyt·tu

I'd like the bill/menu, please.
Ma sooviksin   ma saw·vik·sin
arvet/menüüd, palun.   ar·vet/me·newt pa·lun

I'll have a ...   Ma tahaksin ...   ma ta·hak·sin ...

Cheers!   Terviseks!   tair·vi·seks

Emergencies

Help!	Appi!	ap·pi
Go away!	Minge ära!	ming·ke air·ra

Call the doctor/police!
Kutsuge arst/   ku·tsu·ge arst/
politsei!   po·li·tsay

I'm lost.
Ma olen ära eksinud.   ma o·len air·ra ek·si·nud

Where are the toilets?

Numbers – Estonian

1	üks	ewks
2	kaks	kaks
3	kolm	kolm
4	neli	ne·li
5	viis	vees
6	kuus	koos
7	seitse	say·tse
8	kaheksa	ka·hek·sa
9	üheksa	ew·hek·sa
10	kümme	kewm·me

Kus on WC?   kus on ve·se

Shopping & Services

I'm looking for ...
Ma otsin ...   ma o·tsin

How much is it?
Kui palju see maksab?   ku·i pal·yu sey mak·sab

That's too expensive.
See on liiga kallis.   sey on lee·ga kal·lis

bank	pank	pank
market	turg	turg
post office	postkontor	post·kont·tor

Transport

boat	laev	laiv
bus	buss	bus
plane	lennuk	len·nuk
train	rong	rongk

One ... ticket	Üks ... pilet	ewks ... pi·let
(to Pärnu),	(Pärnusse),	(pair·nus·se)
please.	palun.	pa·lun
one-way	ühe otsa	ew·he o·tsa
return	edasi-tagasi	e·da·si·ta·ga·si

HUNGARIAN

A symbol over a vowel in written Hungarian indicates it's pronounced as a long sound. Double consonants should be drawn out a little longer than in English. Note also that aw is pronounced as in 'law', eu as the 'u' in 'nurse', ew as 'ee' with rounded lips, and zh as the 's' in 'pleasure'. Finally, keep in mind that r is rolled in Hungarian and that the apostrophe (') indicates a slight y sound.

Basics

Hello.	Szervusz. (sg)	ser·vus
	Szervusztok. (pl)	ser·vus·tawk
Goodbye.	Viszlát.	vis·lat
Excuse me.	Elnézést	el·ney·zeysht
	kérek.	key·rek
Sorry.	Sajnálom.	shoy·na·lawm
Please.	Kérem. (pol)	key·rem
	Kérlek. (inf)	keyr·lek
Thank you.	Köszönöm.	keu·seu·neum
Yes.	Igen.	i·gen
No.	Nem.	nem

What's your name?
Mi a neve/   mi o ne·ve/
neved? (pol/inf)   ne·ved

My name is ...
A nevem ...   o ne·vem ...

Do you speak English?
Beszél/Beszélsz   be·seyl/be·seyls
angolul? (pol/inf)   on·gaw·lul

I don't understand.
Nem értem.   nem eyr·tem

Accommodation

campsite	kemping	kem·ping
guesthouse	panzió	pon·zi·āw
hotel	szálloda	sal·law·do
youth hostel	ifjúsági szálló	if·yū·sha·gi sal·lāw

Do you have a single/double room?
Van Önnek kiadó egy   von eun·nek ki·o·dāw ed'
egyágyas/duplaágyas   ej·a·dyosh/dup·lo·a·dyosh
szobája?   saw·ba·yo

How much is it per night/person?
Mennyibe kerül egy   men'·nyi·be ke·rewl ej
éjszakára/főre?   ey·so·ka·ro/fēū·re

Eating & Drinking

What would you recommend?
Mit ajánlana?   mit o·yan·lo·no

Do you have vegetarian food?
Vannak Önöknél   von·nok eu·neuk·neyl
vegetáriánus ételek?   ve·ge·ta·ri·a·nush ey·te·lek

I'll have ...
... kérek.   ... key·rek

Cheers! (to one person)
Egészségedre!   e·geys·shey·ged·re

Cheers! (to more than one person)
Egészségetekre!   e·geys·shey·ge·tek·re

I'd like the ...   *... szeretném.*   ... se·ret·neym

bill	A számlát	o sam·lat
menu	Az étlapot	oz eyt·lo·pawt

Emergencies

Help!	Segítség!	she·geet·sheyg
Go away!	Menjen innen!	men·yen in·nen

Call the doctor!
Hívjon orvost!   heev·yawn awr·vawsht

Call the police!
Hívja a   heev·yo o
rendőrséget!   rend·ēūr·shey·get

Numbers – Hungarian

1	egy	ej
2	kettő	ket·tēū
3	három	ha·rawm
4	négy	neyj
5	öt	eut
6	hat	hot
7	hét	heyt
8	nyolc	nyawlts
9	kilenc	ki·lents
10	tíz	teez

I'm lost.
Eltévedtem.   el·tey·ved·tem

I'm ill.
Rosszul vagyok.   raws·sul vo·dyawk

Where are the toilets?
Hol a vécé?   hawl o vey·tsey

Shopping & Services

I'm looking for ...
Keresem a ...   ke·re·shem o ...

How much is it?
Mennyibe kerül?   men'·nyi·be ke·rewl

That's too expensive.
Ez túl drága.   ez tūl dra·go

market	piac	pi·ots
post office	postahivatal	pawsh·to·hi·vo·tol
tourist office	turistairoda	tu·rish·to·i·raw·do

Transport

bus	busz	bus
plane	repülőgép	re·pew·lēū·geyp
train	vonat	vaw·not
One ... ticket to (Eger), please.	Egy ... jegy (Eger)be.	ej ... yej (e·ger)·be
one-way	csak oda	chok aw·do
return	oda-vissza	aw·do·vis·so

LATVIAN

A line over a vowel in written Latvian indicates it's pronounced as a long sound. Note that air is pronounced as in 'hair', aw as in 'law', ea as in 'ear', ow as in 'how', wa as in 'water', dz as the 'ds' in 'adds', and zh as the 's' in 'pleasure'. The apostrophe (') indicates a slight y sound.

Basics

Hello.	*Sveiks.*	svayks
Goodbye.	*Atā.*	a·taa
Excuse me.	*Atvainojiet.*	at·vai·nwa·yeat
Sorry.	*Piedodiet.*	pea·dwa·deat
Please.	*Lūdzu.*	loo·dzu
Thank you.	*Paldies.*	pal·deas
Yes.	*Jā.*	yaa
No.	*Nē.*	nair

What's your name?
Kā Jūs sauc? kaa yoos sowts

My name is ...
Mani sauc ... ma·ni sowts ...

Do you speak English?
Vai Jūs runājat vai yoos ru·naa·yat
angliski? ang·li·ski

I don't understand.
Es nesaprotu. es ne·sa·prwa·tu

Eating & Drinking

What would you recommend?
Ko Jūs iesakat? kwa yoos ea·sa·kat

Do you have vegetarian food?
Vai Jums ir veģetārie vai yums ir ve·dye·taa·rea
ēdieni? air·dea·ni

I'd like the bill/menu, please.
Es vēlos rēķinu/ es vair·lwas rair·tyi·nu/
ēdienkarti, lūdzu. air·dean·kar·ti loo·dzu

I'll have a ...
Man lūdzu vienu ... man loo·dzu vea·nu ...

Cheers!
Priekā! prea·kaa

Emergencies

Help! *Palīgā!* pa·lee·gaa

Numbers – Latvian		
1	*viens*	veans
2	*divi*	di·vi
3	*trīs*	trees
4	*četri*	che·tri
5	*pieci*	pea·tsi
6	*seši*	se·shi
7	*septiņi*	sep·ti·nyi
8	*astoņi*	as·twa·nyi
9	*deviņi*	de·vi·nyi
10	*desmit*	des·mit

Go away! *Ej prom!* ay prwam

Call the doctor/police!
Zvani ārstam/policijai! zva·ni aar·stam/po·li·tsi·yai

I'm lost.
Esmu apmaldījies. es·mu ap·mal·dee·yeas

Where are the toilets?
Kur ir tualetes? kur ir tu·a·le·tes

Shopping & Services

I'm looking for ...
Es meklēju ... es mek·lair·yu ...

How much is it?
Cik maksā? tsik mak·saa

That's too expensive.
Tas ir par dārgu. tas ir par daar·gu

bank	*banka*	ban·ka
market	*tirgus*	tir·gus
post office	*pasts*	pasts

Transport

boat	*laiva*	lai·va
bus	*autobus*	ow·to·bus
plane	*lidmašīna*	lid·ma·shee·na
train	*vilciens*	vil·tseans

One ... ticket (to Jūrmala), please.	*Vienu ... biļeti (uz Jūrmalu), lūdzu.*	vea·nu ... bi·lye·ti (uz yoor·ma·lu) loo·dzu
one-way	*vienvirziena*	vean·vir·zea·na
return	*turp-atpakaļ*	turp·at·pa·kal'

LITHUANIAN

Symbols on vowels in written Lithuanian indicate they are pronounced as long sounds. Note that aw is pronounced as in 'law', ea as in 'ear', ow as in 'how', wa as in 'water', dz as the 'ds' in 'adds', and zh as the 's' in 'pleasure'.

Basics

Hello.	*Sveiki.*	svay·ki
Goodbye.	*Viso gero.*	vi·so ge·ro
Excuse me.	*Atleiskite.*	at·lays·ki·te
Sorry.	*Atsiprašau.*	at·si·pra·show
Please.	*Prašau.*	pra·show
Thank you.	*Ačiū.*	aa·choo
Yes.	*Taip.*	taip
No.	*Ne.*	ne

What's your name?
Koks jūsų vardas? kawks *yoo*·soo *var*·das

My name is ...
Mano vardas ... *ma*·no *var*·das ...

Do you speak English?
Ar kalbate angliškai? ar *kal*·ba·te *aang*·lish·kai

I don't understand.
Aš nesuprantu. ash ne·su·*pran*·tu

Eating & Drinking

What would you recommend?
Ką jūs rekomenduo- kaa yoos re·ko·men·*dwo*·
tumėte? tu·*mey*·te

Do you have vegetarian food?
Ar turite vegetariško ar *tu*·ri·te ve·ge·*taa*·rish·ko
maisto? *mais*·to

I'd like the bill/menu, please.
Aš norėčiau ash no·*rey*·chyow
sąskaitos/meniu saas·kai·taws/me·*nyu*

I'll have a ...
Aš užsisakysiu ... ash uzh·si·sa·*kee*·syu ...

Cheers!
Į sveikatą! ee svay·*kaa*·taa

Emergencies

Help! *Padėkit!* pa·*dey*·kit

Go away! *Eikit iš čia!* ay·kit ish chya

Call the doctor/police!
Iškvieskit gydytoją/ ish·*kveas*·kit gee·dee·to·ya/
policiją! po·*li*·tsi·ya

I'm lost.
Aš pasiklydau. ash pa·si·*klee*·dow

Where are the toilets?
Kur yra tualetai? kur ee·*ra* tu·a·*le*·tai

Shopping & Services

I'm looking for ...
Aš ieškau ... ash *eash*·kow ...

How much is it?
Kiek kainuoja? keak kain·*wo*·ya

That's too expensive.
Per brangu. per *bran*·gu

bank	*bankas*	*baan*·kas
market	*turgus*	*tur*·gus
post office	*paštas*	*paash*·tas

Transport

boat	*laivas*	*lai*·vas

Numbers – Lithuanian

1	*vienas*	*vea*·nas
2	*du*	du
3	*trys*	trees
4	*keturi*	ke·tu·*ri*
5	*penki*	pen·*ki*
6	*šeši*	she·*shi*
7	*septyni*	sep·tee·*ni*
8	*aštuoni*	ash·twa·*ni*
9	*devyni*	de·vee·*ni*
10	*dešimt*	*de*·shimt

bus	*autobusas*	ow·to·*bu*·sas
plane	*lėktuvas*	leyk·*tu*·vas
train	*traukinys*	trow·ki·*nees*

One ... ticket	*Vieną*	*vea*·naa
(to Kaunas),	*bilietą ...*	bi·lye·taa ...
please.	*(į Kauną),*	(ee kow·naa)
	prašau.	pra·*show*
one-way	*į vieną*	ee *vea*·naa
	pusę	pu·sey
return	*į abi*	ee a·*bi*
	puses	pu·*ses*

MACEDONIAN

Note that dz is pronounced as the 'ds' in 'adds', r is rolled, and zh as the 's' in 'pleasure'.

Basics

Hello.	Здраво.	*zdra*·vo
Goodbye.	До гледање.	do gle·da·nye
Excuse me.	Извинете.	iz·*vi*·ne·te
Sorry.	Простете.	*pros*·te·te
Please.	Молам.	*mo*·lam
Thank you.	Благодарам.	bla·*go*·da·ram
Yes.	Да.	da
No.	Не.	ne

What's your name?
Како се викате/ *ka*·ko se *vi*·ka·te/
викаш? (pol/inf) *vi*·kash

My name is ...
Јас се викам ... yas se *vi*·kam ...

Do you speak English?
Зборувате ли zbo·*ru*·va·te li
англиски? an·glis·ki

I don't understand.
Јас не разбирам. yas ne *raz*·bi·ram

Accommodation

campsite	камп	kamp
guesthouse	приватно сместување	pri·vat·no smes·tu·va·nye
hotel	хотел	ho·tel
youth hostel	младинско преноќиште	mla·din·sko pre·no·kyish·te

Do you have a single/double room?

Дали имате
еднокреветна/
двокреветна соба?
da·li *i*·ma·te
ed·no·*kre*·vet·na/
dvo·*kre*·vet·na *so*·ba

How much is it per night/person?

Која е цената за
ноќ/еден?
ko·ya e *tse*·na·ta za
noky/e·den

Eating & Drinking

What would you recommend?

Што препорачувате
вие?
shto pre·po·ra·*chu*·va·te
vi·e

Do you have vegetarian food?

Дали имате
вегетаријанска храна?
da·li *i*·ma·te
ve·ge·ta·ri·*yan*·ska *hra*·na

I'd like the bill/menu, please.

Ве молам сметката/
мени.
ve *mo*·lam *smet*·ka·ta/
me·*ni*

I'll have ...

Јас ќе земам ...
yas kye *ze*·mam ...

Cheers!

На здравје!
na *zdrav*·ye

Emergencies

Help!	Помош!	po·mosh
Go away!	Одете си!	o·de·te si

Call the doctor/police!

Numbers – Macedonian

1	еден	e·den
2	два	dva
3	три	tri
4	четири	che·ti·ri
5	пет	pet
6	шест	shest
7	седум	se·dum
8	осум	o·sum
9	девет	de·vet
10	десет	de·set

Викнете лекар/
полиција!
vik·ne·te le·*kar*/
po·*li*·tsi·ya

I'm lost.

Се загубив.
se za·*gu*·biv

I'm ill.

Јас сум болен/
болна. (m/f)
yas sum *bo*·len/
bol·na

Where are the toilets?

Каде се тоалетите?
ka·de se to·a·*le*·ti·te

Shopping & Services

I'm looking for ...

Барам ...
ba·ram ...

How much is it?

Колку чини тоа?
kol·ku *chi*·ni *to*·a

That's too expensive.

Тоа е многу скапо.
to·a e *mno*·gu *ska*·po

market	пазар	*pa*·zar
post office	пошта	*posh*·ta
tourist office	туристичко биро	tu·ris·*tich*·ko·to *bi*·ro

Transport

boat	брод	brod
bus	автобус	*av*·to·bus
plane	авион	a·*vi·on*
train	воз	voz

One ... ticket (to Ohrid), please.	Еден ... (за Охрид), ве молам.	e·den ... (za oh·rid) ve *mo*·lam
one-way	билет во еден правец	*bi*·let vo e·den *pra*·vets
return	повратен билет	*pov*·ra·ten *bi*·let

POLISH

Polish vowels are generally pronounced short. Nasal vowels are pronounced as though you're trying to force the air through your nose, and are indicated with n or m following the vowel. Note that ow is pronounced as in 'how', kh as the 'ch' in the Scottish *loch*, and zh as the 's' in 'pleasure'. Also, r is rolled in Polish and the apostrophe (') indicates a slight y sound.

Basics

Hello.	*Cześć.*	cheshch
Goodbye.	*Do widzenia.*	do vee·dze·nya
Excuse me.	*Przepraszam.*	pshe·*pra*·sham

452

LANGUAGE POLISH

Sorry.	Przepraszam.	pshe·*pra*·sham
Please.	Proszę.	*pro*·she
Thank you.	Dziękuję.	jyen·*koo*·ye
Yes.	Tak.	tak
No.	Nie.	nye

What's your name?
Jak się pan/pani nazywa? (m/f pol) — yak shye pan/*pa*·nee na·*zi*·va
Jakie się nazywasz? (inf) — yak shye na·*zi*·vash

My name is ...
Nazywam się ... — na·*zi*·vam shye ...

Do you speak English?
Czy pan/pani mówi po angielsku? (m/f) — chi pan/*pa*·nee moo·vee po an·*gyel*·skoo

I don't understand.
Nie rozumiem. — nye ro·*zoo*·myem

Accommodation

campsite	kamping	*kam*·peeng
guesthouse	pokoje gościnne	po·*ko*·ye gosh·*chee*·ne
hotel	hotel	*ho*·tel
youth hostel	schronisko młodzieżowe	skhro·*nees*·ko mwo·jye·*zho*·ve

Do you have a ... room? — Czy jest pokój ...? — chi yest *po*·kooy ...
  single — jednoosobowy — yed·noo·so·*bo*·vi
  double — z podwójnym łóżkiem — z pod·*vooy*·nim *woozh*·kyem

How much is it per night/person?
Ile kosztuje za noc/osobę? — ee·le kosh·*too*·ye za nots/o·*so*·be

Eating & Drinking

What would you recommend?
Co by pan polecił? (m) — tso bi pan po·*le*·cheew
Co by pani poleciła? (f) — tso bi *pa*·nee po·le·*chee*·wa

Do you have vegetarian food?
Czy jest żywność wegetariańska? — chi yest *zhiv*·noshch ve·ge·tar·*yan*'·ska

I'd like the ..., please.
Proszę o rachunek/jadłospis. — *pro*·she o ra·*khoo*·nek/ya·*dwo*·spees

| I'll have ... | Proszę ... | *pro*·she ... |
| Cheers! | Na zdrowie! | na *zdro*·vye |

Emergencies

| Help! | Na pomoc! | na *po*·mots |
| Go away! | Odejdź! | o·deyj |

Call the doctor/police!
Zadzwoń po lekarza/policję! — zad·zvon' po le·*ka*·zha/po·*lee*·tsye

I'm lost.
Zgubiłem/Zgubiłam się. (m/f) — zgoo·*bee*·wem/zgoo·*bee*·wam shye

I'm ill.
Jestem chory/a. (m/f) — *yes*·tem *kho*·ri/a

Where are the toilets?
Gdzie są toalety? — gjye som to·a·*le*·ti

Shopping & Services

I'm looking for ...
Szukam ... — *shoo*·kam

How much is it?
Ile to kosztuje? — ee·le to kosh·*too*·ye

That's too expensive.
To jest za drogie. — to yest za *dro*·gye

market	targ	tark
post office	urząd pocztowy	oo·zhond poch·*to*·vi
tourist office	biuro turystyczne	*byoo*·ro too·ris·*tich*·ne

Transport

boat	łódź	wooj
bus	autobus	ow·*to*·boos
plane	samolot	sa·*mo*·lot
train	pociąg	po·chonk

Numbers – Polish

1	jeden	*ye*·den
2	dwa	dva
3	trzy	tshi
4	cztery	*chte*·ri
5	pięć	pyench
6	sześć	sheshch
7	siedem	*shye*·dem
8	osiem	*o*·shyem
9	dziewięć	*jye*·vyench
10	dziesięć	*jye*·shench

One ... ticket (to Katowice), please.	Proszę bilet ... (do Katowic).	pro·she bee·let ... (do ka·to·veets)
one-way	w jedną stronę	v yed·nom stro·ne
return	powrotny	po·vro·tni

ROMANIAN

Note that ew is pronounced as 'ee' with rounded lips, oh as the 'o' in 'note', ow as in 'how', uh as the 'a' in 'ago', and zh as the 's' in 'pleasure'. The apostrophe (') indicates a very short, unstressed i (almost silent).

Basics

Hello.	Bună ziua.	boo·nuh zee·wa
Goodbye.	La revedere.	la re·ve·de·re
Excuse me.	Scuzaţi-mă.	skoo·za·tsee·muh
Sorry.	Îmi pare rău.	ewm' pa·re ruh·oo
Please.	Vă rog.	vuh rog
Thank you.	Mulţumesc.	mool·tsoo·mesk
Yes.	Da.	da
No.	Nu.	noo

What's your name?
Cum vă numiţi?   koom vuh noo·meets'

My name is ...
Numele meu este ...   noo·me·le me·oo yes·te ...

Do you speak English?
Vorbiţi engleza?   vor·beets' en·gle·za

I don't understand.
Eu nu înţeleg.   ye·oo noo ewn·tse·leg

Accommodation

campsite	teren de camping	te·ren de kem·peeng
guesthouse	pensiune	pen·syoo·ne
hotel	hotel	ho·tel
youth hostel	hostel	hos·tel

Do you have a ... room?	Aveţi o cameră ...?	a·vets' o ka·me·ruh ...
single	de o persoană	de o per·so·a·nuh
double	dublă	doo·bluh
How much is it per ...?	Cît costă ...?	kewt kos·tuh ...
night	pe noapte	pe no·ap·te
person	de persoană	de per·so·a·nuh

Eating & Drinking

What would you recommend?
Ce recomandaţi?   che re·ko·man·dats'

Do you have vegetarian food?
Aveţi mâncare vegetariană?   a·ve·tsi mewn·ka·re ve·je·ta·rya·nuh

I'll have ...	Aş dori ...	ash do·ree ...
Cheers!	Noroc!	no·rok

I'd like the ..., please.	Vă rog, aş dori ...	vuh rog ash do·ree ...
bill	nota de plată	no·ta de pla·tuh
menu	meniul	me·nee·ool

Emergencies

Help!	Ajutor!	a·zhoo·tor
Go away!	Pleacă!	ple·a·kuh

Call the ...!	Chemaţi ...!	ke·mats' ...
doctor	un doctor	oon dok·tor
police	poliţia	po·lee·tsya

I'm lost.
M-am rătăcit.   mam ruh·tuh·cheet

I'm ill.
Mă simt rău.   muh seemt ruh·oo

Where are the toilets?
Unde este o toaletă?   oon·de yes·te o to·a·le·tuh

Shopping & Services

I'm looking for ...
Caut ...   kowt ...

How much is it?
Cât costă?   kewt kos·tuh

That's too expensive.
E prea scump.   ye pre·a skoomp

market	piaţă	pya·tsuh
post office	poşta	posh·ta
tourist office	biroul de informaţii turistice	bee·ro·ool de een·for·ma·tsee too·rees·tee·che

Numbers – Romanian

1	*unu*	*oo*·noo
2	*doi*	doy
3	*trei*	trey
4	*patru*	pa·troo
5	*cinci*	cheench'
6	*şase*	sha·se
7	*şapte*	shap·te
8	*opt*	opt
9	*nouă*	no·wuh
10	*zece*	ze·che

Transport

boat	*vapor*	va·por
bus	*autobuz*	ow·to·booz
plane	*avion*	a·vyon
train	*tren*	tren

One ... ticket (to Cluj), please.	*Un bilet ... (până la Cluj), vă rog.*	oon bee·let ... (pew·nuh la kloozh) vuh rog
one-way	*dus*	doos
return	*dus-întors*	doos ewn·tors

RUSSIAN

In Russian – also widely used in Belarus – the kh is pronounced as the 'ch' in the Scottish *loch* and zh as the 's' in 'pleasure'. Also, r is rolled in Russian and the apostrophe (') indicates a slight y sound.

Basics

Hello.	Здравствуйте.	zdrast·vuyt·ye
Goodbye.	До свидания.	da svee·dan·ya
Excuse me./ Sorry.	Извините, пожалуйста.	eez·vee·neet·ye pa·zhal·sta
Please.	Пожалуйста.	pa·zhal·sta
Thank you.	Спасибо	spa·see·ba
Yes.	Да.	da
No.	Нет.	nyet

What's your name?
Как вас зовут?   kak vaz za·vut

My name is ...
Меня зовут ...   meen·ya za·vut ...

Do you speak English?
Вы говорите
по-английски?   vi ga·va·reet·ye pa·an·glee·skee

I don't understand.
Я не понимаю.   ya nye pa·nee·ma·yu

Accommodation

campsite	кемпинг	*kyem*·peeng
guesthouse	пансионат	pan·see·a·*nat*
hotel	гостиница	ga·*stee*·neet·sa
youth hostel	общежитие	ap·shee·*zhi*·tee·ye

Do you have a ... room?	У вас есть ...?	u vas yest' ...
single	одноместный номер	ad·nam·*yes*·ni *no*·meer
double	номер с двуспальней кроватью	*no*·meer z dvu·*spaln*·yey kra·*vat*·yu

How much is it ...?	Сколько стоит за ...?	*skol*'·ka *sto*·eet za ...
for two people	двоих	dva·*eekh*
per night	ночь	noch'

Eating & Drinking

What would you recommend?
Что вы
рекомендуете?   shto vi ree·ka·meen·*du*·eet·ye

Do you have vegetarian food?
У вас есть
вегетарианские
блюда?   u vas yest' vi·gi·ta·ri·*an*·ski·ye *blyu*·da

I'd like the bill/menu, please.
Я бы хотел/хотела
счёт/меню. (m/f)   ya bi khat·*yel*/khat·ye·la shot/meen·*yu*

I'll have ...	..., пожалуйста.	... pa·*zhal*·sta
Cheers!	За здоровье!	za zda·*rov*·ye

Emergencies

Help!	Помогите!	pa·ma·*gee*·tye
Go away!	Идите отсюда!	ee·*deet*·ye at·*syu*·da

Call the doctor/police!
Вызовите врача/
милицию!   *vi*·za·veet·ye vra·*cha*/mee·*leet*·si·yu

I'm lost.
Я потерялся/
потерялась. (m/f)   ya pa·teer·*yal*·sa/ pa·teer·ya·las'

I'm ill.
Я болею.   ya bal·*ye*·yu

Where are the toilets?
Где здесь туалет?   gdye zdyes' tu·al·*yet*

Numbers – Russian

1	один	a·*deen*
2	два	dva
3	три	tree
4	четыре	chee·*ti*·ree
5	пять	pyat'
6	шесть	shest'
7	семь	syem'
8	восемь	vo·*seem*'
9	девять	dye·veet'
10	десять	dye·seet'

Shopping & Services

I'd like ...
Я бы хотел/
хотела ... (m/f) — ya bi khat·*yel*/ khat·ye·la ...

How much is it?
Сколько стоит? — skol'·ka *sto*·eet

That's too expensive.
Это очень дорого. — e·ta o·cheen' *do*·ra·ga

bank	банк	bank
market	рынок	*ri*·nak
post office	почта	*poch*·ta
tourist office	туристическое бюро	tu·rees·*tee*· chee·ska·ye byu·ro

Transport

boat	параход	pa·ra·*khot*
bus	автобус	af·*to*·bus
plane	самолёт	sa·mal·*yot*
train	поезд	po·yeest

One ... ticket (to Novgorod), please.	Билет ... (на Новгород).	beel·*yet* ... (na *nov*·ga·rat)
one-way	в один конец	v a·*deen* kan·*yets*
return	в оба конца	v o·ba kant·sa

SLOVAK

An accent mark over a vowel in written Slovak indicates it's pronounced as a long sound. Note that air is pronounced as in 'hair', aw as in 'law', oh as the 'o' in 'note', ow as in 'how', uh as the 'a' in 'ago', dz as the 'ds' in 'adds', kh as the 'ch' in the Scottish *loch*, and zh as the 's' in 'pleasure'. The apostrophe (') indicates a slight y sound.

Basics

Hello.	Dobrý deň.	do·bree dyen'
Goodbye.	Do videnia.	do vi·dye·ni·yuh
Excuse me.	Prepáčte.	pre·pach·tye
Sorry.	Prepáčte.	pre·pach·tye
Please.	Prosím.	pro·seem
Thank you.	Ďakujem	dyuh·ku·yem
Yes.	Áno.	a·no
No.	Nie.	ni·ye

What's your name?
Ako sa voláte? — uh·ko suh vo·la·tye

My name is ...
Volám sa ... — vo·lam suh ...

Do you speak English?
Hovoríte po anglicky? — ho·vo·ree·tye po uhng·lits·ki

I don't understand.
Nerozumiem. — nye·ro·zu·myem

Accommodation

campsite	táborisko	ta·bo·ris·ko
guesthouse	penzión	pen·zi·awn
hotel	hotel	ho·tel
youth hostel	nocľaháreň pre mládež	nots·lyuh·ha·ren' pre mla·dyezh

Do you have a single room?
Máte jedno-posteľovú izbu? — ma·tye yed·no·pos·tye·lyo·voo iz·bu

Do you have a double room?
Máte izbu s manželskou posteľou? — ma·tye iz·bu s muhn·zhels·koh pos·tye·lyoh

How much is it per ...?
Koľko to stojí na noc/osobu — kol'·ko to sto·yee nuh nots/o·so·bu

Eating & Drinking

What would you recommend?
Čo by ste mi odporučili? — cho bi stye mi od·po·ru·chi·li

Do you have vegetarian food?
Máte vegetariánske jedlá? — ma·tye ve·ge·tuh·ri·yan·ske yed·la

I'll have ...
Dám si ... — dam si ...

Cheers!
Nazdravie! — nuhz·druh·vi·ye

Numbers – Slovak

1	jeden	ye·den
2	dva	dvuh
3	tri	tri
4	štyri	shti·ri
5	päť	pet'
6	šesť	shest'
7	sedem	se·dyem
8	osem	o·sem
9	deväť	dye·vet'
10	desať	dye·suht'

I'd like the ..., please.	Prosím si ...	pro·seem si ...
bill	účet	oo·chet
menu	jedálny lístok	ye·dal·ni lees·tok

Emergencies

Help!	Pomoc!	po·mots
Go away!	Choďte preč!	khod'·tye prech
Call ...!	Zavolajte ...!	zuh·vo·lai·tye ...
a doctor	lekára	le·ka·ruh
the police	políciu	po·lee·tsi·yu

I'm lost.
Stratil/Stratila som sa. (m/f) — struh·tyil/struh·tyi·luh som suh

I'm ill.
Som chorý/chorá. (m/f) — som kho·ree/kho·ra

Where are the toilets?
Kde sú tu záchody? — kdye soo tu za·kho·di

Shopping & Services

I'm looking for ...
Hľadám ... — hlyuh·dam ...

How much is it?
Koľko to stojí? — kol'·ko to sto·yee

That's too expensive.
To je príliš drahé. — to ye pree·lish druh·hair

market	trh	trh
post office	pošta	posh·tuh
tourist office	turistická kancelária	tu·ris·tits·ka kuhn·tse·la·ri·yuh

Transport

bus	autobus	ow·to·bus
plane	lietadlo	li·ye·tuhd·lo
train	vlak	vluhk

One ... ticket (to Poprad), please.	Jeden ... lístok (do Popradu), prosím.	ye·den ... lees·tok (do pop·ruh·du) pro·seem
one-way	jedno-smerný	yed·no-smer·nee
return	spiatočný	spyuh·toch·nee

SLOVENE

Note that uh is pronounced as the 'a' in 'ago', oh as the 'o' in 'note', ow as in 'how', zh as the 's' in 'pleasure', r is rolled, and the apostrophe (') indicates a slight y sound.

Basics

Hello.	Zdravo.	zdra·vo
Goodbye.	Na svidenje.	na svee·den·ye
Excuse me.	Dovolite.	do·vo·lee·te
Sorry.	Oprostite.	op·ros·tee·te
Please.	Prosim.	pro·seem
Thank you.	Hvala.	hva·la
Yes.	Da.	da
No.	Ne.	ne

What's your name?
Kako vam/ti je ime? (pol/inf) — ka·ko vam/tee ye ee·me

My name is ...
Ime mi je ... — ee·me mee ye ...

Do you speak English?
Ali govorite angleško? — a·lee go·vo·ree·te ang·lesh·ko

I don't understand.
Ne razumem. — ne ra·zoo·mem

Accommodation

campsite	kamp	kamp
guesthouse	gostišče	gos·teesh·che
hotel	hotel	ho·tel
youth hostel	mladinski hotel	mla·deen·skee ho·tel

Do you have a single/double room?
Ali imate enoposteljno/ — a·lee ee·ma·te e·no·pos·tel'·no/

dvoposteljno sobo? dvo·*pos*·tel'·no so·bo

How much is it per night/person?
Koliko stane na ko·lee·ko *sta*·ne na
noč/osebo? noch/o·*se*·bo

Eating & Drinking

What would you recommend?
Kaj priporočate? kai pree·po·ro·*cha*·te

Do you have vegetarian food?
Ali imate *a*·lee ee·*ma*·te
vegetarijansko hrano? ve·ge·ta·ree·*yan*·sko *hra*·no

I'll have ...	*Jaz bom ...*	yaz bom ...
Cheers!	*Na zdravje!*	na *zdrav*·ye

I'd like the ..., please.	*Želim ...,* *prosim.*	zhe·*leem* ... pro·*seem*
bill	*račun*	ra·*choon*
menu	*jedilni list*	ye·*deel*·nee leest

Emergencies

Help!	*Na pomoč!*	na po·*moch*
Go away!	*Pojdite stran!*	poy·*dee*·te stran

Call the doctor/police!
Pokličite zdravnika/ pok·*lee*·chee·te zdrav·*nee*·ka
policijo! po·lee·*tsee*·yo

I'm lost.
Izgubil/ eez·*goo*·beew/
Izgubila sem se. (m/f) eez·goo·*bee*·la sem se

I'm ill.
Bolan/Bolna sem. (m/f) bo·*lan/boh*·na sem

Where are the toilets?
Kje je stranišče? kye ye stra·*neesh*·che

Shopping & Services

I'm looking for ...
Iščem ... *eesh*·chem ...

How much is this?
Koliko stane? ko·lee·ko *sta*·ne

That's too expensive.
To je predrago. to ye pre·*dra*·go

market	*tržnica*	*tuhrzh*·nee·tsa
post office	*pošta*	*posh*·ta
tourist office	*turistični urad*	too·rees·*teech*·nee oo·*rad*

Numbers – Slovene

1	*en*	en
2	*dva*	dva
3	*trije*	*tree*·ye
4	*štirje*	*shtee*·rye
5	*pet*	pet
6	*šest*	shest
7	*sedem*	*se*·dem
8	*osem*	*o*·sem
9	*devet*	de·*vet*
10	*deset*	de·*set*

Transport

boat	*ladja*	*lad*·ya
bus	*avtobus*	av·to·boos
plane	*letalo*	le·*ta*·lo
train	*vlak*	vlak

One ... ticket to (Koper), please.	*... vozovnico* *do (Kopra),* *prosim.*	... vo·*zov*·nee·tso do (ko·pra) pro·seem
one-way	*Enosmerno*	e·no·*smer*·no
return	*Povratno*	pov·*rat*·no

UKRAINIAN

Vowels in unstressed syllables are generally pronounced shorter and weaker than they are in stressed syllables. Note that kh is pronounced as the 'ch' in the Scottish *loch* and zh as the 's' in 'pleasure'. The apostrophe (') indicates a slight y sound.

Basics

Hello.	Добрий день.	*do*·bry den'
Goodbye.	До побачення.	do po·*ba*·chen·nya
Excuse me.	Вибачте.	*vy*·bach·te
Sorry.	Перепрошую.	pe·re·*pro*·shu·yu
Please.	Прошу.	*pro*·shu
Thank you.	Дякую.	*dya*·ku·yu
Yes.	Так.	tak
No.	Ні.	ni

What's your name?
Як вас звати? yak vas zva·ty

My name is ...
Мене звати ... me·*ne* zva·ti ...

Do you speak English?
Ви розмовляєте vy roz·mow·*lya*·ye·te

англійською мовою?	an·*hliys'*·ko·yu *mo*·vo·yu

I don't understand.

Я не розумію.	ya ne ro·zu·*mi*·yu

Accommodation

campsite	кемпінг	*kem*·pinh
double room	номер на двох	*no*·mer na dvokh
hotel	готель	ho·*tel'*
single room	номер на одного	*no*·mer na o·*dno*·ho
youth hostel	молодіжний гуртожиток	mo·lo·*dizh*·ni hur·*to*·zhi·tok

Do you have any rooms available?

У вас є вільні номери?	u vas ye *vil'*·ni no·me·ri

How much is it per night/person?

Скільки коштує номер за ніч/особу?	*skil'*·ky ko·shtu·ye *no*·mer za nich/*o*·so·bu

Eating & Drinking

What do you recommend?

Що Ви порадите?	shcho vy po·*ra*·dy·te

I'm a vegetarian.

Я вегетаріанець/ вегетаріанка. (m/f)	ya ve·he·ta·ri·*a*·nets'/ ve·he·ta·ri·*an*·ka

Cheers!	Будьмо!	*bud'*·mo
I'd like ...	Я візьму ...	ya viz'·*mu* ...
bill	рахунок	ra·*khu*·nok
menu	меню	me·*nyu*

Emergencies

Help!

Допоможіть!	do·po·mo·*zhit'*

Go away!

Іди/Ідіть звідси! (pol/inf)	i·*di*/i·*dit'* zvid·si

Call the doctor/police!

Викличте лікаря/ міліцію!	*vi*·klich·te li·ka·rya/ mi·*li*·tsi·yu

I'm lost.

Я заблукав/ заблукала. (m/f)	ya za·blu·*kaw*/ za·blu·*ka*·la

I'm ill.

Мені погано.	me·*ni* po·*ha*·no

Numbers – Ukrainian

1	один	o·*din*
2	два	dva
3	три	tri
4	чотири	cho·*ti*·ri
5	п'ять	pyat'
6	шість	shist'
7	сім	sim
8	вісім	*vi*·sim
9	дев'ять	*de*·vyat'
10	десять	*de*·syat'

Where's the toilet?

Де туалети?	de tu·a·le·ti

Shopping & Services

I'd like to buy ...

Я б хотів/хотіла купити ... (m/f)	ya b kho·*tiw*/kho·*ti*·la ku·*pi*·ti ...

How much is this?

Скільки це він/вона коштує? (m/f)	*skil'*·ki tse vin/vo·*na* ko·shtu·ye?

That's too expensive.

Це надто дорого.	tse *nad*·to do·ro·ho

ATM	банкомат	ban·ko·*mat*
market	ринок	*ri*·nok
post office	пошта	*po*·shta
tourist office	туристичне бюро	tu·ri·*stich*·ne byu·*ro*

Transport

I want to go to ...

Мені треба їхати до ...	me·*ni* *tre*·ba *yi*·kha·ti do ...

bus	автобус	aw·*to*·bus
one-way ticket	квиток в один бік	kvi·*tok* v o·*din* bik
plane	літак	li·*tak*
return ticket	зворотний квиток	zvo·*ro*·tni kvi·*tok*
train	поїзд	*po*·yizd

Behind the Scenes

SEND US YOUR FEEDBACK

We love to hear from travellers – your comments keep us on our toes and help make our books better. Our well-travelled team reads every word on what you loved or loathed about this book. Although we cannot reply individually to your submissions, we always guarantee that your feedback goes straight to the appropriate authors, in time for the next edition. Each person who sends us information is thanked in the next edition – the most useful submissions are rewarded with a selection of digital PDF chapters.

Visit **lonelyplanet.com/contact** to submit your updates and suggestions or to ask for help. Our award-winning website also features inspirational travel stories, news and discussions.

Note: We may edit, reproduce and incorporate your comments in Lonely Planet products such as guidebooks, websites and digital products, so let us know if you don't want your comments reproduced or your name acknowledged. For a copy of our privacy policy visit lonelyplanet.com/privacy.

OUR READERS

Many thanks to the travellers who used the last edition and wrote to us with helpful hints, useful advice and interesting anecdotes:

Alannah Cusin, Andreja Skerl, Anna Conley, Dom Van Abbe, Donald Pochowski, Emma White, Hector Del Olmo, Jeff Angermann, Louise Dalton, Marcus Pailing, Marie Goetzke, Marisa Luque, Rosanne Churchouse, Sain Alizada, Sam Pulfer, Suzannah Conway, Tony Collins, Tyler LeBlanc, Vera Wedekind, Victor Jones.

AUTHOR THANKS
Mark Baker

In Lithuania, I would like to thank my friends Simona and Doug for tips on dining and drinking in Vilnius. Indraja Germanaite was kind enough to show me around beautiful Trakai and the amazing Curonian Spit. Evelina Vanclovaite introduced me to new places in Kaunas. In the Czech Republic where I live, I would like to thank my friend Katerina Pavlitova at Prague City Tourism. In Poland, friends Beata Szulęcka and Olga Brzezinska helped me to research Warsaw and Kraków. For Romania: in Timișoara, the crew at Hostel Costel. In Cluj-Napoca, photographer Crina

Prida and Madalina Stanescu at the Fabrica de Pensule. In Sighișoara, dear friends Raluca and Mark Tudose. Finally, in Moldova, Diana Railean's enthusiasm for Chișinău was infectious.

Marc Di Duca

Huge *dyakuyu* goes to Kyiv parents-in-law Mykola and Vira for looking after sons Taras and Kirill while I was on the road. Big thanks to Markiyan in Lviv, all the staff at the Lviv tourist office and of course my wife Tanya, for suffering my long absences from our home in Sandwich, Kent.

Peter Dragicevich

It's a special treat to be able to meet up with friends on the road. On this trip I was lucky enough to have Kaspars Zalitis and his crew show me all of their favourite haunts in their home town of Rīga. And many thanks to Ivica Erdelja for accompanying me on the road in Montenegro.

Mark Elliott

Many thanks to Kate, Amra Begić, Miloš at Srebrenica, Jan, Boro, Branislav, Nermina, Davor at Matuško, Sanja in Banja Luka, Shoba and Leslie for the most remarkable series of coincidences, and the Aussie bridge divers (hope you survived). Endless thanks to my ever inspiring parents who, four decades ago, had the crazy idea of driving me to Bosnia in the first place.

Steve Fallon

In Hungary, my thanks to Bea Szirti and Ildikó Nagy Moran for company and suggestions. On the road, I am indebted to András Cseh (Eger), Zsuzsi Fábián (Kecskemét) and Shandor Madachy (Budapest). *Nagyon szépen köszönöm mindenkinek!* In Slovenia, *najlepša hvala* to the fab trio at the Ljubljana Tourist Board (Petra Stušek, Tatjana Radovič and Verica Leskovar) and Saša Špolar at the Slovenian Tourist Board. Along the way, hats off to Andreja Frelih and David May (Piran), Aleš Hvala (Kobarid) and Kellie and Peter Gasperin (Bohinj). It was a delight spending time with old mates Domen and Barbara Kalajžič in Bled, especially with my partner, Michael Rothschild, in tow.

Tom Masters

Thanks to Catherine Bohne, Ardi Pulaj, Dmitry Sakharov, Lena Durham, Amy Sedaris, Vesna Maric, Jan Morris, Svetlana Aliliuyeva and Edith Durham, all of whom accompanied me in some form on this journey through the Balkans and Belarus.

Anja Mutić

Hvala mama, for your inspiring laughter. *Obrigada* Hoji, for being there before, during and after. A huge *hvala* to my friends in Croatia who gave me endless recommen-

dations – this book wouldn't be the same without you. Special thanks go to Mila in Split. Finally, to the inspiring memory of my father who travels with me still.

Simon Richmond

Many thanks to Brana, fellow editors and the top-class team of authors who pulled together this edition.

Tamara Sheward

Hvala/blagodarya to the combined populations of Serbia and Bulgaria: your warm-hearted ways and inspired lunacy make it harder for me to leave the Balkans every time. Specifically, thanks and *rakija/ rakia* clinks go out to the Lučić family, Dragana Eremić, Gvozden Marinković, Tsvetelina, Alexander and Tanya, Hristo, Andy, kum Ćomi, Nikola and Djordje, Gordana and Srdjan, and the brilliant Brana Vladisavljević. *Naravno, najviše se zahvaljujem mojim partnerima u kriminalu Dušanu i Maši!*

Luke Waterson

A hearty *ďakujem* to Erik Ševčik in Poprad – I hope one day all tour operators are as informative and helpful. Thanks go out to the myriad late-night taxi drivers, train restaurant car staff, cafe waiters and tourist information representatives that got me from A to B and helped me out when I got there. Finally, appreciative nods to the knowledgeable girls of the Human Rights League in Bratislava: how would I have discovered half the city hangouts I've listed without you?

ACKNOWLEDGEMENTS

Climate map data adapted from Peel MC, Finlayson BL & McMahon TA (2007) 'Updated World Map of the Köppen-Geiger Climate Classification', Hydrology and Earth System Sciences, 11, 163344.

Cover photograph: Malá Strana, Prague, Czech Republic. Walter Bibikow/AWL ©

THIS BOOK

This 13th edition of Lonely Planet's *Eastern Europe* guidebook was researched and written by Mark Baker, Marc Di Duca, Peter Dragicevich, Mark Elliott, Steve Fallon, Tom Masters, Anja Mutić, Simon Richmond, Tamara Sheward and Luke Waterson.

This guidebook was produced by the following:

Destination Editor Brana Vladisavljevic

Product Editors Elin Berglund, Jenna Myers, Amanda Williamson

Assisting Editors Sarah Bailey, Michelle Bennett, Andrea Dobbin, Carly Hall, Kellie Langdon, Jodie Martire, Anne Mulvaney, Rosie Nicholson, Kristin Odijk, Charlotte Orr, Susan Paterson, Monique Perrin, Erin Richards, Kathryn Rowan, Kirsten Rawlings, Saralinda Turner, Jeanette Wall

Senior Cartographer Valentina Kremenchutskaya

Assisting Cartographer Alison Lyall

Book Designer Cam Ashley

Assisting Book Designer Jessica Rose

Cover Researcher Campbell McKenzie

Thanks to Imogen Bannister, Brendan Dempsey, Ryan Evans, Gemma Graham, Anna Harris, Kate James, Elizabeth Jones, Claire Naylor, Karyn Noble, Sunny Or, Anna Tyler, Lauren Wellicome, Tony Wheeler

Index

INDEX C

castles, fortresses &
    palaces continued
Râşnov Fortress 320
Rector's Palace 127
Reök Palace 195
Royal Castle
    (Warsaw) 281
Royal Palace
    (Budapest) 179
Royal Palace (Sofia) 87
Royal Palace
    (Visegrád) 188
Royal Wawel Castle 287
Rozafa Fortress 48-9
Rundāle Palace 221
Sighişoara Citadel 321
Sigulda Medieval
    Castle 222
Soroca Fortress 262
Špilberk Castle 151-2
Spiš Castle 388
Sponza Palace 127
Toompea Castle 161
Trakai Castle 234-5
Tsarevets Fortress 98
Turaida Museum
    Reserve 222
Tvrđina Kale
    Fortress 245
Visegrád Citadel 188
Vratnik 73-4
Vyšehrad Citadel 142
cathedrals, see churches &
    cathedrals
cave art, see frecoes
caves
    Dobšinská Ice Cave 389
    Kyevo-Pecherska
        Lavra 414
    Lake Matka 248
    Orheiul Vechi 261
    Postojna Cave 406
    Škocjan Caves 406
cell phones 22, 432
cemeteries, see also
    mausoleums
    Capuchin Monastery
        (Brno) 152
    Jewish Cemetery
        (Warsaw) 284
    Lychakivske Cemetery
        (Lviv) 418
    Old Church & Cemetery
        (Zakopane) 295
    Old Jewish Cemetery
        (Lublin) 293

Old Jewish Cemetery
    (Prague) 141
cell phones 22, 432
Cēsis 223
Český Krumlov 21, 31, 149-
    51, **150**, **21**
Cetinje 275-6
changing of the guard
    ceremony (Sofia) 88-9
Charles Bridge 141, **4**,
    10-11
Chateau Cojuşna 262
children, travel with 426-7
Chişinău 256-61, **258**
    accommodation 257-9
    drinking & nightlife 260
    entertainment 260
    festivals & events 32
    food 259
    medical services 260
    sights 256-7
    travel to/from 260
    travel within 260-1
christmas trees 216
churches & cathedrals
    Aleksander Nevski
        Church (Sofia) 87
    Alexander Nevsky
        Cathedral (Tallinn) 161
    Annunciation
        Cathedral 339
    Assumption
        Cathedral 339
    Basilica of St
        Stephen 183
    Benedictine Abbey
        Church 191
    Biserica Evanghelică 323
    Black Church 318
    Bogorodičina Crkva 371
    Boyana Church 94
    Cathedral of Christ the
        Saviour 340
    Cathedral of SS John
        the Baptist & John the
        Evangelist 306
    Cathedral of
        St Barbara 147
    Cathedral of
        St Domnius 121
    Cathedral of
        St Elizabeth 390
    Cathedral of
        St George 407
    Cathedral of St John the
        Baptist (Lublin) 293
    Cathedral of St John
        the Baptist (Wrocław)
        297-8
    Cathedral of
        St Sophia 345

Cathedral of Sts Peter &
    Paul (Brno) 152
Cathedral of Sts Peter
    & Paul (Kamyanets-
    Podilsky) 419
Cathedral of the
    Assumption
    (Dubrovnik) 127
Cathedral of the
    Assumption of the
    Blessed Virgin Mary
    (Zagreb) 110
Church of Our Lady
    Before Týn 140
Church of
    St Elizabeth 297
Church of
    St Euphemia 118
Church of
    St Jacob 387
Church of St John the
    Baptist 404
Church of St Mary
    Magdalene 297
Church of Sveta
    Bogorodica
    Perivlepta 248
Church of Sveti Jovan
    at Kaneo 248
Church of Sveti
    Konstantin & Elena 95
Church of the
    Annunciation 127
Church of the Holy
    Cross 281
Church on the Hill 322
Church on the Spilled
    Blood 346
Eger Basilica 196
Esztergom Basilica 188-9
Holy Spirit Church 163
Kraljeva Crkva 371
Latin Cathedral 418-19
Matthias Church 179
Metropolitan
    Cathedral 328
Mosque Church 193
Nativity of Christ
    Cathedral 216
Old Church & Cemetery
    (Zakopane) 295
Plaošnik 248
Poznań Cathedral 300
Rīga Cathedral 213
St Anne's Church
    (Vilnius) 229-30
St Anne's Church
    (Warsaw) 281
Stavropoleos
    Church 313
St Basil's Cathedral 338
St Casimir's Church 230

St Isaac's Cathedral
    346-7
St John's
    Church 171
St Mark's
    Church 111
St Martin's
    Cathedral 377, 379
St Mary's Basilica
    (Kraków) 287, 289
St Mary's Cathedral
    (Tallinn) 161
St Mary's Church
    (Gdańsk) 302
St Michael's Church 325
St Nicholas Church
    (Prague) 141
St Nicholas' Church
    (Kotor) 271
St Nicholas' Church
    (Perast) 274
St Olaf's Church 164
St Peter's Church 216
St Sophia's
    Cathedral 414
St Teresa's Church 230
St Tryphon's
    Cathedral 271-2
St Vitus Cathedral 137
Sts Peter & Paul
    Cathedral 235
Sveta Nedelya
    Cathedral 89
Sveta Petka Samardzhi-
    iska Church 89
Sveta Sofia
    Cathedral (Ohrid) 248
Sveta Sofia Church
    (Sofia) 87
Sveti Georgi Rotunda
    (Sofia) 87-8
Sveti Sava
    (Belgrade) 363
Sveti Spas Church
    (Skopje) 243-4
Sveti Stefan Church
    (Varna) 102
Vilnius Cathedral 229
Wawel Cathedral 287
citadels, see castles,
    fortresses & palaces
city walls
    Brașov 318
    Budva 269
    Dubrovnik 15, 126, **15**
    Kotor 271
    Levoča 387
    Sarajevo 73-4
    Sighişoara 321-2
    Sopron 189
    Sozopol 104

474

Map Legend

Sights

- Beach
- Bird Sanctuary
- Buddhist
- Castle/Palace
- Christian
- Confucian
- Hindu
- Islamic
- Jain
- Jewish
- Monument
- Museum/Gallery/Historic Building
- Ruin
- Shinto
- Sikh
- Taoist
- Winery/Vineyard
- Zoo/Wildlife Sanctuary
- Other Sight

Activities, Courses & Tours

- Bodysurfing
- Diving
- Canoeing/Kayaking
- Course/Tour
- Sento Hot Baths/Onsen
- Skiing
- Snorkelling
- Surfing
- Swimming/Pool
- Walking
- Windsurfing
- Other Activity

Sleeping

- Sleeping
- Camping

Eating

- Eating

Drinking & Nightlife

- Drinking & Nightlife
- Cafe

Entertainment

- Entertainment

Shopping

- Shopping

Information

- Bank
- Embassy/Consulate
- Hospital/Medical
- Internet
- Police
- Post Office
- Telephone
- Toilet
- Tourist Information
- Other Information

Geographic

- Beach
- Gate
- Hut/Shelter
- Lighthouse
- Lookout
- Mountain/Volcano
- Oasis
- Park
- Pass
- Picnic Area
- Waterfall

Population

- Capital (National)
- Capital (State/Province)
- City/Large Town
- Town/Village

Transport

- Airport
- Border crossing
- Bus
- Cable car/Funicular
- Cycling
- Ferry
- Metro station
- Monorail
- Parking
- Petrol station
- S-Bahn/S-train/Subway station
- Taxi
- T-bane/Tunnelbana station
- Train station/Railway
- Tram
- Tube station
- U-Bahn/Underground station
- Other Transport

Note: Not all symbols displayed above appear on the maps in this book

Routes

- Tollway
- Freeway
- Primary
- Secondary
- Tertiary
- Lane
- Unsealed road
- Road under construction
- Plaza/Mall
- Steps
- Tunnel
- Pedestrian overpass
- Walking Tour
- Walking Tour detour
- Path/Walking Trail

Boundaries

- International
- State/Province
- Disputed
- Regional/Suburb
- Marine Park
- Cliff
- Wall

Hydrography

- River, Creek
- Intermittent River
- Canal
- Water
- Dry/Salt/Intermittent Lake
- Reef

Areas

- Airport/Runway
- Beach/Desert
- Cemetery (Christian)
- Cemetery (Other)
- Glacier
- Mudflat
- Park/Forest
- Sight (Building)
- Sportsground
- Swamp/Mangrove

Simon Richmond

Russia UK-born writer and photographer Simon first ventured into Eastern Europe shortly after the Berlin Wall fell for an eventful rail trip including Prague and Budapest. Many subsequent, always fascinating, journeys across the region have followed, with work assignments in Russia and the Baltic States. Follow him on Twitter, Instagram and at www.simonrichmond.com. Simon also wrote the Plan and Survive chapters.

Tamara Sheward

Bulgaria, Serbia After years of freelance travel writing, rock'n'roll journalism and insalubrious authordom, Tamara joined Lonely Planet's ranks as the presenter of LPTV's *Roads Less Travelled: Cambodia* documentary. Since then she's stuck to covering decidedly less leech-infested destinations including Russia, Serbia and Bulgaria. Tamara is currently living in Australia's far north with her husband (whom she never would have met were it not for some late night 'researching'), and daughter.

Luke Waterson

Slovakia Luke fell in love with Slovakia and these days lives in its quirky capital, Bratislava, beside vineyards that yield some of the country's finest white wines. He's constantly planning hikes into Slovakia's forests and hills – particularly if they go via a ruined castle or a rustic *krčma* (pub). As well as writing a bunch of content about Slovakia for Lonely Planet and the BBC, he also runs the quirky travel/culture blog on all things Slovak: www.englishmaninslovakia.com.

Mark Elliott

Bosnia & Hercegovina British born travel writer Mark Elliott was only 11 when his family first dragged him to Sarajevo and stood him in the now defunct concrete footsteps of Gavrilo Princip. Fortunately no Austro-Hungarian emperors were passing at the time. He has since visited virtually every corner of BiH, supping fine Hercegovinian wines with master vintners, talking philosophy with Serb monks and Sufi mystics, and drinking more Bosnian coffee than any stomach should be subjected to.

Steve Fallon

Hungary, Slovenia Steve, who has written every edition of Lonely Planet's *Hungary* guidebook, lived in Budapest for three years in the early 1990s. From there he also researched and later wrote LP's first Slovenia guidebook. He maintains close contacts with both countries, returning often to Magyarország for thermal baths, Tokaj wine and *bableves* (bean soup) and to Slovenija for a glimpse of the Julian Alps in the sunshine, a dribble of *bučno olje* (pumpkinseed oil) and a dose of the dual. Find out more about Steve at www.steveslondon.com.

Tom Masters

Albania, Belarus, Kosovo, Macedonia Tom has been travelling in Eastern Europe since the early '90s when, as a young teenager, he travelled by train across the newly liberated 'Eastern Bloc' with his mother, an experience not unlike a Graham Greene novel. Having studied Russian, lived in St Petersburg and currently residing in the former East Berlin, Tom knows this part of the world like few others, though it constantly manages to surprise him. You can find more of his work at www.tommasters.net.

Anja Mutić

Croatia It's been more than two decades since Anja left her native Croatia. The journey took her to several countries before she made New York City her base 15 years ago. But the roots are a-calling. She's been returning to Croatia frequently for work and play, intent on discovering a new place on every visit, be it a nature park, an offbeat town or a remote island. She's happy that Croatia's beauties are appreciated worldwide but secretly longs for the time when you could head to Hvar and hear the sound of crickets instead of blasting music. Anja is online at www.everthenomad.com.

OUR STORY

A beat-up old car, a few dollars in the pocket and a sense of adventure. In 1972 that's all Tony and Maureen Wheeler needed for the trip of a lifetime – across Europe and Asia overland to Australia. It took several months, and at the end – broke but inspired – they sat at their kitchen table writing and stapling together their first travel guide, *Across Asia on the Cheap*. Within a week they'd sold 1500 copies. Lonely Planet was born.

Today, Lonely Planet has offices in Franklin, London, Melbourne, Oakland, Beijing and Delhi, with more than 600 staff and writers. We share Tony's belief that 'a great guidebook should do three things: inform, educate and amuse'.

OUR WRITERS

Mark Baker

Czech Republic, Lithuania, Moldova, Poland, Romania Mark Baker is an independent travel writer based in Prague. He's lived in Central Europe for more than 20 years, working as a writer and editor for the *Economist*, Bloomberg and Radio Free Europe/Radio Liberty, and is an enthusiastic traveller throughout the region. He's author of several Lonely Planet guides, including *Prague & the Czech Republic*, *Estonia, Latvia & Lithuania*, *Romania & Bulgaria*, *Poland* and *Slovenia*. Tweet him @markbakerprague.

Marc Di Duca

Ukraine Driven by an urge to discover Eastern Europe's wilder side, Marc first hit Kyiv one dark, snow-flecked night in early 1998. Many prolonged stints, countless near misses with Kyiv's metro doors and a few too many rides in seatbelt-less Lada taxis later, he still gets excited about exploring this immense but troubled land. A busy travel writer, Marc has penned guides to Moscow, Siberia's Lake Baikal, Russia and the Trans-Siberian Railway, as well as countless other destinations around Europe.

Peter Dragicevich

Estonia, Latvia, Montenegro After a dozen years working for newspapers and magazines in both his native New Zealand and in Australia, Peter ditched the desk and hit the road. He wrote Lonely Planet's first guide to the newly independent Montenegro and has contributed to literally dozens of other Lonely Planet titles, including the *Estonia, Latvia & Lithuania* guidebook and five successive editions of *Eastern Europe*.

OVER MORE
PAGE WRITERS

Published by Lonely Planet Publications Pty Ltd
ABN 36 005 607 983
13th edition – October 2015
ISBN 978 1 74321 466 4
© Lonely Planet 2015   Photographs © as indicated 2015
10 9 8 7 6 5 4 3 2 1
Printed in China

Although the authors and Lonely Planet have taken all reasonable care in preparing this book, we make no warranty about the accuracy or completeness of its content and, to the maximum extent permitted, disclaim all liability arising from its use.